SCATTERED
AMONG
THE PEOPLES

SCATTERED AMONG THE PEOPLES

THE JEWISH DIASPORA IN TWELVE PORTRAITS

ALLAN LEVINE

OVERLOOK DUCKWORTH
NEW YORK • WOODSTOCK • LONDON

First published in paperback in the United States in 2004 by
The Overlook Press, Peter Mayer Publishers, Inc.
Woodstock & New York

WOODSTOCK:
One Overlook Drive
Woodstock, NY 12498
www.overlookpress.com
[for individual orders, bulk and special sales, contact our Woodstock office]

NEW YORK:
141 Wooster Street
New York, NY 10012

LONDON:
Gerald Duckworth & Co. Ltd.
Greenhill House
90-93 Cowcross Street
London EC1M 6BF
www.ducknet.co.uk

Grateful acknowledgement is made to the following for permission to use
extended quotations from copyrighted works:

The Diary of the Vilna Ghetto: June 1941–April 1943 by Yitzhok Rudashevski,
copyright © 1972 by Ghetto Fighters' House, D.N. Western Galilee, 25220 Israel.
Excerpts are used by permission of Ghetto Fighters' House.

The Zionist Idea: A Historical Analysis and Reader, copyright © 1959 by Arthur Hertzberg.
Excerpts are used by permission of Arthur Hertzberg.

Library of Congress Cataloging-in-Publication Data

Levine, Allan.
Scattered among the peoples : the Jewish diaspora in twelve portraits / Allan Levine.
p. cm.
1. Jews—Biography. 2. Jewish diaspora. I. Title
DS1153.3 .L47 2003   909'.04924—dc22   2004268242

Printed in the United States of America
ISBN 1-58567-606-3 US
ISBN 0-7156-3392-9 UK
1 3 5 7 9 8 6 4 2

CONTENTS

For my children,
Alexander and Mia,
their children,
and the generations who follow them

So they should know where they come from . . .

"And the Lord shall scatter you among the peoples, and ye shall be left few in number among the nations, whither the Lord shall lead you away."
– Deuteronomy 4:27

"We are a people – one people."
– Theodor Herzl

EXILE AND DISPERSION

We must revitalize the idea of the national renascence [sic], and use every possible means to strengthen its hold and deepen its roots, until it becomes an organic element in the Jewish consciousness and an independent dynamic force. Only in that way . . . can the Jewish soul be freed from its shackles and regain contact with the broad stream of human life without having to pay for its freedom by the sacrifice of its individuality.

            - AHAD HA-AM (ASHER ZVI GINSBERG), 1894

Tisha B'Av

AS LUCK WOULD HAVE IT, I was in Venice, *La Serenissima,* "The Most Serene," on August 10, 2000. My visit here during the hot summer, when the crowds of North American tourists swell in this exquisite Italian city of canals, lagoons, and Renaissance architecture, had a larger purpose than just to bask in Venice's intoxicating beauty and magical ambience. This was one more stop on a journey across Europe that would eventually take me to Amsterdam, Paris, Seville, Vilnius, Kiev, and Vienna, among other places. I had come seeking answers and searching for elusive links in the history of the Jewish people and their unique lives in the Diaspora. How had the Jews survived for so many years? What mysterious power had permitted this remarkable ancient people to withstand centuries of persecution and tragedy?

The term "Diaspora" is derived from the Greek word meaning "scattering." And though it was originally applied to any peoples who were exiled or resettled in the ancient world, the term has come to define the Jewish experience from the time of the Babylonians to the present. This scattering, dispersion, or exile, depending on your perspective, first started in 586 B.C.E. after Nebuchadnezzar and the Babylonians burned to the ground the Temple of Solomon in Jerusalem. In the aftermath of this devastation, the people of Judea, as the region was then called, were sent into exile in Babylon.

The scattering was made permanent more than six hundred years later in 70 C.E. when the Romans, led by General Titus, countering a Jewish revolt, destroyed the Second Temple (built and rededicated in 515 B.C.E. by permission of the Persian rulers who had taken Judea from the Babylonians). According to Josephus, the chronicler who opted to become a Roman citizen rather than die as a Jew, when the Second Temple was razed "1,100,000 people died by fire or famine or sword in the long campaign and siege; another 97,000 were made slaves and scattered throughout the empire." This was their punishment for taking part in an insurrection against the mightiest power in the world. The Romans forced nearly all of the Jews to leave the Holy Land and rebuild their lives wherever they could and in whatever part of the world that would accept them.

It was the birth of the "Wandering Jew," although the term itself was not used until the thirteenth century. According to the accepted myth, a Jewish cobbler taunted Jesus on his way to Calvary. When Jesus asked the cobbler for aid, he was snubbed. For this insolence, the cobbler was doomed to wander until Jesus returned in the Second Coming. "Since then," as Israeli historian Ora Limor has explained, "the Jew has not died – so ran the story – but he continues to roam the world, appearing occasionally in different places, and will continue to do so till Judgement Day." In any event, nearly 1,900 years would pass before Jews would again reclaim the city of Jerusalem.

The tragedies of 586 B.C.E. and 70 C.E. both occurred on the same day in the Jewish lunar calendar, the ninth day of *Av*, or, in Hebrew, Tisha B'Av. For generations, this day was commemorated by fasting, mourning, and prayer. It is a moment for reflection and repentance, akin to grieving for every Jew who has ever perished for maintaining his faith. Next to Yom Kippur, the Day of Atonement, there is no more sorrowful occasion than Tisha B'Av. In the summer of 2000, the ninth day of *Av* fell on August 10.

Normally, I would not have attended morning synagogue services on Tisha B'Av. In fact, to be completely honest, had I been back in Canada I doubt I would even have acknowledged its passing. But here was an unprecedented opportunity to participate in the Tisha B'Av prayers in the Levantine School, one of Venice's oldest synagogues. (In Italian, *Scuole* means a place for learning and prayer; North American Jews from an Ashkenazi background use the East European term, *shul*.) Built in 1583 by Jewish immigrants from the Levant – the Ottoman Empire and other eastern Mediterranean countries – this synagogue, one of five in Venice, is located within the narrow confines of the city's ancient ghetto. (As will be explained further in Chapter Two, the term "ghetto" derives from the Italian word "*geto*," or "foundry," one such operation having been located in this area.)

That Thursday morning, it was only a short ride from my hotel on the crowded *vaporetto*, the city's water bus, to the small ghetto entrance at the Fondamenta di Cannaregio. If you look closely, you can still find the spot where the gate posts were fastened. For almost three hundred years, beginning in 1516, the Jews of Venice would be locked behind the ghetto gate each night – a way to keep them apart from the Christian world on the outside and to protect them from attack. Beside the portico is a stone sign on which is scratched the rules of the community. Swearing was not permitted, nor were converted Jews allowed inside the ghetto.

Through the entrance, leading away from the canal, is a narrow, damp, and dark walkway. The hot August sun barely penetrates.

Once, Jews lived here in the squeezed-together houses and flats of
the Ghetto Vecchio, as this section of the ghetto is called. This was
the second phase of the segregated Jewish quarter, opened for settlement in 1541. Today, the apartments, which on the outside do not
appear all that attractive, have become too pricey for most Italian
Jews. They prefer to live outside the city in nearby Mestre. Only a
few Judaica shops still exist, selling expensive trinkets. There is also
a small centre, for visiting Orthodox Jews from New York, and a
popular Jewish museum that caters mainly to tourists, offering
guided visits to the ghetto's synagogues. Such is the sad fate of
many former Jewish neighbourhoods in Europe; the centuries of
war and destruction have finally taken their toll, relegating once
vibrant and significant Diaspora centres to not much more than
museum exhibits.

The Levantine synagogue is located in a small and charming
square of the Ghetto Vecchio known as the Campiello della Scuole.
As I entered, a young man who stood at the doorway politely
informed me in English that I would not be allowed to leave until
the service had ended. Given the normal amount of commotion
and comings and goings at most North American synagogues, this
struck me as a strange custom, though I agreed to abide by the rules.

The sanctuary is on the second floor of the building, constructed
that way, I presume, to protect it from Venice's famous spring floods.
The synagogue is not large, but it is imbued with history. The room
is rectangular and ornate. A number of magnificent chandeliers hang
from the finely sculpted ceiling. At the east end is the ark, in which
is kept the Torahs, the Holy Scriptures. A circle of black marble
columns surrounds and protects it. On the opposite side, two finely
crafted wooden staircases curve up to the *bimah*, or dais, though
today no one was using it (in Sephardi synagogues this is referred to
as the *tebah*, from the Hebrew word *tevah*, or "ark," which it often
resembles). Four arched windows were sufficiently opened to let in
air and a small ray of light. There is room in the synagogue for at
least 250 to 300 people, though I sensed it had been a long time since
that many Jews attended.

I took a seat in the front wooden bench beside another worshipper, who barely acknowledged my presence. The other dozen or so men sat on the floor around the ark. It is customary on Tisha B'Av to sit in this fashion and avoid any comfort, like a mourner "sitting *shiva*" for a departed family member. Above us, there were a handful of women, their heads covered, seated in the section reserved for them. The service was Orthodox but clearly informal, and the prayers were shared between the various congregants. I followed along as best I could, as their pronunciation of Hebrew was not quite what I am accustomed to. Partway through the service, the keeper of the ark key gently removed one of the Torahs from the ark. The scroll was placed on a table covered by a white cloth, and a short portion was read and chanted.

Throughout the service, the mood in the synagogue was sombre, as befitted the remembrance of the destruction of the temples in Jerusalem. This was not the time for idle or friendly chit-chat, and I did not try to approach other members of the congregation. Yet without so much as saying a word to me, they made me feel welcome. I was in the presence of the last Jews of the Venice Ghetto in an ancient and historic sanctuary, a symbol of both Jewish life and repression, and I might just as well have been home. I may have spoken a different language and belonged to a foreign culture, but as Jews the bond between us was old and strong. It was a spiritual link that was not easily defined, yet it existed nonetheless.

A Typical Child of the Diaspora

THE SIGNIFICANCE OF THIS SPIRITUAL LINK was taught to me many years earlier as a young student at the Talmud Torah, a Jewish day school in Winnipeg, Canada. There, I had been instilled with a love of the Hebrew language, knowledge of prayer and synagogue ritual, a commitment to Zionism and the State of Israel, and a passion for Jewish history. On a few occasions, I had also experienced some anti-Semitic taunts – "kike" and "dirty Jew" were the favourites – from bullies whose names I cannot recall. At the time, these episodes were hurtful, yet they strengthened my character and Jewish identity rather than weakening it. So, too, did several visits to Israel, where I could proudly use Hebrew in the streets. I was, in short, a typical child of the Diaspora.

My roots, like those of thousands of other North American Jews, are in the small villages of the Russian Pale of Settlement, then a forced Jewish enclave in the western region of the Empire. My great-grandparents and grandparents made the difficult decision at the end of the nineteenth and beginning of the twentieth centuries to search for better opportunities in the New World. Decades later, most of their relatives who had opted to remain perished in the Nazi onslaught. Both of my grandmothers, Sarah Rosen (later Kliman) and Clara Hershberg (later Levine) were born in Canada. Their husbands, my grandfathers, Sam Kliman and Aaron Levine, were the first of their families to journey to North America. For better or worse, they landed in Winnipeg on the Canadian Prairies, where they established themselves, met and married my grand-mothers, and had their respective families.

My father, Marvin Levine, and mother, Bernice Kliman, were raised in "Jewish" homes. In the case of my mother, though, who spent her early years in the rural town of Holland, Manitoba (ninety kilometres southwest of Winnipeg), where my grandfather, like many immigrant Jews, owned a general store, and where they were the only Jewish family for miles, keeping a Jewish home proved more challenging. Still, my grandmother, Sarah, had kosher food shipped in from Winnipeg, and the major holidays were cele-brated with relatives, either in the city or in nearby towns. The Kliman family's relationship with their Christian neighbours was good – my grandfather was famous in the town for extending credit to struggling farmers – and their general store became a favourite gathering spot most Saturday nights. When my mother was still young, she was chosen by her teacher at the local elemen-tary school to play the part of the Virgin Mary in the annual Christmas pageant. This did not sit well with my grandmother, who intervened, and no matter how much my mother cried about it, a little "Gentile" girl (as my grandmother would tell it) was selected instead.

My father grew up in Winnipeg's famed North End immigrant quarter and had a more traditional upbringing. He attended *cheder*, or Jewish school, every day after public school and went to synagogue on the Sabbath far more than I ever did. When my grandfather died a few weeks before my father's bar mitzvah (and thirteenth birthday), my father attended synagogue services each morning to recite the Kaddish, the ancient prayer for the dead. Yet this made him late for school each day, and despite the intervention of the rabbi, the principal at Aberdeen School could not be budged. My father was forced to repeat Grade 7, an event he long remembered, one that taught him about the discrimination faced by Jews in Winnipeg in those days.

I grew up in a caring and happy environment in which Jewish values and traditions were always considered important, though perhaps not practised as stringently as Jewish law prescribes. It is true that each generation is more assimilated than the previous one, and this was certainly the case in my family.* My parents sacrificed much to ensure that their children had a Jewish education. Yet as I became older the issue of kosher food in our home, much to the dissatisfaction of my more traditional father, lost importance.

Our family celebrated Passover and Hanukkah and attended a Conservative middle-of-the-road synagogue on the High Holidays. Participating in regular Sabbath prayer services was not something I was interested in, though I have never felt anything but comfortable in a synagogue.

By the time I was fifteen or so, my interest in synagogue had declined — why, I cannot entirely say. At the same moment, my

---

* As one French Jewish writer observed as early as 1840, "The grandfather believes, the son doubts, and the grandson denies. The grandfather prays in Hebrew, the father reads the prayer in French, and the son does not pray at all. The grandfather observes all festivals, the father observes Yom Kippur, the son does not observe any. The grandfather is still a Jew, the father has become an Israelite, and the son is simply a deist . . . unless he is an atheist, a Fourierist, or a Saint-Simonist."

secular Jewish identity and my source of pride in all things Jewish increased dramatically through my association with two important Winnipeg institutions for Jewish youth. The first was Camp Massad, the only Hebrew-speaking summer camp in Western Canada, in which I was involved as a camper, counsellor, administrator, and board member on and off for about eighteen years. And the second was the Chai Folk Ensemble (*Chai* is the Hebrew word for "life"), an Israeli folk-arts, dance, and singing group of semi-professional status, with which I performed for nearly a decade.

Apart from the cultural nationalism inherent in both of these memorable and enduring organizations, they also nurtured in me the deep feeling that being Jewish, however I defined it, was something special to be cherished with honour and dignity. This did not mean that as one of the so-called "Chosen People," a Jew was better than a non-Jew; rather, the message taught and inculcated was that as a Jew you were a member of a worldwide family with a unique mission and heritage.

These have been the values that my wife and I have tried to pass on to our two children. Moreover, this ongoing desire to delve into the meaning of Judaism and Jewish culture has, I am quite sure, propelled my professional life as a teacher, historian, and writer. Several years ago, it led me to write a book on Jewish resistance and survival during the Holocaust.

That in turn sparked the idea for this book: an exploration of twelve key moments in Diaspora history, from 1492 – when the Jewish world in Europe, though never completely stable, was more or less established – to the present time, in which, following the devastations of the Second World War, the centre of the Diaspora shifted from Europe to North America. The birth of the State of Israel in 1948 also altered the focus and purpose of Diaspora communities, but confirmed, too, that Jewish life beyond the borders of the Holy Land was fundamental to Jewish survival in the future.

The Jewish Diaspora in Twelve Portraits

MY INTENTION WAS NOT TO WRITE a definitive history of the Diaspora, or a general survey of Jewish history. Instead, I studied the Jewish historical experience, relying on the voluminous secondary literature, both academic and popular, and arrived at what I would admit is an "unscientific" selection of twelve key periods and places. Some of the choices were fairly obvious. Until the Holocaust, the expulsion of Jews from Spain in 1492 was regarded as one of the greatest tragedies of Jewish history. Thus, the book's first four chapters trace the circumstances of the expulsion and follow the difficult journey of the Sephardi Jews from their homes in Seville (and Cordoba and Toledo) to Venice, Constantinople, and Amsterdam as they struggled with their collective identity as a people.

Likewise, the era of the court Jews in Vienna, and throughout the Hapsburg and German empires in the eighteenth century, marked the end of one phase of Jewish history and the beginning of the next in the story of Haskalah, or Jewish Enlightenment. It also exacerbated tensions between Ashkenazi Jews – that is, Jews who lived mainly in Germany, Austria, and Russia – and led to disputes and further divisions over questions of assimilation and religious beliefs and practices. And the 1881 pogroms in Russia, the Dreyfus Affair in Paris in the 1890s, and the mass immigration to America at the turn of the twentieth century each in their own way shaped Jewish attitudes to assimilation and adaptation, and in general changed the lives of Jews everywhere. Finally, the last three "portraits" tell the tale of Jewish successes in the twentieth century in Berlin and elsewhere in Germany, as well as the terrible tragedies that have resulted from Nazi and Soviet policies.

Each moment I have selected has been placed in the context of the era that moulded it, but my focus is on the personal experiences of individuals. A few, such as Don Isaac Abravanel, Alfred Dreyfus, Abraham Cahan, and Franz Rosenzweig, are well-known; others, like Moses Hamon, Samuel Oppenheimer, and Judah Leib Gordon, are now unjustly forgotten. Each individual shaped and participated in the Jewish experience of his day. Their successes or failures – as teachers, rabbis, merchants, writers, soldiers, and physicians – did not dictate my choice. Instead, what interested me was their interaction – or, in some cases, lack of interaction – with the societies they found themselves in and with other Jews of their era.

In short, how did the spiritual link that has so clearly affected my own life play a part in each of their own?

Seek the Peace of the City

FOR A LONG TIME Jews regarded their dispersion from Jerusalem as retribution by God for their sins. They were being punished for something they had brought on themselves. It was for this reason that the Hebrew word for the Diaspora was *gola*, or "exile." The scattering of the Jewish people was not an event to be celebrated, yet it was a fact that Jews were forced to live with and accept. The prophet Jeremiah, who witnessed the destruction of the First Temple, may have been the first Jewish leader to grasp this subtle distinction. His solution, one debated forever after by Jews, was to adapt, embrace the culture of the conqueror, and survive until the day of redemption arrived. He implored the children of Israel trapped in Babylon to "Build ye houses and dwell in them; and plant gardens, and eat the fruit of them; Take ye wives, and beget sons and daughters . . . that ye may be increased there, and not diminished. And seek the peace of the city whither I have caused you to be carried away captives, and pray unto the Lord for it; for in the peace thereof shall ye have peace."

This advice was followed so scrupulously that approximately seventy years later, when Jews were permitted by the Persians, who now controlled the Holy Land, to return and rededicate the Second Temple, many chose to remain in Babylon. It was not only their success as farmers and traders that compelled them to remain. They had discovered, as Jews in every age would, that being an active member of a foreign society did not necessarily mean forsaking your faith or people. Ironically, this exile and dispersion, which allowed them to build their synagogues, transform their religion, and establish the enduring Jewish law and customs in Babylon and elsewhere as they spread to other lands across the continents, probably saved the Jews from annihilation at the hands of their enemies. By going out into the world and adapting to the geographic, economic, and social forces they encountered, the Jews of the Diaspora ultimately provided the conditions under which the perpetuation of a Jewish identity, religion, and culture was possible.

In time, the Diaspora experience was seen in a more positive light, not as punishment but more as part of a "divine purpose." A group of progressive Central European rabbis put it like this in an official declaration they issued in 1871: "In the view of modern Judaism the destruction of Jerusalem was the end of the preparatory national existence of the Jews and the beginning of their larger mission as missionaries of the truth of the One God in all parts of the earth whither they were scattered."

The secret or mystery was to find the right balance between assimilation and adaptation, between remaining a Jew and accepting the circumstances and conditions of the society you lived in. As will be seen, more often than not this was not a choice that Jews were able to make for themselves, but one directed by the majority who governed, controlled, and all too frequently persecuted them. As early as the reign of Augustus (63 B.C.E.–14 C.E.), and well before the destruction of the Second Temple, Jews had migrated throughout the Roman Empire, a fact that did not sit well with many Romans. Already the "Jewish Question" was being discussed, and the debate would never end. "This people has made its way into every city," one Roman historian and geographer complained, "and it is not easy to find any place in the habitable world which has not received this nation and in which it has not made its power felt." Centuries would pass before Jews would feel completely at ease in the lands in which they settled. And even then, the persecution and disdain for them as the "other" would not totally vanish.

Theodor Herzl, one of the founders of the modern Zionist movement, was more right than he knew when in early July 1895 he
recorded in his diary a conversation he had had with his friend and
colleague Max Nordau. "Nordau and I agreed," Herzl wrote, "that
only anti-Semitism had made Jews of us." Or, put slightly differently
by the French philosopher Jean-Paul Sartre, "It is the anti-Semite
who makes the Jew."

But being Jewish has also meant participating in an ancient
debate for which there do not seem to be acceptable answers or
clear-cut solutions. What is Judaism: a religion, a culture, a nation,
or all three? And who is a Jew? Down through the ages intense dis-
agreements about the response to these basic questions have torn
communities apart. On many occasions, Jews themselves have been
their own worst enemies, divided by religious issues, class, and geography. Orthodox versus Reform, Ashkenazi versus Sephardi, West
European versus East European, German versus Russian, traditionalists versus assimilated, and, today, Israeli versus Diaspora – these
have been persistent disruptive forces that have threatened (and,
some might argue, still threaten) the continued existence of Jews.

The Zionist writer Asher Zvi Ginsberg, known far and wide by
his Hebrew pen name, Ahad Ha-Am, "One of the People," was one
of many Jewish scholars who wrestled with this quandary. In an
article he wrote in 1909 called "The Negation of the Diaspora," he
argued that though "dispersion is a thoroughly evil and unpleasant
thing, [Jews] can and must live in dispersion, for all its evils and all
its unpleasantness." His solution was to strengthen Jewish life in
foreign lands by establishing a "fixed centre" for the nation. "Isolated
groups of Jews wandering about the world here, there, and everywhere," he suggested, "can be nothing more than a sort of formless
raw material until they are provided with a single permanent centre,
which can exert a 'pull' on all of them, and so transform the scattered atoms into a single entity with a definite and self-subsistent
character of its own." He was correct, of course, yet even the establishment of the State of Israel in the twentieth century has spawned

a whole set of fresh problems. Who would have expected anything else of this intellectual, creative, industrious, and stubborn people?

In the course of researching this book, I spoke to many rabbis and scholars, always asking each the same question: Why are there still Jews in the world? By any measure of historical analysis, the Jewish people should have been swallowed up long ago by the forced conversions, tragedies, and persecutions. They should have disappeared, existing now only as a relic for anthropologists and archaeologists to study. As might be expected, almost all of them were quick to provide me with an answer steeped in religious teaching. "We are the Chosen People," I was told repeatedly. "We made the Covenant with God. As long as we follow God's law, he will ensure our survival. We have a role to play in the divine unfolding of history."

This is a comforting thought, and despite any doubts about my own faith in the existence of the Almighty, I do believe that they are partly right. But as the pages that follow demonstrate, there is something more – more mysterious, indefinable, and even baffling – in this inexplicable story of survival. It is a chronicle, above all, of perseverance in the face of overwhelming odds and an uncanny ability to do what is necessary so that each successive generation will endure.

Chapter One

SEPHARDIM

Seville, 1492

As for the Jews, when they heard the decree they all mourned, and wherever the news of the king's word and order was heard, the Jews despaired, and all feared greatly, a fear unequalled since the exile of Judah from its land to a foreign land. Each said to the other, "Let us strengthen one another in our faith and the Torah of our God, against the enemy who blasphemes and wishes to destroy us. If he lets us live, we shall live, and if he kills us, we shall die, but we will not desecrate our covenant and we will not retreat."

– Don Isaac Abravanel, c.1495

The Golden Age

In 1492, when Don Isaac Abravanel was forced to leave his home in Spain, he was nearly sixty years old and already becoming the Moses-like figure we see depicted in an undated portrait: an elderly man with long white hair and a full beard, his eyes deep and penetrating, his face kind, like that of a wise and loving grandfather. On his head is a *kipah*, or skullcap, a symbol of his faith and strong convictions.

In the aftermath of his expulsion from Spain, he found refuge in Naples and later in Venice, where he spent the remaining years of his life writing and philosophizing about the Book of Kings, the Holy Scriptures, and other revered works. While his scholarly output was prodigious – in a ten-year period beginning in 1493, he wrote or completed at least nine major commentaries – he remained fixated on the plight of his people. "Is this world ruled by any moral principle?" he wondered. "Is there reward for virtue, punishment for evil? Is there, indeed, a God in this world? And if God does govern the world, why does He not manifest His powers?" In many ways, Abravanel was a tortured soul. He searched continuously for life's inner meaning, for its purpose and significance. Clearly, he had been profoundly affected by recent events. Far from being a man of the Renaissance, Abravanel was, as Benzion Netanyahu, his biographer, pointed out many years ago, a product of the Middle Ages. A fatalist, he believed to the day he died that God directed man's existence, that everything was pre-ordained, and that human life was "a failure, dismal and hopeless, which can be rectified only by God." It was such a negative view of the world that prompted Abravanel's strong belief that the Messiah's arrival was imminent and that the day of redemption and salvation was at hand. Soon, the Jews would rise up again and rejoice.

That Abravanel could be tormented by feelings of despair and pessimism, yet remain confident that good would ultimately triumph over evil, was due to his family's illustrious history and his own life experiences as a prominent Jew. Indeed, Abravanel's story, with its moments of success and failure, feats of genius and intrigues, mirrors the complex and often tumultuous history of the Jews of the Iberian Peninsula.

He was born in Lisbon, Portugal in 1437, but Abravanel's roots lay to the east, in Seville, the capital and heart of Andalusia.* Historical documents place his esteemed ancestors there in the latter part of the thirteenth century, already occupying positions of power and influence. According to current family folklore, the first Abravanels made their way to the Iberian Peninsula from Palestine after the destruction of the First Temple. And like most members

---

* The family's name is apparently a diminutive of Abravan, a form of Abraham not unusual in Spain, where the "h" sound was commonly rendered by "f" or "v."

of Spain's one-time Jewish aristocracy (or perhaps bourgeoisie would be a more accurate description) – those who ruled the Jewish councils, or *aljamas*, in the twelfth and thirteen centuries – the Abravanels claimed descent from the house of King David. Such a distinction, whether true or not, conferred upon the Abravanels a distinguished and influential status within their synagogues and communities. Wealth and piety often went hand in hand in medieval Spain, and Davidic descent was a symbol of honour, scholarship, religious supremacy, financial success, and leadership. It also instilled in Isaac Abravanel a "sense of historic mission" that imbued and inspired his writings.

Like the history of Spain itself, the saga of Seville is a chronicle of bloody conquest, the bitter clash of religions, and the ruthless manipulations of feudal barons and knights. The Romans were first, followed by the Vandals and Visigoths, and then the Muslims, or Moors, came in 712. They ruled the city and the region for the next five hundred years.

In 1248, King Ferdinand III of Castile finally reclaimed Seville for Christianity, a pivotal moment of the long *Reconquista*. He made the city his new capital, the Almohad mosque his cathedral, and the Alcázar, the Moors' palace, his new residence. Today, that Moorish heritage is still evident in buildings throughout the city, though once you enter into the Alcázar and the nearby Gothic cathedral – the third-largest in Europe – Seville's Christian past is overwhelming. Ferdinand's capture of Seville – preceded by victories at Cordoba in 1236 and Valencia in 1238 – would be hailed throughout the Christian world as a divine triumph, to be eclipsed only by the conquest of Granada more than two centuries later. For the moment, however, the Spanish presence in Seville symbolized the rising power of Castile and its neighbouring rival, the kingdom of Aragon.

Yet Seville's location in the south, so close to the last remaining Spanish stronghold of Muslim rule, also meant that competing religious tensions ran high in the city. And, as will be seen, the Jews were often caught in the middle. "It was Seville that gave the signal, in 1378, for a nation-wide campaign of persecution of the Jews,"

writes historian Benzion Netanyahu. "It was Seville that initiated
anti-Jewish massacres which swept the peninsula in 1391. And
it was in Seville that the Inquisition opened its first tribunals
in 1481."

There were Jews living in Seville certainly as early as 800 and
likely much earlier than that. Jews probably migrated to what would
become Castile from Palestine in 70 C.E. following the destruction
of the Second Temple. In the south of Spain, where Jewish populations tended to be larger, life, then and later, was dependent upon
the whim of the ruler. During the reign of the Visigoths, King
Sisebut decreed in 613 that all Jews in his realm either had to leave
or convert to Christianity. It was an ominous sign of events on the
horizon. While at least ninety thousand Jews were forced to convert
under Sisebut's harsh law, many did so merely to save their lives.
Under threat of severe punishment, they continued to practise their
Judaism, but in secret. Thus began the controversial saga of the *conversos*, crypto-Jews who were destined to become the focus of the
religious upheavals that engulfed medieval Spain.

Other Jews beyond Sisebut's immediate control learned to adapt
and survive under the Visigoths, Muslims, and finally the Christians.
When rigid orthodox Muslim rule pushed thousands from Granada
in 1066, they moved north, establishing vibrant Jewish areas in
Toledo, Seville, Cordoba, and Barcelona. They brought with them
a more modern intellectual tradition – a combination of Torah,
Greek wisdom, and poetry that had a profound impact on the communities in which they settled.

In Seville, these Jews settled in the Judería, the city's Jewish
quarter, still called that to this day despite the absence of a Jewish population in the city for more than five hundred years. At first, the
segregation was voluntary; unlike in other parts of Europe, where
Jews were legally separated from Christian society, the choice of
living together in one area close to the synagogues and other community institutions was mainly their own. In years to come, however,
Jews in Seville and other cities in Castile and Aragon would be
forced to reside in or near the Juderías, most of which by then had

walls and gates that were locked at night for the Jews' own protection. Located in the centre of Seville, in the shadow of the Cathedral and the Alcázar, the Judería eventually became a crowded and over-populated neighbourhood with little room for expansion. The small winding streets spanned by arches were narrow, the houses built close together.

Centuries later, little has changed, except now the Judería is a trendy tourist area with quaint shops, sidewalk cafés, and noisy bars serving tapas. And long ago the three synagogues in the neighbourhood (which originally had been mosques) were converted into Catholic churches brimming with gold and silver.

By the late fourteenth century, the Judería had a Jewish population of perhaps six thousand families, or approximately twenty-five to thirty thousand people.* Culturally, the Jewish community was as rich and diverse as any in Spain, although in many ways their lives were not much different than those of Jews in any other age. Their days were spent as merchants and artisans, tending their orchards and vineyards and caring for their families. Young and old scholars alike studied Arabic, Latin, and Hebrew. They wrote lyrical poetry in the tradition of Solomon ibn Gabriol and Judah Ha-Levi, two of the literary giants of the so-called "Golden Age" of Sephardi Jews.

These various activities were halted each Friday morning in preparation for the Sabbath eve. Bed linens were changed, houses were cleaned, oil lamps were filled, and wicks cut. Sephardi mothers, wives, and daughters prepared special food for dinner – stuffed partridge or roasted chicken with rice and eggplant – and

---

* Jewish population figures for medieval Spain are a matter of great contention among historians. While Abraham Neuman and Benzion Netanyahu, for example, put the population of Seville in 1391 at more than twenty-five thousand people, Norman Roth at the University of Wisconsin maintains that it was much less. He uses a figure of about two thousand. Angus MacKay, a historian from the University of Edinburgh, "cautiously estimates" that the total Jewish population in the various kingdoms of Spain at the start of the thirteenth century was one hundred thousand, which represented about 2 per cent of the total population. Thus a figure of thirty thousand for Seville in 1391 may indeed be too high, particularly when the high rate of death from the Black Plague is accounted for.

for the following day, a mixture of meatballs and vegetables were left simmering in a clay pot on the fire. Influenced by the cuisine of the Muslim and Mediterranean world, these dishes were enhanced by an array of herbs and spices – cumin, coriander, saffron, turmeric, and cinnamon, to name only a few favourites. Once the men returned from a day of work at the market or court, the family would attend synagogue services and then recite the traditional blessings over bread and wine before sitting down to a Sabbath dinner. More often than not, friends and relatives were invited to share in the celebrations and prayers. Invariably, once dinner had concluded, the more learned men would discuss the great religious questions of the day.

In the early part of the thirteenth century a heated debate had erupted throughout the Jewish world, a conflict of faith versus reason, of tradition versus rationalism. It was a fight that mirrored a similar one then being waged among Christian theologians who felt threatened by the writings of the Greek philosopher Aristotle and of Averroës, the visionary of the Muslim world who lived in the late 1100s.

At issue among Jews in Seville and elsewhere, was the work of Moses ben Maimon or Maimonides (1135–1204), a scholar, physician, and philosopher, revered as "the greatest son of Sepharad." He is remembered today by a charming bronze statue of him erected in 1964. It sits quietly in an unobtrusive square, off a narrow walkway in Cordoba's former Jewish neighbourhood and close to the spot where he once lived. Known far and wide as the Rambam, Maimonides, a man of tremendous vision and wisdom, was the author of the *Mishneh Torah*, fourteen enduring Hebrew volumes that codified Jewish law. But in other works, including the *Moreh Nebukhim,* or *Guide for the Perplexed*, which he finished late in his life, Maimonides also sought to introduce rationalism into the study of Torah. Later generations would argue for decades about Maimonides's interpretation of the Holy Scriptures, a battle in which rationalism ultimately prevailed, though not before Jewish communities in Spain and across Europe were nearly torn apart.

Looking back, the most symbolic event of the Maimonides controversy was not the anger it engendered among the sages of the Jewish community, but the reaction of the Christian community. In the heat of the moment, the traditionalists who blamed Maimonides, rightly or wrongly, for the increasing secularization and assimilation of Jews into the larger Christian society, had become frustrated with the rationalists' tactics. They decided to seek the intervention of Christian religious authorities to help solve the dispute, denouncing Maimonides as a threat to both Christians and Jews. The Dominican friars, dedicated to preserving and spreading the word of Christ, immediately agreed. Their solution was certainly not what the rabbis had in mind. In 1233, they decreed that Maimonides' *Guide for the Perplexed* was a work of heresy and burned it. A decade later, by order of the pope, the Talmud received the same treatment and was burned in public ceremonies at Montpellier and Paris.

A century of religious dispute thus may have kept Jewish leaders in Castile and Aragon preoccupied, but it did not alter two fundamental facts of Jewish life in medieval Spain. First, that despite the bans against secularism, the traditionalists were losing the fight. Change, assimilation, even conversion to Christianity became a reality of life in Jewish communities as the fourteenth century progressed; science and philosophy continued to be studied by Jewish youth no matter what the religious elders decreed. And second, and more significantly, the real power exercised by the financiers, politicians, rabbis, judges, and scholars who dominated the Jewish councils flowed from the king, whom they served. As the pioneering scholar of Spanish Jews, Isaac Baer, put it, the Sephardim were nothing less than "the personal property of the King." This was the reality of Jewish life that could not be ignored or debated.

As long as the king remained popular, feared, and able to rule without being too dependent on the Christian nobility for military support, the Jews were protected and tolerated and the power of the Jewish councils was secure. The king depended on the Jews' services as tax collectors, managers of Crown estates, and taxpayers. But in an era of shifting loyalties, fragile alliances, and repressive taxes, the Jews were playing a dangerous game. Few rulers, no matter how powerful or popular, did not at one time or another raise the ire of their subjects. Rebellion, no matter how difficult, was always a possibility. Deals had to be made and new alliances forged. Though the kings greatly valued the revenue raised by their Jewish subjects, there were often more pressing considerations as well. In 1283, for example, Christian noblemen in Aragon demanded that in exchange for their much-needed military aid in a war with France, Pedro III dismiss all Jews from public service. While Pedro and his successor, Alfonso III, resisted such a drastic move, they did limit the power of Jews enough to placate the nobility and their influence at the Spanish court began gradually to decline.

In the towns and villages, the Jews' reputation fared no better. They were the "strangers" who collected taxes, threatened the Church, and symbolized the Devil. Jews were demonized in the popular medieval imagination as perpetrators of blood rituals. During the era of the Black Death in the late 1340s, the falsehood was spread that they had poisoned the wells using concoctions made from "lizards and basilisks." It made no difference that Jews, too, died by the hundreds from the plague. In short, the Jews of Spain were scapegoats, manipulated by the kings to do their bidding, resented by the nobility, and eventually vilified by the commoners.

Contrary to popular belief, not all Jews in Spain (or throughout Europe, for that matter) were moneylenders, but many did willingly perform this essential economic function. The demand for credit by farmers, artisans, and smaller merchants was great. There was a constant need to expand businesses and landholdings in addition to keeping up with aggressive competitors, especially in the cities. As the Church (at least until the early fifteenth century) successfully prohibited Christians from lending money with interest attached, and few, if any, Christians were prepared to loan large sums of money for no return, there was no other choice for Christian merchants and artisans but to turn to their Jewish associates for financial assistance. It was equally true that before the royal court of Alfonso X of Castile intervened in the mid-1200s and set interest rates at about 20 per cent, some, but not all, Jewish moneylenders charged their Christian clients exorbitant sums – perhaps as high as 60 to 70 per cent. Certainly, this contributed to the gradually deteriorating relations between Jews and the rest of the Spanish population.

There was even more money to be made from tax farming. From the king's point of view, it made perfect sense to have Jewish financiers function as their private tax collectors. Why create and operate an expensive bureaucracy when the Jews could conduct the job more efficiently? Hence, "no financial arrangement," according to Netanyahu, "was guarded by [the kings] more jealously than the collection of their revenues by Jewish tax farmers." It was precisely for this reason that until the early 1400s, the Chief Treasurer of the Realm, the person who supervised the tax collection system, "was almost invariably a Jew."

For their part, the Jews regarded tax farming as a financial opportunity not to be missed. The high profits they made derived from the difference between the amount they advanced the king and the total amount they were able to collect. (Tax farmers also collected tolls on highways, custom duties at ports, and "charges . . . laid upon the cattle as they were herded seasonally to the pasture lands.")

In their approach to this enterprise, however, Jews miscalculated. Despite the protection afforded to them by the king, acting as the chief tax gatherers set them against the vast majority of the Christian population. Even when Christian leaders and merchants protested, the kings refused to listen and ensured that the Jews went about their business.

Among that select group of resourceful Jewish tax officials was Judah Abravanel, Isaac's ancestor (and possibly his great-grandfather).

Born in Cordoba in the mid-thirteenth century, he at some point made his way to nearby Seville. By then, he was collecting taxes for the Castillian King Sancho IV. When Sancho died suddenly in 1295 at the age of twenty-six, his infant son Ferdinand IV inherited the crown. In time, Judah Abravanel became Ferdinand's chief tax administrator. His contacts and resources proved invaluable; in 1310, Judah and a group of wealthy Jews helped finance the siege of Algeciras on the southern tip of Andalusia.

Isaac Abravanel's grandfather, Samuel Abravanel, was a prominent financier and diplomat as well. As a leader of the Seville *aljama* he had a well-deserved reputation, in the words of one contemporary chronicler, for being intelligent, a man who "loved wise men" and "was eager to study whenever the stress of time permitted." His various talents did not escape the notice of the royal court. Enrique II appointed him the chief tax official of Castile in 1379, the final year of his reign. It was the beginning of a long career for Samuel in the service of the king and his successors.

But Samuel was living in tense times. More than two decades had passed since the bubonic plague had ravaged Europe. Yet in some quarters Jews were still blamed for the multitude of deaths. Their position in Castillian society was often precarious. Both Christian religious zeal and economic realities contributed to this grave situation. More than ever before, Jews, rich and poor, were coming under the scrutiny of Dominican friars and other Church officials constantly on the lookout for heretics. Like the dreaded Spanish Inquisition that was to terrorize the country during the next century, harsh judgements against Jews, often based on hearsay and unproven allegations, became all too frequent. In one infamous case, a Jewish courtier from Barcelona, Astrug de Piera, was sentenced to life in prison. His crime: he had been accused – with no hard evidence – of "conjuring up demons and eliciting replies from them." Petitions against Jews owning land were brought before the court as early as 1293, while violent attacks on Jews occurred in Seville in 1354 and in Toledo a year later. The violence in Seville was set off by accusations that Jews were guilty of desecrating the host.

At one time, the most important Jew in Castile was Don Samuel Ha-Levi, who served as the Chief Treasurer of the Realm during the reign of Pedro I (1350–66). A creative tax collector, Ha-Levi oversaw the construction of a lavish synagogue in Toledo as well as negotiated trade treaties with Portugal. Ha-Levi, however, had enemies who resented his vast wealth and influence. In 1360, several Jews in Toledo accused him, so the story goes, of cheating the king. After he refused Pedro's request for a large loan, which the king desperately needed to carry on his war of attrition against Aragon, he was arrested and charged with embezzlement. The evidence against him was likely forged. Nevertheless, while incarcerated in a prison in Seville, he was tortured and died a painful death.

The demise of Don Samuel Ha-Levi showed how dangerous it was becoming for Sephardi Jews. All that was required was for someone or something to harness this growing hostility and turn it ugly.

Death or Conversion

THE MAN WHO ALTERED THE LIFE of Samuel Abravanel and Jews throughout Spain was a lowly Franciscan prelate named Ferrant Martínez. A religious zealot, Martínez was a superb orator and a man with an "iron will and unwavering determination." He was also steadfast in his hatred for Jews. Beginning in 1378, Martínez embarked on a vicious anti-Jewish campaign. Despite repeated warnings and condemnations from Castillian rulers, who repudiated both the threats and the disorder that any violent outbreaks would bring, Martínez was unrelenting in his efforts. Whenever and wherever possible, he preached that Jews should leave Spain. By 1383, he was telling his followers that the Spanish monarchs would be "pleased" if Jews were attacked. No such royal declaration had been issued, but the anti-Jewish fervour continued to grow nonetheless.

Jewish leaders in Seville protested Martínez's actions and delivered petitions to the court denouncing his activities. They were generally met with a sympathetic ear, but Martínez remained a difficult opponent to control. Moreover, the death of King Juan I in 1389 and the accession to the Castillian throne of his young son Enrique ultimately left power in the hands of a weak and feuding regency. Martínez was able to take advantage of this opportunity. In December 1390, he issued orders to the clergy in his diocese that synagogues in their areas were to be destroyed. This was the tragic fate of synagogues in Écija and Alcalá de Guadaira.

It was only a matter of time before Martínez and his growing band of supporters triggered an all-out assault. The attack in Seville began in the early hours of June 4, 1391. Hundreds of Jews were murdered in their homes and many more in the streets. Women and children were captured and sold into slavery. The Seville Judería was destroyed and, according to one observer, resembled a wasteland. Some of the city's Jews were able to flee the country, yet many, perhaps a majority, opted to convert to Christianity to escape a certain death.*

With Jewish blood on their hands, the mob moved from one city and town to the next, slaughtering Jews as they went. In Cordoba, near the breathtaking stone-fortress-like Mezquita, or Great Mosque, with its Moorish marble pillars and arches, two thousand corpses lay scattered in the Jewish quarter. As in Seville, in the same narrow streets where Jews were murdered, crowds of tourists now roam through the white-walled Cordoba Judería, oblivious to the quarter's bloody history. Only the ruin of "La Sinagoga" – a thirteenth-century house of worship where, amidst the Moorish brick floor and white tiles, time seems to stand still – is a reminder of the Judería's true past.

---

* It is not clear how many chose this option, since, as noted earlier, historians dispute the exact Jewish population figures in Seville and throughout Spain during this era. The total Jewish population was said to be approximately three hundred thousand, though the number of converts undoubtedly reached into the thousands. Archival records do indicate that Spanish Jews willingly and voluntarily converted to Christianity centuries before the violence of 1391, yet not in such large numbers.

Farther north in Toledo, on June 20, 1391, Jews were burned alive and drowned in the Tagus river. As in other Spanish cities and towns, hundreds converted to Christianity to save themselves. By then the message to the Jews of Spain was clear: either they were to save themselves by accepting the sacred teachings of Jesus Christ or they were to die.

The rioters reached Valencia in the southern tip of Aragon by early July. King Juan I, who had inherited the throne of Aragon four years earlier from his father, Pedro IV, was older and more intelligent than his Castilian counterpart, but he was also more interested in music, poetry, and hunting than he was in the affairs of state. Far and wide he was known as *el Indolente*, "the Idle One." His efforts to stop the riots were to no avail. Without a doubt, community officials in Valencia were more fearful of the Castilian-led mob than they were of their own monarch.

Behind the gates of the Valencia Judería (known in Catalan as the *call*), the Jews were ready for their attackers. In the ensuing fight, several Christians were killed and captured. Yet this victory was temporary. The Jewish resistance only encouraged more attacks from a larger and more hostile mob. By the time it ended, death and destruction engulfed the city. Approximately seven thousand Jews saved themselves by declaring their belief in Jesus Christ.

The Jews in Barcelona confronted the rioters on August 5, the day of the Sabbath. As the Jewish quarter was assaulted, many residents sought refuge in the city's New Castle, a nearby fortress. The rioters, joined by the local townspeople and peasants, wasted no time in burning the *escribanías*, the notarial archives where records of debts owed by Christians to Barcelona Jews were stored. Here may have been the real motive behind much of the Christian zealotry, fuelled by religious propaganda.

Local authorities intervened and arrested many of the ring-leaders, but the mob could not be stopped. Angered by the action taken against their friends, the rioters stormed the jail and freed them. Then, on August 8, they turned on the Jews in the New Castle. Those inside who refused to be baptized – a minority of about four hundred people – were slaughtered and "their corpses, stretched in the streets and the squares, offered a horrendous spectacle."[*]

Back in Seville, among those who chose conversion over death was Samuel Abravanel. Overnight, he became a prominent member of the new *converso* community and took the name Juan Sánchez de Sevilla.

What are we to make of Samuel Abravanel and the thousands of other Jews who opted for Christianity in order to save themselves? One hundred thousand Jews converted, perhaps a third of the total Spanish Jewish population. Why? Clearly, many like Samuel converted to escape death and perhaps retain their wealth and status. Some were undoubtedly *marranos*, or "crypto-Jews": publicly, they were declared New Christians or "conversos," but in private, they continued to practise their Judaism and, like Samuel, contemplated returning to their own faith when it was safe.

Nevertheless, the extent of the conversions was astonishing. Some observers, such as Solomon Alami, an eyewitness to the catastrophe of 1391, maintained that the religious transformation was due to the inner turmoil then being experienced by Jewish communities in Spain.

"If we ask ourselves why all this happened to us," explains Alami, "then we have to accept the truth: we ourselves at are fault. . . . We and our iniquities caused this evil to happen. Our sages were jealous of each other and disrespectful . . . there was much quarrelling among the wise men. . . . The next in line of decadence were the leaders of the communities and those favoured and trusted by the kings. Their riches and their high position made them forsake humility. . . .

---

[*] In mid-June of 1391, Enrique III of Castile ordered further violence against Jews stopped. "The Jews who used to live in [Seville and Cordoba] have been driven out, about which I am very angry, because this does me a great disservice," he wrote in a letter to the Burgos city council. "And I with my Council have ordered [a commission] to be sent . . . to investigate this event and by which person or persons it was started, and to do such great justice with them, and punish them so severely, that . . . no-one [else] may have such wicked and ugly temerity as to go out against these Jews." Several of the ringleaders involved in the riots in Seville and Cordoba were later hanged.

They acquired costly wagons and horses, dressed in precious garments. . . . They gave up study and industry and cultivated idleness, vainglory, and inordinate ambition. . . . Everyone chased after coveted positions; envy estranged a man from his fellow and they didn't mind denouncing one another before the Court. . . ."

Had Jews like Samuel Abravanel become too materialistic? Were they a little too willing to renounce their true faith? The answers to such questions can only be speculated upon.

This much can be said: the riots of 1391 and the *conversos* they gave birth to not only became a significant segment of the Spanish population, but equally set in motion events that would have historic ramifications for the Abravanel family and for thousands of other Sephardi Jews for generations to come.

During the next decade, Samuel, then probably more than sixty years old, lived publicly as Juan Sánchez, serving the royal court, attending church, and living life as a Christian nobleman. And yet he was struggling with his new identity. Finally, near the end of the fourteenth century, after he had liquidated most of his assets, he fled with his wife and several of his sons, including young Judah, the father of Isaac Abravanel, to Portugal. Given his position at the Court, such an escape was dangerous, but he must have been driven by a deep religious conviction to have undertaken such a bold action.

In fact, at that moment Portugal was possibly the only place in Europe where *conversos* wishing to return to Judaism were more or less permitted to do so. Church officials were shocked. Yet King João I, in dire need of revenue, was willing to allow Jews into the country to boost his finances, even if it did anger the members of his clergy. In this way, Juan Sánchez de Sevilla ceased to exist and Samuel Abravanel's life as a Jew was resurrected.

Wealth and Honour

BY THE TIME ISAAC ABRAVANEL WAS BORN in Lisbon in 1437, his father, Don Judah, was in the service of the royal court of Portugal.

He was among the few Jews in the kingdom exempted from wearing a red badge in the shape of a Star of David on his clothes. Later, Isaac, too, was freed from displaying this humiliating symbol.

Judah was especially close to Don Fernando, the king's youngest brother, and advised him on many financial matters. In the summer of 1437, prior to his departure to fight the Muslims in Tangiers, part of Portugal's ongoing attempt to conquer and absorb vast territories in North Africa, Fernando settled his will. This turned out to be a wise decision, since he never returned to his home country. Captured by the Muslim leader Salah ibn Salah, Fernando withered away in a prison when plans to ransom him fell apart. He died in 1443. In his will he ensured that Don Judah Abravanel was properly compensated with a repayment on a loan of 97,100 reals – a considerable sum of money. It was for this reason that Isaac Abravanel reflected many years later that he had been "brought up from childhood in wealth and honour."

The treatment and position of Jews in Portugal had been slightly better than in neighbouring Castile. During the long reign of João I, Jews were more or less protected. But when João died in 1433, his eldest son, Duarte, decided to appease the nobility whom his father had alienated. Many members of the Portuguese nobility resented the privileges and power, whether real or imagined, possessed by the country's Jews. Soon, curfews were instituted, and any Jew found outside the Judería after sunset was severely punished.

Duarte succumbed to the plague in 1438 and was succeeded by his young son Alfonso V. Until Alfonso reached adulthood, however, Duarte's brother Pedro set policy and controlled the court. He, too, wanted to appease the nobility, and anti-Jewish restrictions remained the law, though not consistently enforced. Jews like Don Judah Abravanel continued to wield a certain degree of power and influence, aggravating some Portuguese Christians. "We saw Jews made knights, mounted on richly caparisoned horses and mules, and clothed in fine gowns and hoods . . . so that it is impossible to know what race they belong to," stated one petition submitted to local authorities in Lisbon. "It is a travesty that Spanish Jews, having been driven from their own country on account of perverse heresies, find welcome and protection in this kingdom."

Such anti-Jewish feelings occasionally boiled over. In 1449,
when Isaac Abravanel was only twelve years old, Jews were violently attacked in Lisbon. More than two hundred people died, and
much property in the Judería was vandalized or destroyed. As
young King Alfonso matured, he was more inclined to follow his
grandfather's protective policies, which he believed was more
advantageous for the Portuguese economy. Most members of the
nobility disagreed, but not all. Don Judah, for example, established
a close friendship with the Duke of Braganza, the head of a powerful and wealthy aristocratic family whose members were related
to the king. These connections would prove crucial as well as critical in Isaac Abravanel's life.

As the son of a courtier, Isaac received the best of everything,
including a fine Renaissance education. At a young age, he was
immersed in the Roman classics and Christian theology. He mastered Latin, Portuguese, and Castilian, in addition to being a
Hebrew scholar. Indeed, his parents ensured that Isaac's Jewish
identity and knowledge of his people was strong; he studied Talmud
and explored the mystical kabbalah.

In the late 1450s, Isaac married, and he and his wife (whose
name is not known) had at least three sons and two daughters. The
eldest son, Judah, was born in Lisbon in 1460 and would become a
celebrated physician and writer in Italy. Joseph, who also chose
medicine as a career, followed in 1471. Samuel was born in 1473.
Samuel's wife, Benvenida, would become famous for her tireless
efforts on behalf of Jews in Naples and Ferrara. Abravanel's daughters' names are unknown, although one of them married her first
cousin Joseph (Samuel's son), who worked closely with his father-
in-law (and uncle).

By the time he was nearly thirty, Isaac's passion for writing and
philosophy bore fruit in one of his first of numerous published
works. Written in Hebrew, it was a small booklet entitled *Ateret
Zekenim*, or the *Crown of Elders*, which probed the meaning of God

as evident in the Books of the Prophets. In this brief dissertation can be found the major themes of his later writings: his fascination with the prophets and the kabbalah, and his critical view of such philosophers as Aristotle and Averroës. For the moment, he could not bring himself to condemn Maimonides for his promotion of rationalism in interpreting the scriptures, yet in time that would come as well.

As his father became older, Isaac assumed more direct control over the family's vast business of tax farming and banking and their trade in cloth with Flanders. These various enterprises required more of Isaac's time, and his scholarly pursuits – he had begun a commentary on Deuteronomy – were put on hold. By the early 1470s, Isaac Abravanel was recognized as one of the leaders of the Portuguese Jewish community. (Though Abravanel owned several houses in the Lisbon Judería, as of 1472 the king had rewarded him with a letter of privilege "authorizing him to live in any part of the city, and allowing him to enjoy all the honours and liberties enjoyed by the Christians.") His reputation as a caring man was further enhanced in 1471, when he represented and helped finance the freedom of 250 North African Jews captured and enslaved by Portugal following the conquest of a fortress at Arzila (in Morocco). It took him six months of travel and negotiations with the slave owners and required more than ten thousand gold doubloons to purchase the Jewish slaves, but he persevered and was successful. Admittedly on this issue, Abravanel had some curious double standards, as it is likely that he, like other Jews of the era, kept black slaves. In 1472 Abravanel's wife sent a black female slave as a gift to the wife of Yehiel of Pisa.

His rise at the royal court coincided with a futile attempt by Alfonso V to take over Castile in 1475, an effort that marked the beginning of a four-year war of attrition with the newly crowned Queen Isabel and her husband, Ferdinand, soon-to-be king of Aragon. Over the years, Alfonso had proved himself willing to protect his Jewish subjects' rights as well as utilize the funds and resources that courtiers like Abravanel raised for him. Such resources were, of course, especially valuable in times of war. Isaac's power at court was linked as well to his close relationship with the Braganza family, especially Ferdinand II, who became duke in 1478. For his work on their behalf, the Braganzas rewarded Abravanel with huge tracts of property and lots of money. Consider, for example, that in 1480, when a group of Christians and Jews loaned the Crown twelve million reals to pay for war debts, Abravanel covered more than 10 per cent of this amount himself.

The death of Alfonso V in 1481 at the age of forty-nine from the plague triggered a series of events that changed Abravanel's life. João II succeeded his father to the Portuguese throne and immediately began to assert his authority. Wishing to establish a more amicable relationship with the lesser nobility, he summoned the Cortes, the Portuguese assembly. But he also decided that the Braganza family – who controlled more than fifty cities and could raise an army of three thousand horsemen and ten thousand foot soldiers – had become too powerful. This included the current duke of Braganza, Ferdinand II, who was João II's brother-in-law, the husband of his sister.

First, the king went after two of the duke's three brothers. Then, when he learned that the Braganzas were corresponding with Ferdinand of Aragon in an attempt to forge an alliance and mount an uprising, he had the duke arrested on May 29, 1483. The duke was charged with treason, and a year later publicly beheaded in the main square of the city of Evora. The duke's brother, the duke of Viseu, was murdered in 1485 by King João II himself.

In the spring of 1483, Isaac Abravanel, due to his connections with the Braganzas, now became embroiled in the intrigues and conspiracies that had engulfed the royal court. It is doubtful that Abravanel was directly involved in any planned uprising – he himself proclaimed his innocence – yet the king suspected him nonetheless. Already, Abravanel had seen his power and privileges, and those of other Jewish courtiers, dwindle under João II. And it distressed him that Jews throughout Portugal were once again placed in such a precarious situation.

"What man, subjected throughout his life to the fear of enemies and the strains of distress, would grieve when his last hour arrives?" he had written to a friend in Pisa in October 1482. "It is all the more so with the noble sons of Zion, who repeatedly witness how, with the rise of evil, their honour is besmirched and their name disgraced. How can they attach any value to their life of sorrow and not rejoice over the prospect of the grave? Weep not for the dying among Israel and do not bemoan them! Weep for those who are cast from one misfortune to another, and for whom God has blocked all avenues of relief."

Still, months later Abravanel was not prepared to give up his life. The day after the duke of Braganza was arrested, Abravanel was ordered to appear at the royal court in Lisbon. On the journey there, he learned of the duke's fate and quickly determined that his life was in danger. Without much planning, he fled across the border into Castile on the night of May 31, eluding the King's agents and soldiers, who had orders to apprehend him.

For several months, he remained in the small town of Segura de la Orden, not far from Plasencia. He was able to get word to his sons, who began to liquidate the family's assets, though the king soon seized Abravanel's property. In a letter to the king, Abravanel proclaimed that he was innocent of the charges of treason and that he was not part of any conspiracy. For whatever reason, the king believed him and permitted his family to depart, taking some of their money with them. Yet within two years the royal court issued death sentences on Abravanel and his son-in-law (and nephew) Joseph, who had escaped in 1484. On flimsy evidence, they were now accused of raising funds to be used in a full-scale rebellion. There was no going back to Portugal now.

For nearly a year, Abravanel occupied himself by working on his writing and completing his commentaries on the Prophets. Then one day, in early March 1484, he was informed that he had been granted an audience with Queen Isabel and King Ferdinand. This was a meeting that would alter Abravanel's life once more and place him at the centre of the great Jewish tragedy of the age: the expulsion from Spain.

Jews and *Conversos*

MUCH HAD CHANGED FOR JEWS IN SPAIN since Isaac Abravanel's grandfather Samuel had fled Castile for Portugal, about eighty years before. In some ways, Jewish life had been altered forever by the riots of 1391. In Toledo, Seville, and Cordoba, among other cities and towns, Jews had attempted to rebuild homes, synagogues, and shops that had been devastated in the onslaught. In Barcelona, on the other hand, there was no hope. The city's ancient Jewish community had been wiped away. The surviving Jews there had either fled or, in the case of many wealthier members of the Judería, converted to Christianity. Indeed, Barcelona had become almost overnight a city of *conversos*. Soon, many of the former Jews, who had retained their property and riches, again occupied the upper echelons of the Aragon royal court, causing deep resentment among the old Christian establishment, whose members still regarded them as Jews and heretics no matter what their baptismal certificates said.

In truth, the pressure for Jews to convert to Christianity had never really subsided. Leading the renewed campaign was a sixty-year-old Dominican friar named Vincente Ferrer, a follower of Pope Benedict XIII, the so-called antipope based in Avignon during the Great Schism that split the Roman Catholic Church between 1378 and 1417. Ferrer was as dedicated to the cause as Ferrant Martínez had been in 1391, but acted with more intelligence and restraint. He did not promote violence against Jews. Instead, he believed that the power of his sermons would put the fear of God into them and convince them to choose the path toward purity and salvation. To have real meaning, the conversion had to be voluntary rather than forced, but that did not stop him from forcing Jews to listen to his message, often in their own synagogues, as he made his way across Castile and Aragon.

Confronting the Jews as well were powerful new Christians like Solomon Ha-Levi, a former rabbinical scholar in Burgos. He had converted with most members of this family just before the 1391 riots. Baptized as Pablo de Santa María, he embraced his new religion with zeal matched by few other *conversos*. Guided by Pope Benedict (still then Cardinal Pedro de Luna y Gotor), Ha-Levi not only rose up the ranks of the Christian church to become bishop of Burgos, but was also soon renowned throughout the Catholic world for his passionate anti-Jewish convictions. Other *conversos*, too, feeling the need to prove their devotion to their new faith, often went out of their way to denounce their former friends and neighbours.

It is not easy to generalize about *converso* behaviour. Some forced converts did not completely relinquish their links to the Jewish community, no matter how dangerous. They were truly *marranos*, or crypto-Jews, who attempted to forge a new life and identity against tremendous odds. Returning to Judaism was not out of the question. But those who did were likely a minority. Most *conversos* were content to accept Christianity, assimilate into their new environment, and use their status as new Christians to reclaim their wealth and status. And for a time they succeeded brilliantly, until the Inquisition and other fierce opponents sought to destroy them.

For a zealot like Vincente Ferrer, there was only one possible answer to the Jewish question in Spain: Jews who refused to succumb to his proselytizing efforts had to be separated and segregated from the rest of the population. In his view, the threat they now posed to the public order and to religious stability had become too great. In 1412, supported by the bishop of Burgos, Ferrer convinced Queen Catalina of Castile and her young son, King Juan II (Isabel's father), to pass a long list of repressive anti-Jewish laws (the laws were also aimed at the Moors). Within a few years – following the death of the Martin I in 1410 and the succession to the Aragon throne of the more impressionable Ferdinand I – the kingdom of Aragon largely adopted these measures as well.

By these decrees, Jews were barred from being merchants and traders, banished to walled sections of the city, expelled from public service and administration, and prohibited from dealing with Christians on any type of economic or social level. To set them apart further, Jewish men were ordered not to shave or cut their hair. Disobeying this last rule resulted in a hefty fine and a punishment of one hundred lashes.

In short, the purpose of this legal onslaught was not just economic oppression, but was aimed at severing all contact between Jews and Christians. And what better way to make Christianity more appealing than to make being a Jew almost impossible?

The immediate consequences of the new laws were devastating. "Inmates of palaces were driven into wretched nooks, and dark and lowly huts. Instead of rustling apparel we were obliged to wear miserable clothes, which drew contempt upon us," one Jew who survived the experience later remembered. "Starvation stared everyone in the face. Children died on their mother's knees from hunger and exposure."

Even when this latest attack resulted in more conversions to Christianity, Pope Benedict XIII and his followers were not done with the Jews. In February 1413, the pope convened a special disputation in Tortosa, a small city north of Valencia. Jews throughout Aragon were ordered to send their best scholars to debate the legitimacy of Christianity and Christian beliefs as foretold in the Jewish Scriptures. At this gathering, even more so than at previous ones, the term "disputation" was largely a misnomer, as Israeli historian Ora Limor has observed. The disputation at Tortosa was "not designed to present a balanced, fair confrontation between two rival parties," she writes, "but to deduce Christian truth from Jewish literature – in other words, to batter the opponent with his weapons. There was only possible conclusion: the Jews had to accept Christianity."

The dozen or so Jewish leaders and rabbis faced about twenty Dominican friars led by a daunting and determined individual who until recently had spent his life studying the Talmud. Joshua Halorki of Alcañiz had been a noted physician, scholar, and rabbi. For several years he had carried on a correspondence with the bishop of Burgos in an attempt to understand why the former Solomon Ha-Levi had converted. But in June 1412, after he had heard a sermon by Vincente Ferrer, Halorki finally gave in to his inner doubts and feelings. In an instant, he became Jerónimo de Santa Fe and, like his friend Ha-Levi, quickly turned against his former co-religionists.

In a small room in the Gothic cathedral in Tortosa, with Pope Benedict XIII at his side, Halorki served his new faith very well. For almost a year, he acted as the chief "prosecutor," rebutting Jewish arguments, attempting to use the words of the Hebrew scriptures, which he knew so well, to confirm that Jesus was the true Messiah, and then exposing as he put it, the Talmud's "errors, heresy, villainy, and abuse of the Christian religion." If Jews were being collectively punished for their sins, Halorki concluded, it was because they were guilty of rejecting Jesus.

Pope Benedict was a stubborn and vengeful man. Even after Halorki had declared victory over his Jewish opponents, the pope refused to end the proceedings; more meetings were held throughout 1414 until Benedict was satisfied that he had established beyond any doubt the superiority of Christianity as the "true faith." A papal bull followed, in which, among other repressive measures, the pontiff banned the study of the Talmud and declared, like the laws issued in Castile in 1412, that all economic and social contact between Jews and Christians should cease.

Throughout the period of the disputation, anti-Jewish feelings intensified as local prelates spread the news of the Christian victory and Jews were periodically attacked in the streets. The pressure to convert was sometimes overwhelming, and it has been estimated that close to three thousand Sephardi Jews chose baptism in order to save themselves.

It would be wrong, however, to conclude that Jews suffered continual discrimination and repression during the century prior to the 1492 expulsion. Within a few years, the campaign against the one hundred thousand to one hundred and fifty thousand Jews (from a total population of about six million) who remained in their Spanish homeland and clung to their ancestral religious convictions had subsided. The reign of Pope Benedict XIII ended in 1417 with the election of Martin V, a pontiff acceptable to all of Catholic Europe and a Church leader with less doctrinaire views on the question of Jews. And in both Castile and Aragon, Juan II and Alfonso V, respectively, adopted more moderate policies towards their Jewish subjects. Life for Jews in Spain would never return to the heady days before the 1391 riots, but a degree of normalcy was possible in Christian–Jewish relations. Jewish tax collectors gathered revenue for the Crown and Jewish merchants continued to be involved in overseas trade. The Spanish monarchs even welcomed back a select number of Jewish physicians and financiers to their courts.

It was the thirty-five thousand or so *conversos* and their decisive impact on Spanish Christian society that ultimately determined the fate of Sephardi Jews. To the growing dissatisfaction of old Christians, these former Jews and their children, the majority of whom were entirely at ease with their new Christian identities, set out to reclaim what they regarded as their rightful place among the upper class. They succeeded beyond their expectations.

"As conversion increased throughout the latter half of the fourteenth and entire fifteenth centuries, Jewish power continually declined and was replaced by that of the *conversos*," concludes historian Norman Roth, who has extensively researched the history of *conversos* in Spain. "The *conversos* were able to attain not only positions in government which had been previously held by Jews – as tax officials, treasurers, etc. – but even higher posts, up to and including those of chancellors of the realm." There were, moreover, few aspects of Spanish life, from the Church to the royal court to the markets of Seville and Valencia, which *conversos* did not touch and make their own.

The first real sign of the growing resentment against the new Christians occurred in Toledo in 1449 as part of a power struggle between the ruthless Alvaro de Luna, King Juan II's chief minister, and the local nobility. When de Luna attempted to implement an unpopular tax, using his *converso* tax collectors to gather the levy, a bloody riot and rebellion ensued. Unable to attack the king or his officials directly, the unruly mob targeted the *converso* government bureaucrats, merchants, and shopkeepers living among them.

Accusations were now made that these new Christians were still practising Jewish rituals and that their commitment to Christianity was insincere. The charges were likely not true. On the contrary, the vast majority of *conversos*, suggests Benzion Netanyahu, "were certain that their own Christianity was far purer, nobler and more in accord with the letter and spirit of the teachings of Christ, of the Apostles and the Church Fathers than that upheld by their hate-filled enemies." But jealousy and fear are powerful emotions not easily dismissed. Authorities in Toledo devised a clever policy by which to segregate *conversos* as they had done the Jews.

A statute of exclusion, the Sentencia Estatuto, was instituted with a provision for *limpieza de sangre*, or "purity of blood." Here was a precursor of modern racism: because the *conversos* were born with Jewish blood running through their veins, they were considered to be "unworthy and unfit to hold any public office." As the purity-of-blood laws spread across the Spain, in defiance of papal rulings that condemned them – the Church was willing to accept the legitimacy of any official baptism – the *conversos* more and more found themselves ostracized from both Christians and Jews.

No matter how hard Jews tried to distance themselves from the new Christians, a link was being forged in the blaze of propaganda. Repeatedly, the *conversos* were accused of being "false" Christians, led astray by Jews who were evil to the core. That, at any rate, was the message spread by a popular Franciscan Friar from Aragon named Alfonso de Espina. In the early 1460s, de Espina published a book entitled *Fortalitium fidei* (*Fortress of Faith*) in which he catalogued the various sins of Jews, with graphic tales of blood rituals, well-poisoning, and devil worship. But he reserved his greatest contempt for the *conversos*, for they were guilty of attempting to subvert Christianity from within. As allegations flew, violent attacks against *coversos* became more frequent. In 1473, Cordoba was the site of an especially brutal assault in which many new Christians – men, women, and children – were slaughtered.

It was such views and actions that gave rise to the two final infamous episodes in this long and controversial struggle: the establishment of the dreaded Inquisition and the expulsion of the Jews from Spain in 1492. Both were closely connected to the marriage of Isabel of Castile and Ferdinand of Aragon in 1469, the eventual union of their kingdoms, and the completion of the *Reconquista*, the Catholic reconquest, with their victory in February 1492 over the Moors in Granada.

The Edict of Expulsion

THE CATHOLIC MONARCHS, as Ferdinand and Isabel were later known for their devotion and services to the Church, were as complex as any royal couple in European history. Ferdinand, whose maternal great-grandmother was a *converso*, has been remembered mainly for being the model upon which Niccolò Machiavelli based his book *The Prince*. It was Ferdinand's calculating mind that must have caught Machiavelli's attention, as well as his penchant for pursuing policies, often seemingly contradictory ones, that ultimately enhanced his own power. Still, it is notable that as late as 1487, Jews in Castile referred to Ferdinand as a "just and righteous" king.

Isabel, who also had *converso* ancestry through her paternal grandmother, was no less a resourceful or capable leader. She was determined to keep the public order, lessen the power of the nobility, and ensure that her kingdom's finances were sound. To this end, she did not hesitate to exploit the various talents of such Jewish courtiers as Abraham Seneor and later Don Isaac Abravanel. "All the Jews in my realm," the queen asserted in 1477, "are mine and under my care and my protection and it belongs to me to defend and aid them and keep justice."

Isabel, like her husband, was devoted to the supremacy of the Church. She, too, viewed it as an institution with religious, moral, and particularly political elements that could be cultivated and manipulated to the crown's advantage. And she was driven by a sense of urgency: rumours of "Judaizing" among *conversos* were especially disconcerting. Dealing decisively with this problem would not only stamp out heresy and renew the purity of the nation, but also go far in appeasing and winning over the anti-*converso* faction among the nobility.

It was against this background that Isabel and Ferdinand negotiated with officials in Rome in 1478 for the establishment of an Inquisition under their control. From the moment it began in Seville and then gradually expanded its investigations into all of Castile and Aragon, the Inquisitors pursued the *conversos* with a religious dedication bordering on fanaticism. In the name of doing "God's work," they left a legacy of fear, terror, and death – one which reached its shocking climax under the leadership of the infamous Dominican Tomás de Torquemada, who was appointed Grand Inquisitor by Isabel and Ferdinand in 1483.

Nothing about the Inquisition was just, and every aspect of its operation worked against the accused. Inquisition authorities relied on testimony and evidence of heresy supplied by informers who never had to face those whom they were reporting on. And in most cases, the informers were later rewarded for their actions from the victim's estate. To accuse a rival or enemy of being a crypto-Jew thus became a convenient way of eliminating him. Horrific torture was employed to win confessions that were largely meaningless. Those convicted faced a life in prison or more likely an agonizing death by burning at a public pageant called an *auto-da-fé* ("act of faith"). "There was always a possibility that the condemned would 'repent' at the very last minute," Norman Roth writes. "In this event, he or she would be spared death by the flames and given the special 'grace' (so it was called) of garrotting: death by strangulation. They were just as dead, but their souls went straight to paradise." Death sentences were always carried out by the secular authorities.

By 1490, more than two thousand *conversos* had been burned. Thousands more had died under torture or were left rotting in prison. Their property and money had been confiscated by the state to help finance the final assault against the Moors, while the lives of their surviving family members had been destroyed.

Jews had been beyond the Inquisition's mandate, but they, too, were affected. In 1480, the Cortes in Toledo passed a series of restrictive measures aimed at segregating Jews from old and new Christians. They were required to relocate to isolated areas of cities and towns. In Andalusia, Jews were expelled from Seville, Cordoba, and Cadiz, though many remained and found ways to stay until 1492.

Isabel and Ferdinand may have both regarded Jews with some disdain and apprehension, but they trusted the instincts of courtier Abraham Seneor. Seneor, who was both intelligent and loyal, had begun his distinguished career serving Enrique IV of Castile in the mid-1450s. Two decades later, he was so influential, wealthy, and well known as a tax farmer and administrator that it was enough for him to sign official documents with the name "Abraham." All knew who he was. Like Abravanel, he also used his wealth to help his people. After 450 Jews, mainly women, were captured following the conquest of Malaga in 1487, Seneor, who was then seventy-five years old, raised a huge sum of money to purchase their freedom.

It was likely Seneor who had recommended to the monarchs that they grant an audience to Don Isaac Abravanel in 1484 (Abravanel, himself, may have well initiated the meeting). The war against the Moors in Granada, then in its fourth year, was expensive, and Isabel and Ferdinand needed all the financial help they could get.

The king and queen must have been impressed by Abravanel's credentials as well as his charismatic personality. Within a few years of his arrival in Spain, he had become not only a successful tax farmer — second probably only to Seneor — but also a recognized leader of the Spanish Jewish community. Considering Seneor's advancing years, it is not surprising that more and more Jews came to regard Abravanel as his natural successor. At the court, Abravanel's role was almost entirely financial, and he fulfilled it brilliantly. By 1488, he had been able to build up enough capital (in addition to what he had obtained from Portugal) to lend the crown vast amounts for the war effort in Granada. In fact, Isabel and Ferdinand gave Seneor and Abravanel the important responsibility for supplying and administering the royal army. Years later, Abravanel would remember his time at the Spanish court less fondly and regret that he had spent so much of this time involved with money instead of studying the Torah.

Apart from the war chest loaned to the monarchs by Abravanel, Seneor, and other courtiers, Jews throughout Spain were forced through exorbitant taxes to contribute to the *Reconquista*. (Between 1482 and 1492, Jews contributed approximately fifty-eight million *maravedís* in taxes and another twenty million in forced "loans.") That long conflict ended in late 1491, when Sultan Boabdil finally agreed to surrender to the armies of the Catholic monarchs. In an act of conciliation, Ferdinand and Isabel permitted those Moors who wished to remain to do so. They could stay in their homes and for a time continue to practise their religion; others were free to leave the country. Boabdil chose the latter option. As the sultan departed, he was said to have stood on the last hill that afforded a view of Granada, gazed one final time at his former kingdom, and sighed longingly as his angry mother berated him for losing their precious land. Forever after, that spot on the hill was to be known as *el último suspiro del moro*, The Moor's Last Sigh.

The celebrated conquest of Granada gave momentum to those who wished to resolve once and for all the *converso* problem. The Jewish threat to Christianity, imagined or not, was never far from Grand Inquisitor Torquemada's thoughts. In his view, segregation was no longer an adequate solution. The proceedings of the La Guardia blood libel the previous year had already confirmed that. In this infamous and twisted case, a forty-year-old *converso* named Benito García, a wool-carder from the town of La Guardia, near Toledo, was accused along with a group of Jews of taking part in the ritual murder of a young boy as part of a Passover plot. Despite the fact that no body was ever found – there had never even been any inquiries about the missing child – García and his Jewish accomplices (who were also accused of "seducing" Christians to Judaism) were convicted on forged evidence and confessions obtained under torture. The sentence of death was carried out before a crowd of hundreds of believers at a dramatic *auto-da-fé* in mid-November 1491.

As word of yet another *converso* conspiracy spread across Spain, attitudes against Jews intensified further. Jews, it will be recalled, had already been expelled (at least in theory) from several major cities, including Toledo, Seville, and Cordoba. Still, when Ferdinand and Isabella finally signed the Edict of Expulsion at the end of March 1492, the Jews were shocked. They were given three months to dispose of their property and businesses and make the necessary arrangements to leave their homeland.

Few events in Jewish history have been dissected and debated as much as the 1492 expulsion from Spain. The motives of both monarchs have been questioned: Ferdinand has been portrayed as the callous and manipulative ruler intent on confiscating as much Jewish wealth as possible; Isabel has been often regarded as the main force behind the order and as a pawn of Torquemada. Indeed, in one well-known, though probably not accurate, version of the story, Torquemada was said to have intervened when Isaac Abravanel and Abraham Seneor attempted to convince the king to rescind the edict with a bribe. In the midst of the negotiations, the Grand Inquisitor, holding a crucifix, supposedly stormed into the room and proclaimed, "See here the crucifix of our Saviour, whom the wretched Judas sold for thirty pieces of silver to his enemies and betrayed to their persecutors. If you applaud this action, sell him for a higher price. I, for my part, resign from all power. I will not take any blame; you will be responsible to God for this business deal." That apparently did the trick.

Yet another tale, advanced by Abravanel himself and made more famous by the sixteenth-century writer Elijah Capsali, was that some time in April or early May of 1492 Abravanel wrote a strongly worded letter to Queen Isabel denouncing her for the edict. "He chastised her mercilessly and showed no respect for rank," claimed Capsali. "He then arranged to have the letter delivered to the queen while he fled for his life." This episode seems unlikely to have occurred. There is evidence that Abravanel was still working on behalf of the monarchs in late May and early June 1492. More importantly, once he decided to leave Spain, he was given special permission to take a thousand gold ducats out of the kingdom. This was an exceptional allowance. As well, loans that he and his son-in-law Joseph had made were favourably settled. This was hardly the treatment accorded someone who was supposedly in fear for his life.

The expulsion order itself blamed the Jews for the quandary in which they now found themselves. They were guilty of leading astray "wicked Christians who have deviated from our Holy Catholic Faith." This charge was undoubtedly bogus, but it did provide the edict with a religious, even spiritual, justification. The decision to expel the Jews must be seen against the backdrop of the larger political and economic forces behind Ferdinand and Isabel's empire-building policies. The conquest of the Moors, appeasement of the nobility, the sponsorship of Columbus's voyages, and the expulsion of the Jews were all components of the royal vision to establish a strong, uniform government, based on the tenets of Christianity, and firmly controlled from the centre.

Another, more interesting, theory has been put forward recently by British scholar Henry Kamen. He argues convincingly that the real purpose of the 1492 edict was not expulsion, but compulsory conversion of all Spanish Jews as a long-term solution to the *converso* problem. But in giving Jews a choice and three months to think about it, the plan backfired; many opted to leave the country rather than convert. "The Inquisition desired nothing more complicated than the elimination of choice for the *conversos*, many of whom felt more at home among their Jewish brethren," writes Kamen. "As long as Jews and synagogues existed, they would go on Judaizing, and the task of the Inquisition, to purify the land of heresy, would never be done. The objective could be achieved by forced conversion (as in 1391); expulsion was unnecessary, and had been resorted to before only as a temporary measure. . . . With conversion as the main goal, it is very likely that the expulsion was nothing less than a mistake."

Whatever the true motives, the expulsion created tremendous financial hardships for thousands of Jews. The Crown, not wishing to miss an opportunity to increase the royal treasury, confiscated property in lieu of future taxes. Under short notice, many Jews were forced to sell businesses and property for far less than they were worth and had no other option but to divest themselves of material goods they had acquired during a lifetime. Ancient synagogues and other community buildings were lost forever; later the monarchs gave them to Christian and *converso* favourites. Some clever Jews found ways to smuggle out gold and silver in the hope of starting life anew in another country, but most were not as resourceful or fortunate.

As many as a hundred thousand Jews refused to give away their property for a pittance and uproot their families.* They followed the lead of eighty-year-old Abraham Seneor and converted to Christianity so that they could stay in Spain. According to Baer and other sources, Isabel did not want to lose Seneor as a financial administrator and put great pressure on him to become a *converso*. But it is more likely that he was in fact too old to leave and did not want to lose his wealth and status. Hence on June 15, 1492, at a ceremony in the church of Santa María de Guadalupe, Seneor was baptized and renamed Fernand Pérez Coronel. His son Solomon became Juan Pérez Coronel. The elder Seneor was appointed a chief financial officer for monarchs' son Juan and died a committed *converso*. His descendants, including his grandson Antonio Núñez Coronel, who studied theology in Paris and became a Dominican monk, were fully integrated into Christian society. It has been estimated that another thirty thousand Jews returned within a few years

---

* There is also a great debate among historians as to the precise number of Jews who actually stayed in Spain and how many chose to leave in 1492. Accepted figures of those departing range from around one hundred twenty thousand people to only forty thousand suggested by Henry Kamen.

of their forced departure and also accepted Jesus in order to reclaim their former lives and property.

Abravanel and his family, too, may have been threatened. A short time after Seneor's conversion, word reached Abravanel that there was a plot at the court to kidnap his infant grandson Isaac (Judah Abravanel's son) and convert him to Christianity. Ferdinand, who valued not only Don Isaac's talents but also those of his eldest son, the noted physician, intended to force the family to remain in Spain. Quickly, Judah sent young Isaac with a nurse across the border into Portugal to stay with relatives.

This plan, however, backfired. As soon as Judah Abravanel reached Italy in the summer of 1492, he wanted the nurse to bring Isaac to him. Portuguese King João II, his father's old nemesis, refused to allow it, and instead had the child taken and forcibly baptized. Judah was not to see his son for many years and was understandably tormented by this tragic loss.[*]

The emigration of the Jews from Spain during the summer of 1492 was a terrible ordeal. Few countries in Europe were willing to accept the Sephardi refugees. More than one hundred thousand Jews, mainly from Castile, travelled to neighbouring Portugal, where King João II, after extracting a high entrance fee, allowed them to remain for eight months. About 600 wealthy Jews were permitted to stay for longer. Thousands more found a brief respite to the northwest, in the kingdom of Navarre. But these lands proved only temporary havens. Within a few years, the Jews who had gone there faced repression and discrimination almost worse than they had left behind in Spain. Some ventured farther north, many more converted

---

[*] "My darling child by force was taken," Judah Abravanel wrote in a long Hebrew poem composed more than a decade later. "An infant snatched from his mother's breast; He now is twelve – I have not seen him – My soul is shaken, my heart oppressed." According to A.R. Milburn, writing in 1937, "In 1560, Amatus Lusitanus saw in Salonika in the house of Isaac Abravanel the younger, a book, *De Coeli harmonia*, written by [his father] Leone Ebreo [Judah Abravanel's pen name], and which it is likely, had been given personally by the author to his son."

to Christianity under threat of death, expanding the *converso* communities throughout the region.

Near the end of July, Isaac Abravanel departed for Naples from Spain's Mediterranean port of Valencia. With him was his family and enough money to start over in another land. At least ten thousand Jews followed him. Other Jews in Andalusia attempted to make their way south and across the Mediterranean to North Africa, but confronted innumerable obstacles. Since Spain controlled ports in Algeria and Tunisia, Jews were not allowed to land. Many others who made it onto ships were at the mercy of pirates and exploited by unscrupulous captains.

Eventually, more prosperous Sephardi communities were established in Morocco and other Muslim-controlled lands. "A new Sephardi nexus began to develop," writes historian Jane Gerber, "linking the dispersed Sephardi refugees in North Africa with their co-religionists (often relatives) in the emergent posts of Western Europe and the New World. For a while, the Spanish exiles in Muslim lands provided a unique link between the world of Islam and the world of European diplomacy and commerce. Nowhere was this more apparent than in the heart of the Ottoman Empire."

Indeed, as in the decades following the 1391 riots, the lands of the Ottoman rulers beckoned Jews from Spain. They soon flocked there, finding a more welcome refuge in Rhodes, Crete, Salonika, and Constantinople, where they re-established their lives and businesses and were welcomed by long-lost relatives.

Their experience of exile demanded an explanation and interpretation. Why had such tragedy and sorrow afflicted Jews yet again? Some rabbinical scholars later regarded the events of 1492 as a just punishment for the sins of the *conversos*; they had forsaken God's law, and their brethren were made to suffer for their actions. These were sentiments that Don Isaac Abravanel understood as he spent the remaining years of his life writing biblical commentaries and philosophy and pondering the complexities and tragedies of Jewish history. And yet, there was always the possibility of salvation and redemption. The Messiah would come; it was only a matter of time.

Wherever they later journeyed in the Diaspora – west to Amsterdam and London, east to the Ottoman Empire, or in time across the ocean to North and South America – the Sephardim took this hope for the future with them. While their individual experiences might have varied, these Jews continued to celebrate their Spanish roots and heritage. It was a tradition and culture passed on from one generation to the next. In that treasured, though admittedly selective, memory, the Golden Age of Spanish Jewry lived on, in their folklore, poetry, literature, and collective imagination.

Chapter Two

THE GHETTO

Venice, 1516

*The Jews must all live together in the Corte de Case, which are in the
Ghetto near San Girolamo; and in order to prevent their roaming about at
night: Let there be built two Gates, on the side of the Old Ghetto where
there is a little Bridge, and likewise on the other side of the Bridge, that is
one for each of said two places, which Gates shall be opened in the morning
at the sound of the Marangona, and shall be closed at midnight by four
Christian guards appointed and paid by the Jews at the rate deemed suitable
by Our Cabinet.*

— EDICT OF THE VENETIAN SENATE, MARCH 29, 1516

The Days of the Messiah

FEW EUROPEAN KINGDOMS welcomed the Jewish refugees from
Spain with open arms. They had enough Jews of their own. Why
would they want more? And yet, it was an accepted, if not entirely
proven, fact of life in the fifteenth and sixteenth centuries that Jews
were good for the economy. At least that was what the monarchs,
princes, and dukes who ruled the multitude of states and duchies
of Renaissance Italy believed. Not entirely comfortable with Jews
in their midst, however, they designed a system to keep them in
check. Jewish life was governed by the *condotta*, a contract set by
the ruler or government, which permitted Jews to live and work in
a city or region for a set amount of time, usually three to five years.

51

When the contract expired, heated debates generally ensued about the value of Jewish moneylenders, pawnshop operators, and merchants. Though religious concerns, resentments, and medieval stereotypes – often fanatically promoted by mendicant friars – were ever present in such discussions, the state's self-interest almost always won out. Still, this did not mean that there were no serious problems or conflicts.

As in Spain, the long-term goal of Christian Italy was to absorb and convert the twenty-five thousand to thirty thousand Jews among its population of eight to ten million people. Acculturation as we know it today was not an acceptable or even possible alternative. The stubborn resolve of Jews to maintain a separate identity and religion coupled with the popular image of them as leeches, scoundrels, and devils meant that there were only two choices for Italian rulers: expulsion or segregation. Economically, expulsion made no sense; Jews were "necessary," it was argued. It is thus not surprising that segregation – keeping Jews controlled and apart – eventually became the policy that defined Jewish life in the Renaissance. And so, the era that gave the world such masterpieces as Michelangelo's *David*, Leonardo da Vinci's *Mona Lisa*, and Botticelli's *The Birth of Venus* also left another lasting legacy – the Ghetto.

Ferrante I, the ruler of the kingdom of Naples, always put his own needs before that of his subjects. It was not a strategy that endeared him to his people, but for a brief time it did make him very wealthy. King Ferrante understood the value of Jews. They paid high taxes, they provided credit to the lower classes, and they never posed a political or military threat. While Ferrante is best remembered as being a bit of a tyrant, he did grant Jews full citizenship rights in a charter of 1468. Soon, Jews from Rome, Bologna, and as far away as Provence and the Holy Roman Empire flocked to Naples to take advantage of Ferrante's extraordinary decree.

Convinced of their economic utility, he, more than most Italian rulers, opened his kingdom to Jewish refugees from Spain in 1492. Those Jews who arrived first in mid-August were in a dreadful condition from the arduous voyage. They were hungry, weak, and some were likely ill with typhus. "You would have thought that they wore masks," wrote a Christian eyewitness who saw the arrival of a group of Sephardi Jews in Genoa. "They were bony, pallid, their eyes sunk in the sockets; and had they not made the slight movements it would have been imagined that they were dead." Ferrante, recorded the chronicler Elijah Capsali, wisely instructed the Jews to bury their dead "in the darkest night," so as not to arouse the ire of his Christian subjects. Six months later, a cholera epidemic swept through Naples, and more than fifty thousand people perished. Almost immediately, word spread that the Spanish Jews had brought the disease with them. (Capsali suggests that when King Ferrante learned of the rumours he grew angry and threatened to abdicate. The "people" then relented and told the king to treat the Jews as he pleased. An unlikely scenario.)

Don Isaac Abravanel arrived in Naples in early September. He was accompanied by his wife and his three sons: the youngest, Samuel, destined to be an influential merchant; Joseph, a physician; and Judah, also trained as a doctor, but who, under the name Leone Ebreo, would be remembered as one of the greatest Jewish poets of the Renaissance.

Don Isaac's reputation preceded him, and Ferrante invited him to his court and inner circle. He would later write that during his time in Naples, his "wealth grew immensely" and that he became "as famous as the country's greatest magnates." Apart from his work as a courtier, he found more than enough time to complete his commentary on the Book of Kings in the fall of 1493. But the exile from Spain still troubled him greatly, a fact reflected in his book *Eternal Justice* and later in *The Days of the World*, in which he wrestled with Divine justice and the place and future of the Jewish people. In this, Abravanel, at the age of fifty-six, stubbornly and proudly followed his own traditional philosophical beliefs and was not caught up in the elitist "Humanism" of Renaissance scholars. More appealing was the spiritualism and idealism offered by Neoplatonism, a philosophy embraced by his son Judah.

Political intrigue would again interrupt Abravanel's life. In early 1494, Ferrante died while in the midst of sensitive alliance negotiations with Ferdinand and Isabel of Spain as a protection against a possible threat from the young and ambitious King Charles VIII of France. Charles maintained that his claim through the House of Anjou, which had held Naples from 1268 to 1435, was greater than that of Ferrante's son and successor, Alfonso II. In the end, blood ties meant little to the Spanish monarchs; they decided to back France instead of their Italian relations. In exchange for some disputed territory that was ceded to Aragon, Charles was given permission to travel through Spanish-held regions in Italy on his way to Naples.

The moment Ferrante died, Charles announced his intentions to take back what was rightly his and to use Naples as a base for his coming battle against the Ottomans. By the time, Charles had reached Milan with an army of 40,000 men, 100 siege guns, and 86 ships of war, Alfonso II had fled south to Sicily, taking Don Isaac Abravanel with him.

The arrival of the French into the Italian states did not bode well for the Jews, who more than a century before had been expelled from France. "Everywhere there were scenes of murder, pillage and destruction," wrote the Jewish historian Cecil Roth. Mass forced conversions followed, and Jews who resisted were killed or sold into slavery. Property, including Isaac Abravanel's home and library, much of which he had brought with him from Spain, was destroyed. The Jewish community of Naples was nearly wiped out. Judah Abravanel managed to escape to Genoa, while other members of the family fled to Salonika in the Ottoman Empire, where Isaac's youngest son, Samuel, was then studying.

Charles's adventure in Italy was halted quickly enough. Led by Pope Alexander VI, the rulers of Venice and Milan, along with Ferdinand and Isabel, who now reconsidered their earlier pro-French position, joined in the Holy League of Venice to send Charles back to his own country. In the meantime, Alfonso II had abdicated in favour of his more popular son Federigo III, who was able to reclaim his kingdom in July 1496. Federigo was even more enlightened than his father had been when it came to dealing with Jews. He encouraged them to return, and amongst those who did so were some members of the Abravanel family. He also accepted Sephardi refugees expelled from Portugal in 1497. For a time, he even allowed Jews to forgo wearing the humiliating yellow badge used to identify them.*

Once his services were no longer needed in Sicily, but before Federigo was back in Naples, Don Isaac Abravanel contemplated a permanent move to the Ottoman Empire. He spent much of 1495 on the island of Corfu, then under Venetian control. While he now had the time to resume work on his commentary on the Prophet Isaiah, he was troubled by what he saw around him. In his view, the Sephardi exiles who had made their way to Corfu were consumed by materialism and had abandoned their faith. Worse, he was alone. "My wife, my sons, and my books are far from me," he wrote to a friend, "and I am left alone, a stranger in a strange land." He responded to the problems he perceived with a new book, *Principles of Faith*, in which he admonished Sephardi Jews in Italy and elsewhere for their apparent failings.

A European at heart, Abravanel was unwilling to settle permanently in Salonika or Constantinople. Once the French departed from Naples, he returned to Italy, settling in the town of Monopoli on the Adriatic coast. The serene seaside setting must have appealed to him, for at the age of fifty-eight he began one of the most prolific periods of his literary career. He completed a lengthy commentary on Deuteronomy begun many years earlier in Portugal, and he

---

* The regulations governing Jewish badges and clothing in Italy and elsewhere in Europe were not consistent; they changed over time and from kingdom to kingdom, often depending on the whim of the ruler. In Rome, for example, Jewish men were required to wear short red jackets when they were in public, while women wore special outer skirts. In Milan and Venice, Jews were compelled to wear yellow or red hats and turbans. The badges, too, differed in colour – though yellow or red was most common – as well as in shape, from a circle or wheel, popular in Spain, among other places, to a Star of David–like figure worn in Portugal.

wrote commentaries on the Passover Haggadah (the Passover sacrifice) and *Avot* (*The Inheritance of the Fathers*). In this last work, he again renewed his criticism of contemporary Jewish morals.

In Abravanel's search for life's true meaning, he leaned towards the messianic and kabbalistic (although he continued to claim that he was no follower of the kabbalah). In the first of his so-called "messianic trilogy," *Fountains of Salvation* (his commentary on the Book of Daniel, completed in 1497), he predicted that redemption was probably less than seven years away. Abravanel's magic year for the arrival of the Messiah was 1503, a date he arrived at by detailed calculations based on a mystical interpretation of the Book of Daniel (Abravanel suggested that 1531 and 1573 were also possibilities).

When the Messiah did arrive on earth, predicted Abravanel, the Jews dispersed throughout the world would return to the Land of Israel and their enemies would be vanquished. The "Days of the Messiah" would be at hand and mankind would finally realize its true spiritual potential. Such visions were later to inspire the false messiahs of the sixteenth and seventeenth centuries. *Fountains of Salvation* was followed by two other books: *Salvation of the Anointed*, an interpretation of rabbinical writings dealing with the Messiah, and *The Announcer of Salvation*, a commentary on messianism in the Prophets, finished in early 1498. The messianic trilogy "was the most original, most significant and most inspiring of Abravanel's work and the greatest work that was ever composed on the messianic problem until his time," asserts his biographer Netanyahu.

As Isaac Abravanel contemplated a more permanent reunion with his family in Naples, the French again attacked the kingdom, in June 1501. Though he escaped the war by remaining in Monopoli to complete a work of philosophy, *The Deeds of God*, undoubtedly inspired by his son Judah's developing interest in Plato, his other son, Joseph, urged him to relocate to Venice, where Joseph worked as a physician. There, in *La Serenissima*, the "Most Serene City," Don Isaac found the peace and quiet he needed. The year was 1503, the year of the Messiah.

A Tower of Strength to His People Was He

THE JEWISH POPULATION OF VENICE never had been large, always hovering around a thousand people, but the community had roots that dated back to the mid-twelfth century and perhaps earlier. Moreover, it was diverse as any in the Diaspora. There were Ashkenazi Jews, the "Italians and Germans," whose ancestors had lived in France and Germany. They were followed later by Jews and *conversos* who immigrated directly from Spain, and by Sephardi Jews who came to Italy via the Levant, which was under Ottoman control.

Far from being a united group, however, they were divided by issues of class, language, and religious beliefs – a recurrent theme in Jewish history. For many years, the Ashkenazim spoke Italian or Yiddish (a German-Hebrew dialect), and the Sephardim, Ladino (Judeo-Spanish). Eventually, each sect had its own synagogues, schools, and community organizations. Sephardim tended to look down upon their Ashkenazi brothers, accusing them of being corrupt and impure. Joseph Ha-Kohen, the renowned Sephardi writer of the sixteenth century, never hid the fact that in his view, Ashkenazi Jews were crude and coarse and were to blame for the recent tragedies that Jews had suffered. As Moshe Shulvass writes, Ha-Kohen "never failed to add to the name of a culprit that he was an Ashkenazi."

Even the charitable Isaac Abravanel criticized the Ashekenazim for their practice of awarding titles, and in particular the title of "rabbi," to everyone and anyone. "When I came to Italy I found that the custom of indiscriminate ordination was very widespread, especially among the Ashkenazim," Abravanel later reflected. "They all ordain or are ordained rabbis. I know not whence comes such license, unless they are envious of the Gentiles who give doctorates to everyone, and want one themselves."

To the outside world these distinctions were insignificant. What did it matter where a Jew had been born? Or what language he spoke? Collectively, they were all Jews and subject to the various array of restrictions and taxes deemed essential by Venice's government. For many years, Jews, with the exception of those who were physicians, were generally banned from the main city and were forced to live and work on the island of Spinalunga or at Mestre on the mainland (where today a modern Jewish community has again developed). During the fourteenth century, as Venice emerged as the main commercial centre for the Eastern trade, demand for credit grew. Soon, more moneylenders, Jews as well as Christians, were permitted to set up shop right in the city, but their business was tightly controlled and monitored by the Venetian senate.

During the ensuing decades, Venetian officials continually weighed the popular resentment of Jewish bankers and pawnshop operators against their economic usefulness and high tax and loan contribution. Still, there were many restrictions and mean-spirited regulations imposed. Jews, for instance, from about 1420 onward were not permitted to own property in Venice and thus were subject to the arbitrary rents of Christian landlords. Worse, as in other European centres, they were also required to wear a special circular yellow badge, changed to a yellow hat (called a *baretta* or a *sessa*) in 1492, then changed again to a red hat in 1500. For most Jews, no matter who they were or how much money they possessed, this was humiliating. In the words of the great Jewish historian Heinrich Graetz, it "was an invitation to the gamin to insult the wearers and to bespatter them with mud. It was a suggestion to stupid mobs to fall upon them, to maltreat them, and even to kill them." Or, put another way more recently by Robert Bonfil, "The Jewish group appeared in the eyes of the others with a uniform, compact, monolithic aspect, which made the Christians feel threatened and reinforced their fear – the fear of the Jews." The message conveyed by the badge or hat was clear: Jews were not to be trusted.

Despite this daily degradation, the Jews of Italy embraced the Renaissance with passion and enthusiasm. If they could afford it, they collected fine art and sculpture, attended plays and concerts alongside their Christian neighbours, and dressed in the latest fashions. They not only developed a Hebrew printing industry to rival no other, but also taught the ancient language to Christian scholars, who could now study the Old Testament in its original tongue.

In their leisure time, some Jews had a lot of fun as well: they gambled with cards and dice, drank large quantities of wine, and danced the evening away at masked balls.

By the time he arrived in Venice, Isaac Abravanel had celebrated his sixty-sixth birthday. In a letter to Saul Ashkenazi, a learned rabbi of Candia (now Iraklion, Crete), he complained about his "feeble hands and defective vision." He was, nonetheless, delighted to be in the city, to admire its beauty and share in its high culture. The structure and operation of the Venetian government, unique for the time, impressed him. In Venice, power was shared between the doge, head of the *Collegio* or cabinet, the *Maggior Consiglio*, the aristocratic Great Council, the Senate, and the *Consiglio de Dieci*, or the "Council of Ten," the Senate's influential executive. Overlooking its dictatorial and aristocratic composition, Abravanel later compared the government in Venice to the rule of law passed down by Moses to the people of Israel.

That the Senate recruited Abravanel for a diplomatic mission with Portugal may have helped him reach this favourable opinion. It was to be his last such adventure. Venice had long controlled the profitable spice trade from the East by its dealings with Egypt, which imported the highly valued commodity from India. But the discovery by Portugal's Vasco da Gama of an all-ocean route to India threatened that monopoly. Abravanel's task was to negotiate an agreement with Portugal that would preserve Venice's trading rights. Don Isaac dispatched his nephew Joseph, the son of his brother Samuel, to deal with the Portuguese. The negotiations were difficult, and in the end Portugal refused to agree to Venice's terms. This marked the beginning of Venice's slow decline as the commercial centre of the Mediterranean.

Disappointed, though not dejected, Don Isaac Abravanel returned to his writings, including a major commentary on Maimonides. In late December 1508, he died. He was seventy-one years old. Since Jews were not permitted to be buried inside Venice, he was interred at the ancient Jewish cemetery at nearby Padua. Less than a year later, Venice and the surrounding area was attacked by troops led by

Emperor Maximilian, the German leader of the Holy Roman Empire. He was one of the key members of the League of Cambrai, an alliance he had helped forge with Ferdinand of Spain and Pope Julius II that was intent on conquering Venice. In the melee that ensued, Padua's Jewish cemetery was destroyed and Don Isaac's grave was lost forever.

At Abravanel's funeral, his son Judah, in a moving and poetic tribute, had described his father with these words: "A tower of strength to his people was he, / A buckler and shield in their need; / Repairer of breaches, restorer of paths, / Consoler in word and in deed." His death was mourned by Jews throughout the Diaspora. He was rightly revered by rabbis, scholars, and laymen as a "great eagle" in learning, "as wise as Daniel" in politics, and as a "man of God" in morals and personality. Abravanel had truly epitomized the power, influence, and scholarship now on the wane among Jews in Europe. When the Messiah did not come in 1503, as Abravanel had predicted, he had not attempted to explain it or defend his position, confident that the day would come soon enough. That simple but genuine hope for a glorious future was his legacy to the Jewish world.

Two generations later, his writings were republished in Amsterdam and had a profound effect on the rabbi and scholar Menasseh ben Israel, who also happened to be married to Rachel Abravanel, Don Isaac's great-granddaughter. In several of his books, including *The Hope of Israel* (1650) and *Concilador* (1632), ben Israel's philosophy, his Biblical interpretations, and most significantly his firm belief that there was a place for Jews in the larger world owed much to Abravanel's influence. It could be said that the spirit of Abravanel even played a small part in ben Israel's successful campaign to have Jews readmitted into England in 1656.

Nearly three hundred years later, in 1937, the five-hundredth anniversary of Abravanel's birth, a scholarly book was published in England examining various aspects of his illustrious career. More curious was a museum exhibit celebrating Abravanel launched at the Jewish museum in Berlin under the prying eyes of Nazi officials. Old and rare editions of Abravanel's books were displayed along with paintings and medallions.

In the introduction to a volume of six essays on Abravanel, Paul Goodman, in a lecture originally delivered in German at the University of Tartu in Estonia in April 1937, observed that "The vicissitudes of Don Isaac Abravanel at the Courts of the Christian Kings in Portugal, Spain and Italy represent a very remarkable phenomenon: intensely Jewish though he was, he moved, conscious of his noble Jewish lineage, freely and with an apparently self-assured dignity in an atmosphere that was so impregnated with the mystical glamour and impelled by the temporal might of the Universal Church that it could not tolerate any other religious manifestation." Yet in the end Don Isaac Abravanel was only one man confronting historical realties that he had limited, if any, power to control.

The Foundry

ISAAC ABRAVANEL DID NOT LIVE LONG ENOUGH to witness what was arguably the most significant event in the history of the Jewish community in Venice – an event that would have repercussions throughout Europe for generations. Segregating Jews from Christians was not a new idea, it dated at least back to the Third Lateran Council of 1179, which had ruled that Christians and Jews should not live together. Although there were segregated Jewish quarters in Spain and elsewhere, for a variety of reasons the Council's ruling was never widely enforced until the early sixteenth century.

In the period after 1508, Jews were tolerated in Venice, if barely, because they provided money and goods towards the republic's war effort against powers that threatened it. But each year, the voices raised against the number of Jewish refugees streaming into the city grew louder. Protests were also made by Venetian clerks and others about the activities of Jewish moneylenders, who seemed to be all over the city. Finally, in the spring of 1516, at a meeting of the

Collegio, it was decided that Jews had to be segregated "and pre-vented from contaminating Christian citizens any longer." This ruling, however, lasted only for two years. In 1518, and every two to five years thereafter for the next century, Jews had to keep reap-plying and paying for a new charter in order to remain in Venice. The area proposed for the new Jewish quarter was located in the north part of the city in the parish of San Gerolamo, beside an on old cannon (or copper) foundry no longer in use. In Italian, the foundry was called the *giotto* or *geto*. And so the word "ghetto" was born, first used to describe the Jewish quarter in Venice, called the Ghetto Nuovo, and in time the segregated Jewish neighbourhoods throughout the continent.

The doge immediately approved of the idea; the Christian tenants in the apartments adjacent to the old foundry, on learning they were to lose their homes, were less pleased. Prominent Jewish community leaders like the banker Asher Meshullam also opposed the plan. Meshullam and others argued that Jewish dealers who had leased stalls in the Rialto, and who now had to relocate to the ghetto, would be financially ruined. They also maintained that seg-regating Jews into one area of the city would make them much more vulnerable to attack.

Jewish protests were ignored, and the Senate approved the seg-regation plan on March 29.[*] Jews were given ten days to make the move into the designated area. Apartment windows facing out-wards in the ghetto were closed up. Venetian Jews discovered that their new landlords were permitted to charge them rents about one-third higher then they had previously charged their Christian tenants in the same properties. (Over the years, Jews obtained a legal

---

[*] In 1930, when Cecil Roth wrote about the establishment of the Ghetto Nuovo in 1516 in his *History of the Jews in Venice*, he suggested that at first only Ashkenazi and local Italian Jews were forced to move into the ghetto. According to Roth, the small number of wealthy Sephardi merchants from the Levant in the city were able to avoid the law due to their political connections and status and did not relocate there until 1541. Recent archival research by Benjamin Ravid, among other scholars, however, confirms that the Sephardim were in fact com-pelled to live in the ghetto in 1516 or soon after.

right to live in the ghetto in "a specific place and a specific house." This right could be passed on to their children or even sold.)

From the beginning, the ghetto was overcrowded. By 1600, there may have been as many as five thousand Jews in the original Ghetto Nuovo and its two expansions, the Ghetto Vecchio, an area with older buildings added in 1541, and the Ghetto Nuovissimo, added in 1633. Each addition, as will be seen, significantly altered the character of the Jewish community. Often a peddler used the ground-floor living quarters, while merchants and physicians occupied the more spacious upper floor apartments. Storeys were continually added on to existing buildings to make room for the ever-increasing population.

High walls enclosed the ghetto. Each morning the gates were opened as the bell in San Marco tolled, and each evening at sunset they were shut again, isolating the Jews from the rest of the city. Four Christian guards patrolled the gates and were paid by the Jews themselves. Yet life in the ghetto, as Riccardo Calimani, a Venetian Jewish writer has noted, was never dull. While areas of the ghetto may have been more impoverished than some parts of the city, it was the "Jewish space [and] the scene of all Jewish life." Out in the narrow streets, in pawn shops and trading stalls, could be heard a Babel of languages: Spanish, Portuguese, Ladino, Hebrew, German, and Italian. "The rhythm of daily life," adds Calimani, "was marked by the traditional morning, afternoon and evening prayers."

The large square that still dominates the ghetto was the hub of Jewish and Christian activities during the day. Jewish traders from across Italy and Europe streamed into the ghetto, visiting pawnshops, spreading gossip and news, arranging for the printing of a new manuscript, buying merchandise of every kind and variety – new and used clothes, silk, velvet, spices, books, precious stones and metals.*

---

* Today, the Ghetto Nuovo's main square is an unusually quiet and serene place, where tourists can relax for a momentary respite from the crowds in the shops and restaurants outside the ghetto's walls. Small groups of Jews from North America and Israel gather at the entrance to the Museum of Jewish Art for a visit to the nearby synagogues or have a drink at the lone outdoor kosher café.

At night, the ghetto was transformed into a separate "Jewish republic" in the centre of the city. Families gathered for evening dinner after prayers, and fathers and sons debated the Talmud and Maimonides as well as the writings of Homer, Plato, Pico della Mirandola, and Aldo Manuzio. The celebration of the holiday of Purim (the Feast of Lots), when children paraded through the ghetto in costumes, and plays were staged about the deliverance of Persian Jews from massacre, was a particularly festive occasion. Most evenings, however, unsavoury characters and harlots walked the ghetto's streets. Men in need of further distraction did not have to look very far – gambling with dice and cards was a popular pastime, a reality of life in Venice that Isaac Abravanel, for one, deplored. Leone Modena, a notable and celebrated Venetian rabbi of the early 1600s, was a frequent visitor, and loser, at the gambling tables. Later in his life, he estimated his losses at about 500 ducats a year, nearly enough to start up a small pawnshop. (Apartment rents in the ghetto averaged 30 to 70 ducats per year.) Considering his annual income was never more than about 200 to 250 ducats, he was perpetually in debt and forced to borrow money from whomever would give it to him (mainly Jewish moneylenders and associations he worked for). In 1620, after the untimely death of his older son, Modena gambled even more. Fate, he confessed, "forced me to err in the foolishness of gambling all my life, while my soul knew its faults and evil quite well."

Among the most lavish buildings in the ghetto were, and still are, the synagogues, built between the apartments. Each represented a different sect or region of the Diaspora. From the outside the synagogues are barely distinguishable from the other buildings, but once you enter, the fine workmanship and expense that went into the construction of each is evident in its sophisticated and elegant design. The Scuola Grande Tedesca, the Great Synagogue of the Germans, was opened in 1528 in the far corner of the Ghetto Nuovo. Its hall of worship, asymmetrical and slightly overpowered by gilding which adorns the ark and *bimah*, is a strong reminder of both the faith and pride its congregants once had. Nearby, the

Scuola Canton was built by the affluent Cantoni family in 1532 to service the needs of the Ashkenazim. They spared little expense in building what probably served for some years as their private place of worship. There is also the Scuola Italiano, erected in 1575 by the less wealthy members of the "Italian nation." It is more austere and less elaborate than the other synagogues; fine wood panelling rather than gold predominates throughout the sanctuary.

In the Ghetto Vecchio, Sephardi Jews built two synagogues facing each other in the ghetto's small square, the Campiello delle Scuole: The Scuola Spagnuola, or Spanish Synagogue, was erected in 1584, and it was where many *conversos*, according to Cecil Roth, had "their first experience of real Judaism." Among all of Venice's synagogues it is the most grandiose, with chandeliers, black and white marble floors, and baroque aesthetic – the result of an expansion and renovation done in the 1630s by the famous Venetian architect Baldassare Longhena. Across the square is the Scuola Levantino, the Levant Synagogue, also built in the 1580s and financed by the merchants who had immigrated to Venice from Greece and Turkey.

The synagogues and the daily routine of prayer may have provided some much-needed stability in the lives of the ghetto's inhabitants, but the rules by which the Jews in Venice existed changed according to the political climate of the times. And in this, they had no control. When the republic was at peace, for example, regulations about closing the ghetto gate each evening were less rigorously enforced. Despite the rising tensions in the Christian world following Martin Luther's bold stand against the Catholic Church in 1517, Jews continued to arrive in Venice, necessitating the two major expansions of the ghetto noted above.

The first, in 1541, was after an influx of Jewish and *converso* merchants and traders from the Levant, when the nearby Ghetto Vecchio, with its old dilapidated buildings, was added. Many of the "Levantines," as they were commonly called, were Sephardi Jews who had left Spain and Portugal as new Christians and then returned to Judaism once they were in Salonika and Constantinople.

While Church officials expressed grave reservations about these "heretics," their wide-ranging trade and financial contacts with the Ottoman Empire proved invaluable as Venice desperately tried to maintain its commercial supremacy.

In 1567, when the ambitious Ottoman leader Sultan Selim II challenged that supremacy by seizing Cyprus, a four-year war ensued that was decisively won by the Venetians – assisted by their allies from Spain and the Papal States – following the great naval battle at Lepanto in October 1571. During the conflict, attitudes towards the Levantines changed significantly. They were regarded as Muslim collaborators, and their goods and property were seized. The Venetian fleet also routinely harassed foreign ships transporting merchandise belonging to Jews across the Adriatic.

More than once, the doge publicly proclaimed that Jews were the main instigators of the war, subscribing to the widely held belief at the time that the Sultan's aggressive action was due to the influence of the well-connected Don Joseph Nasi. A prominent Portuguese *converso* financier and diplomat at the Ottoman court, Nasi had returned to Judaism in 1554. On his journey from Portugal to the East, he and his family had not been treated well by Venetian authorities, and it was said that the war was Nasi's revenge. Later, the sultan rewarded Nasi by giving him the island of Naxos (previously under Venice's control) and the title Duke of Naxos (see Chapter Three). The doge's accusations resulted in violent attacks on Jews in Venice and the publication of pamphlets denouncing Jews as "God-killers, traitors and enemies."

The anti-Jewish fervour reached its peak in December 1571, when the Senate, in the wake of the victory at Lepanto, ordered that all Levantine Jews leave the city. As the members of the Senate explained, in a classic statement of Counter-Reformation zealousness, "It is appropriate to demonstrate our gratitude towards Jesus Christ, our blessed defender and protector, by acting against those who are the enemies of his Holy Faith, as are the Jews." The order also pointed an accusatory finger at the Jewish moneylenders, who, it was claimed, practised "fraud, extortion, deceit and dishonesty towards the poor." Still, two years later, when the expulsion was to be enforced, more practical economic considerations won out and the order was repealed.

Another wave of immigrants, mainly *conversos* from Portugal, arrived in the late 1570s. They were referred to as *ebrei ponentini* ("Western Jews") or the "Ponetines." By this time, the population in the ghetto hovered around 1,100. The Ponetines first lived in the Ghetto Vecchio alongside the Levantines, but soon complained about the overcrowded conditions and the thieves, harlots, and seedy individuals who paraded through the ghetto each night.

The ghetto finally expanded for a second time when the adjacent Ghetto Nuovissimo was absorbed in 1633 to accommodate even more Jewish merchants arriving from the Levant and Portugal. Several decades earlier, the Ponetines, by a charter passed that year, "were given the right to trade in areas previously reserved for Venetian Christian merchants." Remarkably, this was a privilege granted to individuals who had converted to Christianity but who had opted to return to Judaism – a sign that in Venice, economic priorities were often placed ahead of religious ones.

It is accepted historical wisdom to regard the Venice ghetto as a "symbol of oppression," yet the opposite may in fact be true. If the alternative to the ghetto was expulsion, then segregation, even with many of the hardships it entailed, may well have been a compromise of sorts. In recent years, historian Robert Bonfil has pointed out that in Venice and other Italian cities, violence against Jews declined after the establishment of the ghettos, suggesting that segregation may have had a positive effect on Jewish–Gentile relations.

The Ghetto was, according to Bonfil, "a halfway house between acceptance and expulsion . . . [and a] compromise between the tendency to welcome Jews practically unconditionally everywhere, characteristic of the period prior to the second half of the sixteenth century, and the tendency to expel them, characteristic of the period following the Council of Trent (1545–1563). . . . The ghetto represented the last expression of the millenary tradition of ambivalence toward the Jews: keeping them separate without actually rejecting them, accepting them only provided they were kept segregated."

Interestingly, even when Jewish moneylenders started to lose their special economic importance – following the establishment in several Italian cities (only for a brief time in Venice) of the Monti de Pietà (Funds of Piety), publicly owned lending institutions that were not in business to make a profit and thus tolerated by the Catholic Church – the expulsion of Jews was not carried out. They were no longer essential to local economies, but were permitted to remain in the cities and towns nevertheless. Jews were merchants too, and time and again Jewish writers like Simone Luzzato (1582–1663) argued that Jews should also be respected for their mercantile skills.

Besides, Jews in Venice and elsewhere in Italy tried to fit in and get along with their Christian neighbours. There was always work for Christians in the ghetto, particularly on the Sabbath, as porters, street-sweepers, and peddlers. For these Venetians, the ghetto was not an area to be feared or ignored.

In some cases, business relationships became more personal. Christian acquaintances attended Jewish weddings and other celebrations, while Jews reciprocated. In discreet corners of the ghetto, Christians and Jews gambled together as "dicing companions." Jewish women, if they could afford it, tried to emulate their Christian friends in clothing and style. "I saw many Jewish women," reported the English traveller Thomas Coryat in 1612, "whereof some were as beautiful as ever I saw, and so gorgeous in their apparel, chaines of gold, and rings adorned with precious stones, that some of our English Countesses do scarce exceede them, having marvailous long traines like Princesses that are borne up by waiting women serving for the same purpose. An argument to prove that many of the Jewes are very rich."

There were two conflicting consequences of this gradual acculturation and social contact. On the one hand, Jewish conversions declined, since it became possible for Jews to advance socially without abandoning their religion and people. But on the other, Church officials grew increasingly uneasy with this turn of events. They demanded that a certain distance between Jews and Christians be maintained. "Business transactions between Christian and Jew could hardly be prevented, conversation could sometimes lead to conversions to Christianity," states American historian Brian Pullan. "But sharing meals, sleeping under the same roof, sexual relationships and any form of association implying equality, hospitality or mutual acceptance: all these things, if not specifically forbidden, were at least highly suspect."

In short, at any given moment, Church officials, especially after the establishment of the Inquisition in the Papal States in 1542, could and did intervene in Jewish–Christian relations. This situation took a turn for the worse less than eight years later, when the seventy-nine-year-old Cardinal Giovanni Pietro Caraffa became Pope Paul IV. By all accounts, he was a rigid, inflexible, and orthodox man. "The Pope," wrote the Florentine ambassador to the Vatican, "is a man of iron, and the very stones over which he walks emit sparks."

In his bull of 1555, *Cum nimis absurdum*, Paul IV railed against the Jews for their audacity and contempt; for their "shamelessness" in Rome and elsewhere for dwelling "among Christians in the neighbourhood of churches without distinction of dress, and even to rent houses in the more elegant streets and squares"; for "hiring Christian maidservants and wet nurses . . . and to perpetrate diverse other misdeeds to the shame and contumely of the Christian name." The aging pope ruled for only four years, but he managed to start a wave of censorship and book burning – including the Talmud – and new ghettos were established throughout the Italian states and kingdoms.

Under his successor, Pius IV, the treatment of Jews marginally improved, yet the yellow badge or hat and the segregated neighbourhoods remained. Jewish life in Renaissance Italy was therefore unpredictable, a reality exemplified by the varied experiences of Don Isaac's Abravanel's children and grandchildren.

The Dialogues of Love

HIS NICKNAME WAS LEO OR LEONE. It was derived from a passage in Genesis referring to Judah as a "young lion." As a noted physician, he was known as Judah Abravanel. As the writer of the humanist literary masterpiece *Dialoghi di amore*, *The Dialogues of Love*, he was, and remains, Leone Ebreo, or "Leone the Hebrew."

Judah Abravanel was only twenty-three years old when he fled to Castile from Portugal with his famous father, though already he was a practising physician. This meant treating his patients, both Jews and Christians, with a mixture of prayers, herbs, and Arabic medicines. Prescribing laudanum was particularly popular among Renaissance doctors and regarded as a miracle cure for any kind of pain or ache. Undoubtedly, Judah also read the latest works on the human anatomy, though it is likely that any training he received did not include dissecting a human body. It would take another generation before European medical schools accepted that dissections should be mandatory for their students.

Most of the other Jewish physicians in Venice received their medical education at the University of Padua, considered in the late sixteenth and early seventeenth centuries to be the finest medical school on the continent. Unlike many other institutions of higher learning, it did not discriminate against Jews. Here, young Jewish students from a variety of backgrounds could study botany, chemistry, clinical medicine, anatomy, and physics. They were fluent in Hebrew, Latin, and Italian. Their professional status was sufficiently valued in Venice that the government did not insist they wear a red or yellow hat or adhere to the ghetto curfew.

Judah was married some months before the expulsion from Spain. The great tragedy of his life occurred the following year, when he and his wife lost their first-born son, Isaac. The young boy, it will be recalled, had been sent to Portugal to protect him from a possible kidnapping by King Ferdinand of Spain. King João II, however, refused to allow the child to leave and had him baptized. Father and son were likely not reunited until many years later.

Once he had reached Naples in 1492, Judah, unlike his more traditional father, embraced the Renaissance and the philosophy of humanism, which exalted man's free will and superiority to the rest of nature. In time this led him to Neoplatonism, a popular ideology of the era that revered God and man's inner spiritual strength and intellectual power. To make a living, Judah lectured in medicine at the University of Naples. He associated with an elite group of Jewish Renaissance thinkers, and likely met Pico della Mirandola before the young philosopher died at the age of thirty-one. Perhaps they discussed Mirandola's most famous oration, *On the Dignity of Man*, or his views on Antonio Benivieni's worldly *Canzoni d'amore*, which made a favourable impression on Judah. Mirandola was alone among the so-called "nobility" of the Renaissance in counting Jews as teachers – he studied Hebrew – and as good friends. Certainly Judah's interest in Plato was significantly influenced by Mirandola's ardent faith that God "endowed man from birth, with the seeds of every possibility and every life."

After the riots in Naples in 1495, Judah and his wife made their way to Genoa, where they lived for several years. There, he studied sciences, wrote poetry in Ladino and Hebrew, and dabbled in metaphysics. He also composed (most likely in Hebrew) the work that would forever link him with the Renaissance, *Dialoghi di amori*, *The Dialogues of Love*. He returned to Naples with his family following the French withdrawal, and he became the personal physician to Gonzalo Fernández de Córdoba, the "Great Captain," who had led the military campaign against the French enemy.

It was about his time that Judah suffered yet another tragedy: his five-year-old son, Samuel, died from an illness. His pain at this loss and his separation from his eldest son, Isaac, imbued Judah's poetry with sorrow any parent could understand. His Hebrew poem "*T'lunah al Ha-Z'man*" ("Complaint against the Time") is a poignant lament about his family's journey from Portugal and Spain. It was written in 1503.

Fate drove my friends away, and scattered
    All of them who were so close, so dear;
No more do I behold the faces
    Of mother, brothers, father dear
My darling child by force was taken –
    An infant snatched from his mother's breast;
He now is twelve – I have not seen him –
    My soul is shaken, my heart oppressed.
O how I long and yearn to see thee,
    My darling precious, young gazelle!
    At thought of thee, my sleep departeth,
The day from night I cannot tell. . . .

Judah spent the remaining years of his life serving as a physician at the royal court in Naples and visiting his father and family in Venice. Judah's stature at the court was such that in 1520, when Naples was under the authority of the Holy Roman Emperor Charles V (the grandson of Isabel and Ferdinand), he was exempt from a special "tribute" or forced loan levied on all Jews in the kingdom. He also found enough time to continue writing poetry – including an introductory poem to his father's commentary on the last Prophets, printed in Pesaro in 1520 – and finished the *Dialogues of Love*. This first Hebrew version of *Dialoghi* may have been disseminated to a select audience of rabbinical sages and scholars, but Judah chose not to publish it for a general audience. Recent speculation is that the work upset traditional Maimonidean philosophers who were not happy with Judah Abravanel's Platonic and kabbalistic interpretations and approach. The negative criticisms apparently were sufficient for him to keep his work private.

It is not known precisely when Judah died. It was most likely in the early 1520s, and certainly well before Mariano Lenzi, a humanist who had been associated with Pico della Mirandola, came upon *Dialoghi di amore* and arranged for the book to be translated into Italian and published in Rome in about 1535. *Dialoghi* was a sensation, a Renaissance bestseller. One of the few copies of this edition that has survived can be found at the British Library in London. The book of 468 pages is bound in a rich black leather, the paper inside almost like silk, and the print an elegant italic style. During the next two decades, five other editions of the book were released in Italy. There were two French versions, three different translations in Spanish, and, much later, a Hebrew edition. Perhaps to make it even more popular, the Venice second edition, released in 1541, included a statement on the title page that Leone or Judah had converted to Christianity. Though the statement was also repeated in the third edition, published in 1545, there is absolutely no evidence to support this. Judah remained a committed, though assimilated, Jew his entire life.

The secret to the success of *Dialoghi di amore* was that it was both a work of literature and philosophy, and appealed to a wide variety of readers. Moreover, Judah's subject was the power and mysteries of love coupled with a religious and spiritual debate about the meaning of life in general. Modelled on the writings of Plato but also influenced by medieval Sephardi philosophers, the dialogue he so brilliantly created was a conversation between two abstract entities: Philo, representing love or appetite; and the woman he loves, Sophia, representing knowledge. Throughout the book, these two characters dissect the nature, ubiquity, and origin of love. It is possibly the finest example of the merging of Jewish and kabbalistic thought with the "cosmic pantheist attitude of the Italian Renaissance."

Nothing, according to Abravanel, "stands outside of love. Nothing can take its place. It is the granite from which all life is built. God is not only identified with love, but He is love." By the end of the dialogue, it is clear that in Abravanel's view, "intellectual beauty – the beauty of order, plan, and harmony – is superior to physical beauty [and] the supreme beauty is the order, plan, and harmony of the universe, which is the outward expression of divine beauty." Or, as he put it so poetically in the language of the day, "It is the splendour of divine love poured forth upon man which first leads him to his highest pleasure and happiness; and in the second places comes his own burning love leading him to his beatitude and to union with the highest beauty. And that you may the better understand this, you may behold its likeness mirrored in the two perfect lovers, man and woman."

Judah's work, like that of his father, reached across the generations and influenced a diverse group, including the Italian philosopher Giordano Bruno, who was burned at the stake for heresy in 1600; the English clergyman and author Robert Burton, who made repeated references to *Dialoghi* in his 1621 study, *Anatomy of Melancholy*; and possibly the great English philosopher and statesman Francis Bacon. Judah's views on love also made a significant impression on the Amsterdam Jewish philosopher Baruch (Benedict) Spinoza, who created a great controversy in the 1650s by challenging the accepted theories and practices of Judaism.

Samuel and Benvenida

WHILE JUDAH ABRAVANEL may have been something of a "dreamer," his younger brother Samuel was definitely not. Following in the footsteps of his father, Samuel was a well-educated, intelligent, and wealthy man who used his influence and connections to improve the lives of his people. Samuel Usque, a poet of the times, who knew Samuel Abravanel, called him "great in learning, great in ancestry, great in wealth."

Born in Lisbon in 1471, Samuel was in his early twenties when he arrived in Naples with his family. He already had been schooled in the Talmud by his father and later studied in Salonika. Returning to Italy, he became a financier and moneylender. He moved in the highest circles in Naples, first as an advisor to the Viscount of Naples and then in a similar capacity for Cosimo de Medici of Florence. Like Isaac Abravanel, Samuel also used his vast wealth to fund Jewish education, assist impoverished members of the community, and provide dowries for orphan girls.

Samuel chose to remain in Naples, even after his father had left the city, though the situation was less than positive. With control of the kingdom in the hands of the Spanish after 1501, the Jewish population was gradually reduced and taxes were raised. Samuel, with assistance from his father-in-law (and uncle) Jacob Abravanel, succeeded in obtaining royal permission for fifty wealthy Jewish families to settle in Naples in 1520. Restrictions on Jewish trading and financial activities were also eased. Recognizing the importance of close royal connections, Samuel befriended the new viceroy sent from Spain in the early 1530s, Don Pedro de Toledo. Meanwhile Samuel's wife, Benvenida, became a tutor for Pedro's demanding daughter Leonora – a close relationship that would play a significant role in the Abravanel family's future after Leonora married Cosimo de Medici, the duke of Florence, in 1539.

Like other Sephardi women of the times, women who were not content to live in the shadow of their husbands, Benvenida Abravanel was a talented and dynamic force. She had a well-deserved reputation for being level-headed, courageous, and an individual who personified virtue, grace, and culture. She was, claimed one person who knew her well, "one of the most noble and highly spirited women who have existed in Israel since the time of our dispersion."

Her only real lapse of judgement seems to have been when she was caught up in the excitement surrounding David Reubeni, one of the first of several false messiahs. When Reubeni swept through Italy in the early 1520s proclaiming that redemption was at hand, Benvenida sent him a silken banner embroidered with the Ten Commandments. It is not known whether she eventually saw through his charade, though like many others she probably mourned his arrest in Spain and his violent death in prison in about 1538.

Benvenida and Samuel were more practical when the viceroy decreed in early 1533 that all Jews were required either to leave the kingdom of Naples or convert to Christianity. They fought the order with petitions, personal pleas, and lots of money.

The strategy worked, and Pedro postponed the order, but the expulsion edict continued to hang over the community. In 1541, when the decree was proclaimed once again, the Abravanels, like many other Jewish families, had had enough. They began to make preparations to leave Naples permanently. Wisely, they accepted

the invitation of the more tolerant Duke Ercole II, the ruler of the
House of Este, and settled further north in Ferrara, a city close to
Venice and burgeoning with commercial opportunities.

Naples's loss was Ferrara's gain. Ercole was no fool and understood that allowing more Jews, especially wealthy ones, to settle in
his duchy made good economic sense. He even looked the other
way when a large number of *conversos* from Milan relocated to
Ferrara and returned to Judaism. By the time the Abravanels
arrived, Ferrara had at least ten synagogues and a vibrant Hebrew
printing business, although it would soon come under attack from
the Vatican. Indeed, while Jews in Ferrara did eventually have to
wear a yellow badge following Pope Paul IV's infamous bull, the
city did not have a ghetto until 1624.

Samuel and Benvenida lived in grand style in an opulent mansion,
befitting their status and wealth. Immediately, Samuel re-established
himself as a merchant and banker. His son Jacob, meanwhile, had
accepted an offer to work for Cosimo de Medici in nearby
Florence. When Samuel died unexpectedly in 1547 – from taking
an overdose of scammony, a gum resin then used as a drastic
purgative – Benvenida, with assistance from Jacob, decided to
carry on the banking business. It was an opportune moment.

To compete more effectively with Venice, Ferrara, and other
Italian states, Cosimo de Medici invited more Jewish moneylenders
to settle in his duchy. One of the first financiers to apply was Ishmael
de Rieti, the head of a prominent Jewish banking family from
Siena. Benvenida and Jacob, utilizing their close connections to the
Medici, were next. By a charter granted in 1547, the Abravanels
were permitted to engage in banking activities in the territories of
Cortona, Borgo San Sepolcro, Castrocaro, San Giovanni, Valdarno,
and Pescia. Prato and Arezzo were added to the list after Benvenida
teamed up with Abraham da Pisa, a brother to Yehiel Nissim of Pisa,
who had been a lifelong friend to Don Isaac Abravanel.

The following year, Jacob Abravanel convinced Cosimo that it
would serve the duke's economic interests to allow Sephardi merchants from the Levant to settle in Tuscany. Despite the fact that

some of the merchants were *marranos* intent on returning to Judaism, Cosimo ensured that their rights as "nobles and citizens" were well protected. It was all part of his grand plan to build the coastal city of Livorno (Leghorn) into a port to rival Pisa. The strategy worked, and within a decade both Livorno and its new Jewish community were thriving. Meanwhile, the Abravanels found themselves in a heated competition with other Jewish bankers throughout Tuscany. Yet by all accounts, Benvenida and Jacob fared well against the Da Rieti family and the influential Mendes family who had extensive financial interests in Venice, Ferrara, and Ancona.

Benvenida died in Ferrara in 1560. She and Samuel, besides their eldest son, Jacob, left three other children: Judah; Gioia, who married her first cousin, also named Jacob, the son of Benvenida's brother; and Letizia, who married her first cousin Isaac, the son of Judah, who had finally reunited with his family. Though the Abravanels continued to prosper from their home in Ferrara, the anti-Jewish laws and restrictions that were imposed after 1555 during the Counter-Reformation era were a detriment.

Gioia and her husband had already left Ferrara for Florence, where they lived in a large house in the Santo Spirito quarter. In February 1563, the two were accused of attempting to pass themselves off as Christians, an allegation that, if true, could have had serious consequences. On their behalf, Cosimo de Medici wrote to Cardinal Alesandrino defending their honour and explaining that Jacob and Gioia had always lived "under the code of Jewish law, and they have never professed themselves Christians." It was later discovered that an individual who was jealous of the Abravanels' power and status had made the false accusation. The cardinal accepted the duke's explanation and the matter was not pursued.

Regardless of Cosimo's positive feelings towards the Abravanels and other Jews, he was overly ambitious and possessed a large ego. What he wanted most was to be named the grand duke of Tuscany, a title that only the Vatican could grant. The price he had to pay was to fall into line in his treatment of the Jews. First, in 1567, Jews were again required to wear yellow hats. Three years later, a year after Cosimo had become the grand duke, several Jewish banks in Florence were shut down. Several months later, ghettos were established in Florence and Siena. It was not much better in Ferrara as the new duke of Este, Ercole III, also accepted the Vatican's lead and permitted the introduction of the Inquisition.

As they witnessed the burning of the Talmud, the mass executions of *conversos* accused of heresy, and the crowding of Jews into ghettos throughout Italy, most of the remaining members of the Abravanel family concluded that their future lay elsewhere. After almost a century in Italy, they turned eastward, following the path of thousands of other Jews to Salonika and Constantinople in the lands of the Ottoman sultan.

Chapter Three

PHYSICIANS, POETS, AND A FALSE MESSIAH

Constantinople, 1666

Brothers and teachers, friends and acquaintances! I, Isaac Sarfati . . . proclaim to you that Turkey is a land wherein nothing is lacking, and where, if you will, all shall yet be well with you. The way to the Holy Land lies open to you through Turkey. Is it not better for you to live under Muslims than under Christians? Here every man may dwell at peace under his own vine and fig tree. Here you are allowed to wear the most precious garments.

— RABBI YITZHAK SARFATI, 1454

The Sublime Porte

MORE THAN A CENTURY before the Abravanel family departed from Italy and arrived in Constantinople and Salonika, events were taking place in the east that were to have profound ramifications on their lives and on the lives of Jews throughout Europe. The conquest of the city of Constantinople in 1453 and the subsequent destruction of the Byzantine empire by the young Sultan Mehmet II, ruler of the House of Osman, or Ottoman, shook the faith of the continent's Christian rulers like few other military campaigns up to that time. It was the culmination of nearly two hundred years in which the Turks gradually but methodically expanded their empire at the expense of the Byzantines. Within five decades, Mehmet and the Ottoman sultans who followed in his footsteps controlled a vast empire that stretched from the Danube to the Nile – from the Balkans north to Hungary, and as far east as Syria and Egypt.

The siege of Constantinople had begun in early March 1453, and though it took close to eight difficult weeks of fighting for Mehmet finally to declare victory, the outcome was never in doubt. Confronting the Greeks, Venetians, and Catalans trapped inside the walled city was a mighty force of three hundred thousand men, including the twelve thousand Janissary troops, the Sultan's personal and highly disciplined guard.* They had at their disposal the finest weapons of the day in addition to monster cannons never before employed in warfare.

When it was over, Mehmet II established his new capital and court in Constantinople, now referred to by the Muslims as Istanbul (though officially it was called Constantinople until 1930). But instead of occupying the Great Palace of the Byzantine Emperor Constantine, Mehmet built his own, the Topkapi Palace, or Saray, on a site overlooking the waters of the Bosporus where the Acropolis once stood. The sultan's new home was of a unique design for the era: a series of four elaborate private courts, enclosed and isolated from each other, with many small low buildings that housed the sultan's retinue of officials, servants, bureaucrats, and the beautiful women of the harem. In order to enter the sultan's sanctum, visitors had to pass through a large ornamented gate, referred to by the French as the Sublime Porte (or High Gate), a term that soon was used to describe the Ottoman government.

Today, Topkapi is Istanbul's most popular tourist attraction, a vast collection of stunning gardens, magnificent archways, towers, and fountains, and a superb collection of historic artifacts. Visitors to the harem are taken through a narrow stone passage and into the sultan's private quarters and the apartments where his "favourite,"

---

* The word "Janissary" was derived from the Turkish phrase yeniçeri, meaning new soldiers. The troops consisted of mainly young Christian boys who had been taken from their families at a young age, converted to Islam, and moulded into a powerful military force that served the Sultan's every whim. The Janissaries played a key role in Ottoman society until the organization was disbanded in 1826.

his ruling wife, and the other concubines (all captured foreigners) were housed. The splendid rooms are decorated mainly in distinctive blue-and-white glazed tiles, and the Sultan's imperial hall, where he entertained, still appears lavish. On the walls throughout the palace, the prayers of the Koran are inscribed in Arabic letters, a testimony to the Sultan's faith and power.

To Christian Europe, however, the Ottomans then and later embodied bigotry, oppression, and intolerance. In the popular imagination, the Muslim conquerors were as the eighteenth-century historian Edward Gibbon first portrayed them: "fanatical warrior[s] riding out of the desert with the [Koran] in one hand and the sword in the other, offering [their] victims a choice between the two."

For Jews, on the other hand, ever since Elijah Capsali wrote about the siege of Constantinople in the sixteenth century, the sultans have been viewed in a more positive light. They alone among the rulers of the world supposedly offered Jews as well as Christians a haven free of the religious persecution that characterized life in almost every other country, kingdom, and empire. Even Cardinal Reginald Pole, the English papal scholar and King Henry VIII's great opponent, was forced to concede that "the Turks do not compel others to adopt their belief. He who does not attack their religion may profess among them what religion he will; he is safe." In fact, three days after Mehmet II had marched into Constantinople, he proclaimed that the then small Jewish community – mainly Romaniotes, or Greek Jews, Ashkenazi Jews from Eastern Europe, and the children of Sephardi Jewish immigrants who had fled Castile and Aragon–Catalonia after the bloody riots of 1391 – were free to resume their work and practise their religion.

So esteemed were the sultans in the opinion of Jewish scholars that in the rabbinical Responsa (religious legal commentaries) they were commonly referred to as "the mighty and the benevolent" and the Ottoman Empire as "our gracious kingdom." Isaac Abravanel, too, despite the fact that he had resisted leaving Europe for Constantinople, regarded the Jewish migration to the land of the Ottomans as a step toward salvation. In 1550, the few Jews still living in Provence, who were threatened with expulsion, sent a small group to ascertain whether they should move to Constantinople. "We have no words," the envoys concluded, "to record the enlargement and deliverance that has been achieved by the Jews in this place."

Still, the historical reality was more complex than rabbis and early historians would admit. Jews were subject to heavy taxation, forced relocations known in Turkish as *sürgün* – only one of the many imaginative ways the sultan increased the Jewish population of Constantinople after 1453 – and occasionally repressive military conscription. There were strict building regulations with respect to renovating or building new synagogues, and Jews as well as Christians were required to wear only certain kinds and colours of clothing, hats or turbans, and shoes.* This last restriction, it should be stressed, was less a sign of subservience or humiliation (as the Jewish badge represented in Christian lands) and more one of designating the proper place and status in Ottoman society of each of the three self-governing religious communities, known as the *millet* system.

From 1453 onward, almost until the fall of the Ottoman Empire in the early twentieth century, religious persecution by the sultans and their officials against Jews was indeed minimal and pressure to convert to Islam was minor, particularly when compared to events in Spain, France, and the rest of the Christian-controlled continent. It was true that Jews were *dhimmi*, non-believers, yet the Ottomans "wanted tax-paying subjects, not Muslims," in the words of British writer Jason Goodwin. They saw in Jews, especially those who migrated to their land after the expulsion from Spain, skilled

---

* While the rules regarding clothing changed over time, the colour green was generally reserved for Muslims, because it was regarded as holy. Muslims usually wore white turbans and yellow shoes. Muslims also wore finer fabrics than Jews or Christians. Jewish clothes thus tended to be of a coarser material and darker. Depending on a variety of circumstances, these rules were not always rigorously enforced and many Sephardi Jews mixed Ottoman dress with the type they also had worn in Spain.

craftsmen, talented artisans, and astute merchants linked to the Sephardi economic network throughout Europe.

Most important of all, Jews were loyal and dedicated subjects willing and able to serve the greater glory of the empire. It was for this reason that a year after the conquest of Constantinople, Mehmet permitted Rabbi Yitzhak Sarfati, the Chief Rabbi of Edirne, to issue his famous open letter urging European Jews to settle in the Sultan's lands. Four decades later, at the time of the Spanish expulsion, Bayezid II, Mehmet's eldest son and successor, held similar attitudes. "They say Ferdinand is a wise king. How could he be? He who impoverishes his country [by expelling the Jews] and enriches our own," the sultan was supposed to have remarked.

From the Jews' standpoint, the Ottoman system of self-government, in which each of the religious communities remained separate and apart, fit perfectly with the overwhelming Jewish desire for economic participation at a high level while retaining cultural and religious independence. Thus the upper and middle classes were able to pursue their own agendas through the *kehillot* (or "congregations"; singular, *kahal*), which were akin to governing bodies and functioned like municipal governments, though with influence from community rabbis.

Meanwhile, the Sephardim, who soon after their arrival dominated all areas of Ottoman Jewish life – much to the dissatisfaction of the older but smaller Ashkenazi and Romaniote communities – stubbornly retained their local Spanish customs and identity for many generations. Their synagogues in name and liturgical practice resembled the synagogues they had left behind in Toledo, Madrid, and Cordoba, and they still do. One of the oldest active synagogues in Istanbul, if not in the world, is the Ahrida Synagogue in the city's crowded Balat neighbourhood, where Jews were living as early as the 1430s. You enter the building through a small doorway directly off a narrow side-street. This leads you first into a charming courtyard and then into the restored synagogue. Built in the Sephardi style, the wood-panelled *tebah* in the middle of the sanctuary where the Chazan stands to chant the prayers is literally a small replica of

Noah's Ark. Men and women sit separately, the men on all sides of the *tebah* and the women on the second level, as is customary. (The one and only sign of modernity in the ancient synagogue is the presence of hundreds of yellow hard hats kept on shelves by the windows for members, a precaution in case of earthquake.)

In the Jewish neighbourhoods in Constantinople and Salonika, women favoured recipes from Seville and Barcelona; while the men usually began a tale with the Spanish phrase *"era'n buenos d'un rey,"* "it was in the good days of the king." Ladino (Judeo-Spanish) was more commonly spoken in Jewish homes than Turkish, and to this day, some older members of Istanbul's small Jewish community still speak it, although their numbers are dwindling each year. In short, the Sephardi identity did not vanish, even among those Jews of Spanish ancestry who had never set foot in Spain. When a Spanish senator paid a visit to Salonika in 1904, "He was naively overjoyed, not only to find himself prattling away on the street in his own tongue, but to feel, in his bones, so perfectly at home."

Beginning in the 1450s and at least for the next century, the aura of the Sublime Porte among Jews did not fade. They came by boat across the Mediterranean or traversed the European continent. Some, like the Abravanel family, reached the empire via Italy; other Spanish Jews settled first in North Africa or in eastern Mediterranean areas before moving further east. As anti-Jewish attitudes grew stronger during the era of the Counter-Reformation, the number of immigrants who arrived at Ottoman ports probably exceeded one hundred and fifty thousand. By the 1530s, more than fifty thousand Jews (about 5 or 6 per cent of the total population) lived in Constantinople, and more than seventy thousand a century later. In Salonika, the "Jerusalem of the Balkans," as it was called, the Jewish population was less, but even more significant. By the middle of the sixteenth century, at least twenty thousand Jews resided in the Aegean port city, the only major urban centre in the world at the time with a Jewish majority.

For at least two generations, they dominated the Ottoman economy like no other group. Pierre Bellon de Mans, a traveller from France, noted on a journey east in 1547 that the Jews "have taken over the traffic and commerce of Turkey to such an extent that the Turk's wealth and revenue is in their hands. [Their tax farmers] set the highest price on the collection of tributes from the provinces and harbor dues from ships." Likewise, Nicolas de Nicolay, a French diplomat and geographer who visited Constantinople in the 1550s, remarked that "At the present day, [the Jews] have in their hands the most and greatest traffic of merchandise and ready money that is in the Levant. And likewise the shops and warehouses, the best furnished with all rich sorts of merchandise, which are in Constantinople, are those of the Jews." He also marvelled at the Jewish printing industry and the skill of Jewish engravers, artists, and writers.

With their numerous contacts across Europe, the Ottoman Jews controlled international trade. Many were multilingual and possessed the accounting skills necessary to succeed across Europe, from London and Amsterdam into Hungary and Poland and east to Russia. Their agents were in every town and port. Their word was their bond, and huge trade deals were usually sealed with a handshake. If there were contractual problems, they often asked rabbis to settle disputes. They held the most lucrative tax farms, collected the Constantinople customs duties, and controlled the traffic in salt. They speculated in commodities like coffee, sugar, and indigo, and reaped huge profits when their gambles paid off. There were also armies of Jewish shopkeepers, artisans, peddlers, and hawkers who serviced the Ottoman economy.

Located near the mouths of the Gallikos and Vardar rivers, Salonika was the natural entrepôt of the region and the access point for trade from the Mediterranean to Central Europe. Jews took advantage of this geographical advantage by maintaining a near-monopoly in the textile industry. In one way or the other, most Jews in the city were involved with cloth – as manufacturers, shippers, tailors, dress and hat makers, dyers, and labourers. The port even shut down on the Jewish Sabbath. Salonika Jews were the chief suppliers of cloth to the Janissaries and exported textiles to Italy and to cities across Europe. From approximately 1568 onward,

Salonika Jews fulfilled a major part of their tax requirement with shipments of cloth. But this could be dangerous. In 1637, the authorities were not pleased with the quality of the cloth they received and promptly arrested Judah Covo, a prominent member of the Salonika Jewish community. He was given a quick trial, condemned to death, and beheaded.

For many years the city was "a kind of vast cloth factory, with most of the families participating as units, working long hours at home, day and night – men, women and children alike, on their terraces, even in the streets, producing the finest and softest quality stuffs," writes American historian Stanford Shaw. "The constant noise of the weaving machines was an immediate reminder of what the city was doing. The water used to wash the woolens joined in rivers with the dye liquids, running through the streets and forming permanent pestilential lakes in the lower areas of Salonika."

Only the onset of the British Industrial Revolution and the shift of European economic power west to Amsterdam and London in the seventeenth and eighteenth centuries ended Salonika's dominance in the textile industry. Thereafter, the community became mired in debt and poverty, suffered through a terrible fire in 1620 that destroyed thousands of Jewish homes as well as twenty-eight synagogues, lost thousands more through immigration, yet continued to persevere right up to the Second World War.

Dr. Hamon

LIKE EVERYWHERE ELSE IN THE DIASPORA, the diplomatic and economic talents and skills of a handful of Jews brought them into the circles of the highest power. From the notable vantage point of the inner court of the sultans at Constantinople, Jews not only influenced European politics and amassed vast personal fortunes (as well as contributed their fair share of taxes, with some exceptions), but equally represented and promoted the interests of the larger

Jewish community. Many of these Jewish courtiers, interestingly enough, were first and foremost physicians. Indeed, it was their medical expertise that had first attracted the sultans' attention.

It had long been a sign of status among the sultans, as well as other rulers and princes across Europe, to have a Jewish personal physician in their service. And there were many to choose from. "Next to moneylending, medicine seems to have been the most preponderant profession among Jews," according to historian Joseph Shatzmiller in his 1994 study of Jewish doctors during the later Middle Ages. In some European locales, Jews represented less than 10 per cent of the population but accounted for more than 50 per cent of the physicians.

As medieval European society became "medicalized" (to use Shatzmiller's term) between 1250 and 1450, in part due to the spread of scientific and biological knowledge – as rudimentary as it was – the demand for well-trained physicians increased dramatically. Jews were well positioned to take advantage of this opportunity. Many of them could read Arabic medical books (in addition to Greek and Hebrew) and they were not stifled by Church interference or opposition to the spread of science. With the onset of the Black Plague in the 1340s, many cities hired physicians in the hope of solving their drastic public health problems. Though in an era when "mummy powder" was still a popular cure and women's breast milk was believed to have magical and medicinal value, this was wishful thinking at best.

It was only natural that the sultans, who entrusted the doctors with their lives and the lives of their families, also sought advice and favours from these learned and talented multilingual men. One of the more famous Jewish physician-courtiers in the years before and immediately after the conquest of Constantinople was Jacob of Gaeta (a province in southern Italy), also known as Hekim Yakub (or Yakub Pasha). He was an ambitious and powerful individual, who served as the chief physician at the courts of Sultan Murad II and his son Mehmet II.

In his day, Yakub was well-known in every European capital, and it was said that Venetian officials who were anxious to meet with Mehmet presented Yakub with "thirty crimson robes" as payment for his assistance and influence. It is likely that the sultan allowed Yakub to become close with his Venetian rivals as way of keeping a close eye on them. So highly regarded was the doctor that he and his descendants received an exemption from taxes (not the last Jewish courtier to be granted this privilege) and he was honoured when a Constantinople neighbourhood was renamed Hekim Yakub Mahallesi.

In the early 1480s, Yakub converted to Islam, an act uncharacteristic of Jewish physicians and courtiers in the Ottoman Empire. He did receive a large grant of land, perhaps a reward from Sultan Bayezid II for his apostasy. As a Muslim, he was now able to serve the court in an even higher capacity and did so first as a *defterdar* (royal treasurer) and then as vizier, or government minister. While Yakub had rejected Judaism, he did not, by all accounts, forget his obligations to the members of the Jewish community, and continued to work on their behalf.

Whether Yakub influenced Bayezid to accept Spanish Jewish immigrants in 1492 is not known. But Yakub's devotion to the court paved the way for the Jewish physicians who followed him as both doctors and diplomats.

Among those who benefited from Yakub's pioneering efforts were Joseph Hamon, his more famous and esteemed son Moses, and their descendants. Well-educated, skilled as physicians, and possessing a clear understanding of European affairs, the Hamon family epitomized the success and influence of Jews in the Diaspora. For more than a century, this unique family of physicians, scholars, and poets helped to shape Ottoman policy at home and abroad as well as work to enhance the lives of Jews throughout the empire.

Joseph Hamon was born in Granada in 1450, the son or nephew of Isaac Hamon, a physician to the last Muslim ruler of the region, King Abdallah, otherwise known as Boabdil (see Chapter One). Not much is known about Joseph's early career in Granada, only that he followed in his father or uncle's footsteps and served for a brief time at the exquisite court inside the Alhambra. Once the Spanish monarchs conquered Granada and issued the Edict of Expulsion, Joseph left with his wife and young two-year-old son Moses. Like so many Sephardi Jews, he found a refuge at Constantinople, where he immediately attracted the attention of Sultan Bayezid II and was appointed as a court physician. Bayezid attempted to persuade Joseph to convert to Islam. He would not. Three days after he had been given an ultimatum, he refused to appear before the sultan wearing a white turban, worn only by Muslims, even under the threat of death. The sultan was surprised, and also impressed.

Bayezid had been a competent ruler, yet he had not lived up to expectations, nor could he compete with the memory of his illustrious father, Mehmet II. After close to three decades of turbulent rule, a rebellion in 1512 forced Bayezid to abdicate in favour of his youngest son, Selim I, who had gained the support of the powerful Janissaries.

Selim's reign lasted only eight years. He is best remembered for two main controversial deeds, one more nefarious than the other. First, he earned his infamous nickname Selim "the Terrible" by permanently eliminating his rivals to the throne. This included murdering his two brothers and eight nephews. And second, ruling with an iron hand, he embarked on an expansionary conquest of Asian lands that would have made his grandfather Mehmet proud. Still, with respect to Jews and other groups in his kingdom, he was more liberal and open-minded than Bayezid had been.

Following great, though costly, victories in Persia, Selim turned his armies on Egypt and Syria. On this campaign, Joseph Hamon joined him, presumably providing medical and moral support. After taking Damascus in August 1516, the Ottomans moved toward Cairo, capturing that city too. On the return journey to Constantinople, Hamon died in Syria of unknown causes during the winter of 1517–18. At his funeral, Rabbi Joseph Garson praised

Joseph and pointed out that even though he had risen to great prominence at the court, he had never forgotten his co-religionists.

Within two years, Selim, too, only fifty-four years old, had died as he contemplated further conquests against the West. He was succeeded by his only son, the wise, just, and revered Suleiman I (or Süleyman), known in the annals of the Ottoman Empire as *Kanuni*, the "Legislator," and the to the rest of the world as "Suleiman the Magnificent." Under Suleiman's rule, which lasted from 1521 to 1566, the empire reached its greatest heights, expanding north into Hungary and extending almost to Vienna and Venice. He was "spare and swarthy" in appearance, according to one Venetian diplomat, but equally a man of "refined and kindly sentiment" – at least most of the time. At the Topkapi Palace, one of Suleiman's legacies is the *Bab-i-Selam*, or Gate of Salutation, an impressive archway built in 1524 that only the sultan was permitted to use.

Suleiman was extremely protective of his position and status, and one of his more nasty legacies is a long list of murdered family members and close friends, individuals who the sultan rightly or wrongly viewed as potential rivals and threats to his authority. In 1536, he most likely disposed of his one-time friend and supporter the Grand Vizier Ibrahim, because, in his opinion, Ibrahim had grown too powerful for his own good. Less than two decades later it was the turn of Prince Mustafa, his eldest son, a child from his first wife, the Sultana Gülbehar. After Suleiman was told by his second wife, the beautiful and conniving Roxelana, and her ally and son-in-law the Grand Vizier Rustem Pasha, that Mustafa was attempting to usurp his throne, he arranged for his son to be strangled while he watched from behind a curtain. Mustafa's son, Suleiman's grandson, met the same terrible fate. And then, near the end of his reign, he supported his and Roxelana's eldest son, Selim, over their other son, Bayezid, when the two brothers became embroiled in a bloody feud to succeed their father. In 1561, Bayezid and his five sons were executed on Suleiman's orders.

Such were the times that Suleiman's actions at the court had little effect on his subjects; they loved him all the same. As Will Durant concluded in his assessment of the Sultan, "Suleiman fought too many wars, killed half his progeny, had a creative vizier slain without warning or trial; he had the faults that go with unchecked power. But beyond question he was the greatest and ablest ruler of his age."

"Prince" Moses

SULEIMAN HAD ONE OTHER KEY ATTRIBUTE: he surrounded himself with a group of talented advisors and ministers, including sixteen Muslim physicians and a handful of Jewish ones. The most important of his Jewish doctors was Joseph Hamon's son, Moses, about thirty-one years old and already a skilled physician when Suleiman claimed the throne in 1521. We can imagine Moses later in his life resembling the Jewish doctor portrayed in Nicolas de Nicolay's famous 1550s sketch of the *Médicin Juif*, a distinguished robed courtier with a trimmed beard and on his head a tall scarlet hat that signified his high position. Nicolay might well have used Moses Hamon as his model. The sultan's physicians lived in apartments adjacent to the harem and worked in an outer courtyard in chambers on the far side of the Topkapi overlooking the Sea of Marmara. This building also served as a pharmacy, infirmary, and home to the head tutor.

The living quarters were not as grand as the sultan's, but fine wool carpets spun on imperial looms covered the stone floors and the walls were furnished with the same blue-and-white tiles found in all sections of the palace. Each apartment had a large bathroom decorated in marble and a bath fit for an advisor to the sultan; the Ottomans attached great importance to personal cleanliness. In the nearby sitting room, a physician such as Hamon could study medical texts, consult with patients that the Sultan permitted him to treat, meet with representatives of the Jewish community, keep up with correspondence, likely with strongly brewed coffee on the table beside him. It was a more popular drink than wine, which was generally drunk in taverns outside the Topkapi's walls.

Though he made his mark as a courtier and diplomat, Moses Hamon was also a well-respected physician and the author of several books on medicine and one on dental care and gum disease. This last work was dedicated to Suleiman and may have been the first Turkish work on dentistry ever published. (Though Hamon's book is undated, he most likely composed it soon after the first known treatise on the subject was published in Leipzig in 1530 by an anonymous doctor, but certainly long before Bartolomeo Eustachio's well-known study, *Libellus de dentibus*, was published in Venice in 1563.)

At the court, Hamon's success and influence as an advisor was in part dependent on his outgoing personality and the respect Suleiman had for him. But it was also linked to the friendship he cultivated with the Sultana Roxelana and her son-in-law Rustem Pasha. Moses had not had a warm relationship with the Grand Vizier Ibrahim, and he was probably among those at the court who did not grieve Ibrahim's untimely death. Soon after the grand vizier's execution, Hamon's salary was increased, bringing him closer to what Muslim physicians were paid, though this may just have been a coincidence. In the currency of the day, Hamon's daily salary as a court physician increased from 45 akçe in the late 1520s, to 50 akçe in 1537, to 75 akçe in 1549. Muslim physicians were paid 80 akçe in 1549, while the commander-in-chief of the Janissaries was paid 500 akçe per day.

As his father had done, Hamon accompanied the sultan on his three great expeditions against rebellious Persia, in 1534, 1548, and again in 1553. Each time, he was gone from Constantinople and his family for more than a year and a half. The fighting was fierce. There was a bitter hatred between the Turks and the Persians, one based on religious and national differences that dated back hundreds of years. During the battles in 1534, though the sultan ultimately prevailed, the Turks lost ten thousand men. Hamon was likely at Suleiman's side when he triumphantly marched into

Baghdad at the end of November 1534. He was not able to return to Constantinople until early in 1536, following a difficult trek that took ninety-two days.

By the late 1540s, both his son, Joseph, born about 1527, and his nephew Isaac had become physicians, following the family tradition, and had joined Hamon at Suleiman's court. While he may not have been remunerated to the same extent as the Muslim doctor-courtiers, Nicolas de Nicolay, for one, considered him in the early 1550s to be the "leading court physician." A decade earlier, for example, when fighting took place between the Venetian and Ottoman navies, Hamon played a small diplomatic role. As part of a comprehensive peace treaty negotiated between the two powers in October 1540, Venice, under pressure to agree to terms, was forced not only to cede some small Mediterranean islands, but also to pay the sultan war reparations of three hundred thousand ducats and another thirty thousand ducats to Turkish officials. Hamon's personal gift from the Venetians amounted to a thousand ducats.

There is no disputing that the Hamon family lived the good life in Constantinople. In an age when most Jews were not wealthy, when they resided in small cramped and crowded houses and apartments and scratched out livings as shoemakers, tailors, and peddlers in the Balat neighbourhood in the capital city, the Hamons lived like kings in a grand residence within the walls of the Topkapi Palace, complete with servants and fine furniture. Testament to Hamon's affluence was his valuable library, which included ancient Byzantine manuscripts dating back centuries. One treasured work, which later found its way into the library of the Holy Roman Emperor in Vienna, was *De materia medica*, a Greek study of medicinal plants written by Pedanius Dioscorides, a first-century C.E. herbalist. It remains in the Austrian National Library to this day. On Hamon's death, the books and manuscripts were valued at approximately five thousand ducats.

Hamon also did valuable work on behalf of Jews in Constantinople, Salonika, and outside of the empire, and was a generous supporter of religious and community endeavours. This was all the more notable in an era when the political power of rabbis was declining and the lay leadership was on the rise.*

According to Salomon Atia, a scholar in Constantinople who knew Hamon and presumably benefited from his largesse, he "is greatly respected by his brothers who give him the title of 'prince,' not only because of his high position but also in the figurative sense of the word."

Hamon's mediation skills were tested on at least two occasions, when he helped resolve major disputes in Salonika. Even more so than in Constantinople, the Salonika Jewish community was divided: by the 1550s there were at least twenty-six separate local *kehillot* in the city. Salonika's Sephardim seemed to have continuously argued amongst themselves about synagogue rituals and policies; the only issue that united them was their condescension to Ashkenazi Jews, who in turn regarded the Sephardim with suspicion and questioned their religious convictions, practices, devotion, and piety.

"In Salonika, every [Jewish] man speaks his native tongue," reported Rabbi Joseph ibn Leb, a prominent community leader during Suleiman's reign. "When the exiles arrived, each vernacular group founded an independent congregation, there being mobility from congregation to congregation. Each congregation maintains its poor; each congregation is entirely separate in the Crown register. Thus each congregation appears to be an independent city."

Some years later, even after the publication in 1564 of Rabbi Joseph Caro's *Shulhan Aruch*, a codification of Jewish law and ritual that was intended to act as a unifying force, Sephardim in Salonika

---

* The rabbis' religious and moral influence may have been on the wane as well. Rabbi David ibn Zimra, for instance, among other rabbis, complained about the "religious laxity" of Jews in the sixteenth century. Echoing more modern sentiments, he wrote that "The people of this generation, especially those who come from the cities of the West, are not devoted to religion, nor are they people of faith, nor is it needless to add, are they people of Jewish learning." On another occasion, he noted that "In this time, the generation is very rebellious against our religion standards and impudence is written large on its face." In fact, the rabbis could not stop Jews from committing what they interpreted to be moral laxness as well: gambling, drunkenness, and adultery (despite Ottoman laws to the contrary).

remained divided as ever. As Rabbi Samuel de Medina, the greatest of Salonika's rabbis, observed in a Responsa written in 1594, "There are a large number of Jews in Salonika but they follow different customs: there are differences not only among those with distinct ancestries, but even among those who come from the same land. . . . In other words, no one can say which are the accepted customs of the town of Salonika."

In 1545, an epidemic erupted in Salonika leading to the death of two hundred Jews. Rabbi Joseph ibn Leb was blamed for contributing to the tragedy by his inaction. In fact, his own son was one of those who died. It was at this point that the rabbi appealed to Moses Hamon, who fired off a series of letters to members of the Salonika community demanding that Rabbi Leb be treated fairly and with respect. Following an investigation by a deputation dispatched to Salonika by Hamon, this tense situation was resolved.

A few years later, Hamon was again forced to intervene in the community's affairs. An unscrupulous and powerful tax farmer by the name of Baruch had publicly challenged the authority of Rabbi Leb. Upset about a rabbinical ruling that had gone against him, Baruch berated Rabbi Leb and then, in an unheard-of act of defiance, slapped him across the face in Salonika's main marketplace. Baruch also attempted to collect some questionable taxes from the city's Jews.

After an appeal was made to Hamon, the physician used his connections at court and had Baruch brought before the royal *divan*, the sultan's council of government ministers. Baruch, despite his wealth, had his privileges revoked and was exiled to Cyprus. On yet another occasion, Hamon helped prove the innocence of a Jew accused of murdering a Muslim woman. This earned him the reputation of being the Ottoman Jews' "guardian angel."

The benefits to the Jewish community of having someone of Hamon's stature at the court was proved yet again with an infamous blood-libel accusation. Since it was first propagated in 1173 by a Benedictine monk named Thomas of Monmouth in his *The Life and Miracles of Saint William of Norwich*, the bizarre accusation that

Jews ritually murdered Christian children so that they could use their blood to make Passover matzo (unleavened bread) was responsible for much violence against them. In the Ottoman Empire, many Christian Greeks subscribed to this medieval notion right up to the beginning of the twentieth century.

The sultan's Greek subjects had always been wary, even resentful, of the tolerance and respect accorded Jews by the Muslims, and relations between Greeks and Jews had never been easy. During the Easter holiday period especially, much to the displeasure of Turkish authorities, attacks on Jewish neighbourhoods were frequent, particularly as the power of the Ottomans began to decline in the late seventeenth century.

As late as 1910, H.H. Jessup, an American Presbyterian missionary who had spent more than fifty years in the Middle East, wrote in his memoirs, "[The Jews] are hated intensely by all the sects, but more especially by the Greeks and Latins. In the gradations of Oriental cursing, it is tolerably reasonable to call a man a donkey, somewhat severe to call him a dog, contemptuous to call him a swine, but withering to the last degree to call him a Jew. The animosity of the nominal Christian sects against the Jews is most relentless and unreasoning."

In 1530, without any real evidence, Armenian Christians levelled charges of ritual murder at Jews in the town of Amasya in Central Anatolia (east of Ankara). In the ensuing violence, dozens of Jewish men, women, and children were beaten and killed and their homes ransacked. The local Ottoman governor accepted the Armenians' claims and had the town's rabbi, Yakub Avayu, and several other Jewish leaders arrested. Under torture, they confessed to the crime and were hanged. As was common in these incidents, the Armenian boy whose murder had sparked the incident showed up a few days after the execution.

Some time later another blood-libel accusation was made at nearby Tokat. Again the Jewish neighbourhood was destroyed and many people were killed by angry mobs. This time, however, Moses Hamon took action. He presented his case to Suleiman and persuaded the sultan to issue a *firman*, or imperial decree, denouncing the allegations and barring his local officials from taking any criminal action in such cases. In the future, all blood-libel charges would have to be brought to the attention of the sultan and his council. This was by no means a permanent solution to this ancient problem, but it did quell any further violence of this kind for the rest of Suleiman's reign.

During the same period, Hamon was instrumental in arranging for Beatriz da Luna Mendes and her nephew and son-in-law, João Migues – or respectively Doña Gracia Nasi and Don Joseph Nasi, as they are better remembered – to leave Italy and immigrate to Constantinople (see Chapter Two). The head of a prominent merchant and banking *converso* family from Spain and Portugal, Doña Gracia was by all accounts a remarkably resourceful woman. After her husband, the *converso* Francisco Mendes, a successful diamond importer, died in Portugal in 1536, Doña Gracia was determined to maintain the family business. In fact, with help from her very capable nephew João Migues, she built up and expanded the enterprise into one of the richest merchant houses in Europe.

By the mid-1540s, assisted by her daughter Reyna and nephew Migues, she had set up shop in Italy, where, it will be recalled, the family competed in the banking business for a time with the Abravanels. But unhappy with the Counter-Reformation movements in Venice and accused of being a "Judaizer," Doña Gracia – she officially changed her name from da Luna Mendes to Gracia Nasi after she moved in 1550 from Venice to Ferrara, where *conversos* were as yet not persecuted for reverting to Judaism – eventually wanted to leave for the Ottoman Empire. Hamon knew of her troubles and offered to help.

Aware of the family's riches, Sultan Suleiman did not need too much convincing from Hamon to declare his official support for Doña Gracia. Following about a year in Ferrara, Doña Gracia, facing more serious charges regarding her religious convictions, at last made the necessary arrangements, again with assistance from Hamon, to leave for Constantinople. She arrived at the Sublime

Porte in grand style in the spring of 1553 after a six-month journey through Italy and Greece.

"Four roomy coaches, so magnificent that observers spoke of them as 'triumphal chariots,' bore the ladies of the party, with their own companions and serving-wenches, all richly dressed," as Cecil Roth described it in his 1948 biography of Doña Gracia. "Around them rode an escort of forty armed men, who had their safety in the hazardous journey across the Balkans."

Once she was settled in a large house in Constantinople's fashionable European area in Galata, with a magnificent view of the Bosporus, Doña Gracia became a leading member of the empire's Jewish elite. Like the Hamons, she was a generous benefactor, providing funds for synagogues, scholarly study, and a wide variety of charitable causes. Most notably, she attempted with some success to enlist the support of the sultan in providing aid to the besieged Jews of Ancona, a city northeast of Rome on the Adriatic, then part of the Papal States. Doña Gracia managed to arrange a Jewish and Ottoman boycott of Ancona as punishment for the persecution of the city's Jews. Though the boycott was brief – as the Jewish merchants in Ancona themselves were being penalized – the psychological victory of Jews in the Diaspora retaliating against their oppressors was a powerful symbol for many years to come.

As for Doña Gracia's son-in-law, Don Joseph Nasi, he not only assumed control of the family business, but also became a confidant of Prince Selim, Suleiman's son and the future sultan, who named him the duke of Naxos (see Chapter Two). In his day, Nasi became even more powerful than the Hamons. He controlled some of the most lucrative tax farms (lumber, barrels, and alcohol), attained through Hamon's intervention, and became involved in the Salonika textile industry. Had he opted to convert to Islam, it is likely that the sultan would have made him the grand vizier.

At some point soon after the Nasi family arrived in Constantinople, Moses Hamon became embroiled in a court intrigue that led to a temporary decline in his high status. The details remain sketchy. It appears that Hamon's troubles began when his confidant and close friend at the court Rustem Pasha, the grand vizier, was removed from his position after trouble with the sultan and the Janissaries. The elite troops were still angry over Rustem's role in the assassination of Prince Mustafa two decades earlier. Rustem was reinstated in the latter part of 1555, though by then Hamon had probably died.

Another version of this story was that Hamon was unable to perform his usual medical magic and cure a bad case of gout that had afflicted Suleiman. Responsibility for the sultan's health was transferred instead to a Muslim physician, who did not like Hamon. This turn of events so distressed Hamon that he became ill and died.

But whichever account is true, by the time of Hamon's death in 1554, the court's respect for him had not vanished entirely. A German traveller by the name of Hans Dernschwam, an employee of the Fugger banking house, who visited Constantinople that year, reported that "The sultan has never used any but a certain Jewish physician [Hamon], who probably rendered good service to him and the Court. He was allowed to build a large stone house of three or four stories in the Jewish quarter. He died while we were at Constantinople. His son [Joseph] is also said to be a physician. He now has his father's position; is said to have a prescription to cure a bellyache."

The Children of Moses

A COURTIER OF MOSES HAMON'S STATURE was not easily replaced. The Ottoman Jewish communities, now lacking a leader who could so effectively unite them, were slow to find another individual who could so clearly command the sultan's respect. The obvious person was Hamon's son Joseph, already a physician at the sultan's court. Wealth, power, and influence were all connected at the Ottoman court, and Joseph already had the benefit of one of his father's most important legacies: a tax exemption that was passed on to all of Moses's immediate descendants, who were referred to in official Turkish documents as the "children of Moses."

In fact the most prominent Jew in the empire under Selim II, who inherited the Ottoman crown when Suleiman died fighting the Austrians in the Hungarian campaign of 1566, was Don Joseph Nasi. Selim, otherwise known as "Selim the Sot" for his fondness for drink and debauchery, was nothing like his father. He came to rely greatly on Nasi. And Nasi, in turn, functioning almost as Selim's foreign minister, was responsible, according to one Venetian diplomat of the day, "for stirring the Sultan's naturally sluggish nature and spurring him on to a more vigorous and ambitious policy." This included an ill-advised attack on Venetian-held Cyprus in 1570 that led to further warfare with Venice and Spain at the Battle of Lepanto the following year.

Among the Ottoman Jewish community, Nasi was at least as legendary a figure as Moses Hamon had been. He lavished his money on synagogues, community schools, scholars, artists, and poets. Taking a special interest in the development of Palestine, he was permitted by Selim to redevelop Tiberias and urged European Jews to return there. He also ensured that Joseph Hamon retained his position as a physician at Selim's court. Joseph may not have commanded the influence wielded by his father, but he did adequately represent the interests of Salonika Jews when a debate about the renewal of their rights took place early in Selim's reign. He also proved himself by securing a renewal of the *firman* prohibiting blood-libel accusations that his father had initially negotiated.

But Joseph's real interest lay in poetry and literature. Poetry, in particular, had a tradition among Sephardi writers that dated back to the "Golden Era" of Spanish Jews during the tenth and eleventh centuries. From his Andalusian ancestors, Joseph inherited a lifelong love of verse and prose. He became an important member and benefactor of Constantinople's unique Poetical Academy. Supported by the Hamons, Doña Gracia, and Don Joseph Nasi, among others, such poet luminaries as Moses ben Gedaliah, the academy's leader, Solomon Mazal-Tov, Israel ben Moses Najara, and Saadiah Longo and Judah Zarko of Salonika were able to write and study. Moses ben Gedaliah, a descendant of a prominent Portuguese Jewish family, translated Leone Ebreo's *Dialoghi di amore* from Italian into Spanish in 1570. Other writers worked in Latin, Hebrew, Greek, and Arabic. At regular meetings, they presented their own lyric poems, musical compositions, and liturgical hymns and chants. They mixed Turkish music and poetry with styles that they had brought with them from Spain to produce a new Ottoman-Jewish tradition. Their work soon reached the masses in Constantinople, Salonika, and throughout the Jewish world via the expertise of the vibrant Hebrew presses – among them the successful enterprise operated by the Sonsino family of Salonika.

When Joseph Hamon married his wife, Chryse, in approximately 1550, Zarko composed an eloquent verse to commemorate the happy occasion. "My heart was inflamed when I caught sight of the beautiful one," he wrote about the bride. "When she disappeared my eyes wandered all around to search for her. The songs that I want to sing about her stayed imprisoned in my heart and fell like a fatigued woman. When I saw the beautiful one again, an angel wove a string of love and my songs became alive again."

(Chryse Hamon was related by marriage to the Abravanels, who by then had established themselves in Salonika. Many members of that family would continue to excel in business and other commercial enterprises for generations to come. More than two centuries after Isaac Abravanel's grandchildren had left Italy for the Ottoman Empire, his descendant Jacob Señor Abravanel helped found the Ottoman Bank in Salonika. Jacques Joseph Abravanel, Jacob's son, was an executive of the Turkish division of the Ford Motor Company and the Portuguese Consul in Istanbul during the 1940s.)

Yet the times were beginning to change for the Hamons and the other members of the influential Jewish elite. At the end of Selim II's brief reign in 1574, the centuries-long decline that eventually killed the Ottoman Empire began, dramatically altering the lives of its loyal Jewish subjects. This slow but steady change, transforming the once mighty empire into "The Sick Man of Europe," was marked by weak and ineffective leadership, crippling taxes, and corruption at the court. "The Sultans who succeeded each other on the throne during the three-quarters of a century after Suleiman the Magnificent were degenerate," Joseph Nehama, the historian of Salonika's Jewish community, argued many years ago. "They were incapable of curbing harem feuds, sedition in the army, riots among the population or administrative extortion. Public finances were pillaged and draconian taxes brought about the country's economic exhaustion."

As well-connected, resourceful, and intelligent as Joseph Hamon was, when he died at about sixty years old, in 1577, he left little money or property for his wife and four children – two sons, Isaac and Judah, and two daughters, Chashuva and Veleeda. The one thing of value was his father's extensive library and manuscript collection, but Chryse, initially at least, refused to sell it because of its Judaic content. Instead, she sold her luxurious house and moved into a smaller one. Friends and relatives helped her financially.

Only Joseph's son Isaac carried on the family tradition by becoming a physician and an advisor at the court of Sultan Murad III (1574–95). He became well-known for refusing to accept money from officials of the Spanish court of Philip II, who were attempting to buy his services and influence in an attempt to reach a favourable peace agreement with the empire. His son Aaron, on the other hand, inherited the family's love of poetry and in his day was famous for his devotional verse.

Even if Aaron Hamon had been inclined to serve at the Ottoman court, it would have been difficult. By the end of the sixteenth century, members of the Jewish elite had already started to lose some of their power. Certainly, once Joseph Nasi had died in 1579, the number of key Jewish personalities at the sultan's court began to dwindle. Besides Isaac Hamon, two other physicians, Solomon Nathan Ashkenazi and Moses Benveniste, also made a name for themselves as advisors to Murad III. Young Christians who had converted to Islam had begun to take positions once occupied by Jews. Leading Jewish merchants and bankers, too, soon lost their status as intense competition from Greeks and Armenians gradually curtailed their operations. And in general, a rise of anti-Semitism among Christians in the empire, fully backed by European envoys and traders, brought significant changes for Jews who had enjoyed the tolerance that had characterized Ottoman rule for so many years.

During the seventeenth century, while Jews in Constantinople and Salonika still maintained the profitable European trading network that had served them so well, they were among the first to suffer financially from the shift in commercial power to Amsterdam and London. Many, in fact, seeing little hope for future opportunities in the empire, burdened and even impoverished by excessive taxation, packed up their belongings and their families and journeyed west. It was in this way, for instance, that the members of the extended Abravanel family were eventually spread from one end of the Diaspora to the other. They soon established enduring branches in London, Amsterdam, Paris, and across the ocean in the New World.

Those who remained behind in Salonika endured the serious troubles that afflicted the Ottoman textile industry, including the increased competition from British imports that eventually crippled the city's economic life. (Though it should be pointed out that Jews remained the chief suppliers of cloth for the Janissaries right up until the corps was disbanded in 1826.) No one was affected more than the city's Jews. In 1660, Salonika's Jewish population numbered about forty thousand, but by the end of the century it had declined to less than twenty thousand. Though that number would continue to fluctuate, the Jewish community, already severely hurt by a terrible fire in 1620, soon became a shadow of its former vibrant self.

Long Live the King Messiah

POVERTY WAS RAMPANT, epidemics frequent, and debts piled up. Social unrest grew in Jewish neighbourhoods throughout the empire. These desperate times demanded a solution or a saviour. The prayers of some Ottoman Jews were seemingly answered in the early 1660s with the rise of the remarkable Shabbetai Zevi.

Ever since they had been exiled from Spain, Jews like Don Isaac Abravanel had been predicting salvation and redemption. Generations of rabbinical scholars in Constantinople, Salonika, and Safed had probed the sacred texts and feverishly studied the kabbalah in the hope of discovering in its mystical depths the time and place of the Messiah's arrival. When Selim I conquered Palestine in 1516, kabbalists had believed that the Messiah's arrival was imminent. When on that occasion and each subsequent occasion this divine intervention did not come to pass, or when believers had been momentarily fooled by the likes of David Reubeni – who, it will be recalled, proclaimed himself to be the Messiah in Italy in 1520 – they were not discouraged. Instead, they returned to their studies in an attempt to get it right next time.

Many subscribed to the view of the charismatic Safed scholar Isaac Luria (1534–72), who let it be known that the suffering of the exiled Jews had a purpose. Luria taught that divine sparks "had been scattered everywhere during the initial act of creation and still needed to be reconstituted," explains historian Jane Gerber. "The exiled Jews were now in a unique position to do just that. . . . [By] means of exile and proper fulfillment of the commandments, combined with mystical preparation and implementation, Jews could gather the divine sparks dispersed among the nations and become partners with God, as it were, in liberating the universe."

Luria's disciples spread his message throughout the empire and west to Europe with the help of the Hebrew printers. Certainly the Jewish masses may have not fully understood its mystical and biblical complexities, but all could grasp its prophecy for a better future. So at that moment, when much of the Jewish world was open to the idea of the Messiah's coming – indeed they prayed daily for it – and when the economic conditions were less than favourable, Shabbetai Zevi stepped forward to claim his crown.

He was born, by most accounts, in August 1626, on Tisha B'Av, the sombre day of fasting that commemorates the destruction of the Temples in Jerusalem. That year, the holiday fell on a Saturday, the Sabbath. Hence his name was Shabbetai. Zevi grew up in the Aegean port city of Izmir. His father, an Ashkenazi Jew from Patras,

Greece, was an agent and merchant and provided Zevi, his two brothers, and his wife with all of the comforts money could buy. At a young age, Zevi proved himself to be a superior student of Torah and Talmud. He soon turned to the Zohar and became fascinated with the mysteries of the kabbalah. By the time he was eighteen he had been ordained a rabbi. He married twice in a short period, although neither union was likely consummated, as Zevi claimed he was attempting to preserve his purity. Both marriages ended in divorce.

There was no doubting Zevi's intelligence, charm, and passion. He was tall, stout, strong, and had a warm, slightly swarthy countenance marked later in his life by a full round beard. It was said that his appearance was "beautiful and that there was almost none like him." (There is only one authentic picture of Shabbetai Zevi, sketched by a Christian artist who saw him in 1665 in Izmir. It was included in one of the first books written about Zevi by Thomas Coenen, published in Amsterdam in 1669.) His voice, too, was melodic and sweet, and when he chanted from the prayer book few people who listened to him could not help but be moved.

Yet Zevi was a deeply troubled man. As a child, he was "tortured by nightmarish dreams." He often preferred to be alone, and secluded himself for days on end. He also suffered from devastating mood swings. In an instant, he moved from being exultant to the point of ecstasy into an agonizing depression from which there seemed no escape. His brilliant biographer Gershom Scholem suggests with some justification that Zevi's behaviour was characteristic of bipolar, or manic-depressive, disorder.

As he embarked on his messianic journey, it was while in these "up" periods of exultation that he was said to have experienced his so-called "illuminations." But they also caused him to behave in a strange and erratic manner. He suffered frequent fits and seizures, including periodically frothing at the mouth, reminiscent of epilepsy, in an age when sufferers of the disease were believed to be under the spell of witches or possessed by the Devil.

So how did a man, who in some quarters was regarded as a fool and even mad, suddenly become a prophet and saviour, and emerge as the dominant personality of the Jewish world?

In 1648, one of several years regarded as "momentous" by those who studied kabbalistic numerology, Zevi, still in Izmir, experienced a revelation; he encountered his "burning bush," so to speak. Rabbi Solomon Laniado of Aleppo, Syria, a believer, related it this way in a letter after hearing it from Zevi himself: "The Spirit of God descended upon him one night while he was walking at about two hours' distance from the city in solitary meditation, until he heard the voice of God speaking to him, 'Thou art the saviour of Israel, the messiah, the son of David, the anointed of the God of Jacob, and thou art destined to redeem Israel, to gather it from the four corners of the earth to Jerusalem . . .'"

Later, historians tried to connect Zevi's awakening with the tragic pogroms in Poland of the same year. In 1648, more than one hundred thousand Jewish men, women, and children were slaughtered in attacks instigated by the Ukrainian rebel Bogdan Chmielniki. While some Polish refugees did make their way to the Ottoman Empire, including, as it turned out, Zevi's future wife, Zevi and other Ottoman Jews were probably not aware of the massacres until well after they had taken place.

Zevi's claim that he was imbued with God as the Redeemer led him into an almost immediate confrontation with rabbis and scholars in Izmir. In some circles, his erratic actions and his frequent use of the "Ineffable Name of God" was intolerable. By 1654, he had either been asked to leave Izmir or was forced into exile. Thus began nearly a decade of travel through the empire, into Palestine and back again. Throughout this period, as he experienced new "illuminations," Zevi captured the attention of more and more followers, many rabbis among them. But he also made numerous enemies, who considered him a dangerous fool.

One of his more outrageous acts took place in Salonika in 1657. He invited the city's most prominent rabbis to a banquet in a room where he had set up a bridal canopy. With the rabbis assembled, he performed a marriage ceremony between himself and the Torah. The stunned rabbis, according to one contemporary report, "accused him of madness." In another celebrated episode in Constantinople, Zevi purchased a fish, dressed it in baby clothes, and predicted that the "redemption of Israel would occur under the astrological sign of Pisces." The local rabbis had him arrested and flogged. Yet this hardly deterred the by-now unpredictable and often out-of-control Shabbetai Zevi. Next, he started altering prayers and changing dietary laws and other rituals. He decided to celebrate the three important Jewish festivals, Sukkot, Passover, and Shavuot, all on the same day.

Once he arrived in Jerusalem in 1662, Zevi found more people willing to take him seriously. On a visit to Cairo, he attracted the interest of Raphael Joseph, a prominent and wealthy tax farmer, banker, and the Egyptian viceroy's treasurer. Joseph had a wide range of contacts and friends, and Zevi presumably met many of them.

Two years later, Zevi heard about a mysterious woman in Livorno, possibly a young refugee from Poland named Sarah, who claimed that she wanted to marry the Messiah. There are, however, so many stories about Sarah's background that it is impossible to know the truth about her. In one more-or-less accepted version, she and her brother were orphaned in the Chmielniki massacres. She made her way first to Amsterdam and later to Italy. To support herself, she worked as a prostitute. None of this mattered to Zevi. He brought her to Cairo, where he married her in a lavish ceremony held in Raphael Joseph's house.

The defining moment in Zevi's messianic voyage occurred in the spring of 1665 when he met Nathan of Gaza, a bright and inquisitive twenty-one-year-old student. Nathan, whose parents had come from Poland, was married to a Sephardi woman with a hefty dowry and a generous father. As a consequence, Nathan was free to spend much of his time studying the kabbalah. Well before he met Zevi, he had heard about his messianic exploits. As soon as two men came face to face, Nathan was a believer. He became Zevi's "John the Baptist" (to use Howard Sachar's comparison), delivering his message to the many sceptical members of the Jewish population. By the end of May 1665, he had convinced Zevi to proclaim publicly that he was indeed the Messiah.

With that pronouncement, the movement now took on a life all of its own. Nathan provided the necessary kabbalistic interpretations that gave Zevi credibility he had previously been lacking. Still, many rabbis continued to shun him. But word that the Messiah had arrived spread like a brush fire throughout the empire and beyond. Zevi's "illuminations" and messianic gestures became more frequent. Everyone, it seemed, had a story about another miracle he had performed.

Zevi journeyed from city to city denouncing Jewish laws he did not approve of. He wanted, for example, to change the day of the Sabbath from Saturday to Monday and offered his own version of Talmudic regulations. He began to call himself not only the Messiah but also the king, and considered himself more powerful than the sultan. That was one declaration which would return to haunt him. Back in Izmir in mid-December, he arrived at the Portuguese Synagogue early one morning wearing a gold-braided robe. Two rabbis followed him holding the hem of his garment. Another two men marched in front of him carrying flowers and candies. He held a silver fan with which he touched the heads of his followers. Once inside the synagogue, he bid all of those in attendance to greet him and "kiss the hand of the king." Most complied with his wishes.

So utterly devoted to Zevi were many members of the Izmir community that when Rabbi Haim Penha, a congregant at the Portuguese Synagogue, publicly challenged their "Messiah," a mob tried to destroy the rabbi's house. Zevi supporters also forced the resignation of Izmir's sceptical chief rabbi and replaced him with one of their own, Haim Benveniste. One of Rabbi Benveniste's first acts was to announce that at Friday evening synagogue services Shabbetai Zevi's name would be honoured rather than that of Sultan Mehmet IV. Now officials in Constantinople started to scrutinize Zevi's activities and public pronouncements more carefully.

But there was no stopping him. Prodded on by Nathan, Zevi proclaimed that the Day of Judgement would arrive on June 18, 1666. This pushed his followers into a frenzy of action. In preparation for their redemption, they sold their houses and businesses. They prayed, meditated, held banquets and parades, shouting, "Long live the King Messiah, long live Sultan Zevi." Trade and commerce throughout the empire came to a standstill.

Despite the opposition of many rabbis, word of Zevi's prediction spread all over the continent. Special Shabbetean prayer books were printed in a dozen different countries. There was not a town or city in Italy that did not count a large contingent of Zevi supporters among the members of its Jewish community. They fasted, sang hymns, named their children Shabbetai, and sold their possessions in anticipation of the Day of Judgement. Class differences no longer seemed to matter. All over Europe, rabbis corresponded back and forth about Zevi in a flood of letters. Most were swept away by the sheer frenzy of the movement.

In Amsterdam, the wealthy merchant Abraham Pereira pledged his fortune to the Messiah. He was among the many believers who participated in "wild dancing" around the Torah out in the streets. Their fervour was "beyond description," according to Rabbi Aaron Sarphati, who was also caught up in the movement in Amsterdam. Stories about Zevi and his exploits even reached the New World.

As the New Year approached, Zevi decided to return to Constantinople. But news that Zevi had started handing out "kingdoms" to his followers, out of land that belonged to the sultan, had already reached the Sublime Porte. By the time Zevi's ship entered the Constantinople harbour, on February 8, 1666, Grand Vizier Ahmed Köprülü, a fair, patient, though disciplined leader, had ordered that Zevi be arrested. A quick execution would have been the easiest solution, but the grand vizier showed remarkable self-control. Zevi was put in chains and taken to Edirne, where the sultan was visiting, then locked up in much more comfortable surroundings at the fortress in Gallipoli – dubbed by his supporters Migdal Oz, the "Tower of Strength."

For a few months he continued to live like a king, his accommodations furnished with the finest of carpets. He was permitted to see his many visitors, who flocked to Gallipoli to see him, all bearing gifts. If they were disappointed when the Day of Judgement did not arrive on June 18, they did not show it. Neither did Zevi. "He sat at a table made of silver and covered with gold, and the inkstand on the table was made of gold and jewels," several visitors later recalled. "He ate and drank from gold and silver vessels inlaid with jewels. In his right hand, he held a gold staff . . . embroidered with gold, and in his left hand a fan with a silver handle." At the end of the summer, he issued a decree abolishing the traditional fast on the ninth day of *Av* and once more foretold that the Day of Judgement was at hand.

Among the visitors who came to Gallipoli was Rabbi Nehemiah Kohen, a Polish kabbalist, though not necessarily a highly respected one. Nevertheless, following a heated dispute with Zevi, Kohen went straight to Ottoman authorities, denounced Zevi as an impostor, and accused him of "fermenting sedition." This led to a formal investigation of the charges. When confronted at the court in Edirne on September 15, Zevi denied the accusation. (The sultan allowed his council to conduct the proceedings while he watched from behind a curtain.) Ottoman officials immediately decided on a course of action. Zevi was given a simple choice: convert to Islam or die. The "Messiah" opted to live, and in an instant became Aziz Mehmed Effendi with the honorary title Kapıcı Başi, "Keeper of the Palace Gates." His wife, Sarah, followed him, taking the name Fatima Hanim. Their infant son became Ismail.

And so it ended. Shabbetai Zevi's apostasy sent shock waves throughout the Diaspora. Nathan of Gaza, who was stunned by the events in Edirne, attempted to rationalize Zevi's conversion as part of a preconceived kabbalistic master plan to save the world. Other followers, however, felt depressed, humiliated, and betrayed. Hundreds of documents and letters about Zevi and his movement were burned, and many rabbis denied that they had ever been true believers. A minority of his followers, though, never lost faith. For years after, they continued to practise the bizarre form of Judaism that he inspired.

For a time, Zevi, whose mood swings became ever more erratic, settled in Edirne and then in Constantinople before irritating the grand vizier sufficiently to be exiled to a fortress at Dulcigno in northern Albania. There, he died on September 17, 1676, on Yom Kippur. Seven years later, about twenty-five hundred Jews in Salonika, who still refused to believe either that he was a fake or that he had died, converted to Islam to be closer to their king. They and those who later joined them became known in Turkish as the *Donmeh* (literally "false prophets," though in this case "turncoats" is a better translation). Reminiscent of the *conversos* in Spain, they were Muslim in public but continued to practise Jewish rituals in private. The sect, in a variety of forms, survived into the twentieth century. As late as 1912, just prior to the Greek conquest and occupation of Salonika, each morning a small group of *Donmeh* men made their way to the city gates to peer into the horizon. Perhaps today, they hoped each time, Shabbetai Zevi might at last appear.

It took decades for Jews to recover from the Shabbetean debacle, and that recovery came with serious consequences. For a long time, the kabbalah, which had "demonstrated its explosive power and its capacity to lead, via messianism, to heresy, lost much of its credit," observes historian R.J. Zvi Werblowsky. Beyond that, reactions were diverse. In Eastern Europe, Hasidism (pietism) evolved to fill the spiritual void left by Zevi's demise. Its charismatic founder, Israel ben Eliezer, known as the *Ba'al Shem Tov* ("Master of the Good Name"), preached humility and stressed that spiritual fulfilment would come only through "personal devoutness." While in the West, Jews turned their backs on traditional Judaism and soon embraced a new concept of life: assimilation.

The Jews of the Ottoman empire were never the same after the events of 1666. Lacking the leadership of courtiers like Moses Hamon or Don Joseph Nasi, they drifted listlessly for a time, trying to recapture their days of glory. But in the end, they were unable to do so.

Chapter Four

THE PORTUGUESE NAÇÃO

Amsterdam, 1700

And we, the Portuguese, are witnesses of the benefits of this justice for, deprived of our liberties and stripped of our possessions, we sought refuge under the protection of Your Highness who protects us, permits us to earn our living and allows us to enjoy, like all the inhabitants of this land, the liberty which reigns therein. Our homeland is not longer Portugal or Spain but Holland.

— MENASSEH BEN ISRAEL, 1642

The *Esnoga*

EXCEPT FOR A LONE kosher restaurant run by an Israeli immigrant, you would not know that the Jodenbreestraat — literally, Jew's Broadstreet — was once the centre of Amsterdam's thriving Jewish quarter. A few centuries ago, the Jewish market held in the area each Sunday was a popular destination for all the citizens of Amsterdam, a place where you could barter endlessly with Ashkenazi peddlers and find almost any conceivable item from kosher pickles to fine glassware.

Today, this street around the corner from the bustling Waterlooplein, where hordes of tourists munch on french fries served Dutch-style with mayonnaise, looks like any other in Amsterdam. There are the usual restaurants and shops, and pedestrians compete for space with the army of young cyclists who fill the streets with the constant ringing of their bicycle bells.

At the top of Jodenbreestraat, at number 4–6, sits Rembrandthuis, one of many reminders of the past. In this house, now a popular museum, the great Rembrandt van Rijn produced some of his finest work. He lived and painted here for nearly two decades, from 1639 to 1658, until money problems forced him out. It was an era when Sephardi immigrants from Spain and Portugal, *conversos*, or *marranos*, who opted to return to Judaism upon arriving in the Netherlands, gradually created one of the most unique Jewish communities in the Diaspora.

Rembrandt was fascinated with his Spanish and Portuguese Jewish neighbours. He painted and befriended them, including the wealthy physician Ephraim Bueno, who acted as Rembrandt's faithful patron, and the talented and influential Rabbi Menasseh ben Israel, who lived in a house across the street.

Among the remarkable collection of the master's works on display on the museum's second floor are drawings of the two Jewish community leaders. Wearing wide-brimmed black hats and overcoats, and sporting neatly trimmed short black beards in the style popularized by the Flemish painter Vandyke, both appear to be typical members of Amsterdam's seventeenth-century aristocracy, a sure sign that Jewish life here was different than elsewhere in Europe.

A short distance away is the great Portuguese Synagogue, an enduring symbol of that Jewish presence in Amsterdam and a testament to Jewish and *converso* influence in the seventeenth and eighteenth centuries. Opened in 1675 in a magnificent and moving ceremony with Hebrew prayers and sermons conducted in Portuguese, the language spoken by all of its prominent members, the *Esnoga* ("synagogue" in Portuguese) occupies almost a whole city block. For years it was the largest structure in the neighbourhood, and its opulence publicly announced that the city's Jews were proud of their traditions and heritage. This was an era when assimilation was not yet the problem it would soon become, and Jewish communities in Holland grew and prospered with a sense of identity rare in the history of the West.

The Portuguese synagogue equally signified the tolerance shown by the Dutch rulers and by most of the Protestant population towards the Jews. That tolerance was a product of the religious strife that had engulfed so much of the continent during the Thirty Years War (1618–48) as well as a reflection of how financial concerns dictated and shaped government policy in Holland. Like the Ottomans, the Calvinist leaders of Holland, throughout their lengthy struggle for independence from Catholic Spain during the sixteenth and seventeenth centuries, eventually understood the economic value of a strong Jewish merchant class. Indeed, compared to the treatment meted out to Jews in the rest of Europe, the Netherlands was a true haven.*

There were no ghetto walls in Amsterdam – affectionately called the "Dutch Jerusalem" – and Jews did not have to wear humiliating yellow badges. "Today a tranquil and secure people dwells in Amsterdam," reported a local rabbi to Jewish leaders in Salonika in 1616, "and the officials of the city have sought to expand the settlement and to establish laws concerning it. Among these [laws] they have allowed every man to believe in divine matters as he chooses, and each lives according to his faith, as long as he does not go about the markets and streets displaying his opposition to the faith of the residents of the city. . . . Conversos of our time, great in number and prominence, have gone there and have entered under the wings of the Divine Presence."

The Jewish presence in Amsterdam elicited a mixed response. A year after the *Esnoga* was opened, the papal nuncio at Cologne, on a visit to Amsterdam, was "appalled that so 'vile' a people should be allowed to erect so splendid a structure." William Carr, the English consul in the city, pointed out in his book, *Travellours Guide*,

---

* In 1579, seven northern Protestant provinces of the Netherlands, of which Holland was the largest, broke away from Spain, which retained control of the southern region, the Spanish Netherlands, until after the French Revolution. Though there was a truce between the two rivals from 1609 to 1621, Spain did not officially concede Dutch independence in the United Provinces until the end of the Thirty Years War in 1648.

published in 1680, that "Jewes who are verie considerable in the trade of this citie have two synagogues, one whereof is the largest in Christendom, and as some say in the world, sure I am, it far exceeds those in Rome, Venice, and all other places where I have been."*

Despite Holland's tolerant Jewish policies at the time, Jews were not allowed to be members of most trade guilds. Thus the *Esnoga* was designed by Elias Bouman, a Dutch master architect and mason, who had also been involved in the construction of the nearby Great Ashkenazi Synagogue, built between 1670–71 by German and Polish members of the community. (Today, the Great *Shul* is part of Amsterdam's exquisite Jewish Historical Museum.)

Wealthier, more aristocratic, and more influential than their Ashkenazi brethren, the city's Sephardi leaders refused to be outdone. They were a proud group of merchants, doctors, brokers, and intellectuals, who demanded the best for themselves and each other. By the mid-seventeenth century, many of them had achieved tremendous success in buying and selling such colonial products as tobacco and sugar from Brazil and the West Indies and diamonds from India. Through their ingenuity and hard work they had contributed to the

---

* Centuries later, during the Second World War, the *Esnoga* miraculously escaped damage. Every effort was taken to protect the synagogue. Fire-watchers were posted day and night to guard against attack by local Nazis and collaborators. Even after the German occupation of the Netherlands in May 1940, the synagogue was not harmed and Jews were able to use its sanctuary for nearly three more years until it became too dangerous. As a precaution, the *Esnoga*'s ancient ornaments were hidden, along with its register of births and deaths so that the Nazis could not use the documents to identify members of the community. But other precious objects, including gilt leather wall coverings and three pairs of silver finials, were discovered and looted by the Nazis. When Holland was liberated, the *Esnoga* was reopened with an emotional joint service attended by Ashkenazi and Sephardi survivors (in 1940 there were approximately one hundred forty thousand Jews in Holland, of which close to 85 per cent resided in Amsterdam. In all, twenty thousand Dutch Jews survived the war).

Until 1988, the *Esnoga* was not open to the public, but a dwindling congregation – once, the synagogue had three thousand members, now it has about six hundred – along with financial concerns dictated a change in policy. Since then, a visit to the synagogue has been almost as popular a stop for tourists as Anne Frank's hiding place, the most famous Jewish monument in Amsterdam.

rise of Amsterdam as the reigning commercial centre of the world. That they required a grand synagogue as a sign of their success was not surprising. They raised amongst themselves the handsome sum of one hundred eighty-five thousand guilders, and Elias Bouman set out in 1671 on a building project that was to take him the next four years.

The architect modelled the *Esnoga* after the Temple of Solomon, and inside a row of Roman-style columns run down the middle of the synagogue. During the day, light is provided in abundance by large arched windows that encircle the sanctuary, and illumination at night is by more than a dozen brass chandeliers, which in total hold about 1,000 candles. The floor of the synagogue is covered in fine sand, a Dutch tradition, according to a tourist brochure about the synagogue, "to absorb dust, moisture and dirt from shoes and to muffle the noise of people moving around." In the Sephardi tradition, just as in synagogues in Spain and Portugal, the magnificent Holy Ark (*hechal*), as high as the ceiling, is located at the east end of the rectangular structure. It is made of Brazilian jacaranda wood and dominated by four wooden pillars. Inside are numerous Torahs, the oldest of which dates to the first settlement of Jews and *conversos* in the city in late 1500s.

Directly opposite the ark is the *bimah* (or *tebah*), a raised dais also made of jacaranda wood and used by the synagogue's cantor. Male members of the congregation sit on oak benches that run lengthwise down the synagogue facing each other. There is enough space for 1,200 men. Above and on both sides are the women's galleries with seats for 440. Close to the centre of the sanctuary are several benches reserved for the *parnassim*, at one time the governors and leaders of the *Mahamad*, Amsterdam's Jewish self-governing council.*

---

* As magnificent as the *Esnoga* is, its construction was not entirely perfect. In 1690, Prince William of Orange, recently crowned King William III of England, visited the synagogue. He was surprised to discover that the pillars beneath the galleries were made of wood. When synagogue officials explained that they had had difficulty obtaining stone from Germany and Italy, William arranged for the proper materials to be shipped from England and Ireland. A year later, the wooden pillars were replaced by ones made out of stone.

When the dedication service for the *Esnoga* was held in 1675, there were approximately twenty-five hundred Sephardi Jews living in the city, with another two thousand Ashkenazi Jews, and five hundred more from Lithuania, making for a combined Jewish population of about five thousand people from a total population in Amsterdam of two hundred thousand.

Among those privileged few who sat among the *parnassim* was an illustrious merchant and writer named Abraham Pereira, and his sons, Jacob, Isaac, Moses, Aaron, and David. His wife, Sara, and their daughters, Ribca, Raquel, and Judith, proudly sat at the front of the women's section above. Pereira, who was quite possibly the richest Jew in Amsterdam, was one of the benefactors who had generously contributed to the building of the *Esnoga*. In fact, his son Jacob, in time an accomplished and successful merchant in his own right, had served on the synagogue's planning committee.

In many respects, Abraham Pereira's life and work, as well as the careers of his talented sons and grandsons who followed in his footsteps, typified the Sephardi experience in Amsterdam and the experience of those who were the proud members of the "*portugueses da nação hebrea*," the "Portuguese of the Hebrew Nation" – or simply the "*nação*," the "Men of the Nation." So notable were these individuals that for a long time the terms "Portuguese" and "Jew" were interchangeable.

Their Judaism and traditions were something out of the ordinary, a faith they felt had to be protected against sceptics and secularists within the community and against agitators on the outside. They were not perfect. They could be as small-minded, insincere, and arrogant as the next man, yet their journey back to Judaism did show strength of character that was admirable. Growing up in Spain and Portugal, *conversos* like the Pereiras had been taught, in the secrecy of their homes, Jewish rituals passed on from one generation to the next. And until they had reached the safety of the Netherlands, most of them had led double lives. To the outside world they had been good Christians, but in the privacy of their homes they lit candles on Friday night and celebrated Jewish holidays they did not entirely understand. Always, they were watchful and careful not to arouse the suspicions of their Christian neighbours or, even worse, the Church officials of the dreaded Inquisition. Once they arrived in Amsterdam, this ancient charade finally could be halted and they were able to renew their bonds with the faith of their Sephardi ancestors.

It was this sense of real vulnerability, of a shared oppression, that made Jews like Abraham Pereira not only highly protective of their revived religion and status, but equally driven to succeed. In this regard, the emerging mercantile economy of seventeenth-century Europe proved to be auspicious, a fact recognized even by the Spanish. "This 'nation' has very considerable power with the magistrates of the city councils, and especially that of Amsterdam," reported one Spanish diplomat in a 1658 memo to the royal court in Madrid, "for without doubt it is they who have the greatest commerce and, who consequently, yield the greatest advantage."

The official was exaggerating; not all of the Portuguese Jews in Amsterdam were as wealthy as Abraham Pereira and his closest friends. Still, this elite did take it upon themselves, like other Jewish leaders in the Diaspora, to organize the community, build its synagogues, and establish its key institutions. And their wealth and privilege gave them a power and influence out of all proportion to their numbers.

So it was that during seventeenth century in Amsterdam, as a result of a variety of favourable political and economic circumstances, the "Men of the Nation" played a pivotal role in the life of Jews everywhere. In many ways, it was their experience, quite different and more dramatic than any other, that signifies, according to historian Jonathan Israel, "the real beginning of modern Jewish history."

Liberty of Conscience

AT THE COURT IN SPAIN he was known as Tomás Rodrígues Pereyra. At various times in his life, he had also gone by the names Francisco de Agurre and Gerard Carlos Bangardel. He could trace his family ancestry to Portugal, and before that to pre-1492 Spain. His great-grandparents were among those forced by Portuguese King Manuel I to convert to Christianity in 1497. While many Jews had willingly embraced their new religion, many more refused. They remained crypto-Jews, secretly passing on the ancient traditions to their children and grandchildren as best as they could remember them. Unlike in Spain, where the Inquisition hounded and harassed the new Christians, the Portuguese converts were left alone. Almost a century later – and especially following the annexation of Portugal by Spain in 1580, which lasted until 1640 – when Inquisition authorities finally became more aware of this close-knit *marrano* community, it was too late. Their "underground system of Jewish observance," as French historian Henry Mechoulan has called it, was too well entrenched.

Thomas Rodrígues Pereyra was born in Madrid in the early 1600s, soon after his parents had returned to Spain from annexed Portugal. He grew up in a family of privilege. During the reigns of Philip III (1598–1621) and his son Philip IV (1621–65), the business of running Spain was entrusted first to the duke of Lerma and later to Count-Duke de Olivares. Both leaders, who were desperate to build up the kingdom's commercial power in an age of continual and costly warfare, recognized the economic potential of the Portuguese merchants. (There were rumours that Olivares even contemplated trying to have the 1492 expulsion order of Jews rescinded.) Soon, the new Christians were not only involved in the profitable wool trade, but had also replaced Genoese bankers as tax farmers and holders of the Crown's lucrative contracts. Gradually, some of them, including Pereyra, who made a name for himself as an astute businessman during the Olivares years, accumulated large personal fortunes with financial interests in everything from slaves and silver to the tobacco and sugar of the West Indies. More importantly, they were linked with other new Christians across Europe and established a valuable commercial network unmatched by any of their rivals.

Matters took a turn for the worse after Olivares was forced out of his position in 1645. He was replaced by Don Diego de Arce

Reynoso, a supporter of the Inquisition, who took a more traditional Spanish approach in dealing with the new Christians: the number of *marranos* burned at the stake in public *autos-da-fé* as accused "Judaizers" dramatically increased. Prominent *conversos* were arrested, their assets seized, and fear gripped the community.

Pereyra's brother Isaac was the first in the family to depart, settling in Amsterdam in 1644. Other *conversos* escaped the Iberian Peninsula for new opportunities in Hamburg, building up its community and economy. They went also to Bordeaux and Bayonne, on the southwest coast of France, where a small Portuguese *marrano* population, known to be in fact Jews, existed while French government officials looked the other way. And they travelled as far away as the East and West Indies. Two years later, following an interrogation by Inquisition officials in the jails of the Saint-Office in Madrid, Pereyra decided that his life was in danger. He and his wife, Sara, and their eight children were among about a dozen other wealthy Portuguese *conversos* who fled Spain for the Netherlands, each taking with them large sums of money.

Needless to say, Spanish officials, who happened to be caught in the mid-1640s with a cash-flow problem, were not pleased. Pereyra himself was accused of embezzling Crown money that was intended to pay debts to banks in Antwerp in the Spanish-controlled southern Netherlands. And, in fact, he and his son Isaac may well have channelled Spanish money from Crown contracts they had held to their accounts in Holland. With no paper trail, however, there was little Spanish officials could do but complain.

Spain's loss was Holland's gain. For wealthy *conversos* like Thomas Rodrígues Pereyra – now reborn as the Jew, Abraham Israel Pereira – the timing could not have been better. They arrived in Amsterdam at the end of the Thirty Years War. Following a period of stagnation, Amsterdam's trade was about to explode and dominate the world. By 1646, it was already a bustling and vibrant city of commerce, science, and art – the "emporium of Europe," in the words of American historian Herbert Bloom, writing in 1937, in one of the first books to examine Jewish economic history in

Holland. Indeed, it was the trade in fruits, spices, wine, and salt from the south, and Baltic grain, linen, and wood, that dominated daily life in the city's sheltered port.

René Descartes, the French mathematician who spent some time in Holland, was highly influenced by the economic bustle. In a letter of May 1631 to Guez de Balzac, he wrote that in Amsterdam, "there isn't a single man, except me, who is not busy trading. Everyone is so preoccupied making money that I could live my whole life here without being noticed by anyone."

Yet what truly distinguished Amsterdam from any other city in the seventeenth century and made it possible for the *conversos* to start life over again was its cosmopolitan character. Long before Abraham Pereira settled with his family in a grand house not far from the Jodenbreestraat, Dutch Calvinists had decreed that no man would be persecuted for his religious beliefs. The city became a refuge for a multitude of ethnic and religious groups – French Huguenots, English Anabaptists, Quakers, Remonstrants (followers of the Dutch theologian Jacobus Arminius), and Jews. In time, each became part of the larger Dutch culture, though it was the economic opportunities that had initially attracted them. In this case, tolerance and profit went hand in hand.

Amsterdam's officials, explained the Remonstrant Minister Geraert Brandt in the 1640s, "countenance only Calvinism but for Trade's sake they Tolerate all others except the Papists; which is the reason why the treasure and stock of most Nations is transported thither, where there is full Liberty of Conscience: you may be what Devil you will there, so you be but peaceable; for Amsterdam is an University of all Religions which grow confusedly . . . without either order or pruning."

It is more than likely that Dutch rulers did not have Jews in mind when they enacted their guiding principle of tolerance for their new country, but they were willing to adapt as necessary. Besides, the *conversos'* reputation for business acumen was well known, and there was a wide-held belief in some circles at least that the Jews would eventually see the error of their ways and return to Christianity. The decision to admit Jews into the Netherlands and allow them a degree of freedom not practised anywhere else, therefore, made sense.

Early in the seventeenth century, Henry IV of France complained to the Dutch ambassador that this liberal treatment of Jews was "an indecent thing for Christians to do." In response, the ambassador, expressing the "classic" Calvinist viewpoint of the day, remarked, "Since God could have destroyed the Jews, and did not, this was an indication that He wished these people tolerated on earth, and since they had to be somewhere, it could not be godless to permit them to live in Amsterdam."

Despite the genuine welcome the Portuguese received upon arriving in Holland, they met with certain restrictions. The local bourgeoisie, aware that the *conversos* represented competition for trade, succeeded in barring them from most guilds. The few trades in which the Jews were ultimately allowed to participate, such as tobacco spinning, diamond processing, and chocolate making, were all linked to the nation's increasing colonial interests.

Commerce was one issue, religion quite another, and from the first day Jews settled in Amsterdam, Church officials and others expressed serious concerns about public displays of Judaism. One of the earliest discussions on the place of Jews in Dutch society took place in 1615. Following a petition by Jews to build a synagogue, leaders in Amsterdam asked Hugo Grotius, the eminent jurist and theologian, to examine the issue and prepare a report. His study, called the *Remonstrantie*, completed after a five-month investigation, was a typical example of the ambivalence of Dutch–Jewish policy for the next century.

While Grotius maintained that "nothing was more fundamentally at odds with Christianity than Judaism," he also "refused to regard Jews as enemies or advocate their exclusion from the country." He acknowledged their "economic usefulness" and argued that Jews could assist Calvinists to gain a greater understanding of the scriptures by teaching them to read Hebrew. Yet he advised against the construction of synagogues and ordered that no Christian should ever be allowed to attend a Jewish prayer service. He recommended as well that sexual relations between Christians and Jews be forbidden. At the same time, he did not believe that segregation as practised in other countries was required.

Dutch government officials carefully considered Grotius's study, but they did not immediately implement Jewish legislation, good or bad. Instead, Dutch policy with respect to Jews gradually developed on a case-by-case basis. Until approximately 1660, Jews were treated as foreigners by law, yet in practice they were, as will be seen, accorded certain rights and privileges. Grave concerns were raised from time to time about public displays of Judaism in the streets during holidays like the Feast of the Tabernacles. But more often than not, nothing was said. Sensitive to this issue, members of the Jewish elite in fact made a concerted effort not to draw too much attention to themselves. A 1639 ruling by the *Mahamad* stipulated that "bridegrooms or mourners must travel in procession, to avoid the problems which can occur with crowds and to avoid being noticed by the inhabitants of the city." Children were not allowed to parade in public in their masquerade costumes during the festival of Purim. And a 1700 decree abolished the traditional practice of "carrying the Torah scrolls outside of the synagogue on the exuberant holiday of Simchat Torah because of the resulting 'grave troubles and commotion among the gentiles.'"

The line between the Jewish and Christian communities in Amsterdam was clear, and yet it was not. Sephardi leaders like Abraham and Isaac Peiriera desired to integrate themselves into Dutch society – they built palatial homes, hired servants, purchased the finest in everything money could buy, and dressed no differently from their Christian neighbours – yet still remained separate. This marked the beginning of a long struggle among Jews in the Diaspora about assimilation and their place in Gentile society that persists to the present day. What made the struggle of the Jews in Amsterdam slightly different, however, was that they themselves were locked in an intense identity crisis, the direct result of their *converso* past. Not only did this affect the history of the Amsterdam community in a profound way, but on occasion it nearly tore it apart.

A Crisis of Identity

THE FIRST *CONVERSOS* arrived in the Netherlands from Spain and Portugal near the end of the sixteenth century, when Inquisition persecutions had intensified after 1580. Many settled in Antwerp in the south but soon made their way to Amsterdam when it became clear that nowhere in the Spanish empire was safe for them. Still small in number, they used their family and business contacts in Iberia to develop a profitable trade in colonial products – sugar, diamonds, and jacaranda wood, or brazilwood – helped immeasurably for a brief time by a twelve-year truce between Spain and Holland from 1609 to 1621.

The two decades that followed were not the best for the *converso* merchants as they were more or less cut off from their suppliers and contacts, but once the hostilities of the Thirty Years War ceased, trading resumed, reaching new, unprecedented levels. By 1657, the Portuguese Jews were so prominent on the Amsterdam stock exchange (accounting for 50 of the 430 brokers) that some Christian traders did not do business at the exchange on Saturday, when the Jewish brokers were absent.

Jewish economic influence and the vast network of Jewish trade with Spain, Portugal, and the New World colonies (in particular, Curaçao, Surinam, and the West Indies) was a point not lost on Menasseh ben Israel in his famous appeal to Cromwell in 1655 to readmit Jews back into England. And, indeed, it was the economic incentive that eventually convinced Cromwell of the merits of his argument.

Some years earlier, a French diplomat residing in Amsterdam observed that the Jews in the city "already exert an influence on the stock of the East India Company and are heeded by the city because of their knowledge of foreign news and commerce. In both matters they obtain their information from other Jewish communities with which they are in close contact. . . . By this means the Jews in Amsterdam are the best informed about foreign commerce and the news of all people in the world."

Success in trade and commerce was the backbone of the Amsterdam Jewish community's institutional structure as well. Initially, religious services, "an odd syncretic mix of Catholic and Jewish rituals," were discreet affairs held in private homes. But soon after they arrived, the *conversos* established the city's first synagogues. First in 1607 was Beit Yaakov, led by a Portuguese *converso* named Jacob Tirado and by Moses Uri Ha-Levi, an Ashkenazi rabbi from Emden. Neve Shalom was founded by Joseph and Samuel Palache, Sephardi brothers from Morocco, a few years after that. In 1619 an internal dispute at the Beit Yaakov over the finer points of Jewish law led to the establishment by a group of dissidents of a third synagogue, the Beit Yisrael. It took another twenty years for the three separate Sephardi groups to unite into a single organization, the Talmud Torah.

Other, Yiddish-speaking Jews from Poland and Germany soon settled in Amsterdam too, though they were generally much poorer and less educated than the Portuguese. In the opinion of the *conversos*, then and for generations to follow, the Ashkenazim might as well have been followers of a different religion. For years, they were largely excluded from the institutional structure of the community and in business were relegated to more menial and unskilled work such as tobacco rolling. Ashkenazi Jews worked the streets as lowly peddlers and hawkers. After the Polish massacres of 1648 forced hundreds more Ashkenazi refugees into Holland, the Sephardi community did offer them welfare and charity. Yet behind their backs the Polish and German Jews were often referred to in derogatory terms as *Betteljuden* or *Schnorrjuden* (beggar Jews). The fact that in later years, Ashkenazi Jews far outnumbered the Sephardim in

Amsterdam made no difference (by 1790, there were twenty-five thousand Ashkenazim to only thirty-five hundred Sephardim). Even as late as the 1930s (and, in fact, long after that), Portuguese-Jewish parents regarded a marriage between one of their children and an Ashkenazi Jew as being nearly as bad as if their child had married a Gentile.

Curiously, the *conversos* themselves wrestled with their own identity for decades. What did Abraham Israel Pereira and the members of his family, for instance, truly know about being Jewish? Like other *conversos*, they had grown up in Spain with only the most rudimentary idea about what it really meant to be Jewish. They had a vague understanding about dietary rules and an even vaguer knowledge of the Torah. They might have secretly fasted on Yom Kippur, but their conception of sin was largely based on the Catholic teachings that had dominated their public lives.

Isaac de Pinto, a contemporary of Abraham Pereira, recalled in his autobiography of 1671 that as a child living in Spanish-controlled Antwerp, his grandfather had taught him to whisper to himself the Jewish prayer *Shema Yisrael* ("Hear, O Israel: The Lord is our God, the Lord is One") each time he entered a church. This daily religious obligation had been transformed, as historian Miriam Bodian points out, "into an act of resistance against Catholicism." Another *converso* was brought before the Inquisition in 1637 in Evora, Portugal, for allegedly teaching "to recite two *Pater Nosters* and two *Ave Marias* and offer them to Moses." In short, it was one thing to abandon Christianity and return to Judaism, quite another to live a Jewish life.

Not surprisingly, many "Portuguese," once they arrived in the Netherlands, were uncertain about the step they had taken. Many questioned rabbinical authority and Talmudic law, and more than one man – understandably, given the pain involved in the procedure – refused to be circumcised. Some even decided to abandon their new Jewish identity altogether and return to Spain and Portugal. Considering the lack of understanding shown by Inquisition authorities for this turn of faith, however, this action proved to be very dangerous. (For that matter, the Spanish were obsessed with their former subjects. They employed whatever means possible, including spying, to determine the aliases used by the *conversos* in Holland and, more crucially, the names of their business contacts and family members back in Madrid and Lisbon, who were naturally assumed to be "Judaizers.")

New Jews such as Abraham Pereira, on the other hand, passionately embraced their reclaimed religion. They studied the scriptures, taught themselves Hebrew, translated Jewish theology into Spanish and Portuguese, built synagogues, established religious schools for their children, and dedicated themselves in every conceivable way to their new faith. Wealthy and pious Jews such as the Pereiras took the lead in shaping community values, mores, and creating its enduring institutions. It was in this way that the Ets Haim Society was founded. The society promoted higher Jewish education and maintained a remarkable library of Jewish literature, one of the finest in the world (located today in building adjacent to the *Esnoga*).*

Only a few years after he had arrived in Amsterdam, Pereira's brother Isaac (with some assistance from Abraham) financed the establishment of a small yeshiva, or religious seminary, and employed Menasseh ben Israel to run it. By then, Israel, the former rabbi of the Neve Shalom synagogue, was a well-respected Hebrew printer, acknowledged as a learned member of the Portuguese community. He welcomed the opportunity the Pereiras gave him and the much-needed extra income the job provided.

During the next decade, Abraham as well as Isaac continued to amass a large fortune, in part due to wise investments in Brazil. With the Dutch controlling the northern part of Brazil from 1630 to 1654, many Sephardim, the Pereiras among them, became involved

---

* During the Second World War, the librarian Jacob da Silva Rosa managed to hide some of the most rare and precious books, but the majority were shipped by the Nazis to Germany to the Alfred Rosenberg Institut zur Erforschung der Judenfrage, in Frankfurt am Main, for future study. After the war ended, U.S. soldiers found the collection in Offenbach and returned it to Amsterdam. The library reopened in 1947.

in lucrative sugar plantations and invested heavily in the Dutch West India Company. In 1655, the brothers were also the first Jews in the country to be awarded permission to own and operate a sugar refinery. While Christian refiners tried to halt the Pereiras, the government, basing its decision on a strict interpretation of the law, took the side of the Portuguese merchants. They ran the business for about six years and then sold it in 1664 to a Dutch businessman for a sizeable profit.

It was during these years, when Abraham was doing so well, that he joined with Dr. Ephraim Bueno, another key member of the Portuguese elite, and started yet another yeshiva, the *Torah Or* ("Law is Light"). In 1656, they hired Isaac Aboab to be its director. A rabbi who had spent time working in Brazil, Aboab was born in Portugal but grew up in Amsterdam, where he studied to be a rabbi. Prior to his departure for South America, he had worked at the Beit Yisrael synagogue. He had returned to Holland in 1654.

Pereira, by then a forceful and ardent defender of Orthodox Judaism, soon went even one step further in cementing his religious faith: he endowed a yeshiva in Hebron in Palestine, the *Hesed Le-Abraham*, or "Charity of Abraham." It quickly became caught up in the messianic debate of the era, in which heated discussions erupted between rabbinical scholars about the Messiah's imminent arrival. Many years later, Jacob Pereira, one of Abraham's sons and a successful merchant, followed in his father's footsteps by financing a yeshiva in Jerusalem. Called the Beit Yaakov, it was one of the most economically viable of the yeshivot and enjoyed a positive reputation among learned rabbis in Palestine and throughout the Diaspora.

Despite the development of strong community institutions like the Talmud Torah and the *Mahamad* council, the Portuguese Jews could not entirely escape their troubled past. And in their search for their true place in the world, they became protective, inflexible, and intolerant of views that challenged the status quo and the institutional structure that they had worked so hard to create.

Censorship became a prerogative of the seven *parnassim* who comprised the *Mahamad*. In 1656, for example, the members of the Jewish council, having determined that a book of poems published by a former *converso* named Jacob de Pina was "lascivious," had all the copies of the work seized and burned. In an attempt to set proper moral standards as well as to avoid antagonizing Dutch officials, the *parnassim* besieged men in the community to refrain from interacting with "loose" Christian women. Apparently, they were only partially successful, since such liaisons were frequent. In the view of Isaac de Pinto, "*passion des femmes*" was one of the major weaknesses that threatened Amsterdam Jewish males, young and old alike.

Little tolerance was shown for those *conversos* who refused to be circumcised – as early as 1620, men known not to have been circumcised were banned from synagogue. Similarly, community leaders took a harsh view of those who had become Jews to take advantage of the economic opportunities available, then returned to Spain and Portugal only to arrive back in Amsterdam a few years later to declare themselves worthy Jews once again. Such behaviour from the *relapsos*, as they were called, was denounced in the most vigorous terms. Those who journeyed back to the "lands of idolatry" (*terras de idolatria*) in the Iberian Peninsula and later returned to Amsterdam – about eighty-two people between 1644 and 1724 – were publicly castigated and forced to beg for forgiveness. In some instances, *relapsos* who did not comply with the *Mahamad*'s or synagogue's rulings were not allowed burial in the Jewish cemetery outside the city.

As he entered old age, Abraham Pereira especially was a rigorous critic of such weak behaviour, a point of view he passionately articulated in his first major book, written in Spanish and published in Amsterdam in 1666, *La Certeza del camino* (*The Certainty of the Path*). The *relapsos*, he wrote, were "blind sinners," who "continued to cross themselves as prescribed by a religion qualified as idolatrous; they lived to the rhythm of its festivals, publicly recited its prayers, married, had children and thus impiety consumed them and carried on."

He was just as harsh with those *conversos* who opted for material success over religion. That he himself had lived a fairly upper-class life since he moved to Amsterdam was beside the point. He vehemently criticized those members of the community who preferred worldly goods to God, those who preferred the life of business to the life of the synagogue, and those who called themselves Jews "for their personal convenience." It was not enough, Pereira argued, for *conversos* to say merely they were Jews, he believed they had to experience it in the truest spiritual sense.

Pereira, like other *conversos*, may have resented his former Iberian homeland but he was nevertheless influenced by its Catholic theologians, including their "obsession with sin." "*La Certeza* breathes a Catholic spirit," points out the Dutch writer J. van Praag, "the profound concept of sin, belief in the demon . . . the necessity of faith and good works to attain life eternal . . . his recommendation of mortification and penitence; the vivid representation of the sufferings and agonies of hell — it is particularly curious how in this respect he recalls the torments of the Inquisition's dungeons — and especially his placing above all else 'the salvation of the soul.'"

Redemption, Pereira firmly suggested, was to be found in the yeshiva, where one could study. He claimed that by doing this himself, he had personally found his soul and the "way of faith." A wealthy man, Pereira had the financial resources to abandon his business career and devote himself full-time to rabbinical study. This was a luxury most Amsterdam Jews did not have, a fact of life Pereira seemed not to notice. Indeed his own sons, while adhering to their father's strict religious regimen, continued to prosper as men of commerce.

It is not surprising that Pereira reserved his harshest condemnation for those *conversos* who, having become Jews, dared to question publicly its sacred tenets. And he was not the only one. From the beginning of Portuguese settlement in the Netherlands, the fragile nature of Jewish life, along with the determination of the *conversos* to resolve their identity crisis, left little, if any, room for scepticism toward or criticism of their newly adopted faith. There were Amsterdam Jews, however, who could not ignore the intellectual currents of the day, with its emphasis on secularism, rationalism, and humanism. Nor could they submit quietly to the traditional strict orthodoxy of the rabbis and the authoritarianism of elitist and wealthy *parnassim* like Abraham Pereira.

The Time of Our Redemption

LONG BEFORE PEREIRA MADE HIS JOURNEY NORTH, the first leaders of the Jewish community in Amsterdam were faced with the problem of Uriel da Costa (also known as Acosta). Born into a *converso* family in Oporto, Portugal, in approximately 1585, da Costa fled to Hamburg and then Amsterdam in 1615. He arrived already well-educated in Catholic theology but also more than willing to embrace the religion of his ancestors. Yet as he delved into Talmudic law he began to question the interpretation of Judaism as ordained by the community's rabbis – in fact, it has been suggested that da Costa may have been more familiar with Jewish traditions than he later admitted in his autobiography. "I observed that the customs and ordinances of the modern Jews seemed quite different than those commanded by Moses," he later recalled. In his opinion, one that he was not shy about sharing, the rabbis were "an obstinate and perverse race of men, strenuous advocates for the odious sect of the Pharisees."

Determined that he be allowed to express his views, da Costa wrote a tract incorporating his various thoughts "disparaging the Sages' words and denying Oral Law and rabbinical tradition" and sent it to rabbis in Venice. This set off a wave of investigations and recriminations that resulted in da Costa being put under a *herem*; that is, an excommunication from the Amsterdam community. Isolated, he was punished with exclusion; all contact with him by his family and friends ceased while the *herem* was in force. For the next two decades, da Costa remained a constant thorn in the sides of the rabbis. On several occasions, he repented so that the *herem* could be lifted, only to commit yet another transgression and become embroiled in further controversy.

Finally, in 1640, after several years of excommunication, he agreed to recant at a public ceremony held in one of the Portuguese synagogues. By his account (and it is the only one there is), it was a humiliating experience in which he was told to strip to his waist and then received thirty-nine lashes. "This correction being over, I was ordered to sit down on the ground and then the [rabbi] came to me and absolved me from my excommunication," he recalled. "After this I put on my clothes, and went to the door of the synagogue, where I prostrated myself, the door-keeper holding my head, whilst all both old and young passed over me, stepping with one foot on the lower part of my legs, and behaving with ridiculous and foolish gestures, more like monkeys than human creatures." A short time later, Uriel da Costa committed suicide by shooting himself in the head.

Members of the Amsterdam Sephardi community spoke of da Costa no more, but this was certainly not the end of the issues he had raised. No matter what Jewish leaders like Abraham Pereira thought about the ideal and hallowed nature of Judaism, Christian philosophers such as René Descartes were raising questions about religion and the meaning of the relationship between God and man. In Amsterdam, the person who came to embody these modern intellectual trends was Baruch Spinoza, revered today as one of the greatest philosophers of Western civilization.

He was born in 1632 and raised in Amsterdam. His father, Michael, a *converso* immigrant from Portugal, was a prosperous merchant and a typical member of the Sephardi elite. Spinoza received a proper Jewish education and proved to be a brilliant student with a superb grasp of several languages. He was a voracious reader and delved into Christian philosophy including the theories

of Descartes. "He was charmed," wrote Johann Colerus, a Dutch
Lutheran preacher, whose biography of Spinoza was published in
Amsterdam in 1705, "with that maxim of Descartes which says that
nothing ought to be admitted as true, but what had been proved by
good and solid reasons." This logic sounded sensible enough; except,
when applied to religion and the story of Moses on Mount Sinai,
certain inconsistencies immediately became apparent.

In 1655, the twenty-one-year-old Spinoza came under the
influence of Dr. Juan Daniel de Prado, a bright Portuguese *converso*
who had studied theology, philosophy, and medicine in Toledo. He
was a popular member of the crypto-Jewish community and, like
Abraham Pereira and many others, he had fled Spain to avoid interrogation by the Inquisition. De Prado and Spinoza shared their
mutual doubts about Jewish rituals and laws and more importantly
about the existence of God. They debated whether the Holy
Scriptures were "divinely inspired," denied the authority of the
rabbis, and even suggested that Jews were not the chosen people.
From the standpoint of the community elders, such heresies could
not be left unchallenged.

When Spinoza's views first came to the attention of Amsterdam
rabbis, they tried to reason with him, but he refused to alter his
views. According to his later testimony, he was nearly killed when a
member of his synagogue attacked him with a knife in the streets of
Amsterdam. While de Prado initially repented (he was in trouble
again two years later), Spinoza remained steadfast. Eventually, in
1656 the rabbis and *parnassim*, finding Spinoza guilty of "abominable
heresies" and "monstrous deeds," had no choice but to exile him as
they had Uriel da Costa. He was "cursed by day" and "cursed by
night," and the "anger and wrath of the Lord" was brought down
upon him. Among those who signed the *herem* order was likely
Abraham Pereira, whose signature was also on a later decree banning
de Prado. In the pages of *La Certeza*, Pereira alluded to the destruc-
tive evil caused by both men.

While de Prado suffered from the exile, wallowing in loneliness
and poverty, Spinoza flourished. Changing his name to Benedictus,

he spent his time in exile writing one of his greatest works, *Tractatus theologico-politicus*, his criticism of Judaism published in 1670. In it, he reiterated his firm belief that a literal interpretation of the Torah was impossible, suggesting instead that Bible should be understood "as a reflection of the limited worldview of early Israelites writing for their time." By then, he had left Amsterdam first for Rynsburg and then settled in Voorburg, not far from The Hague.

Cut off from his family and from his inheritance, he lived a frugal life yet soon had attracted a group of intellectual followers as well as more critics. Jewish and Christian clerics alike attacked his writings as blasphemy. He paid them no attention. By the time he died in 1677, still a young man of forty-five, he had left a philosophical legacy of original rationalist thought that future generations would debate for years to come.

Ironically, while the excommunicated Spinoza had more or less come to terms with God and life, Abraham Pereira, one of his most vocal critics, had not. Despite his enormous wealth, which, like Don Isaac Abravanel, he now frowned upon, Pereira continued his search for life's true meaning. In 1665, he thought he had found it when news of Shabbetai Zevi and his messianic mission reached him in Amsterdam (see Chapter Three). In fact, Pereira was already a believer. Long before the events surrounding Zevi and Nathan of Gaza unfolded in the Ottoman Empire, he had been influenced by the work and ideas of his close friend and associate Menasseh ben Israel. And Israel, who – like Isaac Abravanel – had accepted the messianic message in the Book of Daniel and the *Zohar*, had instructed him that the Messiah was on his way; it was merely a question of when. This was a major theme in one of ben Israel's most famous works, *Spes Israel* (*The Hope of Israel*) published in 1650, a few years before he embarked on his expedition to England to convince Cromwell to readmit Jews. "Though we cannot exactly show the time of our redemption," Menasseh ben Israel wrote, "yet we judge it to be near."

Pereira first heard of the fervour around Zevi in a letter from the
head of his yeshiva in Hebron. The rabbi, already swept away by
Zevi, wrote to inform Pereira that "henceforth they no longer
required his gifts, but that they wished that he would come and join
them to behold the beauty of the Lord." Some months later, the first
editions of Zevi's book of prayers in Spanish and Portuguese were
released to an enthusiastic reception in Amsterdam. Most *conversos*
remained somewhat sceptical, although by February 1666, special
prayers about Zevi were being recited in the local synagogues.
Pereira was impatient and decided to embark on a journey to
Palestine with his friend Dr. Isaac Nahar. Their plan was to travel
to Hebron to "await the messiah's final and triumphant manifestation
at the yeshiva." As Pereira later related in his second book, *El Espejo
de la vanidad* (*A Reflection of the Vanity of the World*), written in
1671 after Zevi had converted to Islam, he and Nahar made it as far
as Italy – Pereira to Venice and Nahar to Livorno – where they
remained for the next several months. There, they eventually learned
of Zevi's apostasy and a dejected Pereira returned to Amsterdam.

His recollection of those events in *El Espejo de la vanidad*, published five years after the Zevi debacle, is the work of a harsh and
bitter man. Pereira had become even more doctrinaire, urging his
fellow Jews "to practise self-flagellation and other mortifications of
the flesh." Clearly influenced by Catholic theologians, Pereira,
sounding much like an inquisitor, identified the "five abomina-
tions" that he maintained threatened the Portuguese Jews in
Holland: the arrogance of those who wished to separate the community; the malignancy of those who defied rabbinical authority;
the vanity of those who mocked divine precepts; the ambition of
those who did so; and the stubbornness of those who followed the
"ways of perdition." For those guilty of these transgressions, he felt
there was no option but to impose a *herem* as a just punishment.

Pereira would never have admitted that what he truly sought was
a form of an inquisition. As Henry Mechoulan has noted, he did
yearn for a "closely guarded community in which all heterodox

division becomes impossible [and] in which all attempts against proper custom are repressed." Unforgiving, Pereira waged his private war against secularism and heresy until the day he died at the age of sixty-seven in 1699.

The Approach of Winter

THE REIGN OF THE PORTUGUESE lasted as long as Holland maintained its commercial supremacy. As England gradually encroached on Dutch colonial trade in such commodities as tobacco and sugar, establishing itself at the end of the seventeenth century and into the next as the dominant power in Europe, the merchants of Holland, both *converso* and Christian, suffered an economic decline. By 1799, more than half the members of this once proud and wealthy Jewish elite, now overshadowed by their more numerous Ashkenazi co-religionists, were forced to seek poor relief. It was an astonishing turn of events.

One Portuguese writer lamented this dreadful situation in 1770: "Our nation becomes poorer from year to year. Our principal commercial houses are hurt in many ways, some through bankruptcy and others through every increasing luxury and extravagance. The middle classes have to be very cautious in their expenditure. . . . Taken together the Portuguese Jewish nation has had her summer and approaches her winter, while the Ashkenazi Jews, who for the most part came here in poverty, despised by us at that time . . . are over their winter and see a prosperous time drawing near. We fall and they rise." In fact, this writer was mistaken; the Ashkenazi immigrants who had journeyed to Holland from Germany and Poland were no better off financially than were the struggling Portuguese.

It is also true, however, that some Jewish merchants and traders adapted better than others did to the changing economic climate. As early as 1651, when the British Navigation Acts started hindering Holland's foreign trade, the *conversos* began contemplating ways to establish their businesses in London. This was one of the main motives behind Menasseh ben Israel's journey to England in 1655. While he was not entirely successful – despite Cromwell's positive view about the readmission of Jews, church officials and trade leaders opposed it – no law was passed to prevent Jews from coming to England. Slowly a small community of Sephardim took shape in London (joining the hundred or so Jews who already lived there regardless of the 1290 expulsion decree), gaining some support from the restored monarchy of Charles II after 1660. During his exile, the king had spent time in Holland, and his dealings with the few *converso* merchants he had met had been positive.

By mid-century, Jacob Pereira, Abraham's eldest son, had already added to the family fortune with profitable investments in the diamond trade and other colonial products. In 1672, he and his business partner, Antonio Machado, also of Portuguese descent, went into the army supply business, obtaining a lucrative contract from William of Orange, who was engaged in a battle with the ambitious Louis XIV, absolute ruler of France. In order to fulfill the contract, they established a network of factors and agents throughout Europe and financed their extensive operations "using a combination of advances by the state and capital invested by themselves and fellow Dutch Sephardi Jews." It was a high-risk operation in which payment was often delayed, and a fair bit of ruthless business acumen was required. Taking full advantage of the European intrigues of the late seventeenth century, the firm of Machado and Pereira was ready even to act as a purveyor of the supplies, horses, and munitions of Spanish troops when Spain joined the Dutch in the war against the French at Flanders. While it was true that bribery and kickbacks were routine features of seventeenth-century business practices in this field, and Jewish contractors were certainly not immune to this, they also had a reputation for getting the job done.

In 1688, during England's Glorious Revolution, William III's ultimately successful bid for the British crown was based in part on the backing of a strong army supported by the two Portuguese merchants. They remained connected to the king until he died in

1702. They also made a great deal of money. Both amassed huge estates, and for a time Jacob lived in a magnificent house in The Hague that was later used as the official residence of the Netherlands' queen mother.

The firm worked with the Duke of Marlborough and the Duke of Schomberg, who had appointed Isaac Pereira, Jacob's son, the commissary general to the army in Ireland. "The sums involved in Isaac Pereira's Irish operations were vast," historian Jonathan Israel has noted. "In the year from September 1690 to August 1691 he was paid £95,000 for the supplies and shipping services he provided." Provisioning for this campaign alone, according to one report, "required at least 28 bakers, 700–800 horses, and some 300–400 wagons." In addition, by relocating to England, the younger Pereira assured that the family business would continue to prosper into the next century, whether his grandfather thought that was essential or not.

No doubt Abraham Pereira and other traditionalists of the "*Nação*" would have been shocked by the radical changes inflicted on their community, a consequence of the French Revolution and Napoleon's subsequent conquest of Holland. The old order was swept away and with it the authoritarian self-government of the *Mahamad*. Soon the Portuguese language, too, was nearly lost to the children and grandchildren of the *conversos*; the vast majority spoke Dutch at home and in the street. "In general," writes Miriam Bodian, "the task of perpetuating the 'Portuguese' legacy of the community was increasingly relegated to rabbis, Talmud students, communal librarians, and archivists. It was part of the job of these functionaries to preserve the memory of a collective 'golden age' that was highly valued – but gone."

Jews were officially emancipated in the Netherlands on September 2, 1796, and now it was incumbent on the next generation to meet the challenges of the secularism and liberalism transforming the face of European society. The demanding task of the years ahead would be to determine how to integrate into the modern era without completely forsaking the cherished traditions and identity of the past. That proved to be increasingly difficult, if not impossible; by the beginning of the nineteenth century, many Jews of Portuguese ancestry had converted to Christianity. The *Nação* would live on, but in a very different way.

Chapter Five

COURT JEWS

Vienna, 1730

The Jews and their commerce seem not detrimental to us and to the country but rather beneficial.
- FREDERICK WILLIAM OF BRANDENBERG, THE GREAT ELECTOR, 1671

Every Court Has its Jew

EMPEROR LEOPOLD I had a problem. As the eldest son of Ferdinand III he had inherited the Catholic lands of the Holy Roman Empire in 1657. Just eighteen years old, the reigning head of the Hapsburg family would have preferred to become a priest. Instead, the rule of the sprawling empire was thrust upon him. Now, from the Hofburg, his magnificent palace in the heart of Vienna with its endless hallways, sumptuous ballrooms, and exquisite furniture, he was forced to deal with the contentious religious concerns of the Protestant princes, dukes, and electors who clung to power in the multitude of German states to the north and whose support he required.

The Treaty of Westphalia, signed by the great powers in 1648 after thirty years of bloody conflict, had more or less settled this issue – Calvinist and Lutheran rulers in German areas were granted religious freedom (and, indirectly, so were their subject peoples) – yet territorial and national differences still remained. To the west,

King Louis XIV of France, the dominant monarch of the era, was not willing to accept the map of Europe as it was. And in the south and east, the Ottoman Turks still remained a dangerous threat.

Worse for Leopold, his empire's finances were in a terrible mess. The war had almost wrecked his economy and credit, and ruined his Christian merchants. Other rulers had reluctantly turned to Jewish merchants for assistance. During the Thirty Years War, they had proved their worth as purveyors of massive armies and risk takers able to raise vast sums of money, quickly if necessary. The war had been good for Jews. (Or, put more caustically by Will and Ariel Durant, "Protestants and Catholics were so engrossed in mutual murder that they almost forgot to kill Jews, even when these had lent them money.")

For centuries, most Jews in the region, whether they were merchants or peddlers, had been relegated to the fringes of the German and Austrian economies. It was a consequence of enduring medieval religious beliefs that portrayed them as the Devil as well as more modern notions that regarded them as an economic threat and an unwelcome competitor.

Then and later, like Jews in Spain and Italy, the Ashkenazim were often required to wear badges or yellow "wheels" (although it was not uniformly enforced) and were subject to a wide range of restrictions that affected every aspect of their daily lives – where they could live, which streets they could walk on, even when they could marry. They faced heavy and humiliating taxes, including the *Leibzoll*, or body tax. Every Jew, except those with special privileges, who passed through a city, town, or village was required to pay this toll, a demeaning charge that was not eliminated in the German states until the end of the eighteenth century. At the gates of Mainz, for instance, customs officials greeted visitors to the city with a sign for duties to be paid under the following headings: "Honey, Hops, Wood, Jews, Chalk, Cheese, Charcoal." Jews were still victims of what years earlier was sarcastically called a "sponge policy." As British historian Beth-Zion Abrahams states, they "were allowed to absorb the money required by the rulers, which was then squeezed from them by varying degrees of pressure."*

This is a theme that runs through the remarkable autobiography of a Jewish woman of the era named Glückel of Hameln. In 1689, Glückel, who had been born in Hamburg, began writing her memoirs in *Jüdisch-Deutsch*, a German dialect written in Hebrew that eventually evolved into Yiddish, the language that would define East European Ashkenazi Jewish life (the book was first translated into English in a 1932 edition). Glückel, the daughter of a Hamburg merchant, had been married in 1663 at the age of fourteen to Chaim Baruch, the son of a prominent gem dealer from the town of Hameln, in the Kingdom of Hanover. Their marriage lasted thirty years, until Chaim's untimely death in 1693, and produced thirteen children (only one of whom did not survive into adulthood). As a trader at fairs in Leipzig and Frankfurt, Chaim moved in a circle that brought him into contact with the wealthiest Jews of the age.

Yet for much of their lives together, Glückel and Chaim were largely preoccupied with two related tasks: ensuring their many bills and taxes were paid, and arranging marriages for their children that included large dowries. One of Glückel's finest moments was when her eldest daughter, Zipporah, married the son of a distinguished Jewish family in the Duchy of Cleves. Attending the ceremony and celebrations were young Prince Frederick (the future King Frederick 1 of Prussia) and Prince Moritz von Nassau. "For a hundred years," wrote Glückel, "no Jew had such a high honour."

The happy moments aside, much more of Glückel's writings underline the reality that for most Jews of this time life was rarely easy and almost always dependent on the goodwill and mood of the ruler. During this era, far-reaching changes were taking place,

---

* Jews also suffered from prejudice and discrimination in the legal courts in German territories. And when they were found guilty, the sentence of death was often brutal. In one case, "the condemned prisoner was strung up by his legs, head down, between two live dogs, and left to dangle until he died, a slow death which often took several days."

even if Glückel did not quite grasp them. Beginning in the late 1500s, the transition from a feudal political and economic system to one based on principles of absolutism and mercantilism naturally affected Jews throughout Central Europe. In order to free themselves from the old feudal dependence on the nobility, the various German rulers had to centralize their power at their courts. Armies had to be maintained and trade expanded. Absolutism demanded, in their view, a particular lifestyle of palaces, paintings, banquets, costly furniture, tapestries, balls, and the finest jewellery you could buy. The price tag for maintaining such a lavish court was high indeed. Needless to say, the princes and dukes constantly required money, and lots of it.

The Thirty Years War proved that, given the opportunity, a select group of enterprising Jewish merchants could rise to the challenge. Utilizing their impressive networks of merchants, traders, and peddlers east into Poland and west to Amsterdam, they delivered the food, fodder, and weapons that made war possible. In a real sense, they remained "second-class" citizens and "non-Europeans," but in exchange for protection and privileges they got the job done.

Soon these Jewish court factors, or *Hoffaktorn*, became members of the courts that they largely financed. It was due to the ingenuity of such celebrated entrepreneurs – court Jews, or *Hofjuden*, like Samuel Oppenheimer, Samson Wertheimer, Leffman Behrens, Ruben Elias Gomperz, Behrend Lehmann, and Joseph Süss Oppenheimer, among others – that every court did have its Jew, as the popular saying went in the seventeenth and eighteenth centuries. While they functioned as suppliers, diplomats, and agents, it was their skills in raising money that was truly remarkable. Samuel Oppenheimer and Samson Wertheimer, for instance, found the funds for Vienna's Karlskirche (St. Charles's Church), the baroque church erected to honour the Counter-Reformation, as well as the imperial Schönbrunn Palace, the Hapsburg's grand summer home – not too far from the centre of old Vienna – where Empress Maria Theresa eventually resided in the mid-eighteenth century. In fact, many of the most magnificent buildings and structures in Vienna's

Ringstrasse, the circular boulevard in the heart of the city where the Opera House and Hofburg can be found, were largely financed with Jewish money. Behrend Lehmann, who ably served the elector of Saxony August II, was largely responsible for securing the throne of Poland for his employer in 1694 through the payment of millions of thalers.* Similarly, Leffman Behrens (who was Glückel of Hameln's brother-in-law), the resident court Jew in Hanover, amassed a small fortune so that Duke Ernest August could be named an elector and a member of the Collegium, the select group of princes and dukes who chose the emperor.

To be connected to the court, especially during the eighteenth century, was both an honour and a privilege. The pomp and luxury, power, and influence were intoxicating. Soon after they arrived, many of these elite Jews were caught up in all that the court had to offer. Like the princes they served, they dressed in the finest clothes, built magnificent homes (notably, outside of the ghettos), rode in carriages pulled by half a dozen horses, collected art and books, attended gala balls, and regarded themselves in almost every way as members of a new nobility. Their Passover seders and wedding receptions for their children were legendary. After Ulrike of Sweden, the sister of Frederick the Great, was a guest at a Jewish wedding, she "reported to her brother that she was so impressed by the degree of culture of the Chosen People that she imagined herself among nobility." On occasion, however, they could be arrogant and domineering, driven by the need to maintain their high position and status. Like the wealthy Sephardi Jews of Amsterdam, they went to great lengths to arrange marriages for their children within their small group, so that by the middle of the eighteenth century, a large number of them were related.

In their overwhelming desire for success and acceptance, many, though not all, moved closer to total assimilation. Many shaved their beards, and their children more often than not adopted a

---

* In 1999 currency, one thaler would be worth about U.S. $44 and one florin approximately U.S. $69.

Christian lifestyle. Within a few generations, their descendants had converted to Christianity. In her pioneering study of the court Jews, Selma Stern observed many years ago that such a financier or merchant "possessed a remarkable degree of industriousness and restlessness, a great interest in speculation and action, a strong desire for success, a lust for money and profit, an ambition to climb higher and higher and to assimilate as completely as possible to his environment in speech, dress and manners." Still, they could not entirely forsake the Jewish masses, nor did most of them want to.

In the decades before Jewish emancipation became a reality, the court Jews were, in a real sense, trapped. They lived in two worlds but did not belong fully in either one. They were resented by the Christian populace for being tax collectors, holders of monopolies, and harbingers of the new pre-capitalist economy. In particular, the conservative nobility, who had most to lose in the new absolutist regime, viewed the Jews in the princes' courts as usurpers of their own power. As will be seen, both Samuel Oppenheimer and his relative Joseph Süss Oppenheimer faced strong and bitter opponents who would stop at nothing to poison their relationship with the ruler.

Meanwhile, the larger Jewish community, though obviously grateful for the money and influence wielded by the court Jews on their behalf – most were usually given the title *shtadlan*, or community advocate – and for the synagogues and schools they built, equally took exception to their autocratic manner and ostentatious lifestyle. Mainly, Ashkenazi Jews in Germany and the empire fell into the lower and middle classes. They were traders, peddlers, hawkers, and craftsmen, whose simple lives revolved around the synagogues and their families. There were also Jewish thieves, robbers, and beggars. Nevertheless, the vast majority were fairly well-educated and not anything like the less refined, impoverished, and poorly regarded Jews of the Polish and Russian *shtetlach* – though they would hardly have felt comfortable amidst the pageantry and luxury of the imperial court.

The court Jews were in a different category. "They eat, drink and make merry day in, day out, satisfying their cravings and pursuing their passions," stated Rabbi Jacob Emden, an impassioned critic of the Jewish elite. Despite the controversial view of them in their own communities, however, the very existence of the court Jews, certainly their power and influence, was at the whim of the absolute rulers whom they served. In this way, they were no different from the courtiers in medieval Spain, the Jews of the Ottoman Empire, or the merchants in Amsterdam. Maintaining such an exalted position and searching for their rightful place in society occupied a great deal of their time and effort.

It is fair to say that several of the rulers, Emperor Leopold I among them, were torn about using Jewish talents to enhance their own interests. George II of Hesse-Darmstadt, for instance, expressed all too typical a view. In his last will and testament, he passed on the following advice to his son, who succeeded him in 1661: "In order to plant honest religious faith in the country, our son . . . should be wary of the Jews. For they are an idle and useless people. They do not live by the labor of their hands in accordance with the divine design but rather lie about in indolence, greedy for gain, waiting in the lurch to seize what they may. In the most reprehensible manner . . . they suck the Christians dry, blaspheme, desecrate, and vilify the Son of God and dishonor God with their daily superstitious prayers. . . . If one allows the Jews to implant themselves too firmly in a country, it will later prove difficult to get rid of them." George's son took his father's suggestion to heart and expelled all of the Jews from Upper Hesse during the first year of his reign. This was an attitude that Emperor Leopold probably would have concurred with.

A century later, Frederick the Great of Prussia, ignoring the more tolerant approach of his grandfather Frederick William, the great elector, would echo the sentiment. In 1752, in his *Political Testament*, he "berated the Jews as the most dangerous of all sects:

he alleged they were harmful to Christian trade arguing that the state should make no use of their services."

Indeed, the entire history of Jews in Vienna as far back as the Crusades was filled with anguish, injustice, repression, and atrocities. Jews were the classic scapegoats, blamed for any and all problems. In the popular imagery of the day, they were members of a despised religious group who could not be trusted. In 1420, a Viennese Jew named Israel was accused of buying stolen consecrated hosts and then selling them. This precipitated a brutal assault on the then small community and most of the Jews in the city were arrested, imprisoned, tortured, and finally burned alive. For many years after this, the Jewish presence in Vienna was nearly non-existent. Gradually, the community was re-established as the Hapsburg emperors discovered their financial talents. Still, by the beginning of the Thirty Years War, there were fewer than two hundred Jews in the city.

In 1624, Ferdinand II, Leopold's grandfather, confined most of them to the narrow streets and cobblestone lanes of the ghetto, called the *Judenstadt* (the present day site of Leopoldstadt quarter), then separated from the city by a drawbridge over the Danube. Many also ran shops and stores on Judengasse (Jews' Lane), a bustling street of lowbrow commerce near the Hoher Markt, where Jews were permitted to work and sell their wares, but not live. Segregated, as elsewhere in Europe, the community slowly grew and developed an identity all its own, complete with rabbis, scholars, physicians, and self-governing council. Every Sabbath, however, the emperor insisted that a group of Jews attend a Hebrew sermon in a nearby monastery delivered by a Jesuit monk. He hoped that the Jews would accept and welcome the teachings of Christ and convert. They did not.

By the time Leopold inherited the Hapsburg throne, critics of Jewish advances and integration were making themselves heard. A leading and vehement anti-Jewish spokesman was the emperor's confessor, Cardinal Leopold Kollonitsch, who blamed the Jews for all the evils of the world. When Leopold and his wife, the Empress

Margareta Theresa, lost a child in early 1668, Jews for no reason were held responsible for the calamity. A year later, the report of an imperial commission of inquiry – in reality, a catalogue of every anti-Jewish Christian belief from the previous five hundred years – depicted Viennese Jews as dangerous with a high birth rate that would soon overwhelm the Christian majority. The emperor hardly needed convincing, and despite all economic arguments to the contrary ordered the expulsion of the Jews from the city in 1670. No attempt by the Jews to offer the court money to repeal the order was successful.

Perhaps 3,000 Jews left Vienna, mainly for locales in neighbouring Hungary. Frederick William I of Brandenberg–Prussia, influenced by the spirit of tolerance he discovered in Calvinism, permitted fifty wealthy Jewish families to settle in Berlin. Back in Vienna, the Great Synagogue in the ghetto was converted into a Catholic church, and Cardinal Kollonitsch was satisfied that the city was free of Jews forever. He was mistaken. Within two years, the emperor, faced with military threats from France and the Ottomans, and with his economy in tatters, ignored his own religious convictions. He did what he knew he must do; in fact, he had few options. He turned for help to Samuel Oppenheimer, a renowned Jewish financier and court administrator.

A Jew with Good Credit

HIS OFFICIAL PORTRAIT reveals a man of dignity, prominence, and action. His fine clothes and neatly trimmed white beard signify his noble status. His face is of a kind but determined person. Only the black *kipah* mounted proudly on his head indicates that he is a Jew. Known for his honesty and integrity in business, as "the Jew with good credit," Samuel Oppenheimer was the most important court Jew of his day. His reputation was due in part to the fact that he served the Hapsburg emperor, but it also stemmed from his sheer determination to complete whatever task he had been assigned. Moreover, he was a pioneer of the international banking business and one of the first financiers to convert money and move it around Europe at rapid speed. To be associated with him through marriage – as Glückel of Hameln almost was, when a match between her son Nathan and one of Oppenheimer's daughters was proposed, a disagreement over the dowry ruining the plans at the last moment – was an honour sought by many Jews.

Oppenheimer was not a well-educated man, nor a yeshiva scholar. He could be stubborn and vain; he coveted titles and received many during this career, including the "imperial war purveyor" in 1676. He lived in lavish style in a palatial mansion in Vienna's fashionable Bauermarkt – close to the mammoth twelfth-century Gothic St. Stephen's Cathedral – with his wife and nine children. It was as splendid as any noble's residence. (Today, his former house, many times altered, is an expensive jewellery store.) He employed an entourage of servants and agents and travelled to all corners of the continent to accomplish his work. He was also a loyal and dedicated servant of the Crown, no matter how poorly or shoddily he was treated. His long career illustrates more than most just how vulnerable the position of the court Jew was when confronted by enemies that he was powerless to oppose.

Oppenheimer was born in Heidelberg in 1630. Little is known of his early life, only that by the time he was in his forties he had made a name for himself as a competent financial agent and military contractor for Elector Karl Ludwig of the Palatinate. As France moved against the Holy Roman Empire in 1673, Leopold I reluctantly sought Oppenheimer's assistance. During the next six years, as the conflict was waged, he was given the enormous responsibility of supplying the entire Austrian army. This meant everything from uniforms, food rations, and munitions to horses, fodder, and medicine. He even had to pay officers and soldiers their wages.

He accomplished this difficult assignment by relying on his large network of agents and factors, many of whom were relatives and friends. They miraculously amassed the variety of goods he required by trading at fairs and visiting a hundred different villages and towns. It was by all accounts an impressive operation. By 1676, the

emperor had softened and officially allowed Oppenheimer and his
entourage to settle in Vienna, a decision which brought Jews back
to the city only six years after they had been expelled. Still,
Oppenheimer's request to build a synagogue was turned down, and
prayers had to be held in his house.

While Leopold had named him imperial war purveyor,
Oppenheimer's position was weaker than he would likely have conceded. Once the war with France had ended and the Peace of
Nijmegen had been signed, Oppenheimer was owed more than
200,000 florins, but the imperial treasury refused to pay him. As
his creditors pushed for payment, Oppenheimer made a personal
appeal to the emperor. It fell on deaf ears. Instead of honouring
their commitments, the authorities arrested and imprisoned
Oppenheimer and his eldest son, Emmanuel, on the flimsy charge
that they had defrauded the treasury.

Had the Empire not been confronted with yet another military
threat, the Oppenheimers might have spent years in prison. But the
decision by the Turks in the fall of 1682 to launch an assault on
the Hapsburgs necessitated dealing more justly with Samuel
Oppenheimer. He and Emmanuel were released from prison, they
were partially paid what was owed them, and Samuel once more
was placed in charge of overseeing the Austrian army.

Almost immediately he arranged for a consignment of oats to
be delivered to Linz along with thousands of hand grenades. He
sent eight ships, rafts, and barges down the Danube carrying much-
needed supplies – gunpowder, fodder, bombs, and grenades – for
the emperor's soldiers trapped in Hungary. Later, Emmanuel travelled throughout Europe buying horses by the hundreds. As the
Ottoman forces reached the gates of Vienna the following spring,
joined by Moldavians and Transylvanians, who saw an opportunity to free themselves from Austrian control, Leopold fled west
to Passau.

Samuel Oppenheimer, however, remained in Vienna and continued to mastermind the strategy for supplying the emperor's
besieged army. He was relentless in his duty. "His ships were often

wrecked, his goods confiscated or damaged, his transports were delayed, shipments of money were lost, his funds were depleted, his creditors pressed and even threatened him; yet he never lost his courage," writes historian Selma Stern.

A combined force of Germans, Poles, and Austrians eventually beat back the Ottomans from Vienna and pursued them eastward as Leopold consolidated his control over more of Hungary. But within a few years, Louis XIV of France, resentful of the Holy League formed between Austria, Poland, and Venice, as well as territorial gains by the empire, ignored the peace treaty he had signed with Leopold and once again sent his troops against the Austrians. Now Oppenheimer was made responsible for a two-front war. It may have been his finest hour as a court Jew. He raised hundreds of thousands of florins and provided the necessary supplies – and in addition such luxuries as wine, tobacco and spices – for dozens of garrisons. He even came to the rescue of Hungarian Jews who were under attack by occupying empire forces.

Leopold's allies, Eugene of Savoy and Louis of Baden, praised Oppenheimer's work, recognizing that without him both wars would have been lost. As a reward, he received more titles and became *Oberhoffaktor*, the highest of court Jews. While he welcomed the notable distinction, Oppenheimer must have been slightly wary as well. The debts owed to him from the empire and several German states reached staggering proportions, from 53,000 florins in 1685 to more than three million by 1694. Added to this was the fact that his enemy Cardinal Kollonitsch, made responsible for the treasury in 1692, conspired to destroy his career.

As the war in the Palatinate with Louis XIV came to end in the late summer of 1697, a "swindler" named von Edelack told Cardinal Kollonitsch that Oppenheimer and Ruben Elias Gomperz, a prominent court Jew in Cleves, had hired him to murder Samson Wertheimer. At the time, Wertheimer still worked as Oppenheimer's associate, though he was emerging as the next great court Jew in Vienna. Even though there was little foundation to the charges, the Cardinal decided to take action. First, he convinced Frederick I, the elector of Brandenberg, who had jurisdiction over Cleves, to arrest Gomperz. Warrants for the arrest of Oppenheimer and his son Emmanuel were served soon after, just as France was signing the Peace of Ryswick, near The Hague. His arrest set off a minor financial crisis among Jewish agents and traders throughout Central Europe whose own bills to Oppenheimer had not been paid. Included in this group was Nathan, the son of Glückel of Hameln. In order to prevent Nathan from going bankrupt, Glückel was forced to pawn several cherished items. It was, as she writes in her memoirs, a desperate situation.

The incarceration did not last long. The war against the Ottomans continued, and even Kollonitsch had to concede that Oppenheimer's talents were required. Two weeks after his imprisonment, he and Emmanuel were released. (Gomperz was not vindicated for another six months.) The episode was humiliating and illustrated that despite everything Oppenheimer had done for the imperial court, he was defenceless against anti-Jewish attacks. And this was only the start of his troubles.

He later referred to the six years that followed as "a period of teetering on the brink of the abyss." The wars against France and the Ottomans – settled at last by the Treaty of Karlowitz in 1699 – may have boosted Austrian and Hapsburg pride, but they taxed the imperial treasury beyond its limits. And Oppenheimer was left holding the bill; he even paid the expenses of Austrian delegates at the peace treaties. Owed millions of florins by the Vienna court, he in turn owed countless agents, factors, and suppliers. Still the emperor asked for more, and as a loyal servant of the Crown he found another five million florins for the Austrian treasury in 1700. Both Jewish and Christian financiers advanced him this money, despite his debt problems, solely because of his sterling reputation.

To add further insult to injury, a small riot broke out in Vienna in June of 1700, caused by an innocuous disagreement between two chimney sweeps and an associate of Oppenheimer's, who the two men claimed had insulted them. A group of people gathering in the street near Oppenheimer's house sided with the chimney sweeps, and within moments they had transformed themselves into a mob. Before Oppenheimer's private guards could do anything, the family house was under attack. The Viennese police apparently refused to intervene. While Oppenheimer and his family cowered in a secret passageway, his property on the Bauermarkt was looted and destroyed – his furniture, paintings, and above all his private financial papers.

Three years later, on May 3, 1703, Samuel Oppenheimer died after a brief bout of pneumonia. He was buried in the old Jewish cemetery in Seegasse in the Ninth District.* Ironically, the War of the Spanish Succession, one of the defining conflicts of the eighteenth century, was already underway and the Oppenheimers were back in the war-supply business. But Austrian officials claimed that Samuel Oppenheimer was guilty of embezzlement and refused to honour the debt of some six million florins that Emmanuel Oppenheimer now tried to collect. That refusal by the imperial treasury led to one of the first modern financial crises in Europe. Dozens of claims brought Emmanuel to the brink of bankruptcy as princes and dukes across the continent urged the emperor to deal properly with this economic disaster. After much procrastination, Leopold, as he had done in 1673, when he first made use of Oppenheimer's skills, turned to another court Jew to rescue him: Samuel's relative through marriage, Samson Wertheimer, who inherited the position of chief factor in Vienna.

Emmanuel Oppenheimer, more soft-spoken than his father, recovered sufficiently to continue the family business, though he spent the remainder of his life attempting to claim what was

---

* The cemetery was later destroyed by the Nazis during the Second World War. Many of the 900 or so headstones were actually removed by members of the Jewish community and hidden from the Nazis. Recently, the cemetery, located today in the backyard of a retirement home, was restored. Using a map drawn in 1912, many of the headstones were returned to their original locations. The precise spot of Oppenheimer's grave, however, is unknown.

rightfully his. His name still carried some weight, and he followed his father's example by helping Jews in Prague and Nikolsburg. He died at a relatively young age in 1721, leaving his wife, Judith, and family without much money. Judith attempted to carry on the business, but to no avail. Court officials attempted to have her expelled from Vienna, but she fought them and won. She died in 1738, waiting for a judgement of her case against the treasury. At the time of her death, all she had left was about 11 florins.

Samuel's other heirs fared little better. Another son, Simon Wolf Oppenheimer, who had married the granddaughter of Hanover court Jew Leffman Behrends, had some success as banker, but Emmanuel and Judith's children were impoverished and eventually forced to leave Vienna, the city their grandfather had once saved. The entire Oppenheimer estate, or at least what was left of it, was auctioned off in 1763. It was a sad legacy for a man who had once instructed his sons "to carry out the business affairs of the kind and generous Emperor faithfully, honestly and sincerely – as he had done."

The *Judenkaiser*

IT WAS ONLY A DAY'S JOURNEY southeast from Vienna to the city of Eisenstadt, the capital of the Burgenland. Jews had been living in Eisenstadt since the late fifteenth century, their lives like their co-religionists in Vienna dependent on the mood and policies of the emperor. In 1622, the town and the surrounding region had become part of the fiefdom of the pro-Catholic Count Nicholas (Miklós) Esterházy of Galantha, who built an impressive baroque castle there. Nicholas's son, Paul, who inherited the family's various properties, had proved his loyalty to the Holy Roman Empire as commander-in-chief of the army in southern Hungary and ably defended Vienna against Ottoman encroachment in 1683. As a reward, Leopold elevated him to the rank of prince four years later. An enlightened ruler for the period, Prince Paul valued his Jewish subjects and decided to permit more of them – providing they were wealthy enough – to settle in Eisenstadt.

During the 1690s, as the Turks threatened Esterházy's rule, he relied heavily on the court Jew Samson Wertheimer, who provided him the necessary funds to protect his lands. To show his appreciation for Wertheimer's efforts, he granted him the gift of a large house that came with its own synagogue and exempted him and his descendants from paying any tax. Wertheimer never moved permanently to Eisenstadt, since he already had a home in nearby Vienna, only one of about eight that he owned. But he did ensure that it was properly renovated and that the community of about 600 people could use the small and unostentatious synagogue. It was only one of many good deeds that Wertheimer did for the Jews of Eisenstadt.*

From time to time Wertheimer did use the wooden pulpit in the middle of his synagogue to deliver sermons about Jewish life and the meaning of Jewish existence. For unlike most other court Jews, Wertheimer was not only a financier and factor, the "wealthiest Jew of his day," he was also a pious man and a Talmudic scholar. Whereas Samuel Oppenheimer's portrait appears to be that of an anxious nobleman, Wertheimer, with his deep penetrating eyes and look of compassion, is revealed as a proud soul more at ease with the world. Rich though he was, Wertheimer was not absorbed by the acquisition of goods – various lucrative properties, a fine collection of books, and some jewellery for his wife aside. He kept his beard as any rabbi would have, and was said to have "dressed like a Pole."

---

* After Wertheimer's death, the house and synagogue were purchased by the Wolf family, who continued to use the synagogue for private services. From 1850 on, the building was used as a gathering-place for Eisenstadt's Jewish youth. Somehow the synagogue survived Kristallnacht ("Night of Broken Glass") on November 9, 1938, when the majority of Austria's synagogues were burned and destroyed. (It may have been that because most of the Jews in Eisenstadt were deported in the summer and early fall of 1938 and the synagogue's Torah scrolls already hidden in a secret compartment, the pro-Nazi mobs ignored it.) The Red Cross inherited it in 1945 and then during the following decade, when the city was under Soviet occupation, Russian-Jewish soldiers used it as a prayer room. It has since been restored as a museum.

Wertheimer was born in Worms in 1658. His father was a rabbi and a scholar, and young Samson was sent to study at a yeshiva in Frankfurt. That experience and religious training guided the remainder of his life. But it was his marriage to Frumet Veronica, the daughter of Rabbi Isaac Brillin of Mannheim, and the recently widowed wife of Nathan Oppenheimer, that altered his career path. For it was through Frumet that he was introduced to her first husband's uncle, Samuel Oppenheimer. Recognizing Wertheimer's natural intelligence, Oppenheimer appointed his young protege as the manager of his Vienna business interests. He succeeded brilliantly, and soon proved to be especially adept at arranging large loan packages for the Hapsburg war chest.

Even before Oppenheimer's demise, Wertheimer, more conservative and less of a speculator than his mentor and rival, was destined to become the emperor's new chief court factor. He befriended Crown Prince Joseph, who became emperor following Leopold's death in 1705, as well as his brother Charles, who followed as Hapsburg ruler when Joseph himself died suddenly in 1711. By then, he had earned the gratitude of most of the princes and dukes of Central Europe by raising enough money for the imperial treasury to solve the financial debacle caused by Oppenheimer's near bankruptcy. New sources of funds for the government were found by reorganizing the lucrative salt industry and tinkering with customs and trading regulations.

Above all, it was Wertheimer who sustained the Austrian government and army through the War of the Spanish Succession by advancing millions – for which he was reimbursed steadily but slowly – to the emperor in his battles with both the French and the rebels in Hungary led by Francis Rákóczy. He accomplished this feat by relying on other court Jews throughout the German states, who became part of Wertheimer's wide-ranging network. Known among Jews and others as the *Judenkaiser*, he and his son Wolf were invited to Frankfurt to witness the gala coronation of Emperor Charles VI and presented with gold chains to mark the occasion. So highly regarded was Wertheimer that the emperor posted ten of his guards to watch over his house in Vienna. When the hostilities finally ended in 1713, it was Wertheimer, too, who largely financed the Treaty of Utrecht, including paying for the expenses of the Austrian delegation.

Wertheimer was revered by Jews throughout the empire. His sizeable charitable contributions to their communities were part of it, and his aid in rebuilding Jewish areas adversely affected by the war, and also that he was made the honorary chief rabbi for Hungary, the one title that he truly treasured. In 1720, he and his son-in-law, Moses Kann of Frankfurt, financed the printing of a new edition of the Talmud. He generously gave money to Jews in Palestine. He urged his youngest son to become a rabbi instead of a businessman and to marry the daughter of a rabbi. To this end, he set up a dowry fund to be used by his son's future wife. In 1715, another child, a daughter, married the son of learned Rabbi Gabriel Eskeles, a Viennese religious leader. According to Glückel of Hameln, the dowry and presents totalled more than 30,000 thalers. The wedding itself, writes Glückel, "was celebrated with so much pomp that never before had there been such glory among Jews. . . . It was world renowned."

Glückel, who was privileged enough to enter Wertheimer's inner circle, did not immediately trust him. Some years earlier, Wertheimer had taken a genuine interest in Glückel's son Zanvil. Only fourteen years old, Zanvil had been betrothed to Wertheimer's young niece. It was decided that prior to the wedding, Zanvil would live in Vienna, where Wertheimer would educate him in both religious and financial matters. In the three years he spent with him, Wertheimer probably did not supervise Zanvil as well as he should have. Glückel complained that her son was "still very young and did many childish things," including wasting too much money. Nevertheless, when at long last the wedding took place, Wertheimer ensured the safe transportation of Glückel and her family from their home to Bamberg, with a stay at his house in Vienna along the way. Later, when her son Nathan was having financial difficulties during the Oppenheimer fiasco, the first person Glückel thought of turning to was Wertheimer, since she knew he would not refuse her.

In large part, the high opinion accorded Wertheimer was a response to the real influence he wielded at the court on behalf of Jews everywhere. There was no better *shtadlan*, or community representative. Consider for example how Wertheimer dealt with anti-Jewish attitudes and propaganda. In 1700 a professor in Heidelberg named Johann Andreas Eisenmenger was alarmed by what he perceived to be an unacceptable growth of the Jewish population, its assimilation into the larger community in cities like Amsterdam, and its infiltration into the German economy. In response, he wrote the two-volume, 2,000-page *Endecktes Judenthum*, or *Judaism Unmasked*, which bore the alternative title "A Thorough and True Account of How the Unrepenting Jews Horribly Blaspheme and Dishonour the Holy Trinity." Eisenmenger's work was hardly a "true account," but rather a product of the early German Enlightenment mixed with some medieval anti-Jewish notions about blood libels, well-poisonings, and bogus interpretations of the Talmud. Among anti-Semites, it was a popular source of material for many years.

Writing and publishing the book was one thing, distributing it quite another. Jewish leaders in Frankfurt appealed to Samson Wertheimer to take the matter up with the emperor. Convinced by Wertheimer's argument that the book would inflame the general population, Leopold banned the book from being distributed until it could be studied further. Eisenmenger started legal proceedings and enlisted the help of the elector of Palatine and King Frederick I of Prussia, who were sympathetic to his cause. But the emperor remained firm.

Eisenmenger then let it be known that he would let the issue die for a generous payment. Wertheimer and the other court Jews involved in the fight refused the offer. Eisenmenger died in 1704, though that hardly ended the fight. Members of his family continued to campaign for the book's release, and seven years later, through a bit of deception – supposedly publishing a second edition in Königsberg (now Kaliningrad), an area outside of the Emperor's authority – Eisenmenger's controversial work reached an attentive audience in Berlin and nearby cities and towns. It was not until Charles VI's daughter Maria Theresa inherited the Hapsburg throne in 1740 that *Endecktes Judenthum* was widely available. (The empress's reign was notable for its anti-Jewish policies and for drastically reducing the Jewish population in Vienna.)

By the time he reached sixty years of age, in 1720, Wertheimer, having done all he could to improve the lives of Jews in the empire, decided to retire. He died four years later and, like Samuel Oppenheimer, was buried in the Seegasse cemetery.* His eldest son, Wolf, assumed control of the family's properties and commercial affairs. A competent businessman, albeit one who loaned far too much money, he is best remembered for bravely leading the campaign to save the Jews of Prague after Maria Theresa decided to expel them in 1744, in the middle of the War of the Austrian Succession. He rallied other court Jews in this cause and appealed to rulers and influential merchants throughout the German states. It took three years of writing letters, speaking with friends and associates, and cajoling everyone he could before the Jews – after paying the empress's treasury 240,000 florins – were permitted to return to their homes in the city.

By the mid-nineteenth century Samuel's great-grandsons had become assimilated members of the upper class and hardly recognizable as Jews. In fact, the majority of their descendants converted and grew up as Christians, an occurrence more common than not among families of court Jews.

The *Jud Süss*

As Nazi Germany marched its way through Western Europe in 1940 and continued to inflict terror on the Jews of Poland, a

---

* In 1992, during the cemetery's restoration, an elaborate tomb was constructed to honour him.

select group of Berlin citizens were invited on the evening of September 24 to a showing of a new film by the German director Veit Harlan. Entitled *Jud Süss*, the film was Nazi propaganda at its most sophisticated. In response to Josef Goebbels's call for anti-Semitic artistic works, Harlan found the perfect historical character in Joseph Süss Oppenheimer, a famous and controversial court Jew in Stuttgart in the German state of Württemberg. In a twist of irony, the film's story line was lifted from an acclaimed novel published in 1926 about Süss Oppenheimer by the German-Jewish writer Lion Feuchtwanger.

Played by the German actor Ferdinand Marian, Süss Oppenheimer was depicted as a humane but fundamentally evil Jew who was every single anti-Semitic stereotype the Nazis could think of — corrupt, immoral, manipulative, and greedy. Indeed, all of the Jewish characters in the film — it is believed that approximately 120 Jews from the Lublin ghetto were forced to participate as actors — were "dirty, hook-nosed, or without scruples."

The film traces Süss Oppenheimer's sordid career as he rises from the ghetto to the heights of power at court, cheating and destroying anyone who stands in his way. He lusts after women, and in one infamous scene, he rapes a young Aryan woman (played by the actress Kristina Söderbaum) while her husband is tortured. Unable to stand the pain of the experience, the woman drowns herself. The film ends with Süss Oppenheimer's execution and the exile of Jews from Stuttgart.

The film was an ominous sign of the dark days ahead. So impressed was Nazi police chief Heinrich Himmler with the film that he ordered all of his men in the S.S. to watch it. A showing was arranged for concentration-camp guards as well. After members of the Hitler Youth saw the film in Vienna they kicked and trampled a Jewish man to death.

There was, not surprisingly, little truth in the Nazi portrayal of Süss Oppenheimer, other than the real tragedy of his life and the fact that he was executed at public hanging in Stuttgart in 1738. No court Jew has attracted so much attention, and long before the Nazis discovered him, anti-Semites used his career to illustrate the sinful qualities of Jews everywhere. He became an ugly caricature whose exaggerated exploits were an easy target for contemporary politicians, writers, and artists.

The true story of Süss Oppenheimer is more complex. Born in Heidelberg in 1698 or 1699, he grew up not in an impoverished ghetto but in a well-to-do family in a small, tight-knit community. His father, a relative to Samuel Oppenheimer, was a merchant and tax collector, and his mother was the daughter of a prominent Frankfurt Jewish family. Besides Joseph, they had two daughters. After Oppenheimer's father died in 1707, his mother remarried and had three more children. She died in 1753.

At a relatively young age, Süss Oppenheimer was sent across Europe to learn from his various relatives how to be a financier. Ambitious, shrewd, and intelligent, he excelled at his studies. By the age of eighteen, he had obtained a position as a commercial agent and army purveyor at the court of the Landgrave Ernest August of Hesse-Darmstadt.

His reputation as a "born speculator" eventually caught the attention of Prince Karl Alexander of Württemberg, who in 1732 employed him as his factor and spy in Stuttgart. A year later, the reigning ruler of Württemberg, Duke Eberhard Ludwig, died and Karl Alexander succeeded him. Among his first acts was to appoint Süss Oppenheimer as Württemberg's new chief financial administrator. But there was a problem. The new ruler was a Catholic (he had converted in 1712) and a supporter of the Hapsburgs, while most of his subjects were Lutheran. The Peace of Westphalia in 1648 may have ended the religious warfare in Europe, though in Württemberg Catholic–Protestant differences were still very much alive.

Süss Oppenheimer relished his work and was utterly loyal to the duke. Utilizing his various banking contacts in Vienna, Frankfurt, and Amsterdam, he poured money into the court at Stuttgart. There were jewels and expensive dresses for the duchess, spectacular receptions and oil paintings, fine furniture and extravagant feasts.

Today we would call Süss Oppenheimer a workaholic. "He was always hurried and always restless," writes Selma Stern. "He spurred on both horses and servants, dispatched couriers and dashed off letters. . . . He was the repository of hundreds of secrets, a fact which lent his character a certain air of taciturnity and impenetrability." Still, he did know how to enjoy himself.

Unlike Samuel Oppenheimer, Samson Wertheimer, and many other first-generation court Jews, Süss Oppenheimer disregarded his Jewish upbringing, even though he obviously could not escape it. He did not visit the synagogue, not on the Sabbath or the High Holidays. Nor did he keep kosher. His library contained many volumes and reference works, but none were Hebrew. "Pertaining to his belief, that he was a Jew," Henrietta Luciana Fischer, one of his many female companions, told authorities, "I never knew for sure, because he never wanted to be mistreated because of being Jewish." (Typical of his contradictory and complex life, he did at one time want to marry the daughter of an Orthodox Jewish banker from Metz, Nathan Caen.)

He revelled in the luxuries that his position offered him. He dressed in the finest of clothes and purchased thousands of engravings and paintings that he displayed in his magnificent homes in Frankfurt and on the fashionable Seestrasse in Stuttgart. At the auction after his death, there were among his belongings in Frankfurt alone: ten coats, twenty-eight vests, twenty-four pair of pants, ten silk stockings, twenty-five shirts and thirty-one ties, six pair of shoes, thirty-one napkins, four bathrobes, and eight night-shirts. The lone Jewish article was a bag containing *tefillin*, or phylacteries, likely not used for decades, if ever.

He was also, as his critics later charged, a notorious womanizer and bedded countless women – rich or poor, Christian or Jewish, it made no difference. He did prefer them young, single, and with a full figure. He was especially attracted to young widows, since, in his view, "they brought experience." Among his favourites was the lovely eighteen-year-old Henrietta Luciana Fischer, for whom he arranged a job working for Duke Karl Alexander's wife so she would be close to him. At the time of his arrest in 1737, Henrietta was five months pregnant with their son. Oppenheimer was overly protective of her and once beat a servant for taking her out of the house without his permission.

Later, at his trial, it was claimed that Oppenheimer had at least twenty-six mistresses, which was perhaps a slight exaggeration. He was hardly the only man of this era to exhibit such behaviour; illicit love affairs were a staple of baroque culture. But he was a Jew, and therefore somehow more guilty than his Christian peers.

If his autocratic nature and ostentatious lifestyle were not enough to earn the disapproval of large numbers of people, then the plans he devised for reforming the state administration surely were. Ahead of his time, Süss Oppenheimer understood that economic advancement must be accompanied by political change. But he was no advocate of democracy. A Machiavellian through and through, he believed that absolutism was the only form of government worth practising. To this end, at the urging of the duke, he instituted reforms that drastically curtailed the power of the Estates, Württemberg's feudal and Protestant oligarchy, which had prevented Karl Alexander from establishing the centralized administration he desired so much. He removed court advisors, reorganized the accounting and tax system, created state monopolies on salt, wine, and tobacco, and imposed new, higher, and more visible taxes – all without the consent traditionally required from the Estates.

Even worse, he dispensed court patronage at an alarming rate in return for money, favours, and support for the duke. He likely accepted payments from businesses in return for government contracts, not an entirely unheard-of practice at the time. Nonetheless, he was playing a dangerous game. Süss Oppenheimer's unpopularity, rather than the duke's, increased each day, and he knew that many members of the nobility close to Karl Alexander were conspiring against him. There were rumours, too, that he was involved in a secret plan to expand Catholic rights at the expense of Protestant ones. (In fact, there may have been some truth to this, as

Duke Karl Alexander was influenced by the aggressive ecclesiastical policies of his friend the bishop of Würzburg. It also seems likely that Süss Oppenheimer was aware of the duke's intentions.)

The duke, still appreciative of Oppenheimer's talents, ignored the criticism and in 1737 appointed him his Privy Councillor of Finance. The new title may not have given him all that much more authority, but in the eyes of Christian Europe, whether it was true or not, the *Jud Süss* was a power to be reckoned with, and a dangerous one at that.

His fall came quickly. On March 19, 1737, Duke Karl Alexander suddenly died. That evening, Süss Oppenheimer was arrested, charged with corruption, treason, "bleeding the country through various nefarious schemes . . . setting up monopolies, manipulating the currency, violating the constitution and oppressing religion." He was imprisoned at the fortress of Hohenneuffen and his properties and possessions seized. Then or later, no amount of pleading, explanations, or even proper interpretations of the law made any difference to his many accusers. He was, in short, made the lone scapegoat for the duke's detested rulings and trading policies. He was treated like a common criminal, given a trial in which the verdict was never in doubt. His declaration of innocence fell on deaf ears; his few supporters were all but ignored. An offer to buy his freedom made by several members of the Jewish community was rejected. On December 13, 1737, the Württemberg court judges sentenced him to death by hanging.

In prison, he refused to eat and grew sickly. More remarkable was his sudden spiritual awakening. As he awaited his fate, he rediscovered Judaism. He began praying daily in Hebrew, studying the scriptures, and when he began to accept food again it had to be kosher. When various priests visited him in his cell urging him to convert, perhaps as a way to have the death sentence commuted, he rebuffed them. "I am a Jew and will remain a Jew," he told one clergyman. "I would not become a Christian even if I could become an Emperor. Changing one's religion is a matter for consideration by a free man; it is an evil thing for a prisoner."

He was hanged before a large crowd in Stuttgart on April 2, 1738, an event later celebrated in paintings and other artistic works. Before he was placed on a knacker's cart to take him to the gallows, he bequeathed what was left of his possessions to his family and beseeched Rabbi Mordechai Schloss to let the Jewish world know that "he had died for the Holy Name of God." On the last day of his life, it was later reported by eyewitnesses, he "wore a scarlet coat with a small golden lace, also a jacket and trousers of the same color, a fine dress shirt without cuffs, silk white stockings, a wig and a hat without braids." Four hundred guards marched with him. Spectators had travelled from far and wide to attend the pageant. Unlike in the Nazi film, however, as he was hanged he uttered the Hebrew prayer words of the *Shema*: "Hear, O Israel; The Lord is our God, the Lord is one." His body was then placed in a large iron cage so his remains could be exhibited. Even in death he was humiliated.

Was Joseph Süss Oppenheimer the architect of his own demise? To a certain extent the answer must be yes. The lesson of his tragic life is clear: members of the Jewish elite in the Diaspora who alienated the people with whom they lived in order to serve their own personal interests, as well as the interests of an unpopular absolute ruler, suffered dire consequences. The Jud Süss was as Jonathan Israel has put it, "a complex double-being, the courtier in him coexisting uneasily with his Jewish background. He was well-aware that his polished manners and elegant attire both smoothed his path and added to his enemies."

At the same time, court Jews like Samuel Oppenheimer, Samson Wertheimer, and even Süss Oppenheimer himself helped pave the way for the emancipation of Jews in the decades ahead. It was not strictly because of the great wealth some them generated – although nineteenth-century bankers like the Rothschilds, Oppenheims, and Seligmanns did have court Jews and factors as ancestors – but rather the way in which they opened up Jewish society to the outside world. The secular acculturation that governed their lives, frowned upon in the early 1700s, found greater support among intellectuals like Moses Mendelssohn and other adherents of the *Haskalah*, the Jewish Enlightenment.

Less than twenty years after the execution of Süss Oppenheimer, the German Christian philosopher and playwright Gotthold Ephraim Lessing wrote a controversial play entitled *Die Juden* (The Jews). Lessing had met Mendelssohn in Berlin, and despite the fact that the young Mendelssohn suffered from poor health and had a humpback caused by a bout of rickets, Lessing was impressed with his mind. In his play, Lessing showed his fellow Christians a different kind of Jew than they had met before, one who was wise and sophisticated. When challenged that no such Jew existed, he pointed to Mendelssohn, whose prodigious writing career he later helped. Mendelssohn was Lessing's model Jew, a Jew who was not part of the world of the court, but who could, if given the opportunity, become a neighbour and perhaps even a friend.

It was the kind of thinking that appealed to Emperor Joseph II, who succeeded his more doctrinaire mother, Maria Theresa, in 1780. In his view, the only way to make Jews "useful citizens of the state" was to remove the institutions and laws that kept them separate.

Even if most Christians were not yet ready for such a transition, Mendelssohn himself was. Well before the emperor had instituted his enlightened reforms, Mendelssohn had urged his fellow Jews to take a different approach. "Adopt the mores and constitution of the country in which you find yourself, but be steadfast in upholding the religion of your fathers, too," he advised them. "Bear both burdens as well as you can." He and his followers argued that obtaining a Western education was the first step in this path to enlightenment and acceptance.

That would be the challenge for the next generations: was it possible to leave the ghetto but still retain a Jewish identity and culture? There was no single answer to this dilemma, nor did the Christian world provide much guidance in assisting Jews to solve it. Many younger Jews in Austrian and German regions who attended university shaved off their beards, abandoned the synagogue, spoke German rather than Yiddish, and ate what they wanted when they wanted. For their entertainment they gambled, visited brothels, and consumed large amounts of wine and beer. The rabbis and older members of the community were shocked by this behaviour, yet even more dramatic changes were on the horizon.

The rise of nationalism, the changes brought by the French Revolution, and Napoleon's march across the continent had repercussions in the lives of Jews everywhere in the Diaspora, as they did for all Europeans. In Berlin, Paris, and London, there was one Jewish response to the new political, social, and economic realities and to the quandary of assimilation and secularism. In the *shtelach* of the Russian Pale of Settlement, there was quite another.

Chapter Six

THE AGE OF EMANCIPATION

Frankfurt, 1848

From now on we do not recognize our cause as being special . . . We are Germans and want to be nothing else! We have no other fatherland than the German fatherland and we wish for no other! Only by our faith are we Israelites, in every other respect we belong with devotion to the state in which we live.

— RABBI LEOPOLD STEIN, 1848

The *Judengasse*

IN MID-JUNE 1796, THE FRENCH ARMY under the command of Napoleon Bonaparte bombarded the Austrian garrison inside Frankfurt am Main. One casualty of the battle was the small Jewish quarter, the *Judengasse* or Jews' Alley.* A French artillery shell exploded and caused a devastating fire that destroyed at least 150 houses. For a brief time, some of the city's 3,000 Jews (7.5 per cent of the total population) were permitted to live outside of the old ghetto – but only temporarily.

The vast majority of Frankfurt's Jews remained as they had been in Glückel of Hameln's day more than a hundred years earlier: second class citizens whose lives were governed by a myriad of

---

* Readers can assume that all references to Frankfurt refer to Frankfurt am Main. The smaller city Frankfurt-on-the-Oder, east of Berlin, will be denoted by name.

restrictions and rules, discriminatory taxes, arbitrary justice, and humiliating regulations read aloud each year in the synagogue.

Jews had been required to live in the *Judengasse* since the mid-1400s. If they ventured beyond the high walls and gates of the *Judengasse*, they were at the mercy of drunks and gangs of rowdies who could be and often did turn violent. Medieval superstitions about well poisonings, blood rituals, and depictions of Jews as the Devil were to persist into the nineteenth century. In fact, in the south part of Frankfurt, on the wall of a bridge extending over the river Main, the city's own officials had commissioned the infamous and derogatory painting *Judensau* (Jews' Sow). "The caricature," historian Amos Elon writes, "depicted a fat sow holding up its tail for a Jew, with his tongue hanging out, to lick its excrement. Several other Jews, dressed in the obligatory round and pointed Jews' hats, were showed sucking the sow's teats, while the whole scene was watched over approvingly by a devil." It was not removed until 1802.

Outside their proscriptive quarter, Jews were not allowed to walk on public footpaths, nor visit parks, inns and coffee houses – rules that would be used again by the Nazis little more than a century later. And if a Christian, even if no older than a child, approached a Jew with the words *"Mach mores Jud"* ("Jew, do your duty"), the person so addressed had to remove his hat and respectfully bow.

Although a haven from such abuse, there was little redeeming about daily life in the *Judengasse*. Located in the northeast section of the city, it was a narrow and dark muddy street less than a half a mile long – "somber, humid, and filthy," as one visitor described it in 1747. At night, its three gates were locked and guarded, and on Sundays and Christian holidays, its inhabitants were not permitted to leave at all.

As in other ghettos, its living conditions were often abysmal – small apartments and houses crowded together with little space for the residents. Jews were not allowed to farm or trade in grain, spices, or weapons. Most peddled second-hand goods and ran pawnshops, or were shoemakers or tailors; some were small-scale moneylenders.

Their shops were usually found on the bottom floors, stories added as necessary for residents as the population expanded. (In Frankfurt, as a way of controlling the non-Christian population, Jewish men could not marry before the age of 25.)

Fires ravaged the *Judengasse* several times during the 1700s, not only in 1796, leaving many people homeless. Two centuries later, allied bombing attacks during the Second World War permanently destroyed its last remnants. Today, at the *Judengasse* Museum (opened in 1992 and affiliated with the city's larger Jewish Museum), visitors can walk through partial excavations and reconstructions of the ghetto's houses and synagogues. The streets in the surrounding area offer a sharp conrast, bustling with traffic, office buildings, shops, restaurants, and parking lots characteristic of present-day Frankfurt. In a sense, little has changed. For the Jews as well as for curious Christians who dared visit, the *Judengasse* was always an eyesore of poverty, squalor, and congestion.

Johann Wolfgang von Goethe, Germany's most revered poet and playwright who was born in Frankfurt in 1749, recalled passing by the *Judengasse* as a boy. "The lack of space, the dirt, the throng of people, the disagreeable accents of the voice – altogether, it made the most unpleasant impression, even upon the passer-by who merely looked through the gate," he wrote. "It was a long time before I dared to venture in there alone, and I did not return there readily when once I had escaped from that multitude of people, all of them with something to hawk, all indefatigably buying or selling."

Ludwig Börne, a noted political writer of the era, had similar recollections. He was born Judah Baruch, the son of a prosperous Jewish merchant, but later changed his name and converted to Christianity. The *Judengasse*, as Börne remembered it, was "a long, dark prison in which the highly celebrated light of the eighteenth century has not been able to penetrate." He noted that children "swim about in the gutter, creep about the filth innumerable as vermin hatched by the sun from the dung heap."

Despite their hardships and the bleakness of ghetto life, Frankfurt's Jews, like Jews throughout Germany, created a world for themselves replete with synagogues, schools, *yeshivot* for higher rabbinical learning, music, and a rich *Judendeutsch* or Judeo-German (the German-Hebrew dialect of the *Judengasse*) culture distinct from that of Jews in the *shtetlach* of the Russian Pale of Settlement (who spoke what would be more commonly referred today as Yiddish). Traditionalists within the community avoided assimilation with the Christian majority, accepting and, indeed, preferring segregation and rejecting the modern approach of the *Haskalah* (Jewish Enlightenment) proposed by Moses Mendelssohn and his followers, the *maskilim* (singular, *maskil*). How else, they asked, could Jews safeguard the customs and rituals of the past? In their view, integrating themselves into the German national culture along the lines suggested by Mendelssohn was too great a sacrifice. But the tide of progress could not be halted.

As traders, merchants, and bankers, some German Jews were able to take advantage of the economic and social transformations associated with the Industrial Revolution. Gradually, more moved from towns to the larger cities of Berlin, Hamburg and Frankfurt in search of new opportunities in industry, manufacturing, retail, and financial services. Within a generation, they became members of an urbanized middle class in both outlook and appearance.

Still, neither they nor their Christian neighbours and associates ever forgot they were Jews. Unlike in France and Holland, the liberty and equality heralded by the French Revolution proved more elusive in Germany. Gaining entry into law, academia, education, the civil service, and other professions, for instance, was a slow process, and the social acceptance of Jews took even longer. In 1807, when a group of Jewish men in Frankfurt wanted to become members of the Freemasons, they were compelled to create their own lodge since no Christian lodge would admit them.

Napoleon and his army may have brought the Revolution's ideals with them, but the backlash against French-style democracy – especially following the Congress of Vienna and Napoleon's defeat at Waterloo in 1815 – did not bode well for the German Jewish bid for equal civil rights. Indeed, the struggle for emancipation, as it became known, occupied

Jewish politicians, businessmen, intellectuals, and religious leaders for much of the nineteenth century. Any substantial success took decades to reach fruition – for example, not until the 1848 revolutions and after were the endless number of restrictions that governed the Jews of Frankfurt abolished – yet a new desire for change from within, not only from without, impacted dramatically, often sharply, on Jewish life. The practices and beliefs of religious institutions were questioned and then transformed in profound ways giving rise to new schools of Judaism, to radical ideas about the meaning of faith. Thus, while Jews' attempts to find their rightful place in a German society were imbued with the spirit of Teutonic nationalism, their own consciousness of what it meant to be a Jew was forever changed in the process.

This much can be said: at the beginning of the nineteenth century, they were simply "Jews who lived in Germany"; fifty years later, they would be more appropriately described as "German Jews" – acculturated and proud of the fatherland, though not quite in agreement of their proper place within that larger society.

The House of Rothschild

WITHOUT QUESTION, the Frankfurt *Judengasse*'s most famous residents were Mayer Amschel Rothschild and his family – especially his five sons, Amschel, Nathan, Carl, Salomon, and James – whose remarkable and unique story of success was celebrated throughout the Diaspora.* The majority of German Jews were hardly affluent, and mighty bankers, particularly the Rothschilds' deeds and machinations, were a source of endless fascination and gossip. Yet it was not only the family's fabulous wealth, their access to the rich and powerful, and their inernational connections that made them so extraordinary. It was also that they remained dedicated Jews when quite a few others in like situations turned away from their faith and converted to Christianity, to further their careers and gain the

* Years later the Nazis, too, linked Frankfurt with the family, denouncing it as "the city of the Rothschilds" – despite the fact that the Frankfurt branch of the business was wound up in 1901, three decades before Hitler came to power.

much-coveted acceptance by German Gentiles. Apostasy may well have been the necessary "entrance ticket to European society," as Heinrich Heine, the Jewish poet and writer who did convert to Christianity, stated, but denying their heritage was not the Rothschilds' solution to the problem of discrimination.* Contrarily, they openly supported Jewish charities and schools, and embraced the cause of Jewish emancipation.

Mayer Amschel was a traditional Jew who regularly attended synagogue services, did not work on the Sabbath, celebrated Jewish holidays, and followed dietary laws. He was not a great supporter of religious reforms, although he did provide money for a modern *Haskalah* school, was (at least according to one painting) clean-shaven, and wore an unpowdered wig, as was typical for a wealthy Jewish merchant. His sons may not have been as orthodox in their beliefs as he (with the exception of Amschel), but being Jewish was central to their family identity. However palatial their homes and magnificent their attire, as the Rothschild's wealth increased, they never forgot the lessons their father had taught them.

"If everything depends, as it does, on God, if we want, as we do, to be fortunate, then dear Nathan [the interests of the entire Jewish people] must be as important to you as the most important business deal once was," wrote Salomon Rothschild to his brother Nathan

---

* Two of the more significant acts of apostasy during this period concerned Benjamin Disraeli and Karl Marx. Disraeli's father had him baptized in 1817, when he was 12 years old. Had he remained a Jew, Disraeli would have not have been permitted to take a seat in the British Parliament in 1837 nor to become Prime Minister in 1868. Marx was only six years old in 1824 and living in the German town of Trier, when his father had him converted. The elder Marx, whose own father had been a rabbi, was trained as a lawyer, but his status as a Jew had prevented him from practicing law. Converting to Christianity improved his career aspirations as well as the impact his young son – who went on to high school rather than a yeshiva – eventually had on modern history. It is estimated that, between 1800 and 1870, approximately 11,000 German Jews converted to Christianity. While apostasy did open doors to a career, it was not a panacea. As Ludwig Börne discovered, a convert was always a convert in the eyes of Jews and Christians. "For eighteen years I have been baptized," he complained, "and it doesn't help at all."

in early 1818, several years after their father had died. "How can we show more respect for our blessed father, than by supporting that work which he laboured at for years."

The family patriarch was born in the *Judengasse* in 1743 or 1744, where his family had resided for generations. At one time, Mayer Amschel's ancestors had lived in a house with a red coat of arms or shield (in German, *zum Roten Schild*) hanging over the front door – a common practice in those days, to identify a particular property, as there were no numbers on the doors. The name stuck even when the Rothschilds, as they became known, later moved into different houses, including one distinguished by a green shield. (In the *Judengasse*, Jews could own their houses, but not the land on which it stood.) By the mid-1700s, the Rothschilds were slightly better off than the typical *Judengasse* family. Mayer Amschel's father, Amschel Moses, made a decent living as a textile merchant. A pious man, he taught Mayer Amschel about the importance of family, loyalty, and being a good Jew.

At a young age, Mayer Amschel was sent to Fürth, near Nuremberg, to obtain a religious education, though his father did not intend for him to be a rabbi, as is commonly believed. When his parents died in a smallpox epidemic before he was thirteen years old, Mayer Amschel was sent to live with Wolf Jakob Oppenheim, a family friend and financial agent in Hanover. There he learned more about the intricacies of business, forged important contacts with aristocrats and court officials, and took a special interest in rare coins and medals.

It was, in fact, his coin dealing that brought him to the attention of William, the Prince of Hesse-Kassel, heir and son of the Landgrave Frederick II (William became Landgrave as William IX in 1803 and Elector in 1810), following Mayer Amschel's return to Frankfurt in 1764.* Within a decade, Mayer Amschel became an agent to the

---

* William, who was married to his first cousin Caroline of Denmark, was also infamous for having numerous other women in his bed and siring many illegitimate children. Or, as the British writer Virginia Cowles once put it, William was apparently "so potent that almost every woman he slept with became pregnant." His favourite mistress was Rosalie Dorothea Ritter, who bore him eight children.

court in Hesse-Kassel (famous for supplying mercenaries to armies in Europe and North America) and set up shop as a dealer in rare coins and medals. He married Guttle Schnapper, the daughter of a prosperous court agent, and together they eventually had ten children: five sons and five daughters.

Early on, Mayer Amschel decided that the only way to protect the family business and assets was to have his sons and, in turn, theirs run the firm. (His five daughters, their families, and descendents had no claim or involvement, and had to be content with whatever funds they were given.) In later years, the Rothschilds further ensured their dynasty by arranging marriages between first cousins, a fairly common practice in early nineteenth-century Europe. After 1824, as Niall Ferguson, the family's most recent biographer, notes, "Rothschilds tended to marry Rothschilds. Of twenty-one marriages involving descendants of Mayer Amschel between 1824 and 1877, no fewer than fifteen were between his direct descendants." In 1836, for example, Nathan's son Lionel, the first Jew to take a seat in the British Parliament, married his first cousin, Charlotte, Carl's daughter. The oddest match, however, even for that era, was when James Rothschild, the youngest son of Mayer Amschel, in 1824 married his niece Betty, daughter of his brother Salomon. He was thirty-two years old, and she was nineteen.

Mayer Amschel's move into moneychanging and banking was a natural progression for him, from having extended credit and small loans to many of his business and aristocratic clients. Due in part to his connections with William of Hesse-Kassel (or more accurately, with Carl Friedrich Buderus, one of William's financial advisors whom he had befriended), he also became involved in discounting and trading currency bills, a fairly profitable venture. His success was rapid. "At the beginning of the 1790s," writes Ferguson, "Mayer Amschel Rothschild was not more than a prosperous antique dealer. By 1797, he was one of the richest Jews in Frankfurt and a central part of his business was unmistakably banking."

Taking advantage of the hostilities in Europe, Mayer Amschel began supplying grain and money to the Austrian army. Then, in 1799, in an astute move, he sent his son Nathan to Manchester to scout out business prospets in the lucrative British textile industry that was based there. Before long, Nathan emerged as a key financial player in London, establishing a branch of the family banking firm there, while his other brothers eventually set up similiar offices in Paris, Vienna, and Naples. It was, however, the Rothschilds' continuing success from their home base in Frankfurt that allowed them to become masters of the developing international bond market.

Given its prime geographic location to link trade and business within virtually all of Europe, Frankfurt's growing importance as one of the continent's key financial and trade centres was not surprising. During the city's bustling spring and autumn fairs (annual events there since the Middle Ages), traders, merchants, and travellers converged on Frankfurt – and still do. The city was transformed into "Germany's department store," offering deals in cloth, cattle, wool, flax, hemp, silk, and glassware among other goods.

The expensive war against the French and Napoleon left many states and rulers scrambling for cash. Frankfurt's investment bankers, such as the Oppenheimers, Seligmans, and Habers, were the descendants of court Jews, and were quick to respond to the high demand for money and credit. For the Rothschilds, in addition to their direct loan of funds to such aristocrats as Prince Metternich, the Austrian statesman who led the Congress of Vienna, dealings in foreign exchange bills and, later, investment in railways, the sale of high-yield government bonds proved especially lucrative. As long as the states could meet their bond interest payment obligations, both the investors and the bankers remained happy. Nevertheless, the frequently unstable political climate of the early 1800s often made these ventures very risky indeed. This was the reason that the Rothschilds spent so much of their time collecting political intelligence and dispatching correspondence to each other at their various branches. Their couriers were carrier pigeons – a message with the letters AB on it meant buy stock on the exchange, while CD was a code for selling stock. Later, they would also communicate via telegraph.

The war against Napoleon presented many challenges for the

Rothschilds. Once regions of Germany were under French control, the importation of British goods was not permitted, forcing Nathan to smuggle textiles and commodities from the colonies, using forged documents. The Rothschilds also came to the assistance of William of Hesse-Kassel, helping him to protect and manage his fortune when the Landgrave, who backed the British and Prussia against Napoleon, had to flee his small kingdom.

Astutely, they took advantage of whatever situation they could. One dangerous, dazzling move was to befriend the enlightened Baron Karl von Dalberg, who took control of Frankfurt on behalf of the pro-French Confederation of the Rhine (sixteen German states allied with the Emperor Napoleon), and became his chief banker. They convinced him, too, with money and words, to abolish some of the restrictions on the city's Jewish community and in 1811 to proclaim his intent to grant Frankfurt's Jews full citizenship. The decree came into effect the following year, only months before Mayer Amschel died. The total cost to the Jewish community for this privilege was four hundred forty thousand gulden (approximately $3.2 million in today's currency), of which the Rothschilds paid one hundred thousand gulden. Meanwhile, the Rothschilds were also loaning large sums of money to the Austrian army for their next round of battles against the French.

Back in London, young Nathan, stocky and robust, played a key role in raising much-needed funds for Wellington and the British – between 1811 and 1815 possibly as much as $98 million (about $1.4 billion today) – in their ongoing struggle to defeat Napoleon. One famous story in the annals of the Rothschilds is that Nathan, who supposedly first learned of Napoleon's defeat at Waterloo by his private couriers or carrier pigeons – though in some versions, he is actually present on the battlefield – reaped huge profits from a brilliant stock market speculation in which he anticipated the immediate rise in British government securities. Despite its persistence in encyclopedic references, Niall Ferguson's research in the family archives indicates that this story was more myth than reality. Nathan was richly rewarded, but he had probably made more money in exchange-rate transactions and bond speculations before Waterloo, than immediately after.

By the time the diplomats and noblemen at the Congress of Vienna had completed their deliberations, the Rothschilds were in a key position to finance the post-Napoleanic European powers as the latter reclaimed the continent and reasserted nationalistic, conservative rule.

In 1817, when Emperor Francis II had granted them nobility status – this meant that the Rothschilds in Germany could, if they chose, to put the prefix "von" in front of their last name, and those in England and France could use "de" – they regarded it proudly as a "mark of distinction for our nation" – that is, the Jewish nation. As the eldest brother, Amschel, put it, "If one Jew is a baron, every Jew is a baron." They held in contempt wealthy Jews like a Hamburg banker, Oppenheim, who baptized his children in 1818. "When they convert to Christianity," said Carl, "they adopt only what is bad but nothing that is good in it . . . I forsee that Oppenheim's lead will be followed. Well, we are not custodian of others' souls. I will remain what I am and my children, too."

Despite their refusal to convert, Rothschild wealth continued to multiply such that by 1836, the year of Nathan's death, they were "the richest family in the world." Nathan, himself, was likely the wealthiest individual in the world, worth approximately $16.8 million (approximatelly $322 million today) – in comparison, the total capital of Baring Brothers Bank in the same period was $3.7 million (about $72 million today).

"The Rothschilds are the wonders of modern banking," observed the European correspondent for one American newspaper in 1836. "We see the descendants of Judah, after a persecution of two thousand years, peering above the kings, rising higher than emperors, and holding a whole continent in the hollow of their hands. The Rothschilds govern a Christian world. Not a cabinet moves without their advice." Or, put more succinctly by the French writer Alexandre Weill in 1840, "there is but one power in Europe and that is Rothschild."

But this was not quite the whole story. The Rothschilds were as rich as royalty, and counted the most powerful European rulers and politicians among their business associates and clients, but in Germany (and the Austrian Empire), they remained Jews first and foremost, and, for many years, were treated as outsiders. In 1809, they had only been permitted to buy a warehouse on the outskirts of the *Judengasse*, though a significant change came in 1811 when Amschel was able to purchase a house with a lovely garden, outside of the city. Despite such advancments, Carl Rothschild's son Mayer Carl's grand mansion in Frankfurt, on the banks of the Main River, which he bought in 1846, is now the city's Jewish Museum (opened only in 1988). Their mother, Guttle, preferred to remain in the family's house in the *Judengasse* until she died in 1849 at the age of 96.

Socially, the family remained in the ghetto. The Frankfurt Casino, a club for the city's "gentlemen" refused them a membership and the popular press portrayed and lampooned them as greedy Jews intent on controlling the world.*

Typical was the attitude of Friedrich von Gentz, secretary to Metternich, who wrote in 1818 that: "The Rothschilds. . . . are vulgar, ignorant Jews, outwardly presentable in their trade the sheerest Emperialists [sic], without the remotest inkling of any higher relationship. But they are endowed with a remarkable instinct, which causes them always to choose the right and of the two rights the better. Their enormous wealth (they are the richest in Europe) is entirely the result of this instinct, which the public are wont to call luck." They tolerated the critical comments in the press, and the snide remarks they surely must have known were being made about them, with an air of indifference – it was the price to be paid for their remarkable rise to the top of the commercial world. What they refused to accept, however, was the continuing discrimination against them as Jews.

---

* Nathan Rothschild, who living in London had the luxury of being able to be more pompous, had a well-deserved reputation for being "intimidating and coarse." A famous Rothschild joke inspired by Nathan's imperial demeanor is as follows: "An eminent visitor is shown into Rothschild's office; without looking up from his desk, Rothschild casually invites him to "take a chair." "Do you realize whom you are addressing?" exclaims the affronted dignitary. Rothschild still does not look up: "So take two chairs."

In 1839, the Rothschilds were scandalized from within their own ranks, when Nathan's daughter Hannah renounced her Judaism to marry a Christian, the Honourable Henry Fitzroy, son of Lord Southampton. "Nothing could possibly be more disastrous for our family, for our continued well-being, for our good name and for our honour," James wrote to Nathan's son Lionel. Hannah was ostracized by her relatives for publicly besmirching the family's reputation, and never really forgiven. Even the *Times* of London noted in its story of the wedding that "this is the first instance of a member of the Rothschild family abandoning the faith of their fathers."

We Want to Belong to the German Fatherland

IRONICALLY, THE VERY SAME rulers and aristocrats who depended on the Rothschilds' largesse were those who thwarted the cause of Jewish civil rights. At first, Jews in Germany hoped that the liberal spirit of the French Revolution – with its belief in man's natural rights – that had been somewhat evident in Frankfurt under Baron von Dalberg's reign, as well as in other regions of Germany, would continue.

In fact, among the more enlightened humanitarian thinkers of this era, to treat Jews as equal citizens was not a novel concept. Christian Wilhelm von Dohm, a high-ranking Prussian official and scholar, had persuasively advocated this change in policy as early as 1781. Although he had been impressed by the writings of Moses Mendelssohn, he approached this complex issue from a more practical point of view than Mendelssohn would have preferred. In his book published that year, *On the Civil Improvement of the Jews*, Dohm argued that depriving Jews of civil rights made no sense, not only because it discriminated against the Jews themselves, making them more "corrupt" than need be but, more importantly, because it was a detriment to the progress and well-being of the societies in which they lived. "More than anything else a life of normal civil happiness in a well ordered state, enjoying the long withheld freedom, would tend to do away with clannish religious opinions," wrote Dohm. "The Jew is even more man than Jew, and how would it be possible for him not to love a state where he could freely acquire property and freely enjoy it . . . Certainly the Jew will not be prevented by his religion from being a good citizen, if only the government will give him a citizen's rights . . . The Jews could become happier and better members of civil societies."

Dohm's ideas as well as those about liberty, equality, and fraternity advanced in Paris during the early years of the Revolution, gained some favour even among the more enlightened despots of Germany. But theory was one thing, and action another. Any restrictions that were lifted before 1815 probably had more to do with the "economic utility" of Jews as opposed to "abstract considerations of political morality." Frederick William III of Prussia implemented the most favourable legislation in an edict of 1812 that gave Jews in his kingdom the status of "native citizens," with all of the liberties that entailed. Welcome now in the army, Jews in Berlin and throughout Prussia showed their loyalty to the "fatherland" by enlisting to join the battle against Napoleon. "My heart pounded with joy; I was so thankful to be able to prove myself to ruler and fatherland," recalled Löser Cohen, a young Jewish volunteer from Mecklenburg. "I approached my beloved parents with the words, 'the time has come when we Jews have the opportunity to faithfully serve the fatherland. I am committed to sacrifice myself for the beloved fatherland.'"

Cohen and others like him missed their chance to further the cause of Jewish emancipation. Before many of the reforms were put into practice or gained public acceptance, Napoleon was defeated, and the victors in redrawing the map of Europe adopted a reactionary posture. Had they chosen to, the delegates at the Congress of Vienna could have proclaimed their support for Jewish emancipation. Instead, the conservative plan devised by Metternich put a halt to the spread of liberalism and any other progressive notions about democratic rule. The articles of the newly constituted German Confederation (comprising about 40 states and cities, including an expanded Prussia) decreed that each state was empowered to grant its Jews any rights it wanted – or to withhold rights. And thus, in an instant, those civil rights that had been gained as a result of the French conquest were largely swept away. Jews were, for the most part, faced with a return to their previous apartheid-like second-class status.

In Frankfurt (Dalberg had been forced to abdicate in 1814), for example, Jews were excluded again from political life and the bureaucracy; restrictions were placed on their economic pursuits; and the rules governing Jewish marriages were re-instated. As a signal of the new regime's "enlightenment," however, it was decided that the Rothschilds and other Jews already so situated could continue to reside outside of the *Judengasse*. In Prussia, Jews fared slightly better, although they still faced numerous hurdles in their newly won status as citizens. Prussia's expansion into territories that did not support emancipation complicated the situation further.

If German officials needed more proof of how unpopular it was to grant full civil rights to Jews, they got in 1819 when a series of anti-Semitic riots broke out. In truth, the major cause of the protests probably had more to do with the general economic malaise, crop failures, and the high price of bread during the first few years of the post-Napoleonic era, than with Jewish emancipation. But like many such events, Jews – long-convenient scapegoats during times of economic tensions – suffered the brunt of the mobs' wrath.

The riots started in early August in the Bavarian town of Würzburg. The trouble was spurred on by a heated argument in the newspapers over the publication of an anti-Jewish book, between those who favoured civil rights for Jews and those who did not. The violence then shifted to Heidelberg, then Frankfurt, then north to Hamburg and Copenhagen and east to Danzig and a dozen villages in between. As Jewish property was vandalized and Jews attacked in the streets, the mob shouted *"Hep-Hep, Jud verreck!"* (Hep! Hep! Jews drop dead!) It became the rallying cry of the agitators. The strange *"Hep-Hep"* chant either referred to the call commonly used by goat herders – comparing the beards of Jews to those of billy goats – or it was an acronym for the Latin,

"*Hieroslyma est perdita*" – "Jerusalem is lost." While the local police at the behest of alarmed burghers everywhere moved quickly to quell the disorder, Jews were still being attacked in September.

Jewish writers, intellectuals, secular community leaders, and other "ideologues of emancipation" (to use historian David Sorkin's apt term) refused to be thwarted by the inflexibility of the ruling elite nor by the mob violence of 1819. There were two ways, they believed, to accomplish their objectives without converting to Christianity. First, they had to become better Germans: valued members of the bourgeoisie, dedicated to the fatherland, supportive of the national vision, and therefore entitled to equal rights. Second, the Jewish religion, steeped in the orthodox, and some argued medieval, traditions of the past, needed to become more relevant to and appropriate for the times. In other words, Jews needed to reform Judaism in the same way that Martin Luther had reformed Christianity.

Given the present political climate, the campaign for emancipation was viewed as urgent. To spread their message to Jews as well as to receptive non-Jews, the ideologues gave public lectures, delivered sermons in synagogues, and wrote books and pamphlets. *Sulamith*, which was founded in 1806, was the first Jewish journal published in the German language and was devoted to the promotion of emancipation.

The ideologues were the first generation of Jews who embraced what the Germans referred to as *Bildung* – "self-cultivation" or "self-improvement." In an age that treasured reason, morality, and humanity above organized religion and redemption, to live a life guided by *Bildung* was crucial for Jews who were trying to prove their worth in a Gentile society that frequently rejected them. For much of the nineteenth century, the Jewish intelligentsia maintained that, the more cultivated all Jews became – the more theatre and musical concerts they attended, the more books they read, and the more art they collected – the sooner they would be rewarded with emancipation and maybe even a degree of respect they felt

they were entitled to.* "Living means being active, working use-
fully, creating good things, developing the spirit, guiding the sentiments, improving oneself and everything around," wrote the
maskil Joseph Wolf in an 1812 article in *Sulamith*. "Every other life
is dead for man, is merely animalistic, without consciousness, self-
discipline, or spirit."

Those who ascribed to *Bildung* sent their children to Jewish
schools with secular curriculums, or in many cases to German
Christian schools, and adopted the lifestyle of the Western
European bourgeoisie. For a brief period in the late eighteenth and
early years of the nineteenth centuries, lively intellectual discussions took place among young Jewish and Christian men and
women who intermingled at the salons in Berlin hosted by such
Jewish dilettantes as Moses Mendelssohn's daughter, Dorothea
Mendelssohn, Henriette Herz, and especially the celebrated and
charismatic Rahel (Levin) Varnhagen, whose fascination with
Goethe's work started a small cult among her friends and followers.
(It should be noted that all three women did not share the faith in
the ideologues' German-Jewish future and eventually converted to
Christianity.)

Since *Bildung* was soon "synonymous with emancipation," as
Sorkin shows, Jewish dedication to its highest as well as practical
ideals was evident. Wilhelm Riemer, a friend and contemporary of
Goethe, recalled that, "the educated among them [the Jews] were
on the whole more obliging and steady in the veneration of
[Goethe's] person as well as his writings than many his own coreligionists. They do reveal in general more pleasing attention and
flattering participation than a national German."

---

* German Jews were also great fans of the composer Richard Wagner, even after
his anti-Semitic views were made public in his notorious pamphlet "Judaism in
Music," published a second time in 1869 under his real name (it had been first
published anonymously in 1850). By then, many states had granted Jews full civil
rights. And as historian Jacob Katz explained, "Wagner's pamphlet seemed out of
tune with the prevailing trend. Jews could afford – or so they thought – to ignore
the inopportune nastiness of an artist whose work was just beginning to win
general recognition."

At the same time, the almost obsessive quest for *Bildung* led to even wider divisions in the larger community between the so-called "acculturated Jews," who accepted the need for change and productivity and the "ghetto Jews," many of whom had immigrated to Germany from points in the east, and who clung to old traditions and garb. In 1820, Leopold Zunz, a leading figure among the "enlightened," visited Leipzig. He later wrote that his travels there were ruined by his encounter with a group of Hasidim who "screamed and raved and sang like the savages of New Zealand."

Zunz's reaction was predictable. A year earlier, he had helped found in Berlin the *Verein für Cultur und Wissenschaft der Juden* (Association for Culture and Scholarly Study of the Jews). It was a small of group of university-educated intellectuals who endeavored to give new meaning to the study of Jewish history and, in turn, to resolve their own conflicted identities as Jews. Or, as they stated, "to bring Judaism . . . to self-awareness, to make the Jewish world known to itself." When the members of the group did not obtain the results they desired, several, including Eduard Gans and Heinrich Heine, opted to convert to Christianity. By that means Heine, in particular, achieved wide recognition as a scholar and writer. Zunz, on the other hand, remained a Jew and persevered with his theoretical studies of Jewish history and literature, on his earnings as a teacher at a Jewish school and as a journalist. His admittedly complex scholarship was often a lonely and trying exercise that confronted enmity among some Jews, who did not appreciate or understand it, as well as among Gentiles who rejected the separate study of Judaism as an academic discipline.

More pragmatic was the political writer and jurist Gabriel Riesser, an independent and original proponent of Jewish emancipation. His father Lazarus, the son of a rabbi, was involved in the early efforts to reform Hamburg's synagogue. Born in Hamburg in 1806, the younger Riesser grew up in an enlightened home environment where the ideas of Moses Mendelssohn and the *Haskalah* were discussed and debated alongside those of the great German philosophers and thinkers of the day – Immanuel Kant, Johann

Wolfgang von Goethe, Friedrich von Schiller, and Georg Wilhelm Friedrich Hegel. Riesser, like many middle-class Jews of this era, received both a Jewish as well as secular, German education that stressed the Greek and Roman classics, history and literature.

He went on to study at university and, in 1826, graduated at the top of his class with a doctorate in law from the University of Heidelberg. Then he was faced with the inevitable choice of most educated German Jews: If he wanted to practice law or be hired for an academic position, he would have to convert to Christianity. (Until 1848, most German states did not allow Jews to practice law, and the first Jew to receive a full professorship was the mathematician Moritz Stern, ten years later, at the University of Göttingen.) That, he refused to do and instead became a vocal advocate of Jewish emancipation.

A prolific writer influenced by the ideals of the French Revolution, he forcefully argued that Jews were entitled to natural rights and that, to attain them, they should not be required to give up their religious and traditional beliefs and practices. As he reminded Jews in 1831, in his first of many political pamphlets: "Faith in the power and ultimate victory of the just and the good is our messianic belief: let us hold fast to it."

Yet he was also thoroughly convinced of the validity of a future for German-born Jews to be German citizens. Championing a theme taken up by numerous Western European writers and scholars during the 1800s, Riesser maintained that Judaism was not a nation but a religion. To his way of thinking, *Bildung*, coupled with his own love for all things German, would bring together Jews and Christians in common cause. He declared, "The mighty tones of the German language, the songs of German poets, have kindled and nurtured the holy fire of freedom in our breasts. We want to belong to the German fatherland . . . We can and may ask anything of us that it is entitled to ask of its citizens; willingly will we sacrifice everything for it – except faith and loyalty, truth and honor; for Germany's heroes and Germany's wise men have not taught us that through such sacrifices one becomes a German!"

Riesser's approach, with its universal appeal for justice and civil rights, was popular among Jews of every political and ideological stripe. He was well-liked by his peers and respected for his tireless work. Stout and broad with a crop of dark curly hair, he took his mission seriously, helping to prepare petitions and legal briefs for a number of Jewish communities. The periodical he established, *Der Jude* (The Jew) gave him the platform to espouse his personal views on a multitude of political issues, though his primary focus was on civil rights. It was later said of him that, "in Riesser, justice became a quality of character."

He never lost sight of the broader political climate: the link between Jewish emancipation and the establishment of a liberal capitalist system. His opportunity to work towards that lofty goal came during the revolutionary period of 1848 after, as he described them, the "liberal, enlightened bourgeoisie" of the northwest duchy of Lauenburg elected him one of their representatives to the first German National Assembly. In this position, he helped craft the German Constitution of 1849, whose aim was to institute a constitutional monarchy for a united Germany. This unification did not come to pass, but Riesser's efforts helped lay the foundations for passage of more democratic laws in the country culminating in the eventual granting of civil rights for Jews. In the final phase of his career, he was the first Jew to be appointed a judge to the Hamburg Superior Court. Although Riesser may not have single-handedly won emancipation for Jews, but as historian Michael Meyer asserts, he successfully "elaborated for the first time an ideology of insistence upon the right to define and retain one's Jewishness without thereby suffering any civil or political disability. That ideology remained the broadest common denominator among German Jews."

Traditionalists and Modernists

IF AS RIESSER and others suggested, Judaism was no longer a "state within a state" but a religion, what took place within the walls of the synagogue had profound consequences for shaping the new German-Jewish identity. Ashkenazim followed a strict code of conduct and hierarchy, one based on a traditional, orthodox interpretation of the Torah and the Talmud. Rabbis were educated at a yeshiva, not a university. Each rabbi's interpretation of *Halakah* (that part of the Talmud dealing with rabbinical law) was not to be disobeyed or openly challenged. Male-dominated synagogue prayers followed the same format that had been practiced for generations: There was no music or choir singing, nor any sermon. Sitting separately from their wives and daughters (who were usually relegated to the synagogue's second-floor balcony), men swayed back and forth, chanting loudly in Hebrew, in response to the rabbi's announcement, in Yiddish or Hebrew, of the weekly Torah portion to be studied aloud. Each man prayed at his own pace, creating a chaotic thundering of male voices. These communal prayers were interrupted now and again so that congregants could bid for the honour of being called up to the dais as the Torah was being chanted. Such were rituals that had evolved within a ghetto environment, a religious service that was closed and deliberately oblivious to the outside world.

Once many Jews in Germany made the decision to fully participate in a Protestant society and to live their lives according to the principles of *Bildung* – with its emphasis on secularism, education, and a universal standard of morality – altering Jewish religious institutions to more resemble German models became the obvious next step. And what better example to follow than the Lutheran Church itself, which displaced the sacred hierarchical structure of the Roman Catholic Church with a more liberal interpretation of faith? "When Samuel Holdheim, the radical rabbi of the Berlin Reform Society, argued that the modern life of the Jew demanded an end to rabbinical autonomy, the separation of religious affairs from civil and political issues, the recognition of marriage as a civil act," states Howard Sachar, "he was reflecting the Protestant view of the supremacy of State over Church."

Few issues, however, arouse passions and emotions more than the tampering with man's relationship with God, and with how the boundaries and rules of that relationship are defined. So it would be in the case of reformation of German synagogues. Many Jews, particularly those living in rural areas of Germany, who were not as caught up in the race to become part of the bourgeoisie as were Jew living in cities, regarded any changes to long-standing traditions – whether it was the structure of the synagogue service or the role of the rabbi – as unacceptable, even blasphemous. Finding common ground proved difficult, if not impossible, and soon led to an enduring divisiveness within Jewish communities not only in Germany, but throughout the Diaspora.

On an evening in late December 1817, a group of Jews in Hamburg gathered to listen to the words of Eduard Kley, a Jewish "preacher" who had recently arrived in the city from Berlin. Kley was representative of a new generation of religious leaders, young men who had studied at university rather than at a yeshiva, and who more often than not, like Kley, had a doctorate. Most opted not to grow a beard and wore black priestly robes in synagogue, like their Gentile contemporaries at church. They shared in the vision of *Bildung*, campaigned for emancipation, and promoted Jewish education and the study of Judaism as a secular subject. They spoke German in their synagogues to deliver Protestant-style sermons about ethics, morals, and the Jewish "'mission' to reconstitute the non-Jewish world."

At the meeting that night in Hamburg, sixty-five members of the local Jewish community, the majority of them merchants, had agreed to establish the "New Israelite Temple Association," a synagogue that would, as its charter document stated, "restore public worship to its deserving dignity and importance." Less than a year later, the temple held its first Sabbath service in a rented space. It inaugurated a completely new style of prayer that was soon adopted to different degrees by small pockets of Jews in other cities and towns. By 1821, the Hamburg Temple had a congregation of more than 100 families, representing less than ten per cent of the city's Jewish population; whereas Berlin's initial Reform congregation in the period from 1815 to 1823 attracted perhaps 1,000 people or about 25 per cent of the community.

In these Reform temples, men and women were still seated separately (as they were in Christian services at the time). The attendees were met with an organized, formal program. Loud chanting and swaying were banned, young children who might disrupt the service were not to be brought to the synagogue, and opportunities for making excessive noise were no longer permitted, such as when the Book of Esther was read during the holiday of Purim (orthodox congregants are traditionally encouraged to show their displeasure each time the name Haman, the king's advisor who wanted to kill the Jews of Persia, is said). The traditional bar mitzvah, in which a thirteen-year-old boy was called up to read from the Torah, now became more like a confirmation, focusing on the child's public commitment to live a life guided by the highest Jewish principles. In some synagogues, girls were now able to participate in a "bat mitzvah" ceremony. Hamburg reformers were the first to use a non-orthodox prayer book, complete with German-language hymns. They reduced emphasis on the return to Zion – indicative of their loyalty to their German fatherland.

Male choirs were introduced and, at the Berlin and Hamburg Temples, organ music was played during Saturday morning and holiday services. Since playing a musical instrument is considered a form of work and not allowed on the Sabbath, the organ emerged as one of the most controversial issues to divide the traditionalists from the modernists. The introduction of music was usually the final straw for the more orthodox members of a congregation who were unwilling to tolerate such a blatant violation of the Sabbath commandments; they had no choice but to leave the synagogue and start an organ-free one of their own. The cacophony of voices raised against the reformers by orthodox rabbis, scholars, and community officials was virulent and unrelenting. Yet this was merely the beginning of a long debate among German Jews in which four basic points of view as regarded correct observances, eventually arose. Brilliantly, with clarity and zeal, the spokesmen for each position advocated the road that Jews should take.

Samson Raphael Hirsch was only ten years old and living in Hamburg where he had been born, when the New Israelite Temple convened its first prayer service. Little did he know that he would become one of Reform Judaism's great adversaries. His father Raphael was a pious though enlightened Jew, as Hirsch later described him. Raphael was not a supporter of the Israelite Temple, but did ensure that Samson received both a religious as well as secular education. After studying Talmud with the prominent rabbi and scholar Jacob Ettlinger in Mannheim, Samson Hirsch enrolled at the University of Bonn in 1829. There, he became friends with Abraham Geiger, a future leader of the Reform movement. The two would eventually have a falling out after Geiger publicly criticized Hirsch's first book.

His family would have been happy if he had pursued a life in trade and business, yet Hirsch felt a personal calling to become a rabbi – albeit a more modern one. In this, he was probably influenced by Rabbi Isaac Bernays, a popular and erudite religious leader in Hamburg. Bernays, too, combated the city's nascent reform movement, although he had received a university education and delivered sermons in German peppered with elements of German philosophy, literature, and mythology.

Before he had finished his rabbinical studies, Hirsch accepted a synagogue posting in Oldenberg (in Saxony) where he worked out his particular brand of Judaism. In time, this came to be known as neo-Orthodoxy. In his black rabbinical gown accentuated with a white winged collar, and modestly bearded, Hirsch certainly did not look or behave like a traditional rabbi – he supported synagogue choirs and preached in German – and yet early in his career he fervently repudiated Reform Judaism. He articulated his ideas in his first popular German-language work, *Igrot tsafun: Neunzhen Briefe über Judenthum* (Epistles of a Hidden One: Nineteen Letters Concerning Judaism). Published in 1836, it became more notable and talked about than either Hirsch or his publisher had anticipated.

The book is devised around an exchange of letters between Naphtali, an orthodox Jew like Hirsch himself, and Benjamin, "the perplexed," who becomes caught up in reforming Judaism to satisfy the objectives of *Bildung* and the quest for emancipation.

Hirsch did not dismiss *Bildung*. On the contrary, he believed that it was important to become part of the modern world, not to hide from it as the Hasidim of Eastern Europe did. He maintained that it was possible to be a devout Jew and also receive a secular education, attend theatre, and read German literature. He was influenced by Kant and Hegel and cited Schiller in his sermons. His model "man of Israel" (*Jissroel-mensch*) was "an enlightened Jew who observes the precepts," a theory he put into practice in the various Jewish schools he was involved with. His motto was, in Hebrew, "*Torah im derekh eretz*": Torah, or Jewish law, could coexist with *derekh eretz*, the general norms of the non-Jewish world.

However, for Hirsch there was a line that could not be crossed. The Law of the Torah was sacred, he argued. Altering its meaning and tampering with its rituals (including dietary laws and the use of Hebrew in prayers), as the reformers did, were in his view deplorable. Their program of "religion allied to progress" meant, as he later wrote in a critical essay, "sacrificing religion and morality to every man's momentary whim. It allows every man to fix his own goal and progress in any direction he pleases and to accept from religion, only that part which does not hinder his 'progress' or even assist it. It is the cardinal sin which Moses of old described as 'a casual walking with God.'" The only acceptable path for a Jews to take, he believed, was not to make their religious observance dependent or subordinate to progress, but the other way around. "Progress is valid," he wrote, "only to the extent that it does not interfere with religion."

In 1841, Hirsch departed with his family from Oldenberg, and worked in several communities until settling in Frankfurt in 1851. He served there, until his death in 1888, as the leader of the Israelite Religious Society, a newly organized congregation of Jews who, like Hirsch, opted for a more traditional approach. Soon after he arrived, Hirsch found a willing supporter in Wilhelm Carl Rothschild (Carl's third son), who donated enough money for the Society to build its own synagogue on Schutzenstrasse. After that, Hirsch put aside some of his beliefs in the interest of enlarging the congregation's membership (he did not turn away those who did not keep kosher or the Sabbath), while also establishing a viable school that adopted his philosophy of *Torah im derekh eretz*. Most notably, through his lectures and prolific writings – not lacking in confidence, he fancied himself a "modern Maimonides" – he told orthodox Jews in Germany that it was possible to live in the modern world without sacrificing their most sacred articles of faith.

Another influential Jewish scholar of this era who offered a slightly more moderate interpretation was Zacharias Frankel. Born in Prague in 1801, Frankel, like Hirsch, received an education steeped in Talmudic learning, coupled with a secular one at the University of Pest (now Budapest) that focused on philosophy, natural sciences, and especially philology (literature and linguistics) – in which last he obtained his doctorate. In 1836, he became the chief rabbi of Saxony, based in Dresden, and later was appointed the director of the Jewish Theological Seminary at Breslau, "the first modern rabbinical seminary in Germany." He envisioned the role of the rabbi beyond that of the word-is-law figure of the Talmud and yeshiva, as more "a teacher and guide of the people," a conception that is current today.

Frankel hoped to find a middle, acceptable ground between Orthodox and Reform Judaism. But that proved impossible; both sides criticized him. In reaction, he developed his so-called "positive-historical" school that laid the foundations for the Conservative branch of Judaism. Frankel agreed with Hirsch, as Michael Meyer explains, that the "core of Jewish religion was 'positive,' that is revealed, and therefore not subject to traditional criticism or to change. However, Judaism also developed within history and hence its traditions, including even its postbiblical laws, had been and could still be subject to reinterpretation." In short, Frankel wanted to "improve" Judaism rather than "reform" it. As with Hirsch, faith came first for him, and progress second, though the two men differed in their interpretation of rabbinical law.

For a time, Frankel was willing to listen to the reformers and their critiques of rabbinical rulings. He attended a major rabbinical conference in Frankfurt in 1845 (the second of three held between

1844 and 1846), but left the conference before it finished its deliberations, unwilling to accept the proposition that the use of
Hebrew in prayer should be phased out. To him, the reformers had
become too extreme in their demands for change. As he prepared
to depart from the conference, he declared of the participants, "By
limiting Judaism to some principles of faith, they place themselves
partly outside the limits of Judaism."

Two of Frankel's main opponents in Frankfurt were Abraham
Geiger and Samuel Holdheim, who in different ways shaped the
modern Reform movement. Geiger, who grew up in Frankfurt's
Judengasse where he had been born in 1810, was a brilliant student
of the Talmud and then went on to achieve academic success at universities in Heidelberg and Bonn (where he became friends with
Hirsch). His study of philosophy, particularly that of Johann Gottfried
Herder, who stressed the universal development of human culture,
left an imprint on Geiger. After he became a rabbi in Wiesbaden, a
town just southwest of Frankfurt, in 1832, he searched for a variety
of ways to make Judaism more meaningful for his congregants. He
altered the prayer services along lines already instituted in Berlin
and Hamburg, and in 1835 was instrumental in establishing the
Wissenschaftliche Zeitschrift für jüdische Theologie (Scholarly Journal for
Jewish Theology), that became the organ for reform-minded rabbis
and academics. Geiger, clean-shaven with long hair and round,
wire-rimmed glasses, looked more like a university professor than a
rabbi. He desired to rebuild Judaism from the bottom up, to alter its
archaic rules and rid it of any national sentiments. He regarded circumcision, for example, as a "barbaric, bloody act, which fills the
father with fear." Yet he was also torn about abandoning Judaism's
inner spirit. He castigated the use of Hebrew, considering it "a
foreign dead language," but did not eliminate it from the synagogue
services he conducted in Wiesbaden, and later in Breslau and
Frankfurt, nor from the prayer book he edited.

If Geiger represented the liberal wing of the reform movement,
then Samuel Holdheim was its radical voice. He was born in the
town of Kempen, in the Prussian province of Posen, in 1806. His

family observed orthodox Jewish traditions (until 1793, Kempen had been under Polish rule) and he spent his early years learning only the Talmud. Unlike Hirsch, Frankel, and Geiger, he began his secular studies much later in life at universities in Prague and Berlin. In 1836, he was appointed a rabbi at an orthodox synagogue in Frankfurt-on-the-Oder. It was here, and later in his position as rabbi of the Grand Duchy of Mecklenburg-Schwerin from 1840 to 1847, that he gradually began to move across the religious spectrum to the reform position – delivering sermons in German, seeking new ways to attract youth, bringing order to the prayer services, and questioning rabbinical laws. He spent the last years of his life as head of a radical Reform congregation in Berlin, where he eventually held Sabbath services on Sunday instead of Saturday.

Not surprisingly, some considered his writings and speeches controversial and even heretical, and his ideas extreme, even among those who accepted the need for reform. "The Talmud speaks with the standpoint of its time, and that time it was right," he declared at the first Reform rabbinical conference in Brunswick in 1844. "I speak from the higher level of consciousness of my time, and for this age I am right." Religious law, he argued, had to be appropriate for the age. Thus there were few aspects of Judaism he was not prepared to alter in the name of modernity, progress, and acculturation. This included working on the Sabbath if necessary, approving of marriages between Jews and Gentiles, and accepting uncircumcised males as Jews. Yet, like Geiger, he remained devoted to its highest religious principles and mission. He believed that Judaism had a message of humanity applicable to all peoples. It was his "task," he said, sounding very much like Hirsch, to spread its fundamental teachings of equality and morality "amongst the nations [and] to protect the sense of Jewish unity and life and faith without diminishing the sense of unity with all men." Holdheim's radical views were to find supporters beyond Germany in England and the United States, where Jews there – many of whom were immigrants from Germany – were also struggling with questions of faith and assimilation.

You Do Not Emancipate the Jews

IN THEIR OWN WAYS, each of these four rabbis guided their congregants in meeting the challenges of being a Jew in the modern world. In reality, they were already battling a movement toward secularization that characterized all of Western society – a revolution that kept many synagogues largely empty except on the High Holidays; which drastically reduced the number of Jews who followed dietary rules; and that, in many cases, no longer disowned children for marrying out of the faith. Future generations of Jews would continue to face these problems.

Beyond issues concerned with the synagogue, the rabbis were in agreement that emancipation was a necessary positive step forward for Jews. This was despite the challenges they anticipated such freedom would pose in the future, for maintaining Judaism as the faith of a minority in the midst of a vocal and nationalistic majority. They believed that Germany (at least as a national concept) was truly their homeland, as Rabbi Leopold Stein of Frankfurt so clearly articulated, even as revolutions demanding real political change and an end to reactionary rule erupted throughout Europe in the spring of 1848.

Yet the turmoil of that momentous year, in which Jews initially were confronted by mob violence as they had been in 1819, was still another reminder of how difficult the road ahead would be. Half the population of Germany blamed Jews for supporting the reactionary status quo, while the other half portrayed them as gaining too much power under a revolutionary regime that they claimed were only the representatives of a capitalistic conspiracy masterminded by the Rothschilds. (Ironically, many of the Rothschilds, who feared the chaos, disorder, and property destruction, regarded the 1848 upheaval as "the worst revolution that ever happened.") For the conservatives, "the issue at stake was no longer emancipation of the Jews, but rather [as the popular anti-Jewish slogan declared] 'emancipation from the Jews.'" This became a classic conundrum to be exploited by anti-Semites throughout the following decades.

More than 100 Jews – students, intellectuals, writers, teachers, and political activists – did play an active role in the armed revolutionary struggles in the towns and cities of Germany. The revolutions, however, did not produce the desired results: Germany was not united or democratic when the barricades came down. Still, Jews like Gabriel Riesser, along with his colleague Johann Jacoby in Frankfurt, Dr. Sigismund Stern in Berlin, Moses Schreiber in Breslau, Ludwig Bamberger in Mainz, and Rabbi Abraham Adler of Worms, made major contributions to the debates about liberalism and gained more support for the Jewish emancipation that was finally fully achieved with the unification of Germany in 1871.

Gradually, as more and more Jews advanced from the ranks of the poor to become members of the middle and upper classes, Jews' integration into the larger German society, though not yet total, was substantially increased by mid–century. *Bildung* had succeeded. Whatever their particular religious affiliation or economic status, most German Jews now shared in a new-found confidence and pride in being "German citizens of the Jewish faith."

Not even the heavy-handedness of Prussian authorities, who in 1850 repealed recently granted Jewish rights, could deter progress. "You do not emancipate the Jews, they emancipated themselves long ago" suggested Rabbi Ludwig Philippson, the editor of the popular Reform newspaper, *Allgemeine Zeitung des Judenthums* (German Jewish Times). "All you do is to complete the outward emancipation. From that moment when the Jews emerge from the Ghetto, when they participate in all the industrial and intellectual endeavors of mankind, when their children attend schools . . . when their men are active in science and learning, the arts, industry, and trades, when their women acquire culture and education – from that moment they are emancipated and have no need to wait for a few words written in a constitution." As true as Philippson's words may have been, how the newly "emancipated" Jew – psychologically, politically, economically, and socially – would fit into the larger German landscape remained to be seen.

Chapter Seven

THE PALE OF SETTLEMENT

St. Petersburg, 1881

Awake, my people! How long will you slumber? The night has passed, the sun shines bright. Awake, lift up your eyes, look around you; Acknowledge your time and your place. . . . To the treasury of the state bring your strength; Take your share of its possessions, its bounty; Be a man in the streets and a Jew at home; A brother to your countryman and a servant to your king.

— JUDAH LEIB GORDON, 1863

The *Shtetl*

THE PRIMITIVE HAMLET, or *shtetl*, of Kasrielevky was located in the province of Poltava, east of Kiev in the western part of the Russian empire known as the Pale of Settlement. Created by Catherine the Great through successive partitions of Poland in 1772, 1792, and 1795, the Pale was the largest ghetto in the world. By the mid-nineteenth century its fifteen provinces, which stretched north from present day Lithuania and south to the Black Sea, were home to nearly three million Jews, the majority of whom were of Polish descent. In time, many of these Jews would migrate to the urban centres of the region — Vilna, Minsk, Kiev, and Bialystok — and later across the ocean to the United States and Canada. Yet many still resided in *shetlach* like Kasrielevky.

In fact, this *shtetl*, like dozens of others, was nothing more than a collection of wooden houses clustered around a market square. Its muddy, narrow, unpaved streets made progress difficult for man and horse alike. The town's few-hundred Ashkenazi Jewish inhabitants — peddlers, tradesmen, artisans, and salesmen — did not even dream of having proper water or sewage facilities. Many homes still had mud floors. For the most part, the inhabitants spent their time praying in their wooden synagogue, or *shul* (the largest structure in the *shtetl*), doting over their children, studying the mysteries of the Talmud, gossiping, and conducting business with the large population of Christian peasant farmers who toiled the land in the surrounding countryside. By tradition, parents arranged their children's marriages, often brokered by a *shadchan*, or "marriage broker," or by a young man's *melamed*, or "teacher."* Daily routines and the yearly calendar of events were defined by the cycle of Jewish holidays. Whenever there was a *simcha*, a happy occasion, such as a *bris* ("circumcision") or wedding, most everyone in the town was invited. The same went for funerals. There were few wealthy men here. Indeed, the richest men, wrote American writer Maurice Samuel, "could be bought out on the lower margin of four figures."

With both the Russian serfs and the Jews subsisting on a diet of bread, herring, vegetables, and occasionally chicken and meat, it was debatable who was worse off. For example, a tailor and his wife living in Brisk in 1863 had one son and two daughters to feed. The tailor's average yearly rent, taxes, food, wood, and other goods cost him about 153 rubles. His maximum earnings were at most 120 rubles per year. His wife sold whatever she could to make ends meet, though the odds were that the family was always in debt. Similarly, Hyman Wolf, who was born in a small town in the Pale in 1897, recalled that his grandmother, with whom he lived, would soak bread in water "and we called it a meal." An official inquiry in

---

* A bride and groom often met each other for the first time only days, sometimes hours, prior to the wedding ceremony and were left alone only briefly to discuss their future together before the rabbi pronounced them husband and wife.

the 1880s determined that 90 per cent of the Jews in the Pale existed as "a proletariat living from hand to mouth, in poverty and under the most trying and unhygienic conditions."

Generally, Kasrielevky was a quiet and unassuming place, save for a few strange peddlers and old women, who carted around rags, bottles, pickled herring, and dried fish. But as in other *shtetlach* that dotted the countryside of the Pale, two days of the week were special. Wednesday in Kasrielevky was market day. As the sun rose, a parade of Christian peasants with their wagons packed with vegetables, eggs, fruit, grain, and assorted other goods would stream into the town. Often they brought cows, horses, and chickens with them. The Jews working in their marketplace stalls greeted their neighbours and customers, and the day's trading and bartering would begin in earnest. By early evening on most Wednesdays, the Jewish merchants and peddlers had filled their wagons and warehouses with produce, grain, and livestock, and the peasants had departed more or less contented with new high boots, fur hats, fine linens, spices, leather goods, and, more than likely, several bottles of vodka from the tavern.

Friday evening, *Erev Shabbas*, the beginning of the Sabbath, was the other special day in any *shtetl*. Everyone in the town put on their finest clothes. Mothers and daughters worked hard on Fridays. Homes had to be scrubbed clean, and the women prepared a Sabbath meal: freshly baked *chalah* (egg bread), *gefilte* fish, roast chicken or goose, plucked and cleaned a day earlier, chopped liver, *tsimmes* (mashed carrots), and sweet *kugel* (baked noodles with raisins and cinnamon) for desert. The entire family, along with their guests, relatives, or visitors from nearby *shtetlach*, would sit down for dinner following the evening's prayer service welcoming in the Sabbath at the synagogue.

Conversation around the table would undoubtedly focus on the boys' *cheder* lessons with the town's *rebbe*. For the teachings of the Torah strictly guided the lives of these Jews. They may not have been more pious or orthodox than Jews elsewhere, but as in Spain before the expulsion, the Ottoman empire in the 1660s, or Amsterdam in the

seventeenth century, the synagogue was the most significant institution in their lives. It shaped their daily activities and its rabbi was their
life-long teacher and moral instructor. (And if they forgot to attend
one day, the *shul klopfer*, or "synagogue knocker," usually a little old
man, would remind them with his cry in the streets: "to *shul*, to *shul*.")

Connected to the synagogue was a *cheder*, or school, where young
boys, often beginning at the age of five, would receive a rigorous
education in Talmudic law. (Sometimes the daughters as well as sons
of wealthier or religious men attended *cheder*.) The day this education began for a child was an emotional one, as Max Lilienthal, a
prominent Jewish educator, recalled after a visit to the city of Brest
(Belarus) in the 1840s. "A poorly clad couple entered, the man carrying a young boy of about six, wrapped in a *talit* [prayer shawl].
Both father and mother were weeping with joy, grateful to God who
had preserved them that they might witness this beautiful and
meaningful moment. Having extended a cordial welcome to the
newcomers, the *melamed* took the hero of the celebration into his
arms and stood him on a table. Afterwards, the boy was seated on a
bench and was the first to receive cake, nuts, raisins and dainties."

The students' memories of their *melamdim*, or "teachers," were
not as fond. The first day's celebration aside, the young Jewish boys
received a demanding education that usually began in the early
morning and did not end until after the sun had set. Lessons were
often reinforced with physical abuse, including frequent whippings
for errant behaviour. The *melamed* became, in the words of Shmarya
Levin, who had grown up in the town of Swislowitz, "the lord and
master of the Jewish child, and the *cheder*, the narrow one-roomed
school, lightless, unclean, laid its stamp on the Jewish child and
brought ruin and misery on its tenderest years."

Chaim Aronson, who grew up in a small town of Serednik near
Kovno, did not have fond recollections of his *cheder* days either. In
his memoirs, which he wrote after he had emigrated to United
States in 1888, he recalled that his father had sent him at the age of
four to study under the town's *shochet*, or ritual slaughterer. This
brutish man served as the *shtetl*'s synagogue cantor and *melamed*. His

father had told the teacher that his son was not to be whipped. But after a time, Chaim did something to annoy his *melamed.* "The slaughterer sought a pretext for complaint against me," he wrote, "and struck me once or twice with his whip."

Despite the abuse, Aronson proved to be a superior student, and when he was sixteen he was sent to study in a yeshiva in Vilna. His memories of that period in his life were not much happier. The yeshiva *bocherim*, as the students were called, faced long hours of study and inflexible teachers. Worse, the majority of students, including Aronson, had little money and were forced either to find wealthy sponsors to take pity on them or beg in the streets for bread. Many of them slept in the school, since no other quarters could be found. Aronson, who was blessed with beautiful handwriting, made some much-needed money working as a scribe, writing letters for his friends.

As a student in Vilna, Chaim Aronson was caught in the middle of a passionate religious feud that engulfed the Jewish world for more than five decades. It was an intellectual and emotional battle that pitted the Hasidim against the *Mitnagdim*, or "opponents." Jewish life, in the view of the followers of Israel ben Eliezer (1700–60), the esteemed *Ba'al Shem Tov* (Master of the Good Name) and founder of Hasidism, was full of suffering and disappointment. To counter this, daily prayer and orthodox observance of the Torah and Talmud were essential, of course, yet Hasidism demanded of its believers a total commitment that was both intense and far-reaching. It was a religious movement – some might even say a cult – which stressed joy and infused a mystical experience into everyday life. Even today, its practitioners, whether in New York, Montreal, or Jerusalem, still wear the wide fur-trimmed hats, long, black coats, and *peyes*, or long sideburns of their ancestors and live very separate from the larger Jewish and non-Jewish communities. Hasidism was, and still is, deliberately insular.

One of the first scholars to challenge Hasidism's rigid and traditional teachings was Rabbi Elijah ben Solomon Zalman of Vilna (1720–97), known far and wide as the Vilna Gaon, or "Vilna Sage."

His followers were known as the *Mitnagdim* for their outspoken opposition to Hasidism. A brilliant man, Elijah spoke ten languages and, unlike the Hasidim, maintained that knowledge of secular subjects – history, geography, mathematics, and science – could only benefit Jews. Not that he was any less pious or devoted fewer hours to studying the Torah – in fact, Elijah often slept only two hours a night so he could spend more time reading, debating, and contemplating – it was just that his approach was more intellectual than that of the Hasidim. The great rabbi equally objected to the way in which Hasidic leaders, the so-called righteous *tsadikim*, used their positions for personal gain. Most Hasids lived in poverty, yet Hasidism encouraged rabbinical dynasties, and some *tsadikim* resided in lavish homes, complete with servants and much extravagance.

Following Elijah's death in 1797, the conflict between Hasidism and its opponents declined slightly, though both had a powerful impact on Jewish life in the *shtetlach*. True, not every Jew lived a moral life, but in the predominately Jewish villages and towns of the Pale, violent crimes were extremely rare, as were infidelity and drunkenness. The Jews of the *shtetl* were genuinely good people – simple, poor, pious, superstitious, and immersed in a shared and powerful Yiddish culture.* They preferred to be left alone by the Russian

---

* The extent of those superstitions knew no bounds when it came to illness. As a young child, Chaim Aronson became ill with a bout of malaria, and there were no physicians in his small town. At first the boy's distraught parents sought the advice of rabbi, who had them write all over doors and windows of the house in chalk, "The boy Chaim is not at home." "The idea was that, when the demon of malaria came to visit me," Aronson recalled, "he would see written everywhere that the boy he was seeking was not at home, and would therefore turn away and go back to wherever he came from. Unfortunately, the demon of malaria did not understand Yiddish which had been written for him, and so paid me constant visits." After that failed to work, his desperate parents followed the suggestion of an old woman and put him in a bread oven. When he cried out for something to drink, the woman, with his parents' blessing, gave him a concoction of urine mixed with crushed bugs. His parents then forced him to hold a roasted hen's egg in his hand all day. At dusk, he was told to throw it into the street. If someone found the egg and ate it they would supposedly take away Chaim's illness. Eventually, and despite his parents' efforts, Aronson recovered on his own.

government. On the surface, at least, life was apparently free of serious problems. In this instance, however, ignorance was not bliss.

On the subject of Jews and their Christian neighbours, Shmarya Levin observed, "True we lived in two distinct worlds, but it never occurred to us that *their* world was the secure one, while the foundations of *ours* were shaky. On the contrary, we accounted our world the nobler, the finer, and the higher. Of course, we learned even as children that we Jews were a people in exile, such being the divine decree, but that had nothing to do with the details of our daily life. . . . In the interim we did not stand on a lower level than the Gentiles."

Orthodoxy, Autocracy, and Nationalism

THE RUSSIAN RULERS saw the Jewish question slightly differently. "From the enemies of Christ, I desire neither gain nor profit," declared Empress Elizabeth in 1742. Her various successors, from Catherine the Great in the 1760s to Nicholas II more than a century later, may not have been as devoutly disparaging of their Jewish subjects – changing economic, political, and social issues demanded a whole range of policies – but in general Jews were regarded as dangerous exploiters of the peasant masses and a threat to Russian stability. Their function in the economy as middlemen, and especially their selling of liquor and small-time moneylending, were significant concerns for officials back in St. Petersburg. Undoubtedly, Jews did exploit some peasants, but few became very rich in the process. Russian government commissions investigating the Jewish question in the Pale of Settlement between 1883–88, for example, found "no conclusive evidence to show that either the incidence of drunkenness or interest rates were higher than in the rest of the country."

Controlling the relationship between Jews and peasants became the focus of Czarist policy for many years; or, put another way by British historian John Kleir, "the government sought to 'save the peasants' and to 'improve the Jews,' but always in that order." Thus, in

the end, it was the peasants as well as the Czar and his officials' perception of exploitation that ultimately counted. As a consequence,
during the course of the nineteenth century, Jews faced an onslaught
of government legislation, some fourteen hundred different statues
and regulations that restricted their occupations, place of residence in
the Pale, right to own land, and movement. There were special taxes,
double taxes, taxes on Sabbath candles, each contributing to the debilitating poverty most Jews found themselves in. The Pale of Settlement
was, says historian Orlando Figes, the czarist "version of the Hindu
Caste system, with the Jews in the role of the Untouchables."

Alexander I (1800–25) attempted to restrict Jewish self-
government and encouraged Jews to become farmers. But that
did not change anything. His brother, Nicholas I (1825–55)
adopted a more reactionary and, from his point of view, practical
policy. A military man, Nicholas's motto, which he followed reli-
giously, was "Orthodoxy, Autocracy, and Nationalism." He applied
this to Jews in the Pale in 1827 with his infamous "cantonist"
decree, by which Nicholas immediately became Russian Jewry's
greatest ever oppressor.

Until the Czar intervened, Jews had not normally served in the
Russian military. In most quarters, they were regarded as weak
cowards who could not be trained to become effective soldiers (this
was a belief that persisted throughout the twentieth century among
the men of the Red Army). By the new law, all Jewish men, on
turning eighteen years of age, were to be conscripted for a period
of twenty-five years. As if that were not bad enough, Jewish youths
as young as twelve were also to be drafted in order to prepare them
properly for military service. These boys, who were essentially sentenced to upwards of thirty miserable years in the army, were
referred to as "cantonists."* Separated from their families and in the
custody of harsh military taskmasters, the youngsters became an

---

* The word was derived from a Prussian term for a recruiting district and used in
Russia "to denote children taken into military service and sent to cantonal or
district schools far removed from contact with their families."

easy target for proselytizing and severe physical and mental abuse. "The chief benefit to be derived from the drafting of Jews," read a confidential memo from the Czar to military commanders, "is the certainty that it will move them most effectively to change their religion."

To further test the Jews' resolve, it was ordered that local communities themselves would be responsible for furnishing their quota of conscripts. Few government decrees caused as much bitterness and divisiveness. Wealthier Jews could and did save their sons by paying for substitutes. "Rich Mr. Rockover has seven sons," a popular folk song went, "Not a one a uniform dons; But poor widow Leah has an only child, And they hunt him down as if he were wild."

Fulfilling quota obligations in fact proved impossible. Jewish community leaders, therefore, had no choice but to employ gangs of men, *khappers* they were called in Yiddish (from the Yiddish verb *khapn*, "to catch"), whose job it was to ensure that those quotas were filled. The *khappers* were ruthless, callous, and despised. Woe betide any young Jewish boy caught alone on the street of a *shtetl*. Yehuda Levin, a Hebrew writer and poet, recalled in his memoirs that one day while he was visiting Minsk, he witnessed six men, *khappers* as it turned out, barge into a Jewish house. "A few moments later the men came out, dragging a child whom they had gagged. The child's mother soon followed, screaming and sobbing, but the *khappers* threw her to the ground."

Once they were captured, the children were marched sometimes hundreds of miles to military barracks. On a journey through the province of Vyatka, the Russian writer Alexander Herzen happened on a group of Jewish cantonists. It was, he later remembered, "one of the most awful sights I have ever seen. Pale, worn out, with frightened faces, they stood in thick, clumsy soldiers' overcoats, with stand-up collars, fixing helpless, pitiful eyes on the garrison soldiers, who were roughly getting them into ranks. The white lips, the blue rings under the eyes looked like fever or chill. . . . No painting could reproduce the horror of that scene."

From the moment they arrived, the children were not permitted to practise any Jewish custom or ritual. They were regularly fed pork and beaten if they did not co-operate. It is estimated that among the hundred and fifty thousand Jews drafted into the army approximately half converted to Christianity and the vast majority were under the age of eighteen when they did so. It was for this reason that on the day in 1855 when Nicholas I died, Jews throughout the Pale wept for joy.

Let There Be Light

TWO DECADES EARLIER, Nicholas I had codified all laws dealing with Jews in a statute passed in 1835. The boundaries of the Pale were slightly narrowed and permanently set (remaining more or less intact until the revolution in 1917) and strict rules were established with respect to Jewish travel outside of the area. For the moment, Jews were still allowed to operate taverns. What the Czar truly desired, however, was for the Jews to be absorbed into the larger society; that is, their assimilation and conversion. A detested decree of 1845, referred to as the *gzeyreh* ("the harsh edict"), for instance, ordered Jews to dress in public in modern European clothing rather than in their traditional costumes. Those who did not follow the new law were often humiliated and punished. As Pauline Wengeroff, who was then about fifteen years old and living in Brest, remembered, one day a Jewish man appeared in the marketplace wearing a long black kaftan and was apprehended by the local authorities. "The policeman mocked him and calling a second policeman over for support, cut the long skirts of [the kaftan] into the shape of a jacket with a huge pair of shears that he carried at all times. Not enough that this exposed the Jew's underpants. Now the policeman tore off the man's hat and cut off his *peyes* so close to the ear that poor man screamed in pain. Then he let him go. The people in the market accompanied this 'corrected' Jew with loud jeers and insults."

Nicholas's government abolished the *kehillot*, the Jewish self-government community councils, which, as a result of *khappers* and high taxes, were hardly popular at any rate. More importantly, Count Sergei Uvarov, the minister responsible for education, devised a secular educational policy that was aimed at Jewish absorption into the empire.

On a visit to Berlin, Uvarov had seen with his own eyes how Jews there had become like all other citizens in appearance as well as attitude, though it never occurred to him that it was the more moderate German policies that had permitted this transformation. Uvarov did meet with several followers of Moses Mendelssohn and the *Haskalah*, the Jewish enlightenment, and was reasonably impressed. He quickly decided that employing Jews to assist him in his educational project made sense.

While the *Haskalah* had made inroads in Russia during the early part of the nineteenth century with a select group of young and idealistic Jewish intellectuals, most Jews in the empire, especially those in the *shtetlach*, had segregated themselves for their own protection. Becoming full participants in Russian society was about the last thing on their minds.

The first real Russian *maskil* or follower of the Jewish enlightenment, was Isaac Ber Levinsohn, a middle-aged teacher, translator, and writer from the town of Kremenets in the province of Volhynia. In 1820, Levinsohn composed a Russian grammar book in Hebrew and began writing satires about traditional Jewish life. In particular, he lampooned the trials and tribulations of the Hasidim, a theme that was to become popular among Russian *maskilim*. He also completed his first book, *Teudah Be-Yisrael* ("Testimony in Israel"), published in 1828. In it he made the case for Jews to study secular subjects and take on more "productive" careers.

For Levinsohn, as for those who followed him, the Jewish religion was not at issue; indeed, Levinsohn, like other *maskilim*, was an observant Jew. The problem was, in their opinion, the way in which the rabbis, through their strict teachings, had helped keep Jews backward for far too long. And in order to become worthy citizens of the empire, it was necessary, they argued, to abandon the primitive Yiddish culture of the *shtetl*. Osip Rabinovich, the founder in 1860 of the Russian Jewish weekly *Razsvet* ("Dawn") put it like this: "We in Russia . . . instead of learning the glorious Russian language, persist in speaking our corrupted jargon, that grates on the ears and distorts . . . it is our obligation to cast off these old rags, a heritage of the Middle Ages." Rabinovich, who was based in Odessa, at that time a centre of the Jewish enlightenment, adopted the motto "Let there be light." He published articles that were designed, as Jacob Raisin explained (in the first English-language survey of the Russian *Haskalah*, written in 1913) to "elevate the masses by teaching them to lead the life of all nations, participate in their civilization and progress, and preserve, increase and improve the national heritage of Israel."

Russian bureaucrats may not have understood the foundations of the *Haskalah*, nor did they likely want to. Yet Uvarov searched for a young and enthusiastic Jewish educator who could oversee his plans to "improve" Jewish life by creating a new Crown school system that would deliver a modern curriculum. In early 1840, he settled on Max Lilienthal, a bright and accomplished twenty-five-year-old German Jew with a doctorate in philosophy who had also been trained as a rabbi. He found Lilienthal in Riga, where the young man had recently been hired by the wealthy members of that Jewish community to establish a secular school for their children.

Lilienthal accepted the offer, though he did not truly appreciate the pattern or burdens of Jewish life under Nicholas I. He may have misunderstood the government's ultimate aim as well. "His Majesty, the Emperor has favoured the plan of the high-minded Minister of Education to emancipate the Jews," he wrote to one rabbi in a letter of February 1841. "Two hundred schools are to be opened through-out the Empire. . . . The young people who pass through these schools are to receive all the rights of citizenship without trammel. This is a great and glorious thing, the like of which our history has not produced."

Despite Lilienthal's wishful thinking, citizenship and emancipation for Russian Jews were not part of Uvarov's program. On visits to Vilna and Minsk to promote his new school program, Lilienthal was confronted with scepticism and at times outright hostility to the Czar's real intentions. "Doctor, are you fully acquainted with the leading principles of our government?" the elders in Vilna asked him after listening to one of his presentations. These Jews immediately understood the true motive behind the creation of the new schools: conversion to Russian Orthodoxy and total assimilation. In Minsk, the community was less polite. Rabbis and teachers drove Lilienthal right off the stage with their protests. Back in Vilna, Lilienthal was referred to as the "infidel" whose eyes should be gouged out. He received a better reception in Brest, where even Pauline Wengeroff's pious and orthodox father (although not her mother) was more accepting of educational reform.

Not one to be intimidated, Lilienthal publicized his ideas and hopes for the schools in a Hebrew pamphlet entitled *Maggid Yeshuah* ("Herald of Salvation") that was distributed throughout the Pale. He attempted to reassure his opponents that Judaism would not disappear, that they had nothing to fear from the proposed changes. In 1844, with the support of several rabbis and *maskilim*, the government introduced the Jewish Crown School system. No Jewish child was forced to attend, though doing so gave the student an exemption from conscription into the army. The curriculum Lilienthal designed included a wide range of secular studies, including learning Russian, Hebrew, and Jewish religion.

Regardless of Lilienthal's great hopes for the Crown Schools, most Jews remained highly suspicious of the government's policies and did not fail to notice that the schools were nearly all run by Christian principals. In some families, however, the schools and the desire they created for a secular education caused much tension. Some parents even disowned their children. When Rabbi Israel Salanter, for example, learned that his son had departed for Berlin to attend medical school, he "removed his shoes and sat down on the ground to observe *shivah*" (seven days of mourning).

By 1855, there were approximately seventy-one Crown Schools with an enrollment of about 3,000 students, a tiny percentage of the Jewish student population in the Pale. A decade later, the number of students attending had increased to 5,700 (the program eventually ended in 1873). Lilienthal himself abruptly left Russia only a year after the program had begun in 1845. Years later, after he had emigrated to the United States, he claimed he had departed when he realized he had been duped and that the schools were meant only to be a Christianizing agency. In fact, it was more likely a career move.

And yet the secular schools, coupled with the continuing fight of a new generation of *maskilim*, did have a significant impact on the history of Jews in Russia. This intellectual renaissance was about to enter its most critical phase, encouraged by the era of the "Great Reforms" that characterized the first years of the reign of Alexander II, the so-called "Czar Liberator." With Alexander's abolition of the cantonist decrees and the emancipation of the serfs, young Jewish intellectuals believed now more than ever in the future of Jews within the Russian empire.* They shaved their beards, learned Russian, and wore clothes like those of their Russian neighbours, much to the shock of their parents. The traditional authoritarian rule practised by Jewish fathers and mothers for generations was beginning to break down. Their sons and daughters advocated a new style of Judaism unlike that practised by the Hasidim – quieter, more refined, more orderly. It hardly mattered to them, observes historian Michael Stanislawski, that most Jews in the empire were more concerned with the "over-arching dilemma of how to cope with the mundane demands of daily life in a dignified manner" than with changing and reforming the world.

"Our fatherland is Russia," an editorial in *Razsvet* declared in 1860, and the editors of the weekly meant it. Jews could attend universities and under certain circumstances even settle in St. Petersburg

---

* In actuality, the emancipation of the serfs in 1861 was not all that positive for Jews in the *shtetlach*. Those Jews who had been employed as overseers for absentee landlords found that the members of the nobility hurt financially by the emancipation no longer required their services. In urban areas, Jews also found themselves competing for the first time with peasants who had migrated into the cities.

and Moscow. They "were thoroughly convinced that they were going to bring about a complete revolution in the world view of the Jewish people," reflected one *maskil* in 1895, "and they impatiently awaited their moment of action." Among those caught up in the optimism and fervour of the times was Judah Leib Gordon.

Awake My People

HE WAS THE RUSSIAN *Haskalah's* leading Hebrew poet, who in a few stanzas could capture the deep-felt convictions of his generation. A brilliant writer and essayist, he was, claimed the prolific writer Chaim Nachman Bialik, who followed in his footsteps, "the mighty hammer of the Hebrew language." Judah Leib Gordon was a moderate and intelligent man who was equally passionate, even stubborn, about his beliefs. For more than forty years, he argued that the emancipation of Jews in Russia was at hand, but only if they adhered to the pattern set in the west: "religious reform, economic modernization, linguistic acculturation, loyalty to the monarch and state, legal emancipation, social integration." Gordon, however, miscalculated. He was a man born at the wrong time in the wrong age and would experience in old age the great disappointment felt by all of Russia's Jews at the repression and violence that so quickly followed the assassination of Alexander II in 1881.

Gordon was born in Vilna in 1830. He grew up in the city when it already contained a thriving Jewish community of twenty thousand (from a total population of about fifty-five thousand) with an intellectual climate to rival few other East European urban centres. Gordon's parents ran an inn and tavern to support their three children. Gordon was their middle child and their first son. At a young age, he was given a traditional education with a touch of the modern and tutored in the Torah, Talmud, and Hebrew grammar. Gordon was a hard-working and talented student, who at a young age showed his flair for the Hebrew language.

In 1839, Mikhl Gordon (many Jews in Vilna, when ordered by the Russian government of Alexander I to adopt a surname, had chosen Gordon) married Judah's sister. Mikhl, who was soon caught up with his friends in the early *Haskalah* movement, helped to stimulate Gordon's interest in studying European culture and foreign languages. By the age of fourteen, Gordon was beginning to dabble in poetry, the start of a lifelong passion.

A pragmatic young man, Gordon realized that he also needed to make a living. In 1852, he graduated from the government teachers' seminary in Vilna. Soon after, he was hired to teach at Jewish Crown School in the town of Ponevezh (Panevėžys), 150 km northwest of Vilna. He stayed at this school for seven years before being transferred to several other ones in the surrounding area. He married a woman named Bella Orinshtam, and together they would have three children, two daughters and a son. Bella, who suffered from a variety of ailments throughout her life, does not seem to have played a large role in Gordon's literary career, though she did provide the poet with a stable home environment.

Dissatisfied with his low salary as a teacher of 225 rubles per year, Gordon offered private tutoring. He also continued to write. In 1857 he published his first book of poetry, *The Love of David and Michal*, in which he examined the love between the future king of Israel and his first wife. Though not his best work, it was well received in the Jewish intellectual community. More importantly, he had already published his first article on Jewish life in Lithuania. It was a brief piece, but in it Gordon touched on the theme that would shape his essays for the next few decades: that only with Jews and Russians co-operating and working together for a common purpose could the Jewish situation in the empire change for the better.

In his essays and journalism that followed, Gordon focused on what he and other *maskilim* perceived to be the inadequacies of Jewish society in Russia – its backwardness, self-segregation, and domination by traditional rabbinical authorities. "Must Jewish life forever be identified with the squalid *shtetl*?" these young intellectuals wondered. Like many *Haskalah* supporters, Gordon initially regarded Yiddish as a detriment to Jewish advancement (although he did come to understand that using Yiddish was the only way to reach the masses) and urged Jews to learn Hebrew and Russian. It was this idealistic vision of Jewish acculturation that he articulated in one of his most famous poems, "Awake, My People!" composed in 1863. It was a challenge to Jews everywhere to seize the moment: "The night has passed, the sun shines bright. Awake, lift up your eyes, look around you; Acknowledge your time and your place. . . ." The poem also included the line that Gordon is best remembered for. "Be a man in the streets and a Jew at home," he wrote, a motto that quickly was adopted as the clarion call of the *Haskalah*.

Later, after the pogroms, when all hope for Jews in Russia appeared to be lost, Gordon's message was misinterpreted and condemned. Critics like Moses Lieb Lilienblum and Perez Smolenskin, both early Zionists, suggested that Gordon had advocated total Jewish assimilation. In fact, explains his biographer, historian Michael Stanislawski, his intentions were very different. What Gordon meant was that "Russian Jews must at one and the same time partake of the shared culture of civilized European man – which for them meant assimilating to the local version of that genus by adopting the Russian language, Russian mores, and Russian patriotism – *and* remain vibrantly attached to the specific tradition of the Jews." Moreover, Gordon did not dismiss the idea of a Jewish return to the Holy Land, but he did argue that westernization and emancipation were prerequisites to that migration. In short, Gordon was promoting a type of acculturation that has come to characterize Jewish life in many parts of the Diaspora. In the mid-nineteenth century, however, the Russian Jewish world was not yet ready for it.

Meanwhile, to the east in St. Petersburg, a group of wealthy Jewish financiers, merchants, and progressive intellectuals combined their money and talents to form the Society for the Promotion of the

Enlightenment among the Jews of Russia. This new organization had among its founders such luminaries as banker Joseph Gunzburg, his son Horace, who would become Baron Gunzburg, and Leon Rosenthal, the society's first secretary. The group's mandate was "to spread the knowledge of the Russian language among the Jews; to publish and assist others in publishing, in Russian as well as Hebrew, useful works and journals; to aid in carrying out the purposes of the Society; and further, to assist the young in devoting themselves to the pursuit of science and knowledge." As Leon Rosenthal so aptly stated, "We constantly hear men in high positions, with whom we come in contact, complain about the separatism and fanaticism of the Jews and about their aloofness from everything Russian, and we have received assurances on all hands that, with the removal of these peculiarities, the condition of our brethren in Russia will be improved, and we shall become full-fledged citizens of this country."

Gordon had links with the society almost from the beginning. In 1872, when Rosenthal retired as secretary, it made sense to offer Gordon the job. His reputation as poet, essayist, and journalist was by now well-established. Only a year earlier, he had published another popular Hebrew poem, which gave him further notoriety. It was entitled "For Whom Do I Toil?" a serious and somewhat distressing musing on the continual disappointments of the *maskilim* to effect real change. "For whom, then, do I toil, I mere mortal," he pondered. "For the handful remaining lovers of Hebrew; Who have not yet mocked her and scorned her? . . . Yes, to you I sacrifice my soul and my tears . . ."

Once he had made the decision to leave the teaching profession and move with his family to St. Petersburg in June 1872, he immersed himself in the culture of the Russian capital and relished in his new administrative functions on behalf of the Society. Finally, Gordon was among educated and refined Jews who kept one foot in the Old World and the other in the New. He continued to churn out new poems, stories, and editorial articles, including his satirical and witty Hebrew verse "The Tip of the *Yud*," an irreverent poem about the foolishness of rabbinical rules and the shoddy treatment of Jewish women under Talmudic law. This work made Gordon something of a celebrity in the Jewish world. He had reached a point in his life when he felt settled and financially comfortable. He embarked on various new activities in St. Petersburg – assisting young Jewish women who wanted to enroll in medical school, arranging for rabbinical students to attend a more "modern" seminary in Breslau – confident that at long last there was hope of progress.

But his confidence was misplaced. For within the city itself and beyond its boundaries were bands of young revolutionaries, Jews among them, who were dissatisfied with the pace of change and reform offered by the czar. Nor were they pleased by a series of reactionary policies adopted by the government in the decade after the failed Polish uprising of 1863. In *Haskalah* circles, the behaviour of these individuals was frowned upon. Their rejection of Jewish values and assimilation was not what Gordon and his colleagues had been fighting for.

Gordon gained first-hand experience of the new harsher mood in and around St. Petersburg late one evening in March 1879. He returned home from a meeting to find ten armed police officers had invaded his house. His wife and children were terrified. After the police had ransacked his valuables and books, Gordon and his family were taken by the police back to their station. He was certain that this was a case of mistaken identity. The police were surely targeting the wrong man. Instead of receiving a proper hearing, Gordon, his wife, and two of his children (his eldest daughter had recently married a lawyer) were thrown in jail. Only in the morning did Gordon learn that the police, who had also arrested a young revolutionary from Vilna named Mark (or Max) Gordon, had assumed that all of the Gordons from Vilna were connected. Recent threats on the czar's life had made government officials and the police more anxious, overly suspicious, and hence more repressive.

While their children were soon released, Gordon and Bella languished in prison for nearly five weeks. Despite pleading with the
authorities that he was no relative of this Max Gordon, he and Bella
were informed that they were to be exiled to the town of Pudozh,
about 350 km northeast of St. Petersburg. It took more than three
days to reach their destination, a journey made more difficult by
Bella's poor health. Within a few weeks in their primitive new
quarters, Gordon discovered more about the case against him. He
had been charged with providing "stipends to revolutionary students," with "collecting monies for revolutionary propaganda," with
being "in contact with foreign socialists," and lastly with being "the
brother of Max Gordon."

Back in St. Petersburg, his oldest daughter's husband, a lawyer,
tried to sort out the family's legal mess, but his employers at the
Society were not that patient. Much to Gordon's distress, they more
or less disowned him and searched for a new secretary. Powerless to
do much of anything, he looked after Bella and wrote a series of
poems and short stories to occupy the time. Finally, near the end of
the summer, a cable arrived informing him that at long last the
ordeal was over: his exile had been rescinded and he was free to
return to St. Petersburg. Only much later did he determine that his
arrest and exile had been precipitated by a Jewish tailor named
Rosenberg, who had taken great offence at what he thought was
Gordon's anti-religious attitude and was angry about a recent
dispute Gordon had had with the Hasidic community. Rosenberg
had bribed a St. Petersburg secret policeman by the name of Pursov,
who then framed Gordon, linking him to the revolutionary Max
Gordon. Once the head of the secret security services learned the
truth, he had Gordon exonerated.

The six-month exile had taken its toll on Gordon, embittering
him further to those who stood in the way of Jewish progress, both
the Orthodox on the right and the revolutionaries on the left. Faced
with no job prospects, Gordon accepted Alexander Zederbaum's
offer in the spring of 1880 to become editor of the Hebrew weekly

newspaper *Ha-Melitz*. While Gordon had initially hesitated about working for the unpredictable Zederbaum, having a full-time access to a newspaper allowed him to produce some of his finest journalistic commentaries and feel like he was making a real difference. In a series of stories, he condemned the growing revolutionary movement, discounted any Jewish participation in such activities (which in fact was rather minor) and expressed his faith that Alexander II would be the ultimate saviour of Russian Jews.

Gordon was not alone. Such optimism was shared by many Jews. True, more than thirty thousand already had abandoned Russia for America in search of better economic opportunities and freedom from persecution of the kind unleashed on Jews in a riot or "pogrom" in Odessa in 1871. But for most, leaving Russia was not feasible, or, like Judah Leib Gordon, they truly believed that the future would bring progress and emancipation.

They were wrong.

Death in This Case Could Not Be Considered a Misfortune

ON SUNDAY MARCH 1, 1881 (the eve of the Jewish festival of Purim), Czar Alexander II departed from his palace in St. Petersburg for his weekly outing and review of his guard. His personal security forces were more cautious than usual that day. Twice in the past months there had been attempts on the czar's life, and the young revolutionaries of the Narodnaia Volia, or People's Will, had made no effort to hide their hatred for the monarch. In their propaganda he was the "embodiment of despotism, hypocritical, cowardly, bloodthirsty and all-corrupting." They had vowed to end his reign one way or the other.

That day in March, as Alexander's carriage rounded a corner close to the Neva River, a young member of the Narodnaia Volia approached the royal entourage and threw what appeared to be a snowball under the horses' legs. The snowball was, in fact, a homemade bomb. In an instant it exploded, killing the horses, wounding bystanders, and injuring the czar. In the confusion that followed, Alexander got out of his carriage to investigate. At that moment, another revolutionary rushed forward with a package. There was another explosion, and this time the czar was seriously hurt; both his legs had been blown off. An hour later, back at the Winter Palace in his blood-soaked bed, the "Czar Liberator" was dead and telegrams began to spread the bad news across the empire.

In the *shtetl* of Swislowicz, southeast of Bialystok, Jews had gathered in the synagogue to hear the reading of the scroll of Esther, as is customary on the eve of Purim. "Suddenly the doors were flung wide open," Shmarya Levin recalled, "and at the entrance stood the district commissioner and the sergeant. A shudder ran through the congregation, the hereditary terror, the memory of evil decrees. Without introduction, the commissioner read out the telegram he held in his hand. 'Alexander the Second has fallen, a victim of a revolutionary plot. Alexander the Third sits on the throne of all the Russias.'"

Alexander's assassin died without providing the names of his accomplices. But the revolutionary who had thrown the first bomb was made to talk. Among the names he offered was that of one Jewish woman, Gesia Gelfman, a young girl who had run away from her home because she did not want to marry the man her parents had chosen for her. With a group of her friends from the Narodnaia Volia, she was arrested by the police. They were all sentenced to be hanged, but because Gelfman was pregnant, her death sentence was commuted to life in prison. She died several months later in childbirth under suspicious circumstances, and her baby died soon after that.

Alexander III succeeded his father to the throne. A large man, the new czar "possessed almost nothing in the way of intellectual curiosity." Nor did he concern himself with the march of progress, economic or political, that had occupied his father. "He knew his mind, what he should do, and what his policy ought to be," notes historian W. Bruce Lincoln. That policy was to gain order as his grandfather Nicholas I had done.

The czar was as shocked as everyone else in St. Petersburg when in the weeks following the assassination of Alexander II there was a series of violent and ruthless attacks on Jews in the southwest region of the empire. The first attack occurred late in the evening in the Ukrainian town of Elizavetgrad (now Kirovohrad), south of Kiev. It began with a dispute in a Jewish tavern. When the Jewish innkeeper ejected a rowdy Christian troublemaker, his friends in the street began to shout, "the Zhydy [a derogatory Russian term for Jews] are beating our people." Within minutes, the unruly and undoubtedly half-drunken crowd began smashing windows and beating any Jew they could find. The small Elizavetgrad police force attempted to intervene, but without much success, and the pogrom became worse. In the morning, peasants from the surrounding area joined in and more Jewish property was destroyed. The military arrived, but they, too, could not, or would not, quell the violence. In a few cases, eyewitnesses later testified that some soldiers "drank liquor with rioters and plundered Jewish taverns or accepted gifts of looted clothing and household items."

By evening, Elizavetgrad was quiet, yet this was only the beginning of violence that persisted for the next sixteen months. Railway workers and peasants soon spread the word of the pogrom, sparking more devastating riots throughout the region, including in the city of Kiev. One Jewish eyewitness described what transpired there in a report published in the newspaper *Razvet* on May 8, 1881:

> At twelve o'clock noon, the air echoed with wild shouts, whistling, jeering, hooting, and laughing. An enormous crowd of young boys, artisans and labourers was marching. The entire street was jammed with the barefoot brigade. The destruction of the Jewish houses began. Windowpanes and doors began to fly about, and shortly thereafter the mob, having gained access to the

houses and stores, began to throw upon the streets absolutely everything that fell into their hands. . . . Shortly afterwards the mob threw itself upon the Jewish synagogue, which, despite its strong bars, locks and shutters, was wrecked in a moment. One should have seen the fury with which the riff-raff fell upon the [Torah] scrolls, of which there were many in the synagogue. The scrolls were torn to shreds, trampled in the dirt, and destroyed with incredible passion.

In addition, there were reports of assaults, beatings, and rapes on women and young girls. The Jews of the Pale, most notably in the southern provinces, were terrified. They could not leave their homes, nor could they work. Like classic scapegoats, they were blamed for everything, from a child gone missing to the late delivery of the mail. The blood of Czar Alexander II was on their hands, it was claimed, despite the fact that few Jews had participated in the assassination plot. At a funeral held in St. Petersburg in April 1882, Rabbi Yitzhak Elhanan Spektor of Kovno undoubtedly expressed the sentiments felt by many Russian Jews, when he said, "Death in this case . . . could not be considered a misfortune, since for a Jew, in present circumstances, death is much better than life."

Ever since the great Jewish historian Simon Dubnow – a young Jewish intellectual of the day, a follower of *Haskalah*, and the first real chronicler of Russian Jewry – published his three-volume history between 1916 and 1920, the notion has persisted that the pogroms were planned and carried out as part of a larger government conspiracy against the Jews. This included compliance by the police and the participation of a secret military counter-revolutionary faction. Dubnow, who at eighty-one perished in 1941 at the hands of the Nazis in Riga, wrote about a mysterious "hidden hand [that] pushed the masses of people to a great crime."

Why would the czar and his officials, who cherished stability and order to such a degree, support and encourage widespread violence?

The answer is, they did not. "There is, in fact, not a single document that has come to light which comes even close to revealing such government orders, or for that matter, any government involvement in the pogroms," writes historian Stephen Berk. "The government was as shocked as everyone else; its immediate response was one of fear that outside forces – revolutionaries – were responsible for the outbreak of violence." It seems clear that there was no conspiracy; the riots were spontaneous and sporadic outbreaks led by discontented urbanites. Upon reading reports about the pogroms, Alexander III jotted in the margins, "very sad," and "extremely sad and perplexing." As he told a Jewish delegation in mid-May 1881, he believed the riots were "the work of anarchists."

This is not to say that the czar was overly fond of Jews – he was not. For many years, he had been under the influence of his tutor: the anti-Jewish and anti-liberal Konstantine Pobedonostov, the leader of Russia's Orthodox Church. In 1879, in a discussion with the Russian writer Fyodor Dostoyevsky (who also believed that Jews were exploiting peasants), Pobedonostov had asserted that the Jews "undermined everything. . . . They are at the root of the revolutionary socialist movement and of regicide; they own the periodical press; they have in their hands the financial markets; the people as a whole fall into financial slavery to them; they even control the principles of contemporary science and strive to place it outside of Christianity." Later, when asked to explain the impact of the pogroms, he was reported to have remarked that Russia's Jewish problem would be solved like this: "One-third of Jews would emigrate, one-third would convert to Russian Orthodoxy, and one-third would die off." Still, it needs to be repeated that neither Pobedonostov nor the czar endorsed the pogroms or condoned the rioting and violence.

Why, then, did the clerks, shopkeepers, railway workers and peasants join with the rabble-rousers from the nearby cities and turn on their Jewish neighbours and with such viciousness? Certainly, medieval beliefs about Jews endured, as well as a powerful conviction

that Jews were exploiting peasants through liquor sales and trade.
All revolutionaries, too, were Jews — at least that is what much of
the Russian press tried to convince its readers. Vague notions about
a Jewish conspiracy to rule the world were equally popular.[*]

But an even stronger reason for the riots lay in the poverty of
peasants and workers. Their taxes were too high; they had little
money and limited prospects for the future. To make ends meet,
some peasants became home craftsmen, others took low-paying
jobs on railway construction gangs. The frustration level was high.
Finally, there was widespread antipathy, even hatred, felt in the
Ukrainian countryside towards Jews. True, bartering and trading
took place each market day in the *shtetlach*, yet the Jews, in the peasants' eyes, remained alien. "The laws of the empire marked the Jews
as distinctly inferior by discriminating against them even more than
against the peasants themselves," observes historian Michael
Aronson. "Yet the peasants found that they were often dependent
on Jews in many ways, and they naturally resented this."

That Tangled Knot Called the Jewish Question

ALL THINGS CONSIDERED, it should not be surprising that the Czar
and his government ministers eventually determined that the Jews
had brought the pogroms upon themselves. Failing to comprehend
the strong urban element involved in the riots — the arrival of rail
workers and the unemployed from the cities — they blamed Jewish
exploitation of the peasants as the main factor. That, and the Jews'
"tribal seclusion" and their "religious fanaticism." As Count Nikolai

---

[*] The idea of a Jewish conspiracy was promoted in no small way by a convert, a
former Jew named Iakov Brafman. In 1869 Brafman published his book *Kniga
Kagala*, "The Book of the Kahal." He argued that Jews were a law unto themselves, a state within a state. The Talmud was their evil book and in it lay their
devious plans for world domination. Later editions were published and translated
into French, English, Polish, and German. Stephen Berk suggests that, "it is not
out of the realm of the possible that subsequent publications that purported to
be the writings of Jewish cabals, such as the *Protocols of the Elders of Zion* drew their
inspiration form Brafman's work."

P. Ignatiev, the minister of the interior, explained in a report to the Czar, because of the Jews' "clannishness and solidarity, all but a few of them have bent every effort not to increase the productive forces of the country but to exploit the native inhabitants, and primarily the poorer classes."

After some initial inquiries, the government arrived at a partial solution. On May 3, 1882, the czar issued the "Temporary Rules" or "May Laws" governing the life of Jews in the Pale. There was, however, nothing temporary about them; they remained more or less intact until the 1917 revolution. Behind the rules lay the government's paternalistic attitude toward the peasants and the firm belief that the Jews were exploiting them. Thus, Jews were now not allowed to settle in rural areas, nor could they transact business on Sundays and principal Christian holy days. The "Temporary Rules" were not as strict as Ignatiev and others wanted – Jewish ownership of taverns, for instance, was not forbidden – but the Pale, already small and overcrowded, was reduced in size. Moreover, a rigid interpretation of the laws imposed by zealous local officials often meant that when a Jew left his rural village for any length of time, he was not allowed to return.

A more extensive investigation into the Jewish question was conducted for five years during the mid-1880s led by Count Konstantine I. Pahlen, who eventually acknowledged the urban character of the pogroms. In other words, the May Laws missed the point. By restricting Jews to the cities and towns of the Pale, the laws only served to intensify antagonisms towards them.

In the meantime, more regulations and restrictions followed, causing additional hardship for Russian Jews. Quotas were placed on Jewish enrolment in secondary schools and universities. And then, in 1891, in an act that drew condemnation throughout the Western world, thousands of Jews were ordered out of Moscow.

The pogroms of 1881–82 and the new restrictive regulations led to two significant developments. A large portion of the intelligentsia and the general population decided, first, that there was no future for Russian Jews and, second, that the solution for this problem lay either in emigration to America or in the establishment of a Jewish homeland, preferably in Palestine. Hence, more than a decade before Theodor Herzl joined the nationalistic crusade, the Zionist movement was born in Russia.

The reaction to events in Russia of a Moscow Jewish student named Chaim Chissin was typical. He recorded in his diary on February 10, 1882: "Until these pogroms began I myself had thrust aside my Jewish origins. I considered myself a devoted son of Russia. I lived and breathed a Russian life and every new Russian scientific discovery, every new creation of Russian literature, every victory of Russian imperial power, everything filled my heart with pride. . . . Then suddenly, with no warning, we were shown the door. . . . Yes, whether I wish it or not, I am a Jew."

The pogroms had a profound effect on Judah Leib Gordon, too, though in the face of hostile opposition he stubbornly maintained his faith in Jewish life in Russia long after others had conceded that there was no hope. Initially, Gordon had placed blame for Jewish problems with young misguided revolutionaries like Gesia Gelfman, and he was more shocked than resigned to the fact that Russification was a failure. "Who could have predicted that such horrors and devastation could happen in our days! Even in St. Petersburg there are fears that the mobs would rise against the Jews," he wrote in a letter of May 2, 1881, to a close friend. A few weeks later, in an editorial in *Ha-Melitz*, he advised prudence, even suggesting that reports about the pogroms from the Ukraine may have been exaggerated.

As more details of the rioting reached St. Petersburg, Gordon took another approach, as he explained in a lengthy editorial published at the end of July. Now he argued that while emigration to America was acceptable for thousands of Russian Jews, the vast majority would have to remain in Russia and adapt. "In the end," he argued, "our country is Russia, where over half of world Jewry lives. . . . [But] there is no hope for them if they do not set themselves to unraveling that tangled knot called 'the Jewish Question' by our enemies, to blaze a new path and to remove all obstacles in their way, to remove deceit from their hearts and build a new educational system, a new mode of life and earning a living." Privately, he was more despondent, later conceding to a friend that "we are a nation without solutions, with no help in our times of need."

As for the dream of a homeland in Palestine, Gordon was sceptical, particularly since he maintained (somewhat prophetically) that the orthodox rabbinical community would have too much power in such a new state. If leaving Russia was the choice, then relocating to America made more sense in his view. In a new poem he composed in 1882, *Ahoti Ruhama* ("My Sister Ruhama"), he began "Arise, let us go to a place where the light of freedom will shine on everyone and will illuminate every soul."

This was a theme he vigorously set forth in one of his most famous *Ha-Melitz* editorials entitled "Our Redemption and Spiritual Salvation." Published on March 12, 1882, the editorial again stressed that spiritually the movement of Jews to Palestine could be defended, but practically it was more difficult to support. Moreover, given what Gordon considered to be the immaturity of Jewish spiritual development, a result, he suggested, of the backwardness of religious leaders, the time was not yet right for such a move to the Holy Land. "It is preferable to direct the Jews to America," he reasoned, "or other enlightened lands, for there they will learn how to be free men. . . . Then they will appreciate their people and their land, they will return to the Holy Land and fill it with cultured, intelligent, eager and well-trained people."

Thousands heeded the words of Gordon and others. Soon the "great migration" from the *shetlach* and towns of the Russian empire to the United States began. In his annual address to Congress in December 1891, American President Benjamin Harrison expressed his concern about "the harsh measures now being enforced against the Hebrews in Russia." Harrison estimated that "over 1,000,000 will be forced from Russia within a few years." That estimation was low. Between 1880 and 1914, more than two million Russian Jews journeyed across the Atlantic to the United States, and thousands more to Canada and Argentina. The majority ended up in cities like New York, Chicago, Montreal, and Toronto, where they soon established new lives under difficult circumstances and laid the foundation for the vibrant North American Jewish communities that exist today. A smaller number of hardy souls set out from Russia to work the land in the American and Canadian west and Argentina on Jewish agricultural colonies financed by philanthropists like Baron Maurice de Hirsch.

But for some members of the Russian Jewish intelligentsia, the only destination was Palestine, even if the Ottoman Turks, who then controlled the region, did not support the idea. In its nascent stages in Russia, Palestinophilism (the term "Zionism" would not be used until the late 1890s) was first and foremost a powerful and emotional movement with religious and nationalistic overtones. Its early proponents, like Dr. Yehuda (Leon) Pinsker and Moses Leib Lilienblum, who argued that in Palestine Jews "could exist as masters and not as aliens" were passionate and adamant advocates. Criticisms and practical objections like those raised by Judah Lieb Gordon were not acceptable.

In April 1882, Lilienblum submitted a long article to *Ha-Melitz* called "Let Us Not Confuse the Issues," denouncing his old friend Gordon. In Lilienblum's opinion, Gordon's argument about religious reform before migration to Palestine missed the point.

> The nation as a whole is dearer to all of us than all the divisions over rigid orthodoxy or liberalism in religious observance put together. Where the nation is concerned there are not sects or denominations, there are neither modern nor old-fashioned men, no devout or heretics, but all are Children of Abraham, Isaac and Jacob! . . . Let us gather our dispersed from eastern Europe and go up to our land with rejoicing; whoever is on the side of God and His people, let him say: I am

for Zion. . . . Let us pay not heed to the renegades trying to lead us away from our fatherland. Let us not divide into *Mitnagdim*, Hasidim, and *Maskilim*. This is the land in which our fathers have found rest since time immemorial – and as they lived, so will we live. Let us go now to the only land in which we will find respite for our souls that have been harried by murderers for these thousands of years. Our beginnings will be small, but in the end we will flourish.

Even more influential was the pamphlet "Auto-Emancipation" written in German in 1882 by Pinsker, a sixty-year-old physician from Odessa. He is remembered as one of the fathers of Zionism, proclaiming that the "Jewish nation" required "a home, if not a country of our own" more than a decade before Theodor Herzl discovered the movement. Pinsker also attempted to theorize on the reasons for anti-Semitism. "Judeophobia is a form of demonopathy," he wrote, "with the distinction that the Jewish ghost has become known to the whole race of mankind, not merely to certain races, and that it is not disembodied, like other ghosts, but is a being of flesh and blood, and suffers the most excruciating pain from the wounds inflicted upon it by the fearful mob who imagine it threatens them. Judeophobia is a psychic aberration. As a psychic aberration, it is hereditary; as a disease transmitted for two thousand years, it is incurable." Two year later, at a conference in Kattowitz (Katowice) in Upper Silesia, thirty-six delegates from all corners of Europe met to organize the association Hibbat Zion, the "Lovers of Zion."

The stubborn and principled Gordon was not then, nor for the remaining decade of his life, swayed by the ideas of the Zionist writers and philosophers. He continued his fight for a religious transformation and never did give up hope that the survival of Jews would take place in the Diaspora rather than the Holy Land. Yet when he died from cancer in 1892 at the age of sixty-two, Gordon was far from optimistic that the future of Jews was secure. Neither Zionism nor the Yiddish revival inherent in the literary works of Sholom Aleichem and Yehuda L. Peretz held great appeal for him. His faith in an assimilated and emancipated but still very much Jewish community would eventually materialize in the Diaspora, but in another time and place.

Chapter Eight

L'AFFAIRE

Paris, 1895

Until now I have worshiped reason, I have believed there was a logic in things and events, I have believed in human justice! Anything irrational and extravagant found difficult entrance into my brain. Oh, what a breaking down of all my beliefs and of all sound reason!

– ALFRED DREYFUS, 1895

We Are Not a People, We Are a Religion

TO BE A JEW IN FRANCE IN 1889 was to be blessed. It meant being a privileged member of a society where for a century the sacred principles of the Revolution – Liberty, Equality, and Fraternity – were applied to all. Nowhere else in Europe were Jews treated as equal citizens. It was for this reason that the approximately seventy-five thousand Jews living in France at the end of the nineteenth century, a tiny minority in a country of thirty-nine million, enthusiastically joined in the celebrations to commemorate the hundredth anniversary of the fight for liberty and justice.

"To be Jews . . . and only Jews, that did not suffice for you," Rabbi Arnaud Aron, grand rabbi of Strasbourg, told congregants who had gathered to pay tribute to the events of 1789 in a temple in nearby Lunéville, "to that title of nobility you sought to add that of Frenchmen, of children of France, that is what the Revolution made of you." Rabbi Zadoc Kahn, the chief rabbi of France, expressed similar sentiments at a synagogue in Paris. "France will not repudiate her past, her traditions, her principles which constitute the best of her moral patrimony," he declared. "As for us . . . we will continue to love our country . . . and bear witness, in all circumstances to our gratitude and devotion."

Despite the true sincerity of such statements, the French Revolution had posed particular problems for Jews. Was it possible to be both a Frenchman and a Jew? Were Jews a nation and a people or merely adherents to a religion? In December 1789, during the revolutionary debates about whether the Declaration of the Rights of Man and Citizen would apply to French Jews, the Girondist Count Stanislas de Clermont-Tonnerre succinctly answered this troubling question. "The Jews," he stated, "should be denied everything as a nation, but granted everything as individuals." In short, there was room in France for only one "people," and if Jews wanted to be treated equally then their only option was assimilation. The degree to which they maintained a separate religious identity was an issue they would wrestle with throughout the nineteenth century and later.

The process of acculturation was made all the more difficult by some Frenchmen who refused to accept Jews into their fraternal brotherhood, no matter how much they adopted the customs and mores of other citizens. For these individuals, the Jews would always be outsiders, "the other." It was first in France therefore, that Jews were emancipated, that there were no restrictions on their occupations or residence, and that a virulent anti-Semitism, unseen before, took shape.

At the time of the Revolution, pockets of Jews lived in four outlying areas in France. On the southwest coast in Bayonne and further north in Bordeaux, there were about five thousand or so Sephardim, descendants of Portuguese *conversos* who had discreetly slipped back from Portugal into France during the mid-1500s. Initially, these merchants had disguised their Jewish identities, going so far as to have their children baptized in local parishes. Their ruse fooled few French officials, who valued the merchants' economic power enough to ignore it. Regulations set down in royal "*Lettres Patentes*" (Letters of Naturalization and Dispensation), renewable at a price every few years, governed their lives. But like the Sephardi community in Amsterdam, to whom they looked for leadership and guidance, they became acculturated Frenchmen long before this was officially and legally acknowledged in the Declaration of the Rights of Man and Citizen.

In fact, they went to great lengths in 1788 to differentiate themselves from their Ashkenazi brethren (referred to as "German"), whom they regarded, then and for decades later, with snobbish disdain. According to the accepted Sephardi wisdom of the day, "the Germans almost everywhere have long beards; their dress distinguishes them everywhere they live; the Portuguese, on the other hand, except for their religious belief, differ in no respect from the peoples among whom they live. . . . A Portuguese Jew is English in England and French in France, but a German Jew is German everywhere with regard to customs." Revolutionary politicians in Paris were convinced, and in late January 1790, the five thousand Jews of Bayonne and Bordeaux were the first Jews of France to obtain full civil rights.

An even smaller number of Jews lived in Provence, which had been under Papal control until 1791, and about five hundred Jews resided in Paris. Soon, though, as a result of a lost war with Prussia in 1870 and immigration from Eastern Europe, the Jewish population in the French capital would grow at a rapid pace. By the 1890s, 60 per cent of all French Jews, about forty-five thousand, lived in Paris. The vast majority resided in the Saint Paul–Marais neighbourhood in the third and fourth *arrondissements* in the area known as the Pletzel (in Yiddish, "Little Place"). This district had been home to Jews as early as 1198 right up until their expulsion from France in 1394.

When Jews were able to return, they gradually relocated again around the Pletzel, and the Rue des Rosiers, a narrow cobblestone street that was once the main street of Paris's East European ghetto with kosher shops and synagogues. Contemporary descriptions always emphasized the poverty and squalor, no different than

London's East End or New York's Lower East Side. "The alleys are frightfully dirty, the houses mostly old ruins," one American Jewish journalist reported after visiting Paris in 1912. "Without exaggeration one can find from twelve to fifteen persons living in two small rooms." Paris's assimilated bourgeois Jewish community condemned the entire community as an eyesore and criticized its inhabitants for not understanding "French customs."*

Well before Paris became the centre of French Jewry, the heart and soul of the community could be found to the northeast, in the towns and villages that dotted the countryside of Alsace and Lorraine. Here, in the late eighteenth and early nineteenth centuries, lived more than thirty thousand Ashkenazi Jews. Nearly all were of German origin. They spoke Yiddish in their homes, regularly attended synagogue, arranged marriages for their children, and had more in common with Jews in the *shtetlach* of the Russian Pale of Settlement than they did with other Jews in France. Since they were not permitted to own land, be members of artisanal guilds, or sell new items, many became cattle- and horse-traders, small-scale moneylenders, or more frequently peddlers of old clothes. Each Sunday morning the men would bid farewell to their families and with their packs on their backs set off to trek throughout the region, arriving back in time for the beginning of the Sabbath on Friday night. "Living on black bread and water or, in good times, on potatoes and eggs, they bought and sold old clothes, small pieces of furniture,

---

* Today, the Rue des Rosiers is a fashionable and expensive Paris tourist area with Jewish bakeries, high-priced Judaica shops such as Diasporama, and famous landmarks like Jo Goldenberg's restaurant (the site of a terrorist attack on August 9, 1982, in which six people were killed and twenty-two wounded). With the arrival of thousands of North African Jews during the 1950s and 1960s, following the end of French colonial rule in Algeria, Tunisia, and Morocco, and more recently Israeli immigrants, the neighbourhood has acquired a unique Middle Eastern flavour as well. Typically, as in the Venice ghetto, few Jews who work in the Pletzel can afford to live anywhere near it. Still, the area's Jewish character was bolstered with the recent opening of the nearby Musée d'art et d'histoire du judaïsme, the exquisite Jewish museum housed in the palatial mansion that was once home of duc de Saint-Aignan in the mid-1600s.

(*Encyclopedia Judaica* vol.1, original source unknown)

Don Isaac Abravanel (1437–1508)
He was rightly revered as a "great eagle" in learning, "as wise as
Daniel" in politics, and as a "man of God" in morals and personality.
Abravanel truly epitomized the power, influence, and scholarship
that was on the wane among Jews in Europe after the expulsion
from Spain.

Moses Maimonides (1135-1204)

A scholar, physician, and philosopher of tremendous vision and wisdom, Maimonides was revered as "the greatest son of Sepharad." He is remembered today by this charming statue of him erected in 1964. It sits quietly in an unobtrusive square off a narrow walkway in Cordoba's former Jewish neighbourhood, close to the spot where he once lived.

The Cordoba Judería

The Jews of Cordoba worked and lived in buildings like this. The community was part of a great Sephardi culture destroyed in the riots of 1391 and the expulsion from Spain a century later. This neighbourhood of shops and restaurants, now popular with tourists, is still called the Judería more than 500 years after the Jews were either killed or forced to convert to Christianity.

(Author's photo)

Entrance to Venice ghetto
For almost three hundred years beginning in 1516, the Jews of Venice were locked behind the ghetto gate each evening as the bell in San Marco tolled – a way to keep them isolated from the Christian world on the outside and to protect them from attack.

(Roberto Milano Collection, Italy)

The Jewish Square in the Venice ghetto
This square, which still dominates the ghetto, was a hub of Jewish and Christian activity during the day. Traders from across Italy and Europe streamed into the ghetto, visiting pawnshops, spreading gossip and news, arranging for the printing of a new manuscript, and buying merchandise of every kind and variety. Engraving by Joseph Vazi, 1747.

The Ghetto Vecchio

By 1600, there may have been as many as five thousand Jews in the original Venice ghetto and its two expansions – the Ghetto Vecchio, added in 1541, and the Ghetto Nuovissmo, added in 1633. Often, a peddler used the ground-floor living quarters, while a merchant or physician occupied the more spacious upper-floor apartments. Storeys were continually added to existing buildings to make room for the ever-increasing population. Today, this narrow alleyway in the Ghetto Vecchio is cool and quiet.

Entrance to the Scuola Levantino (the Levant Synagogue) in the Venice ghetto

The synagogue was built in the 1580s, financed by the merchants who had immigrated to Venice from Greece and Turkey. The synagogues and the daily routine of prayer may have provided some much-needed stability in the lives of the ghetto's inhabitants, but the rules by which the Jews in Venice existed changed according to the political climate of the times. And over this, they had no control.

Jewish Physician, 1570s

This is likely Moses Hamon (1490-1554), physician and advisor in the court of Sultan Suleiman the Magnificent. The illustration is from Nicolas de Nicolay's *Les Navigations, pèrègrinations et voyages faicts en la Turquie*, published in 1576. Hamon wears a tall red hat, a trademark of Jewish doctors.

Shabbetai Zevi (1626-1676)

It was said of the self-proclaimed Messiah that "his countenance was beautiful and that there was almost none like him." This portrait of him is from a sketch by a Christian artist who saw him in 1665 in Izmir.
The inscription, in Dutch and French, reads, "An authentic likeness of Shabbetai Zevi, who claims to be the restorer of the kingdom of Israel and the Jews."

Menasseh ben Israel (1604-1657)

A writer, teacher, rabbi, and leading citizen of the Portuguese Jewish Community in Amsterdam, ben Israel is best remembered for his successful appeal to Cromwell to readmit Jews to England in 1655.

Amsterdam Jewish Quarter, 1783

Amsterdam was the "emporium of Europe" and a place where the Portuguese Jews were able to immerse themselves in trade and commerce. This view is from the Jodenbreestraat, with the *Esnoga* on the right.

The *Esnoga*

Opened in 1675, the *Esnoga* (or Portuguese Synagogue) was a symbol of Sephardi affluence in Amsterdam. This 1721 engraving, by Bernard Picart, shows the official dedication and opening of the synagogue. The most important members of the Sephardi community in Amsterdam have gathered to pray, rejoice, and especially, it seems, socialize.

Samson Wertheimer (1658-1724)
Known as the *Judenkaiser* (the "Jewish Emperor"), the court Jew Wertheimer was a brilliant financier, "the wealthiest Jew of his day," but also committed to the Jewish community in Vienna and the Hapsburg Empire.

Samuel Oppenheimer (1630-1703)
Known for his honesty and integrity in business, Oppenheimer was the most important court Jew of his day and was responsible for re-establishing the Jewish community in Vienna.

Joseph Süss Oppenheimer (1698-1738)
Oppenheimer was executed before a large crowd in Stuttgart, an event later celebrated in depictions such as this. His body was placed in an iron cage so his remains could be exhibited.

Moses Mendelssohn (1729-1786), c. 1760
A leader of the Haskalah (the Jewish Enlightenment), the intellectual Mendelssohn was a model Jew, one who could be both a Jew and a German.

Frankfurt's ghetto
The *Judengasse* in the 1880s. Located in the northeast section of the city, it was a narrow and dark muddy street less than a half a mile long—"somber, humid and filthy," as one visitor described it in 1747. At night, its three gates were locked and guarded, and on Sundays and Christian holidays, its inhabitants were not permitted to leave at all. During the eighteenth century, its most famous residents were the members of the Rothschild family.

Gabriel Riesser (1806-1863)
An independent and original proponent of Jewish emancipation in Germany. Riesser was a prolific writer, who argued that Jews could maintain their religion and still be worthy German citizens. "The mighty tones of the German language, the songs of German poets, have kindled and nurtured the holy fire of freedom in our breasts," he once declared. "We want to belong to the German fatherland."

Judah Leib Gordon (1830–1892)
A brilliant poet and essayist, Gordon
was called "the mighty hammer
of the Hebrew language." He never
gave up the hope that the survival
of Jews would take place in the
Diaspora rather than the Holy Land.

Kiev marketplace, 1900
The market was the lifeblood of any Jewish community, an opportunity for
Jewish peddlers and artisans to sell their wares. The inscription reads:
"The house where L. Shapiro was a poet: where he was born and grew up."

ALFREDO DREYFUS   3271

**Alfred Dreyfus
(1859-1935), c. 1905**
Dreyfus was a Jewish army captain
wrongfully convicted of betraying
military secrets to the Germans.
The case roused anti-Semitism in
France and embroiled the country
in controversy for more than
a decade.

Lucie Dreyfus, Alfred's wife
Lucie worked tirelessly to free her
husband.

**George Picquart, the intelligence
officer who found the real traitor**
"What does it matter to you if this
Jew stays on Devil's Island?" the army's
deputy-chief of staff asked Picquart.
"If you don't tell anyone, no will
know." Picquart was shocked. "General,
what you have said is abominable;
I don't know what I will do, but I
will not take this secret to the grave."

"Le traître" Dreyfus as an exhibit in the *Musée des horreurs*, 1900
"I need no one to tell me why Dreyfus committed treason," wrote journalist Maurice Barrès. "That Dreyfus is capable of treason, I conclude from his race."

The degradation of Dreyfus, January 5, 1895, at École Militaire
"Soldiers, an innocent man is being dishonoured," Dreyfus declared that day. "Long live France! Long live the Army!"

Abraham Cahan (1860-1951), 1926

Cahan was the long-time editor of the Yiddish newspaper *Der Forverts (The Forward)* and author of several novels about Jewish immigrants. "If one had to select a single person to stand for East European Jews in America, it would be Abraham Cahan," wrote Nathan Glazer in 1957.

Hester Street near Essex, Lower East Side, New York, 1899

Abraham Cahan, who lived in the quarter for many years, described it as "the most densely populated spot on the face of the earth - a seething human sea fed by streams, streamlets, and rills of immigration flowing from all the Yiddish-speaking centers of Europe."

Sweatshop in a Hester Street tenement, from Jacob Riis,
How the Other Half Lives, **New York, 1889**

"Every open window of the big tenements gives you a glimpse of one of those shops," reported Jacob Riis in his study of the Lower East Side. "Men and women, bending over their machines or ironing boards at the windows, half-naked. . . . The road is like a big gangway through an endless workroom, where vast multitudes are forever laboring. Morning, noon, and night, it makes no difference; the scene is always the same."

Franz Rosenzweig (1886-1929)

A brilliant German-Jewish writer, philosopher and educator. "The story of Franz Rosenzweig," his friend and biographer Nahum Glatzer observed many years ago, "is the story of a rediscovery of Judaism. A European intellectual and assimilationist breaks with his personal past and becomes a Jew by conviction, rediscovers his people's existence, and becomes the modern interpreter of this existence."

Jacob Gens (1905-1943), head of the the Vilna ghetto Judenrat

Gens believed that compliance with Nazi orders was the most prudent policy. "Work, especially work for the military, is the order of the day. . . ." he declared in 1942. "Jewish workers must give up easy, convenient jobs and take on more difficult work, in order to increase their usefulness. . . . This is essential for the collective interest of the ghetto."

Ghetto entrance, Rudninku Street in the Vilna ghetto, 1941–42

"Here is the ghetto gate," wrote young Yitzhok Rudashevski the day he arrived. "My freedom is being robbed from me, my home, and the familiar Vilna streets I love so much."

The Yatke meat market, Vilna, 1923

Vilna, once home to a thriving Jewish community, was known as the "Jerusalem of Lithuania." "The sound of Yiddish resonated throughout the city," recalled Lucy Dawidowicz. "You heard Yiddish in the streets, the shops, and the market-place. . . . You could live a full life in Vilna for a year, as I did, or even a lifetime, as many Vilna Jews did, speaking only Yiddish."

The Ponary, or Ponar, forest near Vilna
At this location, between 1941 and 1944, the Nazi death squads murdered approximately 70,000 to 100,000 people. This photograph was taken when the bodies were being exhumed after the war so they could receive proper burial.

Vilna Partisans at the city's liberation, July 1944
Abba Kovner is standing at centre. Beside him (wearing a beret) is Rozka Korczak, and on extreme right is Vitka Kempner, Kovner's wife. At the end of December 1941, as Vilna's Jews were being murdered by the Nazis, Kovner declared the immortal words "Let us not be led as sheep to the slaughter!"

(Moshe Decter, *A Hero for Our Time*, original source unknown)

Boris and Larisa Kochubiyevsky
Inspired by the Israeli victory in the Six Day War, Kochubiyevsky tried to leave the Soviet Union for Israel in June 1967. "I am a Jew," he wrote to Leonid Brezhnev after his request was refused. "I want to live in the Jewish State. As long as I live, as long as I am capable of feeling, I will do all I can to get to Israel." He was sentenced to three years in a labour camp, and his plight came to symbolize the struggle of Soviet Jews.

(Author's photo)

The Great Synagogue of Kiev
Built in 1898, the synagogue was the pride of the city's large Jewish community. During the Second World War, the Nazis, who occupied Kiev, used it as a horse stable, and in the post-war period the Soviets turned it into the Kiev State Puppet Theatre. The Jewish community did not regain total control of the property until 1997.

Bibles, tools, and trinkets, and they slept along the roads or in the homes of other Jewish families," historian Michael Burns relates. "Their daily call, *'Nix zu handel?'* ('Nothing to sell?') had echoed across the Rhine Valley and Vosges Mountains for centuries."

Life for Jews in France became more structured under the rule of Napoleon Bonaparte. The emperor was more concerned than revolutionary leaders had been with the persistence of Jewish distinctiveness and with horror stories of exploitation by Jewish moneylenders who supposedly charged 75 per cent interest. After consulting with Jewish leaders, he created in 1808 a new and enduring legal framework for Jews in Alsace and Lorraine and elsewhere: the Consistoire, or Consistory, a central governing body along with local organizations whose task it was to bring order to Jewish communities. But the ultimate goal was assimilation. Jews now had to adopt surnames legally and serve in the army (unlike other French citizens, they could not find a substitute). Napoleon also attempted to restrict and regulate Jewish economic activities. In this he was less successful.

Despite the fact that relations between Christians and Jews in Alsace and Lorraine were not always affable or even peaceful – as during the 1848 revolutions, when bands of young hoodlums used the political upheaval as an excuse to attack Jews – the process of assimilation, or at least acculturation, had a transforming effect. This was particularly true for the generation born after 1850, the first to be more French than German, or Jewish, for that matter. Decrees by the Consistoire Central in Paris not only altered synagogue services, adding organ music, choirs, and dress codes, but a new mindset also developed. "We are not a people, we are a religion," declared Rabbi Lazare Wogue, and many French Jews, who now regarded themselves as "Israelites," eagerly concurred.

Urbanization and industrialization equally changed Jewish life in France. Over the course of a few generations, the educated children and grandchildren of peddlers became the members of an assimilated middle-class business elite, who often put their patriotism ahead of their religious beliefs. Nothing was valued more, it seemed, than contributing to the life of the nation as full-fledged citizens. Through philanthropic and educational organizations like the Alliance israëlite universelle, established in 1860, French Jews still maintained links and assisted their brethren in the Ottoman Empire and the Pale of Settlement, yet their orientation and focus was definitely more French. Consider as only one example of this decisive economic and cultural process, the story of Alfred Dreyfus's family.

My Childhood Passed Gently

ABRAHAM ISRAEL DREYFUSS, Alfred's great-grandfather, was born in 1749 in the village of Rixheim in the southern part of Alsace. Rixheim did not have a large Jewish community, but there was a synagogue that employed its own rabbi. Abraham learned to be a kosher butcher and at age thirty married a woman named Brandel Meyer from nearby Mülheim. They had two children, although only one, a son whom they called Jacob, survived.

Young Jacob witnessed the Revolution, the Terror, and the rule of Napoleon Bonaparte. In official government documents he became "Jacques Dreyfus," yet he preferred Jacob Dreyfuss and maintained, like other Jews of Alsace, a strong connection to his German-Jewish roots. In the late 1790s, Jacob became a peddler and moneylender. Later, he took advantage of the new opportunities open to Jews by investing in small properties. By the time he turned thirty-two, he felt successful enough to marry Rachel Katz, also from Rixheim. Jacob and Rachel had three children, but, as in his own family, only one son survived.

Raphael, Alfred Dreyfus's father, was born in mid-May 1818 and grew up a French citizen. At home he spoke Yiddish and German, and in school he was taught in French. As was customary, he attended *cheder* classes, and though perhaps not as Orthodox as his grandfather Abraham had been, Raphael was raised in a Jewish environment. In 1835, when Raphael was still a teenager, his father Jacob, seeking better opportunities, decided to relocate his family to Mülhausen, one of Alasace's main cities. Mülhausen, known after the 1848 revolutions by its French name Mulhouse, was a centre for the textile industry.

Jacob purchased a small apartment in the city's growing Jewish neighbourhood and set out to become a textile merchant. In 1838, just as Jacob and Raphael, who was now his father's business partner, were beginning to establish themselves, Jacob died. He is buried in the new "Israelite" section of the Mulhouse cemetery. Engraved on his headstone is the name Jacques Dreyfus, yet with the Frenchified name appears the date from the Hebrew calendar, 5598 – a good example, as Michael Burns points out, of "the mingling of French and Ashkenazic cultures."

Within two years, Raphael had married Jeanette Libman, a seamstress and the daughter of a middle-class Jewish couple from the nearby town of Ribeauville. Jeanette gave birth to Jacques, the first of their many children, in 1844. Their youngest and eighth child, Alfred, was born on October 9, 1859. By then, Raphael, a distinguished-looking man, tall and broad-shouldered, who sported whiskers but no moustache, had officially changed the family's last name to the French Dreyfus.

Like his father, Raphael was a hard-working and savvy businessman. In Mulhouse, he toiled for many years as a commission agent, a middleman between textile manufacturers and prospective buyers. Slowly, he started investing in his own textile business as well as purchasing property. Finally, in 1862, Raphael was able to buy a cotton mill and almost immediately Raphael Dreyfus et Compagnie was a resounding commercial success. Jeanette was able to stop working as a seamstress, and the family moved into a larger house in a more fashionable Mulhouse neighbourhood. It was here that Alfred grew up.

"My childhood passed gently," Alfred Dreyfus later recalled, "amid the gentle influences of mother and sisters, a father deeply devoted to his children, and the companionship of older brothers." In particular, Alfred was close to his brother Mathieu, two years older. Mathieu would play a pivotal role in the tragic ordeal that would soon make the name Alfred Dreyfus known around the world.

While Raphael and Jeanette kept a kosher home and taught their children about their Jewish traditions and heritage, they led more acculturated lives than their parents and grandparents had. French was the primary language spoken in the Dreyfus house, and Alfred and his brothers and sisters were typical French Jews — assimilated, patriotic, and proud. Young Alfred was a shy and reserved boy, especially with people he did not know. He was described as having a "rigid manner." "He is stoic," said Mathieu Dreyfus of his brother in 1902, "with a cold appearance but a warm heart." He was even a bit of a dreamer, so much so that his sisters nicknamed him "Don Quixote."

Alfred's first sorrow, as he later called it, was the day the Prussian Army marched into Mulhouse soon after the brief Franco-Prussian War had ended in September 1870 in the Germans' favour. This experience instilled in him a fear and even a hatred of foreigners as well as deepening his feelings for France. With Alsace and Lorraine ceded to Germany in the Treaty of Frankfurt the following year, the Dreyfus family had a dilemma. Raphael had no desire to become a German citizen, nor did he want his sons drafted into the Germany army. But neither did he want to lose his textile business. The only solution was for the family to split up. Jacques Dreyfus, the eldest son, remained in Mulhouse to watch over the business along with Jeanette, who was ill. Raphael took the rest of the family to Basel, Switzerland. In 1873, Raphael sent his two youngest sons, Mathieu and Alfred, to Paris to complete their schooling.

After a few years in a rigorous French boarding school, Mathieu Dreyfus decided to join his father and brothers Jacques and Leon in the family's textile enterprise. Alfred, on the other hand, opted for a career in the military. In 1878, he was accepted as a student at the École Polytechnique, the French military academy. When he joined the army the humiliating loss to the Prussians eight years earlier was still not forgotten or forgiven. The French military establishment wanted revenge and insisted the only way to obtain it was to adopt a rigid, conservative, and disciplined approach not always in agreement with the liberal principles of the Revolution. "The republican and military points of view are two contradictory and incompatible states," explained one French general at the time. "The Republic represents the sovereignty of public opinion, the absolute equality of all, the crushing of the elite by the majority. It is a pyramid stood on its head. By its motto alone, the Republic is the negation of the Army, for liberty, equality, and fraternity are tantamount to indiscipline, the oblivion of obedience, and the negation of hierarchical principles."

These were sentiments that Alfred Dreyfus could understand. His son Pierre later wrote that his father chose a military career because he never stopped thinking of "Alsace quaking beneath the foreign yoke, of those whose heart had remained French and who so suffered from oppression." The fact that Dreyfus was Jewish was not an obstacle; there were other Jews in the army before he joined. Besides, given his background, it never would have occurred to him that his religion would have been a significant factor, one way or the other, in his career.

In 1880 he graduated as a lieutenant – 128th in his class of 235 recruits. He had matured and was more confident. He now had a distinctive neatly trimmed moustache and a reputation for being an excellent horseman. Lt. Dreyfus, however, decided to specialize in artillery. He was transferred to the Horse Batteries of the First Independent Cavalry Division at Paris. On September 12, 1889, he received his commission of captain in the Twenty-first Regiment of Artillery and was appointed on special service at the École Centrale de Polytechnique Militaire at Bourges.

Through a fellow Jewish officer, the thirty-year-old Dreyfus met Lucie Hadamard, the nineteen-year-old daughter of a diamond merchant and a wealthy assimilated Jewish family. Lucie stood to inherit a great deal of money and be presented with a large dowry on her wedding day. She was also beautiful. The two were married in mid-April 1890 by the Grand Rabbi of France, Zadoc Kahn, at the synagogue on Temple de la Rue de la Victoire, not far from the Opera, in a fashionable area of Paris that was home to many bourgeois Ashkenazi families.

Soon after, Dreyfus, having passed a difficult entrance exam, was accepted to the École Supérieure de Guerre in Paris, the school for staff officers. While he studied and worked, he and Lucie lived in a roomy apartment on a quiet street in the eighth *arrondissement*, not too far from the Champs Élysées. By 1892, Dreyfus had completed his special training and was appointed to the Bureau of General Staff in the Intelligence section.

Only once during the previous two years had Dreyfus been reminded that he was Jewish, a fact all the more interesting given the rise of anti-Semitism in France at this time. One military instructor, General Pierre Bonnefond, made no attempt to hide his dislike of Dreyfus as well as the several other Jewish officers at the École de Guerre. For no apparent reason, at least in Dreyfus's opinion, the general gave Dreyfus a poor evaluation (which lowered his overall ranking in class from third to ninth). He lodged a formal complaint against Bonnefond. At a tense meeting with his commanding officer, General Lebelin de Dionne, Dreyfus asked, "Is a Jewish officer not capable of serving his country as well as any other soldier?" The matter was dealt with quietly. Bonnefond did not receive a reprimand, but General de Dionne gave Dreyfus his assurance that a Jewish officer was valued as highly as any other.

General de Dionne did, however, note in a report that Dreyfus had a "brusque demeanour." He pointed out, too, that Dreyfus was not especially popular with his teachers and classmates and apparently had been seen in the company of prostitutes. "I have seen many Israelite officers at the École de Guerre," wrote de Dionne. "I can affirm that none of them had been the object of the animosity of his superiors and colleagues. If this was not the case for Dreyfus, it was due to his detestable character, his immodesty of language, and his undignified private life, not at all to his religion."

If Dreyfus suspected that his superiors and fellow officers were not overly fond of him, that they regarded him as "cunning, colourless, awkward," he did not mention it. Nor was he bothered by the fact that he had few real friends or a mentor of a high rank whom he could trust. He and Lucie had two children, Pierre, born in

1891, and Jeanne, born two years later. "A brilliant and easy career was open to me," he later wrote about those years in Paris, "the future appeared under the most promising auspices."

A Race of the First Order

IT IS THE GREAT IRONY OF JEWISH HISTORY that, had hate in the form of anti-Semitism not intervened, the acculturation process that had shaped the life of Alfred Dreyfus, his family, and the majority of Jews in France would likely have been completed. There were many in France who rejected the idea that Jews could become active and equal participants in society like anyone else. And the more Jews attempted to assimilate without actually converting to Christianity, the more they were resented. It is important to keep in mind, as historian Paula Hyman points out, that the anti-Semitism of the Dreyfus Affair "coexisted with a higher degree of integration of Jews within the institutions of French society than was possible in Germany or Austria at the time. Indeed neither Germany nor Austria could have had a Dreyfus Affair, since no German or Austrian Jew had achieved a parallel position in their respective armies."

In France, Jews were more visible. The Rothschilds, among other wealthy Jewish banking families, played a high-level role in French finance. In 1882, they were unfairly blamed for the collapse of the Union Générale bank, a Catholic financial institution that failed mainly due to mismanagement. A decade later, the Rothschilds and other Jews were again held responsible for the fiasco surrounding the unsuccessful attempt by a French company to construct the Panama Canal. Thousands of French investors lost money, and the Jewish bankers were a convenient scapegoat.

By the early 1890s, German intellectuals like Heinrich von Treitschke and the more radical Wilhelm Marr – who in 1879 coined the term "anti-Semitism" in a pamphlet entitled *Der Sieg des Judentums über das Germanentum* ("The Victory of Judaism over Germanism") – wrestled with the "Jewish Question." They decided that Jews were now a "race" rather than merely a religion, a position that in the new age of nationalism was in their view unacceptable. Thereafter, the loyalty of Jews toward the nation in which they resided was in doubt. From the left side of the political spectrum, Jews were attacked for being capitalists, and from the right for being "aliens."[*] For both groups, Jews, represented everything wrong with the modern world, and were a threat that could not be tolerated.

Many of these anti-Jewish ideas were brought together in a two-volume treatise by an obscure French journalist named Edouard Drumont. In 1886, Drumont attained fame with the publication of *La France juive*, promoted as the definitive chronicle of Jews in Christian France. While official government policy in the republican administration of the day was not anti-Semitic, the book was an immediate bestseller. Within a year of being released, it had sold more than one hundred thousand copies, had been reviewed in all of the major newspapers, and by 1912 had been translated into six languages and reprinted more than 200 times. Drumont, who in 1892 founded the popular anti-Semitic daily newspaper *La Libre parole*, modestly noted that his "only merit had been to put into print what everyone was thinking."

Hardly original, Drumont linked the medieval variety of anti-Semitism with its more modern social Darwinist racial variety. Jews were ugly, with hooked noses, body odour, and contorted fingers. They were spies, traitors, and carriers of disease. They were cunning and threatened France's future. All Jews, Drumont observed, were wealthy exploiters like the Rothschilds. He recommended creating the "Office of Confiscated Jewish Wealth," which in his estimation would generate for the country ten to fifteen billion francs. Finally, he expressed serious concern about the Jewish presence in the French military. How could Jewish soldiers and officers be entrusted

---

[*] Historian Eugen Weber writes: "In 1694 the Dictionary of the French Academy cited the word 'juif' (or Jew) specifically for its figurative uses: 'It is used for usurers, for the rich, for the wanderer — the juif errant — who has no home and no stability.' . . . In 1863, the great positivist dictionary of Émile Littré does not offer a very different image [in its definition for "juif"]: 'To be rich as a Jew, to lust for gold, to be a usurer.'"

with protecting the nation? And were they not preventing French officers from advancing? In response to Drumont's book, thousands of Frenchmen joined newly organized anti-Semitic organizations and the subject was frequently debated in the press.

Insulted by these derogatory public pronouncements and accusations, Ernest Crémieu-Foa, a Jewish army captain, challenged Drumont to a duel, a common way for French gentlemen to settle their differences. In the ensuing fight, both men were slightly wounded. Ironically, Captain Crémieu-Foa's second was Captain Ferdinand Walsin Esterhazy, who was soon to have a dramatic impact on Alfred Dreyfus's life. Another, more serious, duel took place between the anti-Semite Marquis de Morès, a railway promoter and the financial supporter of the Ligue nationale antisémitique de France, and Armand Mayer, another young Jewish captain. In the altercation, Mayer was killed. This duel in particular sent shockwaves through the Jewish community, and thousands attended Mayer's funeral in Paris.

In general, Jews in Paris and elsewhere were caught off guard by the rise of anti-Semitism in France. Because they saw themselves as French first and Israelites (as opposed to Jews) second, they tended to downplay its effect. Some years later, the Parisian Jewish writer Julien Benda explained the middle-class Jewish dilemma like this: "[We] wanted to prove that we were not an inferior race as detractors claimed, but on the contrary a race of the first order." Hence, they regarded the attacks of Drumont and others with a "silent disdain" and chose not to demonstrate publicly against it. Their logic was akin to the current dilemma in dealing with Holocaust deniers – whether to ignore or draw attention to them? Jews in France, for the most part, who regarded anti-Semitism as a German import, opted for the former tactic and hoped the movement would eventually dissipate.

At the beginning of the 1890s, anti-Semitism had lost some of its momentum, yet the rapid secularization of France worried many members of the Catholic and military establishments who considered Jews part of the problem. Paradoxically, a crisis of religious belief and secularism had also effected the Jewish community. Why, the Grand Rabbi Zadoc Kahn asked on Yom Kippur in 1899, did the "expression of sincere faith arouse indecent laughter?" Although conversion and intermarriage rates were low, synagogues were empty except on the High Holidays. When it was suggested to Geneviève Straus, the wife of Émile Straus, the Rothschilds' lawyer, that she might as well convert to Christianity, she responded cleverly, *"J'ai trop peu de religion pour en changer"* ("I have too little religion to change"). Emmanuel Berl, a French Jewish writer, recalled that his grandmother actually "apologized" for fasting on Yom Kippur, saying with a shrug that it was "for old times' sake." Berl, who admitted he did not know how to recite the Kaddish, the prayer for the dead, conceded that "the idea that I was a Jew, so loaded with meaning and with consequences, had for me a resonance that was sharp, but thin. For a long time, indeed, I did not register this important fact."

Mme Straus, Emmanuel Berl, and many others may not have had religion, but they did have faith. They believed with all their hearts in the principles of Liberty, Equality, and Fraternity. France had replaced the synagogue. Justice was divine. As a modern French Jew, Alfred Dreyfus understood such attitudes. Yet as he was to learn painfully one day in late 1894, life was often more complicated.

Death to Judas

THE ÉCOLE MILITAIRE, France's grand military academy, sits between Avenue de Lowendal and Avenue de la Motte Picquet, not too far from the Eiffel Tower on the left bank of the Seine. Its neo-classical buildings are hidden from public view by ten-foot-high stone walls. Outside, cafés and bars line the sidewalks, as in any Paris neighbourhood, and traffic is heavy all day long. Inside the walls exists a more disciplined world. As it was a century ago, young recruits are taught the code of the French military: honour, loyalty, and love of the republic.

It is possible, with permission from the commandant of the base, to visit the inner sanctum of the École. You enter off Avenue

Lowendal through a large guarded gate. Turning right, you walk down the cobblestone paths as young soldiers, men and women, march smartly by. Half a block farther, you arrive at another, smaller gate and enter into a magnificent and serene area with lush green fields. Ancient stone walls surround the yard on one side and a fenced area for equestrian training is located at the far end. More than a century ago, early in the morning on Saturday January 5, 1895, the courtyard was the scene of one the great injustices of European history.

The series of events that turned Alfred Dreyfus's life, and in time France itself, upside down began in late September 1894. Thanks to a loyal cleaning woman at the German embassy in Paris, Major Hubert-Joseph Henry of the French military's Statistical Section – the codename for the intelligence service dealing with espionage and counter-espionage – was given a small batch of papers that belonged to the German attaché, Lieutenant-Colonel Maximilien von Schwarzkoppen. Among those papers was a one-page hand-written memorandum, a *bordereau*, offering Schwarzkoppen information about a few innocuous military matters. This included "a note on a modification of Artillery formations," and "a note on the hydraulic brake of the 120 and the manner in which that part has performed." The notes were unsigned. Henry immediately deduced that there was a traitor, a French officer selling military secrets to the Germans. He aimed to solve the mystery, but the only way to accomplish that would be to match the handwriting on the *bordereau* with that of the culprit. From the type of information said to be available in the memorandum, Henry and others in intelligence decided that the traitor had to be a high-ranking artillery officer who was most likely connected to the general staff. In other letters Henry had intercepted from the German embassy, he was already aware that Schwarzkoppen was in contact with a French soldier referred to by him as "*ce canaille de D*" ("that scoundrel 'D'"). Within a few weeks, after comparing various handwriting samples, Henry and the members of the intelligence service had narrowed their list of suspects to one individual. He was an artillery officer, he had access to information in the *bordereau*, he had a last name with the initial "D," and, most notably of all, he was Jewish – Captain Alfred Dreyfus.

Following consultations with the minister of war, August Mercier, and the chief of staff, General Raoul de Boisdeffre, further investigations were undertaken by Major Marquis Mercier du Paty de Clam (Boisdeffre's cousin and an amateur handwriting expert). President Jean Casimir-Perier and Prime Minister Charles Dupuy were also advised of the case, and a professional grapholo-gist examined the incriminating evidence. All agreed that Dreyfus was their man. He was watched and then arrested on the morning of October 15.

A barrage of interrogations was next. Major du Paty De Clam hounded Dreyfus day and night for weeks. He was not initially told what crime he had supposedly committed, nor was he permitted to contact his family. Treated like a common criminal, he was forced to give handwriting samples and was locked up in the Prison of the Cherche-Midi. Dreyfus maintained his innocence throughout this ordeal; indeed, throughout his next five years of hell.

The public learned about the case at the end of October, when information about Dreyfus was leaked, most likely by Henry, to the anti-Semitic Edouard Drumont. On November 1, Drumont's paper, *Le Libre parole*, denounced Dreyfus as a "Judas," speculating that "the affair will be hushed up because this officer is a Jew. . . . He had made a full confession. There is absolute proof that he sold our military secrets to Germany." Other newspapers like *Le Figaro* were not as insulting, but they all assumed he was guilty – that much was "absolute, certain," – and that justice was being done.

Meanwhile, pressured to ensure that the military's case against Dreyfus was airtight, the Statistical Section began manufacturing evidence. This was the first of many such illegal forgeries designed to ensure that Dreyfus was found guilty with no hope of appeal. Intelligence officers also intimidated his wife, Lucie, who didn't know her husband's fate until two weeks after his arrest.

The court-martial trial took place in a closed session in mid-December. Over the course of four days, there were false accusations, absurd testimonies about Dreyfus's handwriting – which in reality bore no real resemblance to the handwriting in the *bordereau* – suggestions that he had been paid off by the Germans, and that he was a gambler and a womanizer. The most damning action, however, one that sealed his fate, took place after the last session had ended. The tribunal was contacted privately by War Minister Mercier and shown a "secret dossier" with more unsubstantiated information about Dreyfus and his possible connections to other spying activities. The seven members of the tribunal read the file and then returned it to the minister. Even considering the fragile state of French foreign affairs at the time and the fear of a future war with Germany, Mercier's actions were rather shocking. Only one thing was left for the tribunal to do: find Alfred Dreyfus guilty of treason and sentence him to degradation, deportation, and imprisonment for life on the penal colony of Devil's Island, off the coast of French Guiana.

Guards entered Alfred Dreyfus's cell in the Prison of Cherche-Midi at 7:30 in the morning. In preparation for the degradation ceremony, they loosened his epaulettes, brass buttons, and gold officer's braid, making them easier to remove once the time came. He was taken by a prison wagon to the École Militaire, where they made him wait in a small room for an hour. "During these long minutes," Dreyfus later wrote, "I gathered up all the forces of my being." He did have one conversation with Captain Charles Lebrun-Renault, which later returned to haunt him; Lebrun-Renault would claim that Dreyfus had confessed to his crime. The degradation ceremony had been planned to take place a day earlier, but at the last moment it had been changed to Saturday morning. In the view of many Parisians who had followed the events surrounding Dreyfus's case, it was "fitting that the traitor be publicly condemned on the Jewish Sabbath."

Out on the street, a noisy crowd had formed. "Death to Judas!" some of them shouted, "Death to the Jew!" Inside, waiting patiently in the cold, were about 4,000 French soldiers and a large contingent of invited guests. Among them were the famous French actress Sarah Bernhardt and the journalist Maurice Barrès of *La Patrie*, who would later remember the event as "more exciting than the guillotine." Watching and waiting, too, was a thirty-five-year-old Hungarian Jew named Theodor Herzl, who was covering the story for the Austrian newspaper the *Neue Freie Presse*. What he would see that day was to leave a lasting impression on him. "If such things could happen in republican, modern civilized France, a century after the Declaration of Human Rights," he later reflected, "then the Jews needed their own country, nation, and land."*

Finally the prisoner, Captain Alfred Dreyfus, with his head held high, was led out to the courtyard by a brigadier and four gunners, each with a sabre in hand. As the drums rolled, Dreyfus marched toward General Darras, who was mounted on his horse. The clerk of the court martial read the verdict of the military court. The general then held his sword high and proclaimed the indictment: "Alfred Dreyfus, you are no longer worthy of bearing arms. In the name of the people of France, we dishonour you." Weakened by the emotion of this terrible moment, Dreyfus, barely audible, replied, "Soldiers, an innocent man is being degraded; soldiers, an innocent man is being dishonoured. Long live France! Long live the Army!"

All that was left to do was the final humiliation. Sergeant-Major Bouxin of the Republican Guard stepped toward Dreyfus. He tore the decorations from his cap, the red stripes from his military pants, and the epaulettes from his tunic. Everything was tossed to the ground in a heap. He grabbed Dreyfus's sword and broke it over his knee, throwing it down with the rest of his belongings. With his clothes now in shreds, Dreyfus shouted this time, his voice catching, as he marched past the assembled troops, "Long live

---

* Despite the persistence of the myth, the humiliation of Alfred Dreyfus did not turn Herzl into a Zionist – he had already broached the "Jewish Question" well before Dreyfus had been arrested. In fact, he may have exaggerated its importance a few years later when he first made the connection in his writings. Still, it is reasonable to conclude that it did have a significant impact on his perception of the place of Jews in European society.

France! I am innocent! I swear it on the heads of my wife and my children!" The crowd outside could not be won over. "Coward," "Judas," "Dirty Jew," they yelled.

Reporting the event for *Le Figaro*, the journalist Léon Daudet wrote that Dreyfus appeared as a "rigid puppet, pale and weasel-faced . . . with a body . . . stripped piece by piece of all the things that had given him social value and rank. . . . He no longer had an age, a name, a complexion. He was the color of treason . . . a wreck from the ghetto." The assessment of the anti-Semitic newspaper *La Libre parole* was harsher still: "It was not a man being degraded for an individual error, but an entire race whose shame was laid bare." *La Patrie*'s Maurice Barrès felt the same way: Dreyfus was guilty because he was a Jew. "I need no one to tell me why Dreyfus committed treason. . . . That Dreyfus is capable of treason, I conclude from his race."

Back at his prison cell, Dreyfus wrote a brief letter to his wife: "In promising you to live until my name is rehabilitated, I have the greatest sacrifice that can be made by an honest man. . . . I seemed to myself to be the victim of an hallucination. Then, my torn, dishonored garments would bring me back to reality."

My Only Crime Is to Have Been Born a Jew

LOOKING BACK MORE THAN A CENTURY LATER at the case against Dreyfus, it is almost inconceivable that he could have been found guilty. The evidence was so slim that it is laughable. So how much of what transpired owed to the fact that Dreyfus was Jewish? The case, at least in the beginning, was not an anti-Semitic conspiracy, yet Dreyfus's background was enormously significant from the moment his name was first mentioned as linked to the *bordereau*. As Edgar Demange, the high-profile lawyer hired to defend Dreyfus, told Alfred's brother Mathieu after looking at the evidence, "If Captain Dreyfus were not Jewish he would not be at Cherche-Midi." Similarly, historian Martin Johnson concludes that "It is fair to say that the interested officers did not search for a Jewish traitor and then hit upon Dreyfus; however, given their mistaken assumption about the author of the *bordereau*, once Dreyfus's name was found upon the list of *stagiaires* [officers in training in the general staff] their prejudices led them to assume the worst."

For that matter, even most prominent members of the Jewish community in Paris assumed that Dreyfus was guilty as charged. Why would the army they revered so much convict an innocent man? They were blinded by their abiding faith in the values of the French Revolution. "Having emphasized for so long that they were French, they could scarcely assert with any vigour their right to be Jews," suggests historian Michael Marrus. "In this, as in everything else they did, they showed themselves truly to be the Frenchmen they claimed to be."

Yet they were wrong. It is difficult to dispute the wisdom of the Jewish writer Bernard Lazare. In November 1897, once more of the truth about the injustice of Dreyfus's trial had been revealed, he argued that "It was because [Dreyfus] was a Jew that he was arrested, it was because he was a Jew that he was tried, it was because he was a Jew that he was found guilty, and it is because he is a Jew that the voice of truth and justice is not allowed to speak out on his behalf."

Nonetheless, during the ensuing five long years that Dreyfus spent on Devil's Island, the Consistoire Central barely discussed his case. Its bourgeois members were afraid to act and felt that a show of Jewish solidarity would merely fan the flames of anti-Semitism. In general, they maintained that the "Dreyfusards," the so-called group of Jewish and non-Jewish lawyers, intellectuals, journalists, and family members who fought for Dreyfus's freedom, were merely exacerbating the Jewish position in France.

Léon Blum, a Dreyfusard and the first socialist and Jewish premier of France in 1936, later expressed his disdain for the official Jewish community's response to the affair. "They did not talk of the Affair among themselves; far from raising the subject they studiously avoided it," he wrote. "A great misfortune had fallen upon Israel. One suffered with it without a word, waiting for time and silence to wipe away the effects."

Equally outspoken were working-class East European Jewish immigrants in the area around the Rue des Rosiers, who were more familiar with anti-Jewish treatment than were their Parisian co-religionists. They condemned the injustice of the case, denounced the rise of anti-Semitism in the country, and in 1899 organized one of the lone Jewish public demonstrations during the affair.

As for Alfred Dreyfus himself, owing to his ardent faith in his country and in his deep-felt convictions in the principles of French justice, he did not believe that his Judaism played any part in his arrest and guilty verdict. So assimilated was Dreyfus that in his memoirs he does not even indicate that he was born a Jew. Likewise, in the numerous letters he wrote to Lucie from his prison hut on Devil's Island, he never mentioned that it was anti-Semitism that was mostly responsible for the tragic injustice done to him. (Although, knowing that his mail was being read, perhaps he did not want to antagonize his accusers further.)

Only once, upon returning to his prison cell after the verdict was announced, did he make reference to his status as a Jew. "My only crime is to have been born a Jew," he yelled to the commandant at Cherche-Midi. "To this a life of work and toil has brought me. Great heavens! Why did I enter the War School? Why didn't I resign as my people wished?" Later, when it was all over, Bernard Lazare wrote to Dreyfus, "You are more a Jew than you may think, with your incoercible hope, your faith in the best, your almost fatalistic resignation. This indestructible fund comes to you from your people; it is your people who have sustained you." If Dreyfus understood this, he never showed it.

He arrived on Devil's Island on April 14, 1895, after spending about a month at the prison on nearby Île Royale. Year after year, Dreyfus endured a terrible ordeal. His life, if one could call it that, consisted of treacherous heat, torrential rain, bugs, and malarial fever. At six each evening, he was locked in his small hut and not permitted to talk to the guards. The loneliness was unbearable. "Still alone, never speaking to a single person, never hearing a human voice," he wrote in his journal in June 1895. Within less than two years, his voice was nearly inaudible. He wrote constantly to Lucie and occasionally to his children. Months would often pass before he received a reply, but it was his letters from Lucie and the packages of food, tobacco, and coffee she sent that kept him alive. Month after miserable month, he was barely able to maintain his sanity.

In early September 1896, there were rumours in the French press – planted and encouraged by Mathieu Dreyfus, who was then looking for any way to publicize his brother's legal troubles – that Dreyfus had escaped from Devil's Island. The government denied the stories, yet it did have the desired effect: journalists again began writing about the case. The plan, however, backfired. Now officials were suddenly concerned about the possibility of escape of others from the penal colony, something which in fact was highly unlikely given the island's location in the shark-infested waters off French Guiana. Nevertheless, the order came from Paris that, starting immediately, Dreyfus was to be shackled in his bed at night. It was akin to a medieval torture.

On Devil's Island they built a special bed for him with an "iron bar of justice" so that his legs could be clamped in each night. Having no idea what had transpired back in France, he was shocked by the brutal treatment. In the morning his ankles were bleeding and his body covered with insect bites. "Yesterday evening I was put in irons," he wrote in his journal on September 7. "Why, I know not. Since I have been here, I have always scrupulously observed the orders given me. How is it I did not go crazy during the long dreadful night?"

Yet one more unnecessary precaution was taken to prevent Dreyfus from fleeing. His guards constructed a high wooden stockade around his hut, taking away his view of the ocean. "Nearly two years of this have worn me out," he wrote to Lucie. "I can do no more. The very instinct of life falters. It is too much for mortal man to bear. Why am I not in the grave? Oh, for that everlasting rest!"

J'Accuse

UNKNOWN TO DREYFUS, two events were unfolding back in Europe that were to offer him hope and transform his case into the "Dreyfus Affair" – the *cause célèbre* of France. Almost from the moment of Dreyfus's imprisonment, his brother Mathieu, assisted by Lucie, began a tenacious campaign, talking to sympathizers, listening to advice, searching for allies. In late 1896, Bernard Lazare, one of the original "Dreyfusards," helped initiate the Dreyfus Affair with the publication and wide distribution (paid for by Mathieu) of a controversial pamphlet: "A Judicial Error: The Truth about the Dreyfus Affair." It is interesting that Mathieu insisted that Lazare not focus on the anti-Semitic aspect of the case, but instead on the injustice of trial. In the second edition, released a year later, Mathieu had relented and Lazare included his view that anti-Semitism was at the root of the Affair.

Soon the two men were joined in their struggle by a distinguished group of Jewish and non-Jewish supporters that included Joseph Reinach, Léon Blum, Charles Scheurer-Kestner, the journalist Émile Zola, and Georges Clemenceau, then political editor of *L'Aurore*, and within a decade, the prime minister of France. This powerful and opinionated band of statesmen, intellectuals, and journalists did not always agree on tactics or strategy. In the early days of the fight, the family was especially wary of stirring up too much trouble. But as the years dragged on and Alfred Dreyfus languished away on Devil's Island, they decided to fight any way they could.

At the same time as Mathieu and his friends were pushing forward, the new head of the Statistical Section, forty-two-year-old Lieutenant-Colonel Georges Picquart, was investigating the Dreyfus case as well. Picquart was a bright, cultured, and slightly arrogant officer. He had taught Alfred Dreyfus at the military academy and did not personally like him. He had always assumed, like most everyone else in the army, that Dreyfus was guilty as charged.

That conclusion was challenged in the spring of 1896 when Picquart was presented with a new piece of the puzzle, another suggestive letter from the German embassy written on a piece of lightweight blue paper, thus called in the annals of the Dreyfus Affair the *"petit bleu."* This time, the document had a name on it: Commandant Marie-Charles Ferdinand Walsin Esterhazy – gambler, womanizer, scam artist, and all around lout. Acting cautiously, it took Picquart a few more months to arrive at the conclusion that Esterhazy and not Dreyfus was the traitor. A comparison of Esterhazy's handwriting and that found on the incriminating *bordereau* proved, in Picquart's opinion, to be a perfect match.[*] Yet when Picquart wrote his official report identifying Esterhazy as the real culprit, his superiors were not pleased. The generals were not about to admit that they had made a serious error. In this case appearance counted more than justice did. "What does it matter to you if this Jew stays on Devil's Island?" General Charles-Arthur Gonse, deputy-chief of staff asked Picquart. "If you don't tell anyone, no one will know." Picquart was shocked. "General, what you have said is abominable; I don't know what I will do, but I will not take this secret to the grave."

While the generals soon turned against Picquart, he continued his fight for justice. He was aided by Mathieu Dreyfus's decision in mid-November 1897 to name Esterhazy as the author of the *bordereau* in a public letter to the new minister of war, General Jean-Baptiste Billot. Mathieu's campaign was further supported at this time by the decision of Georges Clemenceau to publish in *L'Aurore* a series of pro-Dreyfus articles. Particularly effective were those penned by the flamboyant novelist Émile Zola.

---

[*] *Le Matin* published a photo of the *bordereau* on November 10, 1896, which Mathieu Dreyfus blew up into a poster and distributed widely. Many people who knew Esterhazy also made the connection that linked him to the memorandum. This included the son of Grand Rabbi Zadoc Kahn, who was employed by a lawyer attempting to collect a debt from Esterhazy. When he showed the rabbi a copy of the *bordereau* next to one of Esterhazy's letters, the rabbi refused to see the similarity and instead pointed to the fact that Esterhazy was a friend of the Jews because he had supported Ernest Crémieux-Foa in his duel with Edouard Drumont. "There is no officer more deserving of sympathy and respect than Commandant Esterhazy!" he admonished his son.

Finally this uproar led to an official inquiry into Esterhazy's activities, but the army maintained its view that he was innocent. In an appalling comedy of errors, a military court, ignoring all the evidence to the contrary, declared Esterhazy not guilty. The Affair reached its climax when Zola published his famous article in *L'Aurore* on January 13, 1898. Clemenceau had come up with its immortal title – "*J'Accuse*." In an approximately five-thousand-word public letter to the president of the republic (and anti-Dreyfusard) Félix Faure, Zola brilliantly dissected the government and military's cover-up. He ended the lengthy piece with a series of accusations against everyone from the former minister of war, General Mercier, to the handwriting experts, alleging that they had committed fraud, colluded in a massive cover-up, convicted an innocent man, and acquitted a guilty one. Needless to say, the article, on the front page of *L'Aurore*, with the huge headline "*J'Accuse*," was a sensation. Clemenceau could not keep up with demand and more than 200,000 copies of the paper were sold.

The government subsequently sued Zola for libel, and the well-publicized legal proceedings compelled Frenchmen to take sides in the Affair. In January and February of 1898 riots broke out, some with as many as 500 participants, pitting Dreyfusards against anti-Dreyfusards in Paris and in more than fifty other cities and towns around the country. In at least thirty instances, Jews were set on by mobs. Synagogues were stoned, and on February 11 about a thousand demonstrators attacked the Dreyfus family home (Lucie and the children were not there at the time). The most extreme violence occurred in the French colony of Algeria, where shops were burned and looted and Jews were assaulted.

Taking the view that the French order and justice they cherished so much would eventually prevail, most French Jews, though shocked by the hostility towards them, did not fight back. Many even blamed the Dreyfusards for stirring up so much trouble. Others, like Isaïe Levaillant, the outspoken editor of the weekly Jewish periodical *Univers israélite*, had already acknowledged that no matter what Jews believed, the Affair had profoundly altered social relations with their fellow citizens. "Truly, this lamentable story," he concluded in an article in mid-November 1897, "weighs heavily upon the situation of the Jews in France." At the same time, and quite naturally enough, the attacks on Jews strengthened bonds within the community.

The Affair played itself out during rest of year. There was worldwide reaction, most of which was negative. It took about eighteen more months of legal and political wrangling until at long last, in June 1899, the appeals court annulled Alfred Dreyfus's 1894 conviction and ordered him to stand trial again.

Still being tormented on Devil's Island, Dreyfus had only obtained snippets of information about the various events back in France. He was told on June 5, 1899, that his appeal had been successful. "My joy was boundless, unutterable," he wrote shortly after. "At last I was escaping from the cross to which I had been nailed for nearly five years, suffering as bitterly in martyrdom of my dear ones as in my own." The long voyage home took him first to the military prison at Rennes in northwestern France (for security reasons it was decided to hold his second trial in Rennes instead of Paris). Here, at long last, he saw his wife again. "It is impossible for words to express in their intensity the emotions to which my wife and I both felt at seeing each other again," he later remembered. "Joy and grief were blended in our hearts."

But Dreyfus's ordeal was not over yet. When he walked into the courtroom in Rennes, there was a collective gasp from the spectators. Five years on Devil's Island had nearly destroyed him. He was gaunt and weak. The years of forced silence made it difficult for him to talk. His teeth were rotted and he walked with a stoop, only the most noticeable effect of being chained in his bed each night. He was only thirty-nine years old but he appeared to be seventy.

Dreyfus again declared his innocence, and the court martial proceeded but slowly. Five years had added a lot of paper, most of it manufactured forgeries, to the "Dreyfus File." Each document had to be considered. All the key actors in this drama, the former war minister Mercier and the generals, did a good job of sticking to their original story. They denied any wrongdoing and maintained that the original verdict had been correct: Dreyfus was guilty, although they conceded that he might have been a partner with Esterhazy in the espionage. Some of them had told these lies so much they probably believed they were true.

The trial dragged on for five weeks. Despite their best efforts to expose the weakness of the circumstantial evidence, Dreyfus's lawyers, Edgar Demange and the famed litigator Fernand Labori, fell short. They attempted to have Schwarzkoppen, who was back in Germany, testify, but German officials would not allow it. All they would state for the record, as they had done earlier, was that the embassy in Paris had never had any dealings with Dreyfus. Sensing a slight shift in momentum, the chief prosecutor in his closing argument suggested that in lieu of life imprisonment, Dreyfus could be found guilty with "extenuating circumstances" and receive a lesser sentence. That was precisely what the judges did. Disregarding the absurdity of much of the evidence, the tribunal, by a vote of five to two, found Dreyfus guilty with "extenuating circumstances" and sentenced him to a total of ten years' imprisonment. He would have to return to Devil's Island for another five years.

Lucie, Mathieu, and the Dreyfusards were stunned. Alfred was merely resigned to his hopeless fate. Mathieu Dreyfus, who had spent the past five years of his life dedicated to this brother, had one last fight left in him. He appealed to the new republican president of France, Émile Loubet, for a presidential pardon. Several of the more radical Dreyfusards, such as Clemenceau, Jaures, Picquart, and Labori, who did not truly appreciate how Dreyfus had suffered, regarded such a tactic as a sign of weakness tantamount to conceding guilt. In what must be the most ironic statement of the Affair, Labori told Alfred that "he had betrayed Dreyfussism."

Mathieu, however, was attempting to save his brother's life. He knew that Alfred could not survive another five years on Devil's Island. Loubet signed the pardon on September 19, 1899. The worst of the Affair was over. All that was left for Dreyfus was an emotional reunion with his two children at his sister's home in Carpentras, where he could recuperate and begin his life again.

In the ensuing years, Dreyfus wrote his memoirs and worked to have the Rennes verdict overturned. That would take another six years. In July 1906, the Court of Appeals, after yet another examination of the evidence, finally declared him innocent. The original court-martial verdict of 1894 was quashed. Within a few weeks, at a quiet ceremony in the Cour Desjardins at the École Militare, not too far from main courtyard where the humiliating degradation ceremony had taken place twelve years earlier, Alfred Dreyfus was reinstated as a major and a chevalier of the Legion of Honour. Even Picquart, who, fittingly, was soon to be the new minister of war, came to watch. The event was, in Dreyfus's words, "a splendid day of restitution . . . for France and the Republic."

Still, some myths die hard. In 1994, a century after Dreyfus had been arrested, Colonel Paul Gaujac, head of the French army's history section, wrote in an article about the Affair in the army magazine *Actualité* that "Dreyfus's innocence is the thesis generally accepted by historians," casting some doubt on that innocence. So loud was the outcry from France's Jewish community and others that the Defence Minister François Léotard was forced to fire Gaujac. A year and half later, the newly appointed head of the army's historical service, General Jean-Louis Mourret, stood at a ceremony before 1,700 people and acknowledged for the first time that the army had indeed convicted an innocent man.

"The general said things before us that never had been said by a military man," remarked Jean Kahn, then president of the Jewish Consistoire Central. "That is indisputably progress."

Assimilation Is Not and Cannot Be a Solution
IN 1914, ON THE EVE OF THE FIRST WORLD WAR, Alfred Dreyfus, nearly fifty-five years old, was sent back into the field as an artillery officer. His son Pierre also fought, in the French Army that had

once condemned his father. Both men survived. Alfred Dreyfus not only lived to see the end of the war, he outlived nearly all of the Dreyfusards, including his brother Mathieu, who died of a heart attack in 1930. Standing by the coffin, Alfred, by then seventy-one, said in farewell to his brother, "*Je te dois tout*" ("I owe you everything").

In his old age, Dreyfus felt vindicated, as did most members of the Jewish community. There is no denying that the entire Affair with its anti-Semitic outbursts was unsettling, disruptive, and disillusioning for the assimilated Jewish community in Paris. The propaganda that portrayed them as rats and traitors was particularly hurtful. Apart from the riots in early 1898, Jews were barred from clubs, Jewish businesses were boycotted, Jewish children were bullied at schools, and Jews were publicly insulted with no repercussions.

This situation had convinced Bernard Lazare and a tiny minority of French Jewish intellectuals that the Dreyfus case was all about anti-Semitism. In the last years of his life, Lazare, who died in 1903, became an ardent Zionist. The Affair had shown him the "limits of assimilation." "Assimilation is not and cannot be a solution," he had written in the magazine *Zion* in late May 1897. Lazare had been impressed with the Zionist vision that Theodor Herzl outlined in his pamphlet *Der Judenstaat* ("The Jewish State"), published in 1896. He concurred with Herzl's view, quite contrary to accepted beliefs, that assimilation was both unattainable and detrimental to the future of the Jewish nation. As Herzl put it, "The distinctive nationality of the Jews neither can, will, nor must perish. It cannot, because external enemies consolidate it. It does not wish to; this it has proved through two millennia of appalling suffering. It need not; that, as a descendant of countless Jews who refused to despair, I am trying once more to prove."

Lazare assisted Herzl in having *Der Judenstaat* published in two parts in a French journal. The two men met in Paris during the summer of 1896, and Lazare struck Herzl as being a "fine intelligent French Jew." Lazare attended the First Zionist Congress, held in Basel, Switzerland, in August 1897, but soon after, he and Herzl had a falling-out in a dispute over Zionist tactics.

Few French Jews, including Mathieu and Alfred Dreyfus, would have agreed with the Zionist position or with Herzl's contention that assimilation was a failure. True, the Affair had put Jews in France in an impossible situation, as Mathieu had understood from the moment of Alfred's arrest. Any action would be interpreted by the anti-Semites as an attack by Jews on France, and that they could not accept. Besides, as loyal and obedient members of the bourgeoisie, the Jews hated public disorder like everyone else. Anti-Semitism, in the words of Paula Hyman, thereby "paralyzed the political will of Jews." But when Dreyfus was freed and then re-instated, their faith in France was restored. "The Affair . . . had particularly fortunate results for our co-religionists," declared the *Univers israélite*, "for in giving birth to the Dreyfus Affair, anti-Semitism had died." The tragic events of the Second World War and the role of the Nazi-collaborationist Vichy government in deporting thousands of French Jews would prove that statement tragically wrong. Among those deported was twenty-six-year-old Madeline Levy, the daughter of Jeanne Dreyfus, and granddaughter of Alfred. She died in Auschwitz from typhus in 1944 after being arrested a year earlier for resistance activities.

Anti-Semitism in France was not dead in 1906 – it was merely dormant. It is instructive that, when asked in a 1947 survey whether Jews were Frenchmen "like all the rest," only 37 per cent of those polled answered "yes."

Alfred Dreyfus did not live to see the calamity of the Second World War or the real effects of anti-Semitism. He died in 1935 at age seventy-five at his apartment in Paris surrounded by his family. Right up until the end, like most French Jews, he maintained his faith in the integrity of the French state. Yet unlike most French Jews, he equally subscribed to the conservative nationalism and militarism espoused by the anti-Dreyfusards.

"I was only an artillery officer, who a tragic error prevented from following his normal career," he had told one Dreyfusard many years earlier. "Dreyfus the symbol . . . is not me. It is you who created that Dreyfus."

Chapter Nine

THE GOLDEN LAND

New York, 1913

*The streets swarmed with Yiddish-speaking immigrants. The sign-boards
were in English and Yiddish, some of them in Russian. The scurry and
hustle of the people were not merely overwhelmingly greater, both in volume
and intensity, than in my native town. It was of another sort. The swing and
step of the pedestrians, the voices and manner of the street peddlers, and a
hundred and one other things seemed to testify to far more self-confidence
and energy, to larger ambitions and wider scopes, than did the appearance of
the crowds in my birthplace.*

       - ABRAHAM CAHAN, *THE RISE OF DAVID LEVINSKY*, 1917

America Was in Everybody's Mouth

AMIDST THE POVERTY AND THE PERSECUTION that defined Jewish
life in the Russian Pale of Settlement, there was one potential way
out of the misery – emigration to America, *di goldeneh medina*, the
Golden Land. Even in the northern regions, where there were no
pogroms after Czar Alexander II was assassinated in 1881, people
saved for their departure.

One day in the summer of that year, Jewish university students
visited a synagogue in Kiev, the site of an attack only days earlier.
The small group mounted the *bimah*, or dais, to address the congregation. Their message was clear: "We are only step-children
here, waifs to be trampled upon and dishonoured. There is no hope

for Israel in Russia. [Let us go to] a land beyond the seas which knows no distinction of race or faith, which is mother to Jew and gentile alike. . . . To America, brethren! To America!"

Mary Antin, who arrived in the United States in 1891 with her family, similarly recalled that in the Pale, "America was in everybody's mouth. Businessmen talked of it over their accounts; the market women made up their quarrels that they might discuss it from stall to stall . . . all talked of it, but scarcely anybody knew one true fact about this magic land."

That was beside the point. Excitement mounted, especially among the young, as letters arrived in Russia from the first group of emigrants, almost always exaggerating life in the New World, where the streets were paved with gold. (Later, when more negative letters were dispatched, or even when a small number of Jews returned to Russia, their reports of hardship in the United States were dismissed.)

It was such a letter mailed to Podberezy, a small village outside Vilna in Lithuania, that enticed Abraham Cahan to leave. An illiterate woman had brought the letter, sent to her by a relative, to the synagogue. She asked Cahan if he could read it. "The concrete details of that letter gave New York tangible form in my imagination," he recalled many years later. "The United States lured me not merely as a land of milk of honey, but also, perhaps chiefly, as one of mystery, of fantastic experiences, of marvelous transformations. To leave my native place and to seek my fortune in that distant weird world seem to be just the kind of sensational adventure my heart was hankering for."

Cahan was twenty years old in 1880, when he read that letter. He came from a distinguished family. His grandfather was a noted rabbi, and his father, Shakhne, was a *melamed* who taught young children the Torah and Talmud. Shakhne also had a small financial interest in a Vilna distillery and tavern, which allowed his family to live fairly comfortably. Cahan had a typical *shtetl* childhood. He attended *cheder*, and as a youngster showed promise as a Torah scholar. There was talk that he would follow in his grandfather's footsteps and become a rabbi.

But Cahan, a somewhat shy intellectual, though with a zeal for life and learning, had other ideas. His father, more progressive than his own parents, insisted that his son receive a secular education. This exposed Cahan to Russian literature and politics. In 1877, to avoid military service, he enrolled at the Jewish Teachers' Institute in Vilna. There, he discovered one of the great passions of his life: socialism. He immersed himself in Marxist thinking and sought new ways to express his Jewish identity within a Russian context. The pogroms of 1881 did not immediately concern him: "Even though the pogrom brought dread into the heart of every Jew, I must admit that the members of my group were not disturbed by it. We regarded ourselves as human beings, not as Jews. There was one remedy for the world's ills and that was socialism."

His involvement in Vilna with his young revolutionary friends introduced him to the anarchist ideology of Narodnaia Volia (The People's Will) and with Nikolai Chernyshevskii's revolutionary tract *What Is to Be Done?* (1863). After the St. Petersburg members of Narodnaia Volia engineered the czar's assassination in 1881 and were captured and executed, Cahan came under the scrutiny of the police. He considered fleeing to Switzerland, but as fate would have it he came into contact with the young Jewish socialists from Am Olam (Eternal People), who were embarking on a journey to establish a Communist utopia in America. Cahan decided that his future lay in the United States. One night in early 1882, he illegally crossed the Russian border into Austro-Hungary and began his journey to the New World.

Abraham Cahan was only one among many. Between 1880 and 1930, 2.5 million Jews came to America. In 1906 alone, 154,000 East European Jews arrived, and until the start of the First World War, about 100,000 people continued to come each year. Only the Germans, Italians, and Irish deposited more people on America's shores. By the time Congress passed its restrictionist immigration policy in 1924, Jews represented 9.4 per cent of all immigrants who had arrived in the United States. And by 1925 the country's Jewish population was four million – 3.5 per cent of the total population (just slightly less than the percentage today).

More significant is that in 1880, 75 per cent of the world's 10 million Jews lived in Eastern Europe and the Russian empire. Forty years later, this figure had declined to 46 per cent of a total of 15.5 million. In the same period, North and South America (mainly Argentina) had an increase from 3.5 per cent of the world's Jews in 1880 to 30 per cent by 1930.

The vast majority of Jews from the Pale of Settlement who came to America in the years before the First World War were, like Abraham Cahan, between the ages of fourteen and forty. Most were not excessively religious, since America was regarded by the Orthodox as being a *treyfa* (unholy or unkosher) land. Some, but not all, had already migrated from rural areas to urban centres. Yet unlike the erudite Cahan, most Jews who left the Pale after 1880 were not well-read or worldly. They were largely poor and superstitious tailors and peddlers seeking better economic opportunities for themselves and their families in the New World.

Leaving was never easy. "Just before train-time [mother] put the gold-clasped prayer book into my grip. . . . She seemed calm and resigned," recalled Marcus Ravage, who immigrated to New York in 1900. "But when the train drew into the station she lost control of her feelings. As she embraced me for the last time her sobs became violent and father had to separate us. There was a despair in her way of clinging to me which I could not then understand. I understand it now. I never saw her again."

No matter which part of the Pale they had come from, the journey to America was fraught with danger. Corrupt border guards and rail and ship agents made a taxing experience worse for immigrants with little money. From the northern part of the Pale, Jews smuggled themselves into East Prussia and made their way to Hamburg, where they could catch a ship to Liverpool or the United States. From the south, they headed toward Brody in Austro-Hungarian controlled territory (now western Poland). A small city,

Brody overnight was swarmed with more Jewish refugees than its impoverished community could handle. Day after day, they arrived in an endless stream. They required shelter and food, both of which were limited. People slept in barns and factories, adding to the turmoil.

Abraham Cahan reached Brody as part of a small group of Jews who had paid several peasants to guide them across the Russian border. Once he was in the city, he was able to find a place to sleep in a dilapidated house owned by a poor Jewish family – a man, his wife, and her twenty-year-old niece. So desperate was this family that during the evening, the woman offered her "small and skinny" niece to one of the men travelling with Cahan. "She is a poor orphan and wants to earn a few pennies," her aunt pleaded.

To continue on their journey, the Jews required a registration card and a train ticket, both of which cost money and were mired in bureaucratic regulations. Somehow, most of them managed to scrape together enough cash – probably close to one hundred dollars for a family of four, no small amount in the 1880s – to board a train for Hamburg or Bremen, where ships were waiting to take them to America. The process was stressful, chaotic, and a struggle for even the strongest of individuals.

Eastern and Western Civilization

WATCHING THIS MASS MOVEMENT of people with more than a little trepidation were the Jews of Western Europe as well as those already living in the United States. While organizations like Alliance israélite universelle did attempt to offer aid to the impoverished immigrants, it was inadequate. Charles Netter, an official of the Alliance who visited the city of Brody, recommended sending the Jews back to Russia. "The emigrants must be checked, otherwise we shall receive here all the beggars of the empire," he reported to the Paris office. That was a solution which no Russian Jew would have accepted.

Meanwhile, in New York and other eastern American cities, the predominately German-Jewish community – assimilated and acculturated to the same degree as were the bourgeois Jews in Paris – were understandably distressed about the impending immigrant onslaught.* How would their charities cope with the arrival of so many "backward" and "utterly helpless" people, as one American Jewish leader put it in late 1881? In their minds, the newcomers were "half-barbarians" and "wild Asiatics" who were about to upset the delicate balance of Jewish life in America, a life they had struggled to create and which they cherished. Even though, as will be seen, the German Jews themselves were targets of anti-Semitism, they, too, were guilty of stereotyping and using crass slurs to describe the Poles, Romanians, and Russians. Indeed, according to one theory it was German Jews in the United States who originated the derogatory term "kike," because so many of the East European Jews had last names that ended in the letters "ki."

When the German Jews had arrived from Europe in the 1830s and 1840s, they worked as merchants, bookkeepers, peddlers, and cigar makers. They were as industrious as any other immigrant group, and many, like the Straus family, found the economic opportunities in the New World to their liking. Lazarus Straus came to the United States from Bavaria. He made a respectable living as a travelling peddler and settled in New York City at the end of the Civil War. With his eldest son, Isidor, he gradually expanded his business and purchased a wholesale enterprise in a building owned by one Captain R.H. Macy. Within a few years, the Strauses had made enough money to pay off any debts they owed, buy Macy's building, and turn it into a department store. In time, they moved to larger quarters on Thirty-fourth Street and established Macy's as the "largest department store in the world."

---

* It is a myth that these "German Jews" were all actually from Germany. Many, as Arthur Hertzberg has pointed out, "came from other places in Central Europe such as Bohemia and Moravia; some came from Posen, the easternmost province of Prussia, which had been Polish until the late eighteenth century."

Lazarus and Isidore Straus were not the only successful German Jews. William Seligman in New York, Max and Harry Hart in Chicago, among others, became the kings of the American garment and clothing industry. A few, such as Joseph Seligman, Heinrich Lehman, Marcus Goldman, and his partner Samuel Sachs, emerged as successful investment bankers. By the 1880s, the wealthiest of them had left the slums of the Lower East Side for the grand brownstones of Fifth Avenue.

Like the Jews in France at the time of the Dreyfus Affair, the German Jews of New York, Philadelphia, and Chicago soon saw themselves as "Israelites" rather than "Jews." It was only religion, they maintained, that separated them from their Christian neighbours. And this religion had to be "progressive," in keeping with the modern world. Orthodox rules on food, dress, and synagogue rituals created in the Old World in an earlier more "primitive" era no longer were applicable. This was the underpinning of the Reform Judaism movement, which would have great success in the United States. Rabbi Bernard Felsenthal, a German Reform rabbi in Chicago, defined his personal identity like this: "Racially, I am a Jew, for I have been born among the Jewish nation. Politically, I am an American, as patriotic, as enthusiastic, as devoted an American citizen as it is possible to be. But spiritually, I am a German, for my inner life has been profoundly influenced by Schiller, Goethe, Kant, and other intellectual giants of Germany."

The great irony is that (as in France) the more the assimilated German Jews tried to transform themselves into "Americans," the more the Christian society they emulated resented them. From the perspective of the upper-class Gentile elite, it was one thing to do business with the German Jews, quite another to socialize with them. In June 1877, the investment banker Joseph Seligman and his family arrived for their vacation at Saratoga Springs in Upstate New York. When they attempted to check in at the luxurious Grand Union Hotel, where they had stayed before, they were told by the hotel manager that on the order of Judge Henry Hilton, the hotel's administrator, "no Israelites shall be permitted in the future to stop at this hotel." Seligman and other Jews protested, but Hilton stood firm. He believed, and probably rightly so, that the Grand Union was losing money because his Gentile clientele objected to the ever-growing number of Jews who frequented the hotel.

This episode marked the start of anti-Semitic restrictions faced by American Jews. During next two decades, wealthy and prominent German Jews found that social clubs were closed to them, elite private schools refused to admit their children, and they could not purchase property at various summer resorts. At hotels and beaches, Jews were met with signs declaring everything from "No Jews or Dogs Admitted Here" to the more subtle "Altitude 1,860 ft. Too high for Jews." Such anti-Semitism was rampant throughout the United States and Canada well into the 1950s. Jews responded by building their own resorts in the Catskills and creating such organizations as B'nai Brith and the Young Men's Hebrew Association (YMHA) for holding political, social, and cultural events. But they remained deeply troubled by this rejection, and the arrival of thousands of backward East Europeans could only make things worse. At least so they thought.

In a real sense, they were trapped. American Jews were sympathetic to the plight of the Russian Jewish immigrants from the Pale, yet they felt that their position would be further threatened if they were identified with these bizarre strangers from the East. Nor could they comprehend the desire of the Russian Jews to retain — admittedly in a new Americanized form — their Old World values, even for one generation.

A typical reaction was that of Morris Loeb, a professor at New York University and a son of Solomon Loeb, a founder of the investment bank Kuhn, Loeb, & Co. "The struggle with which we are faced is one between Eastern and Western civilization," he explained in a 1903 article. "Russian civilization is diametrically opposed to Western ideals. It is our duty to care for [the Russian Jew's] speedy Americanization even more than for his physical welfare. Experience has shown that the Jewish immigrant, once he was able to leave [Russia], could prosper without any outside help . . . but the entry to the land will be forbidden, if it becomes clear that they want to eat American bread, without acquiring American ways."

The East Europeans saw things differently.

Greeneh

AFTER AN EXHAUSTING AND USUALLY MISERABLE week-long ocean voyage, they landed in America without knowing where they would live or work. All they knew for sure was that, unlike Italians, Chinese, or Irish immigrants, they had no desire to return to their Russian homeland one day. (Between 1880 and 1930, approximately 95 per cent of all Jewish immigrants from Eastern Europe and Russia remained in America.) The first wave of Jewish immigrants during the 1880s arrived at Castle Garden in Battery Park at the south end of Manhattan. After 1890, when the U.S. federal government assumed control over immigration, Ellis Island, in the shadow of the Statue of Liberty, became the immigrants' first stop.

When he stepped off the ship at Castle Garden on June 6, 1882, Abraham Cahan could not believe he was truly in America. Many years later he described this moment in his classic immigrant novel *The Rise of David Levinsky*, published in 1917. "The magnificent verdure of Staten Island, the tender blue of sea and sky, the dignified bustle of passing craft – above all, those floating, squatting, multitudinously windowed palaces which I consequently learned to call ferries," Cahan wrote. "It was so utterly unlike anything I had ever seen or dreamed of before. It unfolded itself like a divine revelation."

This idyllic scene ended as soon as he entered the government processing centre at Castle Garden. There were medical examinations to endure as the newcomers were processed and lined up like cattle. Officials were especially on the look out for eye illnesses such

as glaucoma and for tuberculosis, regarded as the "Jewish disease."
"The stench was terrible," Cahan recalled about the night he spent
there, "as if a thousand cats were living there." In *David Levinsky*,
he compared inspectors to Cossacks. The Yiddish pun "a regular
keslgarten," – the word *kesl* means cauldron – came to depict the
tumult and filth of Castle Garden.

At Ellis Island, officials working in its mammoth hall used chalk
to mark the immigrants who required further checking by physicians: the letter "H" denoted a heart problem, "K" was for hernia,
"Sc" for scalp, and "X" for suspected mental problems. The new
arrivals faced a barrage of questions about the amount of money
they had and whether they had a job waiting for them. An 1885
law prohibited importation of contract labour, so even if they had
guaranteed employment it was often better to lie. It usually took an
entire day to get through the ordeal on Ellis Island, providing you
had no serious health problems.

Jewish organizations like the Hebrew Emigrant Aid Society
(HEAS), organized in New York in 1881, had good intentions but
not nearly enough financial resources to deal properly with the
immigrants' basic needs. As a result, conditions at the refugee centre
manned by HEAS officials on nearby Wards Island were terrible. The
food was dreadful and accommodations worse than on the ship.
One day, when a HEAS worker slapped an old woman, the tension
became palpable. That evening at dinner a fight broke out, forcing
the HEAS supervisor to call the police. In the ensuing melee, the
centre was nearly destroyed.

The society disbanded a few years later and it wasn't until 1902
that the Hebrew Immigrant Aid Society (HIAS) was established by
Russian Jewish immigrants themselves to help new arrivals. The
new society proved much more effective than its predecessor. By
then, too, many newcomers had relatives, husbands, and sons already
in the United States, which made the transition much easier.

Still, for the *greeneh*, as the immigrants were called in Yiddish,
adapting to life in America was difficult. They had few marketable

job skills and virtually none could speak a word of English. They were ripe for exploitation by the unscrupulous characters who waited beside the loading docks near Ellis Island. "The greenhorn is fair game and prey," wrote Elyakum Zunzer in his Yiddish poem of 1894, *For Whom Is the Gold Country?* "To every gang that's seen;/the policeman turns his head away;/how helpless the man who's green."

There were really only two options for most Jewish immigrants. First, they could search for shelter and a job in New York or in another nearby city. Chicago, St. Louis, Cincinnati, and even San Francisco attracted many of the newcomers. A second possibility, but one chosen by only a small minority, was to attempt to become a farmer on an agricultural colony established through the generosity of Baron Maurice de Hirsch, a wealthy European financier and philanthropist. This was an idea that found favour with the established American Jewish community.

"The Russian Jew first and foremost needs physical restoration which [he] can find on the American prairies and forests," argued the editors of *American Israelite*. "The atmosphere, the exercise, the food and feelings of security and liberty to be found there will restore and invigorate the immigrants." Similarly, a committee of New York rabbis suggested that, "in colonizing [the immigrants] and settling them as agriculturists, we feel . . . every moral assurance that they will become worthy citizens repaying the protection and rights they receive by becoming faithful and loyal denizens of the soil." Maybe so, but the pioneer life on the American prairies was a dream that could not be achieved. Sixteen Jewish agricultural colonies were established in the 1880s in Oregon, South Dakota, Kansas, and elsewhere, but only one, near Vineland, New Jersey, lasted for any length of time. The rest were dismal failures.

Jews had always been an "urban people," and nowhere more so than in the New World. More than 60 per cent of the Russian immigrants remained in the ever-expanding cities of the eastern seaboard, and the vast majority of them strayed no farther than a few miles from where they first landed. It was in New York's Lower East Side that the real story of Jews in America was born.

Where to live? For those who came in the mid-1890s and after, the answer was easy. You found the neighbourhood where your *landsmen*, your relatives and friends from your Old Country town or *shtetl*, had settled. And that meant the area of New York City that extended from the bottom of Manhattan north to Tenth Street and east past the Bowery. There you could find the streets – Grand, Delancey, Allen, Hester, Orchard, and Houston – that the Jews of Europe quickly made their own.

The chain migration was something to behold as Old World links were forged again in the Lower East Side. As Moses Rischin explained in *The Promised City*, his brilliant 1962 study of New York, "Galicians lived to the south between Houston and Broome, east of Clinton, on Attorney, Ridge, Pitt, Willett and the cross streets. To the west lay the most congested Rumanian quarter, 'in the very thick of the battle for breath' on Chrystie, Forsythe, Eldridge and Allen streets, flanked by Houston Street to the north and Grand Street to the south.... The remainder of the great Jewish quarter, from Grand Street reaching south to Monroe, was the preserve of the Russians – those from Russia, Poland, Lithuania, Byelorussia and the Ukraine – the most numerous and heterogenous of the Jewries of Eastern Europe."

Referred to then more often as the "Jewish Quarter" or the "Jewish East Side," the Lower East Side, was, in fact, never solely a Jewish area. German, Irish, and Polish immigrants were visible on its streets as well. Nor was everyone who resided there mired in poverty. Poverty was widespread, yet there were many Jews on the East Side who did quite well. They were, Hasia Diner points out in her historical survey of the neighbourhood, consumers "of new clothes, good food, pianos [and] vacations at Jewish hotels in the Catskills."

Sender Jarmulowsky, for instance, a Russian Jew who arrived in the first wave of immigration well before the pogroms of 1881, was a wealthy man by the mid-1870s, when he opened the doors to his thriving bank on Canal Street. A prominent East Side citizen, Jarmulowsky was elected the first president of the Eldridge Street Synagogue in 1887; he had also contributed a large amount of money for the synagogue's construction. Designed by a German Protestant, the sanctuary had a distinctive Moorish influence with its arched windows and Roman-style columns.*

For most, the poverty and misery they found in New York's overcrowded immigrant quarter was only intended to be a temporary haven, a place that, one day soon, they could leave for better prospects elsewhere in America.

Still, there was no denying the East Side's unique Jewish character. Abraham Cahan, who resided in the quarter for many years, depicted it as "the most densely populated spot on the face of the earth – a seething human sea fed by streams, streamlets, and rills of immigration flowing from all the Yiddish-speaking centres of Europe." Milton Reizenstein, the superintendent of the Hebrew Educational Society of Brooklyn observed in 1905 (perhaps with some exaggeration) that "no walls shut in this Ghetto, but once

---

* As the character of the East Side changed in the years after the Second World War and Jews gradually deserted the neighbourhood, the Eldridge Street Synagogue, like nearly all of the synagogues in the area, shut its doors and was left to decay. In 1986, a group of concerned citizens, both Jews and non-Jews, began a massive campaign to raise sufficient funds to restore the building. Fifteen years later, that process is ongoing, and much work is still needed to bring back the synagogue to its former grandeur. But it is invariably to Eldridge Street that Jewish visitors to New York flock to in an effort to connect with the area's past. Indeed, no other neighbourhood in the United States, perhaps in the world, remains so fixed in the Jewish imagination as the Lower East Side, a fact celebrated in song, plays, movies, and television shows. The area was even celebrated in 1991 episode of the animated TV show *The Simpsons*. In a takeoff of the 1927 film *The Jazz Singer* (starring Al Jolson), in which a young man struggles with his Jewish identity and his father's traditional outlook, so too does Krusty the Clown. Lisa and Bart Simpson help bridge the gap between Krusty, who was born "on the Lower East Side of Springfield," and his father, Rabbi Krustofski. As Hasia Diner rightly observes, "no other space could have been invoked by Krusty, and the cartoon's creators, than [the Lower East Side]. No other space would have served as well to clue the audience in to the Jewish content and the depth of Krusty's travail."

within the Jewish quarter, one is as conscious of having entered a distinct section of the city as one would be if the passage had been through massive portals, separating this portion of the lower East Side from the non-Jewish districts of New York." For Jacob Riis, a New York journalist who wrote about the area in the 1890s, the Lower East Side was simply "Jewtown."

Besides the people themselves, the neighbourhood's most distinctive feature was (and still is) the rows and rows of crowded tenement housing. The structures had been built, before the immigrants arrived, in a "dumbbell" shape plan. The typical East Side tenement was six to seven storeys high on a small lot. A New York journalist writing in 1888 described them as "great prison-like structures of brick with narrow doors and windows, cramped passages and steep rickety stairs. In case of fire they would be perfect death-traps, for it would be impossible for the occupants of the crowded rooms to escape by the narrow stairways, and the flimsy fire-escapes."

Each floor of a tenement had four apartments, with about three to four rooms in each. But only one or two rooms in each apartment received direct light and air from the street or from a small yard at the back of the building. The residents shared toilet facilities, with one toilet for every two families. The ventilation from narrow air-shafts that ran through the centre of the building actually added to the general discomfort by spreading foul smells.*

As Dr. George Price, himself an immigrant who became a New York sanitary inspector, reported in 1908 after an inspection of a thousand tenements that housed about ten thousand Jewish families, "The rooms were damp, filthy, foul and dark; the air was

---

* Maurice Fishberg, a medical examiner with the United Hebrew Charities, reported in 1905 that "the air that [the shaft] does supply is foul, because it contains the air coming from the windows of the other apartments (there are as many as sixty windows opening in some of these air-shafts). Moreover, the air-shaft is used by some as a convenient receptacle for garbage and all sorts of refuse and indescribable filth thrown out of the windows, and this filth is often allowed to remain rotting at the bottom of the shaft for weeks without being cleaned out."

unbearable, the filth impossible, the crowded conditions terrible, particularly in those places were the rooms were used as work-shops. The life of the children was endangered because of the prevailing contagious diseases, and children died like flies." More than a century later, the musty, dark, and damp atmosphere remains in the tenement at 97 Orchard Street, which was opened in 1988 as part of the Lower East Side Tenement Museum. The claustro-phobic distress endured by its residents is palpable.

Despite the cramped conditions, many immigrants took in boarders to help pay the rent; others used rooms in their homes to work ten to twelve hours a day as tailors, shoemakers, and seam-stresses for paltry wages. A *New York Tribune* news item in 1900 also noted the proliferation of Lower East Side brothels, or "red-lamp places" as the paper called them, popular with those who had first-floor apartments. Nine years later, a government survey found that in New York, there were more than two thousand prostitutes, 75 per cent of whom were Jewish. In many cases, poverty, pressure from pimps, and even the women's own families forced them into a life in the brothels.

Money was indeed hard to come by. During the late 1890s, a husband and wife toiling over a sewing machine sixty or seventy hours a week might have brought in twenty-five dollars. After the cost of renting the sewing machine and the rent for their apart-ment, the couple would be left with only about eight dollars. This meant that they subsisted on bread, coffee, tea, herring, and a small amount of inexpensive meat, milk, and potatoes.

Out in the streets, there was a teeming mass of human activity. The Old World *shtetl* marketplace had been transplanted to Delancey and Hester streets, where amidst the stalls, crowds, and peddlers with pushcarts there was nothing you could not buy or barter for. It was, as the turn-of-the-century journalist Hutchins Hapgood put it, an "eager, militant business, expressing itself in eternal haggling over a thousand kinds of diminutive articles." Abraham Cahan's protago-nist David Levinsky found the life of a Lower East Side peddler a challenge: "Often I would load my push-cart with cheap hosiery, collars, brushes, hand-mirrors, note-books, shoe-laces, and the like. . . . I also learned to crumple up new underwear, or even to wet it somewhat, and then shout that I could sell it 'so cheap' because it was slightly damaged. . . . I hated the constant chase and scramble for bargains and I hated to yell and scream in order to create a demand for my wares by the sheer force of my lungs."

The children who grew up in the ghetto, who spoke English and embraced the American culture as their own, found all the adventure they could wish for on the streets. "There were gang wars to be fought, policemen to annoy and outwit, and sentimental couples to be teased and ridiculed," recalled Samuel Chotzinoff about his childhood in the Lower East Side. "There were great games of leave-e-o, prisoner's base, and one-o'-cat to be played, the last limitlessly peripatetic, so that one might start to play on East Broadway and wind up, hours later, on the Bowery."

Not every Jewish adult male immigrant in New York was a peddler, of course, but in 1900 there were, by one estimation, about twenty-five thousand plying the streets, selling and buying rags, bottles, old clothes, and used furniture. Jews with skills as artisans worked as shoemakers, bookbinders, and cigar makers, among other trades.

Mostly, though, the Russians and East Europeans gravitated toward work in New York's growing garment industry. Many of them already had the required skills (or took jobs where none was needed), and a large number of the factories were owned and operated by German Jews who felt an obligation to hire their struggling co-religionists. Moreover, the garment trade, especially in women's wear, was booming. In 1880, the business in the United States was worth about $60 million a year; by 1920 that figure had jumped to $900 million. The capitalization was low – the necessary machinery was not expensive, and the labour was cheap and desperate. For those entrepreneurs willing to take a risk, the rewards could be high indeed.

Without trade unions to protect the immigrants, exploitation was a fact of life in New York "sweatshops," as the factories were rightly called. Sub-contracting, which allowed workers to set up small operations in their tenement houses, only made matters worse. In 1906 there were likely sixty thousand children in New York employed in the city's sweatshops earning no more than $1.50 for sixty hours of work each week.

"Every open window of the big tenements . . . gives you a glimpse of one of those shops," reported Jacob Riis in his 1890 study of the Lower East Side. "Men and women, bending over their machines or ironing boards at the windows, half-naked. . . . The road is alike a big gangway through an endless workroom, where vast multitudes are forever laboring. Morning, noon, and night, it makes no difference; the scene is always the same." Similarly, in a *McClure's Magazine* article about sweatshops, journalist Ray Stannard Baker, then just starting his brilliant career, wrote that the immigrants "dared not stop working, knowing that there were plenty of other men ready instantly to take their places; and the contractor himself the victim of frightful competition and the tool of the manufacturer, always playing upon their ready fears, always demanding a swifter pace. . . . Nowhere was there, apparently, any relief for this ferocious waste of human life."

In some rare cases, it was possible for an East European immigrant to rise above the squalor. Louis Borgenicht was an Austro-Hungarian immigrant who arrived in the United States in 1881 at the age of twenty. At first, he worked in the East Side as a peddler, selling everything from herring to bananas to socks. He and his wife started making women's aprons, which he sold as well. The aprons were popular, and Borgenicht wisely looked for new opportunities. Working from early in the morning to late into the evening, he and his wife, along with a young girl they hired to assist them, began churning out children's clothes. And the profits soon materialized.

By 1892, a decade after had moved to America, he was operating a small factory with twenty employees and had obtained a contract for girls' dresses from Bloomingdale's department store. But he had expanded too fast, and within months had gone bankrupt.

Undeterred, he started over with a small clothes shop and gradually built up his manufacturing once again. This time he was successful. Known thereafter as "the king of the children's dress trade," Borgenicht employed 150 people and had annual sales of $1.5 million. He moved out of the East Side to a fashionable uptown neighbourhood and vacationed with his family in the Catskills.

Louis Borgenicht's experience was not typical. Most sweatshop workers did not get ahead, and slowly the immigrants began to organize themselves. The United Hebrew Trades was formed in 1888, but its achievements were few. Many of the workers, particularly those who arrived in the first wave, were resistant to the socialist principles pushed on them by more radical union leaders. Later, after 1900, many of the Jewish immigrants had been imbued with the spirit of the Bund, the Jewish worker's political movement created in Russia in 1897, which inspired them to fight for their rights in America. When immigrants in the garment industry did eventually accept some socialist principles about the need for them to speak with one clear voice, it was because, as Arthur Hertzberg has pointed out, the socialist leaders offered them hope that their miserable lives would improve.

At any rate, the radical element died away once the more moderate American Federation of Labor, under the leadership of Samuel Gompers, of a Dutch-Sephardi background, organized large numbers of workers through its affiliate the International Ladies Garment Workers' Union (ILGWU). But the road to collective bargaining and trade-union representation met with violence, disappointments, and the industry owners' stubborn resolve to stop the unionization process in any way they could – legal or otherwise. Starting in 1909, bitter labour disputes broke out in the East Side as workers attempted to assert their right to fair wages and better working conditions. One of the first protracted strikes involved twenty thousand shirtwaist makers, the majority of whom were young Jewish women. For nearly three months, they protested against their low wages, terrible working conditions, and unfair practices such as being charged for sewing-machine needles, power, supplies, the chairs they sat on, and their lockers. The strike ended with a partial victory for the women.

This was merely the beginning of the garment workers' battle. In July 1910, about sixty-five thousand cloakmakers walked off their jobs demanding better conditions and pay. On the picket lines, they faced strikebreakers and bullies, who thought nothing of breaking a worker's head with a metal pipe. The dispute drew in influential members of the Jewish community, who hired Louis D. Brandeis, then a labour lawyer in Boston (and just six years later the first Jewish judge appointed to the Supreme Court), to negotiate the so-called "Protocol of Peace" that ended the walkout. Again the workers did not win everything they hoped for, but Brandeis did obtain a contract for them with a fifty-hour workweek, paid holidays, and better conditions.

Enforcing these new rules was another matter entirely, as the employees of the Triangle Shirtwaist Factory discovered on Saturday, March 25, 1911. It was the worst moment in the history of the New York garment industry. That day, about six hundred young Jewish and Italian women – most between the ages thirteen and twenty-three – and fifty men were working at the Triangle Shirtwaist Company. Located near Washington Square, the factory was housed in a ten-storey building. Inside, among the rows of machinery, were strewn piles of discarded material and rags.

A careless smoker started the fire at about five o'clock in the afternoon. The workers on the top few floors found themselves trapped behind locked steel doors, unable to escape. (The doors were intended to prevent workers from using the outdoor washroom facilities.) In the time it took to bring the fire under control, 175 employees, mostly women, suffocated or jumped to their deaths. The firemen's ladders were only high enough for the seventh floor; for those on the upper three floors, there was no hope. And so, instead of facing death in a raging inferno, they jumped. The firemen's nets could not save them in a fall from such a height.

"Screaming men and women and boys and girls crowded out on the many window ledges and threw themselves into the streets far below," reported the *New York Times* the next day. "They jumped with their clothing ablaze. The hair of some of the girls streamed up aflame as they leaped. Thud after thud sounded on the pavements." It was later revealed that the company had violated the city's fire codes and regulations. Across the East Side, people mourned and compared the treatment of the Triangle workers to that received by Jews during the Spanish Inquisition.

Der Forverts

IT WAS THE PLIGHT OF THE WORKERS in the other Lower East Side factories that tugged at the heart of Abraham Cahan and motivated him to take action. Still, in 1882, he could not have guessed that the bitter struggle of the New York Jewish immigrants would occupy his life for the next six decades.

As historian Nathan Glazer suggested in 1957, "if one had to select a single person to stand for East European Jews in America, it would be Abraham Cahan." In many ways, he was certainly one of them.

He had arrived in America with an education and a thirst for knowledge. Almost immediately, he enrolled in English-language classes and soon he could read and write. He had already started teaching himself English during his voyage to the United States (using an English-Russian dictionary). His first job was at Stachelberg's cigar factory on South Fifth Avenue (now West Broadway) stripping tobacco. He also tutored young children and freelanced for a Jewish newspaper back in St. Petersburg, supplying stories about the Lower East Side. Cahan's socialist views remained strong. Through contacts with workers at the cigar factory, he eventually attended a Jewish labour meeting. He quickly understood that there was no point in addressing the workers in Russian, a language most of them did not use. In order to reach the Jewish masses, Cahan immediately recognized the power of Yiddish to convey his message.

In the late summer of 1882, Cahan was the featured speaker at a labour rally in a small hall at the back of a German saloon on East Sixth Avenue. Before an audience of four hundred people, he delivered in Yiddish a classic Marxist speech for two hours on the "theory of the class struggle and the inevitability of the coming of socialism." It was at a second lecture held some weeks later that he met Anna (Aniuta) Bronstein, an immigrant from Kiev. She shared his intellectual passions, and the two were destined to be lifelong partners. They were married two years later. They opted not to have children, as Cahan needed to immerse himself in his work and his writing. Anna stood dutifully by his side, offering sound advice at all times.

Cahan continued with his English-language studies during the 1880s. He read newspapers, books, whatever he could get his hands on. In time, he qualified as an English teacher at the YMHA night school, an impressive achievement for any newcomer, and gradually he began freelancing for such newspapers as Joseph Pulitzer's *New York World*, contributing pieces on Russian politics and stories about life in the East Side. He continued speaking publicly, too, making a name for himself as a mind to be reckoned with.

In a speech he gave after a May Day parade in 1890, he told the assembled crowd that "this imposing demonstration . . . [is] the beginning of the great revolution which will overthrow the capitalist system and erect a new society on the foundation of genuine liberty, equality and fraternity." Whether he actually believed this is debatable. Throughout the next decade, he adopted a more moderate socialist approach, one more in line with British Fabianism than Russian Bolshevism. Cahan always had been a humanitarian, an attribute that best characterized his political position. But his humanitarianism was mixed with a secular version of Judaism. For Cahan, and like-minded Jewish socialists, socialism was a religion, or as historian Moses Rischin noted many years ago, "the poetry of the oppressed miserable workman."

The first sign of Cahan's shift from anarchism and rigorous Marxist principle appeared in a wide range of articles he contributed to the *Arbeiter Zeitung* (the Worker's Newspaper), the Yiddish weekly of the Socialist Labor Party. It was in this work that he mastered the no-nonsense Yiddish writing style for which he would become famous. From 1894 to 1897, Cahan also edited the newspaper, but was compelled to resign after a falling-out with Daniel DeLeon, the Socialist Party's more doctrinaire Jewish (Sephardi) leader.

These events led in turn to the establishment in 1897 of a more moderate social democratic Yiddish newspaper by the leading lights of the New York Jewish labour movement: Joseph Barondess, a vocal and popular spokesman and union organizer; Morris Hillquit (Moshe Hilkowitz), a famed Lower East Side labour leader and politician; Louis Miller, a respected social democratic writer and journalist; and Cahan. The paper was to be called *Der Forverts — The Forward —* and Cahan was chosen as its first editor.

The first edition of the *Forward* hit the streets of New York on April 22, 1897. From the start, Cahan wanted to make the newspaper both relevant and populist; the other members of the board envisioned it more as an organ for moderate Jewish socialists. This difference of opinion led to Cahan's resignation after eight months, though he would be back.

Despite the financial and emotional heartache it caused him, leaving the *Forward* was likely the best thing that ever happened to Cahan's career. Almost immediately after, Cahan began freelancing for the New York *Commercial Advertiser*. It was a business-oriented and pro-Republican newspaper, but the editor, Henry Wright, who wanted to give his paper a literary appeal, took a liking to Cahan and did not care about his socialist politics. As for Cahan, he needed the work.

As luck would have it, the new city editor of the *Advertiser* was thirty-one-year-old Lincoln Steffens, just beginning his distinguished career as a journalist renowned for his exposés of political corruption. Steffens had heard of Cahan and appreciated the struggles of East Side immigrants more than most American journalists. Cahan now reported on crime and politics and interviewed a range of notable American personalities, including President William McKinley, Theodore Roosevelt, Richard Croker, the boss of Tammany, the powerful New York Democrat organization, Buffalo Bill, and Russell Sage, the railway and grocery magnate. He wrote about the immigrant experience as well, except now as an observer, which gave his work a new outlook. In the countless articles Cahan prepared for the *Advertiser*, he captured the spirit and excitement in New York City generated by the newcomers. For its day, Cahan's writing, whether about peddlers, synagogues, or Jewish holidays, was fresh, colourful, and informed.

Hutchins Hapgood, one of the bright young journalists at the *Advertiser*, naturally sought out Cahan's assistance for articles he was writing on life in the East Side. Cahan guided him through the neighbourhoods and introduced him to the right people. The result was Hapgood's 1902 book *The Spirit of the Ghetto*, which captured the complexities of Jewish life in New York. Unlike other American writers, who dwelled on the misery and disease experienced by the immigrants, Hapgood had found something positive to write about. "The Jewish quarter of New York is generally supposed to be a place of poverty, dirt, ignorance, and immorality – the seat of the sweatshop, the tenement house, where 'red-lights' sparkle at night, where the people are queer and repulsive," he wrote. But in spending time in the ghetto, Hapgood argued that he also found "charm . . . in men and things there." Visiting an East Side café he watched a group of elderly Orthodox Jewish men. "With their long beards, long black coats, and serious demeanor, they sit about little tables and drink honey-cider, eat lima beans and jealously exclude from their society the socialists and freethinkers of the colony who, not unwillingly, have cafés of their own. They all look poor, and many of them are, in fact, peddlers, shop-keepers or tailors; but some, not distinguishable in appearance from the proletarians have 'made their pile.' Some are

Hebrew scholars, some of the older class of Yiddish journalists."

Cahan had discovered that "charm" for himself many years earlier. Some time before he become involved with the *Forward*, he had begun his foray into fiction writing with short Yiddish stories about immigrant life. In 1892, he happened to meet the noted American writer William Dean Howells, the one-time editor of the magazine *Atlantic Monthly* and a pioneer of American social fiction. He was best known for his 1885 novel *The Rise of Silas Lapham*. Howells, like Steffens and Hapgood, had stumbled upon the Lower East Side, and this eventually brought him to Cahan, already known as the best Yiddish journalist of the day. The two men hit it off and kept in touch.

Cahan continued to write short stories exploring various aspects of ghetto life, except now he wrote in English. Several of his pieces, including "A Providential Match" and "A Sweatshop Romance," were accepted for publication in respected literary magazines. And with Howells's encouragement and contacts, Cahan was able to publish his first English-language novel in 1896, *Yekl: A Tale of the New York Ghetto.*[*]

The novel was the story of typical immigrant life in America and the conflict between the Old and New Worlds. Its theme, the

---

[*] Howells first submitted *Yekl* to *Harper's Weekly* and other magazines in an attempt to have it serialized. But the response he received was negative, which typified the attitude to immigrant stories at the turn of the century in mainstream publications. In fact, *Yekl*, which was published by Appleton's – the same company that published Stephen Crane's *The Red Badge of Courage* in 1896 – did not sell well. American women, the most avid readers then, were not interested in the novel, and Jewish women, who might have been, did not buy English-language books in any large number at the time. "The life of an East Side Jew wouldn't interest an American reader," wrote one *Harper's* editor to Howells. Another editor at a different magazine added, "You know, dear Howells, that our readers want to have a novel about richly-dressed cavaliers and women, about women, about love which begins in the fields while they're playing golf. How can a novel about a Jewish immigrant, a blacksmith who became a tailor here, and whose wife is ignorant interest them?" It took until 1975, decades after Cahan had died, before *Yekl* finally got the audience it deserved, when the novel served as the basis for the well-received Hollywood film *Hester Street*.

problems of acculturation, assimilation, and culture-clash. Cahan's protagonist is Yekl, or Jake Podgorny, who arrives on his own in America. Three years later, his wife, Gitl, and their child join him. But in the brief time he is alone, Jake has been transformed. When he first sees Gitl at Ellis Island, he is shocked at the sight of his Old World *shtetl* wife, who now looks simple and backward. Jake and Gitl's marriage cannot be saved, and they divorce. Jake believes he has found what he is looking for in a second marriage to an "American" woman, but that, too, fails to work out the way he had hoped. Like many of Cahan's stories, *Yekl* is a morality tale that revolves around love and Old World links that can never be broken, not even in faraway New York's Lower East Side.

William Howells wrote a favourable review of the novel for the *New York World* and was one of the first to recognize Cahan's unique position as a man who belonged to three distinct cultures. "He sees things with American eyes, and he brings in aid of his vision the far and rich perception of his Hebraic race," Howells observed. "While he is strictly of the great and true Russian principles in literary art." Even if *Yekl* did not become a bestseller, Cahan believed that he had now established himself as a novelist to be taken seriously. His success as a fiction writer, limited as it was, did give him a certain credibility and status among the Lower East Side intellectual community. For unlike most Jewish writers, Cahan was comfortable working in both Yiddish and English.

By 1900, Cahan had started freelancing again for the *Forward*, contributing articles and short stories. The ideological antagonisms of a few years earlier had been forgotten. In reality, the *Forward*'s readership had declined, partly due to the increase in competition for readers from other Yiddish publications, and partly because the newspaper still did not sufficiently address the concerns of East Side residents. The paper's board decided that the *Forward* needed a new look and focus, and there was no one better to accomplish that than Cahan.

He was, not surprisingly, wary of the offer. He did not want to give up on his literary career, nor did he believe he would have the independence necessary to really change the newspaper. Yet after protracted negotiations, and despite Anna's objections, Cahan rejoined the *Forward* as editor in the spring of 1902. And while there was one brief dispute near the end of his first year back, which caused Cahan to leave the paper for a few months, he was associated with the *Forward* for the next five decades. He continued to write novels – most notably *The White Terror and the Red: A Tale of Revolutionary Russia* in 1905, and his best known novel, *The Rise of David Levinsky*, in 1917 – but his main focus was the newspaper. He almost single-handedly established the *Forward* as the most successful Yiddish daily in the world.

In 1903, the newspaper's daily circulation was approximately 7,500; a decade later it had increased to 113,000; and a decade after that to a high of 250,000 (New York's Jewish population was by then 1.5 million). By the early twenties, the paper, thanks mainly to Cahan's talent and effort, had paid off its debts and the business was valued at $200,000. Located near Seward Park on the corner of Division Street and Rutgers Square, the original ten-storey Forward Building, with its name spelled out in Hebrew letters and a distinctive clock at its top, was the Lower East Side's most prominent landmark. It is fitting that the first thing the visitor sees today on entering the *Forward* editorial offices, now located on East Thirty-third Street, is a portrait of Cahan. He looks serious and sombre, as if he has much work to do. His round wire-framed glasses rest firmly on his nose, his thick bushy moustache is trimmed, and his hair slightly tousled.

Cahan's main goal was to make the paper relevant to his immigrant readers. "If as a Socialist you want to influence real live men you must first become a live man yourself," he stated in a 1911 interview. As editor of the *Forward*, he grasped the important role the paper could play "as an instrument of Americanization." It was his task, as he saw it, to lead and guide the process of *oysgegreent*, the "de-greening" of the Jewish immigrants and helping them adjust to the New World.

Through the *Forward*'s pages, the newcomers learned about the world beyond the East Side. "My father revered the *Forward*," remembered the late author and critic Alfred Kazin. "When he exultantly read from the *Forward* to me, with its news of the international working class, he was not alone. He was full of pride in what he was reading aloud, positively worshipping every item." Cahan ensured there were reviews of American plays and music as well as stories about national and international events, even coverage of sex scandals and crime.

He encouraged immigrants to participate in the political process. When he first arrived in the United States, Cahan had witnessed for himself how the corrupt Tammany machine manipulated ignorant Jewish voters. He aimed to educate them about political America and about becoming active citizens of a democracy. Even if his approach was paternalistic, he succeeded in this endeavour. Indeed, between the education the immigrant workers received on the shop floor, from their union organizers, and from the *Forward*'s columns, they quickly made their votes count. In large part, this accounted for the election in 1914 of Meyer London – who at fifteen years old had come to New York from the Ukraine and later become a lawyer – as the first Jewish socialist in the U.S. Congress.

The daily struggle of life in the East Side was immediately captured in 1906 in one of Cahan's best innovations as editor of the *Forward*. To help his readers understand the New World, he created an advice column. Readers could write anonymously with their multitude of problems and he would supply them with solutions and answers. The column was called "A Bintel Brief" ("a bundle of letters"), and almost overnight it became the *Forward*'s most popular and enduring section, running for the next sixty-five years.

One of the first columns dealt with a letter from an immigrant who had been in New York for only five weeks. He had found a job, paid his room and board, and had a few dollars in his pocket.

Yet he felt guilty about having left his blind father back in the Pale. "I want you to advise me what to do," he wrote to the *Forward*'s editor. "Shall I send my father a few dollars for Passover, or should I keep the little money for myself?" Cahan's reply was typical: "The answer to this young man is that he should send his father the few dollars for Passover because, since he is young, he will find it easier to earn a living than would his blind father in Russia."

Soon, letters by the hundreds poured in, many more than the newspaper could print. Cahan, who in the first few years answered all the letters himself, became a maven on morality, marriage, and child rearing. On one occasion, a young widow wrote in to complain about how her dead husband's best friend had suddenly begun making passionate advances toward her. "I had no will to protest and he held me and kissed me again and again," she stated. Her husband had been dead only two weeks and she felt tremendous guilt about what had transpired. Should she marry the friend? she asked the paper. In matters of this type, Cahan held a rigid set of morals. "The woman's excuse that she was unable to protest against the passionate advances of her husband's friend is a weak one," he noted. "There is no excuse for the disgusting behavior of the young man. He should not have acted so shamefully after his friend's death. It is possible the widow is making a mistake in deciding to marry him, because it is doubtful whether she can be happy with such a man."

Yet when it came to young Jewish boys playing baseball, he took a lighter tack. One irate father wrote that he did not want his son playing baseball. "The children can get crippled. . . . I want my boy to grow up to be a *mensh* [a good and decent person], not a wild American runner." In this case, Cahan tired to find a middle ground between the Old and New worlds and suggested that playing baseball was acceptable "as long as it does not interfere with the [boy's] education."

Cahan could be, as Irving Howe has described, "a dictator as well as a genius." He was known to have a temper and did not easily suffer fools or critics. Once, when he was criticized for the populist tone of the *Forward* by intellectuals who wanted a real socialist paper, he dismissed their objections out of hand. What was the point, he asked, of producing an elitist newspaper that few people read? "I have spent some time in the outside world," he said. "I found that we Socialists have no patent on honesty and knowledge. . . . You and your comrades are steeped in the spirit of sectarianism. Should the *Forverts* remain where its . . . [the] public will not come near it because it doesn't concern itself with all life – interests that concern the great masses. . . . I say to you it's just as important to teach the pubic how to carry a handkerchief in one's pocket as it is to carry a union card."

That he did this for the Jewish community better than any other journalist is self-evident. Such was his stature that he was described in an *American Magazine* profile in 1912, as an "editor, family adviser, lay preacher, comrade, critic, littérateur, teacher, and political leader all in one, to half a million East Siders who read the newspaper daily." He moved with the times, moderating his political position as necessary. Following visits to Palestine in 1925 and 1929, he became an ardent supporter of a Jewish state, despite his earlier reservations about the Zionist movement. He eventually understood that despite his views on religion, his "destiny . . . lay with his own people."

When Cahan died in 1951 at the age of ninety-one, more than 10,000 mourners lined up in front of the Forward Building to hear the eulogies given by politicians and dignitaries at his secular funeral held inside on the second floor. The tributes that day to the "Lower East Side's First Citizen," as the *New York Times* called him, were genuine and sincere.

A Centre of Jewish Culture

THROUGHOUT HIS LONG LIFE, Abraham Cahan's socialism remained "spiritual" as opposed to "programmatic." His secular convictions usually put him between Orthodox Jews, who wanted to retain their traditional beliefs, and pragmatic socialists, who saw Cahan as a leading member of the bourgeoisie. As a Jew who did not step inside a synagogue very often, he understood better how to respond to the criticisms of the latter rather than the former; nor did he fully appreciate the religious challenges that life in America posed for the Orthodox.

Back in the Pale, rabbis had feared that emigration would be the death of Judaism. Jews in America, they declared, cared only for making money and had forsaken the religion and values of their fathers. Soon after he arrived in New York, Cahan, had, in fact, visited an East Side synagogue and was told by an elderly congregant that the sanctuary was full only for Saturday morning Sabbath services. "It isn't Russia," the old man pointed out to him. "Judaism has not much chance here."

Initially, at least, the stature of rabbis did decline in the United States. Congregations did not have sufficient funds to pay for full-time rabbis, and far too many synagogues in the New York immigrant quarter were not adequately maintained. In some circumstances, synagogue officials had to turn to the congregant who was most versed in religious procedure to act as their rabbi. Thus was born the American "reverend" as these Jewish lay preachers were mockingly called.

The conflicting impulse both to be American and also retain Old World values seemed to tear apart many immigrants' sense of values. On the surface, deterioration in morals was the price that was paid. "With every day that passed I became more and more overwhelmed at the degeneration of my fellow countrymen in this new home of theirs," reflected Marcus Ravage. "Cut adrift suddenly from their ancient moorings, they were floundering in a sort of moral void. Good manners and good conduct, reverence and religion, had all gone by the board, and the reason was that these things were not American."

There were other signs as well. Immigrant children, accustomed to life in New York, no longer adhered to their parents' wishes. So many Jewish husbands deserted their wives that the *Forward* ran a feature called "Gallery of Missing Husbands" with photographs of the men accompanied by pleas from their families to return. Lower East Side brothels multiplied, and Jewish gangsters like "Dopey" Benny Fein, Arnold Rothstein, and Max "Kid Twist" Zweibach, who was killed in a shootout, terrorized newcomers.* They started young as pickpockets and thieves and moved up to fencing stolen property, arson (which was a big business on the East Side), and eventually extortion and murder. "Big Jack" Zelig was more inventive than most of the Jewish hoods. He had list of services with prices: "ten dollars for a knife slash on the cheek; thirty-five dollars for a bullet in a limb; and up to one hundred dollars for a murder."

Abraham Cahan also dealt with this apparent crisis of morality in *The Rise of David Levinsky*, possibly the most poignant story of the American immigrant experience ever written. (It was also, notes Cahan's biographer Sanford Marovitz, "the first book about Jewish immigrants to be reviewed on the front page of the *New York Times Book Review*.") In the book, the main character, David Levinsky, has a profound identity crisis. As soon as he arrives in New York, he cuts off his beard and *peyes*, or sidelocks, buys new American-style clothing, and sheds his greenhorn manners. But no matter how much success Levinsky has — as he moves up from the sweatshop to become a wealthy businessman in the garment trade — he is never completely at peace with himself. "My sense of triumph is coupled with a brooding sense of emptiness and insignificance, of my lack of anything like a great deep interest," he says near the end of the novel. "I am lonely. . . . I am not happy." David Levinsky is a man with no future, trapped by both the past and the present.

---

* Arnold Rothstein, who came from a Jewish family already living uptown in the early 1890s, got into corruption in the Lower East Side as a youngster when he started working for Big Tim Sullivan, a Tammany boss. Later, he made a name for himself as a loan shark and high-stakes gambler and became famous as the man who fixed the 1919 World Series. Author F. Scott Fitzgerald immortalized him in his novel *The Great Gatsby* as the character Meyer Wolfsheim.

Was the situation as perilous as Cahan and others portrayed it? Cahan himself was living proof that Jewish life in America could have real meaning. And there were other positive examples as well. Jewish children in the East Side flocked to New York's public schools in record numbers. "[The Jewish children] rank among the highest," one teacher put it in 1905. "They are far more earnest and ambitious [than other scholars] and many of them supplement their school work with outside reading."

It was not only the youngsters who had a "hunger for learning," in the words of one immigrant. There were few outings more popular on the East Side than attending lectures delivered by such luminaries as Chaim Zhitlovsky, Morris Hillquit, Nachman Syrkin, Moissaye Olgin, and Abraham Cahan. There were heated discussions of politics and history and debates about the place of Jews in the world. At cafés along Second Avenue, you could sip a glass of tea, munch on a piece of honey cake, and listen to readings by Yiddish writers. One day at the Monopole café at Second Avenue and Ninth Street, Leon Trotsky even paid a visit while on a tour of the city.

The Astor Place Library was a popular gathering-place where young Jewish newcomers discovered the classics for the first time. Marcus Ravage remembered that his education took place in the sweatshop, his "first university." Toiling ten hours a day, he listened and learned about Marx, Darwin, and Spencer. For the slightly more affluent, there was the city's vibrant Yiddish theatre. At East Side landmarks like the Grand Theatre, immigrant audiences could enjoy performances by Jacob Adler, his wife, Sarah, Bertha Kalisch, and David Kessler, among many others, in such plays as the Yiddish versions of *Hamlet*, the Jewish *King Lear*, and *The Merchant of Venice*.

If it appeared to some observers that all Jewish tradition had been lost in America, it was only because the path that Jews now took had been altered by their new environment. Whether this made them less devout than Jews in the Pale is another matter. True, the focus of their lives in the *shetlach* had been the synagogue, but this may have had more to do with the Old World community structure and tradition than with deep feelings of faith. Still, there was a definite shift away from Orthodox religious practices to the secular, as Judaism in the United States became imbued with the socialist spirit of humanitarianism and a love of liberty. The secret was to find the right point between acculturation and total assimilation. Socialists, Zionists, Orthodox, Conservative, and Reform Jews all grappled with this dilemma for many years and, to a certain extent, still do. What was certain, however, was that the face of Judaism, its culture and religious practices, was transformed forever in America.

Israel Friedlander, professor of religion, ardent Zionist, and representative of the new American Jewish intellectual, identified many of these significant changes as early as 1907: "The only place where . . . Judaism has a chance of realization is America. . . . For America . . . is fast becoming the centre of the Jewish people of the Diaspora. . . . The American Jews are fully alive to the future of their country as a centre of Jewish culture. They build not only hospitals and infirmaries, but also schools and colleges; they welcome not only immigrants, but also libraries. . . . But will a Judaism that endeavors to embrace the breadth and depth of modern life, leave sufficient room in the heart of the Jew for the interests and demands of this country? . . . A full and successful participation in all phases of American life is reconcilable with a deep attachment to Judaism in all aspects. . . . Compromises will be unavoidable. . . . But these compromises will never be such as to obliterate or mutilate the character of either."

That much was evident even amidst the poverty and squalor of the Lower East Side. One Friday evening in 1891, journalist Jacob Riis was on one of his many walks though the neighbourhood when he encountered the magic of the Sabbath in one Jewish home. "I came in . . . at the breaking of bread, just as the four candles on the table had been lit, with the Sabbath blessing upon the home and all it sheltered," he wrote. "Their light fell on little else than empty plates and anxious faces; but in the patriarchal host who arose, and bade the guests welcome with a dignity a king might have envied, I recognized with difficulty the humble peddler I had known only from the street."

Chapter Ten

THE GERMAN-JEWISH 'SYMBIOSIS'

Berlin, 1925

What we mean by Judaism, the Jewishness of the Jewish human being, is nothing that can be grasped in a "religious literature" or even in a "religious life" . . . The point is simply that it is no entity, no subject among other subjects, no one sphere of life among other spheres of life; it is not what the century of emancipation with its cultural mania wanted to reduce it to. It is something inside the individual that makes him a Jew, something infinitesimally small, yet immeasurably large, his most impenetrable secret, yet evident in every gesture and every word.

– FRANZ ROSENZWEIG, 1920

The Spirit of Berlin

ARTHUR LANDSBERGER ALWAYS had a good story. It was one of the reasons he opted not to become a lawyer and instead embarked on a highly successful career as popular writer of detective and adventure tales. In 1922, he became impressed with the Viennese journalist (and converted Jew) Hugo Bettauer's novel *Die Stadt ohne Juden* (The City Without Jews). A best seller in its day, it was a biting satire about the rising anti-Semitism in Austria and the disasters that had transpired following the expulsion of Vienna's Jews: according to Bettauer, the city's culture – its theatre, music, art and literature – vanished overnight, not to mention all of its doctors and lawyers, too. Three years later, in 1925, the same year that

Bettauer was murdered in his Vienna office by a Nazi named Otto Rothstock, Landsberger penned his own version of this saga that he called *Berlin ohne Juden* (Berlin Without Jews). A darker and more tragic satire, Lansberger's novel concerned the expulsion of Berlin's Jews, including its celebrated cultural elite, from the city as part of a Communist-right wing nationalist plot, – and devised similar, extreme consequences: nearly all of the opera houses and movie theatres are closed, and fashion magazines cease publication. In the novel, Berlin's reputation as the "cultural capital of the world" is suddenly threatened. It seemed to be a futuristic fantasy: In 1925, few Jews, Landsberger included, would have believed that the expulsion of Jews from Berlin become a reality less than a decade later. Landsberger, himself, was never to witness the worst of it. Soon after the Nazis came to power in 1933, he committed suicide, as his key fictitious Jewish character Oppenheim does in his novel when faced with the prospect of expulsion.

Was Landsberger's main premise (and that of Bettauer) that far-fetched? Did Berlin's cultural life (or Vienna's) truly depend on its small Jewish population? With its population of 4.3 million people in 1920, Berlin was the third largest city in the world, surpassed only by London and New York. Even though it was still hurting from the devastation of the First World War, the city, according to Carl Zuckmayer, "had a taste of the future about it and as a result people were only too willing to put up with the cold and the dirt of the place." Zuckmayer was a Jewish playwright and one of the approximately 175,000 Jews who called Berlin home.

At most, Jews totalled only about 4.5 per cent of the city's inhabitants. And yet, the list of prominent German Jews during the period from 1900 to 1930 appears endless: Max Liebermann, Otto Brahm, Gustav Mahler, Arnold Schoenberg, Otto Klemperer, Bruno Walter, Leon Feuchtwanger, Kurt Weill, Walter Benjamin, Arnold Zweig, Martin Buber, and Franz Rosenzweig – to list only some of the artists, musicians, playwrights, novelists, philosophers, and critics who seemed to dominate the city and country. Nearly all of these individuals were creative, innovative risk-takers; several were geniuses. Two German-speaking Jews, Albert Einstein, who moved to Berlin from Bern, Switzerland, in 1914, and Sigmund Freud, who resided in Vienna, changed forever the way we understand the world and ourselves in it. Between 1901, when Nobel Prizes were first given out, and 1935, when Hitler was in power, Germany was awarded 40 such medals, the most given to any country. Germans of Jewish origin won approximately 30 per cent of them – among them, Einstein, who received the Nobel prize in physics in 1921, not for his theories of relativity, but for his discovery sixteen years earlier of the law of the photoelectric effect.

Was being Jewish in of itself a factor that propelled these men to achieve such brilliance in the arts, academia, and science? Interestingly, Freud, who detested religion of any kind and who for years chastised his wife Martha (the granddaughter of Hamburg's chief rabbi, Isaac Bernays) when she lit the Sabbath candles each Friday evening, did believe that his "Jewish nature" was partially responsible for his success. In a letter to the B'nai Brith lodge in Vienna, of which he was a life-long member, and which had honoured him on the occasion of his seventieth birthday in 1926, he wrote, "because I was a Jew, I found myself free from many prejudices which limited others in the use of their intellect, and being a Jew, I was prepared to enter opposition and to renounce agreement with the 'compact majority.'"

Being members of a minority and always having to prove themselves may well have accounted for Jews' willingness to explore fresh and original modes of thinking. Max Reinhardt successfully experimented with a new form of theatre; Ernst Toller mastered Expressionism in his plays; Erich Mendelsohn was one of the most creative architects of his generation; Franz Kafka and Walter Benjamin made outstanding and enduring literary contributions; Max Liebermann epitomized German Impressionism; and Arnold Schoenberg revolutionized the world of music. Yet, as historian Paul Johnson argues, there was "no Jewish world outlook, let alone a plan to impose modernism on the world." Johnson also noted that "Jews who were decisive innovators in their own fields [including Freud] were often highly conservative in every other aspect of life."

They lived in a German world where intellectualism was valued; reason and religion were compatible; and philosophy, idealism, and humanism were cherished. It cannot be overlooked that such non-Jewish Germans as Bertold Brecht, Stefan George, Thomas Mann, Erich Maria Remarque, and Ranier Maria Rilke, to list only several – were equally, if not more so, responsible for Germany's cultural renaissance, especially during the years of the Weimar Republic from 1919 to 1933. As historian Walter Laqueur pointed out in the early 1970s, "most German Jews were neither intellectuals nor radicals; indeed, there were far more Jewish tailors than writers and journalists." Consider, for example, that in 1925 close to 25 per cent of Berlin's Jews – about 44,000 – were so-called *Ostjuden*, Eastern European Jews who had immigrated from Poland and Russia. They were impoverished, worked at menial jobs, and as in the United States, were viewed as a detested burden by the more cultured Western European Jews.

Origin and class thus created friction even among German Jews. While local leaders and politicians tried to help the Eastern Europe-born Jews – during the early 1920s, the Berlin Jewish community organized nineteen soup kitchens and seven shelters for the homeless – there was a fair degree of animosity towards the immigrants. In a 1926 speech, one Berlin Reform Rabbi told his congregants that the Eastern Europeans had injected "a certain atmosphere of uncleanliness and slovenliness into German Jewry." During the late 1920s, it was a custom at a Hanover synagogue that, when an Eastern Jew came inside and sat on an empty seat to pray, he was handed card which read, "If you do not leave the synagogue immediately, you will be charged with trespassing and disturbing the holy services."

None of this, of course, stopped the ever-growing number of anti-Semites (and others less politically extreme as well) from raging against Berlin as a "Jew city." They blamed Jews for destroying German culture and taking over the country's economy. "What has become of Berlin?" rhetorically asked Wolfgang Kapp, an early supporter of the National Socialist German Workers' Party (Nazis) in 1920. His own rejoinder: "A playground for the Jews." Later, one popular Nazi slogan declared that, "the spirit of the German people rises up against the spirit of Berlin."

Perhaps it was more the case that, in a city where nearly half the population was blue-collar, many German Jews were envied and resented for living middle-class bourgeoisie urbanized lifestyles in Tiergarten and in "fashionable" Charlottenburg. These Jews proudly valued education and were renowned in their achievements in everything from the arts to business.

The largest department stores in Berlin (and elsewhere in Germany) were owned by such wealthy Jewish entrepreneurs as, Hermann Tietz who operated a magnificent establishment on the Alexanderplatz. His brother Leonard ran stores in other cities. There were the Wertheim brothers who opened a store in 1897 on Leipzigerstrasse, a fortress with no show windows; one Berliner referred to it as "a new cathedral." It took Berthold Israel fifteen years, from 1899 to 1914, to complete construction of his huge department store, which occupied one city block. There were Jewish publishers and the most important newspaper in the city was the *Berliner Tageblatt* owned by Rudolph Mosse, who also employed many Jewish editors and reporters. Likewise, the *Frankfurter Zeitung*, another influential paper, was established by the Jewish banker and industrialist Leopold Sonnenman. "Jews," once remarked Rabbi Leo Baeck, who headed the Liberal Fasanenstrasse synagogue from its opening in 1912 until it was destroyed by the Nazis in 1938, "have the strange characteristic to multiply ourselves; if there might be twenty of us, one would think there were two hundred of us."

Despite the prominence of such men, in the positive sense, they were, too, a visible, indeed "conspicuous," minority within a not-all-together friendly population that did not for a minute let them forget that they were Jews. Even the so-called "*Kaiserjuden*," the select Jewish moguls who moved in Kaiser Wilhelm II's close circle prior to the First World War – the shipping magnate Albert Ballin, banker Max Warburg, and the industrialist Walter Rathenau – were looked upon first and foremost as Jews, albeit valuable ones.*

This was a reality not lost on Moritz Goldstein, a thirty-two-year-old literary writer in 1912 who provoked a major debate among the German-Jewish intelligentsia with his article, "*Deutsch-jüdischer Parnass*" (German-Jewish Parnassus). In it, he argued, "We Jews, among ourselves, may have the impression that we are speaking as Germans to Germans. But however fully German we may feel ourselves to be, the others felt that we are fully un-German. We may be called Max Reinhardt and have raised the theatre to unprecedented heights . . . or as Max Liebermann be in the vanguard of modern painting. We may call all that German, but the others call it Jewish . . . And when they have no choice but to acknowledge the achievement (with reservations, of course), they express the wish that we would achieve less."

Albert Einstein, for one, concurred. He had been brought up in an assimilated bourgeois Jewish family in Munich (before living in Bern and Berlin), where being a Jew was only an issue of birth. The Einsteins considered themselves "Israelites." Albert did not have a bar mitzvah, nor did he learn Hebrew. As a young student, his priority was learning about mathematics and science, not religion. It was only after he was famous for his work in theoretical physics, when he taught at the German University in Prague in 1911 and again later in Berlin, that he embraced his Jewishness and also became a committed Zionist. "When I first came to Germany

---

*The Kaiser, who accepted the racist theories of such "experts" as Houston Stewart Chamberlain (Richard Wagner's son-in-law and the author of the widely-read 1899 book on race and eugenics, *The Foundation of the Nineteenth Century*) was no friend of his Jewish subjects. "I am all in favour of the kikes going to Palestine," he once said. "The sooner they take off the better." He also was quick to blame Jews, "the hated tribe of Judah," as he put it, for the revolutionary upheaval that followed his abdication and the defeat of Germany in World War I. "Let no German ever forget this," he said, "or rest until these parasites have been extirpated and exterminated from German soil. This toadstool on the German oak."

fifteen years ago," he wrote in a 1925 letter to a German government minister, "I discovered for the first time that I was a Jew, and
I owe this discovery more to Gentiles than to Jews . . . If we did not
have to live among intolerant, narrow-minded, and violent people,
I should be the first to throw over all nationalism in favour of universal humanity."

As Einstein and many others came to understand, the crux of
the situation was this: The German Constitution of 1871 might
have made Jews equal citizens of the empire, but that did not mean
they were welcome in all sectors of Germany society. Despite their
political emancipation, it remained difficult for Jews to receive
appointments to the civil service or obtain jobs as teachers,
professors, and judges – just as it had been at the beginning of
the nineteenth century. That many Jews did become lawyers,
doctors, and journalists, was only due to the fact that, unlike those
other careers involving a hierarchy of service, these were self-
employable professions.

In nineteenth-century Germany, anti-Semitism reached its peak
as a political movement during the 1890s (under such demagogues
as the court preacher Adolf Stoecker), as it did in France at the time
of the Dreyfus Affair. As an ideology, it had long been and remained
a commanding and influential force in Germany well before the
Nazis discovered its ultimate potential and power. However much
Jews might consider themselves to be German, the Germans
believed otherwise. As early as 1897, Ernst Hasse, Chairman of the
ultra-nationalistic Pan German League, affirmed with a voice of
authority that, "our future lies in our blood." Many Germans from
the Kaiser on down were intrigued by the notion of a supreme
Aryan race.

It was due to this rising anti-Semitism that the *Centralverein
deutscher Staatsbürger jüdischen Glaubens* (Central Association of
German Citizens of the Jewish Faith, or CV) was established in
1893. Its goal was to protect Jewish civil rights and to defend Jews
in the courts and parliament against unwarranted attacks. The CV
was the first truly secular "modern mass organization" created in

Germany for this specific purpose by acculturated Jews. The leaders of the CV campaigned for human rights, and on many occasions, took anti-Semites to court, winning legal actions against them. One such case concerned Julius Streicher, the notorious publisher of the Nazi propaganda sheet, *Der Stürmer*.

As a community, a majority of Germany's Jews supported the CV's work; but as individuals, many were more circumspect. They were wary; they felt that there were lines that should not be crossed. The artist Max Liebermann grew anxious "when a Jew became all too prominent because he expected with good reason, some adverse reaction to follow," recalled Max Osborn, an art critic. In 1921, Albert Einstein warned his friend Walter Rathenau against taking the foreign affairs portfolio offered to him, because of negative attitudes against Jews at the time. Rathenau, a loyal patriot, did not heed Einstein's advice and was murdered in 1922. His assassination wounded Einstein deeply. "That hatred, delusion, and ingratitude could go so far – I still would not have thought it," he wrote following Rathenau's death.

Berlin lawyer Adolf Asch actively advanced the maxim that Jews had to be above reproach. He was concerned that a minority of Jews who were "ostentatious parvenus" making money from the country's terrible economic problems in the early 1920s, "gave, as usual, a welcome opportunity to anti-Semites to make Jewry as a whole responsible." In 1922, he became head of the *Selbstzuchtorganisation*, a new "self discipline organization" that attempted to mute both Jewish achievements and any notoriety. Among other actions, his group cautioned Jews, as he deemed, "to guard the dignity customary before and after the divine services on the High Holidays, and especially to ask Jewish women to avoid all showy luxury in clothing and jewellery."

Germanness and Jewishness

In hindsight, given all we know about the fate of German Jews, such forms of activism seem futile indeed. Yet at that time, defining the German-Jewish "symbiosis" – their rightful contribution as German citizens; the changing role of religion; their "multiple identities" within an increasingly hostile nationalistic environment – provoked heated discussions, produced countless articles and books, and occupied the minds of some of the era's greatest intellectuals of every faith.

The visionary Jewish philosopher Martin Buber, who lived in Berlin and Frankfurt during this period (he emigrated to Palestine in 1938), sought deeper meanings in being Jewish in a German world. In his early writings prior to the First World War, he probed Eastern European Jewish traditions and in particular the mysteries of Hasidism and Jewish mysticism. He not only strived to dispel negative stereotypes about the *Ostjuden*, but in time concluded that there was such a thing as a Jewish essence that "assimilation could perhaps hide and distort, but never fully eradicate." Being Jewish, Buber lectured and wrote, meant being part of a "community of blood."

The notion of belonging to a race of their own in a positive sense eventually found favour among a number of young intellectuals, who like Buber, turned their backs on their "Germanness" and embraced Zionism – if not the practical aspect of physically emigrating to Palestine, then certainly its cultural concept of a Jewish people. One such individual was Gershom Scholem, who became a leading Israeli scholar, an expert on the Kabbalah, and the biographer of the seventeenth-century false messiah Shabbetai Zevi (described in Chapter Three).

Scholem was born in 1897 into a typical middle-class Jewish family. His father Arthur owned two print shops in Berlin. His mother, Betty, helped out at the shop, but also ensured that young Gershom received a proper German and Jewish upbringing. That meant mandatory attendance at the Schiller Festival as well as in synagogue on the High Holidays. Often the family's identity as Germans overwhelmed their identity as Jews. "There was something in the atmosphere," Scholem later recalled, "that came from the environment, something conscious that dialectically combined a desire for self-relinquishment with a desire for human dignity and loyalty to one's own self; there was a deliberate break with the Jewish tradition, of which the most varied and often peculiar fragments were still present in atomized form; and there was also a drifting (not always conscious) in to a world which was to replace this tradition."

The Scholems did not keep kosher, and Friday evening was regarded as "family night" rather than as the Sabbath. The Shabbat candles were lit, he remembered, and the Hebrew blessing was chanted, but that did not keep some of the men from lighting their cigarettes and cigars off the burning flames – an act of insouciance or perhaps even deliberate mockery, since it is not permitted to smoke on the Sabbath. On Passover, the family had a traditional seder, although, as Scholem remembers, during the remaining seven days of the holiday, "bread and matzos (unleavened bread) were next to each other in two breadbaskets." While Betty Scholem took her children to synagogue on Yom Kippur, her husband Arthur usually went to work "with no thought of fasting." As Scholem tells it, "malicious souls used to say in the years before World War I that a headwaiter stood at the entrance to the well-known restaurant next to the Grosse Synagogue on Oranienburger Strasse and addressed the guests in their holiday finery as follows: 'The gentlemen who are fasting will be served in the back room.'"

Still, in his own secular way, Arthur Scholem was a proud German Jew. He purposely did work for Jewish organizations, socialized almost exclusively with other Jews, and railed against Jews who converted to Christianity. Starting in 1910, the *Gemenide*, Berlin's Jewish Community Council, published the names of the recently baptized in its widely circulated newsletter. It became the talk of the Scholem household. Mixed marriages – between 1896 and 1900, only nine per cent of Jews had taken non-Jewish partners, but the figure rose to 21 per cent during the period from 1916 to 1920 – were frowned on as well.

Politics also generated much debate, and in that regard the Scholems were likely more divided than most families. Indeed, they were a microcosm of the German Jewish experience. As head of the household, Arthur was committed to the vision of the CV: that only within Germany, would Jews find the strength to survive. Only one of his sons, Erich, agreed with his liberal position. Another son, Werner, was a Communist, and from 1924 to 1928 a member of the Reichstag, the German Parliament; the eldest, Reinhold, was a German nationalist and supported right-of-centre parties; while Gershom, much to his father's dissatisfaction, eventually became a Zionist and emigrated to Palestine in 1925.

Like Moritz Goldstein, Gershom Scholem maintained that Jews like his father and members of the CV were deluding themselves. Anti-Semitism would never vanish, and to think otherwise was a form of "self-deception." However, it took some years before he arrived at this conclusion. While growing up, he shared his father's optimistic liberal view in "humanity's spirit of progress," believing that Jews had a right to be German. At that time, it had seemed so simple.

Many had shared in that belief. "Ten years ago," Eugen Fuch, who was later president of CV, wrote in a 1912 Jewish newspaper, "I had already indicated that it was not the shape of the beard, the colour of hair, the curve of the nose, or the size of the body that was decisive, but the energetic dedicated will to be a German . . . we are born into a German fatherland and on German soil . . . and that gives us the right to call ourselves Germans, without baptism and the so-called assimilation . . . "

No one gave a more eloquent defence of this position than Hermann Cohen, a well-respected and much beloved neo-Kantian philosopher, mathematician, and teacher at the University of Marburg (north of Frankfurt). When he was in his seventies, by then a stout man with flowing white hair and a moustache and goatee beard to match, he attempted to reconcile the German-Jewish experience. In 1915, he published two major essays, both entitled *"Deutschtum und Judentum"* (Germanness and Jewishness). Writing in the midst of the war when patriotic zeal was at an all-time high, Cohen argued that there was a strong link between

Jewish messianism and German humanism. "For that reason," he declared, "our German sentiments toward state and people are, as it were, transfigured and confirmed by our religion; our soul flourishes equally and harmoniously both in our German patriotism and in our religious consciousness, which has its root and its pinnacle in the unique God of humanity." Optimistic to the end of his life, in 1918, Cohen rejected Zionism as wrongheaded and insisted that it was only a matter of time before the German-Jewish symbiosis would be "harmonized."

A majority of German Jews predictably tended to agree with Cohen's patriotic position rather than with the Zionist one that stressed that Jews were a separate nation who deserved their own land. While Zionism did attract some followers, they, too, were mostly content to be of the "anti-emigration" variety (as historian Peter Pulzer calls them): they supported the establishment of a Jewish state in Palestine, but preferred to remain in Germany, which they considered their homeland. "I felt thoroughly German," Franz Oppenheimer, a leading Zionist, commented as late as 1930, "but I have never been able to understand why awareness of my Jewish origins should be incompatible with awareness of my sense of belonging to the German people and its culture."

Other Zionists, such as editor Robert Weltsch, questioned whether Jews could ever achieve assimilarity within the present climate of Germany. In the newspaper he edited, *Jüdische Rundschau*, he wrote that anti-Semitism would never permit the degree of unity between Jews and Germans that Hermann Cohen had advocated. "Proclaiming 'unswerving cultivation of German sentiment' does nothing to counteract Judeophobia. On the contrary it only makes non-Jews even more suspicious. A decent non-Jew cannot understand why the Jew, whose specific characteristics are obvious to the non-Jews at a glance and are not to be explained away with 'scientific arguments,' wants to compensate with such loud assertions of his German nationality."

Orthodox Jews held the Zionist vision for the Holy Land in disdain, while the Liberal majority accused Zionists of playing into the anti-Semites' hand, since they provided Gentiles with a ready-made solution to the Jewish problem: deport the Jews. Indeed, only a decade later, Hitler's storm troopers handed out fake one-way tickets to Jerusalem, and a Nazi poster from 1932 declared that Jews should "Get ready for Palestine." Even as the Third Reich came to power, almost all of the Zionists stayed put in their German homes, and thus met the same tragic fate as the Orthodox and Liberal Jews who opposed them.

I Will Remain a Jew

ALL THINGS CONSIDERED, it is not surprising that, as child, Gershom Scholem had felt that being Jewish was a "confused jumble." His family celebrated Christmas as a "German national festival," complete with a tree in their apartment and a roast goose dinner. His mother placed a picture of Zionist founder Theodor Herzl (who also had a Christmas tree in his own house in Vienna) under the tree, the last year Scholem participated in his family's festivities. By then, he was a student of Jewish history with an interest in Zionist literature. He was a member of Young Judea, a Zionist youth group, and was preparing to leave his family for Palestine.

Before Scholem departed, his path crossed that of Franz Rosenzweig, another young gifted Jewish writer and philosopher trying to come to terms with being a Jew in a Christian society. Closer in ideology to Hermann Cohen than to Scholem and the Zionists, Rosenzweig was arguably one of the most original Jewish thinkers of the twentieth century. His personal journey, perhaps more than others', epitomizes the Jewish renaissance that took place within the German community during the twenties, proving that being German and Jewish were not incompatible. As his friend and biographer Nahum Glatzer wrote, "The story of Franz Rosenzweig is the story of a rediscovery of Judaism. A European intellectual and assimilationist breaks with his personal past and becomes a Jew by conviction, rediscovers his people's existence, and becomes the modern interpreter of this existence."

Rosenzweig was born on December 25, 1886 in the town of Kassel, north of Frankfurt. He was the only child of Georg and Adele Rosenzweig. Georg was a prosperous businessman who made a living manufacturing dyes. Adele revered education and, like Gershom Scholem's mother, ensured that her son became a cultivated and cultured individual. Though young Franz had a bar mitzvah and his family dutifully attended synagogue on the High Holidays, he later recalled that, until he was much older, he did not truly understand what it meant to be Jewish. The little he did know about Judaism, he learned from his great-uncle, Adam Rosenzweig, who stayed with his family until his death in 1908. On Franz's first day of grammar school at age six, Adam took him aside and told him: "My boy, you are going among people for the first time today; remember as long as you live that you are a Jew." It was advice that he never forgot.

Rosenzweig continued his education at a prominent *Gymnasium* (secondary school), becoming a sophisticated and culturally aware German. As a young adult, he was an avid reader, perceptive and interested in world around him. With his round wire-framed glasses, dark tousled hair, and wispy moustache, he had the look of a European intellectual who would have been quite comfortable in the cafés of Berlin or Paris. Initially, Rosenzweig followed the typical bourgeois German-Jewish path: he was going to be a physician. He enrolled at the University of Göttingen, transferred to University at Munich, and then, in 1906, to the University of Freiburg. His diary and letters of this period reveal a young man absorbed with the intellectual complexities of the world, including his Jewish heritage, but still in doubt about his career choice.

"Why does one philosophize?" he asked himself in the spring of 1906. His reply: "For the same reason that one makes music or literature or art. Here, too, in the last analysis, all that matters is the discovery of one's own personality."

At the University Freiburg, his interest in philosophy led him into classes and seminars on Kant and Hegel. He passed his exams in medicine, but had already decided to abandon his medical studies in favor or history and philosophy, to he displeasure of his pragmatic father. At Freiburg, during the fall semester of 1908, Franz Rosenzweig began an intensive study of Hegel's life and writings, awakening the keen intellectual curiosity that was to guide him thereafter.

In 1909, his family reacted sharply to the news that Rosenzweig's cousin, Hans Ehrenberg, had converted to Christianity. While his parents condemned the decision, Rosenzweig did not think it was "shameful." In a letter to foreshadow his own personal religious crisis that occurred several years later he wrote to his mother in early November of 1909, "it's an excellent thing, after all, to be able to make contact with religion, even somewhat late." "We are Christian in everything," he wrote the following week. "We live in a Christian state, attend Christian schools, read Christian books, in short, our whole 'culture' rests entirely on a Christian foundation; consequently a man who has nothing holding him back needs only a very slight push . . . to make him accept Christianity."

As Germany inched closer to war, Rosenzweig immersed himself in his work, and he completed his dissertation on Hegel in 1912. (It was published in 1920 in two volumes entitled *Hegel and the State*, and achievd immediate recognition for its substantial contribution to German philosophy.) In 1913, while attending a conference for young philosophers and historians in Baden-Baden, Rosenzweig met Eugen Rosenstock, a converted Jew, who became a life-long friend. Soon after, Rosenzweig began taking courses in law at the University of Leipzig, where Rosenstock was lecturing on medieval constitutional law.

One summer night in July 1913, the two friends debated the pros and cons of conversion. By the time their heated discussion had ended, Rosenzweig had been convinced that becoming a Christian was the only way for a Jew to survive in a Protestant society. Still, several trying months followed, as he came to grips with the most difficult decision he had ever made. He returned home to Kassel in early October in time for Rosh Hashana, the start of the High Holiday services, and informed his mother that he was about to be baptized. "Here is the truth," he told her, holding the New Testament in his hand. "There is only one way, Jesus." She expressed only disappointment; she could not support her son's choice. (There is no record of his father's reaction to the news.)

Rosenzweig then went alone to Berlin and decided to attend Yom Kippur services at an orthodox synagogue. It was to be a last farewell to Judaism. He intended to embrace Christianity as a Jew, the way it was done at time of Jesus and not as "a 'pagan,' [that is,] out of a previously irreligious or rationalistic position."

The experience at the synagogue that day had a profound impact on him. He never revealed to his family nor recorded in his letters or diary precisely what had transpired, other than to declare his peace with himself. "I will remain a Jew," he wrote in a letter to Rudolf Ehrenberg (Hans's brother, who had also converted). The solemn Yom Kippur prayers made him realize that it was not necessary to become a Christian to go through Jesus to God, since – as a Jew observing the holiest of Jewish holy days, he now affirmed that God is always present. He found in the service, "a sense of the reality of God and personal communion with Him which he had been so ardently and had come to believe he would find only in the church." Thereafter, Yom Kippur had a special significance for him.

Once his decision was made, he stayed in Berlin and delved into Jewish religious texts. Soon after his personal epiphany, he met Hermann Cohen, who became his mentor, and also befriended Martin Buber. Later, he and Buber would collaborate on a German translation of the Old Testament. Buber was immediately impressed with Rosenzweig and asked him to contribute an article for a volume of essays on Jewish life that he was assembling. Rosenzweig wrote a piece he called "Atheistic Theology," a first attempt to define his personal religious theology in which he broached the issue of divine revelation that was absent from current Jewish and Christian writings. Rosenzweig believed that revelation was "one of the three indispensable foundations of the structure of Jewish faith", a theme he was to elaborate within a few years in his major work of philosophy, *The Star of Redemption*.

In the summer of 1914, however, the outbreak of World War I interrupted his work. As for all Jews throughout the empire, it was a pivotal moment in their lives as Germans.

The *Judenzählung*

"I NO LONGER recognize any parties," declared the Kaiser. "I recognize only Germans and as a sign that you are firmly determined to stand together with me through thick and thin, through danger and death, without distinction of party, without distinction of rank or religion, I ask that the leader of the parties come forward and swear their solemn oath before me." German Jews could appreciate such sentiments. Their country needed them to halt the British, French, and Russian enemies seemingly threatening their national interests, and they responded the way all loyal German citizens did. Here was an opportunity to prove who and what they really were. As Hermann Cohen was to state a few months after the hostilities began, "in times of war it was . . . the special task of German Jews to spread the supremacy of German culture among their coreligionists in other European countries."

Jews of nearly every religious and political orientation joined in the cause. Special prayer services were held at Berlin's synagogues on August 5, two days after the German declaration of war. At the Fasanestrasse synagogue, so many people showed up that the rabbi had to convene two services to accommodate everyone. The Jews of Berlin listened intently to the words of Rabbi Leo Baeck (who was soon to serve at the front as an army chaplain) about the meaning of duty and morality. "It is not a war over land or influence that is now being waged," said Baeck, "but a war that will decide on the culture and morality of Europe, whose destiny has been placed in the hands of Germany and in the hands of those who stand by its side." A group of Zionists even came back from Palestine to join the German army and defend the fatherland. Thousands of Jewish men volunteered for service and Jewish women helped in whatever way they could at home, in factories, and at hospitals. And, the most popular German war poem was *"Hassgesang gegen England"* (Hate Song against England) composed by thirty-two-year-old Jewish writer Ernst Lissauer. For this work, he was praised by the Kaiser and awarded the Prussian Order of the Red Eagle.

Jewish intellectuals and scientists rallied around the flag as well. Fritz Haber, a renowned chemist, helped develop the chlorine gas weapons utilized so effectively by the German army. Artist Max Liebermann and theatre director Max Reinhardt were among those who signed the 1914 "Manifesto of the Ninety-three" that repudiated allegations of "German atrocities and violations of Belgian neutrality."

Albert Einstein was not as certain and later adopted a more pacifist stance. In Vienna, Sigmund Freud initially supported Austria-Hungary's participation, but soon denounced the war and the futility of its carnage. As the fighting dragged on and the death toll mounted, the general enthusiasm for the war waned. Jewish soldiers in the trenches found themselves the target of old-fashioned scapegoat anti-Semitism, a situation made worse in 1917 when the turmoil in Russia raised the spectre of a Bolshevik-Jewish conspiracy. "The average German simply doesn't care for the Jew," lamented one Jewish volunteer who had enlisted in 1914. "I don't want to be anything here except a German soldier – and yet I am given no choice but to believe that is otherwise." When the Jewish soldier Ernest Toller received his Iron Cross for bravery, he was told, "Now you see, this has made up for the stigma of your ancestry." For the men, this treatment merely confirmed what such writers like Mortiz Goldstein had already discovered – the German-Jewish symbiosis that Cohen had written about was a near impossibility. "We experienced a great disappointment with the Germans and we continue to do so," wrote the novelist Georg Hermann, the author of *Jettchen Gebert*, a popular 1906 novel about an assimilated Berlin Jewish family.

Then, in 1916, arose the most controversial issue of all. From the beginning of the war, anti-Semites had been clamouring that

Jews were not doing their part for the war effort and were refusing to enlist. German government officials quickly dismissed the charges, yet the question of Jewish support would not disappear. Finally, in October 1916, one Reichstag member demanded to know "how many Jews are serving at the front?" The War Ministry announced that it would launch its own investigation by conducting a Jewish census at the front – the so-called *Judenzählung*.

Needless to say, Jewish soldiers were humiliated by the count, "as if the yellow patch had been sewn back on," as one Jewish journalist put it at the time. The Ministry decided to keep the census results secret, but information was leaked to the press suggesting that Jews were indeed shirking their military responsibilities, a charge that, statistically, was false.

Once the war had ended, Jewish veterans went to great lengths to publicize that 12,000 Jews had died fighting for Germany – exactly 1 per cent of the 1.2 million Germans killed, which proportionately corresponded to the percentage of the country's total Jewish population.

Ernst Simon, a seventeen-year-old volunteer who was wounded at Verdun, was so angry with the census debacle that he became a Zionist. (Simon later emigrated to Palestine in 1928, where he became a professor of educational philosophy at the Hebrew University.) "The dream of commonality was over. The deep abyss, which had never disappeared, opened up once more with terrible force," he later remembered. "It could not be bridged by common suffering and bleeding, not by common language and work, not even by common civilization and manners."

While the debate about the census roiled, Martin Buber had already started publishing his German-Jewish language journal that he called *Der Jude* (he deliberately picked the same name that Gabriel Riesser had used for his periodical in the 1830s). Soon it was acknowledged as the "single most influential German-Jewish periodical of its time." It was the war that had compelled him to act. The idea that Jews were fighting each other on both sides of the conflict troubled him deeply. It was his desire, born out of his

Zionist orientation, that his journal would enable Jews to see themselves as one, beyond their particular national groups. In this, Buber
was guided by the cultural Zionist writings of Asher Zvi Ginsberg
(Ahad Ha-Am), whose work was featured in the first edition. Even
those who did not support Buber's views – given that he repudiated the German-Jewish vision advanced by Hermann Cohen –
read Der Jude and, consequently, a veritable who's who of Jewish
writers in Germany, Poland, and Russia: Max Brod, Hugo
Bergmann, Jakob Klatzkin, Fritz Kaufmann, Gershom Scholem,
and Arnold Zwieg, among a long list, all contributed articles.
As their publisher, if not for his own politics, Buber gained many
followers who were later disappointed with the philosopher when
he did not immediately leave for Palestine once the Peace of Paris
was signed.

The Star of Redemption

FRANZ ROSENZWEIG'S JOURNEY of self-discovery continued when
he was, himself, in the trenches. In September 1914, he joined the
Red Cross and worked at the front as a nurse. He had volunteered
because he knew that he would be eventually drafted, rather than
out of a grand sense of duty for German honour. Then, in January
1916, he was sent to the ballistics training School at La Fère, in
France, where he was assigned to an anti-aircraft unit. Soon after,
he was transferred to Balkans on the eastern front, where he was to
stay for the duration of the war.

His duties as soldier did not stop him from reading, writing, and
corresponding with his friends, especially Eugen Rosenstock, who
was with the German army on the western front. The two continued their debate about Christianity and Judaism by mail. Mostly
though, when he had the time, Rosenzweig contemplated his own
existence as a Jew, a German, and a human being.

He continued to hold Hermann Cohen in high esteem, when
others like Buber were critical of him. At the same time, Rosenzweig did not entirely share Cohen's vision of German-Jewish

unity. For him, the Jewish future lay in a different direction. Jews, he argued, remained "aliens" in strange lands among the nations of the world, but their destiny was theirs alone to decide. "It is our lot to remain strangers," he wrote in his review of Cohen's essays, *Deutschtum and Judentum*, "alien to all spiritual possessions of the nations, of which they allow us to partake . . ."

Rosenzweig did appreciate the position of such Jewish organizations as the Centralverein and the importance of cultivating the German-Jewish link, despite its fragile nature. Yet he also understood the inner struggle most Jews felt as minority citizens in a majority society that eyed them suspiciously.

Some years later, reflecting on this issue, he admitted that, "perhaps I am especially innocent with regard to the problem of Germanism and Judaism. I believe that becoming more Jewish has not made me a worse but rather a better German. I really think that those in the generation before us . . . were no better Germans that we are." On another occasion in 1923, he was asked which he would stress more, his being German or Jewish. "I refuse to answer," he responded. "If it should happen that life should put me on the rack and tear me into two pieces, I would get to know with which of the two halves the heart would go, as the heart is placed in the body in a non-symmetrical way . . . But I would also get to know something else, that I would not survive this operation."

Rosenzweig was an intellectual with a practical bent. Refusing to accept that the only solution to the Jewish question was escaping to Palestine – although he was sympathetic to Zionism, he never became a full-fledged supporter – he became an outspoken advocate for a new kind of Jewish education. He first elaborated his thoughts in a long essay entitled, "It is Time." Written as an open letter to Hermann Cohen in March 1917, it was published in *Neue Jüdische Monatshefte* (New Jewish Monthly), the journal Cohen edited. It methodically presented Rosenzweig's ambitious plan for a rebirth of Jewish education for children and adults, which included the study of Hebrew, Biblical Scriptures, and Talmud. He did not want to create another yeshiva. Instead, he envisioned modern-style seminars and discussions led by "teacher-scholars" as well as rabbis, in which Jewish values and ideas would be freely exchanged and incorporated into the day-to-day lives of the students. His ultimate goal was to revitalize the Jewish community through education, and he was determined to see his idea come to fruition.

As the war entered its final months in summer of 1918, Rosenzweig now turned to defining more clearly his interpretaion of Jewish theology. He began to jot down his thoughts on scraps of paper while he was still on the battlefields, and then from his bed in a military hospital in Belgrade, where he recovered first from influenza and pneumonia, and later from a malarial infection. He sent these ideas back home to his mother on postcards and in letters.

Once Germany had surrendered in November 1918 and Rosenzweig was permitted to return home to Kassel, he gathered together and reworked his writings into a book, *The Star of Redemption*, completed in early 1919, and was published less than two years later. It cemented his reputation for what he later humbly called, "The New Thinking." While he referred to the book as merely being "an episode" in his life, Rosenzweig had, according to Gershom Scholem, written "one of the central creations of Jewish religious thought in the [twentieth] century." Scholem regarded Rosenzweig, with whom he became acquainted during the early 1920s, as "a man of genius."

Influenced by such philosophers as Plato, Aristotle, Kant, Hegel, Maimonides, and Spinoza, in addition to Hermann Cohen and Martin Buber, *The Star of Redemption* is as complex a book as Rosenzweig was a person. In his quest to reveal the true meaning of God and faith, Rosenzweig determined that Christian and Jewish theology were linked by three elements: Creation, Revelation, and Redemption. Upon that basis, he then advanced his theory for understanding Jewish history and life.

Rosenzweig argued that Jewish survival was dependent on Jews keeping a certain distance from history, on their refusing "to participate in efforts to perfect the world." As historian Paul

Mendes-Flohr explains, Rosenzweig was putting forth a theory that Jews live beyond history "in a spiritual reality that anticipates the Kingdom of God." Daily Jewish prayers and traditional holiday observances created a universal, timeless Jewish community that eclipsed the events of the world and particulars of nationality. For Rosenzweig, being "chosen" by God meant fulfilling a special, unique mission and experiencing a spiritual existence that rose above of the turmoil of war, revolutions, nationalism, and politics that had engulfed Germany in 1918 and 1919.

"Among the peoples of the earth, the Jewish people is 'the one people,' as it calls itself on the high rungs of its life," Rosenzweig wrote, "which it ascends Sabbath after Sabbath. The peoples of the world are not content with the bonds of blood. They sink their roots into the night of earth, lifeless in itself but the spender of life, and from the lastingness of earth they conclude that they themselves will last . . . We were the only ones who trusted in blood and abandoned the land; and so we preserved the priceless sap of life which pledged to us that it would be eternal."

During the ensuing years, *The Star of Redemption* provoked much discussion as scholars speculated and attempted to decipher its true meaning. Rosenzweig, himself, later called his book "a theory that grew out of an ardent longing;" a longing, adds his biographer Nahum Glatzer, that "was to reach the state of a man who stands before God, and now lives in this faith." Rosenzweig's determination to make his faith a tangible force led him to spend the remaining years of his all-too-brief life offering a new approach to Jewish education.

The *Lehrhaus*

BY 1919, THE WAR had been lost and the Kaiser had abdicated. The Allies who condemned Germany in the Peace of Versailles, now watched as the country they'd punished attempted, against great odds, to become a legitimate democracy: For the next several years, until the Weimar government was in place (though never firmly),

Germany underwent a series of violent revolutions and counter-revolutions marked by a rash of political murders.

Much to the chagrin of some members of the Jewish community, Jews were far too active and conspicuous in these events. The writer Jakob Wassermann saw the situation differently, however. "Jews were and are on the front lines of every iconoclasm, every upheaval or social demand," he wrote in the midst of the troubles. "Jews are the Jacobins of the age."

He was not far off. In January 1919, in Berlin, the Spartacists (later the German Communist Party) led by Karl Liebknecht and Rosa Luxemburg, a Polish-born Jew who rejected her heritage in her fight for social justice, tried to start a proletariat revolution as Lenin and Trotsky had done in Russia. They failed and were both murdered by right-wing army officers. In Munich, Kurt Eisner, briefly the leader of a revolutionary government, was also killed (by Count Anton Arco-Valley, whose mother was Jewish, and who wanted to prove his loyalty to Germany). This triggered even more violence, including, as noted, the killing of Walter Rathenau, following his appointment as the Foreign Affairs Minister. On June 24, 1922, while riding to his office in an open car in Berlin, Rathenau was assassinated by a gang of five veterans.

Once the calm had been more or less restored to Germany – following Hitler's and the Nazi Party's failed putsch in Munich in 1923 – Jewish politicians (with the exception of the economist Rudolf Hilferding, who served as finance minister from 1928 to 1930) were far less influential in the highest ranks of the government. This was despite the fact that the right-wing parties blamed the Jews for the inadequacies of the Weimar Republic, or the "*Judenrepublik*," as they called it with contempt. There was little, it seemed, that was not the fault of the Jews. They were held responsible for just about everything wrong with Germany: the defeat in the war, the hyperinflation that destroyed the country's economy, the terrible unemployment (in 1932, one estimate in a Jewish newspaper recorded that 50,000 Jews were also unemployed in Germany), and for undermining "Christian values."

The twenties were a time of vocal and physical backlash. University campuses in particular became hotbeds of anti-Jewish sentiments, resulting in behaviour ranging from unruliness to violence against Jewish students and professors. As early as 1920, Albert Einstein's work was scorned as being "un-German" and right-wing nationalists interrupted his classes.

Eastern European Jews and Jewish-owned shops were swarmed by mobs in Berlin in early November 1923, after the mark lost much of its value. On trains, at schools, and on the street, many Jews became targets of anti-Semitism.

During the next few years, the number of these incidents increased. The Jewish community believed they could deal with it. They organized self-defence groups and put their faith in democracy. And, why should they not have? Until the onset of the Depression, the political parties and groups of the extreme right – most notably the Nazis – carried little weight. (In the 1928 election, for instance, the Nazis received only 2.6 per cent of the vote and 12 of 493 seats in the Reichstag.) When Walter Rathenau was murdered, thousands of Germans peacefully marched through the streets of Berlin out of respect for him, and Reich Chancellor Joseph Wirth disassociated himself from the assassination, declaring, at a gathering in Rathenau's honour, that the "enemy stands on the right." Yet, as historian Fritz Stern adds, "that enemy remained unappeased."

None of these political machinations or anti-Semitic outbreaks deterred Franz Rosenzweig, dedicated and stubborn as he was idealistic, from continuing with his work to foster Jewish education. In 1919, he met Rabbi Nehemiah Nobel, a prominent orthodox clergyman from Frankfurt and one of the founders of Mizrachi, the orthodox Zionist party. With the help of Nobel as well as other influential Jews in Frankfurt, Rosenzweig was able to establish the *Freies Jüdisches Lehrhaus* (Free Jewish Academy). Located in Frankfurt, the school was open to all, though students did have to pay tuition. Rosenzweig served as its first director.

Rosenzweig believed that the *Lehrhaus* would stimulate a new sense of Judaism among its young adult students, one that would bode well for the future. His main aim was to "revitalize" Jewish life within a modern European setting. To this end, he was a pioneer and visionary. According to Nahum Glatzer, Rosenzweig "succeeded in making known to the *Kultur*-obsessed German Jew that Judaism is not a concern of the backward and the obscurantists."

Rosenzweig explained his ultimate objective at the academy's opening in August 1920: "All of us to whom Judaism, to whom being a Jew, has again became the pivot of our lives – and I know that in saying this here I am not speaking for myself alone – we all know that in being Jews we must not give up anything, not renounce anything, but lead everything back to Judaism. From the periphery back to the center; from the outside, in. This is a new sort of learning."

For the teachers and students alike, both the acculturated as well as the religious, the *Lehrhaus* was a "magical" place where a unique method of education was born. Classes were an intellectual journey, where all of the participants learned from each other. It was the "first time in the history of Judaism," recalled Ernst Simon, who was taught at the school, "that the *Rav* [rabbi and scholar] was sitting on the same bench as the *am-ha'arets* [lay persons without adequate knowledge of the Torah and Jewish traditions], not only in order to hear, in order to learn, but also as instructor."

The *Lehrhaus* attracted not only rabbis but secular, stellar teachers. Using his connections in the intellectual community, Rosenzweig assembled an impressive faculty. At various times, seminars were given by: Rabbi Nobel, Franz Oppenheimer, Bertha Pappenheim (the Jewish feminist and president of the Jewish Women's League), Siegfried Kracauer (a popular journalist and critic from the newspaper, *Frankfurt Zeitung*), Eduard Strauss (a chemist as well as a brilliant orator on the Bible), Gershom Scholem (who led discussions on the *Zohar*), Shmuel Agnon (who later won a Nobel prize), Rabbi Leo Baeck, philosopher Leo Strauss, psychologist Erich Fromm, Nahum Glatzer (later Rosenzweig's biographer), Ernst

Simon (who taught Jewish history), and most notably, Martin Buber (whose lectures on Hasidism in 1922 served as basis for his seminal work of existential philosophy *I and Thou*, published later that year).

Overall, between 1920 and 1926, the *Lehrhaus* employed 64 teachers who offered 90 lecture courses and 180 study groups. At its height, in 1922-23, the academy had an enrolment of 1,100 students. Rosenzweig's model stimulated the organization of other academies and study groups throughout Germany. At the Free Jewish Adult Centre in Berlin from 1919-32, 20,000 people took a wide-range of courses.

The *Lehrhaus* movement envisioned and nurtured by Rosenzweig was instrumental in producing "a new type of Jew, who would proudly identify with a positive content of Judaism instead of reducing his or her Jewish identity to the struggle for equality and against anti-Semitism," says Michael Brenner, a historian of Weimar culture. In essence, Rosenzweig set limits for Jewish assimilation, defining and clarifying the parameters of the German-Jewish symbiosis that Hermann Cohen had introduced to him.

Who knows what else Rosenzweig might have accomplished had he not been struck down so early in his life by a debilitating illness. In early 1922, with his pregnant wife Edith by his side, he learned from his doctors that he was suffering from amyotrophic lateral sclerosis, a paralyzing disease. By August 1922, a month before his son Rafael was born, he already had difficulty writing and his speech began to deteriorate. Four months later, he could no longer hold a fountain pen; four months after that, he could no longer speak.

In the fall of 1923, the degeneration stopped, but he remained on permanent life support. For the next six years, he lived in physical agony, yet he did not surrender to his illness and made the most of his life, which became a richly spiritual existence. The poet Karl Wolfskehl visited him during those years and remembered the experience as follows: "Whoever stepped over the threshold of Franz Rosenzweig's room entered a magic circle and fell under a

spell . . . The solidity and the familiar forms of everyday life melted
away and the incredible became the norm. Behind the desk, in the
armchair sat, not as one had imagined on climbing the stairs, a mor-
tally sick, utterly invalid man, almost totally deprived of physical
force . . . behind the desk, in the chair Franz Rosenzweig was throned.
The moment our eyes met his community was established."

For a time Rosenzweig, with his wife's help, used a special type-
writer to communicate with his friends and colleagues. Amazingly,
he continued to work. He translated sixty hymns and poems of the
eleventh-century Sephardi poet Judah Halevi. Most significantly,
he collaborated with Martin Buber on the German translation of
Bible — "a hallmark of the German-Jewish renaissance," in the
words of Paul Mendes-Flohr — a project they started together in
the mid-twenties, but that Buber was not to complete until 1961.
Buber recalled that he had translated sections and sent the drafts to
Rosenzweig for his commentary. They would then meet to discuss
the text. By the time Rosenweig died at the end of 1929, the two
scholars had reached the Book of Isaiah. Fittingly, Buber spoke at
Rosenzweig's funeral and read the Seventy-Third Psalm, a verse of
which was engraved on Rosenzweig's headstone:

Nevertheless I am continually with Thee;
Thou holdest my right hand.

Wear the Yellow Patch with Pride

GIVEN HIS OPTIMISTIC nature and faith in human goodness and
progress, Franz Rosenzweig would not have predicted nor compre-
hended the terrible tragedy that was to befall the Jews of Europe
within but a decade following his death. In this, he was like most
German Jews who remained committed to what they believed was
an assimilated, yet overly Jewish life in Germany. The remarkable
creativity in the arts, music, theatre, and literature that characterized the Jewish contribution to Weimar culture, they reasoned,
would continue far into the future.

There was trouble on the horizon, but most either ignored the signs or dismissed them as a consequence of the horrendous economic crisis. In mid-September 1931, on Rosh Hashana, a Nazi mob numbering in the hundreds used clubs and truncheons to attack and beat Berlin's Jews while they walked on the fashionable Kurfustendamm dressed in their synagogue clothes. Many people in the community were shaken by this violent, premeditated outburst, yet they did not see it as anything but an isolated incident. And how can we blame them? A fair number of German Gentiles (not to mention most Western political leaders) also underestimated Hitler's penchant for destruction.

Two years later, on April 1, 1933, the Nazis organized their first boycott of Jewish businesses and plastered Jewish stores and shops with the Star of David. At the time, Robert Weltsch, the editor of *Jüdische Rundschau*, advised his readers to "wear the yellow badge with pride!" – "a statement that made sense only on the assumption that Jewish life in Germany would go on for some time to come," observes historian Donald Niewyk.

The fact was that, the Rosh Hashana attack in Berlin notwithstanding, the majority of Jews were not confronted with violence on a daily basis, before 1933. Even then, adds Niewyk, "Anti-Semitism, was an annoying but scarcely terrifying propaganda campaign of charges that ran from the predictable – Jews were traitors, exploiters, and so on – to the preposterous: in a grotesquely twisted anticipation of things to come, Dresden racists accused Jews of stealing the gold fillings from the teeth of corpses in the municipal crematorium." It is notable (as well as sadly ironic) that a week before Hitler's appointment as chancellor on January 30, 1933, the Berlin Jewish Museum first opened its doors. It was located only a few blocks away from the Reichstag, so soon to be burned down. In its entranceway, visitors were greeted by a row of busts of such prominent German Jews as Moses Mendelsohnn and Abraham Geiger – German Jews who symbolized the century old German-Jewish connection.

German Jews had learned to live with anti-Semitism. But they also believed that in the country of Kant, Hegel, and Schiller, anti-Semitism would gradually decline, and democracy and liberalism would reassert themselves. The nuclear physicist and refugee Sir Rudolf Peierls's comment that "in pre-Hitler Germany, being Jewish was a bearable handicap" was not far from wrong. Germany's Jews, in the early thirties, had been dealing with prejudice and discrimination all their lives and had learned to adapt to it. Their coping skills were strong, and their love for Germany blinded them to the hatred surrounding them.

Hitler's stunning rise to power brought with it horrors no one could ever have imagined could occur in a civilized nation. "The expectation was not so much that Germans would behave decently," argues Peter Pulzer, "but that they would behave in accordance with rational self-interest." It was the very imperfection of the German-Jewish symbiosis that made them initially complacent about their prospects, even in a country led by Adolf Hitler.

Chapter Eleven

THE JERUSALEM OF LITHUANIA

Vilna, 1944

City
How mourn a city
Whose people are dead and whose dead are alive
In the heart?

— ABBA KOVNER, *MY LITTLE SISTER*, 1967

Litvaks

WHAT WAS ONCE JEWISH VILNA now exists only in the collective imagination of its aging survivors. Walking the streets of present-day Vilnius, as the Lithuanian city has been called since the end of the Second World War, one searches in vain for a sign of the once thriving Jewish community. There is nothing remaining of the gates to the infamous Vilna ghetto in which the Nazis imprisoned the city's Jews. Most of the ghetto's main buildings were destroyed long ago or renovated beyond recognition. The *Judenrat* (or Jewish Council) headquarters is now an art restoration centre, and the Jewish hospital, a Chinese restaurant and office building. A kindergarten and school occupy the site of the Great Synagogue of Vilna, one of the most famous and impressive in Europe. Only the Choral Synagogue, built in 1903 and now a shadow of its former self, is open for the small Jewish community of perhaps twenty-five hundred. Rabbi Samuel Kahn from London is the synagogue's official rabbi, though he is present in Vilnius only about once a month.

Looking down Rudninku Street, once the ghetto's main avenue where the tragedy of the Holocaust was played out, you can see the tall spires of the Church of All Saints, the same spires that the ghetto's inhabitants viewed each day of their captivity, a sight of both hope and despair.

Since the fall of the Soviet Union and the rebirth in 1990 of an independent Lithuanian state, a Jewish museum has been resurrected in Vilnius and a new and larger structure is being planned. Memorials and markers, too, have been erected to commemorate the fallen Jewish martyrs and heroes of a time that many East Europeans would prefer to forget.* But the city that the "Litvaks," as Vilna's Jews were called, nurtured over the course of many centuries has vanished.

In the years between the two world wars, fifty-five thousand Jews, about 30 to 35 per cent of the city's total population, resided in Vilna. (The city was Vilna to the Russians, Wilno or Vilno to the Poles, and Vilne in Yiddish.) And whether they were living under Russian, Polish, or Lithuanian rule, the Litvaks were a breed apart. You could (and still can) tell a Litvak by his or her Yiddish dialect: they pronounce "oy" as "ey" and "sh" as "s." The women of Vilna were famous for using lots of pepper in their gefilte fish rather than sugar, as was the custom in Poland. Tradition has it that this recipe made the Litvaks sharp, peppery, and sceptical.

---

* It has only been in the past few years that a serious effort has been made to include the Holocaust as a subject of study in Lithuanian schools. Yet the role of Lithuanian collaborators who willingly joined the Nazis remains controversial. At several memorial sites, for instance, the Lithuanian version of the marker omits any reference to the Nazis having "local assistants," a phrase used in the Hebrew, Yiddish, and English translations. As my well-informed guide Stefan told me, there are currently three reactions to Holocaust issues: a small minority, mainly intellectuals, accepts the truth of the collaboration; a more popular view is that the Jews brought their troubles upon themselves as a result of their supposed alliance with the Soviets, who ruled Vilna during 1940–41; and the majority remains ignorant and is happy to be so.

In Vilna, the Litvaks lived around the core of the old Jewish quarter located near Zydowska (Žydų) Street, or "Jew's Street." Here, they had their kosher food shops, old clothes market, book stores, and restaurants like Velfkeh's ("Wolfie's"), a must-stop for Yiddish intellectuals and writers. From the Orthodox to the secular, from Zionist to socialist, every possible religious, ideological, and political philosophy was represented in the dynamic spectrum that defined the city's Jewish community. With its yeshivas, schools, libraries, and theatres, it boasted as rich a Jewish culture as anywhere in Europe.

Few events in the modern history of the Jewish Diaspora are not in some way linked to Vilna. The city was home to the great Hebrew and Yiddish novelists of the day, who celebrated Vilna's special character in their books and plays. It was Vilna's Jewish workers who first conceived of the Bund in 1897, and others rallied to the Zionist cause in later years. There was YIVO, the Yiddish Scientific Institute for the research and study of the Yiddish language and culture, prominent publishing houses, and, at one time, six Yiddish and Hebrew newspapers. Vilna's Jewish character was evident even to Napoleon, who, after marching to the entrance of the Great Synagogue in 1812, proclaimed that the city was indeed the "Jerusalem of Lithuania." It was an epithet that stuck.

The city's special character made an impact, too, on Lucy Dawidowicz, later an eminent historian and chronicler of the Holocaust, who spent a year as an American university student studying in Vilna in 1938. "The sound of Yiddish resonated throughout the city," she recalled. "You heard Yiddish in the streets, the shops, and the marketplace.... You could live a full life in Vilna for a year, as I did, or even a lifetime, as many Vilna Jews did, speaking only Yiddish, without knowing much Polish or knowing it well."

The twentieth century brought new concerns and burdens for Vilna's Jews. Who could blame them? They were caught in the middle of a raging battle between the expansionist and nationalistic desires of Russia, Germany, Poland, and Lithuania. Nine different governments ruled over the city between 1914 and 1922. The economy was in ruins, poverty severe, and persecution a reality of day-to-day life. German troops marched into the city on Yom Kippur, September 18, 1915, driving out the Russians, who had controlled Vilna since Catherine the Great had designated it as part of the Pale of Settlement.

Three years later, when the Germans were defeated, both Lithuanians and Poles claimed Vilna as their own. The Russians, now under a Bolshevik regime, had other ideas. Polish Legionnaires assumed command of the city early in 1919, but were beaten back by the Red Army. It took four more months before the Poles mounted another, this time successful, charge. Believing that the Jews had supported the communists, the Poles went on a rampage. Jewish shops were looted, Jews were attacked in the streets, and at least eighty were shot. In July 1920, the Bolsheviks took Vilna once more with the thought of giving the city to the Lithuanians. Further fighting ensued until treaty negotiations in Riga finally ended the conflict and confirmed that Vilna would be part of the newly expanded independent country of Poland.

Poland Was for Poles

THE POLES NOW GOVERNED over an empire that stretched from Katowice in the west to Rovno (now Rivne, Ukraine) in the east. Within its borders lived a population of 35 million people, 30 per cent of whom were not Polish. There were 5 million Ukrainians, 1.5 million Belarussians, 700,000 Germans, 80,000 Lithuanians, and more than 3 million Jews. Poland had agreed to the terms of the Minorities Treaty, which guaranteed equal rights in culture, education, and language to these various ethnic groups. Still, given the nationalistic passions of the day, this diverse mix did not sit well with many Poles, who regarded their country's minorities as an "affliction."

Many of the problems faced by Poland during the years between the two world wars stemmed from its economic backwardness and political vulnerability. Nearly 75 per cent of its population were peasants, and most were illiterate, trapped in a feudal relationship with the aristocracy that had not advanced for centuries. In the cities, industrial development lagged behind the west, and the economy could not generate the required capital. One cost of independence and the turmoil that followed the First World War was the loss of trade with Lithuania and Russia. The onset of the Depression in the early 1930s made a bad situation worse. Beyond this was the ever-present threat of invasion by the Bolsheviks in the east or Germany in the west. Being Polish meant constantly looking over your shoulder.

In such an anxious climate, it is not surprising that anti-Semitism was prevalent. Jews may have lived among Poles for centuries, but they were generally regarded with disdain. In a country that was essentially rural in character, Jews were urban people. According to a 1931 census, nearly a million Jews lived in the large Polish cities of Warsaw, Łódź, Cracow, Lvov, Lublin, and Vilna, where they accounted for 30 to 40 per cent of each city's population. They were members of the urban middle class – small merchants, middlemen, teachers, lawyers, and physicians. While some Jews did attempt to integrate into the larger Polish society, many by choice led more segregated lives not very different from those of their ancestors in the *shtetlach* of the Pale. How else, they reasoned, could they preserve their religion and heritage? But this attitude merely reinforced the Polish view that Jews were outsiders.

Almost from the beginning of Poland's rebirth until the Germans invaded in September 1939, debate on the "Jewish Question" was constant. There were two basic views. The moderate one was advocated by the socialists and liberals, and by Marshal Józef Piłsudski, the charismatic leader who established a semi-dictatorship in Poland from 1926 until his death in 1935. Piłsudski, who supported a Polish federation for all of its peoples, refused to make anti-Semitism part of his government's official program, yet he could not eradicate or control it.

The political parties of the right, Endecja, the National Democratic Party, and its more extreme offshoot, Naras, or the National Radicals, represented the second, more vocal, view. From their perspective, shared by the Polish Catholic Church, Poland was for Poles. The Right's leading spokesman and personality was Roman Dmowski, the head of Endecja, who maintained that Jews were a threat to the unity of the nation because they could not be assimilated. "The Jew treats with aversion the entire past of European nations," Dmowski declared as early as 1914. "He harbors hatred toward their religions and looks upon all the hierarchies that have arisen in these societies as he does upon the usurpers who have taken the place due his 'chosen people.'" At first, Dmowski wanted to limit Jewish involvement in Polish society, but in the decade before the Second World War, he talked about "de-Judaizing" Poland – pushing the Jews out of the economic life of the country.

During the twenties and thirties, anti-Jewish policies and attitudes manifested themselves in a number of ways. The Polish government nationalized several "Jewish" industries, including liquor, salt, and tobacco. Sunday was declared to be a day of rest for everyone in Poland, which meant that if Jews wanted to keep their own Sabbath on Saturday, they could now work only five days a week. And Jews were subject to oppressive and discriminatory taxation. After Piłsudski died, there was a further shift to the right, and the Endecja had some success with its call for a boycott of Jewish businesses. "*Swój do Swego*," the signs in Vilna proclaimed, "Buy from your own kind." One of the last anti-Jewish measures attempted before the war broke out was a bill introduced in the Sejm, the Polish parliament, to ban the Jewish ritual koshering of meat.

The consequence of these sanctions, along with Poland's stagnant economy, was predictable: Jewish businesses went bankrupt, incomes declined, and unemployment and poverty dramatically increased. During the 1930s, there were few Jewish neighbourhoods in Polish cities in which one did not see beggars and ragged children. Among the young, tuberculosis was rampant.

In the universities, the Endecja and other right-wing groups were consistent in their demand not only for a quota system to curtail enrolment of Jewish students, but also for segregated seating, or "ghetto benches," in classrooms. The pressure worked. In 1923–24, approximately 24 per cent of all students enrolled at Polish universities were Jewish. A decade later the figure was only 8 per cent. Segregating the classrooms took longer, although eventually university administrators caved in to the demands of a growing number of their students. There were "Jewless" days, organized to prevent Jewish students from attending classes, and when professors refused to abide by the new seating rules they were attacked. The bullying of Jewish students was constant.

While the Catholic Church in Poland did not support the violence, it did believe in the segregation of Jews from Christians. "A Jewish problem exists, and will continue to exist as long as Jews remain Jews," Cardinal August Hlond argued in a widely quoted pastoral letter in 1936. "It is a fact that the Jews fight against the Catholic Church, they are free-thinkers, and constitute the vanguard of atheism, of the bolshevik movement and of revolutionary activity. It is a fact that Jewish influence upon morals is fatal and their publishers spread pornographic literature. It is true that the Jews are committing frauds, practicing usury, and dealing in white slavery. It is true that in schools, the influence of the Jewish youth upon the Catholic youth is generally evil, from a religious and ethical point of view. But – let us be just. Not all Jews are like that."

Most Poles agreed with the cardinal's assessment. Violence was not the answer, yet something had to be done with the "surplus" Jewish population. Year after year, Polish politicians sought a viable solution. An official government study released in 1937, one of many on the "Jewish Question," defined the problem as follows:

"The effect of [Jews'] separate political aspirations and the effect of their numbers, plus their major influence over many areas of social and national life, is to make the Jews, in the present state of affairs, an element that weakens the normal development of national and state strength that is currently being achieved in Poland."

General Stanisław Skwarczyński put the issue more succinctly. "We aspire to diminish the number of Jews in Poland," he declared a few months before the war began. The General did not know it then, but the Nazis would soon solve Poland's "Jewish question" for them.

It is dangerous to examine Jewish life in Poland during the inter-war years in relation to the tragedy of the Holocaust that followed. One needs to separate Polish anti-Semitism from the mass murder of Jews by the Nazis. Prejudice and discrimination were part of daily life in Poland for Jews, yet there is absolutely nothing in Polish history to suggest that anything remotely like the Holocaust would have occurred without the German initiative.

Once the war started, millions of Poles were victims of the Nazi brutality and murder, and many risked their lives and the lives of their families to protect Jews. Many have been honoured by Yad Vashem in Israel as being "Righteous among the Gentiles," an award of distinction and humanity. But a minority – the fifteen thousand or so members of the Polnische Polizei, the Polish police, who guarded ghettos, an unknown number of peasant farmers who conducted "Jew hunts" to search out and kill ghetto escapees, and some Polish partisans who were as anti-Semitic as the Nazis – did collaborate and were more than happy to see their Jewish neigh-bours marched off to the death camps. As soon as the Jews were gone, they moved into their former neighbours' homes and rifled their possessions. Informing on Jews to the German authorities was common, routinely done in exchange for a few kilograms of salt.

Polish suffering under the Nazi regime has thus left a mixed his-torical legacy. Today, Poles regard themselves no less as victims of the Nazis than do Jews and will vehemently dispute any claim to the contrary. Stories by Holocaust survivors of Polish complicity in crimes against the Jews are often dismissed as distortions of reality based on anecdotal evidence, or, at worst, as aberrations.[*] Polish writers point to Jewish support for the Soviet regime and instances in which Jewish partisans supposedly attacked and killed Polish civilians.

Needless to say, most Holocaust survivors who grew up in Poland during the thirties do not have fond memories of that time (of course, these memories are partly shaped by the events of the war). Most Jewish children, at one time or another, were called a "dirty Jew" and told to "Go back to Palestine." They were bullied and taunted in school by students and, on occasion, by their teachers. Violence in the streets by roaming bands of anti-Semitic thugs was frequent, and Jewish boys and girls learned quickly that visiting a public place alone was unwise. Jack Sutin, who lived in the town of Mir, southwest of Minsk, states that as a youngster he had a sense that Jews were detested in Poland. One day, he boarded a crowded train. When he finally found a seat and sat down, "The man sitting next to it stared at me and then spat out the words, 'No Jews allowed!'" I remember that moment," says Sutin, who survived the war as a partisan, "because it made me

---

[*] On July 10, 1941, in the town of Jedwabne, northeast of Warsaw, 1,600 Jews, almost the village's entire Jewish population, were rounded up, locked in a barn, and burned to death. For years, this crime was blamed on the Nazis. A stone memorial on the spot where the barn once stood stated, "Place of martyrdom of the Jewish people. Hitler's Gestapo and gendarmerie burned 1,600 people alive, July 10, 1941." Now, owing to the diligent research of U.S. Polish historian Jan T. Gross, the truth has emerged. In his new book *Neighbors*, he has confirmed that this act of murder was in fact undertaken and conducted by the Polish villagers themselves. The book unleashed a storm of protest in Poland when it was released in May of 2000. Its reception in North America in the spring of 2001 has not been much better. Some Poles denounced the work as part of "an international Jewish conspiracy." The stone marker at Jedwabne, however, has been removed. A memorial was held there on July 10, 2001, attended by Poland's President Aleksander Kwaśniewski, who asked for forgiveness. Some Poles, however, believe there is nothing to apologize for.

realize, more than anything that had come before, that in Poland I would never be allowed to live a normal and peaceful life."

Despite these difficulties, life went on. Anti-Semitism did not stifle a thriving Polish-Yiddish culture. There were lectures, plays, political clubs, sports teams, schools, and synagogues. The world was changing and so was the Jewish family. More often, it seemed, children challenged their parents and the traditional Jewish customs. Unlike their fathers, Jewish boys were apt to be clean-shaven, a symbol of this secular generation gap. Anti-Semitism should have united Jews of all ages and political stripes in common cause. Instead it only served to split the community farther apart. Members of the religious Agudat Yisrael political party clashed with the more secular Folkist party, the *Yiddishe Folk-Partey in Polyn*, while arguments about Jewish life raged between communists, socialists, and Zionists, who themselves, as noted, were divided along ideological lines.

The young socialist Bundists regarded the Zionists with disdain. If Jews had problems they should be solved in Poland. Fleeing to Palestine was not the answer. They organized self-defence groups and patrolled the streets to protect Jews from anti-Semitic attacks. Young Zionists felt the same way, though their main focus was the development of Hebrew culture and preparing themselves for the eventual move to Palestine, where Jews truly had a future. At summer camps in the Polish countryside, they created *kibbutzim* and trained for life on an agricultural settlement. Two of the more popular groups were Betar, who followed the right-wing teachings of Zionist leader Vladimir Jabotinsky and his Revisionist Party, and the more socialist and idealistic Ha-Shomer Ha-Tsair, or "Young Guard." It was not uncommon for Jewish teenagers to switch back and forth between the two as their political philosophies changed from one day to the next. Regardless, it was the passionate spirit of the young Zionists, their courage and determination, that provided leadership for the resistance movement during the war and later in the establishment of the State of Israel.

Vilna Is Not Vilna Alone, Ponar Is Not a Unique Episode

AMONG THE LEADERS OF THE HA-SHOMER HA-TSAIR in Vilna in 1939 was a bright and popular twenty-one-year-old named Abba Kovner. He was thin, of medium height, with wavy, thick black hair, a long nose, and penetrating dark eyes. Kovner was serious, compassionate, and a deep thinker. Then and later, he was wise beyond his years with "an extraordinary lack of ego." After the war, these qualities would make him one of Israel's best poets. In the 1930s, he was admired and respected by young Zionists for being a man of vision. Few doubted that one day Abba Kovner really would get to Palestine.

Kovner inherited his Zionist beliefs from his parents. He was born in Sevastopol, in the Crimea, in 1918 during his family's attempt to reach Palestine. But the First World War halted their journey. After Kovner was born, they decided to return to Vilna, where the family had resided for many generations. Young Abba received a Hebrew as well as a secular education. He also developed his artistic abilities as a sculptor, much to the chagrin of his father, who thought his son should spend his time doing something more practical.

As a teenager involved in Ha-Shomer Ha-Tsair, Kovner, like other Jews in Vilna, naturally paid attention to the unsettling events in Germany as the Nazis consolidated their power under Hitler and then proceeded to deny German Jews their civil rights. Following Kristallnacht on November 9, 1938, in which Jews were arrested and Jewish shops and synagogues destroyed, events moved quickly. Within a year, Hitler had neutralized the threat of a war with the Soviet Union by signing a non-aggression pact with Stalin. He then toyed with Western leaders before invading Poland in September 1939. For the Jews of Europe, life was never the same again.

The Jews in Vilna considered themselves fortunate. Under the terms of the Nazi–Soviet pact (slightly modified at the end of September 1939), Poland was divided along the Bug River. The

Nazis occupied the western area, while the Soviets moved into the east. For the moment, the three Baltic states, Lithuania, Latvia, and Estonia, though under the Soviet sphere, were declared to be independent. Vilna was again under Lithuanian control.

During the last months of 1939, a general panic ensued throughout the occupied territories. Jews and Poles in the west immediately felt the brutality of the Nazi regime. As cities and towns were taken over, civilians were routinely beaten, humiliated, and murdered. The first ghetto was established in the town of Piotrkow in early October, and ghettos in the larger Jewish communities of Warsaw and Łódź soon followed. Living conditions were abysmal. There were food shortages, limited provisions for sanitation, and tremendous overcrowding.

For a brief period, Jews in western Poland attempted to flee east into Soviet territory, thinking the situation there would be better. An estimated 300,000 to 350,000 Jews were able to escape from the Nazis in this way before the Soviet border was closed. But the truth was many Jews did not know where to go. One story has it that at the Biała Podlaska train station, the first stop on the German side, "a train filled with Jews going east met a train going west. When the Jews coming from Brisk saw the Jews going there, they shouted: 'You are mad, where are you going?' Those coming from Warsaw answered with equal astonishment: 'You are mad, where are you going?'" Many Jews also tried to get to Vilna, believing that the Lithuanians would treat them fairly. They were wrong. Lithuanians, regarding the Jews as Communist sympathizers, vented their anger, and anti-Jewish riots broke out at the end of October.

Less than a year later, Stalin reneged on his promise to Baltic leaders. Under the pretext of acting to protect Russian citizens from "provocative acts," Stalin's troops moved into the three states. Vilna was now under Soviet control. As Zionism was declared to be illegal, Abba Kovner kept away from the Russians and joined a small though not particularly powerful underground. Other Jews stood by helplessly as their property and assets were seized and they were transformed into Soviet citizens. Children went to school to learn Russian and Soviet catechism. The war, it seemed, was over.

Hitler's decision to attack the Soviet Union on June 22, 1941, not only caught Stalin off guard, but also set in motion the devastation of the Holocaust. It only took a few weeks for the German army to push deep into Soviet territory; by the end of July, Nazi troops were 320 kilometres from Moscow. More than three million Red Army soldiers were captured in the German offensive and imprisoned under brutal conditions in prisoner-of-war camps. Hundreds of thousands died from starvation and illness. Other Soviet soldiers trapped behind enemy lines in time became part of the massive Soviet partisan resistance that would be crucial to Jewish survival in the forests of eastern Poland, Belarussia, and the Ukraine.

German bombs hit Vilna early in the afternoon of June 22, and the onslaught continued until the next day. Desperate to flee from the Nazis, Jews left the city by foot or horse-drawn wagon, or managed to find room on eastbound trains. Most Jews, however, were paralyzed with fear and stayed put. "What to do? What to do with myself?" Herman Kruk wrote in his diary on June 23, 1941. Kruk was the director of a Jewish library in Warsaw. He had fled to Vilna to escape the Nazis two years earlier and now chose to remain there and take his chances. "I lacked the strength to take up the wanderer's staff and start off on the way on foot," he conceded. Instead, he decided to keep a record of the Nazi occupation.

Many Lithuanians were more than happy to see the Soviets flee. Once again, they took out their anger on the Jews in the city who, rightly or wrongly, they believed to be allied with the Soviet cause. On the night of June 25, as many as a thousand Jews were killed in Vilna and several synagogues were burned. A similar backlash erupted in the city of Kovno (Kaunas) and in surrounding towns and villages.

Like Herman Kruk, young Yitzhok Rudashevski, only fourteen at the time, also started a diary. He had grown up in Vilna with his mother, Rose, a seamstress, and his father, Eliahu, who worked as a typesetter for a Yiddish newspaper. He was small for his age – his family called him "Itsele" – and very perceptive. He had a capacity for learning and life that knew no bounds. He was, after Anne Frank, the most famous of Holocaust child diarists, an astute and passionate observer of the war's darkest period.

"I observe the empty, sad streets," he wrote on June 24. "A Lithuanian with a gun goes through the streets. I begin to understand the base betrayal of the Lithuanians. They shot the Red Army soldiers in the back. They make common cause with the Hitlerite bandits. The Red Army will return and you will pay dearly. We shall live to see your end." But only four days later, Rudashevski already recognized the despair and terror that had engulfed the city. "I stand at the window and feel a sense of rage. Tears come to my eyes: all our helplessness, all our loneliness lies in the streets. There is no one to take our part. And we ourselves are so helpless. . . . Life becomes more and more difficult. People do not go out anywhere. . . . We are so sad, we are exposed to mockery and humiliation. . . . Our hearts are crushed witnessing the shameful scenes where women and older people are kicked in the middle of the street."*

All through the summer, as the Nazis put into place their police administration, Jews were abused. Jewish men were arrested on the streets and taken to prison or forced into manual labour. Assisted by local collaborators, Nazis employed the same harsh regulations

---

* Both Kruk and Rudashevski were eventually murdered by the Nazis: Kruk in Estonia in September 1944, and Rudashevski a year earlier, when the Vilna ghetto was liquidated. Before he was deported from Vilna, Kruk buried a copy of his diary in a tin can in a bunker. After Vilna was liberated in July 1944, parts of the manuscript were discovered by Kruk's friend, the poet Abraham Sutskever. Rudashevski's cousin Sore Voloshin was able to escape from the ghetto and survive the war hiding with the partisans. She, too, returned to Vilna and found Yitzhok's diary buried in dirt. Both diaries have been published in various forms. They were sent to the YIVO institute, which had relocated to New York from Vilna after the war, where they are presently preserved.

and restrictions that they had enforced in the western occupied area of Poland – rules designed to segregate and terrorize Jews.

On July 3, the German military commander of Vilna ordered that all Jews were required to wear a yellow badge, four inches in diameter and "prominently placed on the chest and on the back." No Jew was allowed in the streets from 6 p.m. to 6 a.m. Breaking curfew could result in punishment by death. A few days later, another Nazi decree stated that all Jews over the age of ten years now had to wear a white armband with a yellow Star of David or a yellow circle on it with the letter "J" in the centre. More restrictions followed. Jews could only purchase food at special stores; they could no longer walk in most sections of the city; and they were forbidden from using most public facilities. Throughout Vilna, official notices declared "Admission forbidden to Jews." To ensure that their regulations were followed, the Nazis appointed community leaders in Vilna into a Judenrat, or Jewish Council, as they did elsewhere. It was a thankless and impossible job. Still, its first members took their position on the council seriously, believing that negotiating with Nazis was a viable option.

One of Hitler's chief objectives of the eastern campaign was to rid the world of Bolshevism. And that struggle, in the words of Field Marshal Wilhelm Keitel, "demands ruthless and energetic measures above all against the Jews, the main carriers of Bolshevism." As the Jews of Vilna and throughout the eastern territory soon learned, this task was to be accomplished by the Einsatzgruppen, Nazi death squads that followed each battalion of Wehrmacht soldiers as they marched across the Soviet Union. The three thousand members of the Einsatzgruppen were specially recruited from the ranks of S.S. police units and given instructions to cleanse the region of communists and Jews. In short, to make it *Judenfrei*, or free of Jews.

In Vilna, the Einsatzgruppe unit assigned to the city and its environs, arrived in the first week of July. The killing began soon after. In what became known as *Aktionen* (singular is *Aktion*), or actions, groups of Jews were roughly rounded up and taken to prison.

Gangs of Lithuanian thugs, known in Vilna as the *Ypatingas Burys*, or special squads, were also employed and paid a token amount for every Jew they caught. No one who ever witnessed the brutality of an *Aktion* would forget it.

When the Nazis first arrived, Abba Kovner and some of his friends had taken refuge at a Benedictine convent outside the city, where the thirty-five-year-old mother superior and her charge of nuns decided to hide as many Jews as they could. One day, Kovner had slipped back into the city to determine the fate of some of his comrades who had gone missing in Nazi roundups. "I still thought that part of these people, or most of them, would return," he remembered years later. Kovner watched in horror from a small apartment window as Nazis and Lithuanian collaborators invaded homes and apartments to gather their daily quota.

The operation began just as the sun set and lasted for the next four to five hours. People were forcibly taken from their homes and beaten if they did not immediately comply. In one instance, two soldiers had hold of a woman. They grabbed her by the hair and threw her on to the road. As she fell, the infant son she had been desperately clutching, dropped from her arms. One of the soldiers "took the infant, raised him into the air [and] grabbed him by the leg," Kovner later testified. "The woman crawled on the earth, took hold of his boot and pleaded for mercy. But the soldier took the boy and hit him with his head against wall, once, twice, smashed him against the wall."

What Kovner did not know then, and would not have believed, was that this woman, and all the of the Jews who had been apprehended that day, would be taken south from Vilna on the road to Grodno about thirteen kilometres to a spot in the Ponary (or Paneriai) forest (also referred to as the Ponar) where the Soviets had dug huge pits for fuel tanks. In groups of ten or twenty, men, women, and children were ordered to undress and hand over any money or jewellery they were carrying. Then a dozen or so people were marched at a time to the edge of the pit, where the soldiers of the Einsatzgruppen and their henchmen, often drunk, were waiting to do their duty for the Fatherland.* The Jews were shot in the head and their bodies piled up in the pits, one on top of the other, a massive heap of humanity. Often the bullet did not immediately kill its victim and he or she writhed in pain for hours after in a slow and terrible death. Children were often flung into the pits alive and young women abused. Some of the soldiers took photographs of the carnage and used them later as postcards.

Once the killing finally stopped, peasants were ordered to throw dirt over the pit, though it often took days for the ground to stop sinking and the river of blood to be absorbed. Approximately thirty-five thousand of Vilna's Jews were slaughtered in this way during July and August 1941, just a small number of the Jews in the eastern occupied territories who were murdered by the death squads that summer and fall. Among the more notorious acts of the Einsatzgruppen was the killing at Babi Yar, the death pits which were then on the outskirts of Kiev in the Ukraine. During a two-day period at the end of September 1941, 33,711 of the city's large Jewish population were executed. Here the Jews "were ordered to lie face down on the dead bodies while the S.S. men walked on the mounds shooting them at close range with pistols." The head of Einsatzgruppe in charge of the operation could later report to Nazi high command that the job in Kiev "was accomplished without

---

* On one occasion S.S. Chief Hienrich Himmler witnessed a mass killing for himself. According to S.S. General Karl Wolf, "Himmler had the deserved bad luck that from one or other of the people who had been shot in the head he got a splash of brains on his coat . . . and he went very green and pale. . . . After the shooting was over, Himmler gathered the shooting squad in a semi-circle around him and, standing up in his car, so that he would be a little higher and be able to see the whole unit, he made a speech. He had seen for himself how hard the task which they had to fulfill for Germany in the occupied areas was, but however terrible it all might be, even for him as a mere spectator, and how much worse it must be for them, the people who had to carry it out, he could not see any way round it. They must be hard and stand firm. He could not relieve them of this duty."

interference. No incidents occurred." Soon the Nazis would design an even more efficient and less personal method of murder with the use of gas at death camps.

At first, few Jews would believe the rumours of mass murder. How can you blame them? After all these years, the grisly tales of the slaughter are still impossible to comprehend. At the time, it was unthinkable that human beings could kill one another like this. Even the Jews marching to the pits could not comprehend their own demise. "The people who were seized did not believe they were being led to their death, that guiltless people would be killed," recorded Grisha Shur, one resident of Vilna, in his diary. "They thought there would be interrogations and those found to be Communists would be punished, but ordinary people would never be killed. They went to the Ponar with these thoughts on their mind."

Abba Kovner was among the few who did grasp the significance of the events in the Ponary. One of those taken to the death pits on the last day of August was a young woman named Sonia. Naked, she was led with her mother to the edge of the pits. When the shots were fired, she fell on the bodies below, but did not die; the bullet had gone right through her. She was bleeding yet alive. Her dead mother lay beside her. Despite the terrible pain, she remained still and silent for hours until the killing stopped and the soldiers left. She crawled out of the pit, over the bloodied bodies of her mother and the hundreds of other Jews who had been killed that day. Somehow she managed to stumble to a peasant farmhouse, where a Polish woman took her in and treated her wounds. In a few days, she had sufficiently recovered to make her way back to the city.

Soon she began telling her story of the slaughter to anyone who would listen. Many of the Jews in Vilna thought she had gone mad, but not Kovner. He heard her story and did not doubt her. He also understood the terrible ramifications of what was happening at the Ponary. "One thing is clear to me," Kovner explained a few months later to his friends. "Vilna is not Vilna alone, Ponar is not a unique episode. . . . It is a complete system."

The Streets Streamed with Jews Carrying Bundles

THE ORDER FOR THE ESTABLISHMENT of the Vilna ghetto was given one morning in early September 1941. They had been told to take only as much as they could carry. By nine o'clock in the morning on the day of the relocation, the streets were jammed. It was by all accounts a pathetic sight. Carrying what they could, or pushing their belongings in baby carriages and wheelbarrows, thousands of Jews were herded by the Nazi and Lithuanian police into one of three locations. They were ordered into one of two adjacent ghettos separated by Vokiečių street or dispatched directly to Lukiszki prison, where they were beaten and then transported to the Ponary and executed.

"The street streamed with Jews carrying bundles," young Yitzhok Rudashevski recorded in his diary. "People fall, bundles scatter. Before me a woman bends under her bundle. From the bundle a thin string of rice keeps pouring over the street. I walk burdened and irritated. The Lithuanians drive us on, do not let us rest. I think of nothing: not what I am losing, not what I have just lost, not what is in store for me. I do not see the street before me, the people passing by. . . . Here is the ghetto gate. I feel that I have been robbed, my freedom is being robbed from me, my home, and the familiar Vilna streets I love so much."

Relocating close to forty-five thousand Jews took the entire day.* Approximately thirty thousand were sent to Ghetto No. 1 and the remainder across the street into Ghetto No. 2. Large wooden gates, guarded on one side by the Nazis and Lithuanians and on the other by a Jewish ghetto police force (armed with wooden truncheons) operated by the Judenrat, were constructed to seal the area off. At first, the division was purely geographical, but within a few weeks Ghetto No. 1 became the home for those Jews who had been given

---

* While the Jewish population of Vilna in 1939 was approximately fifty-five thousand, at least twenty-five thousand Jews had come to the city from the west and from neighbouring towns and villages. Approximately thirty-five thousand, as noted, had been murdered by September 1941, leaving about forty thousand to forty-five thousand survivors.

work permits. They had been deemed useful for forced labour and thus became slaves for the Third Reich. They were abused and tormented, but for the moment they were permitted to live.

Across the street in Ghetto No. 2 were sent the elderly, many women, and children under the age of sixteen. This was the "unproductive" ghetto, where lives were expendable, in a real sense a temporary holding cell before its inhabitants were put to death at the Ponary. Starting on September 15 and continuing for the next month, Ghetto No. 2 was gradually liquidated and the ten thousand or so Jews behind its fence murdered.

"The most appalling thing in the ghetto was not death," remembered Abba Kovner. "It was infinitely more terrible to be defiled to the depth of your soul every hour of the day . . . and to wait. To look at the funeral pyre of the Jerusalem of Lithuania, to look at life by the mercy of the butcher."

Yitzhok Rudashevski and his family were sent to Ghetto No. 1. So were two close friends of Abba Kovner: Ruzka Korczak, a petite and bright young woman from the village of Plosk (or Płońsk) northwest of Warsaw who had fled to Vilna in 1939; and Vitka Kempner, from the town of Kalisz, west of Łódź. Vitka had light brown hair and could speak impeccable Polish, an important asset that she soon used as a key member of the Vilna resistance. Like Kovner, both women were committed Zionists, and both wanted to stay alive.

Life in the crowded ghetto was harsh. It was no better than a large prison camp. Food and water were extremely limited and proper sanitation facilities lacking. For Rudashevski, the first night in the ghetto was unbearable. "Besides the four of us there are eleven persons in the room," he wrote. "The room is a dirty and stuffy one. . . . The first ghetto night. We lie three together on two doors. I do not sleep. In my ears resounds the lamentation of this day. I hear the restless breathing of people with whom I have been suddenly thrown together, people who just like me have suddenly been uprooted from their homes." Similarly, Liza Ettinger, a young woman from Lida, Poland, who was also in Vilna, remembered that her first night in the ghetto was "hell on earth. Only the tongues of fire were missing. Crying of babies and groaning of sick people filled the air."

Even in the so-called "productive" ghetto, the lives of Jews were never secure. As the Nazis continued to reduce the size of ghetto populations throughout Eastern Europe, more and more Jews became expendable, no matter what skills they might have possessed. In Vilna at the end of October 1941, Nazi officials issued a set number of yellow work permits, or *scheins*. They meant the difference between life and death. People scrambled to obtain one, and the phrase, "as precious as a yellow permit" became a common Yiddish colloquialism in the ghetto. The "Yellow Schein Aktion" that followed, and other roundups during November and early December 1941, led to the death of at least another 5,500 people. By the new year, the population of the Vilna ghetto was about 20,000, of which 7,500 likely did not have correct papers. Perhaps 3,500 Jews had escaped death at the Ponary by fleeing the ghetto and finding a temporary refuge at nearby peasant farms or in the forests.

Throughout this period, the dominating presence in the ghetto was Jacob Gens, first as chief of the Judenrat's ghetto police force, and by July 1942 as chairman of the Judenrat itself. In many ways he is also the ghetto's most tragic figure. Like the heads of several other Judenrats, Gens believed that compliance with Nazi orders was the most prudent policy. "We must show [the Germans] that we are very useful," he declared in early 1942. "Work, especially work for the military, is the order of the day. . . . Jewish workers must give up easy, convenient jobs and take on more difficult work, in order to increase their usefulness. . . . This is essential for the collective interest of the ghetto."

In the end, there was no "collective interest of the ghetto." Gens was a victim of his own poor judgement, governed by the desperation of the times and caught up in his own power and ambition. He did not understand that the Vilna ghetto was never meant to be permanent, only a temporary stop on the way to the Ponary or the death camps.

Gens was born in 1905 in the small Lithuanian village near Kovno (now Kaunas). He served in the Lithuanian army and later attended university in Kovno, where he studied law and economics. He obtained a civil service posting, married a non-Jewish Lithuanian woman, and settled into a middle-class life. Gens did, however, keep active in the right-wing Zionist party the Revisionists.

When the Nazi occupation began, Gens could have remained hidden with his family. Instead, he felt compelled as a Jew to enter the ghetto and serve the Judenrat. A power unto himself, he was both detested and revered. Many ghetto inhabitants believed he had enough influence with the Nazis to save their lives. And on a few occasions, he did manage to do this. After he became head of the Judenrat, he was known as the Commandant and *der stolzer Jude*, "the proud Jew," who could deal directly with the Nazis. As he strolled the streets, he was carefully watched. If he was smiling, ghetto inhabitants relaxed for the moment, knowing all was well. An expression of concern or sadness on Gens's face could have a devastating effect on the entire ghetto.

Despite the hunger, disease, and isolation that defined ghetto life, Gens insisted on trying to make each day as routine as possible under the horrific circumstances – as hopeless a task as that was. For children, there was school and sports and drama clubs. Yitzhok Rudashevski enjoyed the distraction that learning offered. "I think to myself: what would be the case if we did not go to school, to the club, did not read books," he wrote in his diary on October 17, 1942. "We would die of dejection inside the ghetto walls." Five months later he added, "I often reflect, this is supposedly a ghetto yet I have a rich life of intellectual work: I study, I read, I visit club circles. Time runs so quickly and there is so much work to be done. . . . I often forget that I am in a ghetto." Seventeen-year-old Norman Shneidman was active in the various ghetto sports clubs. He recalls that for participating in a series of basketball games, he received a prize of a half-kilogram of sugar, and for taking part in boxing matches the reward was a similar amount of butter.

There was a ghetto newspaper, *Geto Yedies* ("Ghetto News"), which functioned as the Judenrat's official organ. Gens ensured that lectures were organized on diverse historical topics. The ghetto's Jewish library was very popular. Two-thirds of the library's forty-five thousand ancient Judaica collection was intact, and people made good use of the books no matter how much death was around them. The head of the library, Herman Kruk, noted somewhat casually on October 1, 1941, "Some 3,000 Jews taken away. And on the morrow, 390 books changed hands."

One of Gens's favourite institutions was the ghetto's theatre. There were Yiddish music recitals, poetry readings, and drama presentations. Gens and the other members of the Judenrat always got the best seats and even went so far as to invite Nazis and Lithuanians to attend productions. By all accounts the guests enjoyed themselves.

The idea of operating a theatre in the ghetto did not sit well with everyone. When productions were first held, a group of Bundists put up signs that read "*Oyf a besoylem shpilt men nit keyn teater*" ("In a cemetery no theatre ought to be performed"). But the theatre performances allowed a momentary respite from the brutality of life, no matter how illusory it was. "People laughed and cried," recorded Dr. Lazar Epstein in his diary after a performance in mid-January 1942. "They cast off the depression that had been weighing on their spirits. The alienation that had hitherto existed among the ghetto population seemed to have been thrown off . . . people woke from a long difficult dream."

All of these efforts were, of course, futile. Gens's attempt to "normalize" life in a Nazi ghetto was impossible and took him down a tortuous path. Manipulated and trapped by the Nazis, he soon tried to convince Vilna Jews and himself that sacrificing the lives of one thousand Jews to save five thousand was both a required and appropriate policy. In an emotional speech delivered at the presentation of a literary prize in 1942, he tried to explain his untenable position:

Many of you think of me as a traitor, and wonder what
I am doing here among you. . . . I, Gens, order you to
uncover your hiding places; I, Gens, struggle to obtain
work certificates, jobs, and benefits for the ghetto. I take
count of Jewish blood, not Jewish honor. When the
Germans ask me for a thousand persons, I hand them
over, for if we Jews will not give on our own, the
Germans will come and take them by force. Then they
will take not one thousand but thousands, and the whole
ghetto will be at their mercy. With hundreds, I save a
thousand; with the thousands that I hand over, I save ten
thousands. . . . If I survive, I shall come out of here
unclean, my hands dripping with blood. Nevertheless, I
shall willingly declare before a Jewish court: I did my
best to rescue as many Jews as I could to bring them to
the gates of redemption. I was forced to lead some
to their death in order that a small remnant may survive;
in order to have others emerge with a clear conscience,
I had to befoul myself and act without conscience.

Some Jews were so distressed that they accepted without reser-
vation whatever Gens said. Hardly a day went by when one person
or another did not arrive at the Judenrat offices begging him for
help. Yet Gens was merely a Nazi pawn, kept alive just as long he
was considered useful. At the end of 1942, Gens was ordered to
assist in a selection from the nearby town of Oszmiana. The
Germans demanded 1,400 people. Instead Gens gave them 400 sick
and elderly and maintained that he had done the correct thing, a
decision also supported by the town's rabbi. On another occasion,
Gens was fooled into assembling 5,000 Jews from Vilna. He was told
by the Nazi commander that they were being transported to the
Kovno ghetto for a work detail. But the Germans lied. The Jews
were put on trucks and taken directly to the death pits at the Ponary,
where they were all executed. For days afterwards, Gens was so
upset by this tragedy that he refused to speak to anyone.

Beginning in 1942, Gens's policy of appeasing the Nazis put him on a collision course with Abba Kovner and the courageous group of younger Jews in the Vilna ghetto who contemplated either armed resistance or an escape to the nearby forests to join up with the Soviet and Lithuanian communist partisans. In Gens's view, neither option was acceptable; both were highly dangerous and placed all Jews at a tremendous risk. The Nazis use of "collective responsibility," punishing fifty Jews for the minor transgression of one, paralyzed the ghetto inhabitants with fear. Gens did not and would not do anything to upset the delicate balance of survival he believed he had created.

Jews! Defend Yourselves with Arms!

ONCE THE RUMOURS OF THE MASS MURDER at Ponary were confirmed to be true, in the fall of 1941 Abba Kovner left his hiding place at the Benedictine convent and entered the ghetto. At twenty-three he was old beyond his years. His reaction, like the reaction of young Jews in Białystok, Warsaw, and Minsk, was to prepare for an armed uprising, even if the odds were tremendously against them. At first, the young fighters had no weapons, and little help from any local resistance movement outside of the ghetto. But they did have courage, strong Jewish identities, and a determination forged in the bonds of their Zionist or Bundist experiences before the war. The Einsatzgruppen had killed many of their parents, and as few were married and none had children, they did not yet have the familial responsibilities or concerns that often stopped slightly older Jews from resisting or escaping.

All of this provided them with the bold determination to believe that they could succeed in their struggle, or at least die knowing that they had done something. Taking huge risks, they smuggled in weapons and food and moved back and forth between the ghetto and the outside world, actions that if detected would have resulted in torture and death. But their youth equally led them into pointless arguments over ideology and strategy. Right- and left-wing Zionists had to put aside their earlier disputes and forge new alliances with socialists and communists, individuals who saw the Jewish world quite differently. The tragedy of the war forced them to make new choices and view that world from a new perspective. This proved easier said than done.

From the beginning, most of them were determined not to forsake the surviving Jews in the ghetto and flee to the forest, an option that might have kept them alive longer. By late 1943, the Soviets, as well as a small group of Lithuanian communists, had established partisan bases in the three forests closest to Vilna: the Narocz, 100 kilometres to the east; the Rudniki, about 50 kilometres to the south; and the Nacha, 133 kilometres to southwest. These guerilla forces had weapons, food, and contact with Moscow. They planned and successfully carried out sabotage and resistance operations. Their attitude towards Jews, though, was often ambivalent. Anti-Semitism was alive and thriving in the forests as elsewhere. Yet partisan messengers who slipped into the Vilna ghetto, usually young Jewish men from nearby villages, made it clear that newcomers, preferably with weapons, would be welcome.

Debates about whether to join the partisans in the forests or remain in the ghetto raged in Białystok and Vilna. In general, the young Jewish communists felt that joining up with their comrades in the forest was the strategy to adopt. The young Zionists were not as certain. "We knew that there would be no armed resistance [in the ghetto] if it were not led by the most courageous of us," recalled Chaika Grosman, a young Zionist member of the resistance in the Bialystok ghetto. "We did not develop any ideology of dying, of the desperate and demonstrative suicide of a small elite group in the ghetto, but of a national war in the streets."

The plans for a resistance movement in Vilna began on New Year's Eve 1941. That night, 150 young Zionists assembled at a meeting called by Abba Kovner in a public soup kitchen. He hoped that the festivities of the evening would distract the German and Lithuanian police outside the ghetto fence. At this gathering, Kovner made a passionate plea for action, arguing that the mass murder at the Ponary would continue until all the Jews of Vilna – indeed, all the Jews of Poland – had vanished from the face of the earth. Kovner urged his friends and comrades to join him in a united front. Prior to the meeting, he had composed in Yiddish a declaration meant for every Jew in Vilna, words that would forever after link him with the tragic legacy of the Jewish resistance during the war.

"All roads of the Gestapo lead to the Ponar," he stated, "And Ponar means death. Those who waiver, put aside all illusion. Your children, your wives and husbands are no more. Ponar is no concentration camp. . . . Hitler conspires to kill all the Jews of Europe. . . . Let us not be led as sheep to the slaughter! True we are weak and defenseless. But the only answer to the murderer is: To rise up with arms! Bretheren! Better fall as free fighters than to live at the mercy of murderers. Rise up! Rise up until your last breath."

It required a few more weeks of negotiations before the three main factions in Vilna – represented by Kovner from Ha-Shomer Ha-Tzair, Joseph Glazman, the twenty-eight-year-old no-nonsense leader of Betar, and Yitzhak Wittenberg, thirty-three, a respected Jewish communist organizer – could agree on a joint strategy. Putting aside their personal and political differences, they established the Fareynegte Partizaner Organizatsye (FPO), or the United Partisan Organization. The group's aim as set out in its charter was "to establish an armed fighting organization" and to prepare Vilna's Jews for a mass uprising.*

The FPO struggled to amass weapons. Gradually they were able to purchase arms on a black market (even from German soldiers)

---

* It should be noted that not everyone in the Vilna ghetto agreed with the FPO's plans. There were other factions, among them fifteen to twenty young Zionists from the Dror group led by Yechiel Scheinbaum, who remained independent and committed to fleeing for the forest. They argued that resistance in the ghetto was not viable. By the spring of 1943 "Yechiel's Struggle Group," as it was called, had approximately 175 members. They made contact with Soviet partisans in the Rudniki forest and by the fall had started sending fighters there.

and steal from munitions factories, where some young FPO members worked. Guns, grenades, rifles, and bullets were smuggled into the ghetto inside coat pockets or in coffins, or were hidden in garbage trucks. One day, Baruch Goldstein faked a hand injury and in a bandage wrapped a small gun that he had stolen. Young Anna Kremer, a FPO courier at the age sixteen, smuggled in a large pair of scissors under her clothes and hid them in her ghetto room. Detection at the gate was always a risk, and the punishment would have meant torture or death for the perpetrator.

Gens knew of the existence of the FPO, and he and his men watched its activities carefully. At times, he supplied members of the group with money for weapons and approved departures from the ghetto to the forest. But given his priorities, confrontation was inevitable.

Throughout 1942 and in the early part of 1943, FPO fighters kept busy gathering an arsenal and learning how to construct homemade bombs out of gasoline, nails, and light bulbs. One of the group's leaders, Shmuel Kaplinsky, a young communist, explored and mapped the Vilna sewer system for an escape route. Yet two unexpected events in July 1943 determined the course of action and fate both of Gens and the members of the FPO.

On July 7, 1943, the Gestapo in Vilna arrested an eighteen-year-old named Władysław Kozłowski. He was accused of being connected with the communist underground. Interrogated and tortured for hours, Kozłowski finally admitted to his involvement with the resistance and gave the Nazis the name of one of his contacts, Yitzhak Wittenberg, inside the Vilna ghetto. Nothing was mentioned about the FPO or Wittenberg's connections with a Jewish resistance.

The next day, Gens was instructed by the Gestapo to turn Wittenberg over to them. He was also told that if he did not produce Wittenberg, the ghetto and everyone in it would be liquidated. A few days passed before Gens convened a late-night meeting with Wittenberg and Kovner and a few others. (Joseph Glazman, who had had a falling out with Gens over a number of issues, did not attend.) The FPO leaders were as yet unaware that

Kozlowski had been arrested and had provided the Nazis with information about Wittenberg.

Soon after the meeting began, Sala Dessler, the head of the Jewish ghetto police, alerted the Gestapo and two Lithuanian policemen suddenly appeared in Gens's apartment. They apprehended Wittenberg. Kovner and his friends were stunned. Gens explained he had no choice but to lay the trap. The Nazis did not know about the FPO, he explained. Wittenberg had been taken for questioning because of his links to the communist underground. Watching these events outside Gen's quarters was Wittenberg's comrade Shmuel Kaplinsky and a small group of fighters. As Wittenberg was being led to the ghetto gate by Dessler and the two Lithuanian policemen, Kaplinsky and his men attacked the group and freed their friend. Wittenberg then went into hiding in a small room on Straszuna street.

The next few days in the ghetto were more tense than usual. No matter how hard they looked, Dessler and his men could not find Wittenberg. Gens tried negotiating with the FPO, but Kovner and his associates refused to co-operate. Undeterred, he gathered together his supporters and publicized throughout the ghetto what had transpired. Were the twenty thousand Jews still alive in Vilna prepared to die to save Wittenberg? Gens rightly anticipated that they were not. Soon Wittenberg, Kovner, and other members of the FPO realized that Wittenberg had no choice but to surrender. It was a tragic moment for everyone who lived through it. Within hours of being in the custody of the Gestapo, Wittenberg had committed suicide by taking a potassium cyanide tablet most likely given to him by Gens. He died without revealing any information about the ghetto resistance movement. A headstone recently erected in the Vilnius Jewish cemetery commemorates his courage.

Disheartened by these events, Kovner, now the leader of the FPO, reluctantly came to the conclusion that an uprising like the one that had occurred in Warsaw only a few months earlier (he had learned about it through an illegal radio the FPO possessed) was unlikely to take place in Vilna.* Joseph Glazman, who had had several confrontations with Gens, led one of the first FPO groups out of the ghetto. On July 24, 1943, they left the ghetto as part of a labour detail and then fled for the Narocz forest. Gens had learned of their plan and had permitted them to leave, but was not happy about it.

On their journey, Glazman and his group ran into the Nazi police on a bridge over the Vileyka River. Nine of the fighters were killed in the battle. The survivors, including Glazman, managed to reach the forest and find the Soviet partisans, led by Fyodor Markov. Markov permitted the Jews to establish their own unit, called Nekamah – Hebrew for "revenge." Four months later, however, Glazman and eighteen of his men were killed in a battle with Nazi troops.

Back in the Vilna ghetto, Gens's fears about the July escape were realized. Enforcing their policy of collective responsibility, Nazi authorities quickly executed thirty-two friends and relatives of those who had fled with Glazman. Gens announced that no more departures would be permitted. But the members of the FPO and other resistance fighters ignored the Judenrat's orders and continued to depart for the forest.

What Gens did not know (or did not want to admit), but what Kovner and the FPO had guessed, was that the liquidation of the Vilna ghetto was imminent. On the first day of September 1943, as the Nazi plans to deport the remaining inhabitants to labour and concentration camps were announced, the moment for the uprising was at hand. At least that was what Kovner and his comrades believed.

"Jews! Defend yourselves with arms!" an FPO poster beseeched the last Jews of Vilna. "The Germans and Lithuanian hangmen have arrived at the gates of the ghetto. They have come to murder

---

* From April 19 to May 16, an uprising took place in the Warsaw ghetto. Led by Mordechai Anielewicz, the courageous young fighters with few weapons were able to hold out for twenty-seven days against a much larger and more powerful Nazi force. Most of the fighters perished in the battle.

us! . . . There is an organized Jewish force within the walls that
will rise up in arms. Lend a hand to the revolt! . . . Go out into the
street! . . . We have nothing to lose! We shall save our lives only if
we wipe out our murderers. Long live freedom! Long live armed
defense, death to the murderers!" "We only wanted to die," Kovner
later wrote. "But die in order to live on in your memory."

The ghetto's inhabitants were too weak and frightened to
respond; a few committed suicide. Other than a small clash that
resulted in the death of Yechiel Sheinbaum, there was no real uprising in the Vilna ghetto. The FPO members themselves, according to
Norman Shneidman, who was in the ghetto until he escaped to the
forest on September 9, did not really want to fight. "The FPO was
indecisive, hesitant, always waiting," asserts Shneidman. "Even after
its call to arms and the proclamation of 1 September 1943, it
remained apathetic." Yitzhak Arad, who survived the war as a young
partisan and is an authority on the Vilna ghetto, concurs. "The FPO
blame[d] the Jews for not joining their call for resistance," Arad has
written, "when in fact they alone, and only they, could [have] pre-
cipitate[d] the bloody confrontation which no one wanted, not the
Jews in the ghetto nor the FPO, everyone wanted to live and hoped
for survival."

Many decades later, Kovner conceded that had the FPO plan
been implemented, thousands of unarmed and helpless Jews, who
had been beaten down by three years of life in the ghetto, would
have been killed instantly. He finally understood, too, that con-
demning the Jews who had "gone like sheep to the slaughter" at
the Ponary was unjustified. They could only be viewed with sympathy. That was the real tragedy of their shortened lives.

Resistance to the Nazi terror was next to impossible, and the
fact that the FPO and other resistance movements were established
in the ghettos at all, no matter how ineffective they were, was one
of the real miracles of the Holocaust tragedy. The FPO could not
have saved the remaining Vilna Jews in the fall of 1943, but many
did save themselves and fought the Nazis from the forests. As the
deportations to labour camps in Estonia and Latvia were underway,

small groups of fighters continued to escape the ghetto and head for Soviet bases in the Narocz and Rudniki forests.

Right to the end, Jacob Gens attempted to meet Nazi demands, believing he might be able to save the lives of the thousand or so Jews left in the ghetto. His intentions were honest, though terribly misguided. It was too late for such conciliatory deeds, and it was too late for him. A German friend had told him that the Gestapo intended to kill him, but he chose to remain in the ghetto rather than flee. On September 14, he was called to Gestapo head-quarters, where he was held in custody and charged with aiding partisans. That evening he was executed by a shot to the head.

Gens's role in the life of the Vilna ghetto seems naive, fruitless, even foolish. Yet so, too, perhaps was the FPO expectation that ghetto inhabitants would join them in a general resistance. Still, judgements made in hindsight about the actions and behaviour of individuals during the war must be weighed carefully and with all due consideration to the tragedy and terror of the era. True, Gens did not grasp the ultimate designs of the Nazis. Yet instead of escaping from the ghetto, as he could have done on countless occasions, he remained and served what he believed to be the best interests of the community. Can he be faulted for that?

On September 23, Kovner and about one hundred FPO fighters made their way through the treacherous underground sewer system mapped by Shmuel Kaplinsky. (A visitor to Vilnius can still see the manhole covers on Rudninku Street where the FPO members descended.) It took them nearly seven hours to travel only a few kilometres to emerge at a spot outside of the ghetto fence. Within a week, most of the group had reached the swampy Rudniki forest and made contact with Soviet and Lithuanian partisans. They formed the nucleus of several partisan detachments, including Kovner's Ha-Nokem, or "Avenger," while Shumel Kaplinsky led the detachment "To Victory." During the next year, they fought side by side with Soviet and Lithuanians partisans in dangerous sabotage operations, destroying rail lines, blowing up power installations and factories, and harassing Nazi forces retreating west as the Red Army pushed onward.

Later, Kovner recalled his first railway sabotage operation in 1944 like this: "I went out with a small group with Rachel Markevitch as our guest. It was New Year's Eve; we were bringing the Germans a festival gift. The train appeared on the raised railway; a line of large, heavy-laden trucks rolled on toward Vilna. My heart suddenly stopped beating for joy and fear. I pulled the string with all my strength and in that moment, before the thunder of the explosion echoed through the air, and twenty-one trucks full of troops hurtled down into the abyss, I heard Rachel cry: 'For Ponar!'"

Most of the Jews trapped in the Vilna ghetto were deported to labour camps to the north, sent to the Sobibor death camp, where they were executed by gassing, or dispatched to the Ponary, where they were murdered immediately. By the end of September 1943, two thousand Jews – of the fifty-seven thousand Jews living in Vilna in June 1941 – remained in the city, imprisoned in makeshift labour camps.

In July 1944, Kovner, Kempner, Korczak, and other FPO fighters took part in the liberation of Vilna. As the Red Army and the partisans closed in, the Nazis marched 1,800 of the Jews left in Vilna to the death pits at the Ponary and slaughtered them, lest they be freed by the Soviets. After five days of intense fighting in which eight thousand Germans soldiers died and another five thousand were taken prisoner, the city was finally taken on July 13. In the few photographs of them taken at this time (by the Russian Jewish journalist Ilya Ehrenberg) Kovner and his fighters are standing in the ruins of the once great city with machine guns slung over their shoulders. The tragedy of the war is etched into their faces, but so too is the pride and determination that drove the partisan movement.

Approximately two hundred Jews had managed to elude the Nazis in the final weeks of the war in Vilna. Among them were a mother and daughter discovered by Kovner as he walked through the rubble of the former ghetto. At first the poor and dishevelled woman thought Kovner and the partisans with him were Nazis, but they reassured her they were there to help her. She told them the story of how she had survived. For more than eleven months, she and her daughter had hidden themselves in a dark hole in the wall of a dilapidated apartment building and kept silent. Now that they were free, the young girl, who saw the tears on her mother's face, asked a question: "Mommy, mother, may one cry now, mother?" Kovner would remember this episode for the rest of his life.

How Can You Know What We Lost

THE SURVIVORS WHO EMERGED from the forests or who were liberated by Soviet and Allied soldiers in Auschwitz, Majdanek, and the other death camps, soon discovered that there was no place for them in post-war Poland. Their families were dead and their homes destroyed. They were not wanted. Astonishingly, close to fifteen hundred Jews lost their lives in attacks in Europe in the days after the war ended. Anti-Semitism had not evaporated, not even in the ovens of the death camps. And, a once great Jewish civilization of the Diaspora had been obliterated.

Many of the Jewish partisans found themselves fighting in the last battles of the conflict as draftees in the Red Army, as the Soviet troops marched towards Berlin in the spring of 1945. In the end, some Jews who could not escape from Russian territory had no choice but to rebuild their lives in Moscow, Kiev, St. Petersburg, and a hundred more locales. They would soon learn, however, that the totalitarian society created by Joseph Stalin was nearly as bad as life under the Nazis. Jews in the western occupied territories were more fortunate. They drifted into camps for "displaced persons," and from there thousands made their way to cities and towns in North and South America and as far away as Australia.

Abba Kovner understood that there was no place for Jews in Europe. "A sword is dangling over our head," he said at the time. "The Holocaust is not a unique catastrophe that is over and done with. It can happen again. It's our duty to warn our fellow Jews and get them out of this slaughterhouse." Kovner (along with his future wife, Vitka Kempner, and their friend Ruzka Korczak) had no desire to start his life over again anywhere other than in Palestine – no matter what the British, who then ruled the area, had to say about the immigration of Jewish refugees. Never one to be passive, Kovner was instrumental in creating a new movement called Bricha ("escape," in Hebrew), an organization that assisted Jewish Holocaust survivors to reach Palestine and set the stage for the events of 1948.

Kovner first reached Palestine in September 1945. His objective was to raise funds for possible retribution and "revenge operations" on Nazis and collaborators still at large in Europe. One plan devised by Kovner and his friends was an elaborate scheme to poison the bread fed to German POWs then being held in Nuremberg.* When Kovner attempted to return to Europe travelling with fake papers, he was arrested by the British and sent to a military prison in Cairo. He was held there for four months before being transferred to a British jail in Jerusalem. After a few weeks, British authorities let him go without an explanation.

During his stay in prison, he had come to the decision that he would remain in Palestine and fight for its independence as a Jewish state. Following his release, he joined his wife at Kibbutz Ein Ha-Horesh, 80 kilometres south of Haifa, his home until he died in 1987 at the age of sixty-nine. When the Israeli War of Independence finally broke out after the United Nations partition of Palestine in 1948, Kovner served as the education and morale officer of the Givati brigade.

In the last part of his life, Kovner developed his writing career, producing prose and long narrative poetry in the style of Chaim Nachman Bialik. Much of his best work was based on his wartime experiences. In his 1951 poem "The Key Drowned," about his time

---

* In the spring of 1946, the operation was carried out and many of the prisoners became sick from arsenic poisoning. A story on the episode was reported by the *New York Times* with the headline, "Poison Plot Toll of Nazis at 2,238." American authorities never revealed if any of the inmates actually died from the attack.

in the ghetto, he wrote, "In the final account, we were all defeated. The Dead and the Living." He received the Israel Prize for literature in 1970.

Kovner worked as well to preserve the memory of Vilna and the other communities of Eastern Europe. He played a major role in establishing Holocaust archives and was one of the founders of the Beth Ha-Tefusoth, the Diaspora Museum in Tel Aviv, an exceptional institution that has helped preserve the story of the Jewish people. Kovner was most proud of the museum's remarkable and vivid historical synagogue recreations, including one that depicts the Great Synagogue of Vilna as it once was. "How can you know what we lost," Kovner used to say, "if you do not know what we had."

Chapter Twelve

ZIONISTS AND SOVIETS

Kiev, 1967

I am a Jew. I want to live in the Jewish State. This is my right, just as it is the right of a Ukrainian to live in the Ukraine. . . . I want to live in Israel. This is my dream, this is the goal not only of my life but also of the lives of hundreds of generations that preceded me, of my ancestors who were expelled from their land. I want my children to study in a school in Yiddish. I want to read Yiddish papers. I want to attend a Yiddish theatre. What's wrong with that? What is my crime?
  – Boris Kochubiyevsky, in a letter to Leonid Brezhnev, 1968

An Inextricable Vise

They were forever marked, no different than the Jews compelled to wear a yellow star in fifteenth-century Spain, in sixteenth-century Italy, and in twentieth-century Nazi-occupied Europe. Whether they regarded themselves as Jews or not, the state certainly did. And whenever they applied for higher education or for jobs, or dealt with the immense and multi-layered bureaucracy of the Soviet government, their internal passports always revealed their ancestry and heritage. They might have been devoted and assimilated communists, but on line five in the space designated for nationality was stamped *Evrey* – "Jew." It was a label that hindered education and halted job advancement, a term that set them apart from the majority as it had in the days of the czars. It was a constant reminder that they were not true citizens of the state, but rather a second-class minority not to be fully trusted. They were aliens, Zionists, cosmopolitans, and traitors.

Igor Korenzvit, who was born in Kiev in 1946, did not have a bar mitzvah, nor did he receive any Jewish education. His family's celebration of Jewish holidays was minimal. Yet he grew up knowing that he was different than his Russian friends. "We knew we were Jewish," he says today in Toronto, where he has lived since 1973, "because on our passports it said we were."

In the decades that followed the devastation of the Second World War, there was no country in the Diaspora more difficult than the Soviet Union for Jews to live in as Jews. They were trapped in what the American writer Moshe Decter called "an inextricable vise." It was the paradox of being a Jew, even in name only, in a country that institutionalized anti-Semitism, where genuine expressions of nationalism or religion were regarded as tantamount to treason, and where the simple desire to emigrate could lead to criminal prosecution. "They are allowed neither to assimilate, nor live a full Jewish life, nor to emigrate to Israel or any other place where they might live freely as Jews," Decter wrote in a 1961 article on Soviet anti-Semitism in the respected journal *Foreign Affairs*. From a Jewish point of view, the inherent contradiction of Soviet society from Lenin and Stalin to Brezhnev and Gorbachev was this: Jews were expected to assimilate, to be loyal and obedient citizens like everyone else, but even when they attempted to do so the state never let them forget that they were, in fact, Jews first and foremost. The miracle of Soviet Jewish life was that despite years of persecution, one generation after the other still managed to pass on something tangible – a prayer, a religious tradition, a story, a pride in the state of Israel – that kept the Jewish identity from dying.

Like the Russians and other nationalities of the Soviet Union, the vast majority of the country's 3.5 million Jews had welcomed and participated in the revolutionary upheaval of 1917 that ultimately brought Vladimir Ilyich Lenin and the communists to power. The promises of equality and religious and national freedom were hailed as "the deliverance of the people," "a miracle . . . that will be recorded as one of the greatest events in the history of Israel." And though the Bolsheviks had initially pledged that Russia's various nationalities would be accorded the right of self-determination, this is not what Lenin, Stalin, and Trotsky quite had in mind.

Lenin, in particular, resented both the Jewish labour party, the Bund, as well as the more popular Zionist parties and organizations. A Jewish "nationality," the Bolshevik leader had argued more than a decade before his conquest of Russia, "is definitely reactionary not only when expounded by its consistent advocates (Zionists), but likewise on the lips of those who try to combine it with the ideas of Social Democracy (the Bundists). This idea of a Jewish nationality runs counter to the interests of the Jewish proletariat, for it fosters among them, directly or indirectly, a spirit hostile to assimilation, the spirit of the 'ghetto.'" As for Zionism, Lenin, and every Soviet leader who followed him, dismissed it as a dangerous bourgeoisie movement. In Joseph Stalin's opinion, it was questionable that Jews were even a "nation." "What . . . national cohesion can there be . . . between the Georgian, Daghestanian, Russian, and American Jew?" he had asked in a 1913 essay. "If there is anything common to them left it is their religion, their common origin and certain relics of national character." This was a view that was to have devastating ramifications in the dark years ahead.

Slowly but methodically, the Soviets cast their net around Jewish cultural and religious institutions. In 1924, massive arrests and secret trials of prominent Zionists were carried out for "counter-revolutionary acts" in which guilty verdicts were more or less determined before the proceedings began – a soon-to-be familiar feature of the Soviet regime. Hebrew schools were closed. Lenin's war on Russia's churches and synagogues began almost from the start of his reign. Property was seized, and any resistance met with force and death. In the four-year period from 1921 to 1926, close to 800 synagogues were shut and Judaism was publicly denounced.*

Many Jews, like the members of Tsilia Michlin Goldin's family, refused to comply with the new Soviet laws that forbade them to practise their religion. Goldin, who was born in the city of Bobruisk in Belarussia in 1908, endured pogroms, revolution, and a bloody civil war. Her father, Zelig, was a pious man in the community who performed circumcisions as the *mohel* and acted as the *shochet*, the man responsible for the ritual slaughtering of animals for food. During the thirties, both practices were banned, and anyone found guilty of committing these religious acts faced a sentence of ten years in a Soviet prison camp. Neither the threat of such a harsh punishment nor the constant harassment by the secret police deterred Zelig Michlin from fulfilling his duties – he just did

---

* This included the Brodsky, or Choral, Synagogue – now the Great Synagogue of Kiev – in its day a magnificent Gothic style sanctuary built through the generosity of Lazar Brodsky, the entrepreneurial "sugar king," and opened in 1898. The Soviets seized the property, the Nazis, who occupied Kiev during the Second World War, used it as a horse stable, and in the post-war period the Soviets turned it into the Kiev State Puppet Theatre. The Jewish community did not regain total control of the property until 1997 (between 1991 and 1997 they shared the synagogue with the Puppet Theatre). It took years of political manoeuvring and major renovation to transform the building back into the impressive house of worship that it is today under the leadership of its ambitious and brilliant young Lubavitcher Chief Rabbi, Moshe Reuven Azman. Born in Leningrad (St. Petersburg) in 1966, Azman, like other Jewish children, had a minimal Jewish education. He recalls his grandparents speaking Yiddish, but he did not have a bar mitzvah. When he was a teenager, his faith and interest in religion began. It took him eight years to obtain permission to leave the country in 1987. He trained as a rabbi in Israel and returned to Kiev in 1996. When promised American money did not materialize for the synagogue's reconstruction, Rabbi Azman picked up a sledgehammer and began the work himself. Several leading and wealthy members of the Kiev Jewish community, most notably businessman Vadim Rabinovich, eventually helped him, yet he acted as his own contractor, whittling down an initial price for the renovations of U.S. $4 million to U.S. $1.5 million. Today, one of his main objectives is to bring back Jews to the synagogue, Jews who are understandably disconnected from the community. The synagogue also functions as a school and soup kitchen to help the neighbourhood's homeless children and poor.

them discreetly. In a real sense, the Michlins became yet another generation of *marranos*, forced to live two lives, a public one permitted by the state, and a private one guided by Jewish law and ritual. This, too, would be an unfortunate feature of life as a Jew in the Soviet Union.

Throughout her life, Tsilia tried to follow the lessons in perseverance and devotion that her father had taught her. At the age of twenty, she married Mendel Goldin of nearby Gomel in a secret synagogue ceremony and in time tried to raise her own children in a Jewish environment despite the many hardships this entailed. Her family survived the Second World War living in Uzbekistan in Central Asia, with the exception of her father, who died there from malnutrition. When the conflict ended, she and her children returned by train in a cattle car to Gomel, her husband's home town, where she was now confronted by the harsh realities of life during the darkest years of Stalin's long reign.

"If I hadn't been born Jewish," she recalled several years ago from her home in Chicago, where she emigrated in the late 1980s, "obviously life would have been easier." This was an understatement. In the years before the Second World War, Jews in the Soviet Union faced a barrage of regulations and restrictions designed to break their will and crush their faith. Jews were ordered to work on the Sabbath and on other religious holidays. A campaign against matzo, the unleavened bread eaten during Passover, began in the 1920s and continued more or less for the next six decades. Among all of the Jewish holidays, Passover, with its celebration of liberation, became a special target of Soviet repression.

In 1922 in Gomel, Rabbi Raphael Mordechai Barishensky was arrested and imprisoned for two years for delivering a sermon preaching that his congregants should send their children to religious schools. The Yiddish schools that authorities did permit to operate were governed by a strict curriculum and students were indoctrinated in Soviet ideology. As Judah Dardak, one committed Communist teacher of a Yiddish school boasted, "All books with a nationalist coloring were removed. [This] enabled the school to

raise the level of instruction and to include anti-religious and international subject matter in its curriculum. . . . The very concept of
'Jewish history' is alien to the school."

Poverty among Jews was rampant. In a society where any form
of capitalism was stamped out, Jewish traders, merchants, and
artisans suddenly found themselves without a livelihood. Some
attempted to become farmers, yet the results were hardly encouraging. Hundreds of thousands of people lived in terrible destitution,
barely able to survive. Moreover, because they were classified by the
regime as "economically undesirable," they suffered further indigni-
ties and humiliations. They were last to be treated in hospitals, their
children were refused entrance into state schools, and their rents and
taxes were set at a higher rate than for other citizens of the Soviet
Union. Even those Jews who did embrace communism, who did
want to assimilate into Soviet society, who married a non-Jewish
spouse, were never allowed to forget that they were, and always
would be, second-class citizens, members of a despised minority.

A few thousand Jewish pioneers were compelled by the Soviet
government in 1928 to establish what was intended to be an
autonomous Jewish region in Birobidzhan, a remote eastern region
close to the Manchurian border, more than eight thousand kilometres
east of Moscow. Stalin had hoped that granting Jews this "privilege"
might be the cure for Zionism, although the Jewish population at
the primitive settlement never exceeded eighteen thousand. Yet
as the American Jewish journalist Ben Zion Goldberg pointed out
after visiting Birobidzhan in 1934, "here was one spot – indeed
the only spot in the world – where the language and culture of the
Jewish masses was primary, not secondary; dominating, not dominated; and practically exclusive." Nevertheless, Jews in Moscow and
Leningrad did not rush to Birobidzhan. During the early 1950s it
was a place to exile Jews regarded as troublemakers. There were less
than twelve thousand Jews living there in 1970, a tiny percentage of
the Soviet Jewish population, and most of them were elderly. There
were no rabbis or Jewish cemeteries, and a small wooden cabin

served as the lone synagogue. Despite Soviet propaganda to the contrary, Jewish cultural life there was minimal.

The assault on Jewish life reached its peak during Stalin's ruthless purges of 1936 to 1938 in which millions of Russians, including an estimated six hundred thousand Jews, perished in Siberian labour camps or were executed. Paranoid and delusional, Stalin saw a conspiracy against him around every corner. Anyone remotely suspected of questioning the dictator's rule was arrested, given a show trial, and dealt with harshly. The country's intelligentsia was decimated and the Soviet Union was engulfed in fear. The situation became so absurd that many Jewish leaders were accused of collaborating with the Nazis, all the more ironic in view of Stalin's pact with Hitler in 1939. Most Jewish institutions, Yiddish schools, and state-approved newspapers, for instance, were closed and never reopened.

Rootless Cosmopolitans

IF THEY HAD SURVIVED the 1936–38 PURGES and the war with the Nazis that followed after the Germans attacked in June 1941, Soviet Jews faced more hardships once the war ended. With more than 1.5 million dead, there was not a Jewish family in Russia not in someway affected by the mass destruction. As elsewhere in Eastern Europe, the survivors of the death camps and those who had fought in the forests were not welcomed back with open arms. "We came back to Kiev in July 1944," recalled Holocaust survivor Zvi Portnoy, "and went straight to the courtyard were we had lived for fifteen years. I shall not forget that moment as long as I live. Our neighbours met us with furious looks, even . . . those we had been friendly with before the war and had helped to raise and bring up our children. . . . I found a Russian called Kompantsiev occupying my apartment. He refused to vacate it, though we had lived there since 1930. . . . After a long struggle I got my apartment back practically by force."

The memory of the Holocaust struck at the heart of every Jew, even for a Communist as loyal and dedicated as the writer Ilya

Ehrenberg. Born into a middle-class Jewish family in Kiev in
1891, Ehrenberg first embraced the revolutionary movement and
then championed the Bolshevik cause throughout the twenties. For
many years he lived in Paris and Berlin, where he wrote novels –
among them, *The Extraordinary Adventures of Julio Jurenito and His
Disciples* (1922) and *The Stormy Life of Lasik Roitschwantz* (1928) –
and worked as a correspondent for Soviet newspapers. During the
war he gained fame as a roving reporter for the *Red Star* military
newspaper. For his attacks on Fascism, Hitler once referred to him
as the "Commissar of Vengeance."

Ehrenberg was a man of many dimensions. He clearly recognized, for instance, the toll taken by the purges, when, as he
remembered many years later, "the fate of a man did not resemble
a game of chess but a lottery." Yet not even the execution of his
close friend Nikolai Bukharin, in 1938, tried for allegedly being in
league with Trotsky as part of an anti-Bolshevik conspiracy, nor
the Soviet–Nazi Pact (which he strongly disapproved of) could
shake his loyalty in the Soviet system or in Stalin.

His links with the Jewish community were not strong, though
he did work with the Jewish Anti-Fascist Committee during and
after the war. "I was born in Kiev, my mother tongue is Russian,"
he wrote in his memoirs published a few years before he died in
1967. "I know neither Yiddish or Hebrew. I have never prayed in a
synagogue, nor yet in an Orthodox or Catholic Church. . . . I spent
my childhood and early youth in Moscow and my comrades were
Russian." And yet as a Jew, something he was always conscious and
even proud of, he could not but identify with the "great misery of
[the] Jewish people." In 1944, when Nikita Khrushchev was then
the First Secretary of the Ukrainian Communist Party and premier
of the Ukraine Republic, Ehrenberg wrote to him to protest the
plans to build a modern market on the site of the 1941 Babi Yar
massacre outside of Kiev. Khrushchev's reply was terse and to the
point. "I advise you not to interfere in matters that do not concern
you," wrote the First Secretary. "You had better keep to writing
good novels."

In the last days of the war, Ehrenberg and his friend Vasily Grossman, assisted by more than twenty other writers, began collecting diaries, eye-witness accounts, and testimonies of Nazi atrocities against Jews with the idea of publishing a "Black Book." Yet while an English version was published in 1946 and another in Romania the following year, much to Ehrenberg's disappointment Stalin refused to permit the book to be distributed in the Soviet Union. The printing plates for the book were destroyed and the project dismissed by the Soviet propaganda department as being filled with "grave political errors." Indeed, at no time was the Soviet leadership prepared to acknowledge that Jews suffered more during the war than had any other national or religious group. It was for this reason that the first memorials erected at Babi Yar near Kiev, the Ponary outside of Vilnius, the Ninth Fort near Kaunas, and the other sites of Nazi massacres made no reference to the thousands of Jews among those who had perished. And as long as Stalin was alive, they never would.

The harsh reality of Jewish life during the post-war years was established early on by Andrei Zhdanov, a prominent member of the Politburo and Stalin's recognized expert on cultural issues. In a speech he delivered in August 1946, Zhdanov, adopting the sharp tone of Cold War rhetoric, attacked Western ideas and values, promising to drive such negative influences out of Soviet society. Thus was born *Zhdanovshchina*, a cultural policy of repression and censorship.

Every work of art or literature was carefully scrutinized by agents of the state to ensure that it provided the "proper" message. So paranoid was this anti-Western campaign that Soviet authors were warned not to "extol the beauties of foreign landscapes." Every invention, from the light bulb to the airplane, was claimed to have been created by Russian ingenuity. In a curious example of historical revisionism, the Soviets even took credit for giving the world American baseball, which was apparently based on a game called *lapta* played for centuries by Russian peasants.

Zhdanov's policies specifically targeted Jewish intellectuals now castigated for being "rootless cosmopolitans" and for "harbouring anti-patriotic views." Denounced as "citizens of the world," Jews were, as historian Yehoshua Gilboa writes, depicted by the government and press "not merely as wanderer[s] without a homeland, but as servant[s] of American venality and imperialism." In short, loyal Soviet citizens did not produce works about Jewish history or dwell on the atrocities inflicted on Jews during the Second World War.

But condemnations and accusations against the Jewish elite were only the most visible signs of "*Zhdanovshchina*." Stalin's official long-term goal of total assimilation (or, more accurately, disappearance) called for more drastic measures. He wanted to wipe away Russian-Jewish culture altogether.[*]

In 1948, one of the most well-known and admired Jewish figures in the Soviet Union was Solomon Mikhoels, the fifty-eight-year-old actor, director of the Moscow Jewish State Theatre, and chairman of the wartime Jewish Anti-Fascist Committee. No one worked more diligently on behalf of Soviet Jews than Mikhoels, and no one was more respected and loved. Ilya Ehrenberg was correct when he described Mikhoels as "a wise rabbi [and] defender of the oppressed."

In mid-January of 1948, Mikhoels was visiting Minsk to serve on a committee as judge for the Stalin Prize in theatre. One evening, he received a phone call, perhaps inviting him to attend a small gathering at a private home or to attend a meeting. Not much more is known. The last time anyone saw him alive, he departed the hotel accompanied by Vladimir Golubov-Potapov, also a respected Jewish theatre critic. The next morning, the bodies of both men were discovered not far from the Minsk railway station.

---

[*] Even the *Great Soviet Encyclopedia* reflected the harsh change in Stalin's policies. In the first edition, published between 1926 and 1932, the entry for "Jews" ran 108 columns or 54 pages and included sections on religion, Yiddish, and Jewish music and theatre. In the second edition, published in 1952, at the height of Stalin's attack on the community, the entry for "Jews" had been significantly altered to only four columns in which it was made clear that "Jews do not constitute a nation."

The police quickly declared that Mikhoels and Golubov-Potapov had been victims of a traffic accident. Yet an anonymous phone call to the Jewish Theatre in Moscow proclaiming that "we have finished off your first Jew, and now comes the turn of all of the rest of you," suggested that the two men had in fact been murdered.

If Khrushchev is to be believed, Mikhoels was assassinated by agents of the NKVD (later the KGB) under the command of Lavrenti Beria, People's Commissar for the Interior. "They killed him like beasts," he related in his memoirs. "They killed him secretly. Then his murderers were rewarded and their victim was buried with honours. The mind reels at the thought! It was announced that Mikhoels had fallen in front of a truck. Actually he was thrown in front a truck. This was done very cleverly and efficiently. And who did it? Stalin did it, or at least it was done on his instructions."

To maintain the facade, the government permitted Mikhoels's family to give him a magnificent funeral in Moscow in which tens of thousands of people passed by his coffin "lying in state" at the Jewish Theatre. Then five years later, as we shall see, he was implicated as the mastermind of the infamous "Doctor's Plot."

Mikhoels's death signalled the start of a harsh anti-Jewish campaign that ended only with Stalin's death in 1953. Within a year, more than 400 Jewish writers, painters, actors, engineers, and scientists had been arrested. Most would perish in Soviet labour camps. Among those persecuted were the popular Yiddish writers David Bergelson, a one-time member of the Jewish Anti-Fascist Committee, and Itzik Fefer, once a committed Communist and admirer of Stalin. They were arrested in April 1949, beaten, and tortured. Bergelson was forced to sit on a two-legged stool for twenty hours a day, and each time he fell off onto the stone floor, the guards put him back up. Eventually Bergelson and Fefer were imprisoned at a labour camp at Bratsk in the distant southeast part of the country. There they remained for the next three years until the authorities could concoct a case against them.

The ordeal in the camp, the lack of food, and physical abuse, took its toll on the forty-nine-year-old Fefer. "The unfortunate

Fefer looked haggard and dried up – skin and bones, and a bundle of nerves," Bernard Turner, another inmate later recalled. "He trembled all over, nervously bit his lips and looked around with an unseeing stare, mumbling something to himself. . . . He was covered with rags, his trousers were tied with a piece of string from which a military tin flask hung. His spectacles – Fefer's characteristic spectacles – were broken and bound with a string."

Meanwhile, back in Moscow, Leningrad, Kiev, and Odessa, any Jewish schools still operating were closed. Jewish books were seized and destroyed, and Jews everywhere were gripped with fear. Possessing poetry or a novel by the wrong writer was enough to warrant a death sentence. Visits in the middle of the night by KGB agents were routine, though they were something that no Russian family, Jewish or otherwise, ever fully adjusted to.

Gennady Reznikov, then only ten years old in 1948 and living in Moscow, recalls that one day his grandmother came home in tears. The synagogue she regularly attended had been shut down. Gennady was warned not to speak Yiddish in the streets. Despite his grandmother's wishes that Gennady be raised as an observant Jew, the safe route during these dark years was for parents to teach their children to be loyal Soviet citizens and forget about the past. And as Gennady conceded, growing up in the 1950s his "sense of being Jewish was very slight." It was only as an adult that he rediscovered his heritage, an act that was to transform him into a pariah.

If the twentieth century has taught us anything, it is that nationalism and religious belief can never be entirely suppressed. More often than not, the greater the pressure inflicted on a group, the deeper their commitment to their heritage. So it was in this case. The one element of Jewish life that Stalin (and those who followed him) was not able to control was the impact of the birth of the State of Israel. Ironically, the Soviet Union, with a view to ending British power in the Middle East, voted in favour of the partition of Palestine at the United Nations in November 1947. When Israel was officially established six months later, in May 1948, Soviet Jews responded with excitement and pride. And when news of this momentous event finally reached Jews who had been imprisoned in Siberia for their Zionist beliefs, there was great rejoicing. From Leningrad to Kiev, many Jews interpreted the Soviet support for Israel as a sign that anti-Jewish policies were about to change. They were terribly mistaken.

The indomitable Golda Meyerson (later Meir) was appointed Israel's first envoy to the Soviet Union in June 1948. She arrived in Moscow a few months later not sure of the reception she would receive. She visited the Great Synagogue one Saturday morning for Sabbath services. The hundred or so mainly elderly people attending that day took notice of her, but few people made direct contact. The next time was much different. Word about her second visit circulated through the Moscow community, and a few weeks later, on Rosh Hashanah, the Jewish New Year, Meir was overwhelmed by a crowd that was estimated at anywhere from twenty thousand to fifty thousand people.

"For a minute I couldn't grasp what had happened – or even who they were. And then it dawned on me," she later remembered. "They come – those good, brave Jews – in order to be us, to demonstrate their sense of kinship and to celebrate the establishment of the State of Israel. Within seconds they had surrounded me, almost lifting me bodily, almost crushing me, saying, 'Nasha Golda, Our Golda,' over and over again. Eventually they parted ranks and let me enter the synagogue, but there too, the demonstrations went on. . . . Without speeches or parades, without any words really at all, the Jews of Moscow were proving their profound desire – and their need – to participate in the miracle of the establishment of the State of Israel and I was the symbol of the State for them."

Ten days later, on Yom Kippur, a large crowd at the synagogue again greeted her. The twenty-four-hour fast of the Day of Atonement ends with a single blast of the *shofar* (the ram's horn) and the promise of *"L'shana habah b'Yerushalayim"* – "Next year in

Jerusalem." That conclusion to Yom Kippur in Moscow, Meir never forgot. "The words shook the synagogue as they looked up at me," she recalled two decades later. "It was the most passionate Zionist speech I had ever heard."

Stalin and his officials were shocked. "The depth and passion of Jewish feeling was startling – and disquieting," observes historian Nora Levin. "After thirty years of Communist rule, 'sovietization' of Soviet Jews and rapid assimilation, these fires had not been quenched." In an effort to counter this Zionist resurgence, the editors of the government organ *Pravda*, under the direction of Stalin, invited Ilya Ehrenberg to write an article about Israel presenting the Soviet view of such nationalist demonstrations. Ehrenberg did not disappoint. While he did denounce anti-Semitism, he also dismissed the new Jewish state as an Anglo-American bourgeoisie collaborator. "A citizen of socialist society," he concluded, "regards the people of any bourgeoisie country, and that means also the people of the State of Israel, as wanderers in a dark forest who have not yet found their way out."

Five days before the article appeared on September 21, 1948, the first applications for immigration to Israel were received in Soviet government offices. They would be the first of many.

In July 1952, three years after they were first arrested, Itzik Fefer, David Bergelson, and twenty-three other Jewish writers and artists were finally put on trial. Apart from being labelled enemies of the Soviet Union and "agents of American imperialism," they were ultimately convicted – on no evidence – of plotting to establish a separate Zionist republic in the Crimea. On August 12, all but one of the defendants, including Fefer and Bergelson, were executed at Lubyanka prison in Moscow. Only seventy-four-year-old Dr. Lina Shtern, the lone woman among them and a brilliant scientist, was spared. She received a life sentence and was later released during the de-Stalinization period of Khrushchev's early years in power. She died in Moscow in 1968 at the age of 90.

Thus began a new wave of arrests, trials, and lengthy sentences in prison on the most absurd of charges. One Jewish physician in Moscow was sentenced to ten years in a labour camp for having greeted Golda Meir in the Moscow synagogue in 1948. The young Jewish writer Meir Kanevsky was accused of being an Israeli spy, among other charges. He was initially sentenced to death, but later this was commuted to twenty-five years in prison.

In early January 1953, Stalin and his officials launched what would be their final assault against the leadership of the Soviet Jewish community. A group of fourteen (mainly Jewish) physicians was arrested and charged with being party to a conspiracy with the objective of eliminating the higher echelons of the Soviet government. In the so-called Doctor's Plot, as it became known, Stalin, among other high officials, was to have been poisoned. It was claimed that the physicians had "deliberately subjected their patients to harmful treatment" and purposely made false diagnoses. The late Solomon Mikhoels was identified as the mastermind, and the doctors were denounced in the pages of *Pravda* as being "monsters," "despicable creatures," and "hired murderers."

Those arrested, on Stalin's direct orders, according to Khrushchev, were tortured and beaten without mercy. At the same time, Stalin planned to use the Doctor's Plot as an excuse for large-scale deportations of Jews from Soviet cities. His death in early 1953 halted both the executions of the doctors and his campaign to rid the Soviet Union of Jews.

The Jews of Silence

IN MANY WAYS THE REPRESSION during the last years of Stalin's rule had pushed younger Jews to attempt to search for their roots. Small groups of those in their late teens and early twenties gravitated towards synagogues, where they could at least talk about Israel and the future. This simmering Jewish national consciousness left a lasting impression on Israeli ambassador Yosef Avidar during his various travels in the Soviet Union in 1956. Wherever he went, young Jews approached him and tried to speak to him in Yiddish and Hebrew.

No doubt, many Jews believed that the new regime led by Nikita Khrushchev truly would usher in the "thaw" that Ilya Ehrenberg described in his 1954 novel of that name. In fact, Khrushchev was no lover of Zionism or Jews. In responding to a query in 1956 about the possibility of giving Jews more freedom, Mikhail Suslov, a leading Politburo member, spoke for all members of the new government when he said, "We have no intention of reviving a dead culture." Moreover, as the Soviet Union chose to champion the Arab cause in the Middle East at this decisive moment of the Cold War, Russian-Jewish identification with Israel became unacceptable.

Far from being a period of tolerance, the years from 1959 to 1964 were nearly as harsh as they had been a decade earlier. Jews understood that they had "to function on two levels at once," explains the Zionist activist Natan (Anatoly) Sharansky: "what you really thought and what you allowed yourself to tell other people." Sharansky, himself, lived with this duality until 1973, at which time he joined the movement to immigrate to Israel. Later, his prominent work on behalf of Jewish rights would result in nearly ten harrowing years in Soviet prisons and labour camps during the 1970s and 1980s. Synagogues were closed – Soviet officials maintained they were being used for illicit Zionist activities – torahs were confiscated, and circumcisions were again banned, as was the baking of matzo on Passover.

Each Passover, KGB agents were on the alert for packages of matzo and other Passover foods shipped to the Soviet Jews from Israel and North America. As Yuri Andropov, head of the KGB in the 1970s, pointed out in a confidential KGB communiqué in 1975, such parcels were aimed at "stirring up nationalistic attitudes among Soviet citizens of Jewish extraction." They were regarded as a serious threat to the welfare of the state and therefore confiscated.

Almost on a daily basis, the Soviet press denounced Israel as an imperialistic aggressor and as "hell on earth." In the streets, the derogatory term *zhidy* was now heard more frequently, and Jewish cemeteries were vandalized. One of the most popular books of the era was Ukrainian philosophy professor Trofim Kychko's anti-Semitic diatribe *Yudaizm bez prykas* ("Judaism without Embellishment"), published in Kiev in 1963. Similar to propaganda produced by the Nazis, Kychko's book argued that the foundations of the Jewish religion were based on "practical needs [and] egoism. The God of practical need and self-interest is money."

On the one hand, Khrushchev vehemently denied that anti-Semitism existed in the Soviet Union (in fact, Kychko was criticized and expelled from the Communist Party for having gone too far in his work); and on the other, Jews were targeted for alleged "economic crimes." Claiming that they were attempting to cleanse the Soviet system of suspected capitalists, officials arrested and imprisoned Jews for such offences as "speculation in footwear" and "speculation in fruit." A charge of "profiteering" for a Jewish bookkeeper could lead to a death sentence or a long stay in prison. According to one estimate, of the 163 "economic criminals" sentenced to death in 81 trials convened in 48 different cities during the period from July 1961 to August 1963, approximately 55 to 60 per cent were Jewish – a fact not overlooked by the press.

In March 1962, *Pravda* reported on an alleged foreign-currency smuggling ring operating out of a synagogue in Lvov. In another similar case in Vilna, eight people, including a rabbi, were arrested and charged with conducting illegal foreign-currency trading. And, in general, as Moshe Decter, who studied the issue in 1961, argued, rabbis and synagogue leaders were "consistently portrayed as extorting money from the faithful for ostensibly religious purposes, their object in fact being to feather their own nests."

No one who visited the Soviet Union during these years could fail to notice the troubling effect this continual repression had on the country's Jews. The fear was pervasive; it hung in the air of every synagogue. "A strong emotion overtakes you when you enter a synagogue in Russia – a sad, mysterious stillness descends upon you," recorded one visitor from New York in 1962. "One communicates with another with the help of a prayer or just a sigh. . . . Young people also attend synagogue. They stand still. They cannot read the prayers, but in this place they become united, as it were, with other Jews. . . . Where else can they do this?"

Rabbi Stuart Rosenberg of Toronto, who was granted a visa to visit the country in 1961, encountered the same anxious atmosphere. "No words could convey the fantastic fright, which has reduced these people to human caricatures and robbed them of their personality as individuals," he later wrote in an article in the *Toronto Star*. Rosenberg was able to arrange a discreet meeting with Rabbi Yehuda Leib Levin in the Great Moscow Synagogue. In the dark, with the office door locked, they talked in hushed tones in Yiddish and then in Hebrew about the harsh realities that confronted Soviet Jews. When Rabbi Levin heard about the vibrancy of Jewish life in North America, he embraced Rosenberg and said, "You have a great and strong community of Jews in America. You must continue to be strong. We have no voice and your Jews do. You must never forget us. We will be finished if you do."

In a real sense, Soviet Jews in the early 1960s were indeed the "Jews of Silence," as the respected writer and Holocaust survivor Elie Wiesel referred to them in the title of his 1961 book about the Russian community. Yet no matter how harsh the punishment, the embers of the past could not be extinguished altogether. The secret was to be discreet. Since it was against Soviet law to teach religion to children under the age of eighteen, it was difficult, if not impossible, for thirteen-year-old Jewish boys to have their bar mitzvahs. A father, like Nissen Gorelsky in Odessa, however, might gather together ten of his friends for the proper *minyan* quorum one Saturday morning so that his son could read from the Torah as thirteen-year-old Jewish boys did throughout the world. Gorelsky even smuggled in a set of *tefillin*, or phylacteries, from Israel as a gift for his son, Izak.

Likewise, despite the serious consequences of being discovered, Jews consistently defied the ban on matzo and secretly baked it in their basements during Passover. Igor Korenzvit recalls that as a young child in Kiev he accompanied his parents to the home of friends where his family could obtain matzo. For the Korenzvit family, like many Jewish families, however, knowing the rules and rituals of Passover was another matter. "We brought the matzo home," he says, "and put it in the same basket we used for bread."

Away from the safety of the basements and the covered windows, there was a growing minority of younger Jews, writers, lawyers, and teachers, who refused to be silent. Though they did not truly understand their religion and culture, they established a nascent Soviet Jewish underground. Their main weapon was books, reports, and literature. They created the first *samizdat*, underground publications that linked them in a common cause. They devoured and passed among them the speeches of Israeli Prime Minister David Ben-Gurion; Simon Dubnow's two-volume history of the Jews of Russia; reports about the trial of Nazi Adolph Eichmann in Jerusalem; the poetry of Russian Yevgeni Yevtushenko, whose 1961 poem *Babi Yar*, with its condemnation of anti-Semitism, touched the heart of every Soviet Jew; and above all Leon Uris's 1958 novel *Exodus*, the melodramatic account of the establishment of the State of Israel, a book which became their *Tanach*, their Bible.

Uris's novel, when it was surreptitiously given to one group of young Zionists in Riga by the Israeli Ambassador to the Soviet Union, captured their imaginations. It was painstakingly translated from English to Russian (all of it, that is, except the section in the book that deals with the Jewish Ari Ben-Canaan's romance with the Gentile Kitty, thought not to be an appropriate example for Soviet Jewish youth), mimeographed, and widely distributed. "For tens of thousands of Soviet Jews," reflected Leah Bliner, a key member of the Riga Zionist underground, "the *samizdat* version of *Exodus* was their greatest Jewish inspiration." Copies of the novel even made their way to Soviet prison camps, where they gave the inmates a spark of hope for the future.

Suddenly, in Riga, Vilna, Moscow, and Leningrad, the "Jews of Silence" found their voice. Defying the authorities, they constructed a memorial, a barbed-wire Magen David, at Rumbuli, the

Nazi death site outside Riga. They made a point of attending synagogues on Jewish holidays, and cheered enthusiastically when an
Israeli women's basketball team played in a tournament in Riga in
1965. Nothing gave the Jewish spectators more pride than singing
Ha-Tikvah, the Israeli national anthem, after the Israelis won a gold
medal. Demand for tickets surged as well when Israeli musicians
gave concerts in Soviet cities. At such events, the police attempted,
with limited success, to keep the Jews from having any contact with
the Israeli visitors. Though a near riot broke out at one performance given by popular Israeli singer Geula Gil in Riga in 1966 – in
which a fifteen-year-old girl was struck hard by a policeman and
then arrested for resisting – Soviet authorities could not dampen
the fervour that these gatherings generated.

One other defining moment occurred in Moscow in October
1965 on the holiday Simchat Torah (the Rejoicing of the Law), celebrated on the last night of Sukkot (the Feast of the Tabernacles).
That evening, a large crowd assembled at the Moscow Synagogue
on Arkhipova Street to revel in their lost, even unknown, Jewish
heritage as they had never done before. Out in front of the synagogue, they loudly sang the songs *"David Melech Yisrael"* ("David,
the King of Israel") and *"Am Yisrael Chai"* ("The Jewish People
Live") and danced through the night following the traditional procession of Torahs.

Elie Wiesel was there to witness this remarkable awakening.
"The street was unrecognizable. For a second I thought I had been
transported to another world, somewhere in Israel or in Brooklyn,"
he later wrote. "Angels and seraphim were serenading the night;
King David played his harp. The city burst with gladness and joy.
The evening had just begun. . . . I do not know where all these
young people came from. . . . They came in droves. From near and
far, from downtown, and the suburbs, from the university and from
factories. . . . How many were there? Ten thousand? Twenty thousand? More. . . . The crush was worse than it had been inside the
synagogue. They filled the whole street, spilling over into court-
yards, dancing and singing. They seemed to hover in mid-air."

A year later, their prayers appeared to have been answered when Soviet prime minister Alexei Kosygin announced in Paris that Soviet Jews would be allowed to join their families in Israel. The details were vague, yet Jews throughout the Diaspora proclaimed this to be a step in the right direction. The door had opened a little, and approximately three thousand Soviet Jews were able to obtain visas to Israel during the next two years. But it could be shut at a moment's notice. No one knew then that the real struggle of Soviet Jews to reclaim their roots was only beginning.

Why I Am a Zionist

AMONG THOSE PAYING ATTENTION to the series of troubling events taking place in the Middle East in the spring of 1967 was Boris Kochubiyevsky. He was a shy, unassuming thirty-year-old radio engineer living in Kiev, the city of his birth. Kochubiyevsky was a typical Soviet Jew of the era. Members of his family had participated in the 1917 revolution, and his father, who had served in the Red Army, had been murdered at Babi Yar by the Nazis in the fall of 1941. During his teenage years and while he attended the Kiev Polytechnic Institute, Kochubiyevsky had tried to hide his Jewish identity as much as he could. He preferred to be an assimilated Russian; life was safer that way. Besides, his mother had not provided him with much of a Jewish education, nor had he sought to learn himself about his Jewish religion or culture.

In February 1966, Soviet authorities arrested a young Kiev Jew by the name of Iosip Chornobilsky, who had been an active Zionist for several years. He was charged with "slandering" the Soviet government and spreading Zionist propaganda and was sentenced to a lengthy term in Soviet prison. While Chornobilsky was denounced in the press, the injustice of his ordeal deeply troubled Kochubiyevsky, even if he did not readily admit it at the time. Gradually, Kochubiyevsky was drawn to a Kiev synagogue where, among friends, his Jewish identity took shape. He read forbidden literature, spoke with visiting Jews from abroad, and learned that

Israel was not the imperialistic aggressor portrayed in the Soviet press.

Arab nations surrounding Israel had tried to crush the Jewish state when it was established in 1948, and Israel and Egypt had gone to war again in 1956 to contest control of the Suez Canal. In May of 1967, once again the situation in the Middle East appeared bleak. Egyptian president Gamal Nasser had sent his troops into the Sinai, ordered United Nations peacekeepers out of Egyptian territory in the Gaza, and banned Israeli ships from using the Strait of Tiran. On June 5, hoping to avoid a calamity, Israel undertook a pre-emptive strike against its three enemies, Egypt, Jordan, and Syria, destroying much of their air power. Initially, the Soviet press, following Arab propaganda, declared that its Arab allies, using Soviet-supplied weapons, were on the verge of destroying the Jewish state. Nothing could have been further from the truth. Within six days, Israel had made gains in every direction, taking the Sinai in the south, the Golan Heights in the north, and the West Bank in the east, including East Jerusalem and the area around the Western Wall of the Holy Temple. Throughout the Diaspora, but especially amongst Soviet Jews, the seemingly miraculous victory of the Six Day War was vigorously applauded as "an event of almost messianic proportions." It sparked, says Natan Sharansky, "a basic, eternal truth . . . that personal freedom wasn't something you could achieve through assimilation. It was available only by reclaiming your historical roots."

The Soviet Union responded to the Israeli victory by cutting all ties with Israel and ordering its ambassador out of the country. In the press, Israel was compared to Nazi Germany. Meetings were organized at factories and shops throughout the Soviet Union to pass resolutions critical of Israel and supportive of Soviet policies. Such a meeting was held at Boris Kochubiyevsky's factory a week after the hostilities in the Middle East had ended. The employees gathered to hear an anti-Israel lecture delivered by officials from the Soviet Ministry of Information. When it came time to vote on the resolution against Israel, something in Kochubiyevsky snapped. "I want the record to show that I disagree," he declared to the stunned crowd. "I do not consider Israel an aggressor. This was a necessary measure of protection of the Jewish people from total physical annihilation."

Within hours, Kochubiyevsky was called before his superiors and ordered to retract his statement and resign his position. He refused. He had crossed a line and there was no return. A year of pressure and recrimination from his fellow workers followed. He was shunned and isolated for being a "Zionist bourgeois agent."

But nothing would make him change his mind. On the contrary, his support for Zionism was strengthened. Determined to apply for an exit visa to Israel, Kochubiyevsky relented and resigned his position at the factory in May 1968. Feeling the need to set down his views on paper, he composed a long essay entitled "Why I Am a Zionist." It was a powerful condemnation of Soviet anti-Semitism and quickly became a staple of Jewish *samizdat*.

"Why is it that the most active sector of Jewish youth raised and educated in the U.S.S.R. still retains a feeling of Jewish national unity and national identity?" Kochubiyevsky asked. "How is it possible that Jewish boys and girls who know nothing about Jewish culture and language, who are mostly atheists, continue to feel so acutely and to be so proud of their national affiliation? The answer is simple: Thanks for that, in large measure, can be given to anti-Semitism – the new brand which was implanted from above and, as a means of camouflage, is called anti-Zionism. . . . We are convinced that there can no longer be room for Jewish patience. Silence is equivalent to death. . . . If we remain silent today, tomorrow will be too late. . . . More and more Jews are coming to understand that endless silence and patience lead straight down the road to Auschwitz. That is why the leaders of the Soviet Union have anathematized Zionism. That is why I am a Zionist."

A month after he wrote these words, Kochubiyevsky married Larissa Aleksandrovna, who was studying to be a teacher. Of Ukrainian background, Larissa, however, shared her husband's Zionist passions and joined him in submitting an application for a visa to immigrate to Israel. Getting out of the Soviet Union in

1968, and for the next twenty-five years, meant dealing with an even worse-than-usual bureaucratic nightmare of long lines, endless forms, delays, and, more often than not, disappointment.

From the end of Stalin's rule to the Six Day War of June 1967, only 6,000 or so Soviet Jews had been granted permission to leave the country. Many more had been refused. In the 1960s, the process began with a *vyzov*, an invitation, sent by Israeli relatives (or someone posing as a relative, which was more common). As Igor Korenzvit explains, "There was an underground network that supplied the invitations. Once it was known that you needed one, the 'right' people got in touch with you and eventually, sometimes after a long time, the papers arrived in the mail." Next, the applicant required a character reference from work, official permission from parents, notarized birth certificates, money for exorbitant passport fees, and an assortment of other documentation. None of these papers was easily obtained. Managers and unions were furious with an employee who wanted to quit, and fearful parents would often not sign a form that could jeopardize their children's lives.

Once an application was submitted to OVIR, the government agency responsible for visa registration, a prospective emigrant usually lost his or her job and was thus liable for arrest under Soviet law for being unemployed – a "parasite" (*parazit* in Russian) on the system. Sometimes it took six months or more to hear from officials at OVIR, and if an applicant was rejected, he or she was required to wait for a set period, often six months, before trying again. Thus was born the "refusenik" movement, large numbers of Soviet Jews, who, for one reason or another, could not, no matter what they did, obtain the government's permission to emigrate. Officials might claim that as a result of their employment they were privy to state secrets, that they posed a "security risk," or that they lived in an area not open to emigration. Whatever the excuse, they were trapped, harassed by the KGB, desperate, and alone.

Precisely how many Soviet Jews attempted to flee the country after 1967 and for the next two decades is unclear, though the figure was probably more than a million. In this period, the Soviets did allow close to 300,000 Jews to leave. But from year to year, the number fluctuated dramatically – from a high of 51,320 in 1979 to a low of only 896 in 1984 – and was dependent on a dozen different domestic and international concerns. For one thing, the Soviets had made promises to their Arab allies to keep the number of Jews entering Israel to a minimum. But worldwide lobbying by Jewish leaders in North America and Europe, in addition to pressure from various United States administrations, all played a role in what in hindsight seems to have been a callous and contradictory Jewish immigration policy instituted by Leonid Brezhnev (who succeeded Khrushchev in 1964) and his successors.

Boris and Larissa Kochubiyevsky's first application was denied. As they contemplated their next move, they attended an informal gathering of Soviet Jews held each year at the end of September at Babi Yar to commemorate the victims of the Nazi slaughter. In the fall of 1968, Soviet authorities also held a memorial meeting on the site to remember "Soviet citizens, Russians, Ukrainians, and others" who were killed there. As the government ceremony ended, Kochubiyevsky, taking exception to the official speaker's words, added, "Here lies a part of the Jewish people." Later, at Kochubiyevsky's trial, this minor episode was blown out of all proportion and witnesses were produced who claimed that he had slandered the Soviet government and its citizens.

In November 1968, Kochubiyevsky and Larissa resubmitted their emigration application. One morning, Boris received a phone call informing him that his application had been approved. Could he come immediately to the OVIR office? Once they arrived, however, their jubilation turned to deep regret. Instead of receiving exit visas, they were ordered to sign a document stating that they could not leave the country. At first they refused, but after being held in a small room for three hours, they relented. When they returned to their apartment, they discovered that it had been ransacked by the KGB.

Kochubiyevsky was so furious that he sat at his desk and composed a long letter to Brezhnev. There was no logic in his action, yet he felt compelled to do something. "I am a Jew," he began. "I want to live in the Jewish State. . . . As long as I live, as long as I am capable of feeling, I will do all I can to get to Israel. And if you find it necessary to imprison me for this, and I live until my release, I will go to the homeland of my ancestors, even if it means going on foot."

Kochubiyevsky's passionate declaration would circulate through the Soviet underground and eventually be smuggled out to the United States. It was published in the *New York Times* on June 5, 1969, along with the story of his trial. For by then, Kochubiyevsky was in trouble. Soon after he had sent the letter, he was arrested and charged with "slandering" the Soviet system. He was kept in prison for the next five months and brought to trial in mid-May 1969, in the same Kiev courtroom where, decades earlier, Mendel Beilis had been accused of murdering a Christian child in a Passover blood ritual. As he entered, a small crowd taunted him: "You are not a brother, you are a Jew, Jew, Jew."

Few of Kochubiyevsky's relatives or friends were permitted into the courtroom, despite the fact that the trial was supposed to be open. Most of the spectators occupying the room had been planted by the KGB, a tactic that was employed repeatedly in the many Zionist trials that were to come. Kochubiyevsky pleaded not guilty, though he did maintain that what he had written in his letter to Brezhnev was essentially true. Both the prosecutor and the judge denounced Kochubiyevsky and the few witnesses who spoke on his behalf.

The trial was a sham from start to finish, and the verdict never in doubt. It was reminiscent of the show trials held during the Stalin era. Consider this typical exchange between the prosecutor and Kochubiyevsky.

"Do you know what we fought against?" the prosecutor asked.

"Against Fascism," Kochubiyevsky replied.

"And what have we fought for? Freedom?"

"Yes."

"Have we won?"

"Yes."

"So you see, we have freedom."

At another point, the judge told Kochubiyevsky's wife, Larissa, who was pregnant, "to find herself another husband." She had already lost her job at the Pedagogical Institute and had been expelled from the Komsomol (Young Communists League) for associating with a Zionist. Her own parents had disowned her. When Kochubiyevsky attempted to make reference to Yevgeni Yevtushenko's poem about Babi Yar, the court admonished him. "Defendant, the last word is given to you to use for your defense," said the judge, "and not for excursions into the history of literature."

After four days of this, Kochubiyevsky was found guilty and sentenced to three years in a "severe regime" labour camp. As a result of his eloquent writings, his case became known around the world. And for a time he represented all of those Soviet Jews who were oppressed simply because they wanted to emigrate to Israel.

Sent to a labour camp in the north, he found himself the only political prisoner among a large group of criminals. He later said that the guards encouraged the other inmates to beat him. In December 1971, having served his sentence and survived, Kochubiyevsky was released from prison. He and Larissa were granted exit visas and at last could begin their lives anew in Israel.

The Prisoners of Zion

BORIS KOCHUBIYEVSKY was far from the only Russian to be utterly frustrated by the injustice of arbitrary Soviet immigration regulations. The Six Day War had also awakened something profound in twenty-year-old Yasha Kazakov, a student at the University of Moscow. On June 10, 1967, the final day of the Middle East conflict, the impetuous Kazakov dispatched a letter to the supreme Soviet renouncing his Soviet citizenship. "I asked to be freed from the humiliation of being considered a citizen of the Union of

Soviet Socialist Republics. I ask to be given the opportunity to leave the Soviet Union. . . . I am a Jew, and as a Jew I feel that the State of Israel is my homeland." At first, the authorities ignored him, but when he persisted, sending another letter to U Thant, then the secretary general of the United Nations, Kazakov was apprehended and questioned. From that day on he was constantly trailed by KGB agents.

Kazakov's first attempt to secure an exit visa for Israel was rejected. Again he wrote a letter to the government demanding that he be allowed to leave, and again he was threatened with imprisonment. Eventually, he was expelled from university and was forced to take a job as an electrical technician. A year later, no closer to achieving his goal, he decided on a new course of action. He wrote yet another declaration of his case and managed to get copies into the British Embassy addressed to the *New York Times* and other newspapers. He also passed on his letter to Jewish tourists, though he had no assurance that they would assist him in his cause.

Finally on December 19, 1968 Kazakov's appeal was published in the *Washington Post*, as he found out that evening while listening to the radio program *Voice of America*. His parents, who wished only that their son would abandon his foolish scheme and accept the Soviet system, feared for his life. But there was no going back now. Kazakov's passionate cry for freedom was published in newspapers around the world. The *Voice of Israel*, popular among Soviet Jews, transmitted his words, and soon Jews in Russia knew of his bold struggle as well. A month later, in January 1969, the Soviets granted Kazakov his visa for Israel. He has been living there ever since as Yasha Kedmi, an outspoken advocate for Russian immigrants.

It was a different story for Edward Kuznetsov. For many years, Kuznetsov, whose father was Jewish and his mother Russian, campaigned in Leningrad and Moscow against human-rights abuses. He and his friends produced underground literature and organized public readings. In 1961, when he was twenty-two years old, he participated in a protest in Moscow that led to his arrest. He was put on trial and sentenced to seven years in a labour camp. When he was finally released, in 1968, he emerged from the gulag with a renewed sense of purpose and a strong Jewish identity. "I grew up in a Russian family and had practically no knowledge whatsoever of Jewish culture, nor did I know anything of the influence it had had on nearly every culture in the world," he later explained. "Therefore my choice to live and be a Jew was dictated in the early stages by emotional considerations rather than by a conscious feeling of physical identity."

In 1970, he met and married Silva Zalmanson and moved with her to Riga, where he obtained a job. There, he also came into contact with Hillel Butman, a friend to Silva, who introduced Kuznetsov to other young Zionist "refuseniks" intent on going to Israel. These included Mark Dymshits, a trained pilot who could not find permanent work because of his Jewish background. In time, Dymshits and Butman, along with a few others, devised a half-baked plan to hijack a small plane and fly it to Sweden. Once there, the group hoped to reach Israel.

They never got off the ground. Early in the morning of June 15, the police, who had several of the individuals involved under surveillance, were waiting for them at the Leningrad airport. The would-be hijackers carried with them one small gun, which could not be fired, and several truncheons intended to scare the aircrew. The arrest that day of Kuznetsov, Dymshits, Kuznetsov's wife, Silva, her brothers, Israel and Wulf Zalmanson, and eight others (in all, nine were Jewish) marked the start of a KGB clampdown on the "refusenik" and Zionist movement. At least another forty people supposedly linked with this "conspiracy" were apprehended in Riga, Kharkov, and Leningrad. More were arrested in the months that followed.

Eleven of those caught at the Leningrad airport were charged with "betrayal of the fatherland," "responsibility for the preparation of a crime," "anti-Soviet agitation and propaganda," and "participation in anti-Soviet organization." That no crime had actually taken place was beside the point. In December, the defendants were put on trial for high treason – a charge that carried the death

penalty – in more-or-less closed proceedings that were manipulated from beginning to end. Much of the time, the prosecutors
attempted without success to link the accused to the "intrigues of
international Zionism."

Near the end of the trial, when it was her turn to speak, Silva
Zalmanson delivered a poignant plea, arguing that the group's only
crime was that they wanted to live in another country. "Our dream
of living in Israel was incomparably stronger than fear of suffering
we might be made to endure," she stated. "Even now I do not doubt
for a minute that some time I shall go after all and I will live in
Israel." Her words fell on deaf ears. On Christmas Eve 1970, after
eight days of testimony and almost meaningless cross-examination,
the verdict was handed down. Kuznetsov and Dymshits were sentenced to death; the others received prison- and labour-camp terms
of between five and twelve years.

As news of the verdict filtered out and eventually reached the
West, it generated a wave of protest. Inside the Soviet Union, noted
human-rights activist Andrei Sakharov organized demonstrations
and made a direct appeal to U.S. President Richard Nixon. Rallies
and protest meetings against Soviet-style justice were held in a
number of American, Canadian, and European cities. Even the
pope made a plea for mercy. The Soviets had not been prepared for
such a worldwide reaction, and within a week it had made an
impact. Soviet authorities granted the accused an unprecedented
appeal. Then, in a stunning decision, the judges quickly commuted
the death sentences of Kuznetsov and Dymshits to fifteen-year
prison terms – though under a "specially strict regime," which
meant "solitary confinement in a prison cell consisting of a plank
bed, barred windows, and a 'slop tank' (no plumbing)" – and
reduced a number of the other sentences as well.

In one respect, the Soviets had backed down. "The Jews had
won," as American journalist Leonard Schroeter put it several years
ago. "The Soviet State had capitulated." Yet in the years ahead, there
would be many more trials, and much more sorrow and pain before
the Soviets would ever truly acknowledge that the freedom to leave

a country, to live where one wanted, was a universal human right that had to be recognized. This ongoing fight for freedom provided a common cause that would unite as never before Soviet Jews with the Jews of Israel and the Diaspora.

As world pressure mounted to free dissidents and permit more Jews to emigrate, the KGB intensified its efforts in a dangerous game of cat and mouse. *Vyzov* applications continued to flow into Soviet offices, though less than half of those Jews who applied between 1970 and 1976 were successful (284,827 first time *vyzovs* were sent in during this period, while 114,312 Jews were granted permission). The KGB kept track of *samizdat* authors, for example, by making it mandatory for persons purchasing typewriters and carbon paper to show their internal passports. Soviet agents also harassed young Jews for attempting to organize remembrance prayers at Babi Yar and other Second World War death sites.

Yet this was minor compared to the serious charges levelled against Jewish activists on January 22, 1977, in a Soviet television program called *Traders of Souls*. The program purported to be a documentary linking Zionist activities with the U.S. Central Intelligence Agency (CIA). Portrayed as spies were, among others, Anatoly (now Natan) Sharansky, Yuli Kosharovsky, Yosif Begun, and Vladimir Slepak, all prominent "refuseniks" who had been denied exit visas to Israel. Later they learned that one of their own, Dr. Sanya Lipavsky, had reported their activities to Soviet authorities and made the false accusation.* United States President Jimmy Carter denied that these Jews were connected to the CIA, but the Soviets were determined to quash the group.

Sharansky was then twenty-eight years old. Born in the Ukraine, he was trained in mathematics and computer science at the Physical

---

* According to Sharansky, Lipavsky had betrayed him and their friends in a deal with the KGB to save his father, who in 1962 had been convicted and sentenced to death for stealing fabric from a textile factory. In other words, Lipavsky had been working as a KGB informer for more than a decade by the time he came into contact with Sharansky.

Technical Institute in Moscow, but it was his fluency in English and friendly relations with members of the foreign media that ultimately attracted the attention of Soviet officials. He had first attempted to leave for Israel in 1973. Through his involvement in the Jewish movement, he met and fell in love with Avital Stieglitz. The two were married in the summer of 1974, a day before Avital was scheduled to move to Israel. The young couple believed they would be reunited soon in Jerusalem. That reunion would not happen for twelve more years.

Officers of the KGB came for Sharansky on March 15, 1977, marking the start of an ordeal that was not to end until he was freed in a prisoner exchange with the United States in 1986. Like other Soviet Jews, he was subjected to a trial in which black was white and white was black. Charged with espionage and treason, he was sentenced to thirteen miserable years in prisons and labour camps. His friends received similar punishments in prison and exile.

Throughout this ordeal, he endured physical and psychological tortures. In total, he spent 403 days of his incarceration in cold dark "punishment cells." Yet the Soviets could not break his remarkable spirit. For more than a decade, and in the face of extremely difficult circumstances, he kept his sanity, his commitment to his wife, and his faith in his people. As he had declared at the end of his trial, he was certain that the day would soon come when he would be reunited with his family in Jerusalem.

As had happened during the Leningrad hijack trial, the Soviets' treatment of Sharansky set in motion a massive campaign of protest rallies, letter writing, and behind-the-scenes lobbying to win his release. Marches were organized in hundreds of Jewish communities, and few Jews in the Diaspora did not know about the Sharansky case.

The movement soon involved people like Wendy Eisen, a young wife and mother of four children in Toronto, who had attended a meeting about Soviet Jews in 1974. From that point on, she dedicated herself to their cause. She wanted never to be accused, as Jews had in the 1930s and 1940s, of not doing enough. For the next decade, she fought on behalf of Sharansky and other refuseniks. She organized countless meetings and made several visits to the Soviet Union as acts of solidarity.

Sharansky's wife, Avital, also travelled around the globe, fighting for her husband's freedom. In the process, she helped unite Jews in the Diaspora in a common cause. Through her diligent effort this Jewish issue became a matter of human rights. On a visit to Ottawa, one sceptic asked her, "how does putting pressure on the Soviets help? After all, your husband is still in prison." Avital did not hesitate to respond: "Without the pressure, he would be dead."

It was as a result of that pressure that Sharansky was eventually freed in a prisoner exchange on the Glienicke Bridge linking Potsdam and West Berlin on February 11, 1986. To the end, Soviet officials insisted that Sharansky was a spy. That evening, he and Avital had an emotional reunion, and soon he was able to pray at the Western Wall in Jerusalem – just has he had predicted.*

Less high-profile Jews, including those who opted to remain Soviet citizens, continued to live on the "margins" of Soviet society, outwardly maintaining their Jewish identity only as much as the government tolerated. Synagogues were often full on the High Holidays (thought this was still dependent on the whim of the authorities), Jewish music was celebrated in concerts, and small groups of Orthodox Jews studied Talmud. If these Jews could get their hands on Yiddish and Hebrew literature – at international book fairs held in Moscow in the late 1970s, for instance – they did so. "People literally pleaded for any small symbol of Jewish identity," said one publishers after attending one such fair, "a Star of David, a Jewish calendar, a Hebrew alphabet chart."

---

* Not one to be quiet, since his arrival in Israel, Sharansky has fought brilliantly for the interests of Russian Jewish immigrants, and in 1996 he established his own political party, Yisrael B'Aliyah. A year later, Sharansky's party won seven seats in the Israeli Knesset and he was named the minister of industry and trade. In the current government of Ariel Sharon, elected March 7, 2001, Sharansky is Housing Minister. His party holds six seats in the Israeli Knesset.

The rise of Mikhail Gorbachev in 1985 and his policy of *glasnost*, or "openness," did not immediately alter Jewish life in the Soviet Union. True, Sharansky was released in 1986 and activists Andrei Sakharov and his wife, Elena Bonner, were allowed to leave their exile in Gorky later that year. Yet twelve months after Gorbachev assumed control, nearly two-dozen key "Prisoners of Zion" still remained incarcerated in prisons and labour camps under the most extreme of circumstances.

Glasnost and *perestroika* may have started a revolution in the country, but most Jews did not feel its real impact until the historic events of 1989 and 1990 led to the communist regime's demise. Only then were close to half a million Jews allowed to leave the country for Israel and the United States (between 1987 and 1991) and a Jewish religious and cultural life began to flourish in Russia once more. That this Jewish spirit, in some form or another, endured in Russia from the time of the czars, through the brutality of Stalin, to the turmoil of the present day, is testimony to the remarkable resilience that has characterized life in the Diaspora for centuries.

THE DIASPORA IN 2003

For two thousand years the Jewish people, my people, have been dispersed all over the world and seemingly deprived of any hope of returning. But still each year Jews have stubbornly, and apparently without reason, said to each other, Leshana habah b'Yerushalayim *(Next Year in Jerusalem)!*

— Natan Sharansky, 1977

Victims and Heroes

IN NORTH AMERICA, the Second World War is relegated to history books and veterans' clubs, but in Europe it is around every corner. You cannot escape it, especially in the east, in Vilnius and Kiev, where in 1943 and 1944 the fighting between the Nazis and Soviets was fierce. Today in both cities, there are moving memorials to the brave fallen of the Soviet Union, statues and monuments commemorating victory and denouncing Fascism.

For decades, Soviet officials ensured that these various remembrances made little or no mention of the Jewish suffering during the Holocaust. In particular, Babi Yar, only a fifteen-minute car ride from the centre of Kiev, and the site of a horrific slaughter of Jews by the Nazis in 1941, remained unkempt, a forest ravine of trees and tall grass. During the 1960s, a Jewish cemetery in front of the death pits was destroyed and a mammoth television tower built on the land. Across the street, the Soviets did erect a monument in

1976 "to Soviet Citizens, Soldiers, and Officers, Prisoners of War, Who Were Tortured and Killed by the Nazi Invaders in 1941–43." It was not until the declaration of independence by the Ukraine in 1990 that the Jewish tragedy was properly acknowledged.

Today there is a long brick sidewalk leading to the ravine behind the television tower. A simple menorah sits in the square at the end of the walkway with markers in Russian and Hebrew denoting what took place on this spot at the end of September of 1941. At the end of January 2001, Moshe Katsav, the newly elected Sephardi president of Israel, visited Babi Yar and added a new stone plaque with the Hebrew inscription "My pain is always with me." Still, the actual site of the killing remains largely neglected, and it is necessary to make your way through a mud path surrounded by tall grass and weeds, where the locals allow their pet dogs to romp, in order to reach the massive death pits.

The Ponary forest memorial eight kilometres outside of Vilnius, on the other hand, is better cared-for, although it also was not until 1992 that the Jewish victims of the Nazi killings were properly acknowledged. The area is a quiet and serene place. A stone marker tells the story of the murder in the seven pits that the Soviets had begun to develop during the war for fuel storage. The grass is green and manicured, and the paths through the forest to the sites are paved. On my visit, only the playing of a few local children, who were there to pick the wild strawberries, was at odds with the solemnity of the moment. But no Jew, religious or not, who visits either city can avoid paying their respects at these places where death still hangs in the air. They pull on your heart and you are forced to remember. That is, after all, one of the most powerful and compelling tenets of being Jewish – the act of remembering.

The terrible memories of Babi Yar, the Ponary, and the Holocaust continue to cast a shadow over Jewish life around the world. Its tragic impact has had both enormous demographic and psychological consequences. In 1939, there were nearly 17 million Jews in the world, of whom almost 60 per cent resided in Europe. Today, the world Jewish population hovers around 13.2 million, of whom 36 per cent live in Israel, 46 per cent in North America, and only 12.6 per cent in Europe.

This has been only one of the most visible results of the Second World War: the virtual disappearance of many Diaspora communities and a dynamic Yiddish culture along with them. Furthermore, because of a declining birth rate – except among the ultra-Orthodox – the overall number of Jews in the world continues to drop. Israel's present population may be ten times that of the small Jewish settlement in Palestine in 1939, but the Diaspora is more than 22 per cent smaller. Among the many countries I visited in Europe in preparing this book, only France (which lost approximately ninety thousand of its three hundred thousand Jews during the Holocaust) has sustained and increased its Jewish population, mainly the result of immigration by Jews from former French colonies in north Africa.

Approximately 1.5 million European Jews survived the Second World War, and, of those, 250,000 to 300,000 were liberated from Auschwitz, Bergen-Belsen, Majadanek, and the other death and slave labour camps. Many would have been happy to return to the cities and towns in Poland and Lithuania where they had lived before the war, but they soon discovered that, despite the tragedy of their ordeal during the past six years, anti-Semitism had not disappeared in those regions. During the summer and fall of 1945, pogroms against Jewish Holocaust survivors broke out in many Polish cities, including Cracow, Lublin, and Sosnoweic. Hundreds of Jews were killed. In Kielce, south of Warsaw, in early 1946, the disappearance of a young boy led to, appallingly, accusations that he had been abducted as part of a Judaic ritual murder plot. In the riots that followed, forty-two Jews, children among them, were killed. Many of the rioters were later arrested and convicted; nine were sentenced to death for their part in the provocation.

Homeless and impoverished, many Holocaust survivors ended up in displaced person camps as the Western world debated what to do with them. In time, about 200,000 made their way to Palestine, joining in the fight to establish the State of Israel. Others often found long-lost relatives in every corner of the Diaspora and made their way to countries in North and South America, the Caribbean, Mexico, Australia, and South Africa. Argentina, Chile, Brazil, and Mexico, became the new home of thousands of survivors. In these Latin American countries, where pockets of Sephardi Jews had been joined by East European immigrants in the late 1880s and early part of the twentieth century, vibrant Jewish communities existed ready and willing to assist and absorb the refugees.

More than 45,000 Jewish refugees had fled to Argentina, for example, in the decade before the Second World War; another 10,000 arrived after the conflict ended. They settled mainly in Buenos Aires, Santiago, Rio de Janeiro, São Paulo, and other cities eventually fitting into a middle and upper class lifestyle. Still, during the ensuing decades, those who had made it to Argentina and Chile were confronted once more with political and economic instability, anti-Semitism, and fascist military regimes led by such dictators as Juan Perón (who for a time permitted many former Nazis, including Adolf Eichmann to settle in Argentina), Juan Ongania, and Augusto Pinochet. The 1994 terrorist bombing of the Jewish community center in Buenos Aires, that killed eighty-six people (Iranian and right-wing groups were suspected, but no one has ever been arrested for the attack) was the final straw for many Argentinean Jews. If they were able to do so, many opted to immigrate to the United States and Canada and start their lives again . . . once more.

The psychological impact of the Holocaust is not as easy to measure, yet its effect on the Jewish world has been more traumatic. The Nazi assault was the climax of thousands of years of Jewish persecution, worse even than the destruction of the two temples in Jerusalem and the expulsion from Spain. Even if not all Jews were led like "sheep to the slaughter," the image of Jews as helpless victims has persisted. At the same time, owing to the courage of the survivors, the Holocaust has become an essential part of school curricula in North America and Europe, and more significantly has been imprinted on the consciousness of people everywhere. The survivors deliver lectures, write their memoirs, and preserve their life stories in such archival collections as Steven Spielberg's Shoah Foundation, which has amassed more than fifty thousand Holocaust testimonies. Today, in a modern version of the blood libel, only a fringe of extremists and cranks denies that it happened at all. Few days, it seems, pass without some mention of a Holocaust issue in the media – the role of Swiss banks, actions of large corporations, slave labour, war criminals, and compensation for survivors. Many Jews are understandably protective of its memory.[*]

The Holocaust finally confirmed for Jews that they could only count on themselves. No longer would they be treated like the 1,128 German-Jewish refugees aboard the ocean liner *St. Louis*, travelling in 1939 from port to port in North and South America. When no country, including Canada and the United States, permitted them to land, they were forced to return to Europe, where many of them eventually perished. The recollection of this and other similar pathetic events in the Second World War has in recent years spurred Jews to action in the Diaspora and in Israel. They have fought for the rights of their people in the former Soviet Union, Arab countries, and, in fact, wherever prejudice, discrimination, and hatred against Jews have taken place. This has been a direct challenge to the view of Jews as history's continual victims.

The widely held belief among Diaspora Jews that the Holocaust could happen again if they are not vigilant has dictated support of Israel through the good times and bad. (Since 2001, outbreaks of violence between Palestinians and Israelis have been worse than they have been in decades, and many North American Jews have cancelled their travel plans to Israel. This had led to criticism from within Israel and North America that Diaspora Jews have forsaken the country.)

---

[*] In August 2000, Rabbi Ovadia Yosef, then the head of the Shas Party, Israel's ultra-Orthodox Sephardi political party, ignited a powder keg with a remark that the millions of Jews who perished in the Holocaust died because they were re-incarnations of sinners. He later claimed that he had been misunderstood, yet the damage had been done.

Since the Diaspora Jew is no longer regarded as an exile, making *aliya* (immigrating to Israel, but literally "going up") is no longer a priority or a realistic option for most North American Jews. But providing financial aid and defending Israel's position has become an integral part of the identity of most Diaspora Jews. Witness, for example, the almost daily barrage of letters submitted by Jews to North American newspapers to protest real and perceived bias or unfair criticism of Israel. In their collective minds, the existence of a powerful Jewish homeland has strengthened their own position as a minority within their own countries. In short, Israel has made them proud to be Jews again.

Supporting Israel was admittedly an easier task during its first thirty-five years of existence as an independent country. Surrounded by hostile Arab states, which wanted to drive Israel into the Mediterranean Sea, only a military ingenuity that often bordered on the miraculous allowed the Jewish state to survive wars in 1948, 1956, 1967, and 1973. Israel was a "victim" but one which fought back. And the Israeli soldier, suggests the French writer Alain Finkielkraut, "served as proof that Jew and coward, or Jew and victim, are not synonymous terms."

Since the early 1980s, and in particular following Israel's invasion of Lebanon in 1982, the country has emerged as the strongest military power in the Middle East. It is no longer a victim in any sense of the word, a fact that has led some Jews outside of the country to debate its policies – regarded almost as sacrilege in some Jewish quarters. Moreover, the multitude of divisions in Israeli society has also made it vulnerable to Jewish as well as non-Jewish criticism from the outside.

To the rest of the world, Israel is a country of Jews, but in fact it is beset by the same internal problems that have plagued Jews for centuries. The country is divided along a dozen different lines – religious, class, traditional racial, Ashkenazi, Sephardi, Israeli, and Arab (one in every six Israelis is an Arab). The ancient Ashkenazi–Sephardi split has been especially problematic. For many years, Sephardi Jews from Morocco and other North African countries felt like second-class citizens at the hands of the Ashkenazi establishment. Finally, they established their own religious political party, Shas, to combat Ashkenazi control, though this has merely exacerbated the divisions. In August 2000, it was a major political and social upset when Moshe Katsav, a popular Sephardi politician born in Iran, was elected to the ceremonial position of president, defeating Shimon Peres, a former prime minister and a key member of the Ashkenazi elite that has run Israel since 1948.

There have been far worse moments, however. The depth of Israeli divisiveness was evident for the world to witness in November 1995, when a Jewish "zealot," Yigal Amir, murdered Israeli Prime Minister Yitzhak Rabin in response to his land-for-peace policies toward the Palestinians and Arab states. Now, Israeli politicians have to employ bodyguards to protect themselves from Arab terrorists, as well as from attacks by religious ultra-Orthodox Jewish extremists. While many Orthodox rabbis condemned the assassination of Rabin, with Amir's violent act Israel lost its innocence forever. For the first time, Diaspora Jews began to question their support, although that support, in spirit at any rate, nevertheless continues. The legacy of the Nazis demands it.

The Good News and the Bad News

JEWS MIGHT HAVE EXPECTED that worldwide revulsion at the Holocaust would have rid society of anti-Semitism altogether, but this has not been the case. A 1946 opinion poll in France indicated that more than a third of the population did not believe that Jews could ever become "loyal French citizens." Two decades later, many Frenchmen still maintained views that would be considered anti-Semitic. Even the near disappearance of Jews from Eastern Europe did not eliminate anti-Jewish sentiments. There was an anti-Semitic backlash in Poland in 1968, when it was still under Soviet control, and attacks against "Judeo-Communism" in the aftermath of the fall of the Soviet Union in 1989.

Łódź once had a Jewish population of two hundred thousand;

today there are only about two hundred Jews left. Recently a group of young Poles decided to clean the derogatory graffiti off the walls of the city's lone synagogue, where such words as *Jude* and *Zhid* were reminders of the dark days of the past. Yet within twenty-four hours after the students had completed their work, the racist graffiti had reappeared. Similar incidents have also occurred in Russia, and politicians like Vladimir Zhirinovsky – not to mention Jean-Marie Le Pen in France or Jörg Haider in Austria – have used anti-Semitism to appeal to their young ultra-nationalistic followers.

Still, this issue is as complex as ever, and certainly it is impossible to generalize. In Lithuania and the Ukraine, among other Eastern European countries, the officially sanctioned anti-Semitism of the Soviet Union is no more. Synagogues have reopened, Jewish community centres have been restored, Jewish museums present new exhibitions, Holocaust education is being promoted, and in both Vilnius and Kiev Lubavitcher Jews go about their business in the streets and at the airports without any problems. "It is just like being in New York," says Kiev's Rabbi Moshe-Reuven Azman. Perhaps, but stereotypes persist, as does a more subtle version of anti-Semitism. At the same time, Jews no longer pose any type of social or economic threat in these countries as they once were perceived to, nor are they politically powerful. Compared to centuries past, their status as a visible minority is nearly non-existent.

Of late, tensions caused by the unsettling developments in the Middle East and a notable backlash against Israeli policies have led to a rise of anti-Semitism in Eastern and Western Europe. Between early 2001 and the spring of 2002, there were 900 reported anti-Semitic incidents in Paris and its surrounding area. Synagogues in France and Belgium have been fire-bombed and Jews have been assaulted in Paris, Berlin, and Kiev. A poll done by the anti-Defamation League found that among 2,500 Europeans, 30 per cent "believe that Jews have too much power in the business world." Such attitudes even have reached China. In the summer of 2002, Chinese officials (China is one of the few powers in the world to recognize a sovereign state of Palestine) demanded that a travelling exhibition from the Israeli Hebrew University, about Albert Einstein's life and work, omit all reference to the fact that he was Jewish. Israelis responsible for the exhibit were stunned by the request and cancelled its display in Beijing.

Much more seriously in the spring of 2002, came the murder of American journalist Daniel Pearl. The Pakistani extremists who killed him are reported to have forced him to declare, "I am a Jew," before they slit his throat. Western society can now pat itself on the back for having been overly tolerant of regularly-produced Islamic propaganda and state-controlled Arab newspapers that conjure up medieval images of blood libels. Such praised matter depicts Jews as the Devil, either deny the Holocaust ever occurred or regret that it was not more effective, and above all propagate the myth that there is a Jewish conspiracy to take over the world. Along the same lines as the early twentieth-century tract, the "Protocols of the Elders of Zion," the Saudi newspaper *Al-Watan* published a two-part article in December 2001 entitled, "The Jewish Sense of Superiority in the World."

The second part of it began as follows, "At the end of the last century, the Jewish organizations consolidated a hellish plan to takeover the world by sparking revolutions or taking control of the keys in various countries, first and foremost the U.S. and Russia . . . The Jews are incapable of actualizing their influence and control for a simple reason, and that is that they are a demographic minority in every society in the world. For this reason, the Jews are trying by means of trickery to weaken the national allegiance [of the Jews] and thus takeover affairs and direct them to serve their interests." When such ideas are advanced daily to young children, it is easy to understand how hate may be perpetuated by one generation upon the next.

It is a much different story in North America – despite the rising number of anti-Semitic incidents in Canada and the United States since the beginning of 2001. In the summer of 2000, when Democratic presidential nominee (and former Vice President) Al Gore chose as his running mate Senator Joseph Lieberman, a Jewish

politician and an overtly observant man a that, the senator's faith did
not become the issue it certainly would have even a decade ago. In
fact, Gore's popularity rose as a result of he announcement. Two years
later, Lieberman again made history when he declared his intention
to seek the Democratic nomination for presidency in 2004. Whether
he will succeed in this remains to be seen, but the election of a Jewish
President is no longer in the realm of the impossible.

The general attitude to Lieberman was positive and a sure sign
that being Jewish in North America is no longer an obstacle to
career advancement or social acceptance. The quotas at medical
schools and the property restrictions at summer resorts do not exist
any longer. America has become "a home rather than an exile,"
in the words of U.S. scholar Ruth Wisse, and the "Wandering
Jew" is no more. But in the view of many Jews, the absence of
anti-Semitism and the current tolerant multicultural attitudes have
had serious consequences.

"The good news is that American Jews – as *individuals* – have
never been more secure, more accepted, more affluent, and less
victimized by discrimination or anti-Semitism," says Harvard law
professor Alan Dershowitz. "The bad news is that American Jews –
as a *people* – have never been in greater danger of disappearing
through assimilation, intermarriage, and low birthrates. The even
worse news is that our very success as individuals contributes to our
vulnerability as a people." Instead of anti-Semitism, Jews, according to Dershowitz, are now being killed "with kindness."

For many generations, Jews felt that they could control the
acculturation process – adapting, borrowing, synthesizing – and if
they could not, then the host society would surly keep them in line.
Yet acculturation has now given way to outright assimilation in
larger numbers than ever before. Younger Jews do not feel that their
Jewish identity is a factor one way or the other in their careers.
They want to move beyond the old stereotypes and do not perceive
themselves to be "victims," as their fathers and grandfathers did.

This new attitude and acceptance has also meant higher intermarriage rates (or, as Dershowitz wryly notes, "Everyone wants to

marry a Jew, except Jews themselves"). In 1957, only 4 per cent of American Jews married out of their faith. By 1964 it had risen to 12 per cent. Today, more than 50 per cent of Jewish children marry Christians (some of whom will convert to Judaism). It is no longer the taboo it once was, and Jewish parents do not go into mourning when their son or daughter chooses a non-Jewish partner – neither do they disown their child, as Tevye the milkman did in the musical *Fiddler on the Roof*. Thus, from one perspective, Judaism and Jewish rituals have become less critical for the new generation. Synagogue attendance is declining. And while it is also true that many Jewish parents do send their children to Jewish schools, they do not practise what the school teaches in their homes. Will these children pass on the traditions, rituals, and rites that they do not fully understand to their own children? What future can there be for Jews when future generations will have no understanding of what it means to be Jewish?

The Post-Persecution Era

IF THE EIGHT HUNDRED YEARS OF JEWISH HISTORY chronicled in this book provide any lessons, it is that despite the constant hardship and crisis, there is always hope. This was the reason, for instance, that the Jewish partisan fighters during the Second World War believed in the words of poet and partisan Hirsh Glik, who began his popular Yiddish song with the phrase "*Zog nit keynmol az du geyst dem letstn veg*," "Never say that you are on your last journey." The journey of the Jewish people is not over.

The story of the Diaspora has been called "a series of encounters and adjustments." It is equally true that from today's perspective these adjustments were often short-sighted. Clearly, at various moments in history, Jews in Spain, Venice, Constantinople, and to a certain extent Amsterdam, did themselves no long-term good by taking the side of the ruling elite against the people with whom they lived. Yet their choices were limited – better to survive today and worry about the future later – and, of course, they expected that the arrival of the Messiah was imminent, that at the "end of days" they would be rescued from their enemies and tormentors.[*]

When this did not transpire, Jewish life was partly sustained by the prejudice and hatred that prevented Jews from getting too close to their Christian neighbours – the persecution was, in the view of some rabbis, a unifying force. (Alan Dershowitz calls this the *tsuris* theory of Jewish survival, *tsuris* being the Yiddish word for "troubles.") In 1812, as Napoleon was marching eastward against Czar Alexander I, Jews gathered in the synagogue for Rosh Hashanah prayers. Rabbi Shneur Zalman, the father of the Lubavitch movement, rose to offer his blessing for the leader who would most benefit the Jews living in the Pale of Settlement. Everyone in the synagogue that day knew that Jewish life could only improve under Napoleon, while the czar's continued reign offered them nothing but hardship. Yet to the dismay of the congregants, Rabbi Zalman prayed for the Russian emperor. "Should Bonaparte win, the wealth of the Jews will be increased and their [civic] position will be raised," he later explained. "At the same time their hearts will be estranged from our Heavenly Father. Should however our Czar Alexander win, the Jewish hearts will draw nearer to our Heavenly Father, though the poverty of Israel may become greater and his position lower."

There are those who maintain that little has changed from Rabbi Zalman's day (or even the era of Don Isaac Abravanel), that Judaism remains perpetually on the brink, in a "crisis of faith." Jews are the world's "ever-dying people," to use historian Simon Rawidowicz's term. Yet Rawidowicz also argues that there are no people "better equipped to resist disaster" than are the Jews. It has always been this way, and though the creative adaptive powers that have sustained Jews through turbulence and tragedy must now be refocused to

---

[*] As one slightly cynical story about the Messiah's arrival goes: "In a small Russian *shtetl*, the community council decides to pay a poor Jew a ruble a week to sit at the town's entrance and be the first to greet the Messiah when he arrives. The man's brother comes to see him, and is puzzled why he took such a low-paying job. "It's true," the poor man responds, "the pay is low. But it's a steady job."

account for the current conditions in the Diaspora, there is no reason to believe that they will not be successful.

Even in Europe, according to the theory of "Diasporism" espoused by Richard Marienstras, a Polish-born professor of English literature living in France, Jews must be acknowledged as a "national minority with a legitimate culture all their own." This is a direct challenge to the old nationalistic homogeneous order that has been ingrained in European society for more than two hundred years, but in the current politically correct climate one that might finally be feasible and acceptable.

A new state of mind must come from within Jews themselves, suggests Alan Dershowitz, one that reaffirms that Jews will be the chosen people: "They will have chosen to remain Jewish." To this end, Dershowitz writes that Jews "must rediscover, redefine and reawaken Jewish values and approaches that are more suited to the dangers we face from our new friends than our old enemies." Judaism must "move beyond its long history of victimization and into its post-persecution era of Jewish life."

Part of being Jewish is the constant search for answers to questions about faith, life, and existence. At any given time, Jews, whether they define themselves as Orthodox, Conservative, Reform, or otherwise, can now participate in "Shabbatons," inexpensive weekends of religious observance and reflection, and different varieties of Jewish renewal experiences. There are exciting educational initiatives from such Modern Orthodox organizations as Aish HaTorah, which for the past twenty-five years has sought "to bring Jews closer together to their heritage and roots." Based at a yeshiva in Jerusalem, there are currently twenty-six branches of Aish HaTorah in North America and another twelve in Europe. The group holds seminars with religious and secular speakers on such topics as the computer analysis of the Holy Scriptures, and maintains a lively Web site with a live photo feed of the Western Wall in Jerusalem. Articles posted about the Jewish theme in movies like *Gladiator* and *X-Men* ("Are Jews X-Men?") attempt to capture the imagination of Jewish youth as does a popular question-and-answer e-mail component in which queries can be sent to a rabbi.

For adults, there is another technological initiative called the *Kallah*, or "gathering." In the days of Maimonides, it was customary for Jews to gather during the Hebrew months of Elul and Adar to study Jewish topics. It was known as "*Yarchey Kallah*," the months, or moons, of gathering. In March 2000, the first modern version of the *Kallah* was held, and thousands of Jews around North America linked by a live-circuit television joined together for a discussion held in the auditorium of New York's Ninety-second Street Y, the site of many famous lectures. The panellists on the inaugural session included Alan Dershowitz, Anne Roiphe, a columnist for the *New York Observer*, and the well-known radio commentator and writer Dennis Prager. Their topic: "The Future of North American Jewry."

As might be expected, the two-hour debate was often heated, loud, witty, and poignant. Each participant brought a unique perspective to the audience – they spoke of faith, the meaning of God, Hebrew schools, intermarriage, and parenting – but the conversation kept coming back to the two fundamental questions of Jewish history: what does it mean to be Jewish, and who is a Jew?

There may never be satisfactory answers to the ancient conundrums, and perhaps that is as it should be. To be a Jew in North America in the twenty-first century – or in Spain at the time of the exile, or in France when Alfred Dreyfus was sent to Devil's Island – is to be blessed with a special burden. Seeking life's true meaning and coming to terms with the Jewish condition as it pertains to each new age – this is part of the mystery of the Jewish people and always will be.

NOTES

INTRODUCTION: EXILE AND DISPERSION

1 "We must revitalize": Ahad Ha-Am, "The Law of the Heart" (1894), in Arthur Hertzberg, *The Zionist Idea* (New York: Atheneum, 1976), 255; **2 The term "Diaspora"**: Abba Eban, *Heritage: Civilization and the Jews* (New York: Summit Books, 1984), 95; **2 According to Josephus**: Cited in ibid., 87; **2 "Since then [. . .] the Jew has not died"**: Ora Limor, "A Rejected People," in Nicholas De Lange, ed., *The Illustrated History of the Jewish People* (Toronto: Key Porter, 1997), 123; **7 Footnote**: Cited in Annie Kriegel, "Generational Difference: The History of an Idea," *Daedalus* 107 (Fall, 1978), 34; **10 He implored the children**: See Jeremiah 29:4–7; **11 By going out into the world**: Eban, *Heritage*, 95–96; **11 A group of progressive Central**: Cited in Raphael Patai and Jennifer Patai Wing, *The Myth of the Jewish Race* (Detroit: Wayne State University Press, 1989), 41; **11 "This people has made its way"**: Cited in Josephus, *Antiquities* 14, in Oded Irshai, "The Making of the Diaspora," in De Lange, ed., *Illustrated History*, 65; **12 "Nordau and I agreed"**: Cited in Lucy S. Dawidowicz, *The Jewish Presence: Essays on Identity and History* (New York: Holt, Rinehart & Winston, 1977), 26; **12 Or, put slightly differently**: Jean-Paul Sartre, *Anti-Semite and Jew: An Exploration of the Etiology of Hate*, translated by George J. Becker (New York: Schocken Books, 1948; reprint, 1995), 91; **12 In an article he wrote**: Ahad Ha-Am, "The Negation of the Diaspora" (1909), in Hertzberg, *Zionist Idea*, 270–76.

CHAPTER ONE: SEPHARDIM

15 "As for the Jews": Cited in David Raphael, ed., *The Expulsion Chronicles* (North Hollywood, Calif.: Carmi House Press, 1992), 53; **16 "Is this world"**: Benzion Netanyahu, *Don Isaac Abravanel* (Philadelphia: Jewish Publication Society, 1968), 65; **16 Far from being a man of the Renaissance**: Ibid., 147–48; **16 It was such a negative view**: See ibid., 195–257; **16 Footnote**: See "Don Isaac Abrabanel," *Encyclopedia Judaica* vol. 2 (Jerusalem: Keter Publishing House, 1972), 102; **16–17 And like most members**: See the family's Web site: http://www.abarbanel.com, maintained by Jenine Abarbanel, one of many descendants of Don Isaac Abravanel. See also "Variations on a Blue-Blooded Theme,"

Jerusalem Post, October 30, 1992, 8b; **17 It also instilled in Isaac Abravanel**:
Netanyahu, *Don Isaac Abravanel*, 4; **17 He made the city**: Will Durant, *Age of Faith*
(New York: Simon & Schuster, 1950), 697–98; **17 "It was Seville"**: Netanyahu,
Don Isaac Abravanel, 5; **18 Other Jews beyond Sisebut's**: Jane S. Gerber, *The Jews*
of Spain: A History of the Sephardic Experience (New York: The Free Press, 1992), 12;
18 They brought with them: Elka Beth Klein, "Power and Patrimony: The
Jewish Community of Barcelona 1050–1250." Ph.D. diss. Harvard University, 1996,
23; **19 Footnote: Jewish population figures**: See Norman Roth, *Conversos,*
Inquisition, and the Expulsion of the Jews from Spain (Madison, Wis.: University of
Wisconsin Press, 1995), 328–29; and Angus MacKay, "The Jews in the Middle
Ages," in ed. Elie Kedourie, *Spain and the Jews: The Sephardi Experience 1492 and*
After (London: Thames & Hudson, 1992), 33; **19 Bed linens were changed**:
See the fascinating description of Sephardi life and food in Claudia Roden, *The*
Book of Jewish Food (New York: Alfred A. Knopf, 1997), 216–25; **20 At issue**
among Jews: Gerber, *Jews of Spain*, 79–80; **21 A decade later**: Ibid., 106;
21 Change, assimilation, even conversion: Durant, *Age of Faith*, 416;
21 And second, and more significantly: Elka Klein, "The Jewish Community,"
ORB: The Online Reference Book for Medieval Studies. http://orb.rhodes.edu/
encyclop/religion/Judaism/judaism.html; **21 As the pioneering scholar**: Isaac
Baer, *A History of the Jews in Christian Spain* vol. 1 (Philadelphia: Jewish Publication
Society of America, 1961), 95; **22 In 1283, for example**: Yom Tov Assis, *The*
Golden Age of Aragonese Jewry: Community and Society in the Crown of Aragon,
1213–1327 (London: Littman Library of Jewish Civilization, 1997), 53–54; **22 In the**
towns and villages: See Kedourie, *Spain and the Jews*, 42–44; Gerber, *Jews of Spain*,
96, 111; **22 During the era of the Black Death**: Durant, *The Reformation* (New
York: Simon & Schuster, 1957), 730; Gerber, *Jews of Spain*, 112; **22 Contrary to**
popular belief: Leila Berner, "On the Western Shores: The Jews of Barcelona
During the Reign of Jaume I, '*El Conqueridor*,' 1213–1276," Ph.D. diss. U.C.L.A.,
1986, 209–20; Assis, *The Golden Age*, 92–94. See also Stephen Bensch, *Barcelona and*
Its Rulers 1096–1291 (Cambridge: Cambridge University Press, 1994); **22 As the**
Church [. . .] successfully prohibited: Benzion Netanyahu, *The Origins of the*
Inquisition in Fifteenth Century Spain (New York: Random House, 1995), 69–70;
23 Hence, "no financial arrangement": Ibid. 70; **23 It was precisely for this**
reason: Ibid. 71; **23 Tax farmers also collected**: Abraham Neuman, *The Jews in*
Spain vol. 2 (Philadelphia: Jewish Publication Society of America, 1942), 223–24,
243–47; **23 Even when Christian leaders**: Ibid. 243–48; **24 In time, Judah**
Abravanel: Ibid., 247–48; **24 As a leader of the Seville *aljama***: Cited in
"Don Isaac Abrabanel," *Encyclopedia Judaica* vol. 2, 102; Roth, *Conversos, Inquisition*,
118–19; **24 His crime**: Baer, *Jews in Christian Spain* vol. 2, 87; **24–25 The**
violence in Seville: Netanyahu, *Origins of the Inquisition*, 97–100; Kedourie, *Spain*
and the Jews, 47–48; **25 A creative tax collector**: Baer, *Jews in Christian Spain* vol.
1, 362–63; **25 The evidence against him**: Netanyahu, *Origins of the Inquisition*,
107–10; **25 A religious zealot**: Ibid. 129–34, 145–46; **26 In December 1390**:

Ibid. 139; Kedourie, *Spain and the Jews*, 52–54; **26 The Seville Judería was destroyed**: Netanyahu, *Origins of the Inquisition*, 148–49; **27 By the time it ended**: Baer, *Jews in Christian Spain* vol. 2, 99–101; **27 The rioters, joined by the local**: Ibid. 104; Netanyahu, *Origins of the Inquisition*, 157; **27 Those inside who refused**: Cited in Netanyahu, ibid., 159; **28 Overnight, he became**: Roth, *Conversos, Inquisition*, 119; **28 Footnote: In mid-June of 1391**: Enrique III of Castile to Burgos city council, June 16, 1391, in *The Jews in Western Europe 1400–1600*, ed. John Edwards (Manchester: Manchester University Press, 1994), 47–48; **28 "If we ask ourselves"**: Cited in Gerber, *Jews of Spain*, 116–17; Baer, *Jews in Christian Spain* vol. 2, 239–40; **30 It was for this reason**: Netanyahu, *Abravanel*, 10; H.V. Livermore, *A New History of Portugal* (Cambridge: Cambridge University Press, 1966), 112–13; **30 "We saw Jews"**: Cited in Howard M. Sachar, *Farewell España: The World of the Sephardim Remembered* (New York: Alfred A. Knopf, 1994), 159; **31 More than two hundred**: Ibid., 159; **31 He mastered Latin**: Netanyahu, *Abravanel*, 13; **32 In this brief dissertation**: Ibid., 17; **32 Though Abravanel owned**: Elias Lipiner, *Two Portuguese Exiles in Castile* (Jerusalem: The Magnes Press, 1997), 51, 65; **32 In 1472 Abravanel's wife**: Moses A. Shulvass, *The Jews in the World of the Renaissance* (Leiden, Netherlands: E.J. Brill, 1973), 174; **33 Consider, for example, that in 1480**: Netanyahu, *Abravanel*, 25; **33 The duke's brother**: Livermore, *New History of Portugal*, 124–25; **33 It is doubtful**: Netanyahu, *Abravanel*, 263–64; **34 "What man, subjected"**: Cited in ibid., 29; **35 Ferrer was as dedicated**: See, Baer, *Jews in Christian Spain* vol. 2, 166–67; Sachar, *Farewell España*, 50; Erna Paris, *The End of Days* (Toronto: Lester Publishing, 1995), 91–92; **36 Guided by Pope Benedict**: Sachar, ibid., 52–53; Netanyahu, *Origins of the Inquisition*, 172; **36 Some forced converts**: On the *converso* issue, see Haim Beinart, "The Great Conversion and the Converso Problem," in Kedourie, *Spain and the Jews*, 92–122; Sachar, *Farewell España*, 51–52; Gerber, *Jews of Spain*, 121–23; Netanyahu, *Origins of the Inquisition*, 928–42; and Roth, *Conversos, Inquisition*; **36 By these decrees**: Netanyahu, *Origins of the Inquisition*, 194; **37 In short, the purpose of this legal**: Ibid., 193–94; **37 "Inmates of palaces"**: Cited in Heinrich Graetz, *History of the Jews* vol. 4, (Philadelphia: Jewish Publication Society of America, 1891–1898), 220; Paris, *End of Days*, 93; **37 Jews throughout Aragon**: Paris, ibid., 103; **37 At this gathering**: Limor, "A Rejected People," 117; **37 For several years he had**: Sachar, *Farewell España*, 52–53; Paris, *End of Days*, 104–5; Roth, *Conversos, Inquisition*, 139–40; **38 For almost a year**: Sachar, *Farewell España*, 55; Paris, *End of Days*, 107; **38 A papal bull followed**: Ibid., 113–14; **38 The pressure to convert**: Ibid., 113; **39 Jewish tax collectors**: Eleazer Gutwirth, "Towards Expulsion: 1392–1492," in Kedourie, *Spain and the Jews*, 61–68; Sachar, *Farewell España*, 57–58; Yom Tov Assis, "The Jews in the Crown of Aragon and its Dominions," in Haim Beinart, *Moreshet Sepharad: The Sephardi Legacy* vol. 1 (Jerusalem: Magnes Press, 1992), 101; **39 "As conversion increased"**: Roth, *Conversos, Inquisition*, 154; **40 On the contrary, the vast**: Netanyahu, *Origins of the Inquisition*, 936; **40 Here was a precursor of**: Paris, *End* *of Days*, 127; Gerber, *Jews of Spain*, 127; Beinart, "Great Conversion and Converso Problem," 94–95; **40 But he reserved**: Paris, *End of Days*, 156–57; Limor, "A Rejected People," 128; Beinart, ibid., 96, 105; **40–41 In 1473, Cordoba**: Roth, *Conversos, Inquisitions*, 105; **41 Still, it is notable**: Baer, *Jews in Christian Spain* vol. 2, 385. See also, Peggy K. Liss, *Isabel the Queen* (New York: Oxford University Press, 1992), 165; **41 "All the Jews in my realm"**: Cited in ibid., 264; **42 Nothing about the Inquisition**: See, Gerber, *Jews of Spain*, 130–31; Beinart, "Great Conversion and Converso Problem," 106–7; "The Trial of Gonzalo Pérez Jarda, Toledo, 1489–1490," in Edwards, *Jews in Western Europe*, 39–43; **42 "There was always a possibility"**: Roth, *Conversos, Inquisition*, 221; **43 Two decades later**: On March 18, 1488, Ferdinand and Isabella appointed Abraham Seneor the royal treasurer of the *Santa Hermandad* (Holy Brotherhood), a royal agency for law and order. See, Edwards, *Jews in Western Europe*, 81–82; **43 After 450 Jews**: Liss, *Isabel*, 219–20; **43 At the court, Abravanel's role**: See, Netanyahu, *Abravanel*, 50–51; Roth, *Conversos, Inquisition*, 280; Baer, *Jews in Christian Spain* vol. 2, 362. Abravanel may have been appointed chief collector of the royal taxes on livestock. A royal document dated November 30, 1488, refers to the appointment to this important position of "Don Yuçef Abravanel." Given that Isaac's son Joseph (Yuçef) was only seventeen years old in 1488, it seems unlikely that this task was given to him. The individual in question also could have been one of Isaac Abravanel's relatives. See, Edwards, *Jews in Western Europe*, 77–78; **44 Years later, Abravanel would remember**: See letter from Abravanel to Saul Ha-Kohen, 1507, cited in Roth, *Conversos, Inquisition*, 299–300; **44 Between 1482 and 1492**: Sachar, *Farewell España*, 69; **44 As the sultan departed**: Ibid., 68–69; Gerber, *Jews of Spain*, 132–3; Liss, *Isabel*, 227–31; **44 In this infamous and twisted case**: See Paris, *End of Days*, 216–23; Gerber, *Jews of Spain*, 133; "Documents of the Inquisition Trial Held in Avila in 1490–1491," in Edwards, *Jews in Western Europe*, 104–16; **45 In the midst of the negotiations**: Gerber, *Jews of Spain*, 134–35; Netanyahu, *Abravanel*, 55–56; Roth, *Conversos, Inquisition*, 299–300; **45–46 "He chastised her"**: Elijah Capsali, *Seder Eliyahu* Zuta, chapter 69, in Raphael, *Expulsion Chronicles*, 14; **46 More importantly, once he decided**: Roth, *Conversos, Inquisition*, 300–301; **46 They were guilty**: Netanyahu, *Origins of the Inquisition*, 1092; **46 The conquest of the Moors**: Limor, "Rejected People," 129; **46 "The Inquisition desired nothing"**: Henry Kamen, "The Expulsion: Purpose and Consequence," in Kedourie, *Spain and the Jews*, 81–82; **47 Whatever the true motives**: See, Gerber, *Jews of Spain*, 138; Roth, *Conversos, Inquisition*, 305–8; **47 Hence on June 15, 1492**: Beinart, "Great Conversion and the Converso Problem," 114; **47 Footnote: There is also a great debate**: See Gerber, *Jews of Spain*, 139; Roth, *Conversos, Inquisition*, 285; Kamen, "Expulsion: Purpose and Consequence," 85; **48 As soon as Judah Abravanel**: See Netanyahu, *Abravanel*, 60; **48 Footnote: "My darling child"**: See A.R. Milburn, "Leone Ebreo and the Renaissance," in ed., J.B. Trend *Isaac Abravanel: Six Lectures*, (Cambridge: Cambridge University Press, 1937), 134; and Jacob S. Minkin, *Abarbanel and the Expulsion of the Jews from Spain* (New York:

Behrman's Jewish Book House, 1938), 191; **49 Since Spain controlled ports**: Gerber, *Jews of Spain*, 148; **49 "A new Sephardi nexus"**: Jane S. Gerber, "My Heart Is in the East," in De Lange, *Illustrated History*, 183–84.

CHAPTER TWO: THE GHETTO

51 "The Jews must all live together": Cited in Riccardo Calimani, *The Ghetto of Venice* (New York: M. Evans and Company, 1985), 1; **51 Jewish life was governed**: Robert Bonfil, *Jewish Life in Renaissance Italy* (Los Angeles: University of California Press, 1994), 22–23, 85; **53 "You would have thought"**: Cited in Cecil Roth, *History of Jews of Italy* (Philadelphia: Jewish Publication Society of America, 1946), 275–77; **53 Ferrante, recorded the chronicler**: Capsali, *Seder Eliyahu Zuta*, Chapter 71, cited in Raphael, *Expulsion Chronicles*, 19; **53 He would later write**: Netanyahu, *Abravanel*, 64; **54 The moment Ferrante died**: Liss, *Isabel*, 310; **54 "Everywhere there were scenes"**: Cecil Roth, *Jews of Italy*, 280; **55 "My wife, my sons"**: Cited in Durant, *Reformation*, 742; **55 He completed a lengthy**: Netanyahu, *Abravanel*, 74–76; **56 In Abravanel's search**: Ibid., 77–78; David B. Ruderman, "Hope Against Hope: Jewish and Christian Messianic Expectations in the Late Middle Ages," in Aharon Mirsky, Avraham Grossman, and Yosef Kaplan, eds., *Exile and Diaspora* (Jerusalem: Hebrew University, 1991), 190; **56 The messianic trilogy**: Netanyahu, *Abravanel*, 78; **57 Sephardim tended to look down**: Shulvass, *Jews in the World of the Renaissance*, 58; **57 "When I came to Italy"**: Cited in Calimani, *Ghetto of Venice*, 145; **57 For many years, Jews**: Cecil Roth, *History of the Jews in Venice* (New York: Schocken Books, 1975), 9, 28; **58 Soon, more moneylenders**: Calimani, *Ghetto of Venice*, 5–7; **58 In the words of the great**: Graetz, *History of the Jews* vol. 3, 511; Durant, *Reformation*, 738; Brian Pullan, *The Jews of Europe and the Inquisition of Venice, 1550–1670* (Totowa, N.J.: Barnes & Noble Books, 1983), 155; **58 Or, put another way more recently**: Bonfil, *Jewish Life*, 24; **59 In their leisure time**: Sachar, *Farewell España*, 222; Shulvass, *Jews in the World of the Renaissance*, 172–89; **59 In a letter to Saul Ashkenazi**: Cited in Minkin, *Abarbanel*, 181; **59 Overlooking its dictatorial**: Calimani, *Ghetto of Venice*, 43; **59 Don Isaac dispatched his nephew**: Netanyahu, *Abravanel*, 82–84; **60 At Abravanel's funeral**: Sachar, *Farewell España*, 214; Minkin, *Abarbanel*, 198–99; **60 He was rightly revered**: Netanyahu, *Abravanel*, 88–89; **60 In several of his books**: M. Gaster, "Abravanel's Literary Work," in Trend, *Isaac Abravanel*, 69–70. Menasseh Ben Israel's life and work is further discussed in Chapter Four; **60 More curious was a museum exhibit**: Jonathan Skolnik, "The Strange Career of the Abarbanel Family," unpublished English translation, 1999, 1. This essay appeared in Joseph Kruse and Bernd Witte, *Aufklärung und Skepsis: Heinrich Heine zum 200. Geburtstag* (Stuttgart: J.B. Metzler Verlag, 1999); **61 In the introduction to a volume**: Trend, *Six Lectures*, 10; **61 Protests were also made**: Benjamin Ravid, "The Venetian Government and the Jews," in Robert C. Davis and Benjamin Ravid, eds., *The Jews of Early Modern Venice* (Baltimore: Johns Hopkins University Press, 2001), 8; **61 Finally, in the spring of 1516**:

Cecil Roth, *Jews in Venice*, 49–53; Ravid, "The Venetian Government and the Jews," 9; **62 This ruling, however**: Ibid., 10–13; **62 Meshullam and others argued**: Ibid., 49–50; Calimani, *Ghetto of Venice*, 32; Pullan, *Jews of Europe*, 156; **62 Footnote: In 1930, when Cecil Roth**: See Cecil Roth, *Jews in Venice*, 61–62; Shulvass, *Jews in the World of the Renaissance*, 60; Calimani, *Ghetto of Venice*, 46–47; Ravid, "The Venetian Government and the Jews," 8–9; Ennio Concina, "Owners, Houses, Functions: New Research on the Origins of the Venetian Ghetto," in ed. Alisa Meyuhas Ginio *Jews, Christians, and Muslims in the Mediterranean World after 1492* (London: Frank Cass & Company, 1992), 180–89; Benjamin Ravid to the Author, November 19, 2001; **63 Often a peddler used the ground-floor**: Concina, "Owners, Houses, Functions," 181; **63 Four Christian guards**: Ravid, "The Venetian Government and the Jews," 9; **63 Yet life in the ghetto**: Calimani, *Ghetto of Venice*, 132; **63 "The rhythm of daily life"**: Ibid., 133; **63 Jewish traders from across Italy**: Cecil Roth, *Jews in Venice*, 164–65; Shulvass, *Jews in the World of the Renaissance*, 135–39; **64 At night, the ghetto**: See, Roth, *Jews in Venice*, 134; **64 Men in need**: Shulvass, *Jews in the World of the Renaissance*, 179; **64 Leone Modena, a notable**: Ibid., 180. See also ed. Mark R. Cohen, *The Autobiography of a Seventeenth-Century Venetian Rabbi: Leon Modena's Life of Judah* (Princeton, N.J.: Princeton University Press, 1988), 97, 129–30, 155–56; **66 During the conflict**: Benjamin Arbel, *Trading Nations: Jews and Venetians in the Early Modern Eastern Mediterranean* (New York: E.J. Brill, 1995), 65–68; **66 Later, the sultan rewarded**: Ibid., 56, 68–69; Sachar, *Farewell España*, 84–85; **66 As the members of the Senate**: Cited in Arbel, *Trading Nations*, 75; **67 The Ponetines first lived**: Pullan, *Jews of Europe*, 157; **67 The ghetto finally expanded**: Ravid, "The Venetian Government and the Jews," 19. I would like to thank Prof. Benjamin Ravid of Brandeis University for bringing this to my attention; **67 "[The Ghetto was] a halfway house"**: Bonfil, *Jewish Life*, 72–73; **68 Jews were merchants**: Ibid., 74; **68 For these Venetians**: Pullan, *Jews of Europe*, 160; **68 In discreet corners**: Ibid., 160; **68 "I saw many Jewish women"**: Cited in ibid., 159; **69 "Business transactions between"**: Ibid., 153; **69 "The Pope," wrote the Florentine**: Cited in Durant, *Reformation*, 922; **69 In his bull of 1555**: Cited in Cecil Roth, *Jews of Italy*, 294; **70 Most of the other Jewish physicians**: Ravid, "The Venetian Government and the Jews," 25–26; David B. Ruderman, "Medicine and Scientific Thought: The World of Tobias Cohen," in Davis and Ravid, *The Jews of Early Modern Venice*, 191–92; Shulvass, *Jews in the World of the Renaissance*, 315–21; **71 He also composed**: Gaster, "Abravanel's Literary Work," 72; **72 "Fate drove my friends"**: Cited in Minkin, *Abarbanel*, 190–91; **72 Recent speculation is that the work**: See, Arthur M. Lesley, "The Place of the *Dialoghi d'amore* in Contemporaneous Jewish Thought," in ed. Konrad Eisenbichler and Olga Zorzi Pugliese, *Ficino and Renaissance Neoplatonism* (Ottawa: Dovehouse Editions Canada, 1986), 82–85; **72 It is not known precisely**: Milburn, "Leone Ebreo and the Renaissance," 140–41; **73 Modelled on the writings of Plato**: Ibid., 140; **73 It is possibly**: "Leone Ebreo," *Encyclopedia of the Renaissance*, (New York: C. Scribner's

Sons, 1999), 412; **73 Nothing, according to Abravanel**: See, Minkin, *Abarbanel*,
188; Durant, *Reformation*, 742; **73 Or, as he put it so poetically**: Leone Ebreo,
The Philosophy of Love, translated by F. Friedeberg-Seeley and Jean H. Barnes
(London: The Soncino Press, 1937), 461–62; **74 Judah's work, like that of**: See
Cecil Roth's "Introduction" in ibid., xv; **74 Samuel Usque, a poet**: Cited in
Minkin, *Abarbanel*, 192; **74 He moved in the highest circles**: E.H. Lindo, *The
Jews of Spain and Portugal* (New York: Burt Franklin, 1970), 269; **75 Samuel, with
assistance from**: Cecil Roth, *Jews of Italy*, 284–85; **75 She had a well-deserved
reputation**: Minkin, *Abarbanel*, 194; **75 She was, claimed one person**: Cited in
Gerber, *Jews of Spain*, 183; **75 They fought the order**: Roth, *Jews of Italy*, 285–86;
76 His son Jacob: B.D. Cooperman, "A Rivalry of Bankers: Responsa concerning
Banking Rights in Pisa, 1547," in ed. Isadore Twersky, *Studies in Medieval Jewish
History and Literature* vol. 2 (Cambridge, Mass.: Harvard University Press, 1984), 46;
76 When Samuel died: Cecil Roth, *The House of Nasi: Doña Gracia* (Philadelphia:
Jewish Publication Society of America, 1948) 67; **76 By a charter granted**:
"Magistrato Supremo 4449, Dei Capitoli D'Ebrei" ("The Charters of the Jews"),
The Medici Archive Project, www.medici.org/medicior/jewish/docs.html;
Cooperman, "Rivalry of Bankers," 49; Renata Segre, "Sephardic Settlements in
Sixteenth-Century Italy: A Historical and Geographical Survey," in ed. Alisa
Meyuhas Ginio, *Jews, Christians, and Muslims*, 127; **76 Despite the fact**: Ibid;
77 On their behalf, Cosimo de Medici: Archivo de Stato di Firenze, Mediceo
del Principato 219; f. 35r–v; Copy of letter from Duke Cosimo de'Medici (in Pisa)
to Cardinal Alesandrino, February 5, 1563, in Medici Archive Project.

CHAPTER THREE: PHYSICIANS, POETS, AND A FALSE MESSIAH

79 "Brothers and teachers": Cited in Bernard Lewis, *The Jews of Islam*
(Princeton, N.J.: Princeton University Press, 1984), 135–36; **79 Within five
decades**: Jason Goodwin, *Lords of the Horizon: A History of the Ottoman Empire*
(London: Chatto & Windus, 1998), xiii; **80 But instead of occupying**: Ibid.,
51–53; Durant, *Reformation*, 710; **81 In the popular imagination**: Ed. Benjamin
Braude and Bernard Lewis, *Christians and Jews in the Ottoman Empire* vol. 1
(London: Holmes & Meier, 1982), 2; **81 Even Cardinal Reginald Pole**: Cited in
Durant, *Reformation*, 716; **81 So esteemed were the sultans**: Aryeh Shmuelevitz,
The Jews of the Ottoman Empire in the Late Fifteenth and the Sixteenth Centuries
(Leiden, Netherlands: E.J. Brill, 1984), 33; **82 "We have no words"**: Cecil Roth,
House of Nasi, 90; **82 Footnote: While the rules**: Stanford J. Shaw, *The Jews of the
Ottoman Empire and the Turkish Republic*, (New York: New York University Press,
1991), 78–79; ed. Esther Juhasz, *Sephardi Jews in the Ottoman Empire*, (Jerusalem: The
Israel Museum, 1990), 121–26; **82 It was true that**: Goodwin, *Lords of the Horizon*,
95; **83 It was for this reason**: Mark Alan Epstein, *The Ottoman Jewish Communities
and their Role in the Fifteenth and Sixteenth Centuries* (Munich: Klaus Schwarz Verlag,
1980), 22. The letter, in fact, was probably composed by the Istanbul Jewish

philosopher Mordechai ben Eliezer Comtino. See Shaw, *Jews of the Ottoman Empire*, 289 n.10; Gerber, *Jews of Spain*, 304 n.1; **83 "They say Ferdinand"**: Cited Gerber, *Jews of Spain*, 151; **83 Thus the upper and middle classes**: Shaw, *Jews of the Ottoman Empire*, 57, 75; Joseph Hacker, "The Sephardim in the Ottoman Empire in the Sixteenth Century," in Beinart, *Moreshet Sephard* vol. 2, 118–23; **84 In the Jewish neighbourhoods**: Goodwin, *Lords of the Horizon*, 272; Cecil Roth, *House of Nasi*, 104; **84 When a Spanish senator**: Goodwin, *Lords of the Horizon*, 272; **84 In Salonika, the "Jerusalem of the Balkans"**: Gerber, "My Heart Is in the East," 185; **84 Pierre Bellon de Mans**: Cited in Sachar, *Farewell España*, 77; **85 Likewise, Nicolas de Nicolay**: Cited in Cecil Roth, *House of Nasi*, 96–97; **85 Many were multilingual**: Shaw, *Jews of Ottoman Empire*, 94–96; Shmuelevitz, *Jews of the Ottoman Empire in the Late Fifteenth and the Sixteenth Centuries*, 128; **85 They held the most lucrative**: Shaw, *Jews of Ottoman Empire*, 95–96; Epstein, *Ottoman Jewish Communities*, 65, 107, 142–43; Jacob Barnai, "The Jews of the Ottoman Empire in the Seventeenth and Eighteenth Centuries," in Beinart, *Moreshet Sephard* vol. 2, 107; **85 Located near the mouths**: See, Benjamin Braude, "The Rise and Fall of Salonica Woollens, 1500–1650: Technology Transfer and Western Competition," in Ginio, *Jews, Christians, and Muslims*, 219–20; **86 In 1637, the authorities**: Joseph Nehama, "The Jews of Salonica in the Ottoman Period," in ed. R.D. Barnett and W.M. Schwab, *The Sephardi Heritage* vol. 1 (Grendon, Northants.: Gibraltar Books, 1989), 213; **86 For many years**: Shaw, *Jews of the Ottoman Empire*, 93; **87 "Next to moneylending"**: Joseph Shatzmiller, *Jews, Medicine, and Medieval Society* (Berkeley, Calif.: University of California Press, 1994), 1; **87 Many of them could read**: Ibid., 10–13, 38, 141; **88 In his day, Yakub**: Epstein, *Ottoman Jewish Communities*, 79–80; **88 As a Muslim**: Ibid., 80–81; **89 Once the Spanish monarchs**: Henri Gross, "La Famille juive des Hamon." *Revue des études juives* 56 (1908), 4; **89 Like so many Sephardi Jews**: Uriel Heyd, "Moses Hamon, Chief Jewish Physician to Sultan Suleyman the Magnificent." *Oriens* 16 (1963), 155; **89 At his funeral**: Gross, "La Famille juive des Hamon," 7; **90 He was "spare and swarthy"**: Cited in Cecil Roth, *House of Nasi*, 99; Durant, *Reformation*, 716–17; **90 In 1536, he most likely**: Roger Merriman, *Suleiman the Magnificent* (Cambridge, Mass.: Harvard University Press, 1944), 184–87; **90 Mustafa's son**: Ibid., 189; **91 As Will Durant concluded**: Durant, *Reformation*, 718–19; **91 Nicolay might well have used**: See, Cecil Roth, *House of Nasi*, 97; **92 This last work was dedicated**: Heyd, "Moses Hamon," 169; **92 In the currency of the day**: Ibid., 156–58; **92 The fighting was fierce**: Merriman, *Suleiman*, 235. The Turks were orthodox Sunnis, while the Persians (as in modern-day Iran) were devoted Shiites; **93 While he may not have**: Heyd, "Moses Hamon," 158–59; **93 Testament to Hamon's affluence**: Ibid., 166–67; Cecil Roth, *House of Nasi*, 94–96; **94 Footnote: The rabbis' religious and moral**: Israel M. Goldman, *The Life and Times of Rabbi David Ibn Zimra* (New York: The Jewish Theological Seminary of America, 1970), 128–30; **94 According to Salomon Atia**: Gross, "La Famille juive des Hamon," 13; **94 Salonika's**

Sephardim seemed: Shaw, *Jews of the Ottoman Empire*, 52; Hacker, "The Sephardim in the Ottoman Empire," 115; Mair José Benardete, *Hispanic Culture and Character of the Sephardic Jews* (New York: Sepher-Hermon Press, 1982), 65–66; **94 "In Salonika, every [Jewish] man"**: Cited in Leah Bornstein-Makovetsky, "Structure, Organization and Spiritual Life of the Sephardi Communities in the Ottoman Empire from the Sixteenth to Eighteenth Centuries," in Barnett and Schwab, *Sephardi Heritage*, 316; **95 As Rabbi Samuel de Medina**: Cited in Hacker, "The Sephardim in the Ottoman Empire," 114; **95 It was at this point**: Gross, "La Famille juive des Hamon," 15–16; **95 Upset about a rabbinical ruling**: Bornstein-Makovetsky, "Structure, Organization, and Spiritual Life of the Sephardi Communities in the Ottoman Empire," 338; Gross, "La Famille juive des Hamon," 17–18; **95 Baruch, despite his wealth**: Epstein, *Ottoman Jewish Communities*, 87; Gross, "La Famille juive des Hamon," 9; **96 In the Ottoman Empire, many Christian Greeks**: See, Shaw, *Jews of the Ottoman Empire*, 197–204; **96 As late as 1910, H.H. Jessup**: Jessup, *Fifty Three Years in Syria*, vol. 2 (New York: Fleming H. Revell Company, 1910), 424–25; Shaw, *Jews of the Ottoman Empire*, 197; **96 In the ensuing violence**: Shaw, Ibid., 84; Heyd, "Moses Hamon," 161 n.5.; Gross, "La Famille juive des Hamon," 9; **96 He presented his case**: Shaw, *Jews of the Ottoman Empire*, 84–85; Heyd, "Moses Hamon," 16; Gross, "La Famille juive des Hamon," 9; **98 "Four roomy coaches"**: Cecil Roth, *House of Nasi*, 83; **98 Once she was settled in a large home**: See Sachar, *Farewell España*, 80–81; **98 In his day, Nasi became**: Epstein, *Ottoman Jewish Communities*, 89–92; **98 It appears that Hamon's troubles**: Heyd, "Moses Hamon," 164–65; **99 Another version of this story**: Ibid., 163–63; **99 A German traveller**: Cited in Cecil Roth, *House of Nasi*, 94–96; **99 Wealth, power, and influence**: Heyd, "Moses Hamon," 170; "Hamon Family," *Encyclopedia Judaica* vol. 7, 1248. For a contrary view on whether the tax exemption actually applied to the Hamon family, see Bernard Lewis, "The Privilege Granted by Mehmed II to His Physician," *Bulletin of the School of Oriental and African Studies*, University of London, 14 (1952), 560–61; **100 And Nasi, in turn**: Cited in Cecil Roth, *The House of Nasi* 41; **100 He lavished his money**: Sachar, *Farewell España*, 85–86; **100 Supported by the Hamons**: Shaw, *Jews of the Ottoman Empire*, 105–7; Cecil Roth, *House of Nasi*, 93; **101 When Joseph Hamon married**: Cited in Gross, "La Famille juive des Hamon," 21; **101 This slow but steady change**: Barnai, "The Jews of the Ottoman Empire in the Seventeenth and Eighteenth Centuries," 135; **101 "The Sultans who succeeded each other"**: Nehama, "The Jews of Salonica in the Ottoman Period," 216; **102 As well-connected, resourceful**: Gross, "La Famille juive des Hamon," 22–23; **102 He became well-known**: "Hamon," *Encyclopedia Judaica*, 1249; **102 Besides Isaac Hamon**: See Sachar, *Farewell España*, 88; **104 Luria taught that divine sparks**: Gerber, *Jews of Spain*, 173. See also R.J. Zwi Werblowsky, "Shabbetai Zevi," in Beinart, *Moreshet Sephard* vol. 2, 208; Gershom Scholem, *Sabbatai Sevi: The Mystical Messiah* (Princeton, N.J.: Princeton University Press, 1973), 7–8; **104 His father, an Ashkenazi**: Scholem, *Sabbatai*

Sevi, 104–8; **105 By the time he was eighteen**: Ibid., 103–23; Shaw, *Jews of
Ottoman Empire*, 132–33; **105 It was said that his appearance**: Cited in Scholem,
Sabbatai Sevi, 188–90; **105 He suffered frequent fits and seizures**: See ibid.,
125–38; Sachar, *Farewell España*, 136–37; **106 Rabbi Solomon Laniado of
Aleppo**: Cited in Scholem, *Sabbatai Sevi*, 136; **107 The stunned rabbis**: Cited in
ibid., 159–61; Shaw, *Jews of the Ottoman Empire*, 133; **107 There are, however**:
See Scholem, *Sabbatai Sevi*, 193–95; **108 He became Zevi's**: Sachar, *Farewell
España*, 138; **108 Nathan provided the necessary**: Ibid., 139; **108 Back in
Izmir**: Ibid., 140; Scholem, *Sabbatai Sevi*, 393; **108 So utterly devoted to Zevi**:
Ibid., 396–97, 405; Shaw, *Jews of the Ottoman Empire*, 134; **109 Their fervour was
"beyond description"**: Sachar, *Farewell España*, 142–44; **109 A quick execution**:
Werblowsky, "Shabbatai Zevi," 213; **110 "He sat at a table"**: Cited in Scholem,
Sabbatai Sevi, 618; **110 The sultan allowed his council**: Werblowsky, "Shabbetai
Zevi," 213; **111 Hundreds of documents**: Ibid., 214; **111 For years after**: Shaw,
Jews of the Ottoman Empire, 136; **111 They and those who later joined**: Ibid.,
136–37; **111 For a long time**: Werblowsky, "Shabbatai Zevi," 216.

CHAPTER FOUR: THE PORTUGUESE *NAÇÃO*

113 "And we, the Portuguese": Cited in Henry Mechoulan, "Menasseh
ben Israel in Beinart," *Moreshet Sephard* vol. 2, 326; **114 At the top of
Jodenbreestraat**: See Sachar, *Farewell España*, 281; **115 "Today a tranquil
and secure"**: Cited in Miriam Bodian, *Hebrews of the Portuguese Nation*
(Bloomington, Ind.: Indiana University Press, 1997), 63; **115 A year after the
Esnoga**: Jonathan I. Israel, *European Jewry in the Age of Mercantilism 1550–1750*
(Oxford: Clarendon Press, 1989), 220; **116 Footnote: Centuries later**: For a
history of the *Esnoga* see Judith C.E. Belinfante (et al.), *The Esnoga: A Monument to
Portuguese-Jewish Culture* (Amsterdam: D'Arts, 1991), 65–67; **117 They raised
amongst themselves**: Ibid., 45; Israel, *Age of Mercantilism*, 220; **117 Footnote:
As magnificent as the Esnoga**: Wilhemina C. Pieterse, "The Sephardi Jews of
Amsterdam," in Barnett and Schwab, *Sephardi Heritage* vol. 2, 82; **118 So notable
were these individuals**: Gerber, Jews of Spain, 188; Yosef Kaplan, "The
Formation of the Western Sephardic Diaspora," in *The Sephardic Journey 1492–1992*
(New York: Yeshiva University Museum, 1992), 136; Bodian, *Hebrews of the
Portuguese Nation*, 13; **118 They could be small-minded**: Gerber, *Jews of
Spain*, 188; **119 It was this sense**: Ibid., 178; **119 In many ways, it was their
experience**: Israel, *Age of Mercantilism*, 35; Bodian, *Hebrews of the Portuguese Nation*,
27–28; Jonathan Israel, "The Sephardim in the Netherlands," in Kedourie, *Spain
and the Jews*, 208; **119 At various times in his life**: Victor Perera, *The Cross
and the Pear Tree: A Sephardic Journey* (New York: Alfred A. Knopf, 1995), 103;
Jonathan I. Israel, *Empires and Entrepôts: The Dutch, the Spanish Monarchy, and
the Jews, 1585–1713* (London: The Hambledon Press, 1990), 398; **120 Their
"underground system"**: Menasseh ben Israel, *The Hope of Israel*, edited and
with an introduction by Henry Mechoulan (Oxford: The Littman Library, 1987), 9;

120 Soon, the new Christians: Israel, *Age of Mercantilism*, 59–60; Bodian, *Hebrews of the Portuguese Nation*, 38; **120 More importantly, they were linked**: Edgar R. Samuel, "The Trade of the 'New Christians' of Portugal in the Seventeenth Century," in Barnett and Schwab, *Sephardi Heritage* vol. 2, 101; **121 Prominent conversos were arrested**: Israel, *Empires and Entrepôts*, 400–402; **121 He and his wife, Sara**: Ibid., 398–400; Henry Mechoulan, "Abraham Pereyra, Juge de Marranes et censeur de ses coreligionnaires à Amsterdam au temps de Spinoza." *Revue de études juives* 138 (3–4) July–December 1979, 391; **121 Pereyra himself was accused**: Israel, *Empires and Entrepôts*, 399–400; **121 By 1646, it was already**: Herbert I. Bloom, *The Economic Activities of the Jews of Amsterdam in the Seventeenth and Eighteenth Centuries* (1937. Reprint, Port Washington, New York: Kennikat Press, 1969), 9; **122 In a letter of May 1631**: Cited in Menasseh ben Israel, *The Hope of Israel*, 4; **122 Amsterdam's officials**: John J. Murray, *Amsterdam in the Age of Rembrandt* (Norman, Okla.: University of Oklahoma Press, 1967), 25; **122 It is more than likely**: Sachar, *Farewell España*, 278; Bodian, *Hebrews of the Portuguese Nation*, 68–69; **123 In response, the ambassador**: Cited in Marcus Arkin, *Aspects of Jewish Economic History* (Philadelphia: Jewish Publication Society of America, 1975), 89–90; **123 The few trades in which the Jews**: Ed. Yosef Kaplan, Henry Mechoulan, and Richard H. Popkin, *Menasseh Ben Israel and His World* (New York: E.J. Brill, 1989), 146; **123 While Grotius maintained**: Israel, *Age of Mercantilism*, 64; **124 A 1639 ruling**: Bodian, *Hebrews of the Portuguese Nation*, 62; **125 Children were not allowed**: Ibid., 62; **125 Still small in number**: Yosef Kaplan, "The Sephardim in North-Western Europe and the New World," in Beinart, *Moreshet Sephard* vol. 2, 246; **125 By 1657, the Portuguese Jews**: Salo Baron and Arcadius Kahn, *An Economic History of the Jews* (New York: Schocken Books, 1975), 277; **125 Some years earlier, a French diplomat**: Cited in L. Vignols, "Le Commerce hollandais et les congregations juives a la fin du XVIIe siècle," *Revue Historique* 44 (1890), 329; Arkin, *Aspects of Jewish Economic History*, 98–99; **126 Initially, religious services**: Perera, *The Cross and the Pear Tree*, 99; **126 First in 1607 was Beit Yaakov**: See Bodian, *Hebrews of the Portuguese Nation*, 44–46; **126 For years, they were largely excluded**: Ibid., 4; **126 Yet behind their backs**: Gerber, *Jews of Spain*, 179; **127 Isaac de Pinto, a contemporary**: Bodian, *Hebrews of the Portuguese Nation*, 42, 101; **127 Many questioned rabbinical**: Yosef Kaplan, "The Intellectual Ferment in the Spanish-Portuguese Community of Seventeenth Century Amsterdam" in Beinart, *Moreshet Sephard* vol. 2, 289; **128 For that matter, the Spanish**: Israel, *Empires and Entrepôts*, 410–15; **128 They studied the scriptures**: Bodian, *Hebrew of the Portuguese Nation*, 96–99; Kaplan, "Intellectual Ferment," 279; **128 Footnote: During the Second World War**: See Belinfante (et al.), *The Esnoga*, 70–71; **128 He welcomed the opportunity**: Israel, *Empires and Entrepôts*, 406; **129 In 1655, the brothers**: Ibid., 427; Bloom, *Economic Activities of the Jews*, 38–39; **129 It quickly became caught up**: Perera, *The Cross and the Pear Tree*, 104; **129 Many years later, Jacob Pereira**: Gérard Nahon, "Amsterdam and Jerusalem in the 18th Century: The State of the

Sources and Some Questions," in ed. Joseph Michman, *Dutch Jewish History* (Jerusalem: The Institute for Research on Dutch Jewry, Hebrew University, 1989), 95–96; **130 In some instances,** *relapsos*: Sachar, *Farewell España*, 290; **130 As he entered old age**: Mechoulan, "Abraham Pereyra," 392; **131 He vehemently criticized**: Ibid., 396; **131 Pereira, like other** *conversos*: Ibid., 399; **131 "La Certeza breathes"**: Cited in Perera, *The Cross and the Pear Tree*, 106–7; **132 There were Amsterdam Jews**: Sachar, *Farewell España*, 290; **132 Yet as he delved**: Kaplan, "Intellectual Ferment," 294–95; **132 "I observed that the customs"**: Uriel Acosta, *A Specimen of Human Life* (New York: Bergman Publishers, 1967), 13–14; **133 "This correction being over"**: Ibid., 26–27; **133 A short time later**: Perera, *The Cross and the Pear Tree*, 112; **133 No matter what Jewish leaders**: See Sachar, *Farewell España*, 295; **134 "He was charmed"**: Cited in ed. Jacob R. Marcus, *The Jew in the Medieval World: A Source Book 315–1791* (New York: Atheneum, 1969), 336; **134 They debated whether**: Kaplan, "Intellectual Ferment," 306–7; **134 He was "cursed by day"**: Eban, *Heritage: Civilization and the Jews*, 205; **134 Among those who signed**: Perera, *The Cross and the Pear Tree*, 111; **135 In it, he reiterated**: Sachar, *Farewell España*, 297; **135 "Though we cannot"**: Menasseh ben Israel, *Hope of Israel*, 148; **136 The rabbi, already swept**: Scholem, *Sabbatai Sevi*, 358; **136 Their plan was to travel**: Ibid., 529; **136 As Pereira later related**: See Perera, *The Cross and the Pear Tree*, 109; **136 Pereira had become even**: Ibid., 111; **136 Clearly influenced by Catholic**: Mechoulan, "Abraham Pereyra," 395; **136 As Henry Mechoulan has noted**: Cited in Perera, *The Cross and the Pear Tree*, 111; **137 By 1799, more than half**: Israel, "Sephardim in the Netherlands," 209; Bodian, *Hebrews of the Portuguese Nation*, 157; **137 "Our nation becomes poorer"**: Cited in ibid., 158; **138 Slowly a small community of Sephardim**: Israel, *Age of Mercantilism*, 159–60; Sachar, *Farewell España*, 318; **138 In order to fulfill the contract**: Israel, *Age of Mercantilism*, 127–28; **138 Taking full advantage**: Israel, *Empire and Entrepôts*, 444–45; **138 While it was true that bribery**: Israel, *Age of Mercantilism*, 131; **139 "The sums involved in Isaac Pereira's"**: Ibid., 129; **139 "In general," writes Miriam Bodian**: Bodian, *Hebrews of the Portuguese Nation*, 160; **139 The demanding task of the years**: Ibid., 160–61.

CHAPTER FIVE: COURT JEWS

141 "The Jews and their commerce": Cited in David Sorkin, "Into the Modern World," in De Lange, *Illustrated History*, 203; **142 Or, put more caustically**: Will and Ariel Durant, *The Age of Louis XIV* (New York: Simon & Schuster, 1963), 464; **142 Then and later, like Jews**: Eban, *Heritage: Civilization and the Jews*, 222; **142 They faced heavy and humiliating**: Mordechai Breuer and Michael Graetz, *German-Jewish History in Modern Times: Tradition and Enlightenment 1600–1780* vol. 1 (New York: Columbia University Press, 1996), 139; **142 At the gates of Mainz**: Cited in Howard Sachar, *The Course of Modern Jewish History* (Cleveland: The World Publishing Company, 1958), 28; **142 British**

historian Beth-Zion Abrahams: Glückel of Hameln, *The Life of Glückel of Hameln 1646–1724*, translated and edited by Beth-Zion Abrahams (London: East and West Library, 1962), x; **143 Footnote: Jews also suffered**: Breuer and Graetz, *German-Jewish History*, 140; **143 "For a hundred years"**: *The Life of Glückel of Hameln*, 80; **144 In a real sense, they remained**: Paul Johnson, *A History of the Jews* (London: Weidenfeld & Nicolson, 1987), 255; **144 Samuel Oppenheimer and Samson Wertheimer**: Breuer and Graetz, *German-Jewish History*, 107–9; **145 Like the princes they served**: Selma Stern, *The Court Jew* (Philadelphia: Jewish Publication Society of America, 1950), 227, 232–33; **145 After Ulrike of Sweden**: Ibid., 234–35; **146 In her pioneering study**: Ibid., 12; **146 Nevertheless, the vast majority**: Breuer and Graetz, *German-Jewish History*, 248–49; **147 In his last will and testament**: Cited in ibid., 135; **147 In 1752, in his *Political Testament***: Ibid., 147; **148 He hoped that the Jews**: Max Grunwald, *History of Jews in Vienna* (Philadelphia: Jewish Publication Society of America, 1936), 88; **149 Frederick William I of Brandenberg–Prussia**: Breuer and Graetz, *German-Jewish History*, 102; **149 Known for his honesty and integrity**: Stern, *Court Jew*, 18, 86; **149 Moreover, he was a pioneer**: Grunwald, *Jews in Vienna*, 123–24; **150 It was by all accounts**: See Israel, *Age of Mercantilism*, 124; Johnson, *History of Jews*, 256–57; **151 As his creditors pushed**: Stern, *Court Jew*, 20; **151 He sent eight ships**: Ed. Vivian B. Mann and Richard I. Cohen, *From Court Jews to the Rothschilds* (New York: Prestel, 1996), 32–33; **151–52 "His ships were often wrecked"**: Stern, *Court Jew*, 23; **152 He raised hundreds of thousands**: Israel, *Age of Mercantilism*, 125; **152 As a reward, he received**: Ibid., 126; **153 Included in this group**: *The Life of Glückel of Hameln*, 146–47; **153 He later referred**: Stern, *Court Jew*, 26; **153 Owed millions**: Ibid., 87; **154 Before Oppenheimer's private**: Grunwald, *Jews in Vienna*, 119–20; **154 That refusal by the imperial**: Johnson, *History of Jews*, 258; **154 After much procrastination**: Israel, *Age of Mercantilism*, 126; **155 At the time of her death**: Stern, *Court Jew*, 248–49; **155 The entire Oppenheimer estate**: "Oppenheimer, Samuel," *Encyclopedia Judaica* vol. 12, 1431; **155 It was a sad legacy**: Stern, *Court Jew*, 90; **155 As a reward, Leopold**: Ed. Felicitas Heiman-Jelinek and Hannes Sulzenbacher, *Jewish Museum Vienna* (Vienna: Jewish Museum Vienna, 1996), 41–42; **156 Wertheimer never moved**: Ibid., 44–45; **156 Wertheimer was not only a financier**: "Wertheimer, Samson," *Encyclopedia Judaica* vol. 16, 458; **156 He kept his beard**: Israel, *Age of Mercantilism*, 132–33; **157 He succeeded brilliantly**: Ibid., 132–33; **157 By then, he had earned**: Ibid., 133; **157 Above all, it was Wertheimer**: Ibid., 133; **157 Known among Jews**: Ibid., 133; **158 He urged his youngest son**: Stern, *Court Jew*, 221; **158 According to Glückel**: *The Life of Glückel of Hameln*, 176; **158 It was decided that prior**: See ibid., 137–39, 147; **159 In 1700 a professor of Oriental languages**: Israel, *Age of Mercantilism*, 234; **159 In response, he wrote the two-volume**: Breuer and Graetz, *German-Jewish History*, 157; **159 Eisenmenger's work was hardly**: Ibid., 157; **159 Eisenmenger started legal proceedings**: Ibid., 157; **159 Members of his family**: Israel, *Age of*

Mercantilism, 235; **160 A competent businessman**: Stern, *Court Jew*, 95–99,
203–5; **160 In fact, the majority of their descendants**: "Wertheimer,"
Encyclopedia Judaica, 460; **161 Indeed, all of the Jewish characters**: See "Films,
Nazi Antisemitic," *Encyclopedia of the Holocaust* vol. 2 (New York: Macmillan, 1990),
484; **161 So impressed was Nazi police**: Ibid., 484. On the impact of the film,
see also, Jay W. Baird, *The Mythical World of Nazi War Propaganda 1939–1945*
(Minneapolis: Minnesota University Press, 1974); **161 No court Jew has
attracted**: Stern, *Court Jew*, 72–73; **162 He became an ugly**: See Otto Ulbrich,
"Criminality and Punishment of the Jews in the Early Modern Period," in ed.
R. Po-Chia Hsia and Hartmut Lehmann, *In and Out of the Ghetto* (Cambridge:
Cambridge University Press, 1995), 49–50; **162 Born in Heidelberg**: Hellmut G.
Haasis, *Joseph Süss Oppenheimer* (Hamburg: Rowohlt Verlag, 1998), 16–18; **162 By
the age of eighteen**: Stern, *Court Jew*, 45; **162 His reputation as**: Ibid., 116–17;
163 "He was always hurried": Ibid., 46; **163 His library contained**: Breuer and
Graetz, *German-Jewish History*, 117; **163 "Pertaining to his belief"**: Cited in
Haasis, *Oppenheimer*, 392; **163 At the auction after**: Ibid., 268; **163 He was
especially attracted**: Ibid., 219; **163 Among his favourites**: Ibid., 232–59; Mann
and Cohen, *Court Jews to the Rothschilds*, 108; **164 But he was a Jew**: Mann and
Cohen, *Court Jews*, 108; **164 Ahead of his time**: Stern, *Court Jew*, 115–16;
164 A Machiavellian: Ibid., 130–31; **164 He removed court advisors**: Ibid.,
118–25, 130–31; **164 Even worse, he dispensed**: Ibid., 125–33; **165 That
evening, Süss Oppenheimer**: Ibid. 257–63; Breuer and Graetz, *German-Jewish
History*, 116; **165 "I am a Jew"**: cited in Stern, *Court Jews*, 261–62; **166 Before
he was placed**: Ibid., 265–66; **166 The Jud Süss was**: Israel, *Age of Mercantilism*,
246; **166 It was not strictly because**: Mann and Cohen, *Court Jews to the
Rothschilds*, 43; **167 In his play, Lessing**: Eban, *Heritage: Civilization and the Jews*,
224; **167 "Adopt the mores and constitution"**: Cited in ibid., 225; **168 For
their entertainment they gambled**: Israel, *Age of Mercantilism*, 255–56.

CHAPTER SIX: THE AGE OF EMANCIPATION
169 "From now on": Allgemeine Zeitung des Judentums (AZJ), March 27,
1848, 210 as cited in Peter Pulzer, *Jews and the German State: The Political History
of a Minority, 1848-1933* (Oxford: Blackwell Publishers, 1992), 81; **169 A French
artillery shell**: Virginia Cowles, *The Rothschilds: A Family Fortune* (London: Futura
Publications, 1975), 21; Amos Elon, *Founder: A Portrait of the First Rothschild and his
Time* (London: Penguin Books, 1996), 99; **170 "The caricature"**: Elon, Ibid., 33,
104; **170 Outside their proscriptive**: Ibid., 27-8; Niall Ferguson, *The World's
Banker: The History of the House of Rothschild* (London: Weidenfeld & Nicolson,
1998), 39; **170 Located in the northeast**: Elon, *Founder*, 39; 20. **170 Most
peddled**: Elon, Ibid., 27; **171 "The lack of space"**: J.W. Goethe, *Poetry and Truth*,
1 (London, 1908), 129; Cowles, *Rothschilds*, 8; **171 The *Judengasse*, as Börne**: Cited
in Ruth Gay, *The Jews of Germany* (New Haven: Yale University Press, 1992), 71;
172 Within a generation: Michael, Brenner, Sefi Jersch-Wenzel and Michael A.

Meyer, *German-Jewish History in Modern Times: Emancipation and Acculturation 1780-1871* vol. 2 (New York: Columbia University Press, 1997), 55-7 (hereafter Brenner, *GJH*); David Sorkin, *The Transformation of German Jewry, 1780-1840* (New York: Oxford University Press, 1987), 108-9; W.E. Mosse, *Jews in the German Economy* (Oxford: Clarendon Press, 1987), 39. **172 In 1807**: Brenner, Ibid., 193-94; **173 This much can be said**: See, Ibid., 352. **174 Contrarily, they openly**: Ferguson, *World's Banker*, 81. **174 He was not a great supporter**: Elon, *Founder*, 63; 124; **174 "If everything depends"**: Salomon Rothschild to Nathan Rothschild, January 14, 1818 cited in Ferguson, *World's Banker*, 83; **174 Footnote: Two of the more significant**: Johnson, *History of the Jews*, 311-12; **175 At one time**: Cowles, *Rothschilds*, 8; Elon, *Founder*, 43; Georg Heuberger, ed., *The Rothschilds: Essays on the History of a European Family* (Frankfurt: Jan Thorbecke Verlag, 1994), 52; **175 Within a decade**: See, Heuberger, Ibid., 21-35; **175 Footnote: William, who was married**: Cowles, *Rothschilds*, 12; **176 After 1824**: Ferguson, *World's Banker*, 196; **176 "At the beginning"**: Ibid., 48; **177 Given its prime geographic**: Heuberger, *The Rothschilds*, 37; Elon, *Founder*, 21; 30; **177 For the Rothschilds**: Sachar, *Modern Jewish History*, 122-24; **177 This was the reason**: Ferguson, *World's Banker*, 6; **178 The total cost**: Elon, *Founder*, 159; **178 One famous story**: John Reeves, *The Rothschilds: The Financial Rulers of Nations* (London: Sampson, Low, Marston, Searle, and Rivington, 1887), 167-75; Cowles, *Rothschilds*, 46-9; **178 Despite its persistence**: Ferguson, *World's Banker*, 90-104; **Their wealth continued**: Ibid., 323-4; **179 As the eldest brother**: Amschel Rothschild to James Rothschild, October 1816 cited in Ibid., 216; **179 "The Rothschilds are the"**: Cited in Rudolf Glanz, "The Rothschild Legend in America," *Jewish Social Studies* (1957), 20; **179 Or put more**: Reeves, *Financial Rulers*, 101-2; **180 Typical was the attitude**: Cited in Cowles, *Rothschilds*, 51; **180 Footnote: Nathan Rothschild**: See, Ferguson, *World's Banker*, 209-10; **181 "Nothing could possibly"**: cited in Ibid., 338-39; **181 Even the *Times***: *Times* of London, May 18, 1839; Ibid., 33-39; **181 In his book published**: Cited in Paul R. Mendes-Flohr and Jehuda Reinharz, *The Jew in the Modern World: A Documentary History* (New York: Oxford University Press, 1980), 27-34; **182 But theory was one thing**: Werner E. Mosse, Arnold Pauker, and Reinhard Rürup, eds., *Revolution and Evolution: 1848 in German-Jewish History* (Tübingen, Germany: J.C.B. Mohr, 1981), 389; **182 "My heart pounded"**: E. Lindner, ed, *Memoiren des Freiwilligen Jägers Löser Cohen* (Berlin: Edition Hentrich, 1993), 18; Brenner, *GJH*, 257; **183 And thus, In an instant**: H.I. Bach, *The German Jew: A Synthesis of Judaism and Western Civilization, 1730-1930* (London: Oxford University Press, 1984), 79-80; **183 As a signal**: Ferguson, *World's Banker*, 186-87; **183 The strange "Hep-Hep"**: Brenner, *GJH*, 37-8; David Vital, *A People Apart: The Jews in Europe 1789-1939* (Oxford: Oxford University Press, 1999), 212-13; **184 The ideologues were the first**: Sander L. Gilman and Jack Zipes, *Yale Companion to Jewish Writing and Thought in German Culture 1096-1996* (New Haven and London: Yale University Press, 1997), 124-25; Jehuda Reinharz and Walter Schatzberg, *The Jewish Response to German Culture: From the Enlightenment to* *the Second World War* (Hanover and London: University Press of New England, 1985), 86-9; **185 "Living means being"**: Cited in Sorkin, *Transformation of German Jewry*, 87; **185 For a brief period**: Gilman and Zipes, *Yale Companion*, 116-23. See also, Hannah Arendt, *Rahel Varnhagen: The Life of a Jewess* (Baltimore: John Hopkins University Press, 1997); **185 Since *Bildung* was**: Gilman and Zipes, Ibid., 124-25; **185 Wilhelm Riemer, a friend**: Cited in Reinharz and Schatzberg, *Jewish Response*, 87; **185 Footnote: German Jews**: Ibid.,, 89-90; **186 At the same time**: See, Steven A. Aschheim, *Brothers and Strangers: The East European Jew in German and German Jewish Consciousness 1800-1923* (Madison: The University of Wisconsin Press, 1982), 3-5; **186 He later wrote**: Cited in Ibid., 14; **186 It was a small group**: Brenner, *GJH*, 131-36; Salman Rubaschoff, "Erslinge der Entjudng" (Drei Reden von Eduard Gans im Kulturverein), *Der jüdische Wille* 1 (1918): 195-96; **187 He went on to study**: See, Brenner, Ibid., 232-34; Sorkin, *Transformation of German Jewry*, 109; **187 As he reminded**: Gabriel Riesser, Über die Stellung der Bekenner des Mosaischen Glaubens in Deutschland" (1831) in M. Isler, ec. *G. Riesser's Gesammelte Schrifiten* (Frankfurt am Main and Leipzig, 1867) 2:89; Brenner, Ibid., 233; Sorkin, Ibid.,144-45; Moshe Rinott, "Gabriel Riesser-Fighter for Jewish Emancipation" *Leo Baeck Institute Yearbook* (LBIY) 7 (1962) 11-38; **187 "The mighty tones"**: Gabriel Riesser, "Verheidigung der bürgerlichen Gleichstellung der Juden gegen Einwürfe des Herrn Dr. H.E. G. Paulus" (1831) in Isler, *Gesammelte Schriften* 2: 183-84 cited in Brenner, Ibid., 234; **188 It was later said**: Brenner, Ibid., 235; **188 In the final phase**: Ibid., 235; **189 "When Samuel Holdheim"**: Sachar, *Modern Jewish History*, 148; **190 They spoke German**: Sorkin, *Transformation of German Jewry*, 137; **190 At the meeting**: See, Michael A. Meyer, *Response to Modernity: A History of the Reform Movement in Judaism* (New York: Oxford University Press, 1988), 54; Mendes-Flohr and Reinharz, *Jew in the Modern World*, 145; **190 By 1821, the Hamburg**: Meyer, Ibid., 49-54; **191 Loud chanting**: Mosse, *Revolution and Evolution*, 260-62; **191 Hamburg reformers**: Meyer, *Response to Modernity*, 56; **191 The introduction of music**: Mosse, *Revolution and Evolution*, 270; **192 Raphael was not**: Noah H. Rosenbloom, *Tradition in an Age of Reform: The Religious Philosophy of Samson Raphael Hirsch* (Philadelphia: The Jewish Publication Society of America, 1976), 48-9; **192 The book is devised**: Sorkin, *Transformation of German Jewry*, 159; **193 His model**: "Samson Raphael Hirsch," *Encyclopedia Judaica* vol. 8, 510; **193 His motto was**: Reinharz and Schatzberg, *The Jewish Response to German Culture*, 144; **193 Their program**: Mendes-Flohr and Reinharz, *Jew in the Modern World*, 178-79; **194 Most notably through his lectures**: Rosenbloom, *Tradition in an Age of Reform*, 99-105; **194 In 1836 he became**: "Zacharias Frankel," *Encyclopedia Judaica* vol. 8, 80; Brenner, *GJH*, 141; **194 Frankel agreed with Hirsch**: Brenner, Ibid., 141; **195 "By limiting Judaism"**: Mendes-Flohr and Reinharz, *Jew in the Modern World*, 174; **195 Geiger, clean-shaven**: Meyer, *Response to Modernity*, 95; **195 He regarded circumcision**: Abraham Geiger to Leopold Zunz March 18, 1845 cited in Ibid., 91; 95-7; **196 In 1836, he was**: See, "Samuel Holdheim," *Encyclopedia Judaica* vol. 8, 818; Meyer, Ibid., 80-1;

196 "The Talmud speaks": Mendes-Flohr and Reinharz, *Jew in the Modern World*, 143; 196 It was his "task": Ibid., 165-66; 197 Ironically, many of the Rothschilds: Ferguson, *World's Banker*, 475-507; 197 For the conservatives: Mosse, *Revolution and Evolution*, 42. See also, Eleonore Sterling, *Judenhass. Die Anfänge des politischne Antismitismus in Deutschland (1815-1850)* Frankfurt am Main: Europäische Verlagsanstalt, 1969) 140-41; 198 Still, Jews like: Brenner, *GJH*, 284-84; 198 Whatever their particular: Steven M. Lowenstein, Paul Mendes-Flohr, Peter Pulzer and Monika Richarz, *German-Jewish History in Modern Times: Integration in Dispute 1871-1918* Vol. 3 (New York: Columbia University Press, 1997), 284-85. (Hereafter Lowenstein, *Integration in Dispute*.); 198 "All you do is": "Das Judenthum und die Emanzipation, in AZJ, XIV, January 14, 1850, 29 cited in Mosse, *Revolution and Evolution*, 51.

CHAPTER SEVEN: THE PALE OF SETTLEMENT

199 "Awake, my people": Cited in Paul R. Mendes-Flohr and Jehuda Reinharz, *The Jew in the Modern World: A Documentary History* (New York: Oxford University Press, 1980), 312–13. Gordon's key phrase, "Be a man in the streets and a Jew at home," also has been translated as, "Be a man abroad and a Jew in your tent"; 200 In fact, this *shtetl*, like dozens: Shmarya Levin, *Childhood in Exile* (New York: Harcourt, Brace, & Company, 1929), 9; Sachar, *Modern Jewish History*, 191; Roden, *Book of Jewish Food*, 52–53; 200 For example, a tailor living in Brisk: Diane K. Roskies and David G. Roskies, *The Shtetl Book* (New York: Ktav Publishing House, 1975), 105; 200 Footnote: A bride and groom: Pauline Wengeroff, *Rememberings: The World of a Russian-Jewish Woman in the Nineteenth Century* (Bethesda, Md.: University Press of Maryland, 2000), 96–104; 200 Similarly, Hyman Wolf: YIVO Archives, RG 102, Jewish autobiographies, no. 298 Hyman Wolf; 200–1 An official inquiry: Cited in Stephen M. Berk, *Year of Crisis, Year of Hope: Russian Jewry and the Pogroms of 1881–1882* (Westport, Conn.: Greenwood Press, 1985), 25; 201 Generally, Kasrielevsky was a quiet: Roskies and Roskies, *Shtetl Book*, 25; 201 Friday evening, *Erev Shabbas*: See Mark Zborowski and Elizabeth Herzog, *Life Is with People: The Jewish Little-Town of Eastern Europe* (New York: International Universities Press, 1952), 38–48; Roden, *Book of Jewish Food*, 55–56; 202 It shaped their daily activities: Sachar, *Modern Jewish History*, 192–93; 202 "A poorly clad couple": Cited in Louis Greenberg, *The Jews in Russia: The Struggle for Emancipation* vol. 1 (New Haven, Conn.: Yale University Press, 1965), 57; 202 The *melamed* became: Levin, *Childhood in Exile*, 47; Sachar, *Modern Jewish History*, 195; 203 "The slaughterer sought a pretext": ed. Norman Marsden, *A Jewish Life Under the Tsars: The Autobiography of Chaim Aronson, 1825–1888* (Totowa, N.J.: Allanheld, Osmun, & Company, 1983), 12–13; 203 It was a religious movement: Sorkin, "Into the Modern World," 226; 203 Even today, its practitioners: Sachar, *Modern Jewish History*, 77; 204 Most Hasids lived in poverty: Salo Baron, *The Russian Jew Under Tsars and Soviets* (New York: Macmillan Publishing Company, 1964), 121; 204 True, not every

Jew lived: Sachar, *Modern Jewish History*, 197; **204 Footnote: The extent of those superstitions**: Marsden, *A Jewish Life*, 13–14; **205 "True we lived in two distinct"**: Levin, *Childhood in Exile*, 37; **205 "From the enemies of Christ"**: John Doyle Klier, *Russia Gathers Her Jews: The Origins of the "Jewish Question" in Russia, 1772–1825* (Dekalb, Ill.: Northern Illinois University Press, 1986), 28–29; **205 Their function in the economy**: I. Michael Aronson, *Troubled Waters: The Origins of the 1881 Anti-Jewish Pogroms in Russia* (Pittsburgh: University of Pittsburgh Press, 1990), 38; Baron, *Russian Jew Under Tsars*, 76; **205 Russian government commissions**: Hans Rogger, *Jewish Policies and Right-Wing Politics in Imperial Russia* (Berkeley: University of California Press, 1986), 148; **205 Controlling the relationship**: Klier, *Russia Gathers Her Jews*, 184; **206 The Pale of Settlement was**: Orlando Figes, *A People's Tragedy: The Russian Revolution 1891–1924* (London: Jonathan Cape, 1996), 80; **206 Footnote: The word was derived**: See Marsden, *A Jewish Life*, 289 n.22; **207 "The chief benefit to be derived"**: Cited in Baron, *Russian Jew Under Tsars*, 29; **207 "Rich Mr. Rockover has"**: Cited in ibid., 31–32; **207 Jewish community leaders**: Sachar, *Modern Jewish History*, 86–87; **207 "A few moments later"**: Cited in Michael Stanislawski, *Tsar Nicholas I and the Jews: The Transformation of Jewish Society in Russia, 1825–1855* (Philadelphia: Jewish Publication Society of America, 1983), 30; **207 On a journey through the province**: Alexander Herzen, *My Past and Thoughts*, translated by Constance Garnett, vol. 1 (London: Chatto & Windus, 1924), 270; Baron, *Russian Jew Under Tsars*, 31; **208 They were regularly fed pork**: Stanislawski, *Tsar Nicholas I*, 24–25; **208 "The policeman mocked him"**: Wengeroff, *Rememberings*, 94–96; **209 While the *Haskalah* had made**: Stanislawski, *Tsar Nicholas I*, 49–50; **209 In it he made the case**: Greenberg, *Jews in Russia*, 26–28; **209–10 Osip Rabinovich, the founder**: Cited in Eban, *Heritage: Civilization and the Jews*, 241; **210 He published articles**: Jacob S. Raisin, *The Haskalah Movement in Russia* (Philadelphia: Jewish Publication Society of America, 1913), 243–44; **210 He found Lilienthal**: Stanislawski, *Tsar Nicholas I*, 59; **210 "His Majesty, the Emperor"**: Lilienthal to Rabbi Isaac Loewi, February 8, 1841, cited in Baron, *Russian Jew Under Tsars*, 35; **211 "Doctor, are you fully"**: Cited in Sachar, *Modern Jewish History*, 93; **211 In Minsk, the community**: Stanislawski, *Tsar Nicholas I*, 74–75; **211 He received a better reception**: Wengeroff, *Rememberings*, 73–80; **211 When Rabbi Israel Salanter**: Raisin, *Haskalah Movement*, 241; **211 By 1855, there were approximately**: Stanislawski, *Tsar Nicholas I*, 98; **212 Years later, after he had relocated**: Sachar, *Modern Jewish History*, 94–95; **212 Their sons and daughters advocated**: Stanislawski, *Tsar Nicholas I*, 139; **212 It hardly mattered to them**: Michael Stanislawski, *For Whom Do I Toil? Judah Leib Gordon and the Crisis of Russian Jewry* (New York: Oxford University Press, 1988), 5; **212 Footnote: In actuality, the emancipation**: Berk, *Year of Crisis*, 25–26; **212 "Our fatherland is Russia"**: Cited in Greenberg, *Jews in Russia*, 81; **213 They "were thoroughly convinced"**: Cited in Stanislawski, *Tsar Nicholas I*, 108; **213 A brilliant writer and essayist**: "Gordon, Judah Leib," *Encyclopedia*

Judaica vol. 7, 798; **213 For more than forty years**: Stanislawski, *Judah Leib Gordon*, 4; **213 At a young age, he was given**: Ibid., 11–12; **213 In 1839, Mikhl Gordon**: Ibid., 15–18; **214 Though not his best work**: Ibid., 28–30; **214 "Must Jewish life forever"**: Sachar, *Modern Jewish History*, 206; **215 What Gordon meant was**: Stanislawski, *Judah Leib Gordon*, 50–51, 101–2; **216 The group's mandate**: Raisin, *Haskalah Movement*, 237–38; **216 As Leon Rosenthal so aptly**: Cited in Berk, *Year of Crisis*, 31; **216 "For whom, then, do I toil"**: Cited in Stanislawski, *Judah Leib Gordon*, 104; **217 He embarked on various new activities**: Ibid., 114–15; **217 He returned home**: For the story of Gordon's imprisonment, see ibid., 132–41; **219 True, more than thirty thousand**: Berk, Year of Crisis, 34, 156; **219 In their propaganda**: Zvi Gitelman, *A Century of Ambivalence: The Jews of Russia and the Soviet Union 1881 to the Present* (New York: Schocken Books, 1988), 2–3; **220 There was another explosion**: Ibid., 2–5; **220 "Suddenly the doors were flung wide"**: Levin, *Childhood in Exile*, 276–77; **220 With a group of her friends**: Gitelman, *A Century of Ambivalence*, 2–5; **220 "He knew his mind"**: W. Bruce Lincoln, *In War's Dark Shadow: The Russians Before the Great War* (New York: Dial Press, 1983), 27–34; **221 The first attack occurred**: See Aronson, *Troubled Waters*; Simon Dubnow, *History of Jews in Russia and Poland* vol. 2 (Philadelphia: Jewish Publication Society of America, 1918), 249–50; **221 In a few cases, eyewitnesses**: Aronson, *Troubled Waters*, 49–58; **221-2 "At twelve o'clock noon"**: *Razsvet* May 8, 1881, cited in Berk, *Year of Crisis*, 35–36; **222 The Jews of the Pale**: Berk, *Year of Crisis*, 36–38; **222 At a funeral held**: Cited in ibid., 38–39; **222 Ever since the great Jewish historian**: See Dubnow, *History of Jews in Russia*, 247–69; Berk, *Year in Crisis*, 40; Greenberg, *Jews in Russia*, 19–25; Baron, *Russian Jew Under Tsars*, 43–45; Aronson, *Troubled Waters*, 11–15; **223 "There is, in fact, not a single"**: Berk, *Year of Crisis*, 41; **223 It seems clear that there was no**: Aronson, *Troubled Waters*, 108–24; **223 Upon reading reports**: Mark Vishniak, "Anti-Semitism in Tsarist Russia," in Koppel S. Pinson, *Essays on Anti-Semitism* (New York: Conference on Jewish Relations, 1946), 133; **223 In 1879, in a discussion with**: Cited in Robert F. Byrnes, *Pobedonostov: His Life and Thought* (Bloomington, Ind.: Indiana University Press, 1968), 204–7; **224 All revolutionaries, too, were Jews**: Berk, *Year of Crisis*, 54; **224 But an even stronger reason**: Ibid., 51; **224 "The laws of the empire"**: Aronson, *Troubled Waters*, 121; **224 Footnote: The idea of a Jewish conspiracy**: Berk, *Year of Crisis*, 46; **224 That, and the Jews' "tribal seclusion"**: Ibid., 58–59; **224-5 As Count Nikolai**: Ignatiev to Czar Alexander III, August 21, 1881, cited in Rogger, *Jewish Policies*, 135; **225 By restricting Jews to the cities**: Aronson, *Troubled Waters*, 119; **226 He recorded in his diary**: Chaim Chissin, *A Palestine Diary: Memoirs of a Bilu Pioneer 1882–1887* (New York: Herzl Press, 1976), 31–32; **226 "Who could have predicted"**: Cited in Stanislawski, *Judah Leib Gordon*, 160; **226 A few weeks later, in an editorial**: *Ha-Melitz*, May 19, 1881, cited in ibid., 162; **226 "In the end"**: *Ha-Melitz*, July 28, 1881, cited in ibid., 169; **227 Privately, he was more**: Gordon to Ze'ev Kaplan, May, 1882, cited in ibid.,

188; **227 In a new poem he composed**: See, Berk, *Year of Crisis*, 125; **227 "It is preferable to direct"**: *Ha-Melitz*, March 22, 1882, cited in Stanislawski, *Judah Leib Gordon*, 184; **227 In his annual address**: Baron, *Russian Jew Under Tsars*, 49; **228–9 "The nation as a whole"**: Moshe Leib Lilienblum, "Let Us Not Confuse the Issues" (1882), in Hertzberg, *Zionist Idea*, 170–73; **229 He is remembered**: Leon Pinsker, "Auto-Emancipation: An Appeal to His People by a Russian Jew" (1882), in ibid., 184–85.

CHAPTER EIGHT: *L'AFFAIRE*

231 "Until now I have worshiped": Alfred Dreyfus, *Five Years of My Life: The Diary of Captain Alfred Dreyfus* (1901. Reprint, New York: Peebles Press, 1977), 95; **231 "To be Jews"**: Cited in Paula E. Hyman, *The Jews of Modern France* (Berkeley: University of California Press, 1998), 92; **232 "France will not repudiate her past"**: Cited in ed. Norman Kleeblatt, *The Dreyfus Affair: Art, Truth, and Justice* (Berkeley: University of California Press, 1987), 31; **232 "The Jews," he stated**: Cited in Sorkin, "Into the Modern World," 211; **232 Initially, these merchants**: Gerber, *Jews of Spain*, 190–91; **233 According to the accepted Sephardi**: Cited in Hyman, *Jews of Modern France*, 5; **234 "The alleys are frightfully"**: *Der Forverts (The Forward)*, New York, August 31, 1912, cited in ibid., 119; **234 Each Sunday morning the men**: Paula E. Hyman, *The Emancipation of the Jews of Alsace* (New Haven, Conn.: Yale University Press, 1991), 5, 12–13; **234 "Living on black bread"**: Michael Burns, *Dreyfus: A Family Affair 1789–1945* (New York: HarperCollins, 1991), 17; **235 The emperor was more concerned**: Ibid., 18–19; **235 "We are not a people"**: Cited in Sorkin, "Into the Modern World," 219; **235–6 Nothing was valued more**: Hyman, *Emancipation of the Jews of Alsace*, 86–87; Michael Marrus, *The Politics of Assimilation* (Oxford: Clarendon Press, 1971), 34; **236 Abraham learned to be a kosher butcher**: Burns, *Dreyfus*, 5–6; **236 In the late 1790s, Jacob**: Ibid., 20; **236 In 1835, when Raphael was still a teenager**: Kleeblatt, *Dreyfus Affair*, 142; **237 "My childhood passed gently"**: Dreyfus, *Five Years of My Life*, 37; **238 He was described as**: Kleeblatt, *Dreyfus Affair*, 146; **238 Alfred's first sorrow**: See, Burns, *Dreyfus*, 60–63; **238–9 "The republican and military points"**: Cited in Jean-Denis Bredin, *The Affair: The Case of Alfred Dreyfus* (New York: George Braziller, 1986), 18; **239 His son Pierre later**: Cited in ibid., 13; **239 Through a fellow Jewish**: Burns, *Dreyfus*, 79–85; **240 At a tense meeting**: Ibid., 91; Martin P. Johnson, *The Dreyfus Affair* (New York: St. Martin's Press, 1999), 7; **240 "I have seen many Israelite officers"**: Bredin, *The Affair*, 22–23; **240 If Dreyfus suspected**: Ibid., 22; **241 "A brilliant and easy career"**: Dreyfus, *Five Years of My Life*, 38; **241 It is important to keep in mind**: Hyman, *Jews of Modern France*, 99; **241 A decade later, the Rothschilds**: Kleeblatt, *Dreyfus Affair*, 52; **242 From the left side**: Ibid., 50–52; **242 Within a year of being released**: Stephen Wilson, *Ideology and Experience: Antisemitism in France at the Time of the Dreyfus Affair* (East Brunswick, N.J.: Associated University Press, 1982), 171, 733; **242 Footnote: Historian Eugen Weber writes**: Eugen Weber, "Reflections on the Jews of France," in ed. Frances Malino and Bernard Wasserstein, *The Jews in Modern France* (Hanover, N.H., and London: University Press of New England, 1985), 11–12; **242 Hardly original, Drumont**: See Edouard-Adolphe Drumont, *La France juive* vol. 1 (Paris: C. Marpon and E. Flammarion, 1885), 520–26, cited in Mendes-Flohr and Reinharz, *Jew in the Modern World*, 276–78; **243 In response to Drumont's book**: Wilson, *Ideology and Experience*, 734; **243 Another, more serious, duel**: Bredin, *The Affair*, 21; **243 Some years later, the Parisian**: Julien Benda, *La Jeunesse d'un clerc* (Paris: Gallimard, 1936), 43; Marrus, *Politics of Assimilation*, 44; **243 Jews in France**: See Marrus, *Politics of Assimilation*, 99, 122, 141; **244 Why, the Grand Rabbi**: Ibid., 54–57; **244 Emmanuel Berl, a French**: Cited in Wilson, *Ideology and Experience*, 695–96; **245 Among those papers**: Bredin, *The Affair*, 59; **246 On November 1, Drumont's**: Cited in Hyman, *Jews of Modern France*, 101; **246 Other newspapers like *Le Figaro***: Johnson, *The Dreyfus Affair*, 25; **246 This was the first of many**: Ibid., 23–24; **247 The tribunal was contacted**: Ibid., 29; **247 "During these long minutes"**: Cited in Bredin, *The Affair*, 4; **247 In the view of many Parisians**: Burns, *Dreyfus*, 149; **247 Out on the street**: Bredin, *The Affair*, 4; **248 "If such things could happen"**: ed. Marvin Lowenthal, *The Diaries of Theodor Herzl* (New York: Dial Press, 1956), xix; **248 Finally the prisoner**: See Bredin, *The Affair*, 4–5; **248 Footnote: Despite the persistence of the myth**: See Jacques Kornberg, "Theodor Herzl: A Reevaluation," *Journal of Modern History* 52:2 (June 1980), 227–28; **249 Reporting the event for**: Cited in Burns, *Dreyfus*, 152; **249 *La Patrie*'s Maurice Barrès**: Cited in Kleeblatt, *Dreyfus Affair*, 59; **249 Back at his prison cell**: Dreyfus, *Five Years of My Life*, 67; **249 As Edgar Demange**: Cited in ibid., 27; **249 Similarly, historian Martin Johnson**: Ibid., 8–9; **250 They were blinded**: Marrus, *Politics of Assimilation*, 284; **250 In November 1897, once more**: Cited in Eric Cahm, *The Dreyfus Affair in French Society and Politics* (New York: Longman, 1996), 43; **250 Its bourgeois members were afraid**: See Hyman, *Jews of Modern France*, 109; **250 "They did not talk of the Affair"**: See Leon Blum, *Souvenirs sur l'affaire* (Paris: Gallimard, 1935), cited in Marrus, *Politics of Assimilation*, 212; **251 They condemned the injustice**: Kleeblatt, *Dreyfus Affair*, 33; **251 So assimilated was Dreyfus**: Louis L. Snyder, *The Dreyfus Case: A Documentary History* (New Brunswick, N.J.: Rutgers University Press, 1973), 7; **251 "My only crime is"**: Dreyfus, *Five Years of My Life*, 62; **251 Later, when it was all**: Cited in Pierre Vidal-Naquet, *The Jews: History, Memory, and the Present* (New York: Columbia University Press, 1996), 86; **251 "Still alone, never speaking"**: Burns, *Dreyfus*, 199–200; **252 Months would often pass**: Ibid., 197–99; **252 "Yesterday evening I was put"**: Dreyfus, *Five Years of My Life*, 191; **252 "Nearly two years of this have worn"**: Ibid., 191–92; **253 In late 1896, Bernard Lazare**: Hyman, *Jews in Modern France*, 103; **253 In the second edition**: Johnson, *The Dreyfus Affair*, 74; **254 "What does it matter"**: Cited in ibid., 55; **254 Footnote: *Le Matin* published a photo**: Cited in ibid., 55; **255 In an approximately five-thousand-word public letter**: Émile Zola, *The Dreyfus Affair: "J'accuse" and*

Other Writings (New Haven, Conn.: Yale University Press, 1996), 43–53; **255 In January and February**: Wilson, *Ideology and Experience*, 106–20; **256 "Truly, this lamentable"**: Cited in Marrus, *Politics of Assimilation*, 203–5, 220; **256 "My joy was boundless"**: Dreyfus, *Five Years of My Life*, 235; **256 "It is impossible"**: Ibid., 239; **256 He was only thirty-nine**: Kleeblatt, *Dreyfus Affair*, 147; **257 Several of the more radical**: See Johnson, *The Dreyfus Affair*, 144; **258 The event was**: See Dreyfus's account in Snyder, *The Dreyfus Case*, 375–77; **258 In 1994, a century after Dreyfus**: See *Globe and Mail* (Toronto), February 9, 1994; September 8, 1995; Frederick Painton, "A Century Late, The Truth Arrives," *Time* magazine, September 25, 1995, 50; **258 "The general said things"**: Ibid; **259 Standing by the coffin**: Cited in Burns, *Dreyfus*, 417; **259 There is no denying that the entire**: See Hyman, *Jews in Modern France*, 107; **259 Jews were barred from clubs**: See Wilson, *Ideology and Experience*, 609, 700–701; **259 The Affair had shown him**: Nelly Wilson, *Bernard-Lazare: Antisemitism and the Problem of Jewish Identity in Late Nineteenth-Century France* (Cambridge: Cambridge University Press, 1978), 222–24; **259 "Assimilation is not and cannot"**: Cited in Marrus, *Politics of Assimilation*, 238; **259 "The distinctive nationality of the Jews"**: Theodor Herzl, *The Jewish State* (1896. Reprint, New York: American Zionist Emergency Council, 1946), 79–80; **259 The two men met in Paris**: Wilson, *Bernard-Lazare*, 226; **260 Anti-Semitism, in the words**: Hyman, *Jews of Modern France*, 109–10; **260 "The Affair . . . had particularly fortunate"**: Cited in Burns, *Dreyfus*, 314; **260 "I was only an artillery"**: Cited in Burns, *Dreyfus*, 422.

CHAPTER NINE: THE GOLDEN LAND

261 "The streets swarmed with Yiddish-speaking": Abraham Cahan, *The Rise of David Levinsky* (1917. Reprint, New York: Penguin Books, 1993), 93; **261 Even in the northern regions**: See Berk, *Year of Crisis*, 145–46; **261-2 "We are only step-children"**: Cited in Stanley Feldstein, *The Land That I Show You: Three Centuries of Jewish Life in America* (Garden City, N.Y.: Anchor Press, 1978), 118–19; **262 "America was in everybody's mouth"**: Mary Antin, *From Plotzk to Boston* (Boston: W.B. Clarke, 1899), 12; **262 "The concrete details of that"**: Cited in Irving Howe and Kenneth Libo, *How We Lived: A Documentary History of Immigrant Jews in America 1880–1930* (New York: Richard Marek Publishers, 1979), 18; **262 He came from a distinguished**: See Abraham Cahan, *The Education of Abraham Cahan* (Philadelphia: Jewish Publication Society of America, 1969), 53. Translation of Vols. 1 and 2 of Cahan's Yiddish memoirs, *Bleter fun Mayn Lebn* (1926–29); **263 "Even though the pogrom brought"**: Ibid., 158; **263 Only the Germans, Italians, and Irish**: See Abraham J. Karp, *Haven and Home: A History of Jews in America* (New York: Schocken Books, 1985), 376; **264 Forty years later**: Sachar, *Modern Jewish History*, 315; **264 They were largely poor and superstitious**: Arthur Hertzberg, *The Jews in America* (New York: Simon & Schuster, 1989), 153–54, 161; **264 "Just before train-time"**: Marcus E. Ravage, *An American in the Making: The Life Story of an Immigrant* (1917. Reprint, New York: Dover

Publications, 1971), 54–55; **264–5 A small city, Brody**: See Berk, *Year of Crisis*,
148–49; **265 So desperate was this family**: Cahan, *Education of Abraham Cahan*,
200–201; **265 To continue on their journey**: See Irving Howe, *World of Our
Fathers* (New York: Harcourt Brace Jovanovich, 1976), 39; Berk, *Year of Crisis*,
149–50; **265 "The emigrants must be checked"**: Cited in Howe, *World of Our
Fathers*, 30; **266 How would their charities**: Ibid., 31; **266 Indeed, according
to one theory**: Feldstein, *The Land That I Show You*, 187; **266 Lazarus Straus
came**: See Howard M. Sachar, *A History of Jews in America* (New York: Alfred A.
Knopf, 1992), 86; **266 Footnote: It is a myth**: Hertzberg, *Jews in America*, 103;
267 William Seligman in New York: See Sachar, *History of Jews in America*,
87–89, 93; **267 And this religion had to be "progressive"**: See Hertzberg, *Jews
in America*, 146–47; **267 "Racially, I am a Jew"**: Cited in Berk, *Year of Crisis*, 153;
267 In June 1877, the investment banker: See Sachar, *History of Jews in America*,
98; John Higham, *Send These to Me: Jews and Other Immigrants in Urban America*
(New York: Atheneum, 1975), 149; **268 At hotels and beaches**: See Higham, *Send
These to Me*, 138–73; **268 American Jews were sympathetic**: Sachar, *Modern
Jewish History*, 309; Hertzberg, *Jews in America*, 170; **268 "The struggle with
which"**: Morris Loeb, "Eastern and Western Civilization," *American Hebrew*,
March 6, 1903, 592; **269 "The magnificent verdure of Staten Island"**: Cahan,
David Levinsky, 87; **270 "The stench was terrible"**: Cited in Ronald Sanders,
The Downtown Jews: Portraits of an Immigrant Generation (New York: Harper & Row,
1969), 42; **270 The Yiddish pun**: Berk, *Year of Crisis*, 167; **270 At Ellis Island**:
See Howe, *World of Our Fathers*, 43–45; **270 The food was dreadful**: Berk, *Year of
Crisis*, 169–71; Howe, *World of Our Fathers*, 46–48; **271 "The greenhorn is fair
game"**: Cited in Abraham J. Karp, *Golden Door to America* (New York: Penguin,
1977), 122–26; **271 "The Russian Jew first and foremost"**: Cited in Sachar,
History of Jews in America, 134; **271 Similarly, a committee of New York
rabbis**: Ibid., 134–36; **272 As Moses Rischin explained**: Moses Rischin,
The Promised City (Cambridge, Mass.: Harvard University Press, 1962), 76–78;
272 Referred to then more often: See Hasia R. Diner, *Lower East Side Memories*
(Princeton, N.J.: Princeton University Press, 2000), 38–47; **272 They were, Hasia
Diner points**: Ibid., 46; **273 A prominent East Side citizen**: Ibid., 45, 110;
273 Footnote: As the character of the East: See Ibid, 52–126; **273 Abraham
Cahan, who resided**: Abraham Cahan, *Yekl, A Tale of the New York Ghetto* (New
York: D. Appleton and Company), 28–29; Jules Chametzky, *From the Ghetto: The
Fiction of Abraham Cahan* (Amherst, Mass.: University of Massachusetts Press, 1977),
61; **273 Milton Reizenstein**: ed. Charles Bernheimer, *The Russian Jews in the
United States* (1905. Reprint, Jerome S. Ozer Publisher, 1971), 44; **274 For Jacob
Riis**: Cited in Rischin, *Promised City*, 82; **274 As Dr. George Price, himself an
immigrant**: Cited in Sachar, *History of Jews in America*, 142; **274 Footnote:
Maurice Fishberg**: Bernheimer, *Russian Jews*, 284–86; **275 A *New York Tribune*
news item**: Karp, *Golden Door*, 131–33; **275 Nine years later**: Sachar, *History of
Jews in America*, 164; **275 During the late 1890s, a husband**: See Jacob Riis, *How

the Other Half Lives: Studies Among the Tenements of New York (New York: C. Scribner's Sons, 1902), cited in Karp, *Golden Door*, 153–54; **275 It was, as the turn-of-the-century**: Cited in Howe and Libo, *How We Lived*, 65; **275 "Often I would load my push-cart"**: Cahan, *David Levinsky*, 107; **276 "There were gang wars"**: Samuel Chotzinoff, *A Lost Paradise* (New York: Alfred A. Knopf, 1955), cited in Howe and Libo, *How We Lived*, 48–49; **276 Not every Jewish adult**: Sachar, *History of Jews in America*, 144; **276 The capitalization was low**: Karp, *Haven and Home*, 198–201; **277 "Every open window"**: Riis, "How the Other Half Lives," cited in Sachar, *Modern Jewish History*, 320; **277 Similarly, in a *McClure's Magazine* article**: Cited in Howe and Libo, *How We Lived*, 153–54; **277 By 1892, a decade after**: See Howe, *World of Our Fathers*, 159–61; **278 When immigrants in the garment industry**: Hertzberg, *Jews in America*, 172; **278 One of the first protracted**: Howe, *World of Our Fathers*, 300; **279 This dispute drew in influential**: Ibid., 301–2; **279 Inside, among the rows**: Sanders, *Downtown Jews*, 393–95; **280 "Screaming men and women"**: *New York Times*, March 25, 1911; Sachar, *History of Jews in America*, 187; Sanders, *Downtown Jews*, 393–94; Howe, *World of Our Fathers*, 304–5; Howe and Libo, *How We Lived*, 187; **280 Historian Nathan Glazer**: Cited in Chametzky, *From the Ghetto*, 26; **281 Before an audience of four hundred**: Ibid., 8; Cahan, *Education of Abraham Cahan*, 237; **281 It was at a second lecture**: Sanders, *Downtown Jews*, 75; Cahan, *Education of Abraham Cahan*, 306; Sanford E. Marovitz, *Abraham Cahan* (New York: Twayne Publishers, 1996), 17; **281 In time, he qualified as**: Cahan, *Education of Abraham Cahan*, 262, 375; Chametzky, *From the Ghetto*, 10–11; **281 In a speech he gave after a May Day**: Feldstein, *The Land That I Show You*, 223–34; **281 For Cahan, and like-minded Jewish socialists**: Rischin, *Promised City*, 166–67; **282 It was in this work that he mastered**: Chametzky, *From the Ghetto*, 13; Sanders, *Downtown Jews*, 177; **282 The paper was to be called**: Sanders, *Downtown Jews*, 179–80; **282 Steffens had heard of Cahan**: Ibid., 213–17; **283 In the countless articles Cahan prepared**: ed. Moses Rischin, *Grandma Never Lived in America: The New Journalism of Abraham Cahan* (Bloomington, Ind.: Indiana University Press, 1985), xxvi; **283 "The Jewish quarter"**: Hutchins Hapgood, *The Spirit of the Ghetto* (1902. Reprint, Cambridge, Mass.: Harvard University Press, 1967), 5; **283 "With their long beards"**: Ibid., 16–17; **284 Footnote: Howells first submitted *Yekl***: Chametzky, *From the Ghetto*, 67; **285 Cahan's protagonist is Yekl or Jake**: See Sanders, *Downtown Jews*, 200; Chametzky, *From the Ghetto*, 57–59; **285 "He sees things with American eyes"**: Cited in ibid., 68–69; **286 By the early twenties**: Ibid., 20; **286 It is fitting that**: See Seth Lipsky, "Abraham Cahan, the *Forward*, and Me," *Commentary* (June 1997) at http://www.commentarymagazine.com/9706/lipsky.html; **286 "If as a Socialist you want"**: Cited in Chametzky, *From the Ghetto*, 20; **286 It was his task**: Sanders, *Downtown Jews*, 269; **287 "My father revered the *Forward*"**: Alfred Kazin, "Jews," *The New Yorker* vol. 70 (March 7, 1994), 72; **287 Indeed, between the education**: See Sachar, *History of Jews in America*, 177–78; Howe and Libo,

How We Lived, 218; Rischin, *Promised City*, 233; **287 To help his readers**: Marovitz, *Abraham Cahan*, 55; **288 "I want you to advise me"**: Ed. Isaac Metzker, *A Bintel Brief*, (New York: Doubleday, 1971), 37–38; **288 "I had no will to protest"**: Ibid., 45–47; **288 "The children can get crippled"**: Cited in Howe, *World of Our Fathers*, 182; **288 Cahan could be**: Irving Howe, "Becoming American," *Commentary* vol. 49 (March 1970), 88–90; **289 "I have spent some time"**: Cited in Sachar, *History of Jews in America*, 204; **289 Such was his stature**: Joseph Gollomb, "Abraham Cahan," *American Magazine* (October 1912), 672; **289 Following visits to Palestine**: Lipsky, "Abraham Cahan, the *Forward*, and Me," 7; Marovitz, *Abraham Cahan*, xix; Yaacov N. Goldstein, *Jewish Socialists in the United States: The Cahan Debates 1925–1926* (Brighton: Sussex Academic Press, 1998), 13–33; **289 When Cahan died in 1951**: Sachar, *History of Jews in America*, 205; *New York Times*, September 6, 1951, 31; **289 Throughout his long life**: Chametzky, *From the Ghetto*, 22–26; **290 Jews in America, they declared**: Hertzberg, *Jews in America*, 157; **290 "It isn't Russia"**: Cited in Howe and Libo, *How We Lived*, 94; **290 "With every day that passed"**: Ravage, *An American in the Making*, 78–79; **291 So many Jewish husbands**: Howe, *World of Our Fathers*, 179; **291 He had a list of services**: Cited in Sachar, *History of Jews in America*, 169; **291 It was also, notes Cahan's biographer**: Marovitz, *Abraham Cahan*, 162; **291 As soon as he arrives in New York**: Chametzky, *From the Ghetto*, 131; **291 "My sense of triumph"**: Cahan, *David Levinsky*, 526; **291 Footnote: Arnold Rothstein**: See Rich Cohen, *Tough Jews* (New York: Simon & Schuster, 1998), 46–57; **292 "[The Jewish children] rank among"**: Bernheimer, *Russian Jews*, 187; **292 It was not only the youngsters**: See Howe, *World of Our Fathers*, 237–47; **292 Marcus Ravage remembered**: Ravage, *An American in the Making*, 146–50; **292 For the slightly more affluent**: See Howe, *World of Our Fathers*, 467–77; **293 The secret was to find**: Hertzberg, *Jews in America*, 174; **293 "The only place where"**: Cited in Karp, *Haven and Home*, 168–69; **293 "I came in . . . at the breaking of the bread"**: Jacob Riis, *Children of the Poor* (1892. Reprint, New York: Scribner's Son, 1923), 44.

CHAPTER TEN: THE GERMAN-JEWISH 'SYMBIOSIS'

295 " What we mean": Franz Rosenzweig, *On Jewish Learning*, edited by Nahum N. Glatzer (New York: Schocken Books, 1955), 57-8; **295 A bestseller**: See, Dianne R. Spielmann, "German Jewish Writers on the Eve of the Holocaust," in Randolph L. Braham, ed, *Detached From Relections of the Holocaust in Art and Literature* (Boulder, CA: Social Science Monographs, 1990), 61-2; **296 In the novel, Berlin's reputation**: See, Arthur Landsberger, *Berlin ohne Juden* (Bonn: Weidle Verlag, 1998), 100-08; 122; 131; 167-81 (originally published in 1925); **296 Landsberger, himself, never**: Spielmann, "German Jewish Writers," 64-5; **296 Even though it was still** : Cited in Ronald Taylor, *Berlin and its Culture: A Historical Portrait* (New Haven: Yale University Press, 1997), 211; **297 Interestingly, Freud, who detested**: David Aberbach, "Freud's Jewish Problem," *Commentary*,

(June 1980), 37; **297 In a letter to the B'nai Brith**: Ernest Jones, *The Life and Works of Sigmund Freud*, (London: Hogarth Press, 1956) Vol. 2, 162; **297 Yet, as historian Paul Johnson**: Johnson, *History of the Jews*, 412; **298 They lived in a German**: Ibid., 405; **298 As historian Walter Laqueur**: Walter Laqueur, *Weimar: A Cultural History 1918-1933* (New York: G.P. Putnam's Sons, 1974), 72; **298 In a 1926 speech**: Cited in Donald L. Niewyk, *The Jews in Weimar Germany* (Baton Rouge: Louisiana State University Press, 1980), 18; 40; 117-18; 120; **298 "What has become"**: Cited in Johnson, *History of the Jews*, 478; **299 Later, one popular**: Cited in Avraham Barkai and Paul Mendes-Flohr, *German-Jewish History in Modern Times: Renewal and Destruction 1818-1945*, Vol. 4 (New York: Columbia University Press, 1998), 174 (hereafter Barkai, *Renewal and Destruction*); **299 Perhaps it was more**: Leonard Baker, *Days of Sorrow and Pain* (New York: Oxford University Press, 1978), 94; **299 The largest department stores**: See, Ruth Gay, *The Jews of Germany* (New Haven: Yale University Press, 1992), 189; 194; **299 There were Jewish publishers**: Barkai, *Renewal and Destruction*, 176; **299 "Jews," once remarked**: Baker, *Days of Sorrow*, 92; **299 Despite the prominence**: Barkai, *Renewal and Destruction*, 174; **299 Even the so-called**: Ruth Gay, *Jews of Germany*, 169; Mosse, *Revolution and Evolution*, 164-94; **300 "We Jews, among"**: Moritz Goldstein, "Deutsch-jüdischer Parnass," *Der Kunstwart*, 25 (1912), 283-6 cited in Lowenstein, *Integration in Dispute*, 358; **300 The Einsteins considered**: See, Fritz Stern, *Einstein's German World* (Princeton, NJ: Princeton, University Press, 1999), 89-136; **300 "When I first came"**: Cited in Sachar, *Modern Jewish History*, 409. See also, Irving Kristol, "Einstein: The Passion of Pure Reason," *Commentary* (September, 1950), 216-24; **300 Footnote: The Kaiser**: See, Johnson, *History of the Jews*, 400; Pulzer, *Jews and the German State*, 214; **301 In nineteenth-century Germany**: Lowenstein, *Integration in Dispute*, 239-40; Ian Kershaw, *Hitler 1889-1936: Hubris* (New York: Penguin Putnam, 1998), 76-80; **301 As early as 1897**: Cited in Sachar, *Modern Jewish History*, 237; **301 The CV was the**: Michael Brenner, *The Renaissance of Jewish Culture in Weimar Germany* (New Have: Yale University Press, 1996), 19-20; **302 The artist Max Liebermann**: Peter Gay, *The Berlin-Jewish Spirit: A Dogma in Search of Some Doubts* (New York: Leo Baeck Institute, 1972), 13; **302 "That hatred, delusion"**: Cited in Stern, *Einstein's German World*, 140; **302 In 1922, he became**: Gay, *Berlin-Jewish Spirit*, 13-14. **303 The visionary Jewish philosopher**: Gilman and Zipes, *Yale Companion*, 303. **303 Scholem was born**: See, Gershom Scholem, *From Berlin to Jerusalem* (New York: Schocken Books, 1980), 25; **304 On Passover**: Ibid., 10-11; **304 Starting in 1910**: Ibid., 11; **304 Mixed marriages**: See, Lowenstein, *Integration in Dispute*, 14; **305 As head of the household**: Michael Brenner, *Renaissance of Jewish Culture*, 21; **305 Anti-Semitism would never**: Scholem, *Berlin to Jerusalem*, 26; **305 While growing up**: Cited in Lowenstein, *Integration in Dispute*, 252; **305 "Ten years ago"**: Cited in Ruth Gay, *Jews of Germany*, 207; **306 "For that reason"**: Hermann Cohen, *Jüdischer Schriften* (Berlin: C.A. Schwetschke, 1924), vol. 2, 316, edited by B. Strauss cited in Lowenstein, *Integration in Dispute*, 356. See also, Hans Liebeschütz, "Hermann

Cohen and His Historical Background," LBIYB 13 (1968), 3-33; **306 Optimistic to the end**: Cohen, Ibid., 317-18; Lowenstein, Ibid., 357; **306 "I felt thoroughly"**: Cited in Barkai, *Renewal and Destruction*, 160; **306 "Proclaiming 'unswerving cultivation'"**: *Jüdische Rundschau*, September 14, 1926 cited in Niewyk, *Jews in Weimar Germany*, 128-29. See also, Reinharz and Schatzberg, *Jewish Response*, 266-93; **307 Hitler's storm troopers**: Niewyk, Ibid., 139-41; **307 All things considered**: Scholem, *Berlin to Jerusalem*, 28; **307 As his friend and biographer**: Nahum N. Glatzer, *Franz Rosenzweig: His Life and Thought* (New York: Schocken Books, 1953), x-xi; **308 On Franz's first day**: Ibid., xxxvii. **308 His diary and letters**: Ibid., 7-9; **308 "Why does one philosophize"**: Ibid., 9; **308 At the University of Freiburg**: Ibid., 15-18; **309 While his parents**: Ibid., 19; **309 One summer night**: Ibid., 25; **310 He intended to embrace**: Bernard Martin, *Great Twentieth Century Jewish Philosophers*, (New York: Macmillan, 1970), 121; **310 "I will remain a Jew"**: Ibid., 121-22; Franz Rosenzweig to Rudolf Ehrenberg, October 31, 1913 in Glatzer, *Rosenzweig*, 341-44; **310 He found in the service**: Martin, Ibid., 122-23; **310 Rosenzweig wrote a piece**: Ibid., 123; **311 "I no longer"**: Gilman and Zipes, *Yale Companion*, 348; **311 The Jews of Berlin**: Cited in Barkai, *Renewal and Destruction*, 8-9; Baker, *Days of Sorrow*, 70-5; Gilman and Zipes, Ibid., 348; **312 For this work, he**: Lowenstein, *Integration in Dispute*, 363; **312 Artist Max Liebermann**: Niewyk, *Jews in Weimar Germany*, 107; **312 Albert Einstein was not**: Lowenstein, *Integration in Dispute*, 364; **312 "The average German"**: Julius Marx, *Kriegs-Tagebuch eines Juden* (Zurich: Verlag Die Liga,1939), 32 cited in Barkai, *Renewal and Destruction*, 13; **312 When the Jewish soldier**: Cited in Lowenstein, *Integration in Dispute*, 371; **312 "We experienced a great"**: Gilman and Zipes, *Yale Companion*, 349; **313 German government officials**: Pulzer, *Jews and the German State*, 205; **313 Needless to say, Jewish**: Ibid., 205; **313 Once the war had ended**: Gay, *Berlin-Jewish Spirit*, 13; **313 "The dream of commonality"**: Ernst Simon, *Brücken Gesammelte Aufsätze* (Heidelberg: L. Schneider, 1965), 18, 20-22; Barkai, *Renewal and Destruction*, 13-14; **313 Soon it was acknowledged**: Gilman and Zipes, *Yale Companion*, 344; **314 In this, Buber was**: Ibid., 346-47; **314 In September 1914**: See, Glatzer, *Rosenzweig*, 33; 334-48; **315 For him, the Jewish**: Ibid., 33-4; **315 Yet he also understood**: Barkai, *Renewal and Destruction*, 16; **315 Some years later**: Franz Rosenzeig to Rudolf Hallo, January 1923 cited in Ibid., 161; **315 "I refuse to answer"**: Cited in Ibid., 97; **315 He first elaborated**: See, Glatzer, *Rosenzweig*, 39-40; 49-50; Franz Rosenzweig, *On Jewish Learning*, edited by Nahum N. Glatzer (New York: Schocken Books, 1955), 27-54; **316 While he referred**: Scholem, *Berlin to Jerusalem*, 139-40; **316 Influenced by such**: Norbert M. Samuelson, *An Introduction to Modern Jewish Philosophy* (Albany: State University of New York Press, 1989), 214; **316 In his quest**: Martin, *Jewish Philosophers*, 126-7; Glatzer, *Rosenzweig*, xxiii-xxvi; **316 Rosenzweig argued that**: Barkai, *Renewal and Destruction*, 24; **316 As historian Paul Mendes-Flohr**: Ibid., 25; **317 "Among the peoples of the earth"**: Franz Rosenzweig, *The Star of Redemption* cited in Glatzer, *Rosenzweig*, 294; **317**

Rosenzweig, himself later: Glatzer, Ibid., xxvii; **318 "Jews were and are":** Jakob Wassermann, *Mein Weg als Deutscher und Jude* (Berlin: S. Fischer, 1921), 117-18 cited in Barkai, *Renewal and Destruction*, 22; **318 This was despite the fact:** See, Johnson, *History of the Jews*, 471-77; Pulzer, *Jews and the German State*, 272; 344; **318 Once the calm:** See, Niewyk, *Jews in Weimar Germany*, 18-20; **University campuses:** Ibid., 63; Barkai, *Renewal and Destruction*, 49-55; **319 When Walter Rathenau:** Stern, *Einstein's German World*, 195; **320 His main aim:** Michael Brenner, *Renaissance of Jewish Culture*, 71; **320 According to Nahum Glatzer:** Nahum N. Glatzer "The Frankfurt Lehrhaus, " LBIY 1 (1956), 115; **320 "All of us":** Rosenzweig, *On Jewish Learning*, 98; **320 It was the "first":** Ernst Simon, "Franz Rosenzweig und das jüdische Bildungsproblem," in *Brücken: Gesammelte Aufsätze* (Heidelberg: Lambert Schneider, 1965) 399, cited in Michael Brenner, *Renaissance of Jewish Culture*, 79-80; **320 The Lehrhaus attracted:** See, Brenner, Ibid., 86-7; **321 Overall between 1920:** Simon Noveck, ed., *Great Jewish Thinkers of the Twentieth Century*, (Washington D.C: B'nai Brith, 1963), 166; Martin, *Jewish Philosphers*,128; **321 The Lehrhaus movement:** Michael Brenner, *Renaissance of Jewish Culture*, 76; 89; **321 In early 1922:** Samuelson, *Jewish Philosphy*, 213; Glatzer, *Rosenzweig*, 108-09; **321 The poet Karl Wolfskehl:** Cited in Glatzer, Ibid., xxxiii. **322 Most significantly, he:** Barkai, *Renewal and Destruction*, 146; **322 Fittingly Buber spoke:** Glatzer, *Rosenzweig*, 171; **323 At the time, Robert Weltsch:** Niewyk, *Jews in Weimar Germany*, 84-6; **323 Even then, adds:** Ibid., 86; **323 It is notable:** Michael Brenner, *Renaissance of Jewish Culture*, 177-81; **324 The nuclear physicist:** Rudolf Peierls, *Bird of Passage: Recollections of a Physicist* (Princeton NJ: Princeton University Press, 1985), 6; Pulzer, *Jews and the German State*, 345; **324 "The expectation was not":** Pulzer, Ibid., 346.

CHAPTER ELEVEN: THE JERUSALEM OF LITHUANIA
Author's note: A part of this chapter is based on my book, *Fugitives of the Forest: The Heroic Story of Jewish Resistance and Survival During the Second World War* (Toronto: Stoddart, 1998).

325 "City/How mourn a city": Abba Kovner, *A Canopy in the Desert* (Pittsburgh: University of Pittsburgh Press, 1973), xiii; **326 Looking down Rudninku Street:** See Abba Kovner, "A First Attempt to Tell," in ed. Yehuda Bauer and Nathan Rotenstreich, *The Holocaust as Historical Experience* (New York: Holmes & Meier Publishers, 1981), 78–79; **326 You could (and still can) tell:** See Lucy S. Dawidowicz, *From That Place and Time: A Memoir 1938–1947* (New York: W.W. Norton, 1989), 45–46; **327 In Vilna, the Litvaks lived:** Ibid., 121; **327 Few events in the modern history:** See ibid., 37–38; Norman N. Shneidman, *Jerusalem of Lithuania: The Rise and Fall of Jewish Vilnius* (Oakville, Ont.: Mosaic Press, 1998), 15–16; **327 "The sound of Yiddish":** Dawidowicz, *From That Place and Time*, 37; **328 Nine different governments:** See Israel Cohen, *Vilna* (Philadelphia: Jewish Publication Society of America, 1943), 358; **328 Believing that the Jews:** Ibid., 378; **328 There were 5 million Ukrainians:** Ezra

Mendelsohn, *The Jews of East Central Europe between the World Wars* (Bloomington, Ind.: Indiana University Press, 1993), 5; Neal Ascherson, *The Struggles for Poland* (London: Michael Joseph, 1987), 59; **328 Still, given the nationalistic passions**: Dawidowicz, *From That Time and Place*, 104; Celia Heller, *On the Edge of Destruction* (New York: Columbia University Press, 1977), 78; **329 According to a 1931 census**: Mendelsohn, *Jews of East Central Europe*, 23–24; **329 Piłsudski, who supported**: Yisrael Gutman and Shmuel Krakowski, *Unequal Victims: Poles and Jews during World War II* (New York: Holocaust Library, 1986), 4; **330 From their perspective**: Heller, *On the Edge*, 63; **330 "The Jew treats with aversion"**: Cited in Edward D. Wynot, "A Necessary Cruelty: The Emergence of Official Anti-Semitism in Poland, 1936–1939," *The American Historical Review* 76:4 (October 1971), 1036; **330 At first, Dmowski wanted to limit**: Dawidowicz, *From That Time and Place*, 172; **330 During the twenties and thirties**: See Heller, *On the Edge*, 100–101; Gutman and Krakowski, *Unequal Victims*, 13; **330 After Piłsudski died**: Cohen, *Vilna*, 404; **331 During the 1930s, there were**: Sachar, *Modern Jewish History*, 358; **331 In 1923–24, approximately 24 per cent**: Dawidowicz, *From That Time and Place*, 167; **331 There were "Jewless" days**: Heller, *On the Edge*, 120–23; **331 "A Jewish problem exists"**: Pastoral Letter of February 29, 1936, cited in Heller, *On the Edge*, 113; **331 An official government study**: Cited in Wynot, "A Necessary Cruelty," 1049; **332 But a minority**: See Allan Levine, *Fugitives of the Forest*, 30–34; **333 Stories by Holocaust survivors**: See as an example of this debate, Allan Levine, "The Prime Minister, Auschwitz, and the Battle for Memory," *Globe and Mail* (Toronto), January 26, 1999; and Bernard Wisniewski, "What the Polish Christian Stake Is in Auschwitz," *Globe and Mail*, February 11, 1999. The various (mostly critical) letters my article generated are worth noting as well. See *Globe and Mail*'s "Letters to the Editor," for January 27, 28, 30, February 11, 1999. My review of Jan T. Gross's book, *Neighbors: The Destruction of the Jewish Community in Jedwabne, Poland* (Princeton, N.J.: Princeton University Press, 2001) triggered the same negative reaction. See Allan Levine, "When Poles Killed Their Jewish Neighbours," *National Post* (Toronto), June 16, 2001, and "Letters to Books," *National Post*, June 23, 2001; **333 Most Jewish children**: See Heller, *On the Edge*, 225; Jack and Rochelle Sutin, *Jack and Rochelle: A Holocaust Story of Love and Resistance* (St. Paul, Minn.: Graywolf Press, 1995), 5; Martin Gilbert, *The Boys: Triumph over Adversity* (Vancouver: Douglas & McIntyre, 1996), 7; Sylvia Rothchild, *Voices from the Holocaust* (New York: New American Library, 1982), 59; **333 "The man sitting next to it"**: Jack and Rochelle Sutin, *Jack and Rochelle*, 16; **333 Footnote: On July 10, 1941**: See Gross, *Neighbors*; Adam Michnik, "Poles and Jews: How Deep the Guilt?" *New York Times*, March 17, 2001; and "Forgive Massacre, Polish Leader Asks," *Globe and Mail*, July 11, 2001; **334 Unlike their fathers**: Heller, *On the Edge*, 212; Mendelsohn, *Jews of East Central Europe*, 81; **335 Then and later, he was wise**: See the introduction by Irving Greenberg in Abba Kovner, *Scrolls of Testimony* (Philadelphia: Jewish Publication Society, 2001), xii; **335 Kovner inherited his Zionist**: "Kovner,

Abba," *Encyclopedia of the Holocaust*, vol. 2, 822; **336 An estimated 300,000 to 350,000 Jews**: Dov Levin, "The Attitude of the Soviet Union to the Rescue of Jews," in *Rescue Attempts During the Holocaust: Proceedings of the Second Yad Vashem International Historical Conference* (Jerusalem: Yad Vashem, 1977), 228–29; **336 One story has it**: Ed. Norman Davies and Antony Polonsky, *Jews in Eastern Poland and the U.S.S.R. 1939–46* (New York: St. Martin's Press, 1991), 28; **337 Hundreds of thousands died**: Alan Bullock, *Hitler and Stalin* (Toronto: McClelland & Stewart, 1991), 745; **337 German bombs hit Vilna**: Yitzhak Arad, *Ghetto in Flames: The Struggle and Destruction of the Jews in Vilna in the Holocaust* (New York: Holocaust Library, 1982), 30–35; Ed. Lucjan Dobroszycki and Jeffrey S. Gurock, *The Holocaust in the Soviet Union* (New York: M.E. Sharpe, 1993), 96; **337 "What to do?"**: Herman Kruk, "Diary of the Vilna Ghetto," *YIVO Annual of Jewish Social Science* 13 (1965), 9–10; **337 On the night of June 25**: Dov Levin, "On the Relations between the Baltic Peoples and Their Jewish Neighbours Before, During, and After World War II," *Holocaust and Genocide Studies* 5:1 (1990), 55–57; Lucy S. Dawidowicz, *A Holocaust Reader* (New York: Behrman, 1976), 93; **338 "I observe the empty, sad"**: Cited in Laurel Holliday, *Children in the Holocaust and World War II* (New York, Pocket Books, 1995), 140–41; **338 "I stand at the window"**: Yitzhok Rudashevski, *The Diary of the Vilna Ghetto: June 1941–April 1943* (Western Galilee, Israel: Ghetto Fighters' House, 1972), 27–28; **338 Footnote: Both Kruk and Rudashevski**: See Kruk, "Diary of the Vilna Ghetto," 10; Rudashevski, *Diary of the Vilna Ghetto*; and Holliday, *Children in the Holocaust*, 137–83; **339 On July 3 the German military**: Arad, *Ghetto in Flames*, 55–57; **339 And that struggle**: Cited in Lucy S. Dawidowicz, *The War Against the Jews, 1933–1945* (New York: Holt, Rinehart, & Winston, 1975), 166; **340 Gangs of Lithuanian thugs**: Shneidman, *Jerusalem of Lithuania*, 47; **340 When the Nazis first arrived**: "Kovner," *Encyclopedia of the Holocaust*, 823; Rich Cohen, *The Avengers: A Jewish War Story* (New York: Alfred A. Knopf, 2000), 40; **340 "I still thought"**: Testimony of Abba Kovner, Trial of Adolph Eichmann, May 4, 1961, cited in Martin Gilbert, *The Holocaust: A Jewish Tragedy* (London: Fontana Press, 1987), 192; **340 One of the soldiers "took"**: Ibid., 192; **340 Then a dozen or so people**: See Arad, *Ghetto in Flames*, 76; Gilbert, *The Holocaust*, 170; **341 Some of the soldiers**: Daniel Jonah Goldhagen, *Hitler's Willing Executioners: Ordinary Germans and the Holocaust* (New York: Alfred A. Knopf, 1996); **341 Footnote: On one occasion S.S. Chief**: Recollection of S.S. General Karl Wolff, *The World at War*, Thames Television documentary, London, March 27, 1974, cited in Gilbert, *Holocaust*, 191; **341 Once the killing finally stopped**: Yitzhak Arad, *The Partisan* (New York: Holocaust Library, 1979), 48–50; **341 Here the Jews "were ordered"**: Dawidowicz, *Holocaust Reader*, 90; **342 "The people who were seized"**: Cited in Arad, *Ghetto in Flames*, 199; **342 Somehow she managed**: Testimony of Meir Mark Dvorjetsky, Eichmann Trial, May 4, 1961, cited in Gilbert, *Holocaust*, 193–94; **342 "One thing is clear to me"**: Cited in Arad, *Ghetto in Flames*, 227; **343 "The street streamed with Jews"**: Rudashevski, *Diary of the Vilna Ghetto*, 32; **344 They had been deemed**:

Dawidowicz, *War Against the Jews*, 386; **344 So were two close friends**: Cohen, *Avenger*, 13–33; **344 "Besides the four of us"**: Rudashevski, *Diary of the Vilna Ghetto*, 33; **344 Similarly, Liza Ettinger**: United States Holocaust Memorial Museum Archives, RG-02.133, Liza Ettinger, "From the Lida Ghetto to the Bielski Partisans" (1989), 16; **345 People scrambled to obtain**: Dawidowicz, *War Against the Jews*, 386; **345 By the new year**: See "Vilna," *Encyclopedia of the Holocaust* vol. 4, 1573; **345 "We must show [the Germans]"**: Ed. Ada June Friedman, *Roads to Extinction* (Essays by Philip Friedman), (Philadelphia: Jewish Publication Society of America, 1980), 367; **346 Gens was born**: See "Gens, Jacob," *Encyclopedia of the Holocaust*, vol. 2, 555; **346 A power unto himself**: Friedman, *Roads to Extinction*, 366–70; **346 "I think to myself"**: Rudashevski, *Diary of the Vilna Ghetto*, 67–69; **346 He recalls that**: Schneidman, *Jerusalem of Lithuania*, 66; **347 Gens ensured that lectures**: Cohen, *Avenger*, 65; **347 The head of the library**: Solon Beinfeld, "The Cultural Life of the Vilna Ghetto," in ed. Michael Marrus, *The Nazi Holocaust: The Victims of the Holocaust* vol. 6 (London: Meckler, 1989), 107; **347 The idea of operating a theatre**: Ibid., 95–96; **347 "People laughed and cried"**: Ibid., 96; **348 "Many of you think of me"**: Cited in Friedman, *Roads to Extinction*, 370–71; **348 Hardly a day went by**: Arad, *Ghetto in Flames*, 63; **348 At the end of 1942**: Friedman, *Roads to Extinction*, 371–72; **348 On another occasion, Gens**: Ibid., 372; **349 All of this provided them**: See Chaika Grosman, *The Underground Army: Fighters of the Bialystok Ghetto* (New York: Holocaust Library, 1987), 89, 94–95, 189–90; Yisrael Gutman, *The Jews of Warsaw, 1939–1943* (Bloomington, Ind.: Indiana University Press, 1989), 143–44; Levine, *Fugitives of the Forest*, 78–84; **350 "We knew that there would be"**: Grosman, *The Underground Army*, 190; **351 "All roads of the Gestapo"**: Ghetto Fighters's House Archives, Western Galilee, Israel, "Kovner's Declaration," January 1, 1942. See also Arad, *Ghetto in Flames*, 231–32; Kovner, "A First Attempt to Tell," 81–82; **351 The FPO struggled**: See ibid., 82; Shneidman, *Jerusalem o f Lithuania*, 84; Author's interview with Anna Kremer, Toronto, May 8, 1996; **352 Gens knew of the existence**: Arad, *Ghetto in Flames*, 383; author's interview with Moshe Shutan, Tel Aviv, June 17, 1996; **352 Throughout 1942**: Cohen, *Avenger*, 54–59; **352 On July 7, 1943**: On the events surrounding the capture of Yitzhak Wittenberg, see Arad, *Ghetto in Flames*, 390–93; **354 On their journey, Glazman**: Ibid., 396–99; Lester Eckman and Chaim Lazar, *The Jewish Resistance: The History of Jewish Partisans in Lithuania and White Russia during the Nazi Occupation* (New York: Shengold, 1977), 124; Chaim Lazar, "Joseph Glazman: Portrait of a Fighter," *Publications of the Museum of the Combatants and Partisans* 8:9 (September, 1994), 76; **354 Gens announced that no more**: Arad, *Ghetto in Flames*, 399–400; Isaiah Trunk, *Judenrat: The Jewish Councils in Eastern Europe under Nazi Occupation* (New York: Stein & Day, 1977), 456; **354 "Jews! Defend yourselves"**: Arad, *Ghetto in Flames*, 411–12; **355 "We only wanted to die"**: Kovner, *Scrolls of Testimony*, xi; **355 The ghetto's inhabitants**: Gilbert, *Holocaust*, 607; **355 "The FPO was indecisive"**: Shneidman, *Jerusalem of Lithuania*, 106;

355 **"The FPO blame[d] the Jews"**: Arad, *Ghetto in Flames*, 417; 355 **Many decades later, Kovner**: See Cohen, *Avenger*, 135–36; 355 **As the deportations to labour camps**: Arad, *Ghetto in Flames*, 434; Dov Levin, *Fighting Back: Lithuanian Jewry's Armed Resistance to the Nazis, 1941–1945* (New York: Holmes & Meier, 1985), 237–38; 356 **Right to the end, Jacob Gens**: Michael Okunieff, "Witness to the Execution of Jacob Gens," *Publications of the Museum of the Combatants and Partisans* 8:8 (September, 1993), 83–86; 356 **Yet instead of escaping**: See Arad, *Ghetto in Flames*, 426; 356 **It took them nearly seven hours**: *Sefer Ha-Partisanim Ha-Yehudim* (*The Jewish Partisan Book*), (Israel: Sifritah Poalim Ha-Shomer Ha-Tzair, 1958), 50–51; Levin, *Fighting Back*, 237–38; 356 **They formed the nucleus**: Levine, *Fugitives of the Forest*, 206–7; Gilbert, *Holocaust*, 607; 357 **Later, Kovner recalled**: Kovner, "A First Attempt to Tell," 90; 358 **For more than eleven months**: Kovner Testimony at Eichmann Trial, May 4, 1961, cited in Gilbert, *Holocaust*, 703–4; 358 **They drifted into camps**: See ibid, 819; Levine, *Fugitives of the Forest*, 300–304; 358 **"A sword is dangling"**: Cited in Cohen, *Avenger*, 174; 359 **Kovner first reached Palestine**: See ibid., 189–207; 359 **Footnote: In the spring of 1946**: *New York Times*, April 24, 1946; Cohen, *Avenger*, 212; 359 **When Kovner attempted**: Ibid., 214; 360 **Kovner was most proud**: Ibid., 8; 360 **"How can you know"**: Cited in ibid., 240.

CHAPTER TWELVE: ZIONISTS AND SOVIETS

361 **"I am a Jew"**: "Jewish Engineer Who Sought to Go to Israel Gets 3 Years as Soviet Slanderer," *New York Times*, June 5, 1969, 5; Moshe Decter, *A Hero for Our Time: The Trial and Fate of Boris Kochubiyevsky* (New York: Academic Committee on Soviet Jewry, 1970), 13; 362 **"We knew we were Jewish"**: Author's interview with Igor Korenzvit, Toronto, February 7, 2001; 362 **They were trapped**: Moshe Decter, "The Status of the Jews in the Soviet Union," *Foreign Affairs* 41:2 (January 1963), 430; 363 **The promises of equality**: Cited in Nora Levin, *The Jews in the Soviet Union Since 1917* vol. 1 (New York: New York University Press, 1988), 2–3; Baron, *Russian Jew Under Tsars*, 168; 363 **A Jewish "nationality," the Bolshevik**: Cited in Baron, *Russian Jew Under Tsars*, 171; 363 **In Joseph Stalin's opinion**: Cited in Levin, *Jews in the Soviet Union* vol. 1, 16–17; 363 **In 1924, massive arrests**: Ibid., 92, 116–17; 363 **In the four-year period**: Figes, *A People's Tragedy*, 750; 364 **Footnote: This included the Brodsky**: Author's interview with Rabbi Moshe Reuven Azman, Kiev, July 6, 2001; 364 **Many Jews, like the members**: For Tsilia Michlin Goldin's story, see ed. Elaine Pomper Snyderman and Margaret Thomas Witkovsky, *Line Five: The Internal Passport* (Chicago: Chicago Review Press, 1992), 3–10; 365 **"If I hadn't been born Jewish"**: Cited in Snyderman and Witkovsky, *Line Five*, 9–10; 365 **Among all of the Jewish holidays**: Benjamin Pinkus, *The Jews of the Soviet Union* (Cambridge: Cambridge University Press, 1988), 104–5; 365 **In 1922 in Gomel**: Baron, *Russian Jew Under Tsars*, 244–45; 365 **As Judah Dardak, one committed**: Cited in ibid., 227; 366 **They were last**: Levin, *Jews in the Soviet Union* vol. 1, 121–22, 152–53; 366 **Yet as the**

American Jewish journalist: Ibid., 295; 367 "We came back to Kiev": Cited
in Yehoshua A. Gilboa, *The Black Years of Soviet Jewry 1939–1953* (Boston: Little,
Brown, & Company, 1971), 36; 368 Ehrenberg was a man: Joshua Rubenstein,
Tangled Loyalties: The Life and Times of Ilya Ehrenberg (New York: Basic Books, 1996),
171–76; 368 "I know neither Yiddish or Hebrew": Cited in Benjamin Pinkus,
The Soviet Government and the Jews 1948–1967 (Cambridge: Cambridge University
Press, 1984), 43–44; 368 And yet as a Jew: See Rubenstein, *Tangled Loyalties*, 204,
208; 368 "I advise you not": Cited in Gilboa, *Black Years*, 36; 369 Yet while an
English version: Rubenstein, *Tangled Loyalties*, 212–18; 369 Every work of art
or literature: Gilboa, *Black Years*, 149–50; 370 Denounced as "citizens of the
world": Ibid., 160; 370 Footnote: Even the *Great Soviet Encyclopedia*: See ibid.,
209; 370 Ilya Ehrenberg was correct: Cited in ibid., 80; 371 Yet an anony-
mous phone call: Louis Rapoport, *Stalin's War against the Jews* (New York: The
Free Press, 1990), 93; 371 "They killed him like beasts": Nikita Khrushchev,
Khrushchev Remembers (Boston: Little, Brown, & Company, 1970), 262–63; 371 To
maintain the facade: Rapoport, *Stalin's War*, 96; 371 Among those persecuted:
Pinkus, *Soviet Government and the Jews*, 214–16; 371–2 "The unfortunate Fefer":
Ibid., 214–16; 372 Jewish books were seized: Gilboa, *Black Years*, 311; 372
Gennady Reznikov, then only ten: Snyderman and Witkovsky, *Line Five*,
144–49, 157–58; 373 And when news of this: Yaacov Ro'i, *The Struggle for
Soviet Jewish Emigration 1948–1967* (Cambridge: Cambridge University Press, 1991);
373 "For a minute I couldn't grasp": Golda Meir, *My Life* (New York: Putnam,
1975), 246–50; Levin, *Jews in the Soviet Union* vol. 2, 477–79; 374 "The words
shook the synagogue": Cited in Marie Syrkin, *Golda Meir: Israel's Leader* (New
York: Putnam, 1969), 227; 374 "The depth and passion": Levin, *Jews in the Soviet
Union* vol. 1, 483; 374 "A citizen of socialist": Pinkus, *Soviet Government and the
Jews*, 39–42; 374 On August 12, all but one of the defendants: See Martin
Gilbert, *The Jews of Hope* (London: Macmillan, 1984), 55; 375 The young Jewish
writer: Ro'i, *Struggle for Soviet Jewish Emigration*, 46–49; 375 In the so-called
Doctor's Plot: Gilbert, *Jews of Hope*, 55; 375 Those arrested, on Stalin's direct:
Baron, *Russian Jew Under Tsars*, 277; 375 This simmering Jewish national: Ro'i,
Struggle for Soviet Jewish Emigration, 70; 376 In responding to a query: Cited in
Levin, *Jews in the Soviet Union* vol. 2, 577; 376 Jews understood: Natan Sharansky,
Fear No Evil (New York: Random House, 1988), x; 376 Synagogues were closed:
Pinkus, *Jews of the Soviet Union*, 286; 376 As Yuri Andropov, head of the
KGB: Ed. Michael Beizer, "Confiscation of Matzah by the KGB, 1975," *Jews and
Jewish Topics in the Soviet Union and Eastern Europe*, no. 19 (Winter 1992), 43–45;
376 Almost on a daily basis: See Gilbert, *Jews of Hope*, 56; 377 One of the
most popular books: See Pinkus, *Soviet Government and the Jews*, 336–37; 377 A
charge of "profiteering": Decter, "Status of Jews," 430; 377 According to one
estimate: Baron, *Russian Jew Under Tsars*, 285; 377 In March 1962: See *Pravda*,
March 1, 1962, cited in Pinkus, *Soviet Government and the Jews*, 223–25; Levin, *Jews
in the Soviet Union* vol. 2, 616–17; Decter, "Status of Jews," 426–27; 377 "A strong

emotion overtakes you": Cited in Levin, *Jews in the Soviet Union* vol. 2, 628; **378 "No words could convey"**: Stuart E. Rosenberg, "Fear Hangs over Every Jew," *Toronto Star*, April 11, 1961; **378 When Rabbi Levin heard**: Stuart E. Rosenberg, *The Real Jewish World: A Rabbi's Second Thoughts* (Toronto: Clarke Irwin, 1984), 296–97; **378 A father, like Nissen Gorelsky**: Paul Panish, *Exit Visa: The Emigration of Soviet Jews* (New York: Coward, McCann & Geoghegan, 1981), 87–88; **378 Igor Korenzvit recalls**: Author's interview with Korenzvit; **379 They created the first *samizdat***: Leonard Schroeter, *The Last Exodus* (New York: Universe Books, 1974), 64; **379 "For tens of thousands"**: Cited in ibid., 65; **380 Nothing gave the Jewish spectators**: Ro'i, *Struggles for Soviet Jewish Emigration*, 321–27; **380 Out in front of the synagogue**: Sylvia Rothchild, *A Special Legacy: An Oral History of Soviet Jewish Emigrés in the United States* (New York: Simon & Schuster, 1985), 10–20; **380 "The street was unrecognizable"**: Elie Wiesel, "The Rejoicing of the Law," in ed. Ronald I. Rubin, *The Unredeemed: Anti-Semitism in the Soviet Union* (Chicago: Quadrangle Books, 1968), 243–45; **381 He was a shy, unassuming**: See Schroeter, *The Last Exodus*, 39–40; **381 Gradually, Kochubiyevsky was drawn**: Ibid., 42–43; **382 Throughout the Diaspora**: Bernard Wasserstein, "The Age of Upheavals," in De Lange, *Illustrated History*, 366; **382 It sparked, says Natan Sharansky**: Sharansky, *Fear No Evil*, xiv; **382 In the press, Israel**: Schroeter, *The Last Exodus*, 43–44; **382 "I want the record"**: Cited in ibid., 44; Rebecca Rass and Morris Brafman, *From Moscow to Jerusalem* (New York: Shengold Publishers, 1976), 13; **383 He was shunned and isolated**: Ibid., 14; **383 "Why is it that the most active"**: Cited in Schroeter, *The Last Exodus*, 45; **384 As Igor Korenzvit explains**: Author's interview with Korenzvit; **384 Next, the applicant required**: See Panish, *Exit Visa*, 34; **384 Thus was born the "refusenik"**: Levin, *Jews in the Soviet Union* vol. 2, 684; **384 Precisely how many Soviet Jews**: Ro'i, *Struggle for Soviet Jewish Emigration*, 327–28; **385 As the government ceremony**: Decter, *Hero for Our Time*, 22–26; **385 When they returned**: Rass and Brafman, *From Moscow to Jerusalem*, 68; **386 "I am a Jew"**: Cited in ibid., 69; "Jewish Engineer," *New York Times*, June 5, 1969, 5; **386 He was kept in prison**: Ibid.; Schroeter, *The Last Exodus*, 47; **386 "Do you know"**: Decter, *Hero for Our Time*, 17; **387 At another point**: Ibid., 7; Schroeter, *The Last Exodus*, 48; **387 "Defendant, the last word"**: "Jewish Engineer," *New York Times*, June 5, 1969, 5; **387 After four days**: Gilbert, *Jews of Hope*, 71; **387 He later said that the guards**: "Critic of Soviet Stand on Israel Freed," *New York Times*, December 24, 1971; **387 "I asked to be freed"**: Cited in Rass and Brafman, *From Moscow to Jerusalem*, 9–15; **388 Finally on December 19**: Ibid., 70–75; Wendy Eisen, *Count Us In* (Toronto: Burgher Books, 1995), 272; **388–9 When he was finally released**: Schroeter, *The Last Exodus*, 146; **389 "I grew up"**: Cited in Joshua Rubenstein, *Soviet Dissidents: Their Struggle for Human Rights* (Boston: Beacon Press, 1980), 171; **389 There, he also came into contact**: Schroeter, *The Last Exodus*, 141–46; Levin, *Jews in the Soviet Union* vol. 2, 672–73; **389 Eleven of those caught**: Levin, *Jews in the Soviet Union*, 673; **390 "Our**

dream of living in Israel": Cited in Schroeter, *The Last Exodus*, 173; **390 Then,** **in a stunning decision**: Levin, *Jews in the Soviet Union* vol. 2, 678; **390 "The Jews had won"**: Schroeter, *The Last Exodus*, 175; **391** *Vyzov* **applications continued**: Levin, *Jews in the Soviet Union* vol. 2, 715; **391 The KGB kept track**: Leonard Schroeter, "Samizdat and the Struggle of Soviet Jewry," *Jerusalem Post*, March 28, 1972; Levin, *Jews in the Soviet Union*, 667, 776; **391 Later they learned**: Ibid., 732–33; **391 Footnote: According to Sharansky**: See Sharansky, *Fear No Evil*, 91–94; **392 Officers of the KGB**: The complete story is told in Sharansky's memoirs, *Fear No Evil*; **392 The movement soon involved**: See Eisen, *Count Us In*; author's interview with Irving Abella, Toronto, February 9, 2001; **393 On a visit to Ottawa**: Eisen, *Count Us In*, 192; **393 "People literally pleaded"**: Richard Yaffee, "Soviet Jews at the Fair," *Israel Horizons* (December 1979), 25; Levin, *Jews in the Soviet Union* vol. 2, 765.

CONCLUSION: THE DIASPORA IN 2003

395 "For two thousand years": Sharansky, *Fear No Evil*, 224; **397 Israel's present population**: See Robert S. Wistrich, "The Post-War Jewish World," in ed. Wistrich, *Terms of Survival: The Jewish World Since 1945* (London: Routledge, 1995), 15–16; **397 In Kielce:** Levine, *Fugitives of the Forest*, 303-4; Gilbert, *Holocaust*, 819. **397 Others often found**: Dalia Ofer, "Emigration and Aliyah: A Reassessment of Israeli and Jewish policies," in Wistrich, *Terms of Survival*, 67; Ronald Sanders, *Shores of Refuge: A Hundred Years of Jewish Emigration* (New York: Holt and Company, 1988), 586. **398 More than 45,000**: Howard Sachar, *The Course of Modern Jewish History*, (revised edition) New York: Vintage Books, 1990), 689. **398 The 1994 terrorist**: De Lange, *Illustrated History*, 382. **399 Footnote: In August 2000, Rabbi Ovadia Yosef**: See "Rabbi's Holocaust View Creates Uproar in Israel," *International Herald Tribune*, August 7, 2000; "Another Holocaust Lesson: Perhaps It's Time to Pause," *International Herald Tribune*, August 10, 2000; **400 In their collective minds**: Alain Finkielkraut, *The Imaginary Jew* (Lincoln, Nebr.: University of Nebraska Press, 1994), 119–20; **400 And the Israeli soldier**: Ibid., 125; **340 Now, Israeli politicians**: Alan M. Dershowitz, *The Vanishing American Jew* (Boston: Little, Brown & Company, 1997), 221; **401 Two decades later, many Frenchmen**: Robert S. Wistrich, "Anti-Semitism in Europe After 1945" in Wistrich, *Terms of Survival*, 272–76; **402 Recently a group of young**: See Alan Freeman, "A Polish City Whitewashes Its Anti-Semitic Image," *Globe and Mail*, March 22, 2000; Wistrich, *Terms of Survival*, 281–82, 286–91; **402 "It is just like being"**: Author's interview with Rabbi Azman; **402 A poll done**: "Anti-Defamation League Poll," *National Post*, Toronto, July 2, 2002. **402 In the summer of 2002**: "Israel Enraged by China Ban on 'Jewish' Einstein Display," *Daily Telegraph*, London, July 31, 2002. **403 The Pakistani extremists**: See, Michael Kamber, "The Chosen One," *The Village Voice* (New York) February 25, 2002. **403 Along the same lines**: Abdallah Aal Malhi, "The Jewish Sense of Superiority in the World," *Al-Watan*, December 8 and 9, 2001 cited in Anti-Defamation League, December 2001, www.adl.org. See also, The Middle East Media Research Institute, Special Dispatch Series, 321, Report of December 28, 2001, memri.org/bin/articles. **404 The quotas at medical schools**: Dershowitz, *Vanishing American Jew*, 7–9; Hertzberg, *Jews in America*, 380; **404 America has become**: Ruth Wisse, in ed. Robert M. Seltzer and Norman J. Cohen, *The Americanization of the Jews* (New York: New York University Press, 1995), 67; **404 "The good news is"**: Dershowitz, *Vanishing American Jew*, 1–2; **405 It is no longer the taboo**: Paul Ritterband, "Modern Times and Jewish Assimilation," in Seltzer and Cohen, *Americanization of Jews*, 382–83; **406 Footnote: As one slightly cynical story**: Dershowitz, *Vanishing American Jew*, 213; **406 In 1812, as Napoleon was marching**: Dubnow, *History of the Jews in Russia*, 356–57; Dershowitz, *Vanishing American Jew*, 2–3; **406–7 Jews are the world's**: Simon Rawidowicz, "Israel: The Ever-Dying People," in Simon Rawidowicz, *Israel: The Ever-Dying People and Other Essays* (Cranbury, N.J.: Associated University Presses, 1986), ed. Benjamin Ravid, 53–4, 61, 66; Hertzberg, *Jews in America*, 388; **407 Even in Europe, according to the theory**: Hyman, *Jews in Modern France*, 205–6; **407 A new state of mind**: Dershowitz, *Vanishing American Jew*, 65, 246, 336.

SELECTED BIBLIOGRAPHY

GENERAL

Arkin, Marcus. *Aspects of Jewish Economic History*. Philadelphia: Jewish Publication Society of America, 1975.

Baron, Salo W. and Arcadius Kahn. *Economic History of the Jews*. New York: Schocken, 1975.

Chazan, Robert and Marc Lee Raphael, eds. *Modern Jewish History: A Source Reader*. New York: Schocken, 1974.

Dawidowicz, Lucy S. *The Jewish Presence: Essays on Identity and History*. New York: Holt, Rinehart & Winston, 1977.

• De Lange, Nicholas, ed. *The Illustrated History of the Jewish People*. Toronto: Key Porter, 1997.

Dershowitz, Alan M. *The Vanishing American Jew*. Boston: Little, Brown & Company, 1997.

Eban, Abba. *My People: The Story of the Jews*. New York: Behrman House, 1968.

——. *Heritage: Civilization and the Jews*. New York: Summit, 1984.

Elazar, Daniel J. *The Other Jews: The Sephardim Today*. New York: Basic, 1989.

Gerber, Jane S. *The Jews of Spain: A History of the Sephardic Experience*. New York: Free Press, 1992.

Johnson, Paul. *A History of the Jews*. London: Weidenfeld & Nicolson, 1987.

Marcus, Jacob R., ed. *The Jew in the Medieval World: A Source Book: 315–1791*. New York: Atheneum, 1969.

Mendes-Flohr, Paul R. and Jehuda Reinharz, eds. *The Jew in the Modern World: A Documentary History*. New York: Oxford University Press, 1980.

Meyer, Michael A. *The Origins of the Modern Jew: Jewish Identity and European Culture in Germany, 1794–1824*. Detroit: Wayne State University Press, 1979.

Mirsky, Aaron, Avraham Grossman, and Yosef Kaplan, eds. *Exile and Diaspora: Studies in the History of the Jewish People, Presented to Professor Haim Beinart on the Occasion of His Seventieth Birthday*. Jerusalem: Hebrew University, 1991.

Reinharz, Jehuda and Walter Schatzberg, eds. *The Jewish Response to German Culture: From the Enlightenment to the Second World War*. Hanover, N.H. and London: University Press of New England, 1985.

Roden, Claudia. *The Book of Jewish Food*. New York: Alfred A. Knopf, 1997.

Ruderman, David B. *Jewish Thought and Scientific Discovery in Early Modern Europe*. New Haven: Yale University Press, 1995.

Sachar, Howard M. *The Course of Modern Jewish History*. Cleveland: World
    Publishing Company, 1958.
—— . *Diaspora: An Inquiry into the Contemporary Jewish World*. New York: Harper &
    Row, 1985.
—— . *Farewell España: The World of the Sephardim Remembered*. New York: Alfred A.
    Knopf, 1994.
Strom, Yale. *The Expulsion of the Jews: Five Hundred Years of Exodus*. New York: S.P.I.
    Books, 1992.

CHAPTER ONE: SEPHARDIM

Abravanel, Don Isaac. *Opera minora*. Westmead, Farnborough, Hants.:
    Gregg International Publishers, 1972. Reprint with an introduction
    by Louis Jacobs.
Adler, Marcus Nathan. *The Itinerary of Benjamin of Tudela*. New York: Philipp
    Feldheim, 1907.
Assis, Yom Tov. *The Golden Age of Aragonese Jewry: Community and Society in the
    Crown of Aragon, 1213–1327*. London: Littman Library of Jewish Civilization,
    1997.
Baer, Yitzhak. *A History of the Jews in Christian Spain*. 2 vols. Philadelphia: Jewish
    Publication Society of America, 1961.
Benardete, Mair José. *Hispanic Culture and Character of the Sephardic Jews*. New York:
    Sepher-Hermon Press, 1982.
Beinart, Haim, ed. *Moreshet Sephard: The Sephardi Legacy*. 2 vols. Jerusalem: Magnes
    Press, Hebrew University, 1992.
Ben-Sasson, H.H. "The Generation of the Spanish Exiles on its Fate." *Zion* 26:1
    (1961): 23–64 (Hebrew).
Durant, Will. *Age of Faith* (vol. 4 in *The Story of Civilization*). New York: Simon &
    Schuster, 1950.
—— . *The Reformation* (vol. 6 in *The Story of Civilization*). New York: Simon &
    Schuster, 1957.
Faur, José. *In the Shadow of History: Jews and Conversos at the Dawn of Modernity*.
    Albany: State University of New York Press, 1992.
Gampel, Benjamin R. *The Last Jews on Iberian Soil: Navarrese Jewry, 1479 to 1498*. Los
    Angeles: University of California Press, 1989.
Heschel, Abraham. *Don Jizchak Abravanel*. Berlin: Erich Reiss Verlag, 1937.
Kedourie, Elie, ed. *Spain and the Jews: The Sephardi Experience 1492 and After*.
    London: Thames & Hudson, 1992.
Klein, Elka Beth. "Power and Patrimony: The Jewish Community of Barcelona,
    1050–1250." Ph.D. diss. Harvard University, 1996.
Lea, Henry Charles. *A History of the Inquisition of Spain*, vol. 1. New York: A.M.S.
    Press, 1988. (Originally published 1906.)
Lindo, E.H. *The Jews of Spain and Portugal*. New York: Burt Franklin, 1970.
    (Originally published 1848.)
Lipiner, Elias. *Two Portuguese Exiles in Castile: Dom David Negro and Dom Isaac
    Abravanel*. Jerusalem: Magnes Press, 1997.

Liss, Peggy K. *Isabel the Queen: Life and Times*. New York: Oxford University Press, 1992.

Livermore, H.V. *A New History of Portugal*. Cambridge: Cambridge University Press, 1966.

Minkin, Jacob S. *Abarbanel and the Expulsion of the Jews from Spain*. New York: Behrman's Jewish Book House, 1938.

Mocatta, Frederic. *The Jews of Spain and Portugal and the Inquisition*. New York: Cooper Square Publishers, 1973.

Netanyahu, Benzion. *Don Isaac Abravanel: Statesman and Philosopher*. Philadelphia: Jewish Publication Society, 1968.

—— . *The Marranos of Spain, from the Late Fourteenth to the Early Sixteenth Century, According to Contemporary Hebrew Sources*. New York: American Academy for Jewish Research, 1966.

—— . *The Origins of the Inquisition in Fifteenth Century Spain*. New York: Random House, 1995

—— . *Toward the Inquisition: Essays on Jewish and Converso History in Late Medieval Spain*. Ithaca and London: Cornell University Press, 1997.

Neuman, Abraham A. *The Jews in Spain: Their Social, Political, and Cultural Life During the Middle Ages*. 2 vols. Philadelphia: Jewish Publication Society of America, 1942.

Paris, Erna. *The End of Days: A Story of Tolerance, Tyranny, and the Expulsion of Jews from Spain*. Toronto: Lester Publishing, 1995.

Raphael, David, ed. *The Expulsion 1492 Chronicles: An Anthology of Medieval Chronicles Relating to the Expulsion of the Jews from Spain and Portugal*. North Hollywood, Calif.: Carmi House Press, 1992.

Roth, Cecil. *The Spanish Inquisition*. New York: W.W. Norton & Company, 1964.

Roth, Norman. *Conversos, Inquisition, and the Expulsion of the Jews from Spain*. Madison, Wis.: University of Wisconsin Press, 1995.

Sarachek, Joseph. *Don Isaac Abravanel*. New York: Bloch Publishing, 1938.

Trend, J.B., ed. *Isaac Abravanel: Six Lectures*. Cambridge: Cambridge University Press, 1937.

Waddington, Raymond B. and Arthur H. Williamson, eds. *The Expulsion of the Jews: 1492 and After*. New York: Garland Publishing, 1994.

CHAPTER TWO: THE GHETTO

Arbel, Benjamin. *Trading Nations: Jews and Venetians in the Early-Modern Eastern Mediterranean*. New York: E.J. Brill, 1995.

Barnett, R.D. and W.M. Schwab, eds. *The Sephardi Heritage*. Vol. 2. Grendon, Northants.: Gibraltar Books, 1989.

Bonfil, Robert. *Jewish Life in Renaissance Italy*. Berkeley: University of California Press, 1994.

Calimani, Riccardo. *The Ghetto of Venice* translated by Katherine Silberblatt Wolfthal. New York: M. Evans & Company, 1985.

Cohen, Mark R., ed. *The Autobiography of a Seventeenth-Century Venetian Rabbi: Leon Modena's Life of Judah*. Princeton, N.J.: Princeton University Press, 1988.

Curiel, Roberta and Bernard Cooperman. *The Ghetto of Venice*. London: Tauris Parke, 1990.

Davis, Robert C. and Benjamin Ravid, eds. *The Jews of Early Modern Venice*. Baltimore: John Hopkins University Press, 2001.

Ebreo, Leone. *Dialogues di amore*. Edited by T. Anthony Perry. Chapel Hill, N.C.: University of North Carolina Press, 1974.

——. *The Philosophy of Love (Dialoghi di amore)*. Translated by F. Friedeberg-Seeley and Jean H. Barnes. London: Soncino Press, 1937.

Ginio, Alisa Meyuhas, ed. *Jews, Christians, and Muslims in the Mediterranean World After 1492*. London and Portland, Ore.: Frank Cass and Company, 1992.

Goitein, S.D. *Letters of Medieval Jewish Traders*. Princeton, N.J.: Princeton University Press, 1973.

Lesley, Arthur M. "The Place of the *Dialoghi di amore* in Contemporaneous Jewish Thought." In *Ficino and Renaissance Neoplatonism*, edited by Konrad Eisenbichler and Olga Zorzi Pugliese, 69–86. Ottawa: Dovehouse Editions, 1986.

Pullan, Brian. *The Jews of Europe and the Inquisition of Venice, 1550–1670*. Totowa, N.J.: Barnes & Noble Books, 1983.

Roth, Cecil. *History of the Jews of Italy*. Philadelphia: Jewish Publication Society of America, 1946.

——. *History of the Jews in Venice*. New York: Schocken Books, 1975.

——. *The House of Nasi: Doña Gracia*. Philadelphia: Jewish Publication Society of America, 1948.

——. *The House of Nasi: The Duke of Naxos*. Philadelphia: Jewish Publication Society of America, 1948.

Shulvass, Moses A. *The Jews in the World of the Renaissance*. Translated by E.I. Kose. Leiden: E.J. Brill, 1973.

Twersky, Isadore, ed. *Studies in Medieval Jewish History and Literature*, vol. 2. Cambridge, Mass.: Harvard University Press, 1984.

Yerushalmi, Yosef. *From Spanish Court to Italian Ghetto: Isaac Cardoso, a Study in Seventeenth-Century Marranism and Jewish Apologetics*. New York: Columbia University Press, 1971.

CHAPTER THREE: PHYSICIANS, POETS, AND A FALSE MESSIAH

Braude, Benjamin and Bernard Lewis, eds. *Christians and Jews in the Ottoman Empire: The Functioning of a Plural Society*. 2 vols. London: Holmes & Meier, 1980–82.

Epstein, Mark Alan. *The Ottoman Jewish Communities and their Role in the Fifteenth and Sixteenth Centuries*. Freiburg: Klaus Schwarz Verlag, 1980.

Galante, Avram. *Histoire des juifs de Turquie*. 9 vols. Istanbul: Isis, 1985.

Goldman, Israel M. *The Life and Times of Rabbi David Ibn Abi Zimra*. New York: The Jewish Theological Seminary of America, 1970.

Goodwin, Jason. *Lords of the Horizons: A History of the Ottoman Empire*. London: Chatto & Windus, 1998.

Gross, Henri. "La Famille juive des Hamon." *Revue des Études juives* 56 (1908): 1–26.

——. "La Famille juive des Hamon." *Revue des Études juives* 57 (1909): 55–78.

Heyd, Uriel. "Moses Hamon, Chief Jewish Physician to Sultan Suleyman the Magnificent." *Oriens* 16 (1963): 152–70.

———. "The Jewish Community of Istanbul in the Seventeenth Century." *Oriens* 6 (1953): 299–314.

Juhasz, Esther, ed. *Sephardi Jews in the Ottoman Empire: Aspects of Material Culture.* Jerusalem: The Israel Museum, 1990.

Lamb, Harold. *Suleiman the Magnificent: Sultan of the East.* New York: Bantam, 1951.

Lewis, Bernard. *The Jews of Islam.* Princeton, N.J.: Princeton University Press, 1984.

———. "The Privileges Granted by Mehmed II to His Physician." *Bulletin of the School of Oriental and African Studies*, University of London, 14 (1952): 550–63.

Merriman, Roger B. *Suleiman the Magnificent, 1520–1566.* Cambridge, Mass.: Harvard University Press, 1944.

Nehama, Joseph. *Histoire des israélites de Salonique.* Vol. 2 and 3. Thessaloníki: Librairie Molho, 1935 and 1936.

Rodrigue, Aron, ed. *Ottoman and Turkish Jewry: Community and Leadership.* Bloomington, Ind.: Indiana University, 1992.

Scholem, Gershom. *Sabbatai Sevi: The Mystical Messiah, 1626–1676.* Princeton, N.J.: Princeton University Press, 1973.

Shatzmiller, Joseph. *Jews, Medicine, and Medieval Society.* Berkeley: University of California Press, 1994.

Shaw, Stanford J. *The Jews of the Ottoman Empire and the Turkish Republic.* New York: New York University Press, 1991.

Shmuelevitz, Aryeh. *The Jews of the Ottoman Empire in the Late Fifteenth and the Sixteenth Centuries: Administrative, Economic, Legal, and Social Relations As Reflected in the Responsa.* Leiden: E.J. Brill, 1984.

Van Wijk, Jetteke. "The Rise and Fall of Shabbatai Zevi as Reflected in Contemporary Press Reports." *Studia Rosenthaliana*, 33:1 (1999), 7–27.

CHAPTER FOUR: THE PORTUGUESE NAÇÃO

Altmann, Alexander. *Moses Mendelssohn: A Biographical Study.* Philadelphia: Jewish Publication Society of America, 1973.

Amzalak, Moses. *Abraham Israel Pereyra: Noticia Biobibliográfica.* Lisbon: Museo Comercial, 1927.

Belinfante, Judith C.E., Edward van Voolen, David P. Cohen Paraira, Jaffa Baruch-Sznaj, and Julie-Marthe Cohen. *The Esnoga: A Monument to Portuguese-Jewish Culture.* Amsterdam: D'Arts, 1991.

Ben Israel, Menasseh. *The Hope of Israel.* Translated by Moses Wall, edited by Henry Mechoulan. Oxford: The Littman Library, 1987.

Bloom, Herbert I. *The Economic Activities of the Jews of Amsterdam in the Seventeenth and Eighteenth Centuries.* Port Washington, New York: Kennikat Press, 1969. (Originally published in London, 1937.)

Bodian, Miriam. *Hebrews of the Portuguese Nation: Conversos and Community in Early Modern Amsterdam.* Bloomington, Ind.: Indiana University Press, 1997.

Da Silva, Aldina, André Myre, and Tereza Pinto. *Les Juifs portugais: exil, heritage, perspectives, 1496–1996.* Montreal: Mediaspaul, 1998.

De Vries, B.W. *From Pedlars to Textile Barons: The Economic Development of a Jewish Minority Group in the Netherlands*. New York: Netherlands Organization for the Advancement of Pure Research, 1989.

Huizinga, J.H. *Dutch Civilization in the Seventeenth Century, and Other Essays*. London: Collins, 1968.

Israel, Jonathan I. *The Dutch Republic: Its Rise, Greatness, and Fall 1477–1806*. Oxford: Clarendon Press, 1995.

——. *The Dutch Republic and the Hispanic World 1606–1661*. Oxford: Clarendon Press, 1982.

——. *Empires and Entrepôts: The Dutch, the Spanish Monarchy, and the Jews, 1585–1713*. London: Hambledon Press, 1990.

——. *European Jewry in the Age of Mercantilism 1550–1750*. Oxford: Clarendon Press, 1989.

Kaplan, Yosef. *The Alternative Path to Modernity: The Sephardi Diaspora in Western Europe*. Leiden, Netherlands: Brill, 2000.

——. "The Formation of the Western Sephardic Diaspora." In *The Sephardic Journey, 1492–1992*. New York: Yeshiva University Museum, 1992.

Kaplan, Yosef, Mechoulan Henry, and Richard H. Popkin, eds. *Menasseh Ben Israel and His World*. New York: E.J. Brill, 1989.

Mechoulan, Henry. "Abraham Pereyra, juge de Marranes et censeur de ses coreligionnaires à Amsterdam au temps de Spinoza." *Revue des études juives* 138: 3–4 (July–December 1979): 391–400.

——. *Amsterdam au temps de Spinoza: argent et liberté*. Paris: Presses universitaires de France, 1990.

——. *Hispanidad y judaismo en tiempos de Espinoza: edición de "La Certeza del camino" de Abraham Pereyra*. Salamanca: Ediciones Universidad de Salmanaca, 1987.

——, ed. *Les Juifs d'Espagne: historie d'une diaspora*. Paris: Liana Levi, 1992.

Michman, Jozeph, ed. *Dutch Jewish History: Proceedings of the Fourth-Fifth Symposium on the History of the Jews in the Netherlands*. Jerusalem: Institute for Research on Dutch Jewry, Hebrew University, 1989.

Murray, John J. *Amsterdam in the Age of Rembrandt*. Norman, Okla.: University of Oklahoma Press, 1967.

Perera, Victor. *The Cross and the Pear Tree: A Sephardic Journey*. New York: Alfred A. Knopf, 1995.

Price, J.L. *Holland and the Dutch Republic in the Seventeenth Century: The Politics of Particularism*. Oxford: Clarendon Press, 1994.

Sutcliffe, Adam. "Judaism in Spinoza and His Circle." *Studia Rosenthaliana*, 34:1 (2000): 7–22.

Vega, L. Alvares. *The Beth Haim of Ouderkerk aan de Amstel: Images of a Portuguese Jewish Cemetery in Holland*. Schoonl: Pirola, 1994.

CHAPTER FIVE: COURT JEWS

Altmann, Alexander. *Moses Mendelssohn: A Biographical Study*. Tuscaloosa, Ala.: University of Alabama Press, 1973.

Beller, Steven. *Vienna and the Jews 1867–1938: A Cultural History*. Cambridge: Cambridge University Press, 1989.

Breuer, Mordechai, and Michael Graetz. *German-Jewish History in Modern Times: Tradition and Enlightenment 1600–1780*. Vol. 1. New York: Columbia University Press, 1996.

Durant, Will and Ariel Durant. *The Age of Louis XIV* (vol. 8 in *The Story of Civilization*). New York: Simon & Schuster, 1963.

Ferguson, Niall. *The World's Banker: The History of the House of Rothschild*. London: Weidenfeld & Nicolson, 1998.

Glückel of Hameln. *The Life of Glückel of Hameln, 1646–1724*. Translated and edited by Beth-Zion Abrahams. London: East & West Library, 1962.

Grunwald, Max. *History of the Jews in Vienna*. Philadelphia: Jewish Publication Society of America, 1936.

——. *Samuel Oppenheimer und Sein Kreis: Ein Kapitel aus der Finanzgeschichte Österreichs*. Vienna: W. Braumüller, 1913.

Haasis, Hellmut G. *Joseph Süss Oppenheimer, genannt Jud Süss: Financier, Freidenker, Justizopfer*. Hamburg: Rowohlt Verlag, 1998.

Holborn, Hajo. *A History of Modern Germany 1648–1840*. Princeton, N.J.: Princeton University Press, 1964.

Hsia, R. Po-Chia and Hartmut Lehmann, eds. *In and Out of the Ghetto: Jewish–Gentile Relations in Late Medieval and Early Modern Germany*. Cambridge: Cambridge University Press, 1995.

Kaufman, David. *Samson Wertheimer, der Oberhoffaktor und Landesrabbiner (1658–1724) und seine Kinder*. Vienna: F. Beck, 1888.

Lorenz, Dagmar C.G. and Gabriele Weinberger, eds. *Insiders and Outsiders: Jewish and Gentile Culture in Germany and Austria*. Detroit: Wayne State University Press, 1994.

Mann, Vivian B. and Richard I. Cohen, eds. *From Court Jews to the Rothschilds: Art, Patronage, and Power, 1600–1800*. New York: Prestel, 1996.

McCagg, William O. *A History of Habsburg Jews, 1670–1918*. Bloomington, Ind.: Indiana University Press, 1989.

Mosse, W.E. *Jews in the German Economy: The German-Jewish Economic Elite, 1820–1935*. Oxford: Clarendon Press, 1987.

Rozenblit, Marsha L. *The Jews of Vienna 1867–1914: Assimilation and Identity*. Albany: State University of New York Press, 1983.

Stern, Selma. *The Court Jew: A Contribution to the History of the Period of Absolutism in Central Europe*. Translated by Ralph Weiman. Philadelphia: Jewish Publication Society of America, 1950.

——. *Jud Süss: Ein Beitrag zur Deutschen und zur Judischen Geschichte*. Berlin: Akademie Verlag, 1929.

Wistrich, Robert. *The Jews of Vienna in the Age of Franz Joseph*. New York: Littman Library and Oxford University Press, 1990.

CHAPTER SIX: THE AGE OF EMANCIPATION

Aschheim, Steven A. *Brothers and Strangers: The East European Jew in German and German Jewish Consciousness 1800-1923*. Madison: The University of Wisconsin Press, 1982.

Arendt, Hannah. *Rahel Varnhagen: The Life of a Jewess*. Baltimore: John Hopkins University Press, 1997.

Brenner, Michael, Sefi Jersch-Wenzel and Michael A. Meyer. *German-Jewish History in Modern Times: Emancipation and Acculturation 1780-1871*. v.2 New York: Columbia University Press, 1997.

Bach, H.I. *The German Jew: A Synthesis of Judaism and Western Civilization, 1730-1930*. London: Oxford University Press, 1984.

Cowles, Virginia. *The Rothschilds: A Family Fortune*. London: Futura Publications, 1975.

Elon, Amos. *Founder: A Portrait of the First Rothschild and his Time*. London: Penguin Books, 1996.

Ferguson, Niall. *The World's Banker: The History of the House of Rothschild*. London: Weidenfeld & Nicolson, 1998.

Frankel, Jonathan and Steven J. Zipperstein, eds. *Assimilation and Community: The Jews in Nineteenth Century Europe* Cambridge: Cambridge University Press, 1992.

Gay, Ruth. *The Jews of Germany*. New Haven: Yale University Press, 1992.

Gilman, Sander L. and Jack Zipes, *Yale Companion to Jewish Writing and Thought in German Culture 1096-1996*. New Haven and London: Yale University Press, 1997.

Heuberger, Georg, ed. *The Rothschilds: Essays on the History of a European Family*. Frankfurt: Jan Thorbecke Verlag, 1994.

Liberles, Robert Sam. "Between Community and Separation: The Resurgence of Orthodoxy in Frankfurt 1838-1877," Ph.D. dissertation, The Jewish Theological Seminary of America, 1979.

Liptzin, Solomon. *Germany's Stepchildren*. Philadelphia: The Jewish Publication Society of America, 1944.

Meyer, Michael A. *Response to Modernity: A History of the Reform Movement in Judaism*. New York: Oxford University Press, 1988.

Morton, Frederic. *The Rothschilds*. New York: Atheneum, 1962.

Mosse, W.E. *Jews in the German Economy*. Oxford: Clarendon Press, 1987.

Mosse, W.E., Arnold Pauker, and Reinhard Rürup (eds.). *Revolution and Evolution: 1848 in German-Jewish History*. Tübingen, Germany: J.C.B. Mohr, 1981.

Pulzer, Peter. *Jews and the German State: The Political History of a Minority, 1848-1933*. Oxford: Blackwell Publishers, 1992.

Reinharz, Jehuda and Walter Schatzberg. *The Jewish Response to German Culture: From the Enlightenment to the Second World War*. Hanover and London: University Press of New England, 1985.

Reeves, John. *The Rothschilds: The Financial Rulers of Nations*. London: Sampson, Low, Marston, Searle, and Rivington, 1887.

Rosenbloom, Noah H. *Tradition in an Age of Reform: The Religious Philosophy of Samson Raphael Hirsch*. Philadelphia: The Jewish Publication Society of America, 1976.

Sorkin, David. *The Transformation of German Jewry, 1780-1840*. New York: Oxford University Press, 1987.

Vital, David. *A People Apart: The Jews in Europe 1789-1939*. Oxford: Oxford University Press, 1999.

CHAPTER SEVEN: THE PALE OF SETTLEMENT

Aronson, I. Michael. *Troubled Waters: The Origins of the 1881 Anti-Jewish Pogroms in Russia*. Pittsburgh: University of Pittsburgh Press, 1990.

Baron, Salo W. *The Russian Jew Under Tsars and Soviets*. New York: Macmillan Publishing Company, 1964.

Berk, Stephen M. *Year of Crisis, Year of Hope: Russian Jewry and the Pogroms of 1881–1882*. Westport, Conn.: Greenwood Press, 1985.

Byrnes, Robert F. *Pobedonostsev, His Life and Thought*. Bloomington, Ind.: Indiana University Press, 1968.

Dubnow, Simon M. *History of the Jews in Russia and Poland*, vol. 2. Philadelphia: Jewish Publication Society of America, 1918.

Gitelman, Zvi. *A Century of Ambivalence: The Jews of Russia and the Soviet Union, 1881 to the Present*. New York: Schocken Books, 1988.

Greenberg, Louis. *The Jews in Russia: The Struggle for Emancipation*. 2 vols. New Haven, Conn.: Yale University Press, 1965.

Hertzberg, Arthur. *The Zionist Idea: A Historical Analysis and Reader*. New York: Atheneum, 1976.

Klier, John Doyle. *Russia Gathers Her Jews: The Origins of the "Jewish Question" in Russia, 1772–1825*. Dekalb, Ill.: Northern Illinois University Press, 1986.

Klier, John Doyle and Shlomo Lambroza, eds. *Pogroms: Anti-Jewish Violence in Modern Russian History*. Cambridge: Cambridge University Press, 1992.

Levin, Shmarya. *Childhood in Exile*. 3 vols. Translated by Maurice Samuel. New York: Harcourt, Brace, & Company, 1929.

Lincoln, W. Bruce. *In War's Dark Shadow: The Russians Before the Great War*. New York: Dial Press, 1983.

Marsden, Norman, ed. *A Jewish Life Under the Tsars: The Autobiography of Chaim Aronson, 1825–1888*. Totowa, N.J.: Allanheld, Osmun, & Company, 1983.

Neugroschel, Joachim, ed. *The Shtetl*. New York: Overlook Press, 1989.

Orbach, Alexander. *New Voices of Russian Jewry: A Study of the Russian-Jewish Press of Odessa in the Era of the Great Reforms, 1860–1871*. Leiden: E.J. Brill, 1980.

Raisin, Jacob S. *The Haskalah Movement in Russia*. Philadelphia: Jewish Publication Society of America, 1913.

Rischin, Moses. *The Promised City New York's Jews, 1870–1914*. Cambridge, Mass.: Harvard University Press, 1962.

——, ed. *Grandma Never Lived in America: The New Journalism of Abraham Cahan*. Bloomington, Ind.: Indiana University Press, 1985.

Rogger, Hans. *Jewish Policies and Right-Wing Politics in Imperial Russia*. Berkeley: University of California Press, 1986.

Roskies, Diane K. and David G. Roskies. *The Shtetl Book*. New York: Ktav Publishing House, 1975.

Rosman, Moshe. *Founder of Hasidism: A Quest for the Historical Ba'al Shem Tov*. Berkeley: University of California Press, 1996.

Stanislawski, Michael. *Tsar Nicholas I and the Jews: The Transformation of Jewish Society in Russia, 1825–1855*. Philadelphia: Jewish Publication Society of America, 1983.

—— . *For Whom Do I Toil? Judah Leib Gordon and the Crisis of Russian Jewry*. New York: Oxford University Press, 1988.

Wengeroff, Pauline. *Rememberings: The World of a Russian-Jewish Woman in the Nineteenth Century*. Translated by Henny Wenkart. Bethesda, Md.: University Press of Maryland, 2000.

Zborowski, Mark and Elizabeth Herzog. *Life is with People: The Jewish Little-Town of Eastern Europe*. New York: International Universities Press, 1952.

CHAPTER EIGHT: *L'AFFAIRE*

Birnbaum, Pierre. *Anti-Semitism in France: A Political History from Léon Blum to the Present*. Oxford: Blackwell Publishers, 1992.

Bredin, Jean-Denis. *The Affair: The Case of Alfred Dreyfus*. Translated by Jeffrey Mohlman. New York: George Braziller, 1986.

Brennan, James F. *The Reflection of the Dreyfus Affair in the European Press, 1897–1899*. New York: Peter Lang, 1998.

Burns, Michael. *Dreyfus: A Family Affair, 1789–1945*. New York: HarperCollins, 1991.

Byrnes, Robert F. *Antisemitism in Modern France*. New Brunswick, N.J.: Rutgers University Press, 1950.

Cahm, Eric. *The Dreyfus Affair in French Society and Politics*. New York: Longman, 1996.

Chapman, Guy. *The Dreyfus Case: A Reassessment*. New York: Reynal & Company, 1956.

Dreyfus, Alfred. *Lettres d'un innocent: The Letters of Captain Dreyfus to his Wife*. New York: Harper & Brothers, 1899.

Dreyfus, Alfred. *Five Years of My Life: The Diary of Captain Alfred Dreyfus*. New York: Peebles Press, 1977. (Originally published 1901.)

Feldman, Egal. *The Dreyfus Affair and the American Conscience, 1895–1906*. Detroit: Wayne State University Press, 1981.

Graetz, Michael. *The Jews in Nineteenth-Century France: From the French Revolution to the Alliance israélite universelle*. Stanford, Calif.: Stanford University Press, 1996.

Green, Nancy L. *The Pletzl of Paris: Jewish Immigrant Workers in the Belle Époque*. New York: Holmes & Meier, 1986.

Halasz, Nicholas. *Captain Dreyfus: The Story of a Mass Hysteria*. New York: Simon & Schuster, 1955.

Hyman, Paula E. *The Emancipation of the Jews of Alsace: Acculturation and Tradition in the Nineteenth Century*. New Haven, Conn.: Yale University Press, 1991.

—— . *The Jews of Modern France*. Berkeley: University of California Press, 1998.

Isser, Natalie. *Antisemitism During the French Second Empire*. New York: Peter Lang, 1991.

Johnson, Martin P. *The Dreyfus Affair: Honor and Politics in the Belle Époque*. New York: St. Martin's Press, 1999.

Jussem-Wilson, Nelly. *Bernard-Lazare: Antisemitism and the Problem of Jewish Identity in Late Nineteenth-Century France*. Cambridge: Cambridge University Press, 1978.

Kleeblatt, Norman, ed. *The Dreyfus Affair: Art, Truth, and Justice*. Berkeley: University of California Press, 1987.

Kornberg, Jacques. "Theodor Herzl: A Re-evaluation." *Journal of Modern History* 52: 2 (June 1980): 226–52.

Malino, Frances. *The Sephardic Jews of Bordeaux: Assimilation and Emancipation in Revolutionary and Napoleonic France*. Birmingham, Ala.: University of Alabama Press, 1978.

Malino, Frances and Bernard Wasserstein, eds. *The Jews in Modern France*. Hanover, N.H. and London: University Press of New England, 1985.

Marrus, Michael. *The Politics of Assimilation, A Study of the French Jewish Community at the time of the Dreyfus Affair*. Oxford: Clarendon Press, 1971.

Mitchell, Allan. "The Xenophobic Style: French Counterespionage and the Emergence of the Dreyfus Affair." *Journal of Modern History* 52:3 (September 1980): 414–25.

Snyder, Louis L. *The Dreyfus Case: A Documentary History*. New Brunswick, N.J.: Rutgers University Press, 1973.

Vidal-Naquet, Pierre. *The Jews: History, Memory, and the Present*. Translated by David Ames Curtis. New York: Columbia University Press, 1996.

Wilson, Stephen. *Ideology and Experience: Antisemitism in France at the Time of the Dreyfus Affair*. East Brunswick, N.J.: Associated University Press, 1982.

Zola, Émile. *The Dreyfus Affair: "J'accuse" and Other Writings*. Edited by Alain Pages and translated by Eleanor Levieux. New Haven: Yale University Press, 1996.

CHAPTER NINE: THE GOLDEN LAND

Bernheimer, Charles, ed. *The Russian Jew in the United States: Studies in Social Conditions in New York, Philadelphia, and Chicago, with a Description of Rural Settlements*. Philadelphia: John C. Winston Company, 1905. (Reprint by Jerome S. Ozer, 1971.)

Cahan, Abraham. *The Education of Abraham Cahan*. Translated by Leon Stein. Philadelphia: Jewish Publication Society of America, 1969.

——. *The Imported Bridegroom and Other Stories of the New York Ghetto*. New York: Garrett Press, 1968. (Originally published Houghton, Mifflin, 1898.)

——. *The Rise of David Levinsky*. New York: Penguin Books, 1993. (Originally published Harper & Brothers, 1917.)

Chametzky, Jules. *From the Ghetto: The Fiction of Abraham Cahan*. Amherst, Mass.: University of Massachusetts Press, 1977.

Cohen, Rich. *Tough Jews*. New York: Simon & Schuster, 1998.

Diner, Hasia R. *Lower East Side Memories: A Jewish Place in America*. Princeton: Princeton University Press, 2000.

Epstein, Melech. *Profiles of Eleven*. Detroit: Wayne State University Press, 1965.

Feldstein, Stanley. *The Land That I Show You: Three Centuries of Jewish Life in America*. Garden City, N.Y.: Anchor Press, 1978.

Hapgood, Hutchins. *The Spirit of the Ghetto*. Cambridge, Mass.: Harvard University Press, 1967. (Originally published 1902.)

Hertzberg, Arthur. *The Jews in America: Four Centuries of an Uneasy Encounter, A History*. New York: Simon & Schuster, 1989.

Higham, John. *Send These to Me: Jews and Other Immigrants in Urban America*. New York: Atheneum, 1975.

Howe, Irving. *World of Our Fathers*. New York: Harcourt Brace Jovanovich, 1976.

Howe, Irving and Libo, Kenneth. *How We Lived: A Documentary History of Immigrant Jews in America, 1880–1930*. New York: Richard Marek Publishers, 1979.

Karp, Abraham J. *Golden Door to America: The Jewish Immigrant*. New York: Penguin Books, 1977.

——. *Haven and Home: A History of Jews in America*. New York: Schocken Books, 1985.

Liptzin, Sol. *Generation of Decision: Jewish Rejuvenation in America*. New York: Bloch Publishing Company, 1958.

Marovitz, Sanford E. *Abraham Cahan*. New York: Twayne Publishers, 1996.

Metzker, Isaac, ed. *A Bintel Brief*. Garden City, N.Y.: Doubleday, 1971.

Sachar, Howard M. *A History of the Jews in America*. New York: Alfred A. Knopf, 1992.

Sanders, Ronald. *The Downtown Jews: Portraits of an Immigrant Generation*. New York: Harper & Row, 1969.

Yaffe, James. *The American Jews: Portrait of a Split Personality*. New York: Random House, 1968.

CHAPTER TEN: THE GERMAN-JEWISH 'SYMBIOSIS'

Baker, Leonard. *Days of Sorrow and Pain*. New York: Oxford University Press, 1978.

Barkai, Avraham and Paul Mendes-Flohr. *German-Jewish History in Modern Times: Renewal and Destruction 1818-1945*. Vol. 4. New York: Columbia University Press, 1998.

Bernard, Martin. *Great Twentieth Century Jewish Philosophers*. New York: The MacMillan Company, 1970.

Benner, David A. *Marketing Identities: The Invention of Jewish Ethnicity in Ost und West*. Detroit: Wayne State University Press, 1998.

Brenner, Michael. *The Renaissance of Jewish Culture in Weimar Germany*. New Haven: Yale University Press, 1996.

Cohen, Hermann. *Religion of Reason Out of the Sources of Judaism*. Translated by Simon Kaplan. Atlanta: Scholars Press, 1995.

Gay, Peter. *The Berlin-Jewish Spirit: A Dogma in Search of Some Doubts*. New York: Leo Baeck Institute, 1972.

——. *Freud, Jews and Other Germans*. New York: Oxford University Press, 1978.

——. *Weimar Culture: The Outsider as Insider*. New York: Harper & Row Publishers, 1968.

Glatzer, Nahum N. *Franz Rosenzweig: His Life and Thought*. New York: Schocken Books, 1953.

Kaplan, Marion A. *The Making of the Jewish Middle Class*. New York: Oxford University Press, 1991.

Kershaw, Ian. *Hitler 1889-1936: Hubris*. New York: Penguin Putnam, 1998.

Landsberger, Arthur. *Berlin ohne Juden*. Bonn: Weidle Verlag, 1998. (Originally published in 1925).

Laqueur, Walter. *Weimar: A Cultural History 1918-1933*. New York: G.P. Putnam's Sons, 1974.

Liptzin, Solomon. *Germany's Stepchildren*. Philadelphia: The Jewish Publication Society of America, 1944.

Lowenstein, Steven M., Paul Mendes-Flohr, Peter Pulzer and Monika Richarz. *German-Jewish History in Modern Times: Integration in Dispute 1871-1918*. Vol. 3. New York: Columbia University Press, 1997.

Martin, Bernard. *Great Twentieth Century Jewish Philosophers*. New York: Macmillan, 1970.

Mendes-Flohr, Paul, ed. *The Philosophy of Franz Rosensweig*. Hanover, N.H.: University Press of New England, 1988.

Moses, Stéphane. *System and Revelation: The Philosophy of Franz Rosenszwieg*. Detroit: Wayne State University Press, 1992.

Niewyk, Donald L. *The Jews in Weimar Germany*. Baton Rouge: Louisiana State University Press, 1980.

Rosenzweig, Franz. *On Jewish Learning*. Edited by Nahum N. Glatzer. New York: Schocken Books, 1955.

Samuelson, Norbert M. *An Introduction to Modern Jewish Philosophy*. Albany: State University of New York Press, 1989.

Scholem, Gershom. *From Berlin to Jerusalem*. New York: Schocken Books, 1980.

Spielmann, Dianne R. "German Jewish Writers on the Eve of the Holocaust." In Randolph L. Braham, ed. *Detached From Reflections of the Holocaust in Art and Literature*. Boulder, CA: Social Science Monographs, 1990, 55-77.

Stern, Fritz. *Einstein's German World*. Princeton, NJ: Princeton, University Press, 1999.

Taylor, Ronald. *Berlin and its Culture: A Historical Portrait*. New Haven: Yale University Press, 1997.

CHAPTER ELEVEN: THE JERUSALEM OF LITHUANIA

Arad, Yitzhak. *Ghetto in Flames: The Struggle and Destruction of the Jews in Vilna in the Holocaust*. New York: Holocaust Library, 1982.

——— . *The Partisan: From the Valley of Death to Mount Zion*. New York: Holocaust Library, 1979.

Ascherson, Neal. *The Struggles for Poland*. London: Michael Joseph, 1987.

Browning, Christopher R. *Ordinary Men: Reserve Police Battalion 101 and the Final Solution in Poland*. New York: HarperCollins, 1992.

Bullock, Alan. *Hitler and Stalin: Parallel Lives*. Toronto: McClelland & Stewart, 1991.

Cohen, Israel. *Vilna*. Philadelphia: Jewish Publication Society of America, 1943.

Cohen, Rich. *The Avengers: A Jewish War Story*. New York: Alfred A. Knopf, 2000.

Davies, Norman. *God's Playground: A History of Poland*. New York: Columbia University Press, 1984.

Dawidowicz, Lucy S. *From That Place and Time: A Memoir, 1938–1947*. New York: W.W. Norton & Company, 1989.

——— . *The War Against the Jews, 1933–1945*. New York: Holt, Rinehart, & Winston, 1975.

Eckman, Lester and Chaim Lazar. *The Jewish Resistance: The History of the Jewish Partisans in Lithuania and White Russia during the Nazi Occupation*. New York: Shengold, 1977.

Engel, David. *Facing a Holocaust: The Polish Government-in-Exile and the Jews, 1943–1945*. Chapel Hill, N.C.: University of North Carolina Press, 1993.

——— . *In the Shadow of Auschwitz: The Polish Government-in-Exile and the Jews, 1939–1942*. Chapel Hill, N.C.: University of North Carolina Press, 1987.

Friedman, Ada June, ed. *Roads to Extinction: Essays on the Holocaust* (essays by Philip
    Friedman). Philadelphia: Jewish Publication Society of America, 1980.

Gilbert, Martin. *The Holocaust: The Jewish Tragedy*. London: Fontana Press, 1987.

Goldhagen, Daniel Jonah. *Hitler's Willing Executioners: Ordinary Germans and the
    Holocaust*. New York: Alfred A. Knopf, 1996.

Gutman, Yisrael and Shmuel Krakowski. *Unequal Victims: Poles and Jews during World
    War Two*. New York: Holocaust Library, 1986.

Heller, Celia S. *On the Edge of Destruction: Jews of Poland between the Two World Wars*.
    New York: Columbia University Press, 1977.

Holliday, Laurel, ed. *Children in the Holocaust and World War II: Their Secret Diaries*.
    New York: Pocket Books, 1995.

Kovner, Abba. *A Canopy in the Desert: Selected Poems*. Pittsburgh: University of
    Pittsburgh Press, 1973.

—— . "A First Attempt to Tell." In *The Holocaust as Historical Experience*, edited by
    Yehuda Bauer and Nathan Rotenstreich. 77–94. New York: Holmes & Meier
    Publishers, 1981.

—— . *Scrolls of Testimony*. Philadelphia: Jewish Publication Society, 2001. (English
    translation of *Megillot Ha-Edut*.)

Lazar, Chaim. *Destruction and Resistance: A History of the Partisan Movement in Vilna*.
    Translated by Galia Eden Bishop. New York: Shengold, 1985.

Levin, Dov. *Fighting Back: Lithuanian Jewry's Armed Resistance to the Nazis, 1941–1945*.
    New York: Holmes & Meier, 1985.

Levine, Allan. *Fugitives of the Forest: The Heroic Story of Jewish Resistance and Survival
    during the Second World War*. Toronto: Stoddart, 1998.

Mendelsohn, Ezra. *The Jews of East Central Europe Between the World Wars*.
    Bloomington: Indiana University Press, 1983.

Polonsky, Antony. *Politics in Independent Poland 1921–1939: The Crisis of Constitutional
    Government*. Oxford: Clarendon Press, 1972.

Rudashevski, Yitzhok. *The Diary of the Vilna Ghetto: June 1941–April 1943*. Western
    Galilee, Israel: Ghetto Fighters' House, 1972.

Shneidman, Norman N. *Jerusalem of Lithuania: The Rise and Fall of Jewish Vilnius*.
    Oakville, Ont.: Mosaic Press, 1998.

Shutan, Moshe. *Ghetto and Woods* (Hebrew). Tel Aviv: Jewish Partisan and Fighters
    Organization, 1985.

Sutin, Jack and Rochelle Sutin. *Jack and Rochelle: A Holocaust Story of Love and
    Resistance*. St. Paul, Minn.: Graywolf Press, 1995.

Wynot, Edward D. "A Necessary Cruelty: The Emergence of Official Anti-Semitism in
    Poland, 1936–1939." *The American Historical Review* 76:4 (October 1971): 1035–58.

Yahil, Leni. *Holocaust: The Fate of European Jewry, 1932–1945*. New York: Oxford
    University Press, 1990.

CHAPTER TWELVE: ZIONISTS AND SOVIETS

Altshuler, Mordechai. *Soviet Jewry Since the Second World War: Population and Social
    Structure*. New York: Greenwood Press, 1987.

Baron, Salo W. *The Russian Jew Under Tsars and Soviets*. New York: Macmillan, 1964.

Chesler, Evan R. *The Russian Jewry Reader.* New York: Behrman House, 1974.

Decter, Moshe. "The Status of the Jews in the Soviet Union." *Foreign Affairs* 41:2 (January 1963): 420–30.

Ehrenberg, Ilya and Vasily Grossman, eds. *The Black Book: The Nazi Crimes against the Jewish People.* New York: Holocaust Library, 1980.

Eisen, Wendy, *Count Us In: The Struggle to Free Canadian Jews; A Canadian Perspective.* Toronto: Burgher Books, 1995.

Figes, Orlando. *A People's Tragedy: The Russian Revolution, 1891–1924.* London: Jonathan Cape, 1996.

Freedman, Theodore, ed. *Anti-Semitism in the Soviet Union: Its Roots and Consequences.* New York: Freedom Library Press, 1984.

Frumkin, Jacob, Gregor Aronson, Alexis Goldenweiser, and Joseph Lewitan, eds. *Russian Jewry, 1917–1967.* New York: Thomas Yoseloff, 1969.

Gilboa, Yehoshua A. *The Black Years of Soviet Jewry, 1939–1953.* Translated by Yosef Schachter and Dov Ben-Abba. New York: Little Brown and Company, 1971.

Gilbert, Martin. *The Jews of Hope.* London: Macmillan, 1984.

Gilbert, Martin. *Shcharansky: Hero of Our Time.* London: Macmillan, 1986.

Kochan, Lionel, ed. *Jews in Soviet Russia Since 1917.* London: Oxford University Press, 1970.

Levin, Nora. *The Jews in the Soviet Union Since 1917: Paradox of Survival.* 2 vols. New York: New York University Press, 1988.

Panish, Paul. *Exit Visa: The Emigration of the Soviet Jews.* New York: Coward, McCann, & Geoghegan, 1981.

Pinkus, Benjamin. *The Jews of the Soviet Union: The History of a National Minority.* Cambridge: Cambridge University Press, 1988.

——— . *The Soviet Government and the Jews, 1948–1967.* Cambridge: Cambridge University Press, 1984.

Rapoport, Louis. *Stalin's War against the Jews: The Doctors' Plot and the Soviet Solution.* New York: The Free Press, 1990.

Rass, Rebecca with Morris Brafman. *From Moscow to Jerusalem: The Dramatic Story of the Jewish Liberation Movement and Its Impact on Israel.* New York: Shengold Publishers, 1976.

Ro'i, Yaacov. *The Struggle for Soviet Jewish Emigration, 1948–1967.* Cambridge: Cambridge University Press, 1991.

Rothchild, Sylvia. *A Special Legacy: An Oral History of Soviet Jewish Émigrés in the United States.* New York: Simon & Schuster, 1985.

Rubenstein, Joshua. *Tangled Loyalties: The Life and Times of Ilya Ehrenberg.* New York: Basic Books, 1996.

——— . *Soviet Dissidents: Their Struggle for Human Rights.* Boston: Beacon Press, 1980.

Rubin, Ronald I., ed. *The Unredeemed: Anti-Semitism in the Soviet Union.* Chicago: Quadrangle Books, 1968.

Schroeter, Leonard. *The Last Exodus.* New York: Universe Books, 1974.

Sharansky, Natan. *Fear No Evil.* New York: Random House, 1988.

Snyderman, Elaine Pomper, and Margaret Thomas Witkovsky, eds. *Line Five, the Internal Passport: Jewish Family Odysseys from the U.S.S.R. to the U.S.A.* Chicago: Chicago Review Press, 1992.

ACKNOWLEDGEMENTS

I AM A FIRM BELIEVER in taking advantage of the opportunities presented to you. One afternoon in January 1999, I found myself at Dorval Airport in Montreal on my way to a Canadian history conference being held at a downtown hotel. Douglas Gibson, the president of McClelland & Stewart, was there, too, on his way to the same conference. We knew each other well enough for Doug to insist I share a taxi with him to the hotel. Who was I to argue?

Any writer in Canada will tell you that when you find yourself alone in a cab with the head of the country's premier publishing company, you should probably mention your next project. So, after some polite small talk about what to expect at the conference, I gently launched into my pitch for this book. By the time we arrived at our destination, I sensed that Doug was interested – or at least that's what I had convinced myself. I do thank him for the ride that day, for listening to me, and, above all, for his friendship and support.

After that, I put together a more formal proposal, and Jennifer Barclay of Westwood Creative Artists, my dedicated and diligent literary agent at the time, took over. When she left the business, my new agent, Hilary McMahon, also of Westwood, finalized arrangements. I am most grateful to them both for their tireless work on my behalf. My association with Bruce Westwood and the Westwood agency during the past six years or so has been delightful, propitious, and invaluable.

At M&S, my editor, Alex Schultz, was always encouraging, consistently displayed good humour and wit, and was a pleasure to work with. His fine (and meticulous) effort in transforming the manuscript into this book is greatly appreciated. I would also like to acknowledge the work of Marilyn Biderman, director of contracts and foreign rights; copy editor Adam Levin, for having a keen eye; and Gustavo Rymberg, a friend in Winnipeg, for designing the book's cover, with guidance from M&S designer Blaine Herrmann.

At The Overlook Press in New York, my gratitude goes to publisher Peter Mayer, editor Caroline Trefler, and everyone else who helped make the book happen.

My research, especially with French, Spanish, and German sources, was made easier thanks to David Messenger and Han Werner. Mel Kliman, my devoted uncle, drafted the letter to the French military that got me inside the École Militaire in Paris (the site of Alfred Dreyfus's degradation ceremony in 1895). And Rochelle Tenenbein, my sister-in-law, searched out some books and articles for me in New York.

For their generous assistance with funding this research and my extensive travel in preparing this book, I wish to thank the Canada Council, the Manitoba Arts Council, and the Jewish Foundation of Manitoba.

Travelling around Europe, I benefited enormously from the wisdom of many people who helped me in libraries, museums, archives, and synagogues. In particular, my guides to the Jewish sites of Vienna, Dr. Brigitte Timmerman and Eleonore Neubacher, were superb, as was Stephan Luscevic in Vilnius. And I must single out, too, Bonnie Bodner of the Winnipeg Public Library's Inter-Library Loan Department for tracking down countless books for me. Her service is much appreciated.

I had many interesting discussions with several rabbis, historians, journalists, and scholars of Jewish history, and I thank each of them for sharing their views with me. In this regard, I would especially like to acknowledge: Rabbi Dr. Ronald Sobel, the chief rabbi of the Temple Emanuel in New York City; Rabbi Ephraim Mirvis, chairman of the Rabbinical Council in London; Rabbi Moshe-Reuven Azman of the Great Synagogue of Kiev; Rabbi Roy Tanenbaum of Beth Zedek Synagogue in Toronto; Stephen Speisman, Canadian Jewish Congress archivist in Toronto; Moshe Ronen, past-president of the Canadian Jewish Congress in Toronto; journalist and author Seth Lipsky in New York City; journalist Phillipe Boucara in Paris; writer Rifat Bali in Istanbul; Abraham Rosenberg, the librarian of the Ets Haim Library in Amsterdam; and Carine Cassuto, editor of *Nieuw Israelietisch Weekblad* in Amsterdam.

For taking the time to read portions of the manuscript and for their insightful comments, I am indebted to historians Lionel Steiman of the University of Manitoba, Irving Abella at York University in Toronto, and Jane Gerber, a professor of Jewish history at City University in New York. Igor Korenzvit, the president of IKOR Integrated Facilities, a furniture design and supply store in Toronto, shared with me the story of his early years growing up Jewish in the Soviet Union, read Chapter Twelve and offered helpful suggestions about Soviet Jewish life, and helped me arrange interviews on my visit to Kiev.

It goes without saying that all omissions, misinterpretations, and errors of fact and judgement are strictly my own.

As always, my wife, Angie, and our children, Alexander and Mia, offered me encouragement, love, and were more than willing to listen to the usual issues, concerns, and (very occasional) griping in getting a book finished. They remain my most loyal and devoted supporters, and for that, as I have acknowledged many times before, I am most fortunate. If, some day in the future, Alexander and Mia decide to share this book about their people and heritage with their own grand-children, so much the better.

A.L.
Winnipeg
April, 2003

INDEX